S0-APN-365

bf

Titles available from boyd & fraser

BASIC Programming

Applesoft BASIC Fundamentals and Style
BASIC Fundamentals and Style
Complete BASIC for the Short Course
Structured BASIC Fundamentals and Style for the IBM® PC and Compatibles
Structured Microsoft BASIC: Essentials for Business
Structuring Programs in Microsoft BASIC

COBOL Programming

Advanced Structured COBOL: Batch and Interactive
COBOL: Structured Programming Techniques for Solving Problems
Comprehensive Structured COBOL
Fundamentals of Structured COBOL

Database

A Guide to SQL
Database Systems: Management and Design

Computer Information Systems

Applications Software Programming with Fourth-Generation Languages
Business Data Communications and Networks
Expert Systems for Business: Concepts and Applications
Fundamentals of Systems Analysis with Application Design
Investment Management: Decision Support and Expert Systems
Learning Computer Programming: Structured Logic Algorithms, and Flowcharting
Office Automation: An Information Systems Approach

Microcomputer Applications

An Introduction to Desktop Publishing
dBASE III PLUS® Programming
DOS: Complete and Simplified
Introduction to Computers and Microcomputer Applications
Macintosh Productivity Tools
Mastering and Using Lotus 1-2-3®, Release 3
Mastering and Using Lotus 1-2-3®, Version 2.2
Mastering and Using WordPerfect® 5.0 and 5.1
Mastering Lotus 1-2-3®
Microcomputer Applications: A Practical Approach
Microcomputer Applications: Using Small Systems Software, Second Edition
Microcomputer Database Management Using dBASE III PLUS®
Microcomputer Database Management Using dBASE IV®
Microcomputer Database Management Using R:BASE System V®
Microcomputer Productivity Tools
Microcomputer Systems Management and Applications
PC-DOS®/MS-DOS® Simplified, Second Edition
Using Enable®: An Introduction to Integrated Software

Shelly and Cashman Titles

Computer Concepts with Microcomputer Applications (Lotus 1-2-3® and VP-Planner Plus® versions)
Computer Concepts
Essential Computer Concepts
Learning to Use WordPerfect®, Lotus 1-2-3®, and dBASE III PLUS®
Learning to Use WordPerfect®, VP-Planner Plus®, and dBASE III PLUS®
Learning to Use WordPerfect®
Learning to Use Lotus 1-2-3®
Learning to Use VP-Planner Plus®
Learning to Use dBASE III PLUS®
Computer Fundamentals with Application Software
Learning to Use SuperCalc®3, dBASE III®, and WordStar® 3.3: An Introduction
Learning to Use SuperCalc®3: An Introduction
Learning to Use dBASE III®: An Introduction
Learning to Use WordStar® 3.3: An Introduction
BASIC Programming for the IBM Personal Computer
Structured COBOL: Pseudocode Edition
Structured COBOL: Flowchart Edition
RPG II, RPG III, & RPG/400

Order information on page 774.

Mastering and Using LOTUS 1-2-3®

Release 3

H. Albert Napier

Rice University and
Napier & Judd, Inc.

Philip J. Judd

Napier & Judd, Inc.

boyd & fraser publishing company

Dedication

This book is dedicated to our families for their loving support and patience.

Liz, J.B. and Lanham
Valerie, Michelle, Jacob and Heather

Credits:

Publisher: Tom Walker
Acquisitions Editor: James H. Edwards
Editor: Donna Villanucci
Director of Production: Becky Herrington
Manufacturing Director: Dean Sherman

This book was produced using Manuscript®

A Division of South-Western Publishing Company
Boston, MA 02116

Manufactured in the United States of America

Library of Congress Cataloging-in-Publication Data

Napier, H. Albert, 1944-
Mastering Lotus 1-2-3 : release 3 / H. Albert Napier, Philip J. Judd.
p. cm.
ISBN 0-87835-332-1
1. Lotus 1-2-3 (Computer program) 2. Electronic spreadsheets. 3. Business--Data processing. I. Judd, Philip J., 1953- . II. Title.
HF5548.4.L67N364 1990
005.36'9--dc20 89-17395
CIP

1 2 3 4 5 6 7 8 9 10 Ki 4 3 2 1 0 9

BRIEF CONTENTS

CONTENTS

Chapter Four
Creating and Printing Graphs 219

Chapter Eight
Introduction to Database Capabilities 383

Chapter Ten
Special Functions in Lotus 1-2-3 477

Chapter Twelve

PREFACE

INTRODUCTION

Today, there are literally millions of people using personal computers. One of the most popular uses of personal computers, sometimes referred to as microcomputers, is for creating spreadsheets. A spreadsheet is typically completed on what are called "columnar pad" sheets of paper. Spreadsheets are used extensively in accounting, financial analysis and many other business planning and analysis situations.

OBJECTIVES OF THIS BOOK

This book was developed specifically for an introductory course on personal computers or spreadsheet analysis that utilizes IBM PCs or compatible hardware on which Lotus 1-2-3 can be used. The objectives of this book are as follows:

- To acquaint the user with the process of using personal computers to solve spreadsheet analysis type problems.
- To provide a working knowledge of the basic and advanced capabilities of 1-2-3.
- To encourage the use of good problem-solving techniques for situations in which spreadsheet solutions are appropriate.
- To permit learning through examples using an exercise-oriented approach.
- To provide the user with an excellent reference source to advance in the knowledge of 1-2-3.

LEVEL OF INSTRUCTION

This book is designed to introduce the beginning, intermediate and advanced capabilities available in Lotus 1-2-3. It is pedagogically designed. First, the basic skills needed to create a spreadsheet are discussed. Subsequent chapters build on previously presented concepts and developed skills. A variety of practical examples provide an understanding of how Lotus 1-2-3 can be used. The book assumes the user has little or no personal computer experience.

However, individuals with some previous experience can also advance their knowledge of 1-2-3. The book is characterized by its continuity, simplicity and practicality. This book does not replace the Lotus 1-2-3 reference manual that accompanies the software package. Used in conjunction with the reference manual, this book will provide the user with a complete understanding of the capabilities of Lotus 1-2-3.

AUTHORS' EXPERIENCE

The authors have worked with personal computers since they were introduced. More than 20,000 people have participated in personal computer seminars for which the authors have been responsible for providing instruction. Insights from this experience are implicit throughout the book. In addition, the authors have more than 34 years of combined experience in teaching and consulting in the field of information systems and data processing.

LOTUS AUTHORIZED TRAINING COMPANY

The authors' consulting company, Napier & Judd, Inc., is a Lotus Authorized Training Company. The company's training materials, instructors and facilities have been evaluated and approved by Lotus Development Corporation. Only a small number of companies in the United States and Canada have been designated as a Lotus Authorized Training Company. This book is based on materials that have been used in the company's training activities in which more than 12,000 participants have been trained on Lotus 1-2-3.

DISTINGUISHING FEATURES

The distinguishing features of this book include the following:

Research-Based Material

The design of the book is based on how experienced 1-2-3 users actually utilize the software. Napier completed a study of 40 experienced 1-2-3 users from eight large organizations and determined the set of commands used most often by the individuals. The users studied had an average of 2.5 years experience and worked in a variety of corporations and governmental agencies.

The research indicates that 27 commands accounted for 85 percent of the commands issued by the experienced individuals. The materials in this book have been carefully planned to provide extensive coverage of these 27 most frequently used commands.

Proven Materials

This book is based on proven materials that have been used in college and university classes as well as training seminars. More than 10,000 individuals have learned to use 1-2-3 utilizing materials on which this book is based. For example, the authors have been responsible for training more than 4,000 members of the Texas Society of CPAs employing materials from this book.

Featuring Lotus 1-2-3 Release 3

This book features Lotus 1-2-3 Release 3.

Comprehensive Coverage

Major topics represented are: creating and printing worksheets and graphs; templates; using 3-D worksheets; combining and consolidating worksheets; database management; special functions; and macros.

Learning through Examples

The book is designed for learning through examples rather than learning a series of commands. The materials are built around a series of example problems. Commands are learned for one example, then reinforced. New commands are learned on subsequent examples. The example problems are logically related and integrated throughout the book.

Step-by-Step Instructions and Screen Illustrations

All examples include step-by-step instruction. Screen illustrations are used extensively to assist the user while learning 1-2-3.

Extensive Exercises

At the end of each chapter, there are exercises that provide comprehensive coverage of the topics introduced in the chapter. Answers for many of the exercises are provided.

Three-Dimensional Worksheets

Extensive coverage of the use of multiple worksheets in a file is presented. The process for linking worksheets between files is illustrated.

Graphics

One of the most powerful options available in 1-2-3 is graphics. Graphs can be useful in business analysis and presentations. The user learns how to create and print bar, line, stacked bar, XY, pie, mixed and high-low-open-close graphs.

Templates

Most experienced users of 1-2-3 make extensive use of templates. This book covers the process of building and using templates.

Database Capabilities

While 1-2-3 is not a database management system, it does have many database-like commands that can be applied to data in a worksheet. For example, how to sort data, complete queries on information in a worksheet, fill spreadsheets with sequences of data, create tables for decision-making purposes, use data tables created by external database management systems and create frequency distributions are discussed.

Macros

With experience in using 1-2-3, the use of macros increases. Much of the power of 1-2-3 is really available to users of macros. This book introduces the process of building and using macros both at the simple and advanced levels.

Emphasis on Business and Organizational Problem Solving

The book includes many example problems that are similar to spreadsheets that may be encountered in a business or other type of organization.

What You Should Know

Each chapter includes a list of key concepts that emphasize what should be learned in the chapter.

■ ORGANIZATION/FLEXIBILITY

The book is organized in a manner that takes the user through the fundamentals of Lotus 1-2-3 and then builds on the solid foundation to cover more advanced subjects. The book is useful for college courses, training classes, individual learning and as a reference manual.

In Chapter 1, the Lotus 1-2-3 package is described and explained. Typical applications are presented. The process of loading the software package is explained. The various parts of the 1-2-3 worksheet screen are detailed along with methods to move around the screen. The structure of the menu system is described, and the meaning of the function keys is summarized.

Chapter 2 contains a step-by-step process for creating, building and printing a spreadsheet. Operations included are: entering labels, numbers and formulas; copying numbers, formulas and labels; widening columns; inserting rows; entering headings; selecting formats for numeric data; saving and retrieving a spreadsheet; correcting for rounding errors, and more. Special printing options such as selecting various font styles are given, and a method for completing "What-if" analysis is illustrated.

Chapter 3 covers a variety of useful Lotus 1-2-3 commands. Some of the topics covered include: holding a cell constant in a formula; annotating and documenting the contents of cells; printing in the **background** while continuing to use 1-2-3; protecting cells; erasing the contents of cells; correcting errors; various file commands; automatic and percent formatting options; hiding and displaying columns; label prefixes; moving cell contents; creating a page break for printing purposes; using borders, headers and footers; and portrait versus landscape printing options. Other topics represented are: creating and deleting range names; recalculation of a worksheet; searching and replacing data; checking the status of a worksheet; using the system command; freezing titles; using the Undo command; widening multiple columns; creating and clearing windows; inserting and deleting columns, rows and worksheets; and suppressing zero values from appearing.

Numerous types of graphs can be prepared using 1-2-3. In Chapter 4, graphics capabilities are covered, including bar graph, line graph, mixed graph (combined bar and line graphs), stacked-bar graph, pie graph, XY graph and high-low-close-open graph. Other topics discussed are automatic graphing, group graphing, displaying the graph in a window while the worksheet remains on the screen and printing a graph.

In Chapter 5, the process for building and using **template** worksheets is discussed. A template is a worksheet that is constructed and saved as a "shell" for the creation of worksheets at a later time containing the same formulas and/or text.

Sometimes it is useful to have more than one worksheet in a file. Chapter 6 explains a discussion of the use of multiple worksheets in a file and the three-dimensional capabilities. Topics incorporated are: adding worksheets to a file, moving between worksheets, copying information from one worksheet to other worksheets, and formatting data in multiple worksheets. The process of using multiple files at the same time is also presented.

Many practical applications of spreadsheets require that information be combined from one or more spreadsheets into one or more other spreadsheets. The process for consolidating information from one or several worksheets into a summary worksheet within a file is illustrated in Chapter 7. This process is demonstrated using the 3-D capabilities available in 1-2-3. The method for linking worksheets in different files is also covered.

While 1-2-3 does not provide all the capabilities of a database management system, many database-like operations can be applied to data in a worksheet. Chapter 8 includes a discussion of sorting data, completing a query and computing information based on a query. Chapter 9 contains the following topics: filling cells with data, creating data tables that can be used in decision-making situations, using a database table created by an external database management system, combining information from multiple database tables, creating a frequency distribution and graphing a frequency distribution.

There are many pre-programmed functions available in Lotus 1-2-3. In Chapter 10, most of the special functions available in 1-2-3 such as functions for statistical analysis, financial analysis, date and time data, logical analysis, database operations, mathematical computations, special analyses such as lookup table calculations and string functions are discussed and illustrated.

In many situations, the same steps are applied to the development of a worksheet each time it is used. For example, an organization may summarize the budget expenditures of three departments into one worksheet. In 1-2-3, a macro can be developed that instructs the computer to repeat the steps automatically rather than have the user enter the set of steps each time the spreadsheets are summarized. An introduction to the process of creating and using macros appears in Chapter 11. The concept of using a macro library file for storing macros that are used in many types of applications is presented.

Advanced macro commands and examples of using the commands are described in Chapter 12. Some types of macros illustrated are: sorting data, restricting data entry to specific cells, automatically executing macros, interactive macros, changing program flow and looping, and using subroutines. User-designed menus are also created.

Frequently, users need to place explanatory information on their worksheets. Chapter 13 includes an explanation of the simple **text processing** capabilities of 1-2-3.

Appendix A contains menu tree diagrams and a brief summary of the commands covered in this book.

■ ACKNOWLEDGEMENTS

We would like to thank and express our appreciation to the many fine and talented individuals who have contributed to the completion of this book. We have been fortunate to have a group of reviewers whose constructive comments have been helpful in completing the book. Special thanks go to: Professor Nancy Haney, Oakton Community College and PCT Professional Microcomputer Consulting/Training; Mr. Louis Fuxan, Delgado Community College; Professor Barbara Vrana, Oklahoma City Community College; and Professor Mark Griffin, Davenport College of Business.

No book is possible without the motivation and support of an editorial staff. Therefore, we wish to acknowledge with great appreciation the following people at Boyd & Fraser: Tom Walker, vice-president and publisher, for the opportunity to write this book and for his constant encouragement; Jim Edwards and Donna Villanucci, for their keen assistance in the editing process; and the production staff for support in completing the book.

We appreciate the assistance provided by Marla McBryde, Arlene Waterman, Dan Jurden, Nancy Onarheim, Lori Ruzicka, Donna Kainer, Darlene Funderburke and Linda Rice of Napier & Judd, Inc. in the preparation of the initial drafts of the book.

Houston, Texas
August, 1989

H. Albert Napier
Philip J. Judd

CHAPTER ONE

GETTING STARTED WITH LOTUS 1-2-3

OBJECTIVES

In this chapter, you will learn to:

- Load the Lotus 1-2-3 program into the computer
- Identify the basic features of the 1-2-3 worksheet screen
- Move the cell pointer around the worksheet
- Use the 1-2-3 menu
- Identify the use of the function keys in 1-2-3
- Exit Lotus 1-2-3

CHAPTER OVERVIEW

This book assumes that you have little or no knowledge of Lotus 1-2-3. In this chapter, you are introduced to the capabilities of 1-2-3 and typical applications. The hardware requirements for using 1-2-3 and the process for loading the software into a personal computer are explained. The basic items that appear on the worksheet screen are discussed. The process of moving around the 1-2-3 worksheet is defined. The process of entering information into a spreadsheet is introduced. The Lotus 1-2-3 menu structure is explained and illustrated. Finally, an overview of the special functions associated with the function keys is presented.

WHAT IS LOTUS 1-2-3?

Lotus 1-2-3 is an integrated software package. The term integrated means that Lotus has more than one basic capability. Lotus 1-2-3 can be used for creating spreadsheets (interchangeably referred to as worksheets), creating graphs, and executing database operations. In this book, it is assumed that you are using Lotus 1-2-3 Release 3. However, if you are using an earlier version of Lotus 1-2-3, much of the material presented in this book is still applicable.

An example of a worksheet appears in Figure 1-1. In the next chapter, you are shown how to create and print this spreadsheet. Figure 1-2 is a graph that includes some information from the worksheet in Figure 1-1.

A:A1: [W18] READY

A	A	B	C	D	E	F	G
1				ABC COMPANY			
2				BUDGET			
3							
4							
5		QTR1	QTR2	QTR3	QTR4	YR TOTAL	
6							
7	SALES	60,000	61,200	62,424	63,672	247,296	
8							
9	EXPENSES						
10	SALARIES	35,000	35,500	36,200	37,000	143,700	
11	RENT	9,000	9,000	9,000	9,000	36,000	
12	TELEPHONE	1,000	1,050	1,103	1,158	4,311	
13	OFFICE SUPPLIES	750	800	850	900	3,300	
14	MISCELLANEOUS	1,000	1,030	1,061	1,093	4,184	
15		--------	--------	--------	--------	--------	
16	TOTAL EXPENSES	46,750	47,380	48,214	49,151	191,495	
17		--------	--------	--------	--------	--------	
18	GROSS PROFIT	13,250	13,820	14,210	14,521	55,801	
19		========	========	========	========	========	
20							

Figure 1-1

Up to six items such as SALES can appear on a graph. Graphs other than bar charts can be developed.

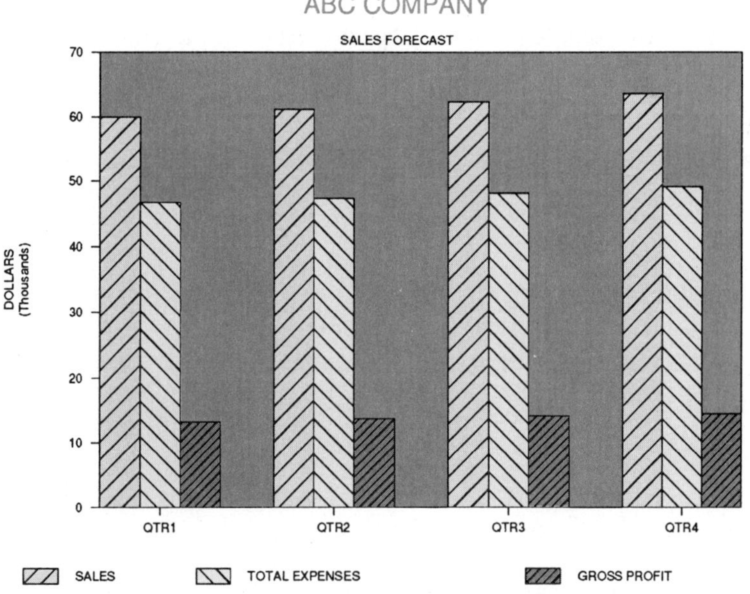

Figure 1-2

Lotus 1-2-3 can also be used to perform operations on a file. For example, information in a worksheet can be sorted by various criteria. Figure 1-3 is a worksheet that has information on salaries for a group of individuals that is not sorted in any particular order.

A:A1: [W11] READY

A	A	B	C	D	E	F	G	H
1				ABC COMPANY				
2				SALARY BUDGET				
3								
4								
5	LAST NAME	FIRST NAME	DIV.	QTR1	QTR2	QTR3	QTR4	TOTAL
6	SPROUT	AL	3	5,950	5,950	6,450	6,450	24,800
7	LYLIE	SUSAN	1	7,800	7,800	7,800	8,580	31,980
8	CHIN	TOMMY	2	5,000	5,000	5,200	5,200	20,400
9	JOHNSON	ERNEST	1	8,000	8,000	8,800	8,800	33,600
10	VALETTI	GEORGE	3	5,900	5,900	6,300	6,300	24,400
11	ARMOUR	CYNTHIA	2	5,200	5,200	5,400	5,400	21,200
12	JONES	NINA	3	6,750	6,750	6,750	7,450	27,700
13				--------	--------	--------	--------	--------
14	TOTAL			44,600	44,600	46,700	48,180	184,080
15								
16								
17								
18								
19								
20								

Figure 1-3

Sometimes it is desirable to sort the information into a particular order. In Figure 1-4, the data that appears in Figure 1-3 has been sorted in ascending order by division number.

A:A1: [W11] READY

A	A	B	C	D	E	F	G	H
1				ABC COMPANY				
2				SALARY BUDGET				
3								
4								
5	LAST NAME	FIRST NAME	DIV.	QTR1	QTR2	QTR3	QTR4	TOTAL
6	JOHNSON	ERNEST	1	8,000	8,000	8,800	8,800	33,600
7	LYLIE	SUSAN	1	7,800	7,800	7,800	8,580	31,980
8	CHIN	TOMMY	2	5,000	5,000	5,200	5,200	20,400
9	ARMOUR	CYNTHIA	2	5,200	5,200	5,400	5,400	21,200
10	SPROUT	AL	3	5,950	5,950	6,450	6,450	24,800
11	VALETTI	GEORGE	3	5,900	5,900	6,300	6,300	24,400
12	JONES	NINA	3	6,750	6,750	6,750	7,450	27,700
13				--------	--------	--------	--------	--------
14	TOTAL			44,600	44,600	46,700	48,180	184,080
15								
16								
17								
18								
19								
20								

Figure 1-4

TYPICAL APPLICATIONS

Lotus 1-2-3 is used in many organizations as well as for personal use. Some examples of Lotus 1-2-3 applications include:

Advertising expense forecast
Balance sheet forecasts
Budgets
Cash flow analysis
Checkbook balancing
Depreciation schedules
Household expenses
Income statement forecasts
Income tax projections
Income tax records
Inventory forecasting
Job bids and costing
Sports analysis
Stock portfolio analysis and records

HARDWARE REQUIREMENTS

To use Lotus 1-2-3 Release 3, you must have a microcomputer with a minimum of 1 megabyte of RAM under DOS and 3 megabytes of RAM under OS/2. A hard disk is required. Your computer should have at least one floppy disk drive. A monochrome or color monitor can be used with Lotus 1-2-3. A color monitor is particularly useful if you want to see better quality graphics.

A printer is also necessary. A dot matrix printer provides the capability of printing spreadsheets as well as graphs. Most laser printers provide a full range of graphics printing capabilities. If high-quality graphics are desired, a plotter is necessary.

Blank diskettes that have been appropriately formatted are also needed. These diskettes can be used to store spreadsheets and graphs on files to be used at a later time.

SOFTWARE REQUIREMENTS

The Lotus 1-2-3 diskettes on which the software is stored are needed. The software package includes several diskettes. The DOS system software disk is also needed. To install the 1-2-3 software on the hard disk, see the Lotus 1-2-3 reference manual that came with your software.

LOADING THE LOTUS 1-2-3 SOFTWARE PACKAGE

Before you attempt to load Lotus 1-2-3 into the memory of the microcomputer, all connections need to be checked. Make sure the monitor and printer are properly installed. The power cord should be connected to an appropriate electric outlet.

Turn on the computer

Assuming that 1-2-3 Release 3 is installed in the directory 123R3 on the **C** drive, use the following steps to load the software.

Type cd\123R3 (to change to directory 123R3)

Press ↵

Type Lotus

Press ↵

In many situations, you may have a menu from which to select Release 3 or some other process for invoking the use of 1-2-3 Release 3. In a few seconds your screen will look like Figure 1-5.

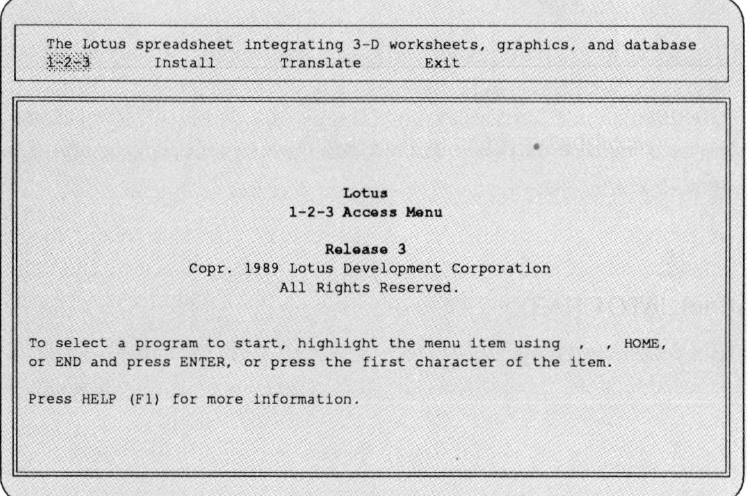

Figure 1-5

The menu at the top of the screen has the sets of characters 1-2-3, Install, Translate, and Exit. Notice that the characters 1-2-3 are highlighted with a rectangle that is referred to as a pointer. Above 1-2-3 appears the message "The Lotus spreadsheet integrating 3-D worksheets, graphics, and database." This indicates that the Lotus program will be entered if the 1-2-3 option is selected from the menu.

The menu structure will be illustrated in more detail later in this chapter. To select "The Lotus spreadsheet integrating 3-D worksheets, graphics, and database" option:

Press ↵

A message with copyright and licensing information then appears on the screen. A blank worksheet such as the one in Figure 1-6 will appear on your screen in another few seconds.

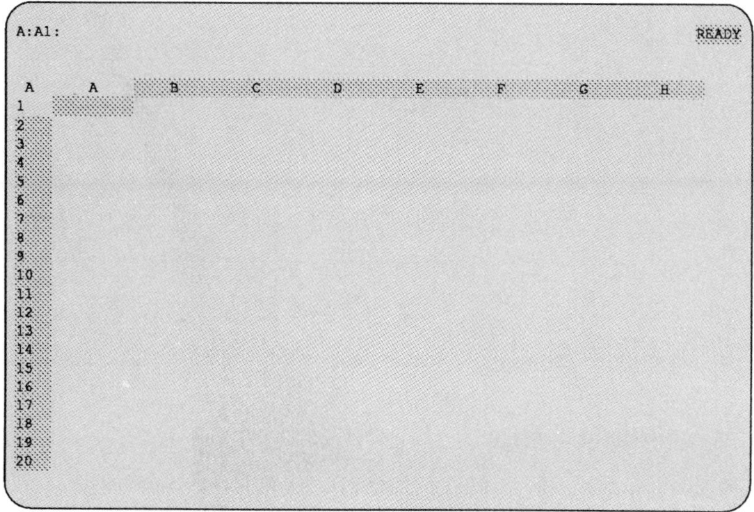

Figure 1-6

THE LOTUS 1-2-3 WORKSHEET SCREEN

Figure 1-6 is the standard form of the initial **worksheet** used by Lotus when it is loaded. In some situations, a worksheet is referred to as a **spreadsheet**. The terms **worksheet** and **spreadsheet** are used interchangeably in this book. A worksheet is a grid-like structure consisting of rows and columns.

Figure 1-7 is a worksheet screen after the main menu of Lotus 1-2-3 has been placed on the screen.

```
A:A1:                                                                    MENU
Worksheet  Range  Copy  Move  File  Print  Graph  Data  System  Quit
Global  Insert  Delete  Column  Erase  Titles  Window  Status  Page  Hide
 A      A        B        C        D        E        F        G        H
1
2
3
4
5
6
7
8
9
10
11
12
13
14
15
16
17
18
19
20
```

Figure 1-7

In this section various items that appear on the worksheet screen in Figure 1-7 are discussed.

Worksheet Letter

A maximum of 256 worksheets can be used at one time. The worksheets are labeled A through Z, AA through AZ, BA through BZ and so forth, until the letter IV is reached. In Figure 1-7, the worksheet letter is A and appears at the intersection of the horizontal and vertical borders near the top left corner of the screen. The use of multiple worksheets is discussed in Chapter 6.

Worksheet Frame

Above and to the left of the worksheet is the **worksheet frame**. This area includes the row number and column letter borders.

Row Numbers

On the left border of the worksheet on the screen is a set of numbers called **row numbers**. Note that there are 20 rows appearing on the screen. There are a total of 8,192 rows available in the worksheet.

Column Letters

Across the top border of the worksheet on the screen is the set of letters A through H. These are the **column letters**. There are 256 columns in the worksheet. The columns are identified with the letters A through Z, AA through AZ, BA through BZ and so forth until the letter IV is reached.

Cell

A **cell** is the area on a worksheet that occurs at the intersection of a column and a row. Data is stored in a cell. A:A1 refers to the cell in worksheet A that is located at the intersection of column A and row 1. Initially, each cell is set to display 9 characters.

Cell Pointer

Notice on the screen that cell A1 in worksheet A is highlighted by a rectangular form. The item highlighting cell A1 is called the **cell pointer**. The cell pointer can be moved from cell to cell in the worksheet. Whenever information is input to the worksheet, it is placed in the cell highlighted by the cell pointer.

Current Cell

The **current cell** is highlighted by the cell pointer. The next data entry or operation affects this cell.

Cell Address

The location of a cell is called the **cell address**. A cell address is defined by a worksheet letter followed by a colon, column letter and row number. For example A:B2 is the cell address for the cell that occurs at the intersection of column B and row 2 in worksheet A.

Control Panel

Above the worksheet at the top of the screen is an area called the **control panel**. The control panel consists of three lines. The first line has the cell address for the current cell and the contents of the cell. Notice at the top left side of the screen, there is a cell address. Assuming you have a blank worksheet and the cell pointer is in cell A1, then the cell address area on the first line of the control panel contains A:A1: and there will be blank spaces immediately to the right. Nothing appears to the right of A:A1: because no data has been entered in the cell.

The second line of the control panel displays the current data when the contents of a cell are being created or edited. It is also used to display the Lotus 1-2-3 menus when the / key is pressed.

The third line of the control panel is used to display either a submenu or a one-line description of the command item currently highlighted on the second line of the control panel.

Even though the control panel always includes the worksheet letter (e.g., A:H1: or D:B4:), in most cases this book refers to the cell address appearing in the control panel using only the column and row location (e.g., H1 or B4).

Mode Indicator

The **mode indicator** appears at the right end of the first line in the control panel area of the worksheet. It indicates the current operating mode. For example, it may say READY indicating that 1-2-3 is ready for you to input information or create a formula. If it says MENU, then a menu appears on the screen and you can make a selection from the menu.

Status Indicator

The **status indicator** specifies the condition of certain keys or of the program. For example, if the CapsLock key is pressed, the characters CAP will appear in the right corner below the worksheet indicating that all alphabetic characters subsequently used are automatically capitalized. To remove the CAP specification, you need only to press the CapsLock key again and the CAP indicator no longer appears on the screen.

File and Clock Indicator

At the bottom left side of the screen the date and time appear. Assuming the current date and time have been entered properly, the current date and time should appear. Lotus 1-2-3 has an option that allows you to suppress the date and time indicator from view. If the current file has been saved, or if the current file has been retrieved, the file name will appear instead of the date and time. Note that in this book only the file name will appear in the screen illustrations.

MOVING AROUND THE WORKSHEET

As mentioned earlier in this chapter, the cell pointer is the highlighted rectangle on the screen that indicates the location on the worksheet. The cell address of the cell pointer's location always appears in the top left corner of the worksheet. In this section, methods to move the cell pointer on the worksheet are discussed and illustrated.

Using the Pointer-Movement Keys to Move the Cell Pointer

The cursor movement keys, which are the basic keys used to move the cell pointer from cell to cell on the worksheet, are located on the right side of the keyboard (see Figure 1-8). The cursor movement keys are placed on the numeric keypad (sometimes called "the ten key") and/or they may be in a separate location as depicted in Figure 1-8.

In Lotus 1-2-3 Release 3, these keys are referred to as the pointer-movement keys.

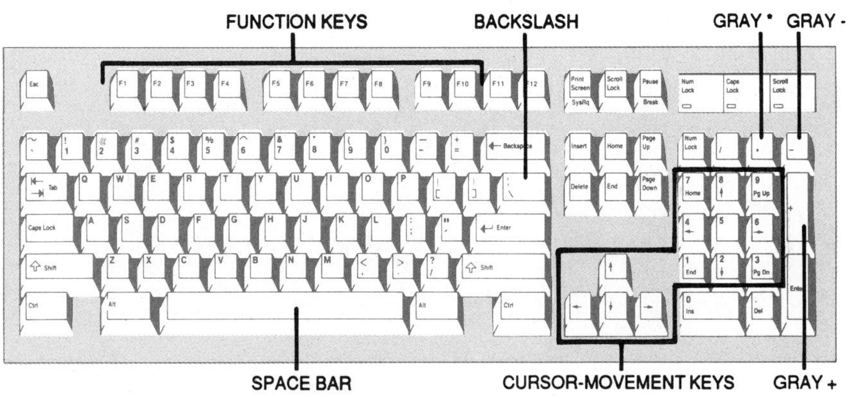

Figure 1-8

To illustrate the use of the pointer-movement keys:

Locate the pointer-movement keys

Press → key seven times

As shown in Figure 1-9, the cell pointer is now in cell H1. This fact is indicated on the first line of the control panel. The process of moving around the screen is sometimes called "scrolling."

As you press the → key, note that the current column letter and row number are highlighted for easy reference as you scan the screen. When the cell pointer is in cell H1, the column label H and the row label 1 are highlighted.

Figure 1-9

To move the cell pointer to cell I1:

Press → key one time

As illustrated in Figure 1-10, the cell pointer has been moved to column I and column A has disappeared. 1-2-3 can only display a total of 72 characters on the screen and no portion of a column is displayed unless the entire column can be shown on the screen.

```
A:I1:                                                        READY

A     B      C      D      E      F      G      H       I
1
2
3
4
5
6
7
8
9
10
11
12
13
14
15
16
17
18
19
20
```

Figure 1-10

To move to cell A1:

Locate the ← key

Press ← key eight times or until the cell pointer appears in cell A1

If the ← key is pressed too many times, a "beep" sound will be heard indicating that you are trying to move to the left of column A. Anytime the "beep" sound occurs, it denotes that you are trying to perform some type of operation that is not permitted at that point.

To move the cell pointer rapidly:

Locate the ↓ key

Press ↓ key and hold it down

After the cell pointer has moved down 20 or 30 rows, stop depressing the ↓ key. Notice that the row number is highlighted for easy reference as you scan the screen.

To return the cell pointer to cell A1:

Locate the ↑ key

Press ↑ key until the cell pointer appears in cell A1

A "beep" sound may be heard if the ↑ key has been depressed after reaching cell A1.

Using the PgDn and PgUp Keys to Move the Cell Pointer

The cell pointer key can be moved up and down one screen at a time using the PgUp and PgDn keys. PgDn stands for "Page Down" and PgUp means "Page Up." These keys permit you to move the cell pointer up and down the screen 20 rows at a time. Note that on many keyboards there is a Page Down key and a Page Up key as well as the PgDn key and PgUp keys. They can be used interchangeably.

To use the PgDn key:

Locate the PgDn key

Press PgDn

Assuming that the cell pointer was in cell A1 prior to pressing the PgDn key, then the cell pointer is now be in cell A21. See Figure 1-11. If the cell pointer was not in cell A1, then the cell pointer is now in a cell that is 20 rows farther down in the worksheet from the cell it was in prior to pressing the PgDn key.

Figure 1-11

To use the PgUp key:

Locate the PgUp key

Press PgUp

Assuming that the cell pointer was in cell A21 prior to pressing the PgUp key, the cell pointer should now be in cell A1. If the cell pointer was not in cell A21, then the cell pointer is now 20 rows up in the worksheet.

Using the Tab Key to Move the Cell Pointer

The cell pointer can be moved to the right or left one screen at a time using the ⇥ (tab) key.

To move the cell pointer one screen to the right:

Make sure the cell pointer is in cell A1

Locate the ⇥ key (it is usually to the left of the letter Q)

Press ⇥

As illustrated in Figure 1-12, the cell pointer has been moved to the right one screen and now appears in cell I1.

Figure 1-12

To move the cell pointer one screen to the left:

Make	sure the cell pointer is in cell I1
Locate	the ⇥ key
Hold	a Shift key down
Press	⇥

The cell pointer has been moved to cell A1 or one screen to the left. The shift key is marked with the word Shift. There are two shift keys on a keyboard.

Another way to move the cell pointer one screen to the right or left is:

Make	sure the cell pointer is in cell A1
Depress	the [Ctrl] key
Press	→

The cell pointer now should be in cell I1. To return to cell A1:

Depress	the [Ctrl] key
Press	←

Using the [GoTo] Key (the [F5] Function Key) to Move the Cell Pointer

Sometimes it is necessary to move the cell pointer to a particular cell in the worksheet. For example, to move the cursor to cell IV8192:

Make	sure the cell pointer is in cell A1
Locate	the [F5] function key (the [F5] key is usually at the top of keyboard or on the left side of the keyboard)
Press	[F5]

As displayed in Figure 1-13, the screen now has a message in the control panel prompting you to enter the cell address desired.

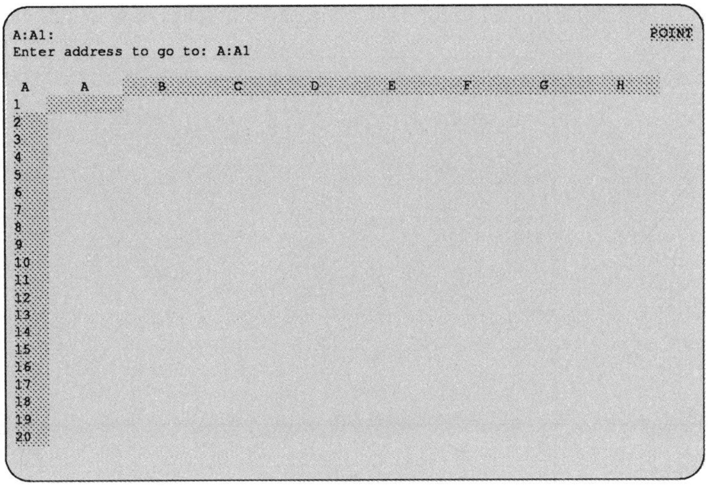

A:A1: POINT
Enter address to go to: A:A1

Figure 1-13

Type IV8192

Note that lowercase or uppercase letters can be used when you type the cell address.

Press ↵

Figure 1-14 depicts the entering of cell address IV8192.

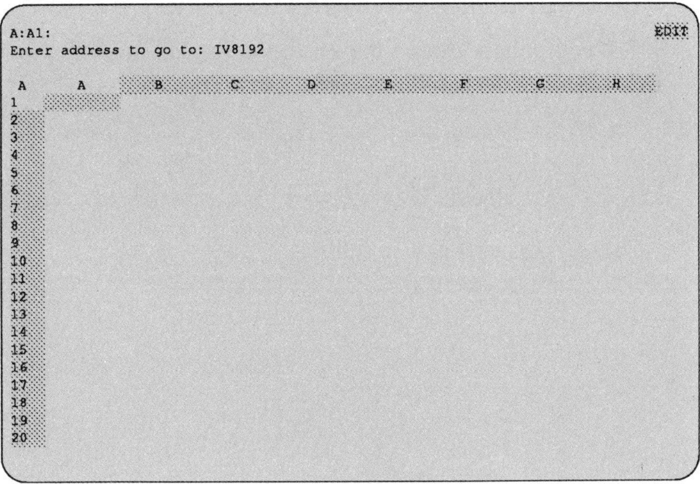

Figure 1-14

As illustrated in Figure 1-15, the cell pointer is now in cell IV8192.

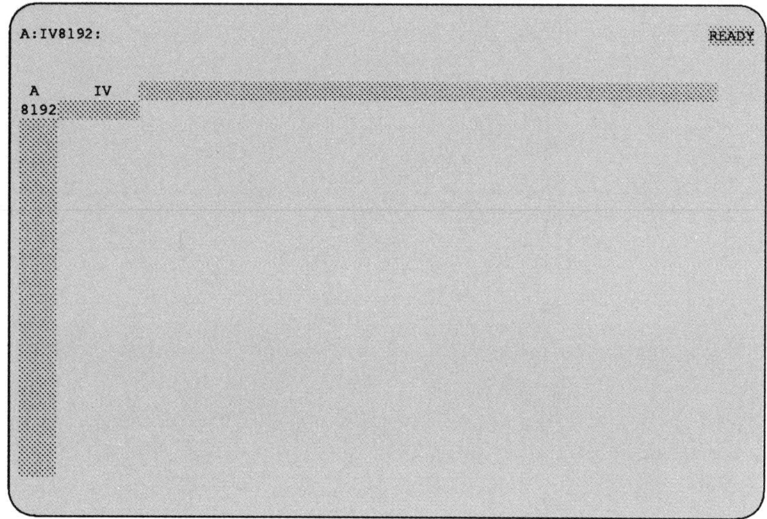

Figure 1-15

Cell IV8192 is the cell in the bottom right corner of the worksheet. In other words, column IV is the last column in the worksheet and row 8,192 is the last row in the worksheet.

Using the Home Key to Move the Cell Pointer

The cell pointer can be moved to the top left corner by pressing the Home key. To demonstrate the use of the Home key:

Locate the Home key

Press Home

The cell pointer is now in cell A1.

Using the End Key in Combination with Other Keys to Move the Cell Pointer

Assume the cell pointer is in a blank cell. If the End key is pressed and a pointer-movement key is then pressed, the cell pointer will be moved to the first nonblank cell in the direction of the pointer-movement key. If a nonblank cell does not exist in the selected direction, the cell pointer will move to the last cell in the selected direction. When the cell pointer is in a nonblank cell and the above action is repeated, then the cell pointer will be moved to the last nonblank cell in the direction selected. If nonblank cells do not exist in the selected direction, the cell pointer will be moved to the last cell in the selected direction.

If the End key is pressed and followed by pressing a Home key, then the cell pointer is moved to the last cell in the worksheet which is defined by the last column and row that have a nonblank entry.

Note that the word End appears at the bottom of the screen when the End key is pressed. If you decide not to press a pointer-movement key after pressing the End key, the End indicator can be removed from the screen by pressing the End key again. The End indicator automatically disappears when a pointer-movement key is pressed.

■ LOTUS 1-2-3 MENU STRUCTURE

Earlier in this chapter, the menu structure was mentioned. In this section, the menu structure is discussed and defined.

To display the main 1-2-3 menu:

Press /

The main 1-2-3 menu is now on the screen. Notice the word MENU now appears as the mode indicator. See Figure 1-16.

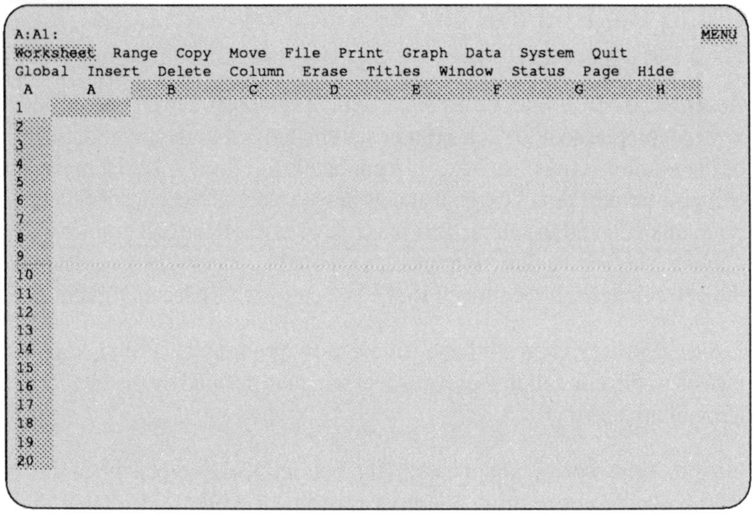

```
A:A1:                                                                    MENU
Worksheet  Range  Copy  Move  File  Print  Graph  Data  System  Quit
Global  Insert  Delete  Column  Erase  Titles  Window  Status  Page  Hide
 A      A          B          C          D          E          F          G          H
1
2
3
4
5
6
7
8
9
10
11
12
13
14
15
16
17
18
19
20
```

Figure 1-16

The menu appears on the second line of the control panel. The Worksheet option on the menu is highlighted. The submenu that will be used if the Worksheet option is selected appears on the third line of the control panel.

Other options on the main menu include Range, Copy, Move, File, Print, Graph, Data, System, and Quit. The options are used to perform a variety of operations on a worksheet. Many of these operations are presented in the remainder of this book.

To remove the Main menu from the screen:

Press Esc

Esc stands for escape. It can be used to "back up" one level in the menu structure. In this situation, since the main menu is displayed on the screen, the main menu will disappear.

Using the Menu Structure

To illustrate the use of the menu structure, you will enter information in cell A1 and then erase the worksheet.

To designate some information to be entered in cell A1:

Make	sure the cell pointer is in cell A1
Type	Lotus

The word Lotus now appears on the second line of the control panel. Notice that when the first character is typed, the word LABEL appears in the mode indicator specifying that a label is being entered. See Figure 1-17.

Figure 1-17

To enter the information in cell A1:

Press	↵

The word Lotus is now shown in cell A1. See Figure 1-18.

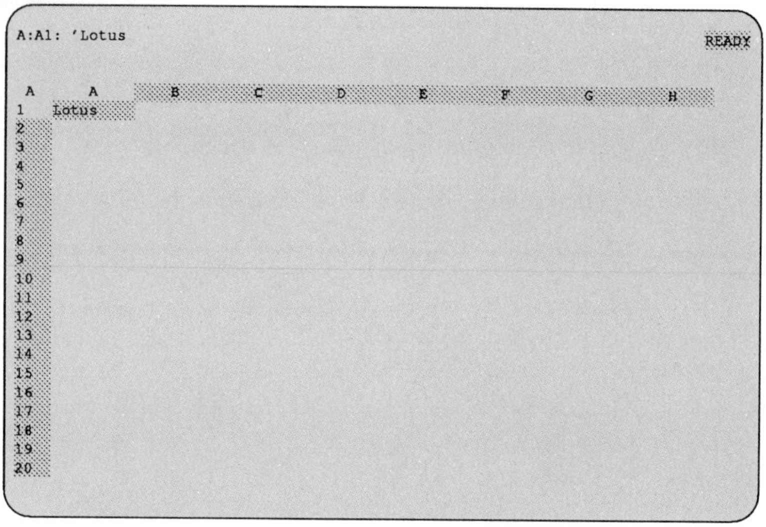

Figure 1-18

Note that all labels are *left-justified* in a cell. In other words, the characters begin at the leftmost position in the cell. When a number is entered, the mode indicator says VALUE and the number is *right-justified* in the cell when the ⏎ key is pressed; that is, the number appears in the rightmost portion of the cell. Notice that the characters **'Lotus** are visible next to the cell address A1 on the first line in the control panel. The **'** is the symbol that means label in 1-2-3 and **Lotus** is the information stored in cell A1.

To erase the entire worksheet:

Press /

At this point the main menu appears on the screen as it is shown in Figure 1-19. The menu structure works by moving the menu pointer to the desired menu option and pressing the ⏎ key.

```
A:A1: 'Lotus                                                                   MENU
Worksheet  Range  Copy  Move  File  Print  Graph  Data  System  Quit
Global  Insert  Delete  Column  Erase  Titles  Window  Status  Page  Hide
 A      A        B        C        D        E        F        G        H
1   Lotus
2
3
4
5
6
7
8
9
10
11
12
13
14
15
16
17
18
19
20
```

Figure 1-19

The menu pointer is a rectangular shape that is similar to the cell pointer. It is used to highlight the options on a menu. Since it is desired to use the Worksheet option, the cell pointer does not need to be moved and the ↵ key can be pressed.

Press ↵

The submenu that previously appeared on the third line of the control panel is now shown on the second line of the control panel and becomes the menu that is in use. See Figure 1-20. Note that the menu pointer is on the word Global.

```
A:A1: 'Lotus                                                              MENU
Global  Insert  Delete  Column  Erase  Titles  Window  Status  Page  Hide
Format  Label  Col-Width  Prot  Zero  Recalc  Default  Group
 A      A        B        C        D        E        F        G        H
1    Lotus
2
3
4
5
6
7
8
9
10
11
12
13
14
15
16
17
18
19
20
```

Figure 1-20

The next step in the process of erasing the worksheet on the screen is to move the menu pointer to the Erase menu option. See Figure 1-21.

To move the menu pointer to the Erase option:

Press → until the menu pointer is on the word Erase

```
A:A1: 'Lotus                                                              MENU
Global  Insert  Delete  Column  Erase  Titles  Window  Status  Page  Hide
Clear all worksheets and files from memory
 A      A        B        C        D        E        F        G        H
1    Lotus
2
3
4
5
6
7
8
9
10
11
12
13
14
15
16
17
18
19
20
```

Figure 1-21

To complete the process of erasing the worksheet:

Press ↵

Figure 1-22 illustrates that 1-2-3 gives you the option of making sure it is desirable to erase the worksheet. If the ↵ is pressed while the No option is highlighted, then 1-2-3 returns to the READY mode and the worksheet is not erased.

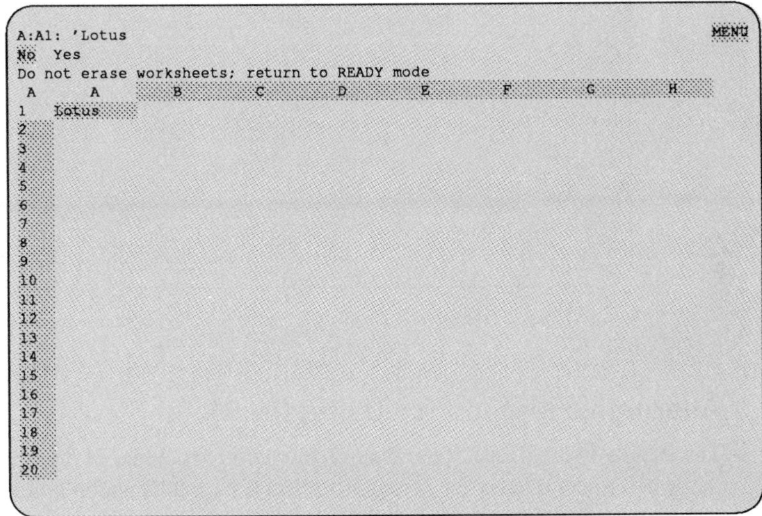

Figure 1-22

The final steps in the process for erasing the worksheet are:

Press → to move the menu pointer to the word **Yes**. Notice the explanation of the option on the third line of the control panel indicates the worksheet will be erased if the Yes menu option is selected.

Press ↵

You will hear a beep sound. A message appears in the control panel indicating you have made changes to the worksheet and have not saved the worksheet. For this exercise:

Press → to move the menu pointer to the word **Yes**

Press ↵

Your screen should have a blank worksheet on it and should look like Figure 1-23.

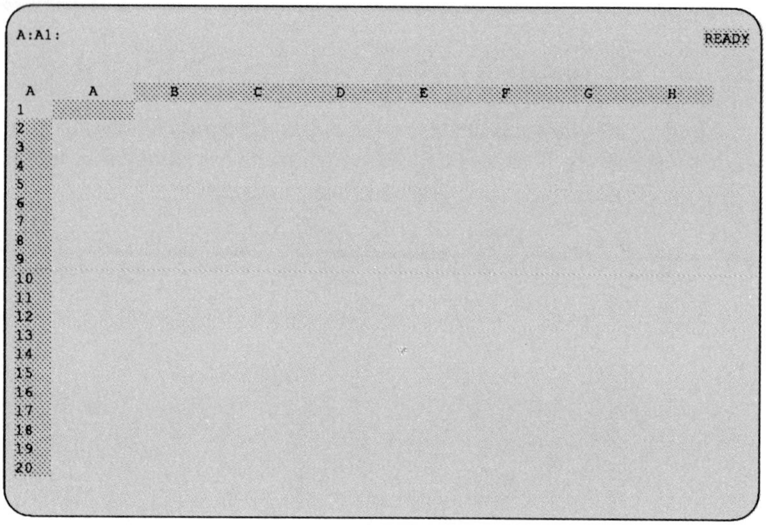

Figure 1-23

Alternative Method for Using the Menu Structure

The standard way of using the menu structure is explained in the previous section. Recall that when a menu is on the screen, to select a particular menu option, you must move the menu pointer to the appropriate menu option and press the ↵ key. In this section, an alternative approach for using the menu structure is presented.

To illustrate the alternative method, the process for erasing a worksheet is repeated. To place the word Lotus in cell A1:

Make	sure the cell pointer is in cell A1
Type	Lotus
Press	↵

The screen now should look like Figure 1-24.

```
A:A1: 'Lotus                                                         READY

 A      A       B       C       D       E       F       G       H
1   Lotus
2
3
4
5
6
7
8
9
10
11
12
13
14
15
16
17
18
19
20
```

Figure 1-24

To begin the process of erasing the screen:

Press /

The slash key is sometimes referred to as the **command key** because the initial set of command options appear as the main menu. The screen now should look like Figure 1-25.

```
A:A1: 'Lotus                                                          MENU
Worksheet  Range  Copy  Move  File  Print  Graph  Data  System  Quit
Global  Insert  Delete  Column  Erase  Titles  Window  Status  Page  Hide
 A      A       B       C       D       E       F       G       H
1   Lotus
2
3
4
5
6
7
8
9
10
11
12
13
14
15
16
17
18
19
20
```

Figure 1-25

Look at the words on the main menu. Notice that none of the words start with the same first character. Rather than move the menu pointer to the desired menu option, you can press the letter on the keyboard corresponding to the first letter of the word in the menu. To illustrate the use of the first letter:

Select Worksheet

by typing a **W**. The letter **W** activates the Worksheet option on the main menu. The screen should now look like Figure 1-26.

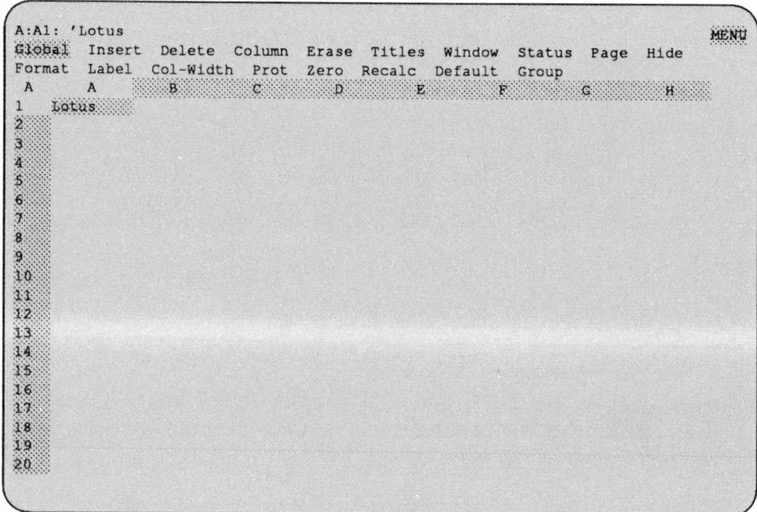

Figure 1-26

To select the menu option to erase the worksheet:

Select Erase

by typing the letter **E** to indicate that you want to select the Erase option on the menu. Your screen now should look like Figure 1-27.

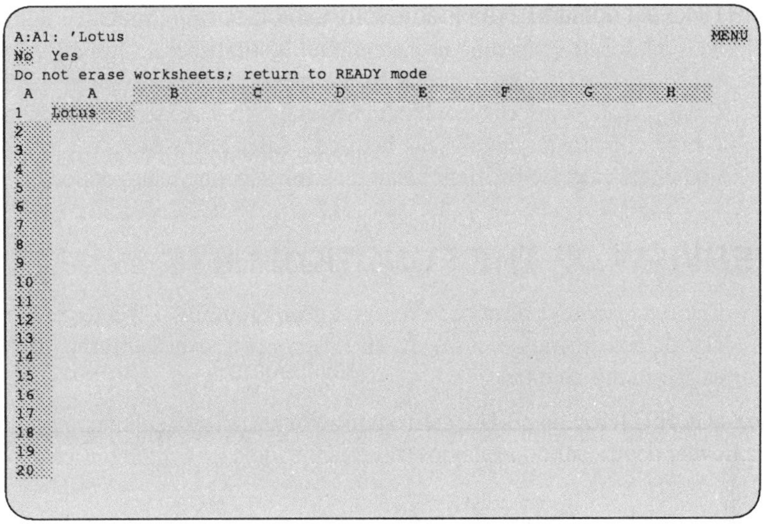

A:A1: 'Lotus
MENU
No Yes
Do not erase worksheets; return to READY mode
A A B C D E F G H
1 Lotus
2
3
4
5
6
7
8
9
10
11
12
13
14
15
16
17
18
19
20

Figure 1-27

To select the menu option Yes, and then complete the process for erasing the worksheet:

Select Yes twice

By typing **Y**, you indicate that the worksheet does in fact need to be erased. A blank screen like the one in Figure 1-28 now should appear on your screen.

A:A1:
READY
A A B C D E F G H
1
2
3
4
5
6
7
8
9
10
11
12
13
14
15
16
17
18
19
20

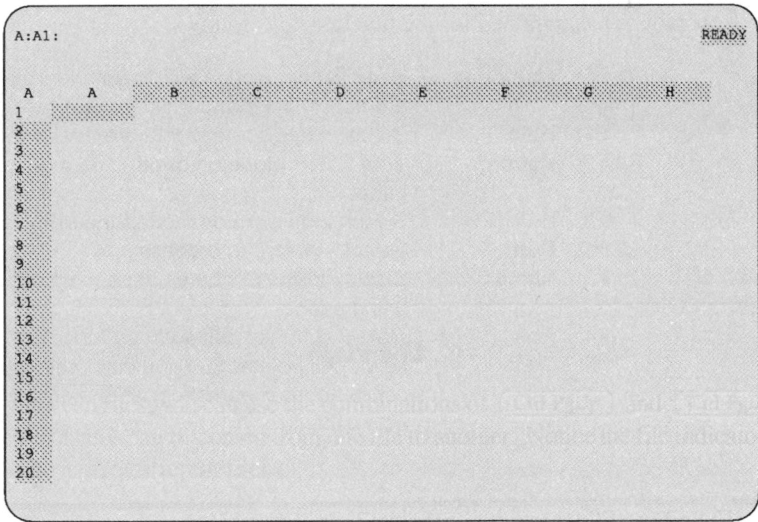

Figure 1-28

In this book, the alternative method for using the menu structure is utilized in the illustrations. This approach saves time in the creation of worksheets. Initially, it may be advantageous for you to move the menu pointer to the appropriate menu option and then press the ↵ key. Once you are comfortable with the way the menus are structured, then the use of first letters for selecting menu options can be used. After Lotus 1-2-3 is used for a short while, most individuals use the first letter approach for selecting menu options.

■ OVERVIEW OF THE FUNCTION KEYS

The function keys have been "programmed" in Lotus 1-2-3 to perform specific operations. One of these operations is the GOTO function, associated with the F5 key, that was presented earlier in this chapter.

The HELP function, located on the F1 key, allows you to access an on-line reference for 1-2-3 features on your screen. To access the Help menu:

Press F1

The Help menu appears. To get assistance on specific topics, choose one of the menu options listed on the screen. Use the arrow keys to move the pointer to the desired option. When the desired option is highlighted, press the ↵ key. To leave the Help option and return to the spreadsheet currently in use:

Press Esc

Many of the function keys will be used in succeeding chapters. A brief description of the operations programmed for the function keys follows.

Alt F1:	**Compose**	Used in conjunction with keystrokes to input characters that are not on the standard keyboard
F1:	**Help**	Display Help screens that are available in Lotus 1-2-3
Alt F2:	**Record**	Turn STEP mode on or off, or use contents of the record buffer
F2:	**Edit**	Switch to / from Edit mode for current entry
Alt F3:	**Run**	Select a macro to process
F3:	**Name**	Display menu of names depending on what command is being used
F4:	**Abs**	Make / Unmake cell address "absolute"
F5:	**GoTo**	Move cell pointer to a particular cell in the worksheet or to a cell in another worksheet or to a different cell in another active file

F6:	**Window**	Move cell pointer when "windows" appear on the screen
F7:	**Query**	Repeat most recent Data Query operation
F8:	**Table**	Repeat most recent Data Table operation
F9:	**Calc**	Recalculate worksheet values
F10:	**Graph**	Draw graph on screen using the most recent graph specifications
Alt F7	**APP 1**	Start an available add-in application assigned to the key
Alt F8	**APP 2**	Start an available add-in application assigned to the key
Alt F9	**APP 3**	Start an available add-in application assigned to the key
Alt F10	**EXTEND**	Display menu of available add-in applications

■ EXITING LOTUS 1-2-3

When you are ready to exit Lotus 1-2-3, perform the following set of operations:

Press /

Select Quit

Select Yes

Select Exit

You now should have an appropriate prompt on the screen.

SUMMARY

In this chapter, an overview of Lotus 1-2-3 is included. Lotus 1-2-3 is often used for business, government, and personal applications. Microcomputer hardware is required to process Lotus 1-2-3. Lotus 1-2-3 can be executed on IBM or IBM-compatible PCs. The actual Lotus 1-2-3 software is on a set of diskettes. The software can be loaded into the main memory by reading from a hard disk. The key items on the worksheet screen are the worksheet letter, row numbers, column letters, cells, cell pointer, current cell, cell address, control panel, mode indicator, status indicator, file indicator, and the clock indicator. The cell pointer can be moved around the worksheet by using the arrow keys, the PgDn and PgUp keys, the ⇥ key and the F5 function key. Lotus 1-2-3 has a set of menus containing various operations that can be applied to a worksheet. There are two ways to use the menu structure in 1-2-3. There are a set of function keys (F1 through F10) that are preprogrammed in Lotus 1-2-3 to perform specific operations such as moving to a specific cell in a worksheet.

KEY CONCEPTS

Cell
Cell Address
Cell Pointer
Clock Indicator
Column Letters
Command Key
Control Panel
Current Cell
End Indicator
Escape Key
File Indicator
Function Keys
GoTo F5 Key
Hardware Requirements for 1-2-3
Help F1 Key
Menu
Menu Structure
Mode Indicator
Pointer-movement Keys
Row Numbers
Software Requirements for 1-2-3
Status Indicator
Time Indicator
Worksheet
Worksheet Erase Yes
Worksheet Letter

CHAPTER ONE
EXERCISE 1

INSTRUCTIONS: Answer the following questions in the space provided.

1. Define the following terms:

   a. Worksheet Letter ______

   b. Row Numbers ______

   c. Column Letters ______

   d. Cell ______

   e. Cell Pointer ______

   f. Current Cell ______

   g. Cell Address ______

   h. Control Panel ______

   i. Mode Indicator ______

   j. Status Indicator ______

   k. File Indicator ______

   l. Clock Indicator ______

   m. Worksheet ______

   n. Worksheet Frame ______

2. Describe the standard way of using the 1-2-3 menu structure.

____

____

____

____

3. Describe the alternative method of using the 1-2-3 menu structure.

____

____

____

____

4. Describe the purpose of using the function keys F1 through F10.

____

____

____

____

CHAPTER ONE
EXERCISE 2

INSTRUCTIONS: Identify the circled and enclosed items on the worksheet in Figure 1-29.

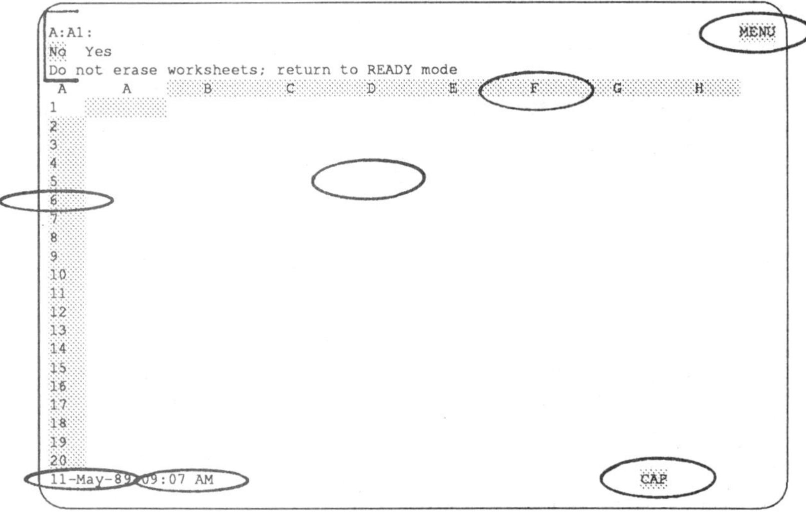

Figure 1-29

CHAPTER ONE
EXERCISE 3

INSTRUCTIONS: 1. Create the worksheet displayed in Figure 1-30.

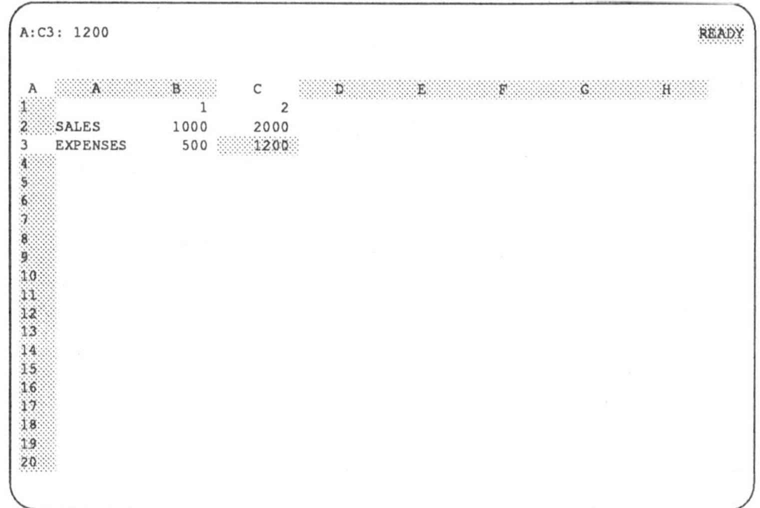

Figure 1-30

2. Erase the worksheet using the standard method.

CHAPTER ONE
EXERCISE 4

INSTRUCTIONS: 1. Create the worksheet displayed in Figure 1-31.

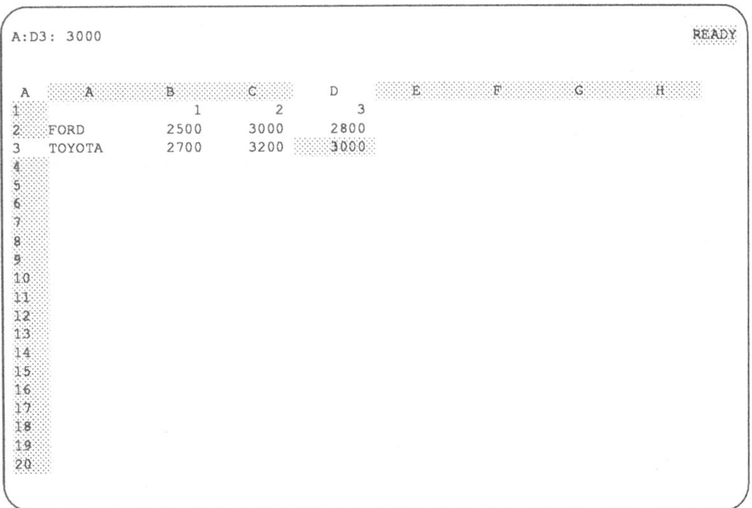

Figure 1-31

2. Erase the worksheet using the alternate method.

CHAPTER TWO

CREATING AND PRINTING A SPREADSHEET

OBJECTIVES

In this chapter, you will learn to:

- Create, print, and save a spreadsheet
- Prevent rounding errors
- Print the cell formulas used to create the spreadsheet
- Use different numeric formats
- Make a backup of the spreadsheet file

CHAPTER OVERVIEW

One of the difficulties facing you as a beginning Lotus 1-2-3 user in learning to create a spreadsheet is how to begin! Chapter 2 cites an example problem and provides a step-by-step procedure on how to solve the problem with a Lotus 1-2-3 spreadsheet. While guiding you through the process for building the spreadsheet, the exercise provides information about 1-2-3 capabilities at the time you need them. After the spreadsheet is created, you can complete subsequent exercises for printing and storing the spreadsheet on a disk.

Additional exercises address typical problems you may have as a beginning user : how to solve rounding problems, how to print the cell formulas used in the spreadsheet, how to change the numeric display of the spreadsheet, and how to make a backup copy of the spreadsheet.

■ EXAMPLE PROBLEM

The spreadsheet you create in this chapter will project sales for the last three quarters of a year based on data from the first quarter. The information from the first quarter and the projections are as follows:

	1st Quarter	Projected Increase Per Quarter
Sales	$60,000	2%
Salaries	35,000	(given below)
Rent	9,000	(constant for all periods)
Telephone	1,000	5%
Office Supplies	750	$50
Miscellaneous	1,000	3%

The salary amounts for the quarters are as follows: $35,000; $35,500; $36,200; $37,000.

To complete the problem cited above, a common procedure for creating a spreadsheet using 1-2-3 will be followed. The procedure you will use is outlined below:

Creating Labels for the Spreadsheet
Correcting Errors
Expanding the Width of a Column
Entering Numbers, Formulas, and Copying Information in a Spreadsheet
Selecting a Format for the Data
Inserting Blank Rows for Headings
Entering Headings
Inserting Blank Rows in a Spreadsheet
Entering Underlines and Double Underlines

The completed spreadsheet is displayed in Figure 2-1.

```
A:A1: [W18]                                                          READY

A            A            B         C         D         E         F         G
1                                      ABC COMPANY
2                                        BUDGET
3
4
5                       QTR1      QTR2      QTR3      QTR4   YR TOTAL
6
7  SALES              60,000    61,200    62,424    63,672    247,296
8
9  EXPENSES
10   SALARIES         35,000    35,500    36,200    37,000    143,700
11   RENT              9,000     9,000     9,000     9,000     36,000
12   TELEPHONE         1,000     1,050     1,103     1,158      4,311
13   OFFICE SUPPLIES     750       800       850       900      3,300
14   MISCELLANEOUS     1,000     1,030     1,061     1,093      4,184
15                 ---------------------------------------------
16     TOTAL EXPENSES 46,750    47,380    48,214    49,151    191,495
17                 ---------------------------------------------
18 GROSS PROFIT       13,250    13,820    14,210    14,521     55,801
19                 =============================================
20
```

Figure 2-1

■ BUILDING THE SPREADSHEET

It is assumed that the microcomputer is turned on and that Lotus 1-2-3 has been loaded. A blank spreadsheet should be displayed on your screen such as the one in Figure 2-2.

Figure 2-2

If your screen needs to be erased, use the **W**orksheet **E**rase command sequence to clear the screen.

Creating Labels for the Spreadsheet

The term **label** refers to nonnumeric data. Note that numbers can be made into labels if they are not needed in computations (refer to the section on label prefixes in Chapter 3). Labels will be entered beginning in cell A1 to describe the contents of each row. Rows will be inserted later for the worksheet titles and headings.

To make all of the labels appear in capital letters, make sure that the CAP indicator appears at the bottom of the screen. If the Caps Lock key needs to be activated:

Press Caps Lock

CAP should appear at the lower right corner of the screen. All of the alphabetic characters typed will be capital letters. (To turn the CAP indicator off, tap the Caps Lock key again to "toggle" the indicator off.)

The cell pointer should be in cell A1. If it is not, use the pointer-movement keys to move the cell pointer to cell A1.

Enter the labels in column A. The first label is SALES. To enter the label SALES in cell A1:

Type SALES

At the upper right corner of the screen, the mode indicator message changes from READY to LABEL. When data is first entered, the 1-2-3 program looks at the first character and judges the entry to be either a LABEL or a VALUE. Since the first character of SALES is nonnumeric, the entry will be considered a label. Never precede numbers that will be used in computation with spaces or other nonnumeric characters because 1-2-3 will interpret the entry as a label.

To enter the label SALES:

Press ↵

SALES has been entered in cell A1. The mode indicator changes back to READY.

To input the label EXPENSES in cell A2:

Move the cell pointer to cell A2

Type EXPENSES

Press ↵

To input the label SALARIES in cell A3:

Move the cell pointer to cell A3

To indent the label:

Press the space bar twice

Type SALARIES

Pressing the space bar is an easy way to indent labels. Note that from this point on, the instructions utilize a "short cut" for entering labels. Instead of pressing the ↵ key, press the ↓ key to enter a label and move to the next cell.

Press ↓

With one keystroke, the label SALARIES has been entered and the cell pointer has been moved to the next cell.

The cell pointer now should be in cell A4. To enter the next label:

Press the space bar twice

Type RENT

Press ↓

The cell pointer now should be in cell A5. To enter the next label:

Press the space bar twice

Type TELEPHONE

Press ↓

The cell pointer now should be in cell A6. To enter the next label:

Press the space bar twice

Type OFFICE SUPPLIES

Press ↓

The cell pointer now should be in cell A7. To enter the next label:

Press the space bar twice

Type MISCELLANEOUS

Press ↓

The cell pointer now should be in cell A8. To enter the next label:

Press the space bar four times

Type TOTAL EXPENSES

Press ↓

The cell pointer now should be in cell A9. To enter the next label:

Type GROSS PROFIT

Press ↵

The ↓ key did not have to be pressed since GROSS PROFIT is the last label on the spreadsheet. The worksheet should look like Figure 2-3. If corrections need to be made, refer to the next exercise.

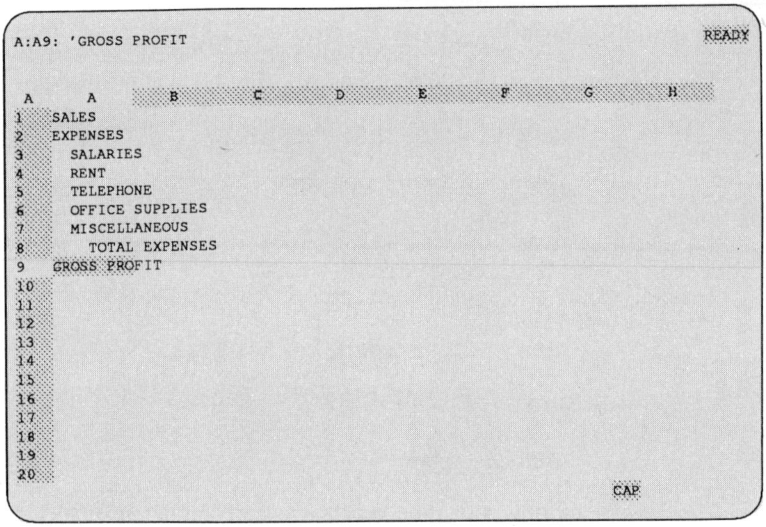

```
A:A9: 'GROSS PROFIT                                                    READY

A     A        B        C        D        E        F        G        H
1   SALES
2   EXPENSES
3     SALARIES
4     RENT
5     TELEPHONE
6     OFFICE SUPPLIES
7     MISCELLANEOUS
8       TOTAL EXPENSES
9   GROSS PROFIT
10
11
12
13
14
15
16
17
18
19
20
                                                               CAP
```

Figure 2-3

Correcting Errors

If an entry has been misspelled:

Move the cell pointer to the cell displaying the error

Type the entry correctly

Press ↵

Refer to Figure 2-4 to see an example. In Figure 2-4, the word EXPENSES in cell A2 is spelled EXPANSES. To correct the error, move the cell pointer to cell A2, type EXPENSES, and press ↵. The error is replaced with the correction.

REPLACING AN INCORRECT ENTRY

Move the cell pointer to the cell containing the error and type the desired entry . . .

```
A:A2: 'EXPANSES                                                    READY

 A     A        B       C       D       E       F       G       H
 1   SALES
 2   EXPANSES
 3     SALARIES
 4     RENT
 5     TELEPHONE
 6     OFFICE SUPPLIES
 7     MISCELLANEOUS
 8       TOTAL EXPENSES
 9   GROSS PROFIT
10
11
12
13
14
15
16
17
18
19
20
                                                        CAP
```

Figure 2-4
Part 1

then press ↵ after typing the correction to replace the previous entry (EXPANSES is changed to EXPENSES in cell A2).

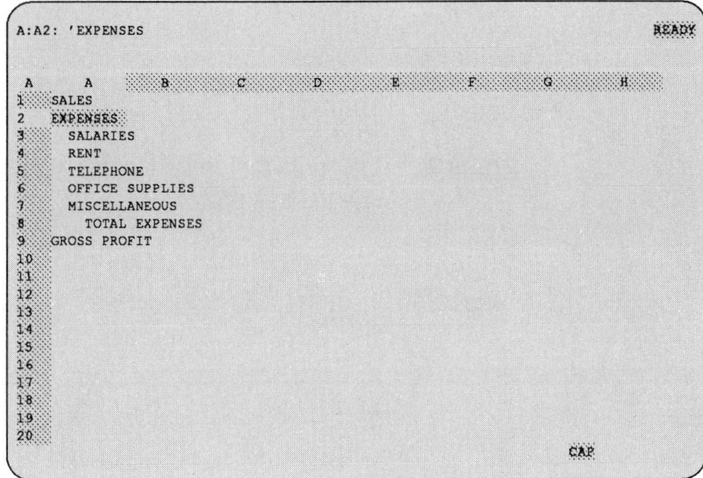

Figure 2-4
Part 2

The [Esc] key can be used to cancel data entered in the control panel if the [↵] key has not yet been pressed. The [Esc] key also may be used to exit from a 1-2-3 menu. An alternative to pressing the [Esc] key several times (for example, to exit several levels of menus) is to hold down the [Ctrl] key and press the [Break] key.

If other errors have been made, clear the screen and begin the exercise again. If necessary, refer to the previous chapter for the instructions to clear a screen. Additional ways to correct errors are discussed in Chapter 3.

Expanding the Width of a Column

Several labels extend into column B. To enter data in column B but still see all of the labels in column A, you must widen column A. To widen column A:

Move the cell pointer to the longest label in the column

In this example, move the cell pointer to cell A8, which has the indented label TOTAL EXPENSES.

Access the Lotus 1-2-3 menu and select the menu options for expanding a column:

Press /

Select Worksheet

Select Column

Select Set-Width

Press [→] until the entire label is highlighted by the cell pointer

In the control panel, the message "Enter column width (1..240): 18" should be displayed as shown in Figure 2-5.

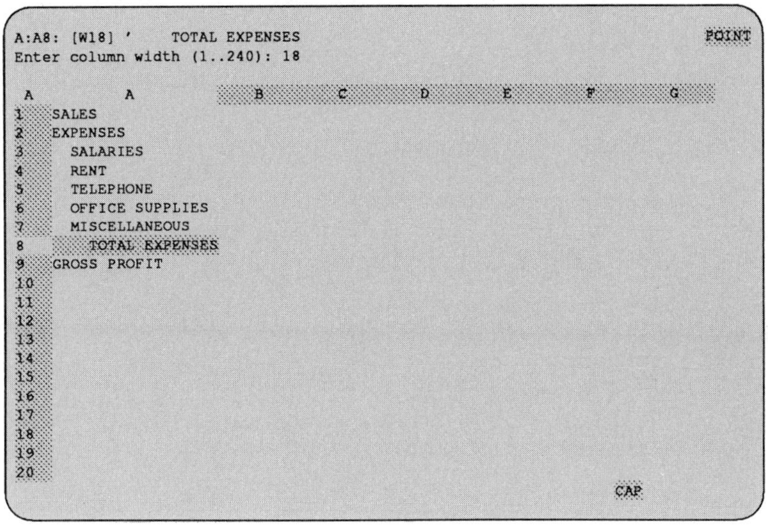

```
A:A8: [W18] '     TOTAL EXPENSES                                          POINT
Enter column width (1..240): 18

 A         A          B         C         D         E         F         G
 1  SALES
 2  EXPENSES
 3    SALARIES
 4    RENT
 5    TELEPHONE
 6    OFFICE SUPPLIES
 7    MISCELLANEOUS
 8      TOTAL EXPENSES
 9  GROSS PROFIT
10
11
12
13
14
15
16
17
18
19
20
                                                                  CAP
```

Figure 2-5

When the entire label is highlighted:

Press ↵

The column width of column A is now 18 characters (refer to Figure 2-6). Column B has shifted to the right and column H no longer appears on the screen, because column A occupies more screen space. Note that when the prompt "Enter column width (1..240):" appears, you do not have to highlight the desired width, but rather you can type the desired column width (such as 18) and press ↵. The column width can be set from 1 character to 240 characters.

When the cell pointer is in any cell in column A, the control panel will display [W18], indicating that a column width of 18 has been set for the column.

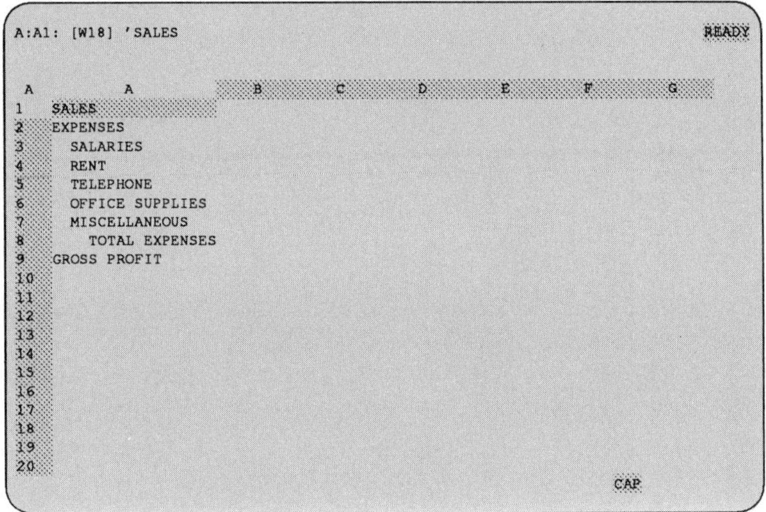

Figure 2-6

Entering the Assumptions

To enter the labels for the ASSUMPTIONS:

Move the cell pointer to cell A11

Type GROWTH RATE

Press ⊕

The cell pointer is in cell A12. To enter the next label:

Type ASSUMPTIONS

Press ⊕ twice

The cell pointer is in cell A14. To enter the next label:

Type SALES

Press ⊕

The cell pointer is in cell A15. To enter the next label:

Type TELEPHONE

Press ↓

The cell pointer is in cell A16. To enter the next label:

Type OFFICE SUPPLIES

Press ↓

The cell pointer is in cell A17. To enter the next label:

Type MISCELLANEOUS

Press ↵

Your screen should look like Figure 2-7.

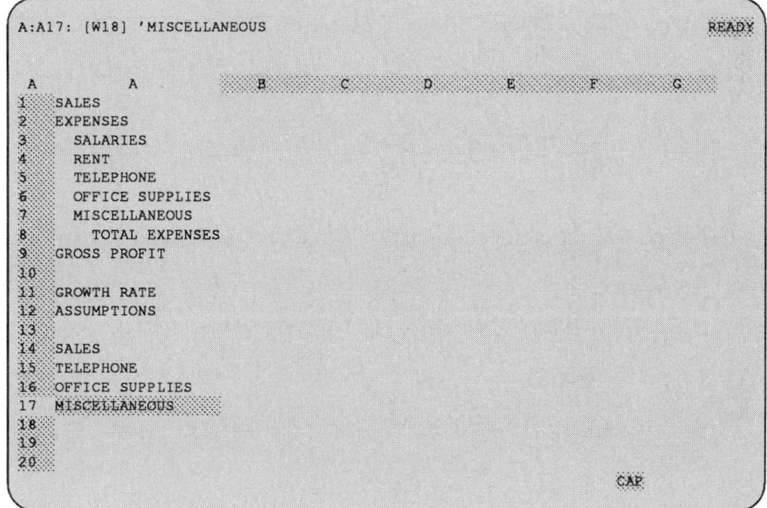

Figure 2-7

To input the assumed sales growth rate for Quarters 2, 3, and 4 in columns C, D and E:

Move the cell pointer to C14

Type 1.02

Because 1.02 is numeric, it is interpreted by Lotus 1-2-3 as a **value**. The mode indicator at the upper right corner of the screen displays the word VALUE. To enter the number:

Press ⊕→

The cell pointer is in cell D14. Notice that the ↵ key did not have to be pressed. Pressing the → key after typing 1.02 did two things: entered 1.02 and moved the cell pointer to cell D14.

Type 1.02

Press →

With the cell pointer in cell E14,

Type 1.02

Press ↵

The sales rate is not placed in column B because the rate is not needed for the first quarter.

Move the cell pointer to cell C15. To input the TELEPHONE expense rate for Quarter 2:

Type 1.05

Press ↓

The cell pointer is in cell C16. To input the OFFICE SUPPLIES expense rate for Quarter 2:

Type 50

Press ↓

The cell pointer is in cell C17. To input the MISCELLANEOUS expense rate:

Type 1.03

Press ↵

You will enter the remaining growth rate for TELEPHONE, OFFICE SUPPLIES and MISCELLANEOUS expenses using a more efficient process in the next section. Your screen should appear as Figure 2-8.

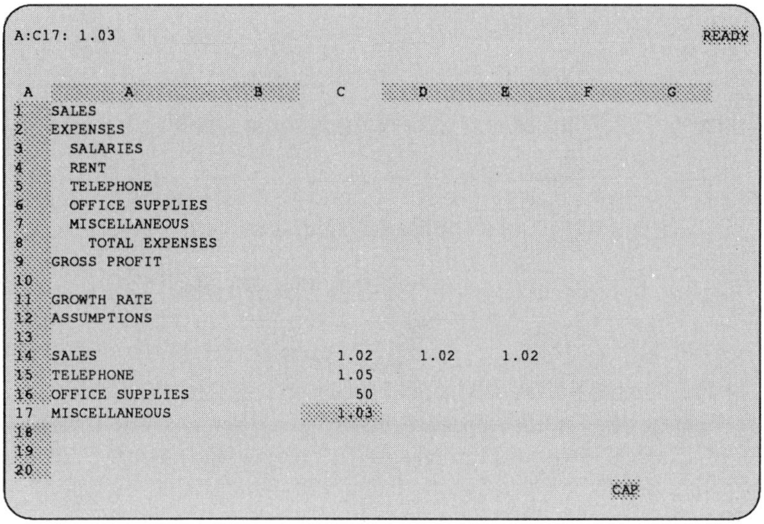

```
A:C17: 1.03                                                        READY

A           A                 B        C        D        E        F        G
1   SALES
2   EXPENSES
3     SALARIES
4     RENT
5     TELEPHONE
6     OFFICE SUPPLIES
7     MISCELLANEOUS
8       TOTAL EXPENSES
9   GROSS PROFIT
10
11  GROWTH RATE
12  ASSUMPTIONS
13
14  SALES                           1.02     1.02     1.02
15  TELEPHONE                       1.05
16  OFFICE SUPPLIES                   50
17  MISCELLANEOUS                   1.03
18
19
20
                                                              CAP
```

Figure 2-8

Entering Numbers, Formulas, and Copying Information in a Spreadsheet[1]

To enter the SALES amount for the first quarter:

Move the cell pointer to cell B1

Type 60000

Press ↵

The formula for the second quarter of SALES multiplies the SALES amount in the first quarter by 1.02 to show a 2% projected increase. First place the cell pointer in the cell where the formula will be entered.

Move the cell pointer to cell C1

[1] See the section at the end of this chapter on Using Formulas in Lotus 1-2-3 for more information on formulas.

Begin typing the formula:

Type +

Move the cell pointer to cell B1 (SALES)

Type *

The asterisk (*) is the symbol for multiplication.

Move the cell pointer to cell C14

Press ↵

The number 61200 now should appear in cell C1. With cell C1 highlighted, look at the control panel at the upper left corner of the screen. The formula +B1*C14 should be displayed. This is the formula used to compute the number 61200 (refer to Figure 2-9). A formula can be typed directly into a cell. For example, by typing +B1*C14 with the cell pointer in cell C1 and pressing the ↵ key, you would obtain the same result. It is *best* to point to the cells when creating a formula, because you tend to make fewer errors in specifying the formula.

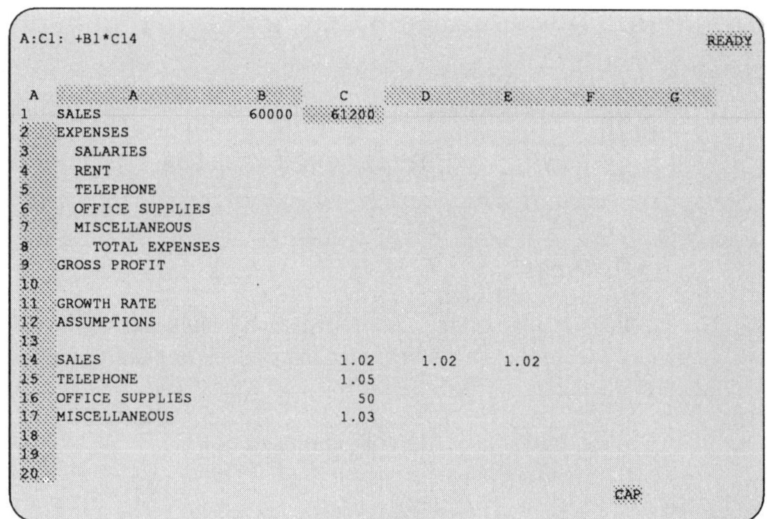

Figure 2-9

The formulas in Lotus 1-2-3 are based upon **relative cell location**. For example, the formula in cell C1, +B1*C14, is interpreted by Lotus 1-2-3 as "multiply the contents of the cell immediately to the left of the formula location by the number appearing 13 cells below the formula location." The Sales for Quarters 3 and 4 also are projected to increase from the previous quarter (the previous cell) by 2 percent. Therefore, the formula +B1*C14 can be **copied** to cells D1 and E1 and adjusted to +C1*D14 and +D1*E14, respectively.

The cell pointer should be highlighting cell C1.

Press /

Select Copy

The Copy command consists of two prompts. One prompt requires you to indicate which cells are to be copied. An easy way to do this is to highlight the cells to copy and press the ↵ key. When the ↵ key is pressed, another prompt requires you to specify the area to which the cell or cells will be copied. When the ↵ key is pressed after the second prompt, the Copy command is completed.

The first prompt asks for the "range to copy FROM." Make sure that the cell or cells to copy are highlighted. Since C1 is the cell to copy and it is already highlighted:

Press 

The second prompt asks for the "range to copy TO."

Move the cell pointer to cell D1

Type . (the period key)

Notice that "A:D1" (in the control panel) changes to "A:D1..A:D1" when the period key is pressed. The period key **anchors** the cell pointer so that more than one cell can be highlighted at a time. In this example, the cell pointer is **anchored** at cell D1 so that it can be **stretched** to cell E1.

Move the cell pointer to cell E1

Press 

The formula in cell C1 has now been copied to cells D1 and E1 (Quarters 3 and 4). Refer to Parts 1 through 5 of Figure 2-10.

USING THE COPY COMMAND - RANGE TO COPY FROM
Step 1 of Copy Procedure: Highlight the cell(s) to copy and press ⏎.

```
A:C1: +B1*C14                                                    POINT
Enter range to copy FROM: A:C1..A:C1

A          A               B        C        D        E        F        G
1   SALES                  60000    61200
2   EXPENSES
3     SALARIES
4     RENT
5     TELEPHONE
6     OFFICE SUPPLIES
7     MISCELLANEOUS
8       TOTAL EXPENSES
9   GROSS PROFIT
10
11  GROWTH RATE
12  ASSUMPTIONS
13
14  SALES                           1.02     1.02     1.02
15  TELEPHONE                       1.05
16  OFFICE SUPPLIES                   50
17  MISCELLANEOUS                   1.03
18
19
20
                                                          CAP
```

Figure 2-10
Part 1

USING THE COPY PROCEDURE - RANGE TO COPY TO
Step 2 of Copy Procedure: Highlight the first cell to which the cell(s) will be copied.

```
A:D1:                                                            POINT
Enter range to copy TO: A:D1

A          A               B        C        D        E        F        G
1   SALES                  60000    61200
2   EXPENSES
3     SALARIES
4     RENT
5     TELEPHONE
6     OFFICE SUPPLIES
7     MISCELLANEOUS
8       TOTAL EXPENSES
9   GROSS PROFIT
10
11  GROWTH RATE
12  ASSUMPTIONS
13
14  SALES                           1.02     1.02     1.02
15  TELEPHONE                       1.05
16  OFFICE SUPPLIES                   50
17  MISCELLANEOUS                   1.03
18
19
20
                                                          CAP
```

Figure 2-10
Part 2

Step 3 of Copy Procedure: When copying to more than one cell, press the period key to **anchor** the cell pointer.

```
A:D1:                                                         POINT
Enter range to copy TO: A:D1..A:D1

A           A              B         C         D        E        F        G
1   SALES                  60000     61200
2   EXPENSES
3     SALARIES
4     RENT
5     TELEPHONE
6     OFFICE SUPPLIES
7     MISCELLANEOUS
8       TOTAL EXPENSES
9   GROSS PROFIT
10
11  GROWTH RATE
12  ASSUMPTIONS
13
14  SALES                              1.02      1.02      1.02
15  TELEPHONE                          1.05
16  OFFICE SUPPLIES                      50
17  MISCELLANEOUS                      1.03
18
19
20
                                                        CAP
```

Figure 2-10
Part 3

Step 4 of Copy Procedure: **Stretch** the cell pointer from its anchored position to the rest of the area to which the cell will be copied.

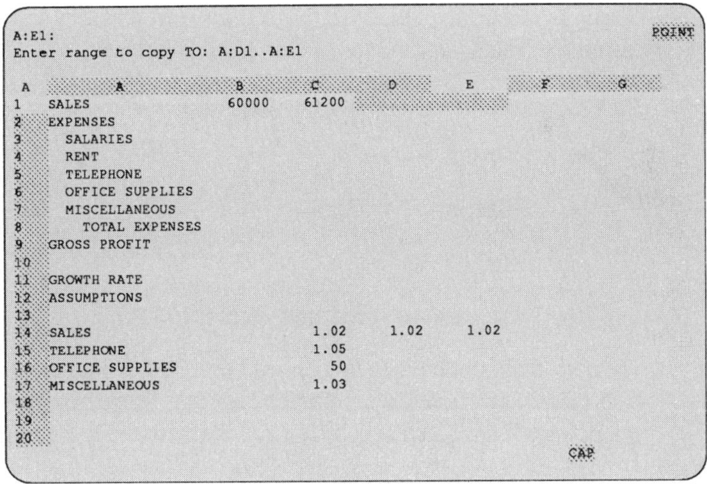

```
A:E1:                                                         POINT
Enter range to copy TO: A:D1..A:E1

A           A              B         C         D        E        F        G
1   SALES                  60000     61200
2   EXPENSES
3     SALARIES
4     RENT
5     TELEPHONE
6     OFFICE SUPPLIES
7     MISCELLANEOUS
8       TOTAL EXPENSES
9   GROSS PROFIT
10
11  GROWTH RATE
12  ASSUMPTIONS
13
14  SALES                              1.02      1.02      1.02
15  TELEPHONE                          1.05
16  OFFICE SUPPLIES                      50
17  MISCELLANEOUS                      1.03
18
19
20
                                                        CAP
```

Figure 2-10
Part 4

Step 5 of Copy Procedure: Press ↵ to copy the desired cell(s) and complete the Copy Procedure.

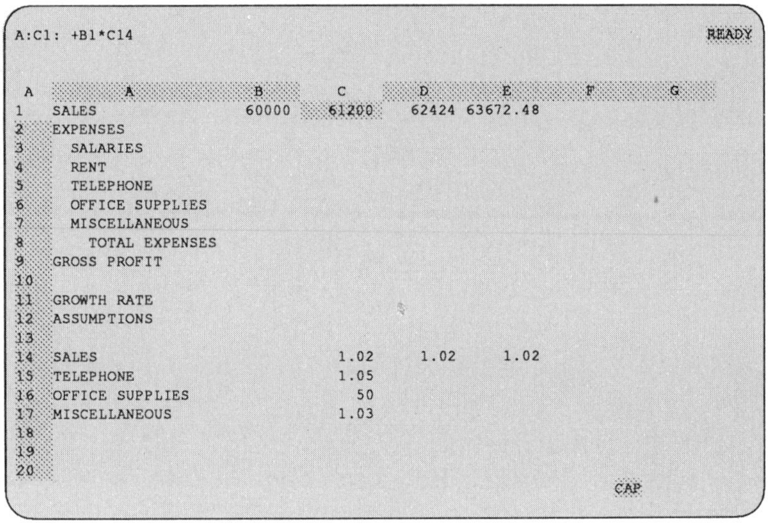

```
A:C1: +B1*C14                                                        READY

A        A                  B         C         D         E         F         G
1   SALES                  60000     61200     62424  63672.48
2   EXPENSES
3     SALARIES
4     RENT
5     TELEPHONE
6     OFFICE SUPPLIES
7     MISCELLANEOUS
8       TOTAL EXPENSES
9   GROSS PROFIT
10
11  GROWTH RATE
12  ASSUMPTIONS
13
14  SALES                               1.02      1.02      1.02
15  TELEPHONE                           1.05
16  OFFICE SUPPLIES                       50
17  MISCELLANEOUS                       1.03
18
19
20
                                                            CAP
```

Figure 2-10
Part 5

To copy the rates for TELEPHONE, OFFICE SUPPLIES and MISCELLANEOUS expense categories from Quarter 2 to Quarter 3 and Quarter 4:

Move the cell pointer to cell C15

Press /

Select Copy

When prompted for the Range to copy FROM:

Move the cell pointer to C17

The period did not have to be pressed because 1-2-3 automatically anchors the cell pointer at its current position when prompting for the "Range to copy FROM." In this example the cell pointer is anchored at cell C15 and is **stretched** to highlight cells C15 through C17.

Press ↵

When prompted for the range to copy TO:

Move the cell pointer to cell D15

Type .

The period anchors the cursor at cell D15.

Move the cell pointer to cell E17

Press ↵

The expense growth rates have now been copied and your screen should look like Figure 2-11, Part 3.

COPYING MULTIPLE FORMULAS TO A RANGE

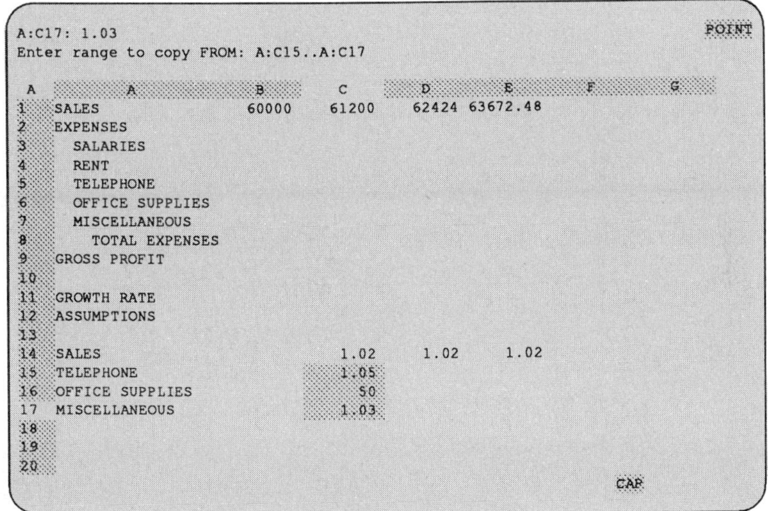

Figure 2-11
Part 1

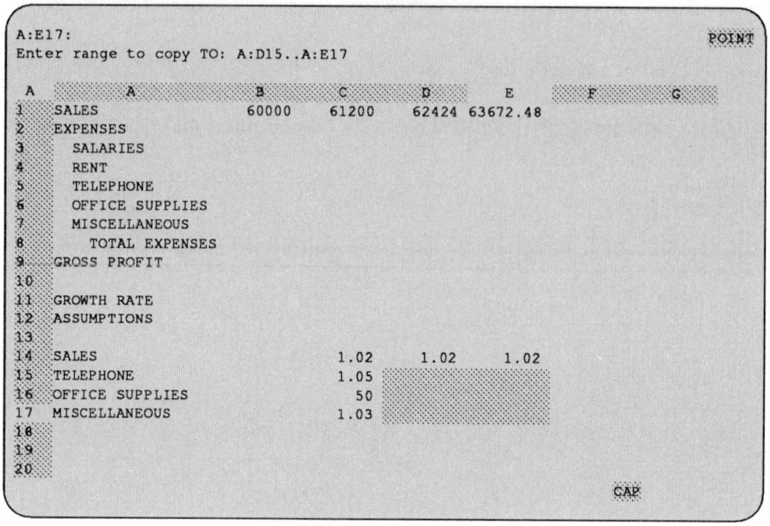

```
A:E17:                                                          POINT
Enter range to copy TO: A:D15..A:E17

 A        A                B        C        D        E        F        G
 1  SALES                60000    61200    62424 63672.48
 2  EXPENSES
 3    SALARIES
 4    RENT
 5    TELEPHONE
 6    OFFICE SUPPLIES
 7    MISCELLANEOUS
 8      TOTAL EXPENSES
 9  GROSS PROFIT
10
11  GROWTH RATE
12  ASSUMPTIONS
13
14  SALES                          1.02     1.02     1.02
15  TELEPHONE                      1.05
16  OFFICE SUPPLIES                  50
17  MISCELLANEOUS                  1.03
18
19
20
                                                      CAP
```

Figure 2-11
Part 2

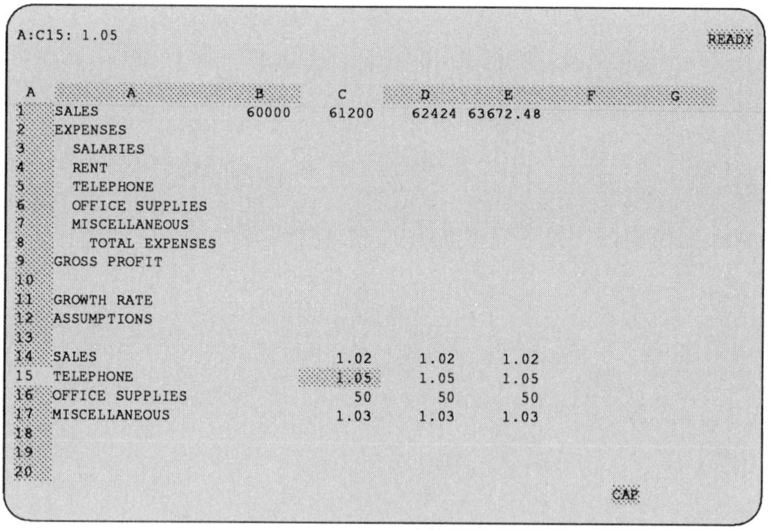

```
A:C15: 1.05                                                     READY

 A        A                B        C        D        E        F        G
 1  SALES                60000    61200    62424 63672.48
 2  EXPENSES
 3    SALARIES
 4    RENT
 5    TELEPHONE
 6    OFFICE SUPPLIES
 7    MISCELLANEOUS
 8      TOTAL EXPENSES
 9  GROSS PROFIT
10
11  GROWTH RATE
12  ASSUMPTIONS
13
14  SALES                          1.02     1.02     1.02
15  TELEPHONE                      1.05     1.05     1.05
16  OFFICE SUPPLIES                  50       50       50
17  MISCELLANEOUS                  1.03     1.03     1.03
18
19
20
                                                      CAP
```

Figure 2-11
Part 3

To input the data for SALARIES:

Move	the cell pointer to cell B3	

Make sure that the cell pointer is in the *third* row.

Type	35000	(First Quarter SALARIES)
Press	→	

The cell pointer is now in cell C3.

To enter the salary amounts for Quarters 2, 3, and 4:

Type	35500	(Second Quarter SALARIES)
Press	→	
Type	36200	(Third Quarter SALARIES)
Press	→	
Type	37000	(Fourth Quarter SALARIES)
Press	↵	

Your screen should look like Figure 2-12.

A:E3: 37000 READY

A	A	B	C	D	E	F	G
1	SALES	60000	61200	62424	63672.48		
2	EXPENSES						
3	SALARIES	35000	35500	36200	37000		
4	RENT						
5	TELEPHONE						
6	OFFICE SUPPLIES						
7	MISCELLANEOUS						
8	TOTAL EXPENSES						
9	GROSS PROFIT						
10							
11	GROWTH RATE						
12	ASSUMPTIONS						
13							
14	SALES		1.02	1.02	1.02		
15	TELEPHONE		1.05	1.05	1.05		
16	OFFICE SUPPLIES		50	50	50		
17	MISCELLANEOUS		1.03	1.03	1.03		
18							
19							
20							

CAP

Figure 2-12

To input the data for RENT:

Move the cell pointer to cell B4

Type 9000

Press ↵

You can use the Copy command to copy the 9000 from Quarter 1 to Quarters 2, 3, and 4. The cell pointer should be in cell B4. To copy the amount:

Press /

Select Copy

When prompted for the range to copy FROM, note that the cell pointer is highlighting cell B4, which is the cell to copy. To indicate that B4 is the cell to copy:

Press ↵

When prompted for the range to copy TO:

Move the cell pointer to cell C4

Type .

Move the cell pointer to cell E4

Press ↵

The number 9000 now should be copied to Quarters 2, 3, and 4. Your screen should look like Figure 2-13.

A:B4: 9000 READY

A	A	B	C	D	E	F	G
1	SALES	60000	61200	62424	63672.48		
2	EXPENSES						
3	SALARIES	35000	35500	36200	37000		
4	RENT	9000	9000	9000	9000		
5	TELEPHONE						
6	OFFICE SUPPLIES						
7	MISCELLANEOUS						
8	TOTAL EXPENSES						
9	GROSS PROFIT						
10							
11	GROWTH RATE						
12	ASSUMPTIONS						
13							
14	SALES		1.02	1.02	1.02		
15	TELEPHONE		1.05	1.05	1.05		
16	OFFICE SUPPLIES		50	50	50		
17	MISCELLANEOUS		1.03	1.03	1.03		
18							
19							
20							

CAP

Figure 2-13

To input the data for TELEPHONE expenses for the first quarter:

Move the cell pointer to cell B5

Type 1000

Press ↵

You can enter the following formula to indicate that TELEPHONE expenses will increase by 5% for the remaining quarters:

Move the cell pointer to cell C5

Type +

Move the cell pointer to cell B5 (TELEPHONE expense for Quarter 1)

Type *

Move the cell pointer to cell C15 (GROWTH RATE factor for TELEPHONE expense)

Press ↵

The number 1050 should appear in cell C5. The formula +B5*C15 is displayed in the control panel and your screen should look like Figure 2-14. The formula for Quarters 3 and 4 will be completed later in this section.

```
A:C5: +B5*C15                                                   READY

A        A                 B        C        D        E        F        G
1  SALES                 60000    61200    62424 63672.48
2  EXPENSES
3    SALARIES            35000    35500    36200    37000
4    RENT                 9000     9000     9000     9000
5    TELEPHONE            1000     1050
6    OFFICE SUPPLIES
7    MISCELLANEOUS
8      TOTAL EXPENSES
9  GROSS PROFIT
10
11 GROWTH RATE
12 ASSUMPTIONS
13
14 SALES                          1.02     1.02     1.02
15 TELEPHONE                      1.05     1.05     1.05
16 OFFICE SUPPLIES                  50       50       50
17 MISCELLANEOUS                  1.03     1.03     1.03
18
19
20
                                                         CAP
```

Figure 2-14

To input the data for OFFICE SUPPLIES expenses for the first quarter:

Move the cell pointer to cell B6

Type 750

Press ↵

OFFICE SUPPLIES expenses increase by $50 for the remaining three quarters. To enter the appropriate formula:

Move the cell pointer to cell C6

Type +

Move the cell pointer to cell B6

Type +

Move the cell pointer to C16

Press ↵

The number 800 appears in cell C6. The formula +B6+C16 is now displayed in the control panel. Your screen should look like Figure 2-15. The formulas for Quarters 3 and 4 are completed later in this exercise.

```
A:C6: +B6+C16                                                         READY

A           A                 B        C        D        E        F        G
1  SALES                    60000    61200    62424 63672.48
2  EXPENSES
3    SALARIES               35000    35500    36200    37000
4    RENT                    9000     9000     9000     9000
5    TELEPHONE               1000     1050
6    OFFICE SUPPLIES          750      800
7    MISCELLANEOUS
8      TOTAL EXPENSES
9  GROSS PROFIT
10
11 GROWTH RATE
12 ASSUMPTIONS
13
14 SALES                              1.02     1.02     1.02
15 TELEPHONE                          1.05     1.05     1.05
16 OFFICE SUPPLIES                      50       50       50
17 MISCELLANEOUS                      1.03     1.03     1.03
18
19
20                                                               CAP
```

Figure 2-15

To input the data for MISCELLANEOUS expenses for the first quarter:

Move	the cell pointer to cell B7
Type	1000
Press	↵

To enter the formula that indicates MISCELLANEOUS expenses are to increase by 3%:

Move	the cell pointer to cell C7
Type	+
Move	the cell pointer to cell B7
Type	*
Move	the cell pointer to cell C17
Press	↵

The number 1030 now appears in cell C7. The formula +B7*C17 is displayed in the control panel and your screen should look like Figure 2-16.

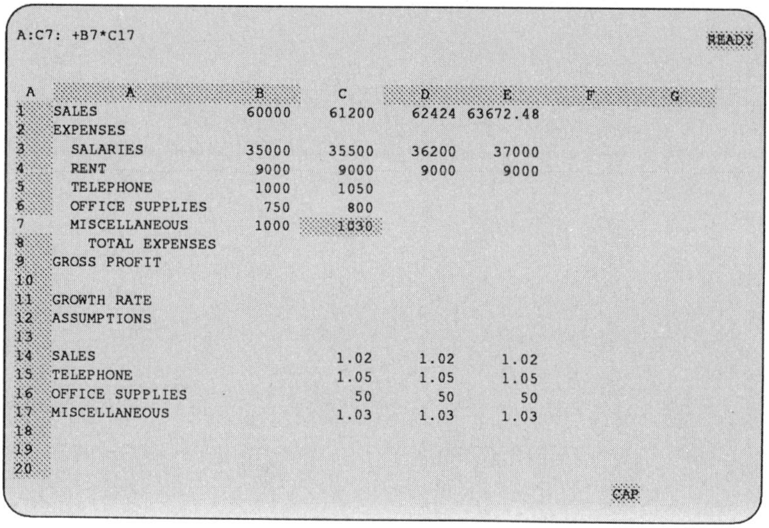

```
A:C7: +B7*C17                                                          READY

 A          A                 B        C         D        E        F        G
 1   SALES                  60000    61200     62424 63672.48
 2   EXPENSES
 3     SALARIES             35000    35500     36200    37000
 4     RENT                  9000     9000      9000     9000
 5     TELEPHONE             1000     1050
 6     OFFICE SUPPLIES        750      800
 7     MISCELLANEOUS         1000     1030
 8       TOTAL EXPENSES
 9   GROSS PROFIT
10
11   GROWTH RATE
12   ASSUMPTIONS
13
14   SALES                            1.02      1.02     1.02
15   TELEPHONE                        1.05      1.05     1.05
16   OFFICE SUPPLIES                    50        50       50
17   MISCELLANEOUS                    1.03      1.03     1.03
18
19
20
                                                              CAP
```

Figure 2-16

To copy the formulas for TELEPHONE, OFFICE SUPPLIES, and MISCELLANEOUS expenses to Quarters 3 and 4:

Move	the cell pointer to cell C5 (the formula for projecting TELEPHONE expenses)
Press	/
Select	Copy

When prompted for the Range to copy FROM:

Move	the cell pointer to cell C7 (the formula for projecting MISCELLANEOUS expenses)

The period key did not have to be pressed because 1-2-3 automatically anchors the cell pointer at its current position when prompting for the "Range to copy FROM." In this example, the cell pointer is anchored at cell C5 and is **stretched** to highlight cells C5 through C7.

Press	↵

When prompted for the range to copy TO:

Move	the cell pointer to cell D5
Type	.

The period key anchors the cursor at cell D5.

Move the cell pointer to cell E7

The screen currently displays a highlighted rectangle that covers cells D5 through E7.

Press ↵

The formulas in cells C5 through C7 that project TELEPHONE, OFFICE SUPPLIES and MISCELLANEOUS expenses, have been copied to cells D5 through E7. Your screen should look like Figure 2-17.

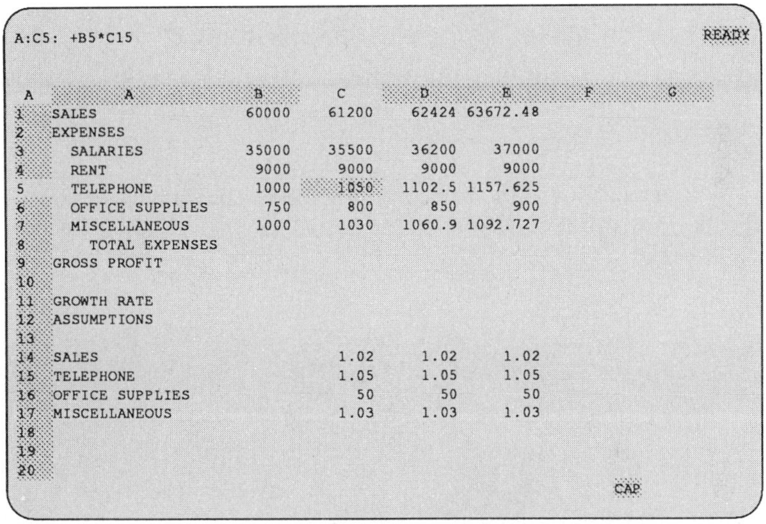

```
A:C5: +B5*C15                                                    READY

A   A                      B          C          D          E          F          G
1   SALES                  60000      61200      62424  63672.48
2   EXPENSES
3     SALARIES             35000      35500      36200      37000
4     RENT                  9000       9000       9000       9000
5     TELEPHONE             1000       1050     1102.5   1157.625
6     OFFICE SUPPLIES        750        800        850        900
7     MISCELLANEOUS         1000       1030     1060.9   1092.727
8       TOTAL EXPENSES
9   GROSS PROFIT
10
11  GROWTH RATE
12  ASSUMPTIONS
13
14  SALES                              1.02       1.02       1.02
15  TELEPHONE                          1.05       1.05       1.05
16  OFFICE SUPPLIES                      50         50         50
17  MISCELLANEOUS                      1.03       1.03       1.03
18
19
20
                                                              CAP
```

Figure 2-17

You now need to sum the quarterly values for the various items to obtain TOTAL EXPENSES for the first quarter. Lotus 1-2-3 has a special function that makes it easy to sum the expense values. The general format for the SUM function is:

@SUM(first cell..last cell)

Note that a range of cells is specified within the set of parentheses. By placing the @ character prior to the word SUM, you have indicated that you want to use the special function @SUM. The many other special functions available in 1-2-3 are discussed in Chapter 9.

To enter the @SUM function for calculating total expenses for the first quarter:

Move the cell pointer to cell B8

Type @SUM(

Move the cell pointer to cell B3 (the first item in column B to total, which is SALARIES)

Type .

The period key anchors the cell pointer in cell B3.

Move the cell pointer to cell B7

Type)

Press ↵

The number 46750 should appear in cell B8. The formula @SUM(B3..B7) is displayed in the control panel, and your screen should look like Figure 2-18.

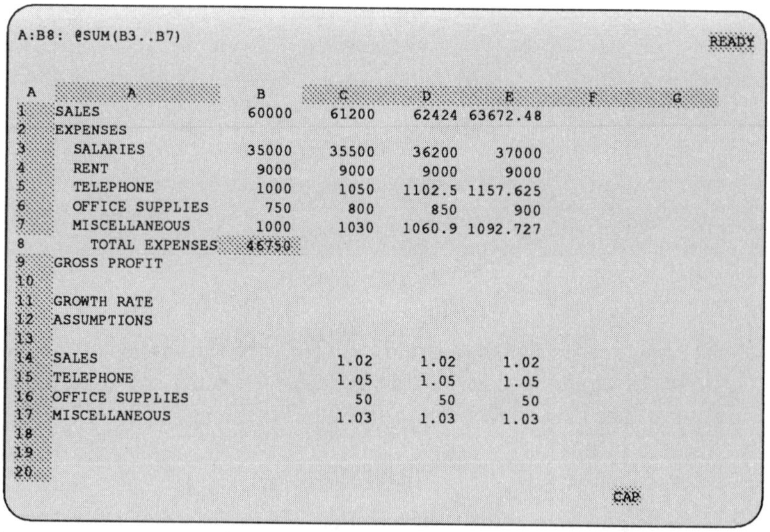

```
A:B8: @SUM(B3..B7)                                                  READY

A          A              B         C         D         E        F        G
1   SALES                60000     61200     62424  63672.48
2   EXPENSES
3     SALARIES           35000     35500     36200     37000
4     RENT                9000      9000      9000      9000
5     TELEPHONE           1000      1050    1102.5  1157.625
6     OFFICE SUPPLIES      750       800       850       900
7     MISCELLANEOUS       1000      1030    1060.9  1092.727
8       TOTAL EXPENSES   46750
9   GROSS PROFIT
10
11  GROWTH RATE
12  ASSUMPTIONS
13
14  SALES                           1.02      1.02      1.02
15  TELEPHONE                       1.05      1.05      1.05
16  OFFICE SUPPLIES                   50        50        50
17  MISCELLANEOUS                   1.03      1.03      1.03
18
19
20
                                                            CAP
```

Figure 2-18

To compute GROSS PROFIT, you must create a formula which subtracts TOTAL EXPENSES from SALES.

Move the cell pointer to cell B9

Type +

Move the cell pointer to cell B1 (SALES)

Type -

Move the cell pointer to cell B8 (TOTAL EXPENSES)

Press ↵

The number 13250 should appear in cell B9. The formula +B1-B8 is displayed in the control panel.

You can use the Copy command to copy the formulas for computing the TOTAL EXPENSES and GROSS PROFIT to the remaining three quarters.

Move the cell pointer to cell B8 (TOTAL EXPENSES)

Press /

Select Copy

When prompted for the Range to copy FROM:

Move the cell pointer to cell B9 (GROSS PROFIT)

The copy FROM range should highlight cells B8 and B9.

Press ↵

When prompted for the Range to copy TO:

Move the cell pointer to cell C8

Type .

Move the cell pointer to cell E9

A highlighted rectangle covers cells C8 through E9.

Press ↵

Your screen should look like Figure 2-19.

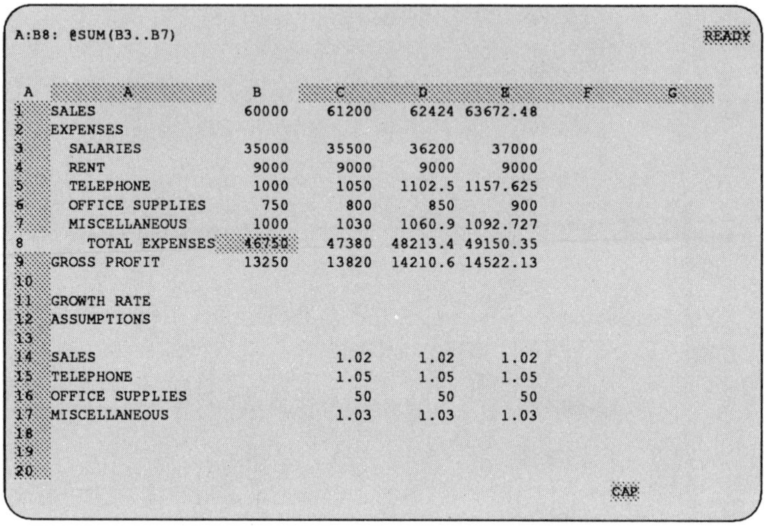

```
A:B8: @SUM(B3..B7)                                                          READY

A            A                   B        C         D        E          F         G
1   SALES                       60000    61200     62424 63672.48
2   EXPENSES
3     SALARIES                  35000    35500     36200    37000
4     RENT                       9000     9000      9000     9000
5     TELEPHONE                  1000     1050    1102.5 1157.625
6     OFFICE SUPPLIES             750      800       850      900
7     MISCELLANEOUS              1000     1030    1060.9 1092.727
8       TOTAL EXPENSES          46750    47380   48213.4 49150.35
9   GROSS PROFIT                13250    13820   14210.6 14522.13
10
11  GROWTH RATE
12  ASSUMPTIONS
13
14  SALES                                 1.02      1.02     1.02
15  TELEPHONE                             1.05      1.05     1.05
16  OFFICE SUPPLIES                         50        50       50
17  MISCELLANEOUS                         1.03      1.03     1.03
18
19
20                                                                    CAP
```

Figure 2-19

To compute the total SALES for the year:

Move the cell pointer to cell F1

Type @SUM(

Move the cell pointer to cell B1

Type .

Move the cell pointer to cell E1

Type)

Press ↵

The number 247296.5 appears in cell F1. The formula @SUM(B1..E1) appears in the control panel.

To copy the @SUM(B1..E1) formula to the appropriate rows below the SALES row:

Press /

Select Copy

When prompted for the range to copy FROM:

Press ↵

Since F1 was already highlighted, the cell pointer did not have to be moved.

When prompted for the range to copy TO:

Move	the cell pointer to cell F3
Type	.
Move	the cell pointer to cell F9
Press	↵

The formula @SUM(B1..E1) has been copied from cells F1 to cells F3 through F9. Your screen should look like Figure 2-20.

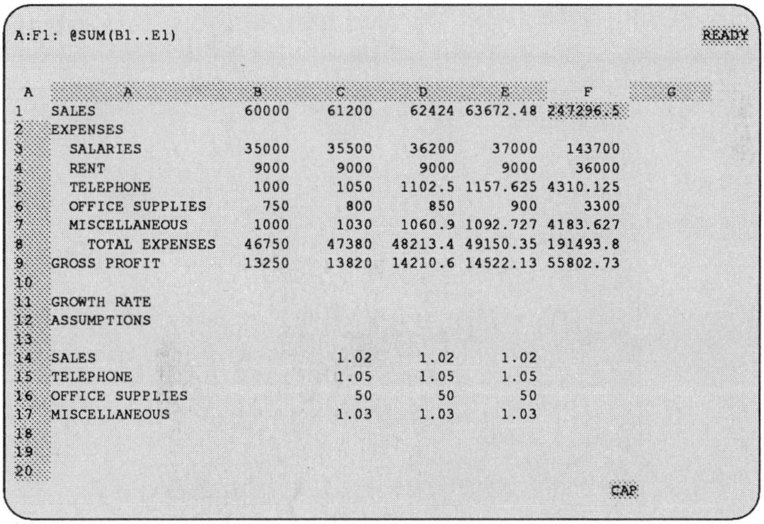

```
A:F1: @SUM(B1..E1)                                                    READY

A         A                B        C         D        E        F        G
1   SALES               60000    61200     62424 63672.48 247296.5
2   EXPENSES
3     SALARIES          35000    35500     36200    37000   143700
4     RENT               9000     9000      9000     9000    36000
5     TELEPHONE          1000     1050    1102.5 1157.625 4310.125
6     OFFICE SUPPLIES     750      800       850      900     3300
7     MISCELLANEOUS      1000     1030    1060.9 1092.727 4183.627
8       TOTAL EXPENSES  46750    47380   48213.4 49150.35 191493.8
9   GROSS PROFIT        13250    13820   14210.6 14522.13 55802.73
10
11  GROWTH RATE
12  ASSUMPTIONS
13
14  SALES                         1.02      1.02     1.02
15  TELEPHONE                     1.05      1.05     1.05
16  OFFICE SUPPLIES                 50        50       50
17  MISCELLANEOUS                 1.03      1.03     1.03
18
19
20
                                                              CAP
```

Figure 2-20

Selecting a Format for the Data

To choose a numeric format (commas, dollar signs, the number of decimal places, and so forth) for the worksheet:

Press	/
Select	Worksheet
Select	Global

Select Format

Select , (comma)

Global means that the selected format will be used as the default for the spreadsheet, unless another numeric format is specified. The , represents the comma format.

When prompted for the number of decimal places:

Type 0

Press ↵

Be sure to type the number "zero" and not the letter "O". Your screen should look like Figure 2-21.

A:F1: @SUM(B1..E1) READY

A	A	B	C	D	E	F	G
1	SALES	60,000	61,200	62,424	63672.48	247,296	
2	EXPENSES						
3	SALARIES	35,000	35,500	36,200	37,000	143,700	
4	RENT	9,000	9,000	9,000	9,000	36,000	
5	TELEPHONE	1,000	1,050	1,103	1,158	4,310	
6	OFFICE SUPPLIES	750	800	850	900	3,300	
7	MISCELLANEOUS	1,000	1,030	1,061	1,093	4,184	
8	TOTAL EXPENSES	46,750	47,380	48,213	49,150	191,494	
9	GROSS PROFIT	13,250	13,820	14,211	14,522	55,803	
10							
11	GROWTH RATE						
12	ASSUMPTIONS						
13							
14	SALES		1	1	1		
15	TELEPHONE		1	1	1		
16	OFFICE SUPPLIES		50	50	50		
17	MISCELLANEOUS		1	1	1		
18							
19							
20							

CAP

Figure 2-21

Notice that the various expense rates no longer have decimal numbers on the screen, because the previous format command indicated that the format for all numbers does not include any characters to the right of the decimal point.

To have the proper format for the growth rate assumption values, you must format a range of cells using the Fixed format menu option.

Move the cell pointer to cell C14

Press /

Select Range

Select Format

Select Fixed

Press ↵ to accept 2 decimal places

Move the cell pointer to cell E17 to highlight the range of cells to be formatted

Press ↵

Your screen should look like Figure 2-22.

```
A:C14: (F2) 1.02                                                      READY

A         A                B        C        D        E        F        G
1   SALES                60,000   61,200   62,424   63,672  247,296
2   EXPENSES
3     SALARIES           35,000   35,500   36,200   37,000  143,700
4     RENT                9,000    9,000    9,000    9,000   36,000
5     TELEPHONE           1,000    1,050    1,103    1,158    4,310
6     OFFICE SUPPLIES       750      800      850      900    3,300
7     MISCELLANEOUS       1,000    1,030    1,061    1,093    4,184
8       TOTAL EXPENSES   46,750   47,380   48,213   49,150  191,494
9   GROSS PROFIT         13,250   13,820   14,211   14,522   55,803
10
11  GROWTH RATE
12  ASSUMPTIONS
13
14  SALES                           1.02     1.02     1.02
15  TELEPHONE                       1.05     1.05     1.05
16  OFFICE SUPPLIES                50.00    50.00    50.00
17  MISCELLANEOUS                   1.03     1.03     1.03
18
19
20                                                         CAP
```

Figure 2-22

Notice that rounding errors occur (e.g., Sales of 247,296 minus Total Expenses of 191,494 should equal 55,802 rather than 55,803). The rounding error occurred because the numbers are *formatted* to *show* 0 decimal places on your screen, but the *values* in the cells are not truly *rounded* to 0 decimal places. Rounding errors are resolved later in this chapter.

Inserting Blank Rows for a Title and Column Headings

To insert six blank rows at the top of the spreadsheet:

Move the cell pointer to cell A1

Press /

Select Worksheet

Select Insert

Select Row

When prompted for the insert range:

Move the cell pointer to cell A6

The period key did not have to be pressed because the **W**orksheet **I**nsert **R**ow command automatically anchors the cell pointer at its current position. The insert range is from rows A1 through A6, or rows 1 through 6. Note that the entire row does not have to be highlighted. Also notice that the cell pointer does not have to be in column A to insert rows; it can be in any column.

Press ↵

Your screen should look like Figure 2-23.

```
A:A1: [W18]                                                              READY

A        A                B         C         D         E         F         G
1
2
3
4
5
6
7  SALES                60,000    61,200    62,424    63,672   247,296
8  EXPENSES
9    SALARIES           35,000    35,500    36,200    37,000   143,700
10   RENT                9,000     9,000     9,000     9,000    36,000
11   TELEPHONE           1,000     1,050     1,103     1,158     4,310
12   OFFICE SUPPLIES       750       800       850       900     3,300
13   MISCELLANEOUS       1,000     1,030     1,061     1,093     4,184
14     TOTAL EXPENSES   46,750    47,380    48,213    49,150   191,494
15 GROSS PROFIT         13,250    13,820    14,211    14,522    55,803
16
17 GROWTH RATE
18 ASSUMPTIONS
19
20 SALES                           1.02      1.02      1.02
                                                                   CAP
```

Figure 2-23

The worksheet formulas and values remain correct and are **adjusted** to the new location. For example, the formula for Quarter 2's SALES have been changed from +B1*C14 to +B7*C20 in C7.

Entering the Spreadsheet Title and Column Headings

When entering the spreadsheet title lines, you must determine where the spreadsheet title will be centered correctly. To input the first title line for this example:

Move the cell pointer to cell C1

Press the space bar five times

Type ABC COMPANY

Press ↵

To enter the second title line:

Move the cell pointer to cell C2

Press the space bar seven times

Type BUDGET

Press ↵

To enter the column heading for the first quarter:

Move the cell pointer to cell B5

Type ^QTR1

Press ↵

The ^ mark causes the label to be **centered** within the column; a **double quote mark** before the heading would cause the label to be **right-justified** in the column.

To enter the column headings for the last three quarters:

Press →

Type ^QTR2

Press →

Type ^QTR3

Press →

Type ^QTR4

Press →

To enter the column heading for the total column:

Type YR TOTAL

Press ↵

Your screen should look like Figure 2-24.

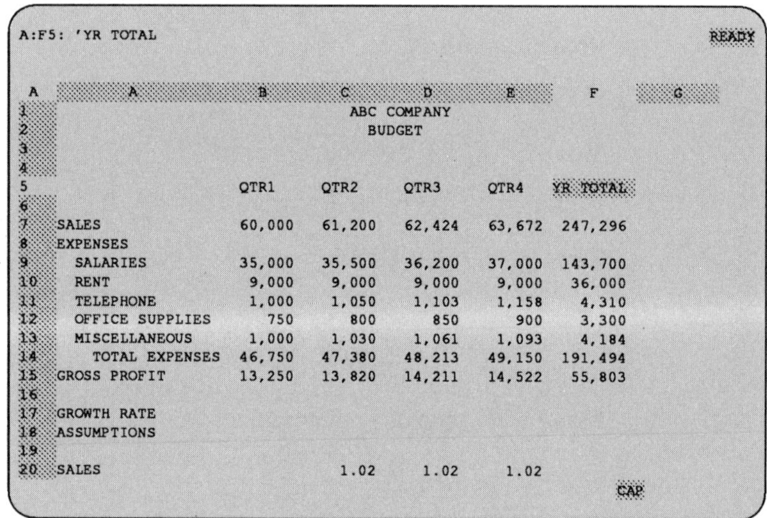

A:F5: 'YR TOTAL READY

A	A	B	C	D	E	F	G
1				ABC COMPANY			
2				BUDGET			
3							
4							
5		QTR1	QTR2	QTR3	QTR4	YR TOTAL	
6							
7	SALES	60,000	61,200	62,424	63,672	247,296	
8	EXPENSES						
9	SALARIES	35,000	35,500	36,200	37,000	143,700	
10	RENT	9,000	9,000	9,000	9,000	36,000	
11	TELEPHONE	1,000	1,050	1,103	1,158	4,310	
12	OFFICE SUPPLIES	750	800	850	900	3,300	
13	MISCELLANEOUS	1,000	1,030	1,061	1,093	4,184	
14	TOTAL EXPENSES	46,750	47,380	48,213	49,150	191,494	
15	GROSS PROFIT	13,250	13,820	14,211	14,522	55,803	
16							
17	GROWTH RATE						
18	ASSUMPTIONS						
19							
20	SALES		1.02	1.02	1.02		

CAP

Figure 2-24

Inserting Blank Rows in a Spreadsheet

To insert a blank row between SALES and EXPENSES:

Move the cell pointer to cell A8 (EXPENSES)

Press /

Select Worksheet

Select Insert

Select Row

When prompted for the row to insert:

Press ↵

Since the cell pointer was already highlighting cell A8, pressing the ↵ key at this point caused one row to be inserted at cell A8. Your screen should look like Figure 2-25.

A:A8: [W18] READY

A	A	B	C	D	E	F	G
1			ABC COMPANY				
2			BUDGET				
3							
4							
5		QTR1	QTR2	QTR3	QTR4	YR TOTAL	
6							
7	SALES	60,000	61,200	62,424	63,672	247,296	
8							
9	EXPENSES						
10	SALARIES	35,000	35,500	36,200	37,000	143,700	
11	RENT	9,000	9,000	9,000	9,000	36,000	
12	TELEPHONE	1,000	1,050	1,103	1,158	4,310	
13	OFFICE SUPPLIES	750	800	850	900	3,300	
14	MISCELLANEOUS	1,000	1,030	1,061	1,093	4,184	
15	TOTAL EXPENSES	46,750	47,380	48,213	49,150	191,494	
16	GROSS PROFIT	13,250	13,820	14,211	14,522	55,803	
17							
18	GROWTH RATE						
19	ASSUMPTIONS						
20							

CAP

Figure 2-25

To insert a blank row between MISCELLANEOUS and TOTAL EXPENSES:

Move the cell pointer to cell A15 (TOTAL EXPENSES)

Press /

Select Worksheet

Select Insert

Select Row

When prompted for the row to insert:

Press ↵

Pressing the ↵ key at this point causes one row to be inserted at cell A15. A blank row can be inserted when the cell pointer is in another column other than column A.

To insert a blank row between TOTAL EXPENSES and GROSS PROFIT:

Move	the cell pointer to cell C17
Press	/
Select	Worksheet
Select	Insert
Select	Row

When prompted for the row to insert:

Press ↵

Pressing the ↵ key at this point caused one row to be inserted at cell C17. Your screen should look like Figure 2-26.

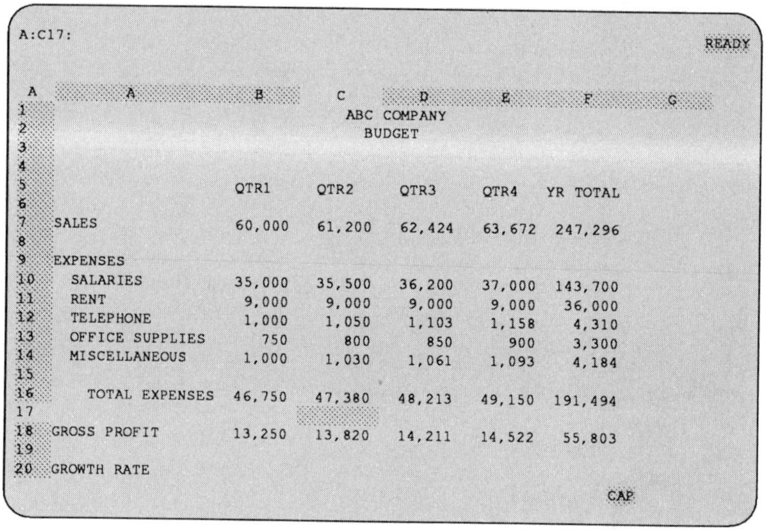

```
A:C17:                                                            READY

A            A               B       C        D        E        F        G
1                                   ABC COMPANY
2                                     BUDGET
3
4
5                          QTR1     QTR2     QTR3     QTR4   YR TOTAL
6
7   SALES                 60,000   61,200   62,424   63,672   247,296
8
9   EXPENSES
10    SALARIES            35,000   35,500   36,200   37,000   143,700
11    RENT                 9,000    9,000    9,000    9,000    36,000
12    TELEPHONE            1,000    1,050    1,103    1,158     4,310
13    OFFICE SUPPLIES        750      800      850      900     3,300
14    MISCELLANEOUS        1,000    1,030    1,061    1,093     4,184
15
16      TOTAL EXPENSES    46,750   47,380   48,213   49,150   191,494
17
18  GROSS PROFIT          13,250   13,820   14,211   14,522    55,803
19
20  GROWTH RATE
                                                          CAP
```

Figure 2-26

Entering Underlines and Double Underlines

To input subtotal underlines for the TOTAL EXPENSES:

Move	the cell pointer to cell B15
Type	\
Type	-
Press	↵

By pressing \ once and then a minus sign or dash, a subtotal line has been created. The \ indicates you desire to fill a cell with whatever character(s) follow the \ .

To copy the subtotal underlines to the rest of the current row:

Press /

Select Copy

When prompted for the range to copy FROM:

Press ↵

By pressing the ↵ key, cell B15 is indicated as the cell to copy.

When prompted for the range to copy TO:

Move the cell pointer to cell C15

Type .

Move the cell pointer to cell F15

Press ↵

Your screen should look like Figure 2-27.

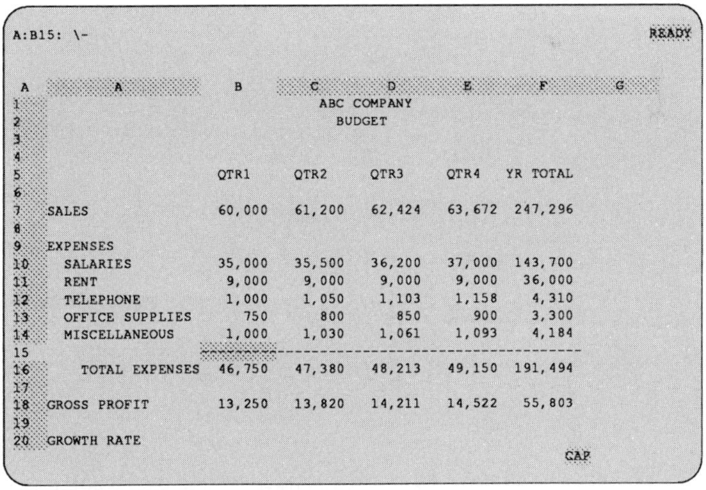

```
A:B15: \-                                                              READY

A   A                      B          C          D          E          F          G
1                                          ABC COMPANY
2                                             BUDGET
3
4
5                          QTR1       QTR2       QTR3       QTR4    YR TOTAL
6
7   SALES                  60,000     61,200     62,424     63,672   247,296
8
9   EXPENSES
10    SALARIES             35,000     35,500     36,200     37,000   143,700
11    RENT                  9,000      9,000      9,000      9,000    36,000
12    TELEPHONE             1,000      1,050      1,103      1,158     4,310
13    OFFICE SUPPLIES         750        800        850        900     3,300
14    MISCELLANEOUS         1,000      1,030      1,061      1,093     4,184
15                     ----------------------------------------------------
16       TOTAL EXPENSES    46,750     47,380     48,213     49,150   191,494
17
18  GROSS PROFIT           13,250     13,820     14,211     14,522    55,803
19
20  GROWTH RATE
                                                                   CAP
```

Figure 2-27

To copy row 15's subtotal underlines to row 17, make sure the cell pointer is in cell B15 and then:

Press /

Select Copy

When prompted for the range to copy FROM:

Move the cell pointer to cell F15

Cells B15 through F15 should now be highlighted.

Press ↵

When prompted for the range to copy TO:

Move the cell pointer to cell B17

Press ↵

Notice that to copy a range of cells, it is not necessary to highlight the entire area to which the cells are to be copied.

To input the double underlines in cell B19:

Move the cell pointer to cell B19

Type \

Type =

Press ↵

To copy the double underlines to the rest of row 19:

Press /

Select Copy

When prompted for the range to copy FROM:

Press ↵

By pressing the ↵ key, cell B19 is indicated as the cell to copy.

When prompted for the range to copy TO:

Move the cell pointer to cell C19

Type .

Move the cell pointer to cell F19

Press ↵

Your screen should look like Figure 2-28.

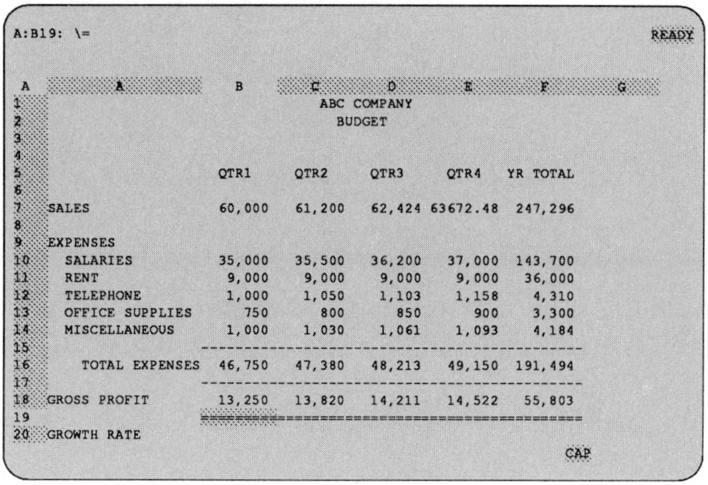

```
A:B19: \=                                                         READY

A          A            B        C        D        E         F        G
1                                  ABC COMPANY
2                                     BUDGET
3
4
5                        QTR1     QTR2     QTR3     QTR4   YR TOTAL
6
7   SALES              60,000   61,200   62,424 63672.48   247,296
8
9   EXPENSES
10    SALARIES         35,000   35,500   36,200   37,000   143,700
11    RENT              9,000    9,000    9,000    9,000    36,000
12    TELEPHONE         1,000    1,050    1,103    1,158     4,310
13    OFFICE SUPPLIES     750      800      850      900     3,300
14    MISCELLANEOUS     1,000    1,030    1,061    1,093     4,184
15                   ---------------------------------------------
16      TOTAL EXPENSES 46,750   47,380   48,213   49,150   191,494
17                   ---------------------------------------------
18  GROSS PROFIT       13,250   13,820   14,211   14,522    55,803
19                   =============================================
20  GROWTH RATE
                                                             CAP
```

Figure 2-28

To place two blank lines between the row with the double underlines and the ASSUMPTIONS:

Move the cell pointer to cell A20

Press /

Select Worksheet

Select Insert

Select Row

Press ↓ one time

Press ↵

Your screen should look like Figure 2-29.

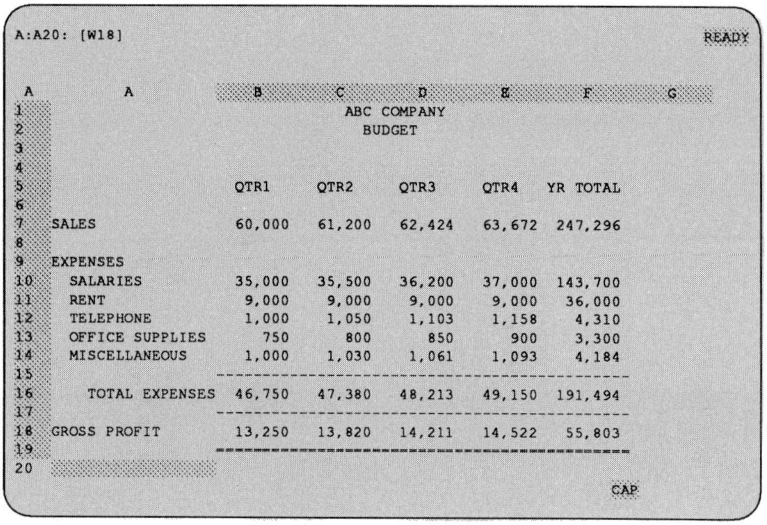

```
A:A20: [W18]                                                           READY

A    A                  B        C        D        E        F         G
1                                    ABC COMPANY
2                                      BUDGET
3
4
5                       QTR1     QTR2     QTR3     QTR4   YR TOTAL
6
7  SALES              60,000   61,200   62,424   63,672   247,296
8
9  EXPENSES
10   SALARIES         35,000   35,500   36,200   37,000   143,700
11   RENT              9,000    9,000    9,000    9,000    36,000
12   TELEPHONE         1,000    1,050    1,103    1,158     4,310
13   OFFICE SUPPLIES     750      800      850      900     3,300
14   MISCELLANEOUS     1,000    1,030    1,061    1,093     4,184
15                  ---------------------------------------------
16     TOTAL EXPENSES 46,750   47,380   48,213   49,150   191,494
17                  ---------------------------------------------
18 GROSS PROFIT       13,250   13,820   14,211   14,522    55,803
19                  =============================================
20
                                                              CAP
```

Figure 2-29

■ SAVING AND NAMING THE SPREADSHEET

Pressing the (Home) key prior to saving a spreadsheet to a file is an optional step. If the (Home) key is pressed, the file will be saved with the cell pointer located in cell A1. When the file is later retrieved, the cell pointer will appear in cell A1.

Press /

Select File

Select Save

When prompted for the file name:

Type BUDGET

Press ↵

File names can be a maximum of eight characters long. Acceptable characters are letters of the alphabet. numbers, and the underline (_) character. (The underline character takes up one space; it cannot be used to underline other characters in the file name.) Do not include **spaces** or **periods** in the file name. The file named BUDGET contains the spreadsheet that was created.

Note that you may set up 1-2-3 to save files on a separate disk or directory on hard disk or a floppy disk drive.

CORRECTING THE ROUNDING ERROR

The worksheet that was just completed did not **foot** or balance correctly. The result in the YR TOTAL column is shown below:

Sales	$247,296	
-Total Expenses	191,494	
Gross Profit	$ 55,803	(does not foot correctly)

When multiplication, division, or exponents are used in a formula, the @ROUND function can be used to round a number to a specified number of decimal places. Otherwise, Lotus uses the "hidden" decimal places in computation, resulting in rounding errors. The @ROUND function will be explained in more detail later in this chapter. For now, the following steps can be used for rounding the appropriate formulas where necessary in this example.

Note that you should *immediately* use the @ROUND function when creating formulas rather than going back to edit. This example was done differently to show the results of *not* using the @ROUND function.

The three sets of formulas for SALES, TELEPHONE EXPENSES, and MISCELLANEOUS expenses need to be edited to use the @ROUND function because the three lines contain multiplication.

Note that the only way rounding errors can occur in a spreadsheet is through multiplying, dividing, exponentiation or through the use of special functions such as the square root.

The @ROUND function's format is as follows:

```
@ROUND(number or formula,number of digits to round to)
```

SALES will be the first formula to be edited. The formula is +B7*C25 for the SALES projection for the Second Quarter. To round the SALES projections to 0 decimal places:

Move the cell pointer to cell C7

Type @ROUND (

Move the cell pointer to cell B7

Type *

Move the cell pointer to cell C25

Type ,

To indicate zero decimal places:

Type 0

Type)

Press ↵

The formula @ROUND(B7*C25,0) is now in cell C7. The formula "B7*C25" is rounded to 0 decimal places. Your screen should look like Figure 2-30.

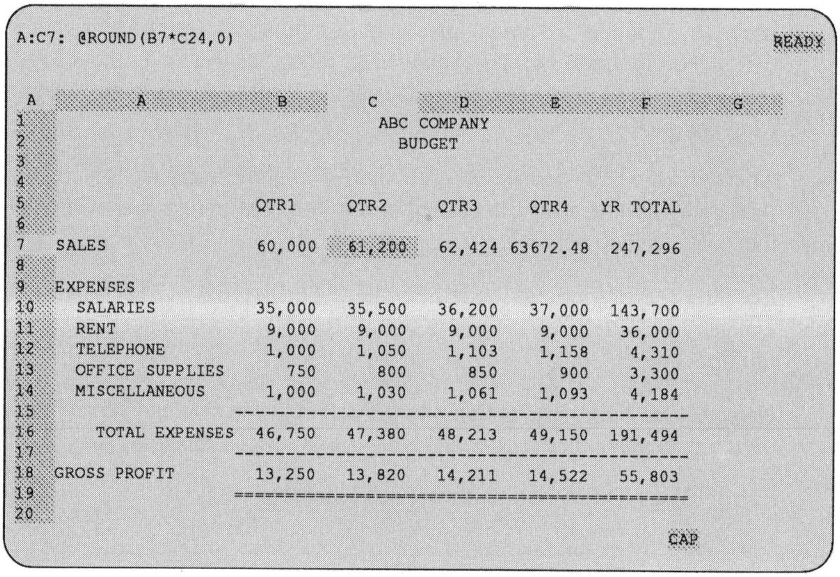

```
A:C7: @ROUND(B7*C24,0)                                                    READY

 A   A                       B          C          D          E          F          G
 1                                     ABC COMPANY
 2                                       BUDGET
 3
 4
 5                          QTR1       QTR2       QTR3       QTR4   YR TOTAL
 6
 7  SALES                 60,000     61,200     62,424   63672.48    247,296
 8
 9  EXPENSES
10    SALARIES            35,000     35,500     36,200     37,000    143,700
11    RENT                 9,000      9,000      9,000      9,000     36,000
12    TELEPHONE            1,000      1,050      1,103      1,158      4,310
13    OFFICE SUPPLIES        750        800        850        900      3,300
14    MISCELLANEOUS        1,000      1,030      1,061      1,093      4,184
15                   ---------------------------------------------------------
16      TOTAL EXPENSES    46,750     47,380     48,213     49,150    191,494
17                   ---------------------------------------------------------
18  GROSS PROFIT          13,250     13,820     14,211     14,522     55,803
19                   =========================================================
20
                                                                  CAP
```

Figure 2-30

To copy the rounded formula to the remaining quarters:

Press /

Select Copy

When prompted for the range to copy FROM:

Press ↵

By pressing the ↵ key, C7 was selected as the cell to copy.

When prompted for the range to copy TO:

Move the cell pointer to cell D7

Type .

Move the cell pointer to cell E7

Press ↵

The projections for SALES are now rounded to 0 decimal places.

The second set of formulas you need to round is for TELEPHONE expenses. The formula for TELEPHONE expenses in the Second Quarter is +B12*C26. To round the TELEPHONE expenses to 0 decimal places:

Move the cell pointer to cell C12

Rather than retyping the formula, use a shortcut to edit the current formula.

Press the F2 key

The F2 function key is often referred to as the "Edit" key when using 1-2-3.

Press the ← key until the cell pointer is under the + sign at the front of the formula—an alternative is to press the Home key to move to the beginning of the formula

Type @ROUND (

Press the Del key one time to delete the + sign if desired

Press the → key to move the cell pointer to the end of the formula—an alternative is to press the End key to move to the end of the formula.

Type ,0)

Press ↵

The formula @ROUND(B12*C26,0) is now in cell C12.

To copy the formula to the remaining quarters:

Press /

Select Copy

When prompted for the range to copy FROM:

Press ↵

By pressing the ↵ key, you selected cell C12 as the cell to copy.

When prompted for the range to copy TO:

Move the cell pointer to cell D12

Type .

Move the cell pointer to cell E12

Press ↵

TELEPHONE expenses are now rounded to 0 decimal places.

The next set of formulas to be rounded is for MISCELLANEOUS expenses. The formula for MISCELLANEOUS expenses in the Second Quarter is +B14*C28. To round the MISCELLANEOUS expenses to 0 decimal places:

Move the cell pointer to cell C14

Press F2 to edit the formula in cell C14

Press Home to move to the beginning of the formula

Type @ROUND (

Press Del one time to delete the + sign if desired

Press End to move to the end of a formula

Type ,0)

Press ↵

The formula @ROUND(B14*C28,0) is now in cell C14.

To copy the formula to the remaining quarters:

Press /

Select Copy

When prompted for the range to copy FROM:

Press ↵

By pressing the ↵ key, you selected cell C14 as the cell to copy.

When prompted for the range to copy TO:

Move	the cell pointer to cell D14
Type	.
Move	the cell pointer to cell E14
Press	↵

The projections for MISCELLANEOUS expenses are rounded to 0 decimal places.

The rounding error in the worksheet has been corrected. The corrected results in the YR TOTAL column are shown below:

Sales	$247,296
-Total Expenses	191,495
Gross Profit	$55,801

Your screen should look like Figure 2-31.

```
A:C14: @ROUND(B14*C27,0)                                              READY

A         A                B        C         D        E         F        G
1                                ABC COMPANY
2                                  BUDGET
3
4
5                        QTR1     QTR2     QTR3     QTR4    YR TOTAL
6
7   SALES               60,000   61,200   62,424   63,672   247,296
8
9   EXPENSES
10    SALARIES          35,000   35,500   36,200   37,000   143,700
11    RENT               9,000    9,000    9,000    9,000    36,000
12    TELEPHONE          1,000    1,050    1,103    1,158     4,311
13    OFFICE SUPPLIES      750      800      850      900     3,300
14    MISCELLANEOUS      1,000    1,030    1,061    1,093     4,184
15                     --------------------------------------------
16      TOTAL EXPENSES  46,750   47,380   48,214   49,151   191,495
17                     --------------------------------------------
18  GROSS PROFIT        13,250   13,820   14,210   14,521    55,801
19                     ============================================
20
                                                              CAP
```

Figure 2-31

■ IDENTIFYING THE SPREADSHEET PREPARER AND DATE THE SPREADSHEET IS CREATED

When a spreadsheet is used in an organization, it is useful to know who prepared the spreadsheet and the date on which it was prepared. One useful place to put the name of the spreadsheet preparer and date is just below the completed spreadsheet.

To indicate who created the BUDGET spreadsheet:

Move the cell pointer to cell A31

Type Prepared by

Type Your name or initials

Press ↵

To enter the current date on the spreadsheet:

Move the cell pointer to cell A32

Type @NOW

Press ↵

Note that a number appears. The number represents the number of days that have passed since December 31, 1899. To format the date so that it is in an appropriate form:

Press /

Select Range

Select Format

Select Date

Type 1 (to select the first format option)

Press ↵

Your name and the current date now should appear in cells A31 and A32. Your screen should look similar to Figure 2-32. Whenever you use the spreadsheet on your computer, the current date will always appear.

```
A:A32: (D1) [W18] @NOW                                                        READY

A        A               B         C         D         E         F         G
13   OFFICE SUPPLIES       750       800       850       900     3,300
14   MISCELLANEOUS       1,000     1,030     1,061     1,093     4,184
15                   ---------------------------------------------------
16     TOTAL EXPENSES   46,750    47,380    48,214    49,151   191,495
17                   ---------------------------------------------------
18  GROSS PROFIT        13,250    13,820    14,210    14,521    55,801
19                   ===================================================
20
21  GROWTH RATE
22  ASSUMPTIONS
23
24  SALES                         1.02      1.02      1.02
25  TELEPHONE                     1.05      1.05      1.05
26  OFFICE SUPPLIES              50.00     50.00     50.00
27  MISCELLANEOUS                 1.03      1.03      1.03
28
29
30
31  Prepared by H. Al Napier
32          06-Jun-89
                                                                   CAP
```

Figure 2-32

SAVING AND REPLACING A SPREADSHEET

The spreadsheet previously created was saved before the rounding errors were corrected. In order to save the changes to the worksheet, you must save it to the disk again.

To replace the BUDGET spreadsheet file that was previously saved:

Press Home

Pressing the Home key is optional.

Press /

Select File

Select Save

When prompted for the file name, the name for the file that is currently on the screen should appear. In this example, BUDGET appears. To keep the file name as BUDGET:

Press ↵

Since the file BUDGET already exists on the disk, a prompt appears requesting whether to cancel the Save command, replace the BUDGET file with the version in memory, or create a backup file named BUDGET.BAK from the previously saved file on the disk and also save the file that is currently in memory as BUDGET.WK3.

When prompted whether to **C**ancel, **R**eplace, or **B**ackup:

Select Replace

The previously saved version of BUDGET has now been replaced with the updated version that is currently displayed on the screen.

■ RETRIEVING A SPREADSHEET

First, clear the screen before beginning the exercise. To clear the screen:

Press /

Select Worksheet

Select Erase

Select Yes

Clearing the screen is not necessary before retrieving a spreadsheet because the screen will be erased automatically when retrieving a spreadsheet file. Note that **W**orksheet **E**rase **Y**es command did **not** erase the file BUDGET from the disk where it was previously saved. **The W**orksheet **E**rase **Y**es command only erases the spreadsheet from main **memory** so that the screen is cleared. The file BUDGET can still be retrieved from the disk. This action was taken to clarify the steps below.

To retrieve the file BUDGET:

Press /

Select File

Select Retrieve

When prompted for the file to retrieve:

Type BUDGET

Press 

An alternative to typing the file name is to press the F3 key and use the pointer-movement keys to highlight the desired file with the pointer. Since BUDGET is the only file on the disk, it is already highlighted. Once the desired file is highlighted, press the ⏎ key to retrieve the file. Another alternative is to press the → key until the desired file is highlighted; then press the ⏎ key.

The spreadsheet BUDGET is visible on your screen. It is now possible to make revisions or print it. Any changes are made *only* to the screen, not to the file on the disk. To save any changes to the file BUDGET, go through the process of saving and replacing the file that is presented in the previous section. To save revisions as a completely separate file, save the file, but type a different file name.

PREPARING THE PRINTER AND PRINTING THE SPREADSHEET

The spreadsheet is complete and the rounding errors have been corrected. The following steps outline how to print the results.

Prepare the Printer for Use

If you are using a dot matrix printer and the paper needs to be aligned, perform the following step before turning on the printer:

Turn	the cylinder that moves the paper so the paper perforation is directly above the print head and ribbon

For many printers, the gears can be damaged if the cylinder is manually turned while the motor is running.

If you are using a laser printer, the previous step is not required.

Before printing:

Check	to see that the printer is connected to the computer
Turn	on the printer

Your printer now should be on.

Printing the Spreadsheet

To specify the range to print:

Press	/

Select Print

Select Printer

Select Range

When prompted for the print range:

Move the cell pointer to cell A1 (if the cell pointer is not already there)

Type .

Move the cell pointer to cell F32

The entire worksheet is now highlighted.

Press ↵

To begin printing the range:

Select Align

Select Go

The printer should begin to print your spreadsheet.

Note that the Align command sets a 1-2-3 counter to 0 (top of page) before it begins to print. This command is especially useful when the paper has been readjusted in the printer or the printer has been reloaded.

To eject the page from the printer:

Select Page

The page is ejected and the printer moves to the top of the next page. 1-2-3 counts the number of lines you printed (32 in this case), and subtracts the number of lines printed from the number that can be printed on a page. The difference is the number of lines that the printhead needs to be moved to reach the top of the next page. For many printers, an additional page needs to be ejected so that the paper remains aligned properly in the printer.

To eject a second page:

Select Page

Tear the perforation to remove the printed page (not necessary if you are using a laser printer)

To leave the Print menu:

Select Quit

The printout should appear similar to the printout in Figure 2-33. If the printout is satisfactory, resave the spreadsheet so that the print setting will be saved with the spreadsheet. Save and replace the spreadsheet on file BUDGET using the **F**ile **S**ave **R**eplace command sequence.

ABC COMPANY
BUDGET

	QTR1	QTR2	QTR3	QTR4	YR TOTAL
SALES	$60,000	$61,200	$62,424	$63,672	$247,296
EXPENSES					
SALARIES	35,000	35,500	36,200	37,000	143,700
RENT	9,000	9,000	9,000	9,000	36,000
TELEPHONE	1,000	1,050	1,103	1,158	4,311
OFFICE SUPPLIES	750	800	850	900	3,300
MISCELLANEOUS	1,000	1,030	1,061	1,093	4,184
TOTAL EXPENSES	46,750	47,380	48,214	49,151	191,495
GROSS PROFIT	$13,250	$13,820	$14,210	$14,521	$55,801

GROWTH RATE ASSUMPTIONS				
SALES		1.02	1.02	1.02
TELEPHONE EXP		1.05	1.05	1.05
OFFICE SUPPLIES EXP		50.00	50.00	50.00
MISCELLANEOUS EXP		1.03	1.03	1.03

Figure 2-33

■ PRINTING THE CELL FORMULAS OF A SPREADSHEET

At times you may want to see the cell formulas which comprise a spreadsheet. To print the cell formulas used to create the spreadsheet BUDGET, follow the steps below. It is assumed that the BUDGET spreadsheet is currently in memory and that the print range for BUDGET has previously been set.

Press /

Select Print

Select Printer

Select Options

Select Other

Select Cell-Formulas

Select Quit

Select Align

Select Go

Assuming that the print range has been set previously, the printer will print the contents of each nonblank cell.

To eject the printout when it is complete, and also to eject a second page (if necessary) to keep the paper aligned in the printer:

Select Page

Select Page

The printout should look like Figure 2-34, Parts 1 and 2.

```
A:C1: '     ABC COMPANY
A:C2: '       BUDGET
A:B5: ^QTR1
A:C5: ^QTR2
A:D5: ^QTR3
A:E5: ^QTR4
A:F5: 'YR TOTAL
A:A7: [W18] 'SALES
A:B7: (C0) 60000
A:C7: (C0) @ROUND(B7*C25,0)
A:D7: (C0) @ROUND(C7*D25,0)
A:E7: (C0) @ROUND(D7*E25,0)
A:F7: (C0) @SUM(B7..E7)
A:A9: [W18] 'EXPENSES
A:A10: [W18] '  SALARIES
A:B10: 35000
A:C10: 35500
A:D10: 36200
A:E10: 37000
A:F10: @SUM(B10..E10)
A:A11: [W18] '  RENT
A:B11: 9000
A:C11: 9000
A:D11: 9000
A:E11: 9000
A:F11: @SUM(B11..E11)
A:A12: [W18] '  TELEPHONE
A:B12: 1000
A:C12: @ROUND(B12*C26,0)
A:D12: @ROUND(C12*D26,0)
A:E12: @ROUND(D12*E26,0)
A:F12: @SUM(B12..E12)
A:A13: [W18] '  OFFICE SUPPLIES
A:B13: 750
A:C13: +B13+C27
A:D13: +C13+D27
A:E13: +D13+E27
A:F13: @SUM(B13..E13)
A:A14: [W18] '  MISCELLANEOUS
A:B14: 1000
A:C14: @ROUND(B14*C28,0)
A:D14: @ROUND(C14*D28,0)
A:E14: @ROUND(D14*E28,0)
A:F14: @SUM(B14..E14)
A:B15: \-
A:C15: \-
A:D15: \-
A:E15: \-
A:F15: \-
A:A16: [W18] '    TOTAL EXPENSES
A:B16: @SUM(B10..B14)
A:C16: @SUM(C10..C14)
A:D16: @SUM(D10..D14)
A:E16: @SUM(E10..E14)
A:F16: @SUM(B16..E16)
```

Figure 2-34
Part 1

```
A:B17: \-
A:C17: \-
A:D17: \-
A:E17: \-
A:F17: \-
A:A18: [W18] 'GROSS PROFIT
A:B18: (C0) +B7-B16
A:C18: (C0) +C7-C16
A:D18: (C0) +D7-D16
A:E18: (C0) +E7-E16
A:F18: (C0) @SUM(B18..E18)
A:B19: \=
A:C19: \=
A:D19: \=
A:E19: \=
A:F19: \=
A:A22: [W18] 'GROWTH RATE
A:A23: [W18] 'ASSUMPTIONS
A:A25: [W18] 'SALES
A:C25: (F2) 1.02
A:D25: (F2) 1.02
A:E25: (F2) 1.02
A:A26: [W18] 'TELEPHONE
A:C26: (F2) 1.05
A:D26: (F2) 1.05
A:E26: (F2) 1.05
A:A27: [W18] 'OFFICE SUPPLIES
A:C27: (F0) 50
A:D27: (F0) 50
A:E27: (F0) 50
A:A28: [W18] 'MISCELLANEOUS
A:C28: (F2) 1.03
A:D28: (F2) 1.03
A:E28: (F2) 1.03
```

Figure 2-34
Part 2

To return the print settings back to their previous setting (i.e., so when Go is selected, the spreadsheet will be printed rather than the cell formulas):

Select Options

Select Other

Select As-Displayed

To leave the current menu:

Select Quit

To leave the print menu:

Select Quit

The print settings have now been returned to their previous setting.

PRINTING THE CELL FORMULAS OF A SPREADSHEET IN TABULAR FORM

To display cell formulas exactly where they appear on the spreadsheet BUDGET requires changing the format of the spreadsheet. Before changing the format to see the cell formulas, make sure the spreadsheet has been saved to the disk in the desired numeric format. In this way, the "final version" of the spreadsheet is safely saved on the disk and can be retrieved for later use.

To change the format of the spreadsheet to see the cell formulas:

Press /

Select Worksheet

Select Global

Select Format

Select Text

The formulas are now displayed on the spreadsheet itself. However, some cell formulas are not fully displayed because the column width is not wide enough to accommodate them. For example, column F is not large enough to fully display the @SUM formulas. In row 16, the @SUM command is not displayed fully. Your screen should look like Figure 2-35.

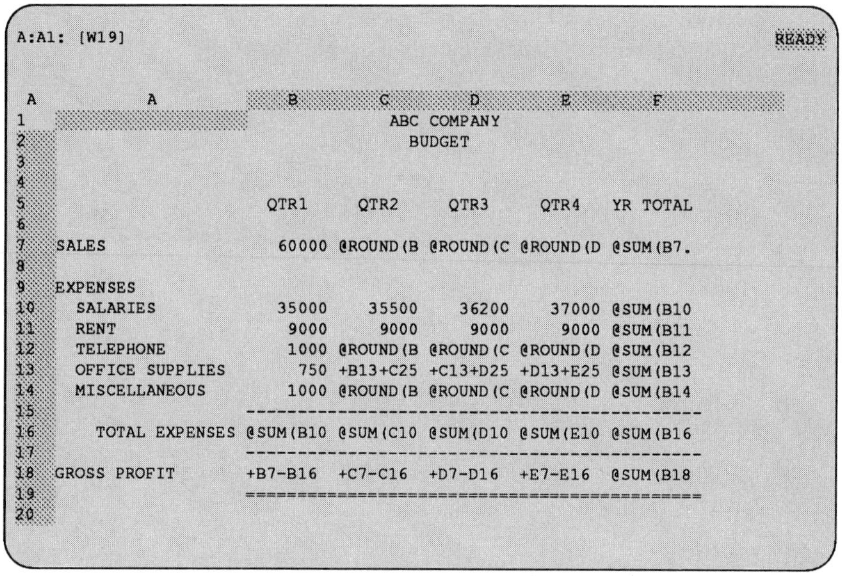

```
A:A1: [W19]                                                    READY

 A         A              B        C        D        E        F
 1                                   ABC COMPANY
 2                                     BUDGET
 3
 4
 5                          QTR1     QTR2     QTR3     QTR4   YR TOTAL
 6
 7 SALES                   60000 @ROUND(B @ROUND(C @ROUND(D @SUM(B7.
 8
 9 EXPENSES
10   SALARIES              35000    35500    36200    37000 @SUM(B10
11   RENT                   9000     9000     9000     9000 @SUM(B11
12   TELEPHONE              1000 @ROUND(B @ROUND(C @ROUND(D @SUM(B12
13   OFFICE SUPPLIES         750 +B13+C25 +C13+D25 +D13+E25 @SUM(B13
14   MISCELLANEOUS          1000 @ROUND(B @ROUND(C @ROUND(D @SUM(B14
15                     ---------------------------------------------
16     TOTAL EXPENSES @SUM(B10 @SUM(C10 @SUM(D10 @SUM(E10 @SUM(B16
17                     ---------------------------------------------
18 GROSS PROFIT        +B7-B16  +C7-C16  +D7-D16  +E7-E16  @SUM(B18
19                     =============================================
20
```

Figure 2-35

For this example, widen column F in order to view the full formula. The only other formulas not fully displayed in columns B through E are the @SUM functions in row 16 used to compute TOTAL EXPENSES and the formulas in which you entered the @ROUND function. For this example, only column F will be altered to fully display the formulas.

To widen column F:

Move	the cell pointer to cell F1 (or any other cell in column F)
Press	/
Select	Worksheet
Select	Column
Select	Set-Width

When prompted for the column width:

Press	the → key until the formulas are fully displayed

In this example, the column width should be 15 characters wide. To accept 15 as the column width:

Press	↵

The entire formula for each cell in column F is now displayed.

To print the cells in tabular form:

Press /

Select Print

Select Printer

Select Align

Select Go

The print range did not need to be specified because it was specified earlier.

To eject the printout, if necessary, and a second page to keep the paper properly aligned in the printer:

Select Page

Select Page

To exit the print menu:

Select Quit

The printout should look like Figure 2-36.

```
                              ABC COMPANY
                               BUDGET

                    QTR1     QTR2     QTR3     QTR4       YR TOTAL

SALES              60000 @ROUND@ROUND@ROUND@SUM(B7..E7)

EXPENSES
 SALARIES          35000    35500    36200    37000 @SUM(SALARIES)
 RENT               9000     9000     9000     9000 @SUM(B11..E11)
 TELEPHONE          1000 @ROUND@ROUND@ROUND@SUM(B12..E12)
 OFFICE SUPPLIES     750 +B13+C27+C13+D27+D13+E27@SUM(B13..E13)
 MISCELLANEOUS      1000 @ROUND@ROUND@ROUND@SUM(B14..E14)
                 ---------------------------------------------------------
  TOTAL EXPENSES@SUM(B1@SUM(C1@SUM(D1@SUM(E1@SUM(B16..E16)
                 ---------------------------------------------------------
GROSS PROFIT     +B7-B16  +C7-C16  +D7-D16  +E7-E16  @SUM(B18..E18)
                 =========================================================


GROWTH RATE
ASSUMPTIONS

SALES                        1.02     1.02     1.02
TELEPHONE EXP                1.05     1.05     1.05
OFFICE SUPPLIES EXP            50       50       50
MISCELLANEOUS EXP            1.03     1.03     1.03
```

Figure 2-36

PRINTING A SPREADSHEET WITH COLUMN LETTERS AND ROW NUMBERS FRAMING THE SPREADSHEET

In some situations, it is useful to have a spreadsheet printed with the column letters and row numbers **framing** the spreadsheet. For example, when you print the cell formulas using text format, it will be helpful to have the column letters and row numbers printed so it is easy to determine which cell contains a particular formula.

Assuming that you have just finished the example in the last section, the steps for printing the spreadsheet framed with the column letters and row numbers are:

Press	/	
Select	Print	
Select	Printer	
Select	Options	
Select	Borders	
Select	Frame	
Select	Quit	(to exit the Options menu)
Select	Align	
Select	Go	
Select	Page	
Select	Page	(if necessary)
Select	Quit	(to exit the Print menu)

The printout should look like Figure 2-37.

```
A    A                  B        C        D        E        F
1                              ABC COMPANY
2                                BUDGET
3
4
5                     QTR1     QTR2     QTR3     QTR4       YR TOTAL
6
7    SALES            60000 @ROUND@ROUND@ROUND@SUM(B7..E7)
8
9    EXPENSES
10    SALARIES        35000    35500    36200    37000 @SUM(SALARIES)
11    RENT             9000     9000     9000     9000 @SUM(B11..E11)
12    TELEPHONE        1000 @ROUND@ROUND@ROUND@SUM(B12..E12)
13    OFFICE SUPPLIES   750 +B13+C27+C13+D27+D13+E27@SUM(B13..E13)
14    MISCELLANEOUS    1000 @ROUND@ROUND@ROUND@SUM(B14..E14)
15                 -----------------------------------------------------
16     TOTAL EXPENSES@SUM(B10@SUM(C1@SUM(D1@SUM(E1@SUM(B16..E16)
17                 -----------------------------------------------------
18   GROSS PROFIT    +B7-B16  +C7-C16  +D7-D16  +E7-E16  @SUM(B18..E18)
19                 =====================================================
20
21
22   GROWTH RATE
23   ASSUMPTIONS
24
25   SALES                      1.02     1.02     1.02
26   TELEPHONE EXP              1.05     1.05     1.05
27   OFFICE SUPPLIES EXP       50.00    50.00    50.00
28   MISCELLANEOUS EXP          1.03     1.03     1.03
29
30
31   Prepared by H. Al Napier
32            08-Aug-89
```

Figure 2-37

To specify that the "Frame" is no longer desired:

Press /

Select Print

Select Printer

Select Options

Select Borders

Select No-Frame

To exit the options menu:

Select Quit

To exit the print menu:

Select Quit

The easiest way to return the BUDGET spreadsheet to its initial format is simply to retrieve the BUDGET spreadsheet that is saved on the disk. However, the following exercise demonstrates how to use 1-2-3 commands to return the spreadsheet to its original format.

To return the format to its original setting:

Press /

Select Worksheet

Select Global

Select Format

Select ,

When prompted for the number of decimal places:

Type 0

Press ↵

Column F needs to be reset so that it once again has a column width of 9. To return column F to its original column width, make sure the cell pointer is within column F.

Press	/
Select	Worksheet
Select	Column
Select	Reset-Width

The width for column F is returned to the default size of 9 characters. Your screen should look like Figure 2-38.

```
A:F7: @SUM(B7..E7)                                                    READY

A          A            B         C         D         E         F         G
1                                    ABC COMPANY
2                                      BUDGET
3
4
5                     QTR1      QTR2      QTR3      QTR4   YR TOTAL
6
7  SALES            60,000    61,200    62,424    63,672   247,296
8
9  EXPENSES
10   SALARIES       35,000    35,500    36,200    37,000   143,700
11   RENT            9,000     9,000     9,000     9,000    36,000
12   TELEPHONE       1,000     1,050     1,103     1,158     4,311
13   OFFICE SUPPLIES   750       800       850       900     3,300
14   MISCELLANEOUS   1,000     1,030     1,061     1,093     4,184
15                ---------------------------------------------
16     TOTAL EXPENSES 46,750   47,380    48,214    49,151   191,495
17                ---------------------------------------------
18 GROSS PROFIT     13,250    13,820    14,210    14,521    55,801
19                =============================================
20
```

Figure 2-38

CHANGING THE FONT USED IN PRINTING

In some situations, you may want to change the print font used for printing a spreadsheet. Initially, 1-2-3 assigns the Serif font as the default font. This font is applied to the print range, headers and footers, borders and the frame created by the column letters and row numbers. You may change the font of any of these items if you so desire.

To specify the use of the bold serif option for the print range of the BUDGET spreadsheet, follow these steps:

Press	/
Select	Print
Select	Printer

Select	Options
Select	Advanced
Select	Fonts
Select	Range

Serif fonts are included in Choices 1 through 4 for standard, bold, italic, and bold italic (in that order). Sans serif fonts are included in Choices 5 through 8 in standard, bold, italic, and bold italic (in that order).

To select the second font option:

Type 2

To exit the font menu:

Select Quit

To exit the advanced menu:

Select Quit

To exit the options menu:

Select Quit

To print the worksheet:

Select	Align	
Select	Go	
Select	Page	twice

To exit the print menu:

Select Quit

The printout should look like Figure 2-39.

The capability to use various fonts depends upon what type of printer you have. You may need to refer to your printer manual for further information.

ABC COMPANY
BUDGET

	QTR1	QTR2	QTR3	QTR4	YR TOTAL
SALES	$60,000	$61,200	$62,424	$63,672	$247,296
EXPENSES					
SALARIES	35,000	35,500	36,200	37,000	143,700
RENT	9,000	9,000	9,000	9,000	36,000
TELEPHONE	1,000	1,050	1,103	1,158	4,311
OFFICE SUPPLIES	750	800	850	900	3,300
MISCELLANEOUS	1,000	1,030	1,061	1,093	4,184
TOTAL EXPENSES	46,750	47,380	48,214	49,151	191,495
GROSS PROFIT	$13,250	$13,820	$14,210	$14,521	$55,801

Figure 2-39

If you are printing headers and footers, borders and/or the frame, a similar procedure can be used to indicate the appropriate font by specifying the range for these cells one at a time and specifying the appropriate number for the desired font.

In some cases, you may wish to print two or more ranges of cells in the spreadsheet using different fonts. In this situation, define the first print range and then specify the desired font for the range using the **P**rint **P**rinter **O**ptions **A**dvanced **F**onts **R**ange **G**o command sequence. You should then define the second range and select the appropriate font by using the same commands. You can continue the process until all the ranges are selected. Then finish printing the spreadsheet.

■ USING OTHER FORMAT SPECIFICATIONS FOR THE SPREADSHEET

When building the spreadsheet BUDGET, you chose the numeric format **W**orksheet **G**lobal **F**ormat **,** **0** from the menus to display numbers with commas and no decimal places. The exercises in this section demonstrate how to use some of the other available format specifications.

Setting the Entire Spreadsheet with Dollar Signs

It is assumed that the BUDGET spreadsheet is displayed on your screen. If not, retrieve the file BUDGET before continuing and make sure your screen looks like Figure 2-38.

To change the numeric format in BUDGET so that dollar signs are added and two decimal places are shown, use the Currency format.

Press /

Select Worksheet

Select Global

Select Format

Select Currency

When prompted for the number of decimal places:

Press ↵

By pressing the ↵ key, the default of two decimal places is accepted. Notice that asterisks fill the majority of the spreadsheet instead of numbers. Due to the addition of a dollar sign, a period, and two decimal places to each cell containing a value or formula, **the columns are no longer wide enough to display many of the cells** in currency format. Sometimes asterisks may appear in only one or two cells in a column rather than throughout the entire worksheet. The columns need to be widened for you to see the contents of the cell(s) containing asterisks (refer to Figure 2-40). Make sure your cell pointer is in cell F1.

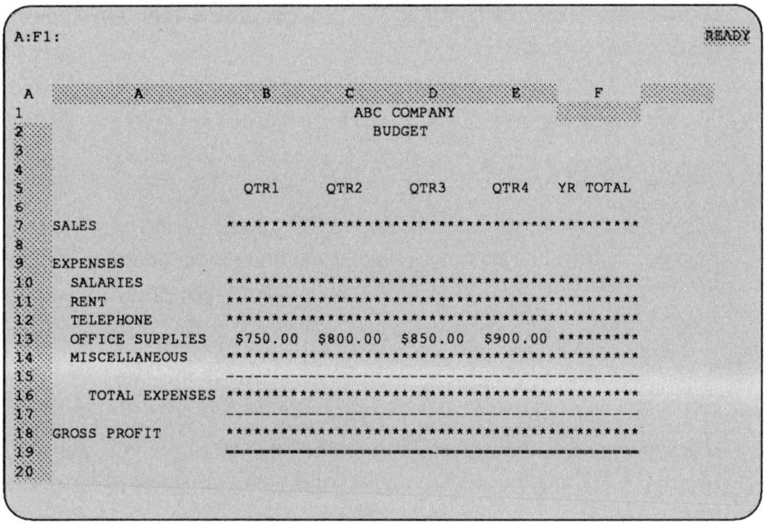

```
A:F1:                                                              READY

A          A          B         C         D         E         F
1                                    ABC COMPANY
2                                      BUDGET
3
4
5                         QTR1      QTR2      QTR3      QTR4    YR TOTAL
6
7   SALES                 *********************************************
8
9   EXPENSES
10    SALARIES            *********************************************
11    RENT                *********************************************
12    TELEPHONE           *********************************************
13    OFFICE SUPPLIES      $750.00   $800.00   $850.00   $900.00 *********
14    MISCELLANEOUS       *********************************************
15                        ---------------------------------------------
16      TOTAL EXPENSES    *********************************************
17                        ---------------------------------------------
18  GROSS PROFIT          *********************************************
19                        =============================================
20
```

Figure 2-40

To widen the columns so that the numbers are visible:

Press	/
Select	Worksheet
Select	Global
Select	Col-Width
Press	the → key until the numbers can be seen in their entirety
Press	↵

The column width should be set to 12 characters. Due to the column width change, columns F and G scroll off the screen. After pressing the Home key, your screen should look like Figure 2-41.

```
A:A1: [W18]                                                              READY

A         A              B            C            D            E
1                                  ABC COMPANY
2                                    BUDGET
3
4
5                        QTR1         QTR2         QTR3         QTR4
6
7  SALES             $60,000.00   $61,200.00   $62,424.00   $63,672.00
8
9  EXPENSES
10   SALARIES        $35,000.00   $35,500.00   $36,200.00   $37,000.00
11   RENT             $9,000.00    $9,000.00    $9,000.00    $9,000.00
12   TELEPHONE        $1,000.00    $1,050.00    $1,103.00    $1,158.00
13   OFFICE SUPPLIES    $750.00      $800.00      $850.00      $900.00
14   MISCELLANEOUS    $1,000.00    $1,030.00    $1,061.00    $1,093.00
15                   ------------------------------------------------
16     TOTAL EXPENSES $46,750.00  $47,380.00   $48,214.00   $49,151.00
17                   ------------------------------------------------
18 GROSS PROFIT      $13,250.00   $13,820.00   $14,210.00   $14,521.00
19                   ================================================
20
```

Figure 2-41

When the global column width is set, any columns that have been set individually using the **W**orksheet **C**olumn **S**et-Width command are *not* affected. This is the reason that the width of column A did not change.

Using More than One Numeric Format in a Spreadsheet

In this exercise, you alter the BUDGET spreadsheet so that only the top and bottom rows of the spreadsheet display dollar signs.

It is assumed that the original BUDGET spreadsheet file is displayed on the screen. If not, retrieve the file BUDGET before continuing and make sure that it looks like Figure 2-38.

The BUDGET spreadsheet's format was set by **W**orksheet **G**lobal **F**ormat **,** **0** which displays all numbers in the spreadsheet with commas and no decimal places. For the majority of the spreadsheet, this format is appropriate. However, another command is needed to change the top and bottom rows of the spreadsheet to show dollar signs.

To change the numeric format of the top row in BUDGET:

Press	/
Select	Range

Select Format

Select Currency

When prompted for the number of decimal places:

Type 0

Press ↵

When prompted for the range to format:

Press Esc

The Range Format command automatically **anchors** the cell pointer at its current position with the period key. To release the cell pointer from its anchored position, press the Esc key.

The first range to format is the top row of numbers of the BUDGET spreadsheet.

Move the cell pointer to cell B7

Type .

Move the cell pointer to cell F7

Press ↵

Cells B7 through F7 now have dollar signs.

To change the numeric format of the bottom row of numbers in BUDGET:

Move the cell pointer to cell B18

Moving to the first cell of the range to format will eliminate the need to press the Esc key when prompted to highlight the range to format.

Press /

Select Range

Select Format

Select Currency

When prompted for the number of decimal places:

Type 0

Press ↵

When prompted for the range to format:

Move to cell F18

Press ↵

Since the cell pointer was in cell B18, moving the cell pointer to cell F18 highlighted cells B18 through F18, which now display dollar signs. Your screen should look like Figure 2-42.

```
A:B18: (C0) +B7-B16                                                READY

A         A              B        C        D        E        F
1                                  ABC COMPANY
2                                    BUDGET
3
4
5                             QTR1     QTR2     QTR3     QTR4  YR TOTAL
6
7   SALES                  $60,000  $61,200  $62,424  $63,672  $247,296
8
9   EXPENSES
10    SALARIES              35,000   35,500   36,200   37,000   143,700
11    RENT                   9,000    9,000    9,000    9,000    36,000
12    TELEPHONE              1,000    1,050    1,103    1,158     4,311
13    OFFICE SUPPLIES          750      800      850      900     3,300
14    MISCELLANEOUS          1,000    1,030    1,061    1,093     4,184
15                       ---------------------------------------------
16       TOTAL EXPENSES     46,750   47,380   48,214   49,151   191,495
17                       ---------------------------------------------
18  GROSS PROFIT           $13,250  $13,820  $14,210  $14,521   $55,801
19                       =============================================
20
```

Figure 2-42

The dollar signs in the Currency format do not align with each other in a column; the dollar signs are placed flush to the formatted number. If the dollar signs need to be aligned, it is not appropriate to use the Currency format. Instead, one-character columns must be inserted before each column of values and the dollar sign "$" must be typed manually. The dollar sign must be entered with the label prefix such as the apostrophe (e.g., '$).

Comparing Worksheet Global Format to Range Format

The **W**orksheet **G**lobal **F**ormat command sequence is used to set the format of how *most* of the numbers in the spreadsheet are to be displayed. The **R**ange **F**ormat command sequence is used to set the format of **specified ranges** of numbers in the spreadsheet.

In the BUDGET worksheet, most of the worksheet was set to display commas; therefore, the **W**orksheet **G**lobal **F**ormat command sequence was used. The **R**ange **F**ormat could have been used, but the former command sequence is faster. Two specified ranges, the top and bottom row of numbers, of the BUDGET worksheet were set to display dollar signs; therefore, the **R**ange **F**ormat command sequence was used.

With the cell pointer in cell B18, look at the information in the control panel. "(C0)" is displayed, indicating that the **C**urrency format with **0** decimal places was chosen with **R**ange **F**ormat. All cells formatted with the **R**ange **F**ormat command will display a similar message in the control panel when highlighted by the cell pointer. No format specification appears in the control panel for cells when the **W**orksheet **G**lobal **F**ormat command is used.

■ USING THE ROUNDING OPTION

As demonstrated in the BUDGET spreadsheet, rounding errors may occur in spreadsheets that have growth rates or percentages. To prevent this problem, use the @ROUND function whenever a formula includes multiplication, division, or exponents. The format for the @ROUND function is as follows:

```
@ROUND(formula,number of digits to round to)
```

Both the formula and the number of digits to round to must be specified.

In the BUDGET worksheet, the original formula for the Fourth Quarter of SALES was:

+D7*E25

The value of the computation was:

63672.48

Later, when the Worksheet Global Format Sequence was used to format the numbers to display commas and 0 decimal places, the number was formatted to *appear* as:

63,672

The number *appeared* as 63,672 but the *value used in computation* was still 63672.48. The use of this number can result in a rounding error.

To truly round the number, use the @ROUND function. Enter the formula above must be entered as:

```
@ROUND(+D7*E25,0)
```

A summary of the differences are below:

Formula	Value	Global Format Appears as Comma 0	Number Used in Computation
+D7*E25	63672.48	63,672	63672.48
@ROUND (+D7*1.02,0)	63672	63,672	63672

The @ROUND function may not remove rounding errors properly for all situations (e.g., percentages). It may be necessary to "plug a number" to get the desired results.

MAKING A BACKUP OF A SPREADSHEET FILE

In 1-2-3 you can make a backup worksheet file on the disk with the **F**ile **S**ave **B**ackup command sequence. You also can place the worksheet on a separate diskette to create a backup file.

To make a backup file on the same disk on which your active files reside:

Press /

Select File

Select Save

Press ↵

When prompted to **C**ancel, **R**eplace or **B**ackup:

Select Backup

A .BAK file has been created.

When you use the Backup menu option again for the BUDGET file, 1-2-3 renames the file on the disk with the .BAK extension and saves the active version of the BUDGET file with its existing file name. To see that a .BAK file has been created:

Press /

Select File

Select List

Select Other

BUDGET.BAK now appears on the list of files with BUDGET.WK3. To continue to the next exercise:

Press ↵

To save the BUDGET worksheet on a separate diskette in drive A, you first need to insert a formatted disk in drive A. Then you can save the worksheet using the following instructions:

Press /

Select File

Select Save

Press Esc three times

By pressing the Esc key three times, you clear the current directory and file name from the control panel.

Type A:BUDGET

Press ↵

You now have saved a copy of BUDGET on the diskette in drive A. Note that the extension .WK3 file has been used. The .WK3 extension will always be used except when you select the Backup menu option mentioned earlier in this section.

CHANGING THE ASSUMPTIONS TO COMPLETE A "WHAT-IF" ANALYSIS

One of the advantages of using 1-2-3 is the ability to change some of the ASSUMPTIONS and see the impact of the changes on the other values in the worksheet. For example, suppose you show your supervisor the BUDGET spreadsheet results. Your supervisor then may ask some "what- if" questions and ask you to complete some further analysis.

Assume that you are asked to determine the impact on GROSS PROFIT if the growth rate for SALES is 5%, 9% and 6% in Quarters 2 through 4 respectively.

To enter the new growth rates for SALES:

Move the cell pointer to cell C25

Type 1.05

Press →

Type 1.09

Press →

Type 1.06

Press ↵

Your worksheet is recalculated to reflect the new growth rates each time you change one of them. You now can see the new values for GROSS PROFIT that were computed using the new ASSUMPTIONS. If desired, you can change some of the other ASSUMPTIONS. Your screen now should look like Figure 2-43.

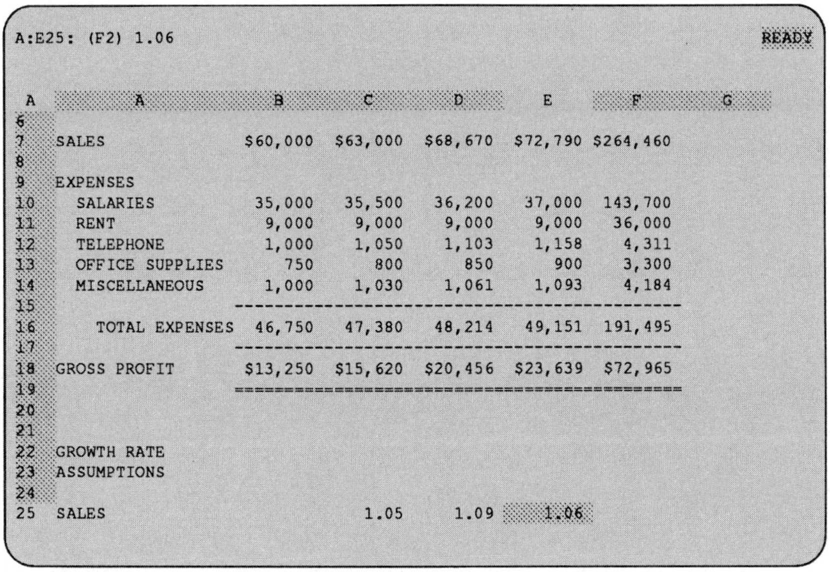

```
A:E25: (F2) 1.06                                                    READY

 A          A                B        C         D         E        F         G
 6
 7   SALES                $60,000  $63,000  $68,670  $72,790 $264,460
 8
 9   EXPENSES
10     SALARIES            35,000   35,500   36,200   37,000  143,700
11     RENT                 9,000    9,000    9,000    9,000   36,000
12     TELEPHONE            1,000    1,050    1,103    1,158    4,311
13     OFFICE SUPPLIES        750      800      850      900    3,300
14     MISCELLANEOUS        1,000    1,030    1,061    1,093    4,184
15                      ---------------------------------------------
16       TOTAL EXPENSES    46,750   47,380   48,214   49,151  191,495
17                      ---------------------------------------------
18   GROSS PROFIT         $13,250  $15,620  $20,456  $23,639  $72,965
19                      =============================================
20
21
22   GROWTH RATE
23   ASSUMPTIONS
24
25   SALES                             1.05      1.09     1.06
```

Figure 2-43

■ USING FORMULAS IN LOTUS 1-2-3

Lotus 1-2-3 allows the use of formulas to indicate operations such as addition and subtraction. The types of formulas and the order in which operations occur in formulas are discussed in this section.

Types of Formulas

The three types of formulas that can be entered into a cell in 1-2-3 are arithmetic, text, and logical.

Arithmetic Formulas

Arithmetic formulas are used to compute numeric values using arithmetic operators. For example, if the cell formula +A3-10 appears in B5, then the value 10 is subtracted from the number appearing in cell A3 and the result will appear in cell B5.

Text Formulas

Text formulas are used to calculate labels using the text operator (&). For example, if the text formula +C5&"EXPENSES" appears in cell K7, then the label that results from combining the label in cell C5 with EXPENSES will appear in cell K7.

Logical Formulas

Logical formulas are used to compare values in two or more cells using logical operators. A logical formula calculates a value of 0 (meaning false) or 1 (meaning true). For example, if the formula +C3<=25000 appears in cell D3, then the value 0 will appear in cell D3 whenever the value in cell C3 is greater than 25,000. A value of 1 will appear in cell D3 if the value in cell C3 is less than or equal to 25,000.

Operators and Order of Precedence

1-2-3 uses various operators in formulas to indicate arithmetic operations. Listed below are the mathematical operators allowed in 1-2-3. The operators are listed in the order of precedence by which operations are completed.

Operator	Definition
^	Exponentiation
- +	Negative, Positive
* /	Multiplication, Division
+ -	Addition, Subtraction

The operators that appear higher on the list are evaluated prior to operators that are lower on the list.

Exponentiation is the highest level operator. For example, if the arithmetic formula 10+5^2 is used for cell A5, then the result that appears in cell A5 is 35 (10 + 5 squared) not 225 (15 raised to the power of two).

Lotus 1-2-3 can tell the difference between the + or - sign that means a positive or negative number as opposed to the + or - sign meaning addition or subtraction. For example, if the formula 10/-5+10 appears in cell B8, then the result that appears in the cell is 8 (-2+10) not 2 (10/5).

Multiplication and division operators are evaluated before addition and subtraction operators. For example, if cell C8 contains the formula 7-3/2, the value that appears in cell C8 is 5.5 (7-(3/2)) not 2 (7-3)/2.

The order of precedence can be overridden using sets of parentheses. If more than one set of parentheses is included in a formula, then the order of execution begins with the innermost set of parentheses and proceeds to the outermost set of parentheses. For example, suppose the formula ((10/2) + 3) * 4 is used for cell E1; the result appearing in cell E1 is 32.

SUMMARY

Creating spreadsheets is faster and more effective using a spreadsheet software package such as Lotus 1-2-3. Creating formulas and values that can be copied, inserting and deleting entire rows and columns with menu commands, and saving the file for easy editing are just a few advantages of the Lotus 1-2-3 spreadsheet software package.

KEY CONCEPTS

Assumptions
@NOW
@ROUND
@SUM
Centering labels
Copy
Ctrl-Break
Esc
File Retrieve
File Save
Font
Format
Formula
Frame
Label
Print Printer Align Go
Print Printer Options Advanced Font
Print Printer Options Border Frame
Print Printer Options Border No-Frame
Print Printer Options Other As-Displayed
Print Printer Options Other Cell-Formulas
Print Printer Range
Range Format Currency
Range Format Fixed
Relative cell location
Replacing a spreadsheet file
Value
Worksheet Column Reset-Width
Worksheet Column Set-Width
Worksheet Global Column-Width
Worksheet Global Format
Worksheet Insert Row

CHAPTER TWO
EXERCISE 1

INSTRUCTIONS: Circle T if the statement is true and F if the statement is false.

T F 1. One way to correct incorrect data is to move to the incorrect data's cell, retype the data correctly, and press the (↵) to enter the correction.

T F 2. The formula SUM(A..A7) will add the data in cells A1 through A7.

T F 3. To round a number to two decimal places, you use the **R**ange **F**ormat command.

T F 4. The **W**orksheet **E**rase **Y**es command sequence erases the worksheet currently in use from memory.

T F 5. A print range must be specified before a spreadsheet can be printed.

T F 6. The "@" character must precede special functions such as the SUM and ROUND functions.

T F 7. Lotus 1-2-3 will automatically save changes that are made to a spreadsheet file.

T F 8. The **F**ile **R**etrieve command is used to look at a previously saved file.

T F 9. "BUDGET 1" is an acceptable file name.

T F 10. The letter "X" is the symbol for multiplication when using Lotus 1-2-3.

T F 11. Fonts cannot be changed.

T F 12. Column letters and row numbers can be used to form a "frame" when a spreadsheet is printed.

CHAPTER TWO
EXERCISE 2

INSTRUCTIONS: Explain a typical situation when the following keystrokes or Lotus 1-2-3 commands are used.

Problem 1:	/ **F**ile **S**ave
Problem 2:	/ **W**orksheet **I**nsert **R**ow
Problem 3:	+B1*1.09
Problem 4:	/ **W**orksheet **G**lobal **C**olumn-Width
Problem 5:	/ **W**orksheet **C**olumn **S**et-Width
Problem 6:	/ **W**orksheet **E**rase **Y**es
Problem 7:	/ **P**rint **P**rinter **R**ange
Problem 8:	/ **P**rint **P**rinter **A**lign **G**o
Problem 9:	F2
Problem 10:	+B7-B6
Problem 11:	@ROUND (+B7*B8,0)
Problem 12:	@SUM(B1..B25)
Problem 13:	/**W**orksheet **G**lobal **F**ormat **, 2**
Problem 14:	/**R**ange **F**ormat **C**urrency **2**
Problem 15:	/ **F**ile **R**etrieve
Problem 16:	/ **C**opy
Problem 17:	/**P**rint **P**rinter **O**ptions **A**dvanced **F**ont
Problem 18:	/ **R**ange **F**ormat **F**ixed **2**
Problem 19:	/ **F**ile **S**ave **R**eplace

CHAPTER TWO
EXERCISE 3
Correcting a Spreadsheet

INSTRUCTIONS: The following example illustrates a common error. Follow the instructions below to create the error and answer the questions.

Clear the screen (use the **W**orksheet **E**rase **Y**es commands).
In cell A1, type 52 and press ↵.
In cell A2, type 30 and press ↵.
In cell A3, type A1-A2 and press ↵.

Your screen should look like Figure 2-44.

Figure 2-44

1. What caused the error in cell A3?

2. How can the error be corrected?

CHAPTER TWO
EXERCISE 4
Correcting a Spreadsheet

INSTRUCTIONS: The following example illustrates a common error. Follow the instructions below to create the error and answer the questions.

Clear the screen (use the **W**orksheet **E**rase **Y**es commands).
In cell A1, type 52 and press ↵.
In cell A2, press the space bar one time. Type 30 and press ↵.
In cell A3, type +A1-A2 and press ↵.

The screen should look like Figure 2-45.

Figure 2-45

1. What caused the error in computing A1-A2?
2. How can the error be corrected?

CHAPTER TWO
EXERCISE 5
Correcting a Spreadsheet

INSTRUCTIONS: The following example illustrates a common error. Use the instructions below to create the error and answer the questions.

Clear the screen (use the **Wo**rksheet **E**rase **Y**es commands).
In cell A1, type 52 and press ⊖.
In cell A2, type 30 and press ⊖.
In cell A3, type +A1 and press ⊖. Then type -A2 and press ⊖.

The screen should look like Figure 2-46.

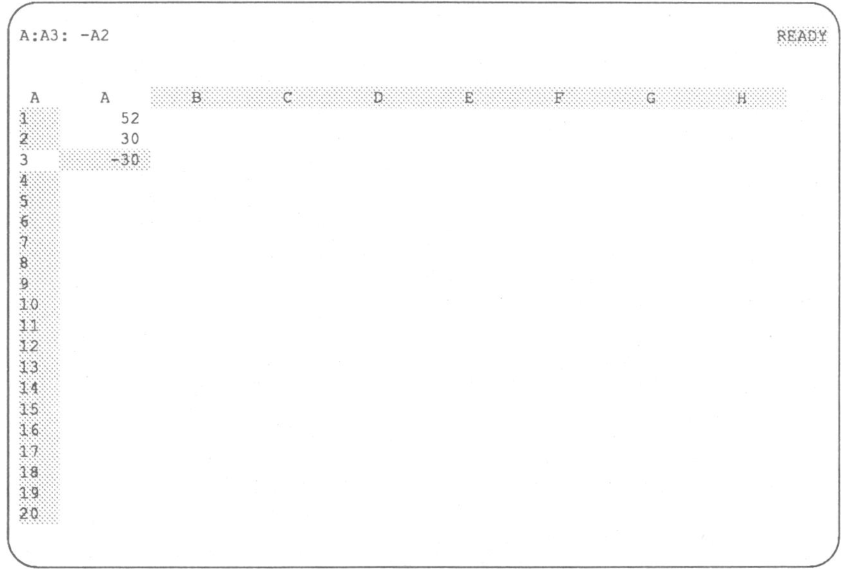

Figure 2-46

1. What caused the error in computing A1-A2?
2. How can the error be corrected?

CHAPTER TWO
EXERCISE 6
Creating a Spreadsheet

INSTRUCTIONS: Create the spreadsheet below. It will be used for exercises in other chapters. The spreadsheet consists of straight data entry (no formulas). Save the file under the name UNITPROD (for Unit Production).

The spreadsheet should look like Figure 2-47.

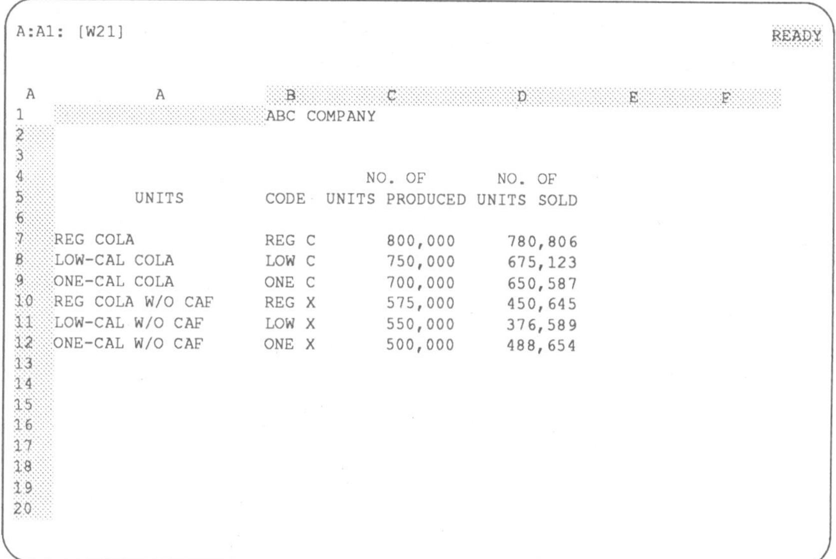

A:A1: [W21] READY

A	A	B	C	D	E	F
1		ABC COMPANY				
2						
3						
4			NO. OF	NO. OF		
5	UNITS	CODE	UNITS PRODUCED	UNITS SOLD		
6						
7	REG COLA	REG C	800,000	780,806		
8	LOW-CAL COLA	LOW C	750,000	675,123		
9	ONE-CAL COLA	ONE C	700,000	650,587		
10	REG COLA W/O CAF	REG X	575,000	450,645		
11	LOW-CAL W/O CAF	LOW X	550,000	376,589		
12	ONE-CAL W/O CAF	ONE X	500,000	488,654		
13						
14						
15						
16						
17						
18						
19						
20						

Figure 2-47

CHAPTER TWO
EXERCISE 7
Creating a Spreadsheet

INSTRUCTIONS: Create the spreadsheet below. It will be used for an exercise in a later chapter. The spreadsheet consists of straight data entry except for the SUM formula in cell C15. Save the file under the name SALES. Format only cells C8 through C13 and C15.

The spreadsheet should look like Figure 2-48.

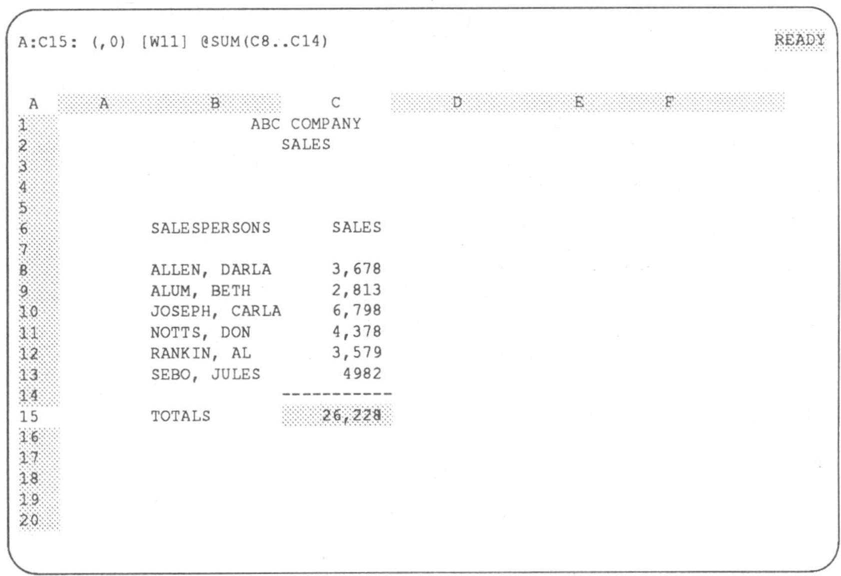

Figure 2-48

CHAPTER TWO
EXERCISE 8
Creating and Printing a Spreadsheet

INSTRUCTIONS: Create and print the spreadsheet below.

REVENUE is 25,000 in YEAR 1 and projected to increase by six percent for YEARS 2 through 5. EXPENSES are 9,500 in YEAR 1 and projected to be twenty-five percent of REVENUE in YEARS 2 through 5. PROFIT BEFORE TAX is REVENUE minus EXPENSES. TAXES are forty percent of PROFIT BEFORE TAX. PROFIT AFTER TAX is PROFIT BEFORE TAX less TAXES. Place your name and the current date on the spreadsheet. Save the file under the name PRACTICE. This file will be used in an exercise in a subsequent chapter.

Before placing your name and the current date on your worksheet, the screen should look like Figure 2-49.

```
A:C5: @ROUND(B5*(1+C14),0)                                          READY

 A        A                B        C        D        E        F        G
 1                               PROJECTED PROFITS
 2
 3                       YEAR 1   YEAR 2   YEAR 3   YEAR 4   YEAR 5    TOTAL
 4
 5  REVENUE              25,000   26,500   28,090   29,775   31,561  140,926
 6  EXPENSES              9,500    6,625    7,023    7,444    7,890   38,482
 7                      ---------------------------------------------------
 8  PROFIT BEFORE TAX    15,500   19,875   21,067   22,331   23,671  102,444
 9  TAXES                 6,200    7,950    8,427    8,932    9,468   40,978
10                      ---------------------------------------------------
11  PROFIT AFTER TAX      9,300   11,925   12,640   13,399   14,203   61,466
12                      ===================================================
13  ASSUMPTIONS
14  REVENUE GROWTH RATE                6%       6%       6%       6%
15  EXPENSE RATE                      25%      25%      25%      25%
16  TAX RATE                 40%      40%      40%      40%      40%
17
18
19
20
```

Figure 2-49

CHAPTER TWO
EXERCISE 9
Editing a Spreadsheet

INSTRUCTIONS: Retrieve the file BUDGET. Edit BUDGET using the instructions below. Use Figure 2-50 as a guide. Note that the file created will be entitled BUDGET2 and will be needed for an exercise in a later chapter.

1. Expand the worksheet to include projections through YEAR 10.

   Insert six columns (F-K) between QTR4 and YR TOTAL using the **W**orksheet **I**nsert **C**olumn command sequence.
   Rename the headings QTR1 through QTR4 with the headings YEAR 1 through YEAR 4 and continue the headings through YEAR 10. Copy the growth rate assumptions to YEARS 5 through 10. Copy the formulas, values, subtotal lines, and total lines from YEAR 4 (E7..E19) to YEAR 5 through YEAR 10 (F7..K19).

2. Change the sums under YR TOTAL to reflect the additional years:

   Change the formula in cell L7 from @SUM(B7..E7) to @SUM(B7..K7). Copy the formula in cell L7 to cells L10..L18. Replace the result of copying the @SUM formula in cells L15 and L17 (which now display zeroes) with subtotal lines.

3. Use the **M**ove command to move the titles ABC COMPANY and BUDGET to column F. The titles will be centered on the new spreadsheet.

4. Save the spreadsheet, being sure to name the new spreadsheet BUDGET2. BUDGET and BUDGET2 are two separate files on the disk.

The final result should look like Figure 2-50 (the entire spreadsheet will not be visible on the screen at one time).

ABC COMPANY
BUDGET

	YEAR 1	YEAR 2	YEAR 3	YEAR 4	YEAR 5	YEAR 6	YEAR 7	YEAR 8	YEAR 9	YEAR 10	YR TOTAL
SALES	$60,000	$61,200	$62,424	$63,672	$64,945	$66,244	$67,569	$68,920	$70,298	$71,704	$656,976
EXPENSES											
SALARIES	35,000	35,500	36,200	37,000	37,000	37,000	37,000	37,000	37,000	37,000	365,700
RENT	9,000	9,000	9,000	9,000	9,000	9,000	9,000	9,000	9,000	9,000	90,000
TELEPHONE	1,000	1,050	1,103	1,158	1,216	1,277	1,341	1,408	1,478	1,552	12,583
OFFICE SUPPLIES	750	800	850	900	950	1,000	1,050	1,100	1,150	1,200	9,750
MISCELLANEOUS	1,000	1,030	1,061	1,093	1,126	1,160	1,195	1,231	1,268	1,306	11,470
TOTAL EXPENSES	46,750	47,380	48,214	49,151	49,292	49,437	49,586	49,739	49,896	50,058	489,503
GROSS PROFIT	$13,250	$13,820	$14,210	$14,521	$15,653	$16,807	$17,983	$19,181	$20,402	$21,646	$167,473

Figure 2-50

CHAPTER TWO
EXERCISE 10
Printing a Spreadsheet with the Column Letters and Row Numbers

INSTRUCTIONS: Retrieve the file BUDGET. Print the spreadsheet so that the column letters and row numbers "frame" the spreadsheet.

CHAPTER TWO
EXERCISE 11
Printing a Spreadsheet with Various Fonts

INSTRUCTIONS: Retrieve the file BUDGET. Print the file so the spreadsheet title lines and column headings are bold serif and the remaining cells are regular serif.

CHAPTER TWO
EXERCISE 12

INSTRUCTIONS: Work the following set of problems using the information provided to make sure you understand the order of precedence in the calculation of formulas. Assume that cell A1=3, cell B2=4 and cell C4=8.

	Formula	Order of Evaluation	Answer
a.	+C4-B2*2	8-(4*2)	____________
b.	+B2-A1-C4/B2	4-3-(8/4)	____________
c.	+B2-(A1-C4)/B2	4-((3-8)/4)	____________
d.	+A1/-3+3	(3/-3)+3	____________
e.	+A1-4*C4/B2^2	3-((4*8)/4^2)	____________
f.	(A1-4)*C4/B2^2	(3-4)*(8/4^2)	____________
g.	+A1*B2/C4-10/2	((3*4)/8-(20/2))	____________

CHAPTER THREE

USEFUL LOTUS COMMANDS

- Hiding a Column
- Redisplaying a Hidden Column
- Hiding a Range of Cells
- Redisplaying a Range of Cells

Label Prefixes

Moving Cell Contents

- Moving the Contents of One Cell to Another Cell
- Moving the Contents of Several Cells to Another Location on the Worksheet

Page Break

Printing

- Borders
- Headers and Footers
- Landscape versus Portrait

Range Names

- Creating a Range Name
- Deleting a Range Name
- Table of Range Names

Recalculation of a Spreadsheet

Search and Replace

Status of a Worksheet

System Command

Titles

Undo

Widening Multiple Columns in One Worksheet

Windows

Worksheet Insertions and Deletions

- Inserting and Deleting Columns
- Inserting and Deleting Rows
- Inserting and Deleting Worksheets

Zero-Value Suppression

Summary

Key Concepts

OBJECTIVES

In this chapter, you will learn to:

- Keep a cell address constant in a formula
- Annotate ranges and formulas
- Print in background
- Protect cells
- Erase cells
- Correct cell errors
- Use various file commands
- Automatically format numbers
- Use the percent format
- Hide columns from view
- Change location of data in a cell
- Move cell contents
- Create page breaks
- Print borders, headers and footers
- Create range names and tables
- Control the recalculation of a spreadsheet
- Search and replace data
- Check status of a worksheet
- Use the system command
- Keep titles on the screen
- Undo a previous entry
- Widen multiple columns
- Create windows
- Insert and delete columns, rows and worksheets

■ CHAPTER OVERVIEW

Chapter 2 provided general procedures for building spreadsheets. Chapter 3 describes a variety of Lotus 1-2-3 commands that are often indispensable when creating and maintaining spreadsheets. For example, one exercise demonstrates how to use the **W**orksheet **T**itles command so that column headings and row labels do not scroll off of the screen when you move the cell pointer around on a large spreadsheet.

■ ABSOLUTE AND RELATIVE CELL ADDRESSES

Use the file SALES in this exercise. SALES was created in an assignment at the end of Chapter 2. To retrieve the file SALES:

Press /

Select	File
Select	Retrieve

When prompted for the file name:

Press	[F3]
Move	the cell pointer to SALES.WK3
Press	↵

To enter a formula that will compute the percentage of SALES for each salesperson:

Move	the cell pointer to cell D8
Type	+
Move	the cell pointer to cell C8
Type	/
Move	the cell pointer to cell C15
Press	↵

Cell D8 now should display the following number: 0.140232

To copy the formula for the rest of the SALESPERSONS:

Press	/
Select	Copy

When prompted for the range to copy FROM:

Press	↵

Since the cell pointer was highlighting cell D8, it is now designated as the range to copy.

When prompted for the range to copy TO:

Move	the cell pointer to cell D9
Type	.
Move	the cell pointer to cell D13
Press	↵

ERR (Error) will appear in cells D9 through D13. Your screen should look like Figure 3-1.

```
A:D8: +C8/C15                                                       READY

 A       A          B           C        D        E        F        G
 1                    ABC COMPANY
 2                       SALES
 3
 4
 5
 6            SALESPERSONS      SALES
 7
 8            ALLEN, DARLA      3,678  0.140232
 9            ALUM, BETH        2,813       ERR
10            JOSEPH, CARLA     6,798       ERR
11            NOTTS, DON        4,378       ERR
12            RANKIN, AL        3,579       ERR
13            SEBO, JULES       4,982       ERR
14                          ---------
15            TOTALS           26,228
16
17
18
19
20
                                                               CAP
```

Figure 3-1

To see why the formula +C8/C15, when copied, did not compute the expected amount:

Move the cell pointer to cell D9

Look in the control panel to see the formula in cell D9. The formula that was *intended* to be copied was **+C9/C15**. However, when the formula was copied, it became **+C9/C16**. The same results occurred for the formulas in cells D10 through D13 (**+C10/C17**, **+C11/C18**, and so on). Formulas are based upon **relative location** in Lotus 1-2-3. Lotus 1-2-3 interprets the formula that was copied not as **C8/C15** but as "divide the number one cell to the left by the number to the left and *seven rows down*". The problem occurs when the formula is copied; cell C16 is not ". . . to the left and seven rows down" for cells D9 through D13. Furthermore, since the cells C16, C17, and so forth are blank and a number cannot be divided by zero, the ERR message appears.

To solve the problem encountered above, keep cell C15 (the address for TOTAL SALES) *constant* in the formula, even when the formula is copied to other cells. Lotus 1-2-3 refers to constant cells as being **absolute**.

To enter a formula that will compute the percentage of SALES for each salesperson and keep the TOTAL SALES constant:

Move the cell pointer to cell D8

Type +

Move the cell pointer to cell C8

Type /

Move the cell pointer to cell C15

Press [F4]

Press [↵]

Look at the formula for cell D8 in the control panel. It should appear as **+C8/$C$15**. The dollar signs in front of the C and the 15 indicate that the column (C) and the row (15) will remain constant, or absolute, when copied. Cell D8 now should display the following number: 0.140232.

Note that $C$15 can be typed directly into the cell without having to use the [F4] ([Abs]) key.

The [F4] key actually has eight **cycles** or ways of changing a cell. The following options provide ways to change rows, columns and worksheets using the absolute feature.

Option	Example	Worksheet	Column	Row
1	$A:$C$8	Absolute	Absolute	Absolute
2	$A:C$8	Absolute	Relative	Absolute
3	$A:$C8	Absolute	Absolute	Relative
4	$A:C8	Absolute	Relative	Relative
5	A:$C$8	Relative	Absolute	Absolute
6	A:C$8	Relative	Relative	Absolute
7	A:$C8	Relative	Absolute	Relative
8	A:C8	Relative	Relative	Relative

You can continue pressing the [F4] key until the desired format has been selected.

To copy the formula for the rest of the SALESPERSONS:

Press /

Select Copy

When prompted for the range to copy FROM:

Press [↵]

Since the cell pointer was highlighting cell D8, it is now designated as the range to copy.

When prompted for the range to copy TO:

Move the cell pointer to cell D9

Type .

Move the cell pointer to cell D13

Press ↵

The correct computation will occur. Your screen should look like Figure 3-2.

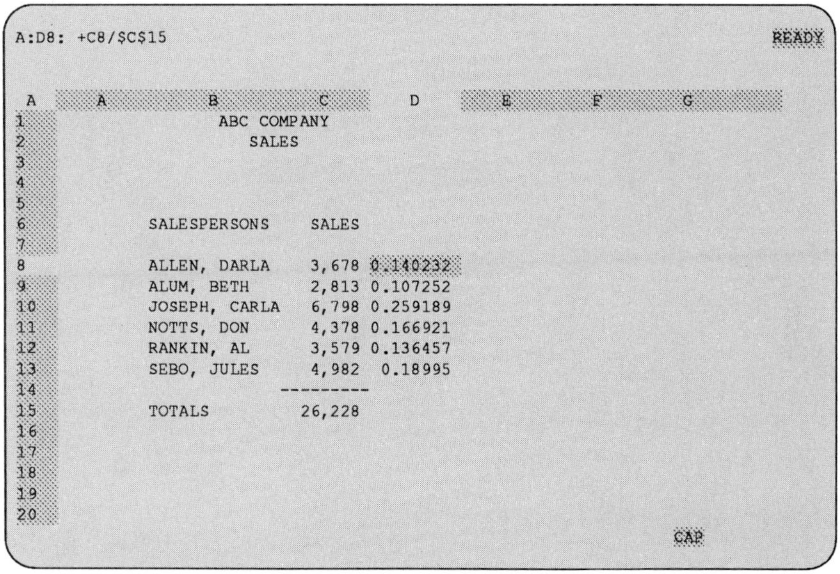

```
A:D8: +C8/$C$15                                                  READY

 A    A         B         C         D         E         F         G
 1                ABC COMPANY
 2                   SALES
 3
 4
 5
 6          SALESPERSONS     SALES
 7
 8          ALLEN, DARLA     3,678 0.140232
 9          ALUM, BETH       2,813 0.107252
10          JOSEPH, CARLA    6,798 0.259189
11          NOTTS, DON       4,378 0.166921
12          RANKIN, AL       3,579 0.136457
13          SEBO, JULES      4,982  0.18995
14                       ---------
15          TOTALS          26,228
16
17
18
19
20
                                                            CAP
```

Figure 3-2

To see how the formula +C8/$C$15 was copied:

Move the cell pointer to cell D9

The formula +C9/$C$15 should be visible in the control panel; $C$15 is held constant. If you so desire, move to cells D10 through D13 to see that $C$15 is held constant in the formulas for the cells.

■ AUDITING CONSIDERATIONS

Worksheets can be documented for ease in understanding by others. Explanatory notes can be added to values as they are entered into the worksheet. These annotations will appear in the control panel only when the cell pointer is on a cell with a notation. They do not show in the cell unless the Text format is used. Notes can also be attached to range names to explain the data in the named range.

Annotating a Formula

Retrieve the BUDGET file. To document that the SALES value in the Second Quarter represents a two percent increase over the First Quarter, you will add a note to the formula.

Move	the cell pointer to C7
Press	F2
Type	; (without any spacing before the semicolon)
Type	represents a 2% increase
Press	↵

Your screen now should look like Figure 3-3.

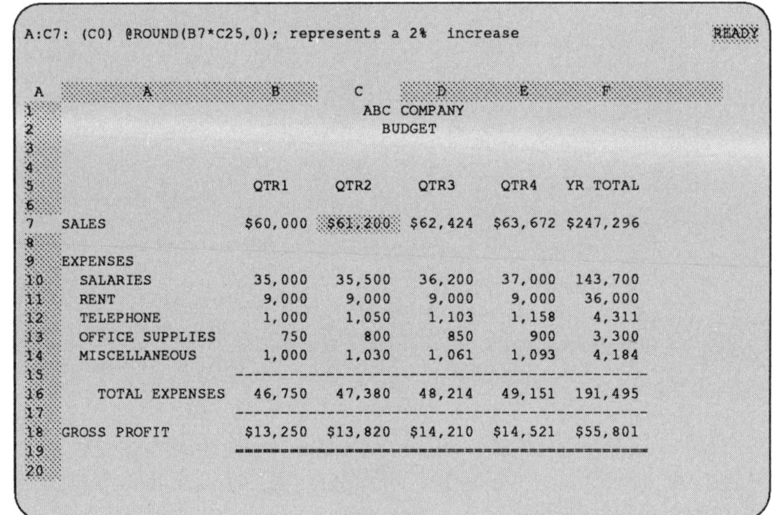

A:C7: (C0) @ROUND(B7*C25,0); represents a 2% increase READY

A	A	B	C	D	E	F
1			ABC COMPANY			
2			BUDGET			
3						
4						
5		QTR1	QTR2	QTR3	QTR4	YR TOTAL
6						
7	SALES	$60,000	$61,200	$62,424	$63,672	$247,296
8						
9	EXPENSES					
10	SALARIES	35,000	35,500	36,200	37,000	143,700
11	RENT	9,000	9,000	9,000	9,000	36,000
12	TELEPHONE	1,000	1,050	1,103	1,158	4,311
13	OFFICE SUPPLIES	750	800	850	900	3,300
14	MISCELLANEOUS	1,000	1,030	1,061	1,093	4,184
15		-------	-------	-------	-------	-------
16	TOTAL EXPENSES	46,750	47,380	48,214	49,151	191,495
17		-------	-------	-------	-------	-------
18	GROSS PROFIT	$13,250	$13,820	$14,210	$14,521	$55,801
19		=======	=======	=======	=======	=======
20						

Figure 3-3

Annotating a Range

Range names which have notes provide an explanation of the data for others. The notes are attached to the range name by using the command **R**ange **N**ame **N**ote **C**reate.

Before illustrating the process for annotating a range name, you need to create a range name that includes cells B7 through E7.

Move	the cell pointer to cell B7
Press	/

Select Range

Select Name

Select Create

When prompted for the range name:

Type SALES

Press ⏎

When prompted for the range to be assigned to the name SALES:

Move the cell pointer E7

Press ⏎

Additional information on creating range names is included in the Range Name section appearing later in this chapter.

To add a notation to the previously named SALES range in the BUDGET worksheet, use the following commands:

Press /

Select Range

Select Name

Select Note

Select Create

Select Sales

When prompted to enter the note:

Type Quarterly Sales increased 2 percent

Your screen should look like Figure 3-4.

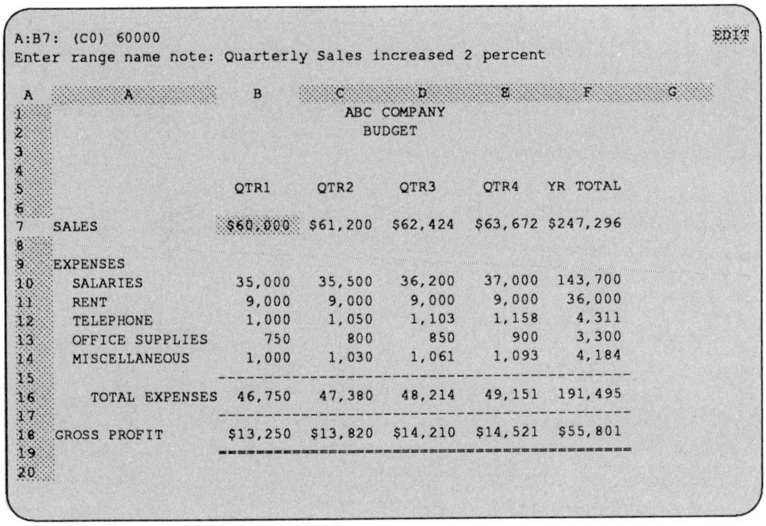

```
A:B7: (C0) 60000                                                          EDIT
Enter range name note: Quarterly Sales increased 2 percent

A        A              B        C        D        E        F        G
1                                  ABC COMPANY
2                                    BUDGET
3
4
5                      QTR1     QTR2     QTR3     QTR4   YR TOTAL
6
7   SALES            $60,000  $61,200  $62,424  $63,672 $247,296
8
9  EXPENSES
10   SALARIES         35,000   35,500   36,200   37,000  143,700
11   RENT              9,000    9,000    9,000    9,000   36,000
12   TELEPHONE         1,000    1,050    1,103    1,158    4,311
13   OFFICE SUPPLIES     750      800      850      900    3,300
14   MISCELLANEOUS     1,000    1,030    1,061    1,093    4,184
15                 ---------------------------------------------
16     TOTAL EXPENSES 46,750   47,380   48,214   49,151  191,495
17                 ---------------------------------------------
18 GROSS PROFIT      $13,250  $13,820  $14,210  $14,521  $55,801
19                 =============================================
20
```

Figure 3-4

To complete the command:

Press	↵
Select	Quit

If you wish to view the notes and range name in a worksheet, use the **R**ange **N**ame **N**ote **T**able command.

Press	/
Select	Range
Select	Name
Select	Note
Select	Table
Press	Esc
Move	the cell pointer to cell A35 (the first cell selected for the table range)
Press	↵
Select	Quit

Press (PgDn)

The table appears in a three-column format with the range name, cell addresses, and range notes. The table location selected should be blank because 1-2-3 writes over any existing data when it generates the table. When there are at least two range names, they are listed in alphabetical order. Your screen should look like Figure 3-5.

```
A:A35: [W18] 'SALES                                                        READY

A         A                  B        C        D        E        F        G
23  ASSUMPTIONS
24
25  SALES                              1.02     1.02     1.02
26  TELEPHONE EXP                      1.05     1.05     1.05
27  OFFICE SUPPLIES EXP               50.00    50.00    50.00
28  MISCELLANEOUS EXP                  1.03     1.03     1.03
29
30
31  Prepared by H. Al Napier
32          19-Jun-89
33
34
35  SALES             A:B7..A:EQuarterly Sales increased 2 percent
36
37
```

Figure 3-5

Press (Home)

Mapping a Spreadsheet

Through the Worksheet Window Map command sequence a view can be obtained of the type of data in the worksheet cells. 1-2-3 creates a map with compressed columns which displays symbols for what appears in the nonblank cells.

Make sure the BUDGET worksheet appears on your screen.

To create a map of the cell information:

Press /

Select Worksheet

Select Window

Select Map

Select Enable

Your screen now appears like Figure 3-6 showing the cell data using these symbols:

"	label cells
#	number cells
+	formulas or annotated numbers

```
A:A1: [W18]                                                          READY

 A  A B C D E F G H I J K L M N O P Q R S T U V W X Y Z AAABACADAEAFAGAHAIAJ
1      "
2      "
3
4
5     " " " " "
6
7   " # + + + +
8
9   "
10  " # # # # +
11  " # # # # +
12  " # + + + +
13  " # + + + +
14  " # + + + +
15    " " " " "
16  " + + + + +
17    " " " " "
18  " + + + + +
19    " " " " "
20
                                                               CAP
```

Figure 3-6

To return to the worksheet, you must disable the Map feature by pressing (Esc) or (↵).

Press (Esc)

Your screen should now display the BUDGET worksheet again.

■ BACKGROUND PRINTING

Background printing stores a printing job in memory so you can continue to work on another job without having to wait for the printing job to finish. Print jobs are processed in the order in which they are created unless they have been marked with one of the print priority options.

The Background printing feature works automatically unless you are printing to a file. In that situation, you must first select the **H**old option before leaving the print menu.

Retrieve the BUDGET file and print it using background printing. Follow these commands:

Press /
Select Print
Select Printer
Select Range

If necessary, highlight the portion of the worksheet to be printed for the print range.

Press ↵
Select Align
Select Go
Select Page

When the MENU mode appears:

Select Quit

Now you can save the file and retrieve a new worksheet or send another print job to the printer. Should you need to prioritize several print jobs, choose the **P**rint **P**rinter **O**ptions **A**dvanced **P**riority command. The **P**riority choices are: **D**efault—prints the current job after other jobs have been printed except those marked with low priority; **H**igh—prints the current job immediately; **L**ow—prints these jobs last.

The **W**orksheet **G**lobal **D**efault **O**ther **I**nternational commands should not be used while a job is printing or waiting to be printed because these commands may affect the way in which date information is printed.

■ CALCULATION SPEED

The **optimal recalculation** technique reduces the recalculation time when data is changed. 1-2-3 skips over cells and formulas which are not affected by the change of data. This feature is especially helpful when you are working with large spreadsheets.

When using the **W**orksheet **G**lobal **R**ecalc command, the data is recalculated automatically in the background. This means that you can continue working in the spreadsheet while the recalculation is taking place. Should you happen to make a correction to a cell while it is being recalculated, 1-2-3 simply stops the procedure and continues the recalculation after you have finished making the changes.

■ CELL PROTECTION

Cells can be locked to prevent changes from being made to them. This protection is accomplished through the **W**orksheet **G**lobal **P**rotect **E**nable command sequence or through a range command.

Once the **W**orksheet **G**lobal **P**rotect **E**nable command is used, it turns on the worksheet protection. Only when cells have been unprotected with the **R**ange **U**nprotect command can they be changed. When you try to enter data or make changes in protected cells, an error message is displayed. 1-2-3 also uses screen colors or highlighting to distinguish between protected and unprotected cells.

Saving files with a password or using the **F**ile **A**dmin **S**eal command are alternate methods for limiting access to files.

Retrieve the BUDGET file to practice protecting cells. Your screen should look like Figure 3-7.

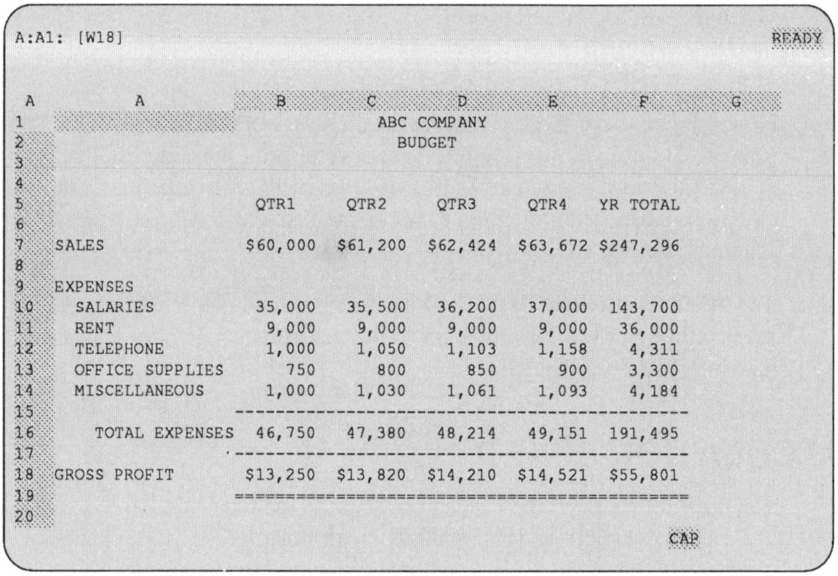

```
A:A1: [W18]                                                       READY

A        A                 B        C        D        E        F        G
1                                ABC COMPANY
2                                  BUDGET
3
4
5                       QTR1     QTR2     QTR3     QTR4   YR TOTAL
6
7  SALES              $60,000  $61,200  $62,424  $63,672  $247,296
8
9  EXPENSES
10   SALARIES          35,000   35,500   36,200   37,000   143,700
11   RENT               9,000    9,000    9,000    9,000    36,000
12   TELEPHONE          1,000    1,050    1,103    1,158     4,311
13   OFFICE SUPPLIES      750      800      850      900     3,300
14   MISCELLANEOUS      1,000    1,030    1,061    1,093     4,184
15                   ---------------------------------------------
16     TOTAL EXPENSES  46,750   47,380   48,214   49,151   191,495
17                   ---------------------------------------------
18 GROSS PROFIT       $13,250  $13,820  $14,210  $14,521   $55,801
19                   =============================================
20
                                                               CAP
```

Figure 3-7

To protect all of the cells in the worksheet, use the following Worksheet global commands:

Press	/
Select	Worksheet
Select	Global

Select Prot

Select Enable

Now all the cells are protected. To unprotect cells A1..B14, use the following Range commands:

Press /

Select Range

Select Unprot

When prompted to enter the range to unprotect, highlight cells A1..B14.

Press ↵

The unprotected area will be a different color or highlighted depending upon the type of monitor being used.

Move cell pointer to cell C10

Type 36000

Press ↵

Your computer will sound a "beep" and a message will appear at the bottom of the screen reminding you that the cell is protected.

Press Esc

Move cell pointer to cell B10

Type 36000

Press ↵

Notice that you are able to change the data in the unprotected cell, and the worksheet recalculates.

Using the Range commands, return the unprotected cells to a protected status again.

Press /

Select Range

Select Prot

When prompted to enter the range to protect, highlight cells A1..B14.

Press	↵

The entire worksheet is protected again and changes cannot be made to any of the cells.

■ ERASING CELLS

Retrieve the file BUDGET2 for this exercise.

To erase the labels ABC COMPANY in cells F1 and BUDGET in F2:

Move	the cell pointer to cell F1
Press	/
Select	Range
Select	Erase
Press	↓

The highlighted cells should appear as in Figure 3-8.

```
A:F2: '       BUDGET                                                    POINT
Enter range to erase: A:F1..A:F2

 A          A               B         C         D         E         F         G
1                                                                    ABC COMPANY
2                                                                      BUDGET
3
4
5                        YEAR 1    YEAR 2    YEAR 3    YEAR 4    YEAR 5    YEAR 6
6
7   SALES               $60,000   $61,200   $62,424   $63,672   $64,945   $66,244
8
9   EXPENSES
10    SALARIES           35,000    35,500    36,200    37,000    37,000    37,000
11    RENT                9,000     9,000     9,000     9,000     9,000     9,000
12    TELEPHONE           1,000     1,050     1,103     1,158     1,216     1,277
13    OFFICE SUPPLIES       750       800       850       900       950     1,000
14    MISCELLANEOUS       1,000     1,030     1,061     1,093     1,126     1,160
15                     -----------------------------------------------------------
16      TOTAL EXPENSES   46,750    47,380    48,214    49,151    49,292    49,437
17                     -----------------------------------------------------------
18  GROSS PROFIT        $13,250   $13,820   $14,210   $14,521   $15,653   $16,807
19                     ===========================================================
20
                                                                      CAP
```

Figure 3-8

Press ⏎

Cells F1 and F2 are now erased. Your screen should look like Figure 3-9.

A:F1: READY

A	A	B	C	D	E	F	G
1							
2							
3							
4							
5		YEAR 1	YEAR 2	YEAR 3	YEAR 4	YEAR 5	YEAR 6
6							
7	SALES	$60,000	$61,200	$62,424	$63,672	$64,945	$66,244
8							
9	EXPENSES						
10	SALARIES	35,000	35,500	36,200	37,000	37,000	37,000
11	RENT	9,000	9,000	9,000	9,000	9,000	9,000
12	TELEPHONE	1,000	1,050	1,103	1,158	1,216	1,277
13	OFFICE SUPPLIES	750	800	850	900	950	1,000
14	MISCELLANEOUS	1,000	1,030	1,061	1,093	1,126	1,160
15		---------	---------	---------	---------	---------	---------
16	TOTAL EXPENSES	46,750	47,380	48,214	49,151	49,292	49,437
17		---------	---------	---------	---------	---------	---------
18	GROSS PROFIT	$13,250	$13,820	$14,210	$14,521	$15,653	$16,807
19		=========	=========	=========	=========	=========	=========
20							

Figure 3-9

■ ERROR CORRECTION AND CELL EDITING

There are various ways to correct errors on a worksheet. Two commonly used methods are illustrated below.

Replacing an Erroneous Entry

Clear your screen. In cell A1:

Type 100

Press ⏎

Your screen should look like Figure 3-10 Part 1.

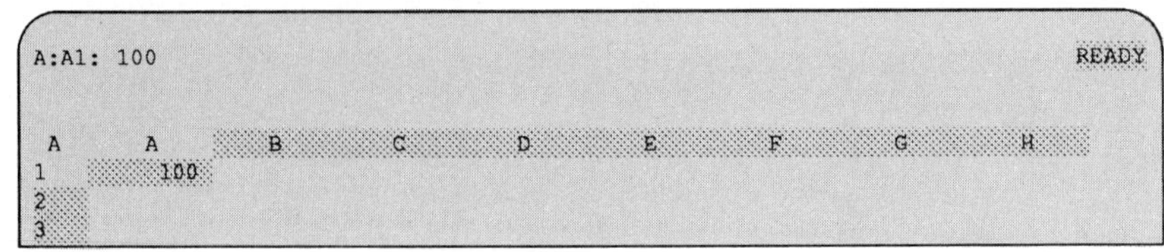

Figure 3-10
Part 1

To change the entry to 1000:

Type 1000

Press ↵

To replace an item that is incorrect, make sure the cell pointer is highlighting the incorrect cell entry and retype the entry. Your screen should look like Figure 3-10 Part 2.

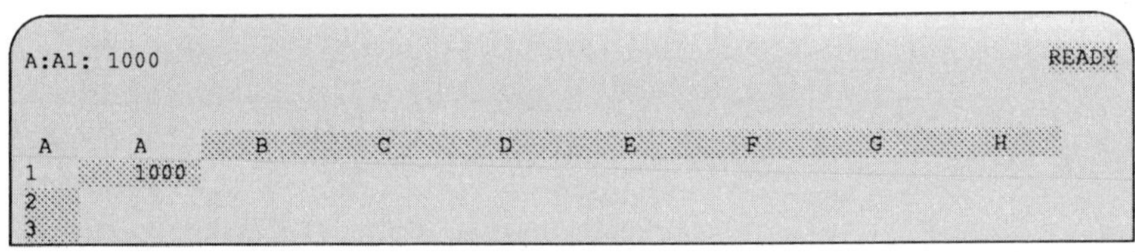

Figure 3-10
Part 2

Editing an Entry Using the F2 Key

To change the cell entry in cell A1 from 1000 to 1000*1.03:

Move the cell pointer to cell A1

Press F2

The entry is displayed in the control panel and a cursor appears at the end of the entry. EDIT appears as the mode indicator to indicate that the EDIT mode has been activated. The screen should look like Figure 3-11 Part 1.

```
A:A1: 1000                                                    EDIT
1000

 A     A       B       C       D       E       F       G       H
 1     1000
 2
 3
```

Figure 3-11
Part 1

To add to the end of the existing entry:

Type *1.03

Press ↵

The entry in cell A1 has now been changed from 1000 to 1000*1.03. Your screen should look like Figure 3-11 Part 2.

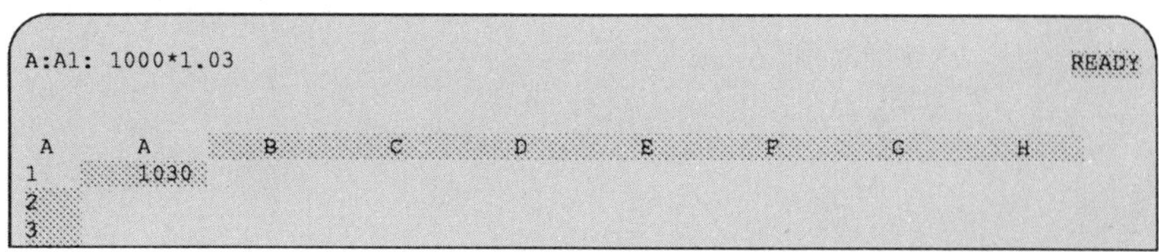

Figure 3-11
Part 2

When the EDIT mode is activated, the left and right pointer-movement keys as well as the [Home] and [End] keys can be used to move to various characters in an entry.

Clear your screen using the **W**orksheet **E**rase **Y**es command sequence..

Move the cell pointer to cell C3

Type ABC COMPANY

Press ↵

To change the entry to THE ABC MANUFACTURING COMPANY, INC.:

Press [F2]

Press [Home]

The cursor is now under the apostrophe, which is the default label prefix. The [Home] key places the cursor at the first position of the cell entry.

Press → to move the cursor to the letter A in ABC

Type THE

Press the space bar

When the additional text is typed, the remaining text **moves over** so that the new text is inserted. To insert MANUFACTURING:

Press → until the cursor appears under the space after ABC

Press the space bar

Type MANUFACTURING

Press the space bar

To move quickly to the end of the line, you can use the End key so that , INC. can be added:

Press End

Type , INC.

Since the entry is completely edited:

Press ↵

The screen should look like Figure 3-12.

A:C3: 'THE ABC MANUFACTURING COMPANY, INC. READY

A	A	B	C	D	E	F	G	H
1								
2								
3			THE ABC MANUFACTURING COMPANY, INC.					
4								
5								

Figure 3-12

When you are in EDIT mode, additional text can be typed and the remaining text is **moved over**, as illustrated in the example above.

The Ins or Insert key can be pressed to activate Overstrike (OVR will appear on the screen).

If the Overstrike function is activated, the new text will overstrike or type over the existing text. For example, to replace the letters ABC with XYZ:

Move the cell pointer to cell C3

Press F2

Press ← to move to the letter A in ABC (or use the Home key and the → key to achieve the same result).

Press Ins

OVR appears at the bottom right corner of the screen.

Type XYZ

Press ↵

The letters ABC now have been replaced with the letters XYZ. Your screen should look like Figure 3-13.

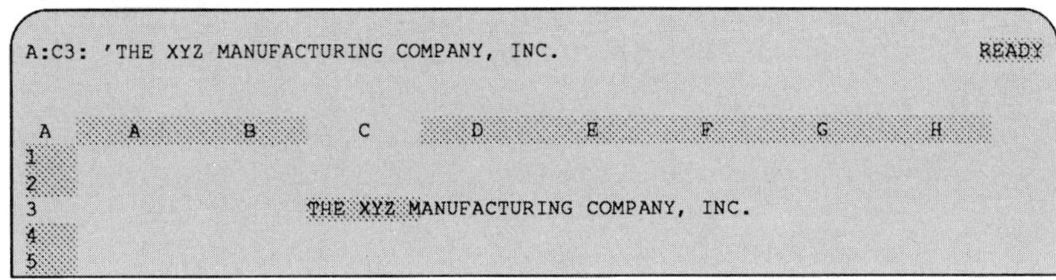

Figure 3-13

FILE COMMANDS

File Directory

The File Directory command changes the drive and path specifications from which files are retrieved and saved. To change from drive C to drive A, for example:

Press /

Select File

Select Directory

Your screen should look similar to Figure 3-14.

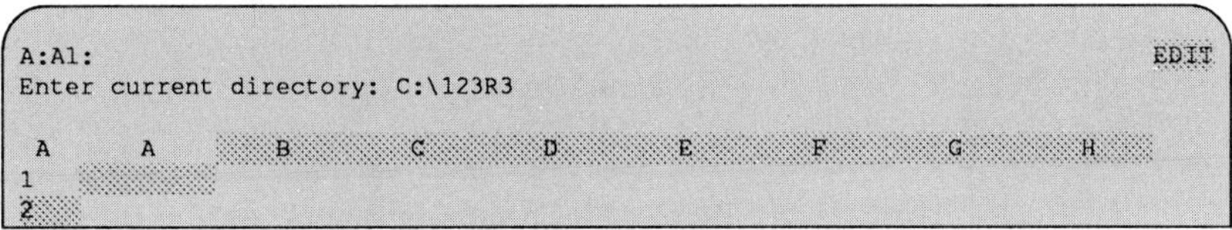

Figure 3-14

The current directory (where data files are being retrieved and saved) should be displayed. If you are currently saving all of the data in the root directory on drive C, your directory setting is C:\ .

To change the directory to drive A, for example, you could type A:\ and press ↵ to save or retrieve files from drive A (do **not** do so at this time). To avoid changing the directory from its present setting:

Press	Esc until the menus disappear from the control panel

Note: To permanently change the directory, issue the **W**orksheet **G**lobal **D**efault **D**irectory sequence. Change the directory to the desired drive or path, press the ↵ key and select **U**pdate to permanently save the directory as a default. Choose **Q**uit to exit the menu.

File Erase

The **F**ile **E**rase command sequence erases a file. To erase a worksheet file:

Press	/
Select	File
Select	Erase

Four types of files are listed on the menu—Worksheet, Print, Graph and Other. When prompted for the type of file to erase:

Select	Worksheet

Your screen should look like Figure 3-15.

Figure 3-15

To erase a file, you can press the F3 key and use the pointer-movement keys to highlight the file to erase and press ↵ (do **not** do so at this time). To escape from this process and not erase a file:

Press	Esc until the menus disappear

File List

The **File List** command sequence lists the files in the directory being used. To list the worksheet files:

Press	/
Select	File
Select	List

Note the six options—Worksheet, Print, Graph, Other, Active or Linked.

Worksheet: lists the worksheet files.

Print: lists print files (created using the **Print File** command sequence and printing a range to a file).

Graph: lists graph files (created using the **Graph Save** command sequence to print a graph from the graph settings in the current file).

Other: lists all files in the directory being used including those that were not created with Lotus 1-2-3.

Active: lists the files that are in memory.

Linked: lists the files that are linked to the current file.

Select Worksheet

Your screen should look like Figure 3-16.

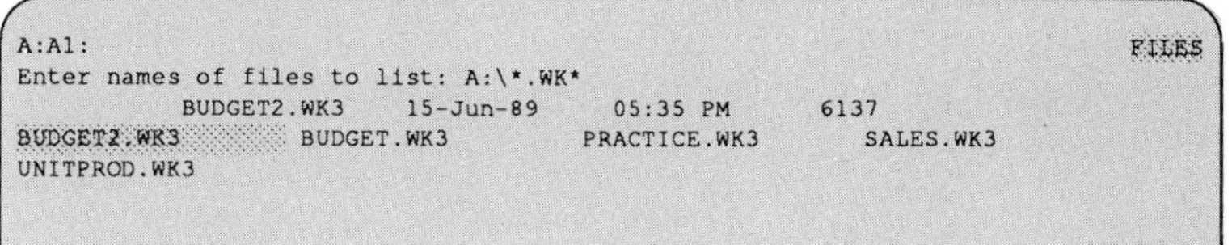

Figure 3-16

To return to the worksheet:

Press ↵

File Admin Seal

In a multiuser situation, several persons may be using a file at the same time. Only one user at a time may make changes to a file. 1-2-3 has a **reservation-setting** which guarantees you changes to a file can be saved. If you do not have a file's reservation status, changes to that file cannot be saved. A read only (RO) indicator alerts you that the reservation status is currently not available.

The Seal feature prevents changes from being made to worksheets, ranges, graphs, or print settings. A file is sealed by using the **File Admin Seal** command sequence. The entire file or just the reservation-settings can be sealed.

The file or reservation-settings are sealed from general use with a password. Only users who know the password can make changes to the file. The password is case sensitive. It is important to remember or keep a record of the exact password and the combination of uppercase or lowercase letters that you used.

When a password is entered at the prompt, 1-2-3 displays an asterisk for each character. Upon entering the password, 1-2-3 again asks you to verify the password. You must enter the exact password again.

Three choices appear when selecting the Seal feature. Each choice performs one of the following functions:

File:	seals the File and the Reservation-Settings.
Reservation-Setting:	seals the Settings only.
Disable:	permits the unsealing of the File or Reservation-Settings.

Retrieve the BUDGET file and use the following commands to seal the file's reservation-settings so they cannot be changed.

Press /

Select File

Select Admin

Select Seal

Select Reservation-Setting

When prompted to enter a password, choose a suitable word and make a notation of it exactly as it was entered.

Press 

When prompted to verify the password, enter the same password exactly as you did before. Your screen should look similar to Figure 3-17.

```
A:A1: [W18]                                                                 EDIT
Enter password: ******                    Verify password: ******_

A    A                    B        C        D        E        F        G
1                                    ABC COMPANY
2                                      BUDGET
3
4
5                         QTR1     QTR2     QTR3     QTR4   YR TOTAL
6
7   SALES              $60,000  $61,200  $62,424  $63,672 $247,296
8
9   EXPENSES
10    SALARIES           35,000   35,500   36,200   37,000  143,700
11    RENT                9,000    9,000    9,000    9,000   36,000
12    TELEPHONE           1,000    1,050    1,103    1,158    4,311
13    OFFICE SUPPLIES       750      800      850      900    3,300
14    MISCELLANEOUS       1,000    1,030    1,061    1,093    4,184
15                     ---------------------------------------------
16      TOTAL EXPENSES   46,750   47,380   48,214   49,151  191,495
17                     ---------------------------------------------
18  GROSS PROFIT       $13,250  $13,820  $14,210  $14,521  $55,801
19                     =============================================
20
                                                            CAP
```

Figure 3-17

Press ↵

To remove the password, the procedure is similar. Use the following commands:

Press /

Select File

Select Admin

Select Seal

Select Disable

When prompted to enter the password, use the password you used before to seal the file or reservation-settings. Your screen should look like Figure 3-18.

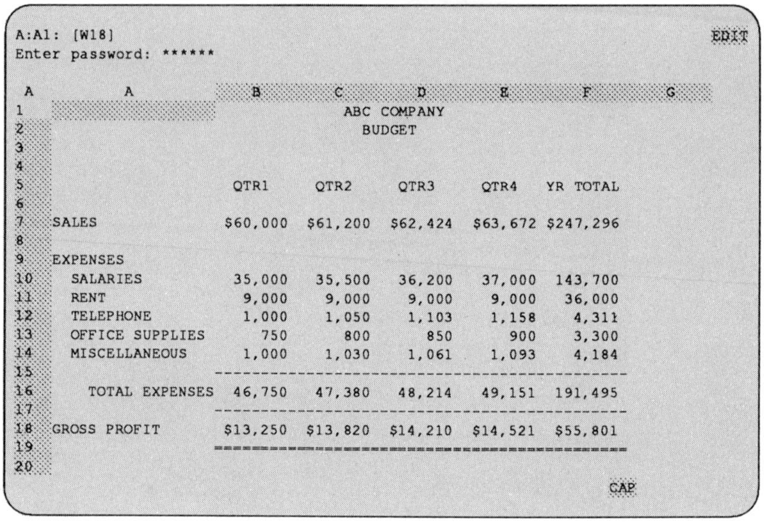

```
A:A1: [W18]                                                              EDIT
Enter password: ******

A         A              B        C        D        E        F        G
1                                ABC COMPANY
2                                  BUDGET
3
4
5                      QTR1     QTR2     QTR3     QTR4   YR TOTAL
6
7  SALES             $60,000  $61,200  $62,424  $63,672 $247,296
8
9  EXPENSES
10   SALARIES         35,000   35,500   36,200   37,000  143,700
11   RENT              9,000    9,000    9,000    9,000   36,000
12   TELEPHONE         1,000    1,050    1,103    1,158    4,311
13   OFFICE SUPPLIES     750      800      850      900    3,300
14   MISCELLANEOUS     1,000    1,030    1,061    1,093    4,184
15                  ---------------------------------------------
16     TOTAL EXPENSES 46,750   47,380   48,214   49,151  191,495
17                  ---------------------------------------------
18 GROSS PROFIT      $13,250  $13,820  $14,210  $14,521  $55,801
19                  =============================================
20
                                                            CAP
```

Figure 3-18

Press ↵

Whether a file is sealed or just the reservation-setting is sealed, the following commands will not work in making changes to the file:

File Admin Reservation-Setting
Graph Name
Print Encoded/File/Printer Options Name
Range Format
Range Label
Range Name
Range Name Note
Range Protect
Range Unprotect
Worksheet Column
Worksheet Hide
Worksheet Global

When the reservation-setting is sealed, changes can be made to everything in the file except the reservation-setting.

Before sealing the entire file, it is wise to unprotect the cells that may have data changes. Use the **R**ange **U**nprot command sequence. If the file is globally protected, data can only be changed in the unprotected cells.

File Save Backup

When saving a file, 1-2-3 will automatically add a three-character extension to a file name. Although there are six possible extensions, only the backup extension (BAK) and the temporary extension (TMP) cannot be overridden by changing the file extension when specifying the file to be saved.

The **F**ile **S**ave **B**ackup command is useful when you want to save the last version of a file without renaming the file. To use this feature, follow these commands:

Press /

Select File

Select Save

When prompted to enter the file name, a file name already appears above the control panel.

Press ↵

Three choices appear on the screen as shown in Figure 3-19.

Cancel: cancels the Save command.

Replace: replaces the original file with the file being used.

Backup: creates a second file with a backup (BAK) extension.

```
A:A1: [W18]                                                              MENU
Cancel  Replace  Backup
Create a backup file from a file on disk (with a .BAK extension)
 A          A              B        C        D        E        F        G
1                                      ABC COMPANY
2                                        BUDGET
3
4
5                          QTR1     QTR2     QTR3     QTR4    YR TOTAL
6
7   SALES               $60,000  $61,200  $62,424  $63,672  $247,296
8
9   EXPENSES
10    SALARIES            35,000   35,500   36,200   37,000   143,700
11    RENT                 9,000    9,000    9,000    9,000    36,000
12    TELEPHONE            1,000    1,050    1,103    1,158     4,311
13    OFFICE SUPPLIES        750      800      850      900     3,300
14    MISCELLANEOUS        1,000    1,030    1,061    1,093     4,184
15                     ---------------------------------------------
16      TOTAL EXPENSES    46,750   47,380   48,214   49,151   191,495
17                     ---------------------------------------------
18  GROSS PROFIT        $13,250  $13,820  $14,210  $14,521   $55,801
19                     =============================================
20
                                                            CAP
```

Figure 3-19

Select Backup

The file is now saved under its original extension and also as a backup file with the backup extension.

File Admin Tables

One of the features of the **F**ile **A**dmin **T**ables command sequence is its capability to create information in table form about active files and files on the disk. From the following six selections, tables can be created which will occupy from four to seven columns.

Worksheet:	worksheet files in a specific directory.
Print:	files in a specific directory with PRN extension.
Graph:	graph files in a specific directory.
Other:	all files in a specific directory.
Active:	all the active files.
Linked:	all files linked by formula references to current file.

To create a table showing all the files on the disk in drive C:

Press /

Select File

Select Admin

Select Table

Select Other

When prompted to enter the current directory:

Type C:*.* (or your directory)

Press ↵

When prompted to enter a range, select an area which is blank since existing data will be written over by the table.

Press ↵

A sample of a table appears in Figure 3-20.

```
A:A1: '123DOS.EXE                                                READY

A     A          B        C           D        E        F        G        H
1   123DOS.EX   32660 0.227269   822447
2   123.CNF     32693 0.506481      184
3   123.DCF     32681  0.62794      313
4   123.EXE     32660 0.267292    54805
5   123.HLP     32660 0.015394   451390
6   ACCTG.WK3   32651 0.783727     2186
7   BC008LBA.   32645 0.569352     6418
8   BC014LDA.   32645 0.569722     8735
9   BC031LDA.   32645 0.570648    20561
10  CONSOL.WK   32623 0.612454     2746
11  DATA.WK3    32644 0.478495     3199
12  DBT13S.WK   32623 0.613171     5540
13  DBT14S.WK   32623 0.613565     5548
14  DR123TXT.   32645 0.506806      395
15  EMPFILE.D   32622 0.480787      666
16  EXPENSES.   32646 0.535509     2315
17  FLATE.RI    32639 0.666042     1078
18  HRCF25MM.   32647 0.846343     1207
19  INC10S.WK   32623 0.614213     2295
20  INC11S.WK   32623 0.614583     5141
```

Figure 3-20

The first column indicates the filename; the second and third columns show the date and time before they are formatted. The last column indicates the file size.

If the date and time are formatted and the columns have been widened to display the information, your table would look similar to Figure 3-21. The process of formatting the date and time is covered in Chapter 9.

```
A:A1: '123DOS.EXE                                                READY

A     A           B              C             D        E        F        G
1   123DOS.EX   01-Jun-89     05:27 AM     822447
2   123.CNF     04-Jul-89     12:09 PM        184
3   123.DCF     22-Jun-89     03:04 PM        313
4   123.EXE     01-Jun-89     06:24 AM      54805
5   123.HLP     01-Jun-89     12:22 AM     451390
6   ACCTG.WK3   23-May-89     06:48 PM       2186
7   BC008LBA.   17-May-89     01:39 PM       6418
8   BC014LDA.   17-May-89     01:40 PM       8735
9   BC031LDA.   17-May-89     01:41 PM      20561
10  CONSOL.WK   25-Apr-89     02:41 PM       2746
11  DATA.WK3    16-May-89     11:29 AM       3199
12  DBT13S.WK   25-Apr-89     02:42 PM       5540
13  DBT14S.WK   25-Apr-89     02:43 PM       5548
14  DR123TXT.   17-May-89     12:09 PM        395
15  EMPFILE.D   24-Apr-89     11:32 AM        666
16  EXPENSES.   18-May-89     12:51 PM       2315
17  FLATE.RI    11-May-89     03:59 PM       1078
18  HRCF25MM.   19-May-89     08:18 PM       1207
19  INC10S.WK   25-Apr-89     02:44 PM       2295
20  INC11S.WK   25-Apr-89     02:45 PM       5141
```

Figure 3-21

With some of the table choices additional columns appear. The fifth column indicates the number of worksheets in a file. The sixth column shows whether changes have been made to a file. A "0" indicates no changes; a "1" shows that changes have been made to the file. The seventh column represents the file's reservation status. A "1" means you have the reservation; a "0" indicates no reservation.

■ FORMATTING

Automatic

Regular formatting uses two operations. First the value is entered; then the cell is formatted. With automatic formatting, data can be entered and formatted at the same time. Automatic formatting can be applied to the entire worksheet or it can be used for a specific range.

With automatic formatting, 1-2-3 recognizes data as it is entered and formats cells in a logical way. Existing numbers are formatted in General format. When a new entry is made, 1-2-3 looks at the number and then formats that cell according to the format used in the number.

Clear your screen. To format a worksheet globally using the Automatic feature:

Press /

Select Worksheet

Select Global

Select Format

Select Other

Select Automatic

Widen column A to 15 spaces. Then place the cursor in cell A1. Include the commas and decimal point as you enter a number.

Type 35,000.00

Press ↵

Additional entries are formatted according to the previous cell unless the new entry uses a different format. If a different format is used, 1-2-3 changes to that format and continues to use it for subsequent entries until a new format is encountered.

Move the cell pointer down column A of the worksheet as you enter these numbers. Include the commas and decimal points.

Type 9,000.00

Type 0,750.00

Type 1,000.00

Your screen should look like Figure 3-22.

```
A:A4: (,2) [W15] 1000                                    READY

A        A           B      C      D      E      F      G
1    35,000.00
2     9,000.00
3       750.00
4     1,000.00
5
6
```

Figure 3-22

In cell A4 0,750.00 was entered. The zero and comma in front of the number 750 are place holders. The numbers have been entered in the Comma format with two decimal places. 1-2-3 immediately recognized the format and displayed (, 2) in the control panel before the value. Another format such as the Currency format could have been used.

To illustrate how you can change formats, move the cell pointer to cell A6.

Type 25%

Press ↵

Look at the control panel in Figure 3-23 and notice that 1-2-3 recognized the format change to **P**ercent with zero decimal places (P0) and stored the number as .25 in cell A6.

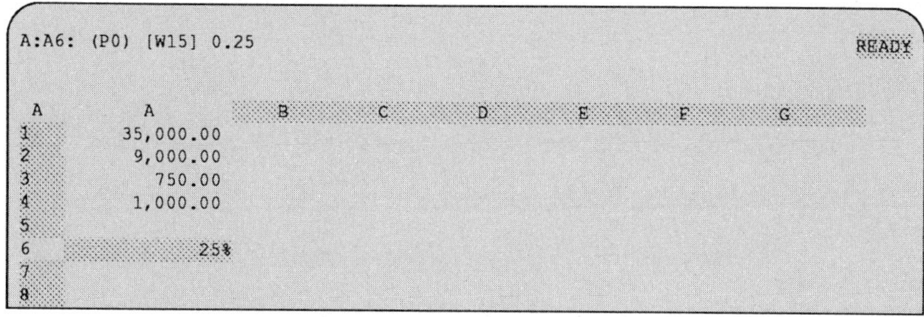

Figure 3-23

Ranges can also be formatted automatically. Erase the current worksheet, then widen column A to 15. To format a range automatically:

Press /

Select Range

Select	Format
Select	Other
Select	Automatic

Highlight the range A1..A4 when prompted to enter the range. Using the Currency format, enter the following numbers in cells A1 through A4 making certain that the dollar sign, comma, and periods are included.

Type	$9,000.00	in cell A1
Type	$1,000.00	in cell A2
Type	$750.00	in cell A3
Type	$1,000.00	in cell A4

The screen should look like Figure 3-24. Notice that 1-2-3 recognized the format as Currency with two decimal places (C2) as shown in the control panel.

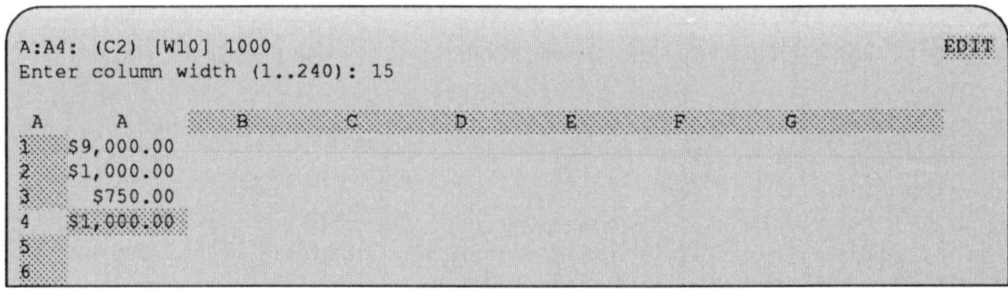

Figure 3-24

Percent

Retrieve the file SALES so that the percent format can be illustrated.

Create an appropriate heading as follows:

Move	the cell pointer to D6
Type	"% SALES

The " symbol right-justifies the label in cell D6. See the Label Prefixes section later in this chapter for additional information.

Press	↵

To format the data in column D so that percent signs and two decimal places are displayed:

Move the cell pointer to D8

Press /

Select Range

Select Format

Select Percent

To accept the default of two decimal places:

Press ↵

When prompted for the range to format:

Move the cell pointer to cell D15

The range to format should be cells D8..D15. If it is not, press the Esc key to release the anchor and set the range to D8..D15. When the range is correct:

Press ↵

To enter percentages in column D:

Type @ROUND(C8/$C$15,2)

Press ↵

To copy the formula to the remaining cells in column D:

Press /

Select Copy

Press ↵

Move the cell pointer to cell D9

Press .

Move the cell pointer down to cell D15

Press ↵

Move the cell pointer to cell D14

Type \-

Press ⏎

The percentages now use the Percent format which multiplies the data by 100, displays the desired number of decimal places, and attaches the % symbol to the end of the data. Note that percentages do not always add up to 100 percent, but may add up to 99 or 101 percent. Using the @ROUND function for percentages (e.g., @ROUND(+C8/$C$15,2) may not solve the problem. It also may be necessary to "plug" a number to obtain the desired results.

Your screen should look like Figure 3-25.

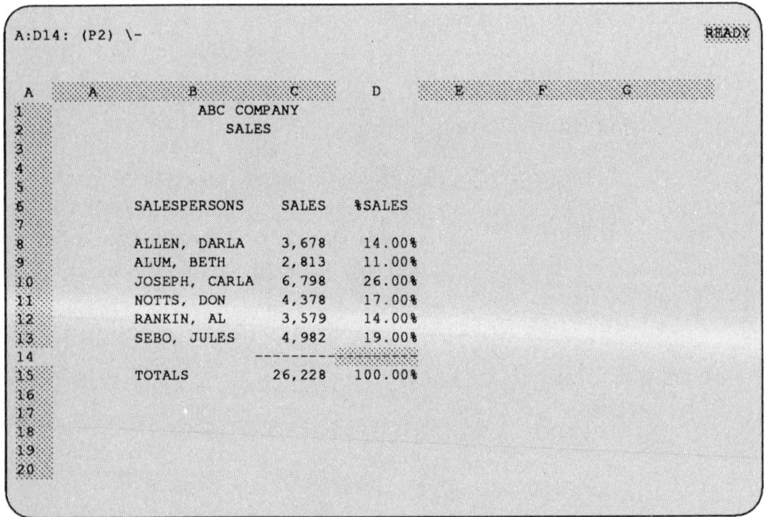

Figure 3-25

HIDING AND REDISPLAYING COLUMNS

Hiding a Column

One or more columns of a worksheet can be suppressed so that any data in them is not displayed or printed, but the data continues to be used in calculations.

Retrieve the BUDGET file. To hide column E:

Press /

Select Worksheet

Select Column

Select Hide

When prompted for the column(s) to hide:

Move	the cell pointer to a cell in column E
Press	↵

Column E is no longer visible on the screen. Your screen should look like Figure 3-26.

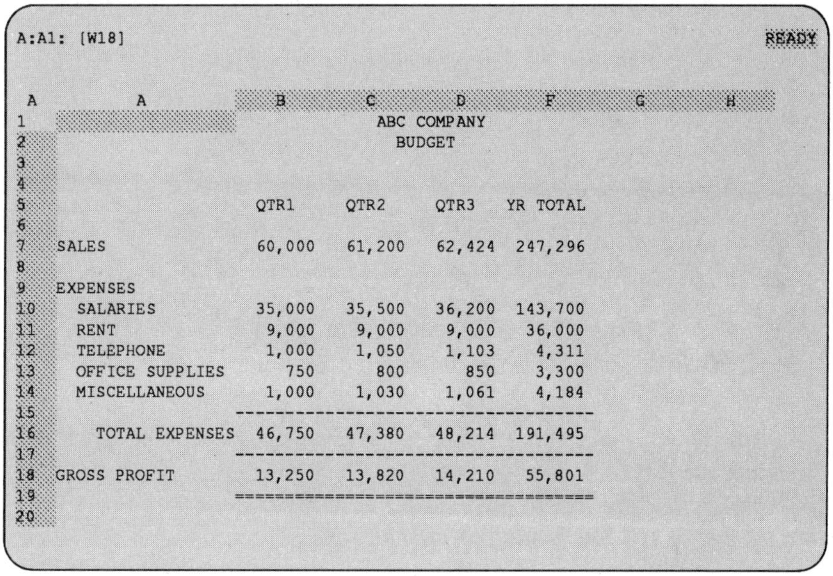

```
A:A1: [W18]                                                        READY

 A         A           B         C         D         F         G         H
 1                             ABC COMPANY
 2                               BUDGET
 3
 4
 5                   QTR1      QTR2      QTR3    YR TOTAL
 6
 7 SALES             60,000    61,200    62,424  247,296
 8
 9 EXPENSES
10   SALARIES        35,000    35,500    36,200  143,700
11   RENT             9,000     9,000     9,000   36,000
12   TELEPHONE        1,000     1,050     1,103    4,311
13   OFFICE SUPPLIES    750       800       850    3,300
14   MISCELLANEOUS    1,000     1,030     1,061    4,184
15                 ------------------------------------
16     TOTAL EXPENSES 46,750   47,380    48,214  191,495
17                 ------------------------------------
18 GROSS PROFIT      13,250    13,820    14,210   55,801
19                 ====================================
20
```

Figure 3-26

Redisplaying a Hidden Column

To make column E visible on the screen again:

Press	/
Select	Worksheet
Select	Column
Select	Display

The columns which had been hidden will now be visible and an asterisk appears beside each column.

When prompted for the column to unhide:

Move	the cell pointer to a cell in column E

Press ↵

Column E now should appear on your screen.

Hiding a Range of Cells

To hide the GROSS PROFIT label and values and double underlines:

Move the cell pointer to cell A18

Press /

Select Range

Select Format

Select Hidden

Move the cell pointer to cell F19

Press ↵

The GROSS PROFIT label and associated values as well as the double underlines have been hidden.

Redisplaying a Range of Cells

To restore the hidden information to your screen:

Move the cell pointer to cell A18

Press /

Select Range

Select Format

Select Reset

Move the cell pointer to cell F19

Press ↵

The hidden data now appears on your screen.

■ LABEL PREFIXES

The use of the caret (the ^ symbol) to center labels was illustrated in Chapter 2. The caret is a **label prefix**. 1-2-3 has four label prefixes that affect the appearance of labels on the screen and when they are printed. In this section, the label prefixes are discussed and demonstrated. Before starting the following exercise, erase your screen.

The apostrophe (the ' symbol located on the double-quote key) is the default label prefix in 1-2-3. When a nonnumeric character is the first character of an entry, 1-2-3 automatically places an apostrophe as the prefix to the label. The entry then appears at the left of the cell in which it is input. Enter the following label in cell A1:

Type	USA
Press	↵

Look at the control panel. Notice that an apostrophe appears in the control panel before USA. In the worksheet, notice that USA appears on the left side of cell A1. Because you did not specify a label prefix, the apostrophe was used. Your screen should look like Figure 3-27.

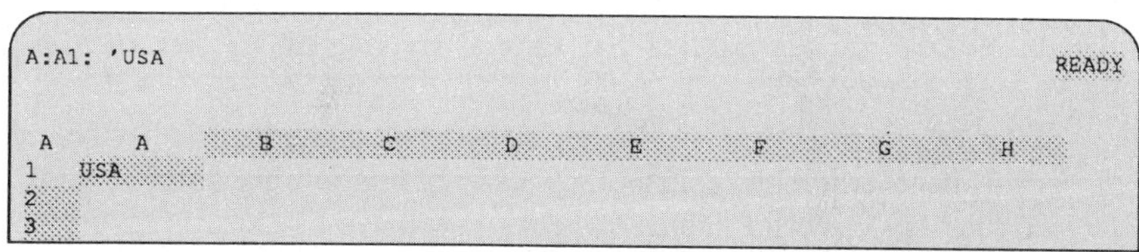

Figure 3-27

Erase the screen using the **W**orksheet **E**rase **Y**es command sequence. In cell A1, manually input the apostrophe before entering USA.

Type	'USA
Press	↵

Again, USA appears at the left side of the cell. The apostrophe appears before USA in the control panel when cell A1 is highlighted.

The caret symbol causes a label to appear in the center of a cell. The caret must be typed as the first character of the entry. To center a label:

Move	the cell pointer to cell A2
Type	^USA
Press	↵

USA appears in the center of the cell. The caret appears before USA in the control panel when cell A2 is highlighted.

The double-quote symbol causes a label to appear at the right side of the cell. The double-quote must be typed as the first character of the entry. To right-justify a label:

Move	the cell pointer to cell A3
Type	"USA
Press	↵

USA appears in the rightmost portion of the cell. The double-quote appears before USA in the control panel when cell A3 is highlighted.

The backward slash (the \ symbol) causes the characters entered after the backward slash to be repeated in the cells. To cause the label USA to be repeated in a cell:

Move	the cell pointer to cell A4
Type	\USA
Press	↵

Cell A4 displays USAUSAUSA throughout the cell. If the width of column A is shortened or lengthened, the repeating label adjusts accordingly. This label prefix is useful for subtotal and total lines. For example, entering \- will cause repeating dashes to appear in a cell. Refer to Figure 3-28 to see how the label prefixes alter the appearance of the label USA.

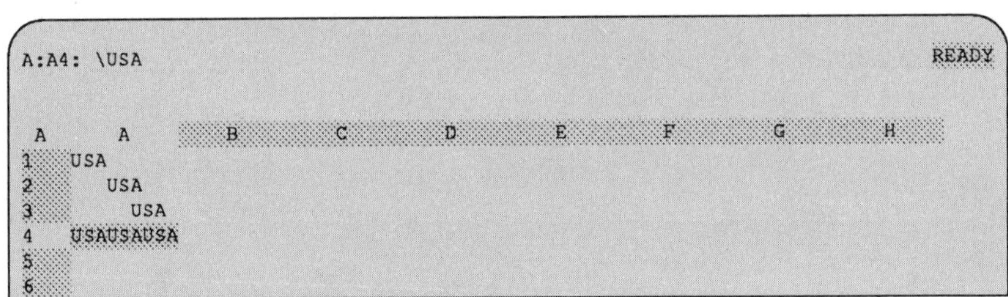

Figure 3-28

Note that label prefixes are to be used only for **labels**. If ^123 is entered in a cell, for example, 123 is centered and treated as a label in a cell and should not be used for computation.

■ MOVING CELL CONTENTS

To prepare to illustrate the process of moving the contents of cells from one location on a spreadsheet to another location, complete the following steps. First erase the worksheet on your screen. Make sure the cell pointer is in cell A1; then:

Type	100
Press	↵
Move	the cell pointer to cell A4
Type	50
Press	→
Type	25
Press	↵

Make sure your screen looks like Figure 3-29.

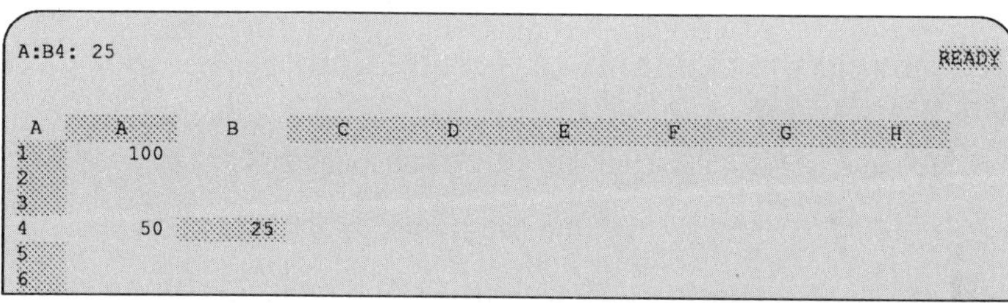

Figure 3-29

Moving the Contents of One Cell to Another Cell

To move the contents of cell A1 to cell H1:

Move	the cell pointer to cell A1

When the cell pointer is already highlighting the cell to move, it is easier to use the Move command.

Press	/
Select	Move

When prompted for the range to move FROM:

Press	↵

The cell to move (cell A1) was already highlighted, so only the ↵ had to be pressed.

When prompted for the range to move TO:

Move the cell pointer to cell H1

Press ↵

Your screen should look like Figure 3-30.

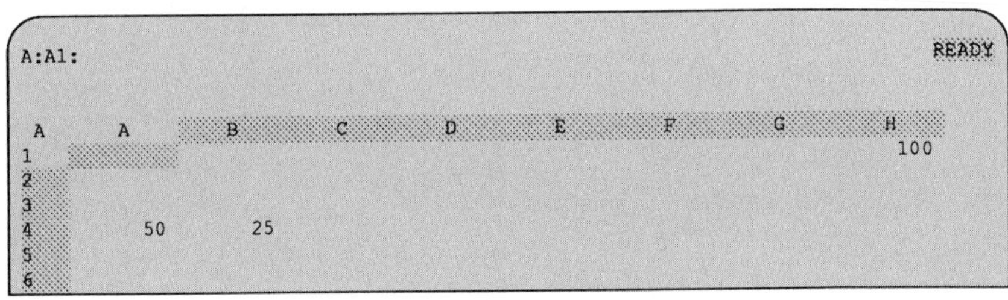

Figure 3-30

Moving the Contents of Several Cells to Another Location on the Worksheet

To move cells A4 through B4 to cells A14 through B14:

Move the cell pointer to cell A4

Press /

Select Move

When prompted for the range to move FROM:

Move the cell pointer to cell B4

Cells A4 through B4 are now highlighted and therefore specified as the cells to move.

Press ↵

When prompted for the range to move TO:

Move the cell pointer to cell A14

Press ↵

The contents of cells A4 through B4 have now been moved to cells A14 through B14. Note that it was only necessary to specify the upper left corner of the range to move to. Your screen should look like Figure 3-31.

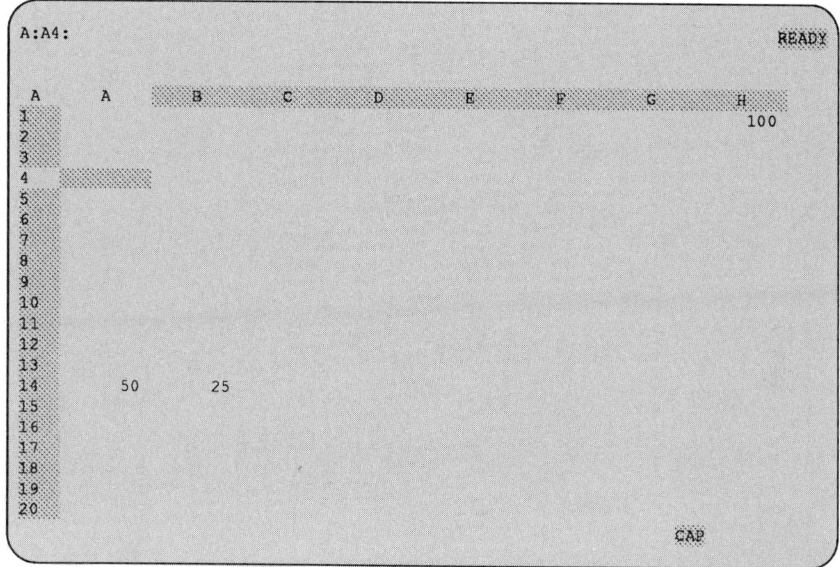

Figure 3-31

■ PAGE BREAK

When printing a spreadsheet in Lotus 1-2-3, Lotus prints as much as it can on a single page based upon the default page length. The remaining rows are printed on the next page or set of pages. Sometimes, you may wish to specify where you want page breaks to occur. The page break command can be used in such situations.

Retrieve the BUDGET2 file for use in the following exercise. To set a print range:

Press /

Select Print

Select Printer

Select Range

If necessary, press the [Esc] key to delete the current print range. When prompted for the range to print:

Press the [Home] key (if the cell pointer is not already in cell A1)

Type .

Move the cell pointer to cell G32

Cells A1. .G32 (the descriptions, data and assumptions for YEAR 1 through YEAR 6) are now highlighted.

Press ↵

Select Quit

To insert a page break at cell A12:

Move the cell pointer to cell A12

Press /

Select Worksheet

Type Page

Note that two colons (: :) now appear in cell A12. The data that was previously in rows 12 through the end of the worksheet has been moved down one row. If the print range for BUDGET2 is printed, the data in row 13 (TELEPHONE expenses) will be printed at the top of the second page. Note that |: : (the pipe symbol and two colons) appear in the control panel as the contents of A12. The symbols |: : can be typed manually on the spreadsheet where a page break is desired. No data should be contained in the row with the designation for the page break if the symbol is typed. Note that the page break symbol can be erased just as though it were a typical data entry using the **R**ange **E**rase command sequence. The **W**orksheet **D**elete **R**ow command sequence may be preferable because a row was added to accommodate the page break symbol. Your screen should look like Figure 3-32 Part 1.

```
A:A12: [W18] |::                                                          READY

A          A               B         C         D         E         F         G
1                                                                 ABC COMPANY
2                                                                   BUDGET
3
4
5                       YEAR 1    YEAR 2    YEAR 3    YEAR 4    YEAR 5    YEAR 6
6
7   SALES              $60,000   $61,200   $62,424   $63,672   $64,945   $66,244
8
9   EXPENSES
10    SALARIES          35,000    35,500    36,200    37,000    37,000    37,000
11    RENT               9,000     9,000     9,000     9,000     9,000     9,000
12  ::
13    TELEPHONE          1,000     1,050     1,103     1,158     1,216     1,277
14    OFFICE SUPPLIES      750       800       850       900       950     1,000
15    MISCELLANEOUS      1,000     1,030     1,061     1,093     1,126     1,160
16                  ------------------------------------------------------------
17      TOTAL EXPENSES  46,750    47,380    48,214    49,151    49,292    49,437
18                  ------------------------------------------------------------
19  GROSS PROFIT       $13,250   $13,820   $14,210   $14,521   $15,653   $16,807
20                  ============================================================
                                                                    CAP
```

Figure 3-32
Part 1

To print the spreadsheet:

Press	/
Select	Print
Select	Printer
Select	Align
Select	Go

After printing:

Select	Page
Select	Quit

Assuming that the printing was performed on 8 1/2 by 11-inch paper, your printout should look like Figure 3-32 Parts 2 and 3.

ABC COMPANY
BUDGET

	YEAR 1	YEAR 2	YEAR 3	YEAR 4	YEAR 5	YEAR 6
SALES	$60,000	$61,200	$62,424	$63,672	$64,945	$66,244
EXPENSES						
SALARIES	35,000	35,500	36,200	37,000	37,000	37,000
RENT	9,000	9,000	9,000	9,000	9,000	9,000

Figure 3-32
Part 2

TELEPHONE	1,000	1,050	1,103	1,158	1,216	1,277
OFFICE SUPPLIES	750	800	850	900	950	1,000
MISCELLANEOUS	1,000	1,030	1,061	1,093	1,126	1,160
TOTAL EXPENSE:	46,750	47,380	48,214	49,151	49,292	49,437
GROSS PROFIT	$13,250	$13,820	$14,210	$14,521	$15,653	$16,807
GROWTH RATE ASSUMPTIONS						
SALES		1.02	1.02	1.02	1.02	1.02
TELEPHONE		1.05	1.05	1.05	1.05	1.05
OFFICE SUPPLIES		50.00	50.00	50.00	50.00	50.00
MISCELLANEOUS		1.03	1.03	1.03	1.03	1.03

Figure 3-32
Part 3

To delete the page break symbol, you must delete the row containing it or erase the cell. In this case you will delete the row.

Move the cell pointer to cell A12

Press /

Select Worksheet

Select Delete

Select Row

Press ↵

The page break symbol no longer appears on your screen.

■ PRINTING

Borders

The **B**orders option is useful when working with large spreadsheets or worksheets of more than one page. This command places headings or labels from the worksheet on every page either to the left of the data or at the top of the page, or both.

Row borders are useful when there are several pages to a report. They provide descriptive information at the top of each page. Column information can be printed on the left side of each page for ease in reading the worksheet.

When using the **B**order feature, there are several options to choose from:

Columns: vertical headings to the left of each print range and at the left side of each page.

Rows: horizontal headings above each print range and at the top of each page.

Frame: prints the column letters above each print range and the row numbers to the left of each print range and printed page.

No-frame: cancels the instructions to print the frame.

Before starting this exercise, retrieve the BUDGET2 file. To print columns on every page of the worksheet:

Press /

Select Print

Select Printer

Select Options

Select Borders

Select Columns

To make the labels in column A appear on every page, highlight a cell in column A; then

Press ↵

Select Quit

When selecting the print range, do not include the borders. This would cause a double printing of the border. For this example:

Select Range

To clear the current print range:

Press Esc

To specify the new print range:

Move the cell pointer to cell B1

Type .

Move the cell pointer to cell L28

Press ↵

To undo a border selection, use **P**rint **P**rinter **C**lear **B**orders.

Headers and Footers

A header is a line of text entered below the top margin of every page. The default reserves three lines for a header: one line for the text followed by two blank lines before the data. Headers may be placed at the left margin, right margin, or centered. Although headers are normally short, they may contain as many as 512 characters.

To place a header at the top of each page, use the following procedure:

Select Options

Select Header

When prompted to enter the header:

Type ABC COMPANY

Notice the control panel in Figure 3-33.

```
A:A1: [W18]                                                          EDIT
Enter header: ABC COMPANY

A          A            B        C        D        E        F        G
1                                                          ABC COMPANY
2                                                            BUDGET
3
4
5                     YEAR 1   YEAR 2   YEAR 3   YEAR 4   YEAR 5   YEAR 6
6
7  SALES              $60,000  $61,200  $62,424  $63,672  $64,945  $66,244
8
9  EXPENSES
10   SALARIES          35,000   35,500   36,200   37,000   37,000   37,000
11   RENT               9,000    9,000    9,000    9,000    9,000    9,000
12   TELEPHONE          1,000    1,050    1,103    1,158    1,216    1,277
13   OFFICE SUPPLIES      750      800      850      900      950    1,000
14   MISCELLANEOUS      1,000    1,030    1,061    1,093    1,126    1,160
15                    -----------------------------------------------------
16     TOTAL EXPENSES  46,750   47,380   48,214   49,151   49,292   49,437
17                    -----------------------------------------------------
18 GROSS PROFIT       $13,250  $13,820  $14,210  $14,521  $15,653  $16,807
19                    =====================================================
20
                                                          CAP
```

Figure 3-33

Press ↵

Headers are entered only once, but they are reproduced on each printed page. Headers can be changed by repeating the procedure. They can be deleted by repeating the procedure and then pressing the Esc key when you are prompted to enter the heading.

Headers and footers may also be entered by using special characters and symbols. The following symbols can be used to format them:

- # (pound symbol) used to place the page number on every page.
- ## (double pound symbol) when followed by a page number specifies that page number as the first page of the printout.
- @ (at symbol) places current date (DD-MM-YY) on every page.
- | (vertical bar) separates footers or headers (left, right, or centered).
- \ (backslash) followed by a cell address or range name whose contents become the footer text.

The vertical bar controls the position of the text on the page. Without the vertical bar, the text is left-justified. With one vertical bar preceding the text, it is centered. With two vertical bars preceding the symbol, the text is right-justified.

To create a footer which will result in a right-justified page number:

Select Footer

When prompted to enter the footer:

Type ||#

Your control panel should match the one shown in Figure 3-34.

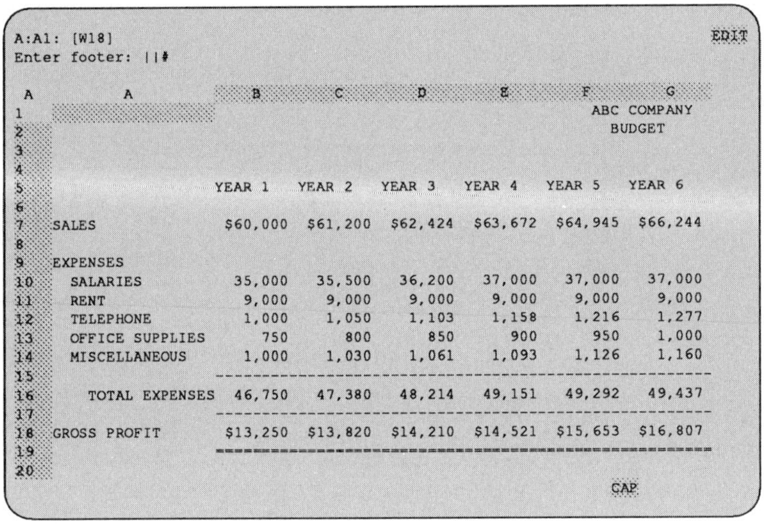

```
A:A1: [W18]                                                                EDIT
Enter footer: ||#

A          A             B        C        D        E        F        G
1                                                               ABC COMPANY
2                                                                 BUDGET
3
4
5                     YEAR 1   YEAR 2   YEAR 3   YEAR 4   YEAR 5   YEAR 6
6
7   SALES            $60,000  $61,200  $62,424  $63,672  $64,945  $66,244
8
9   EXPENSES
10    SALARIES        35,000   35,500   36,200   37,000   37,000   37,000
11    RENT             9,000    9,000    9,000    9,000    9,000    9,000
12    TELEPHONE        1,000    1,050    1,103    1,158    1,216    1,277
13    OFFICE SUPPLIES    750      800      850      900      950    1,000
14    MISCELLANEOUS    1,000    1,030    1,061    1,093    1,126    1,160
15                 ------------------------------------------------------
16      TOTAL EXPENSES 46,750  47,380   48,214   49,151   49,292   49,437
17                 ------------------------------------------------------
18  GROSS PROFIT     $13,250  $13,820  $14,210  $14,521  $15,653  $16,807
19                 ======================================================
20
                                                                 CAP
```

Figure 3-34

Press ↵

Select Quit

Note that the Page command must be issued for 1-2-3 to put a footer on the last page. To print the worksheet with the borders, header and footer:

Select Align

Select Go

Select Page (twice if necessary to advance paper to top of next page)

Select Quit

Landscape versus Portrait

Text and graphs can be printed either horizontally or vertically on the page. The vertical printing position (from top to bottom of the page) is called the Portrait mode and it is the default selection. The horizontal printing position (sideways on the page) is called the Landscape mode which makes the printout wider.

Before printing, the layout for printing from vertical (Portrait) to horizontal (Landscape) can be changed by using the following procedure:

Press /

Select Print

Select Printer

Select Option

Select Advanced

Select Layout

Select Orientation

Select Landscape

Select Quit four times

To place the data attractively on the page, you must adjust the margins and page length. On some printers, you will not be able to use the Landscape mode.

■ RANGE NAMES

Creating a Range Name

Range names can be used rather than cell addresses to make it easier to remember the location of cells. A range name is associated with cell addresses.

Retrieve the BUDGET worksheet. To assign a range name to the cells containing the values of TOTAL EXPENSES for the four quarters:

Press /

Select Range

Select Name

Select Create

When prompted for the range name:

Type TOTAL_EXP

Press ↵

When prompted for the range to be assigned to the name TOTAL_EXP:

Press Esc

Move cell pointer to B16

Type .

Move cell pointer to E16

Your screen should look like Figure 3-35.

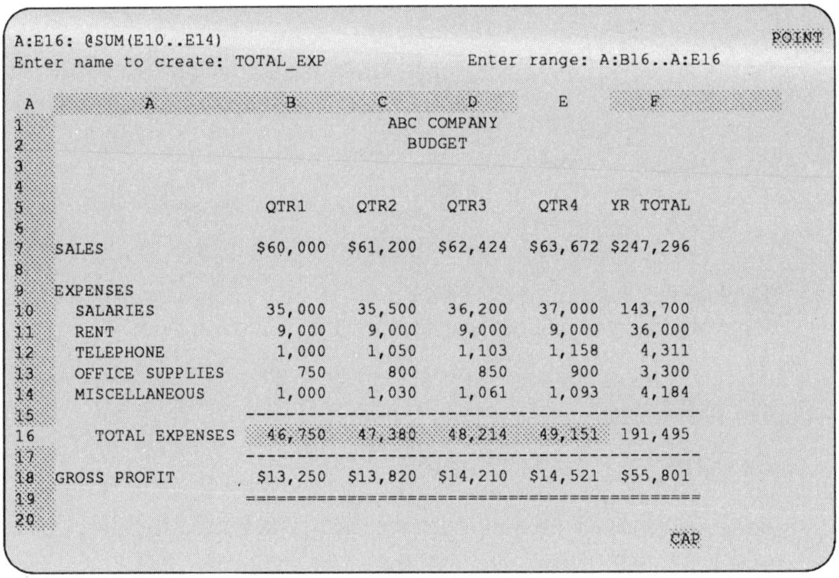

```
A:E16: @SUM(E10..E14)                                                  POINT
Enter name to create: TOTAL_EXP            Enter range: A:B16..A:E16

 A         A              B        C        D        E        F
 1                                   ABC COMPANY
 2                                     BUDGET
 3
 4
 5                       QTR1     QTR2     QTR3     QTR4   YR TOTAL
 6
 7  SALES              $60,000  $61,200  $62,424  $63,672 $247,296
 8
 9  EXPENSES
10    SALARIES          35,000   35,500   36,200   37,000  143,700
11    RENT               9,000    9,000    9,000    9,000   36,000
12    TELEPHONE          1,000    1,050    1,103    1,158    4,311
13    OFFICE SUPPLIES      750      800      850      900    3,300
14    MISCELLANEOUS      1,000    1,030    1,061    1,093    4,184
15                     ---------------------------------------------
16      TOTAL EXPENSES  46,750   47,380   48,214   49,151  191,495
17                     ---------------------------------------------
18  GROSS PROFIT       $13,250  $13,820  $14,210  $14,521  $55,801
19                     =============================================
20
                                                                 CAP
```

Figure 3-35

Press ↵

Range names are used in formulas in place of cell addresses. Cell addresses in formulas are changed to reflect that you have defined a range name.

Move the cell pointer to cell F16

Note that TOTAL_EXP has replaced the B16..E16 in the @SUM function.

Names may be up to 15 characters in length. Do not use special characters. The underline and dash symbols are an exception and may be used.

Deleting a Range Name

When deleting a range name, the range name is replaced in formulas with the cell address. It does not change the range. Remember to delete the name for a range of cells before assigning the name to a different set of cells.

To delete a range name for a range of cells:

Press /

Select Range

Select Name

Select Delete

Press F3

Specify the range name TOTAL_EXP is to be deleted by highlighting it.

Press ↵

Notice that TOTAL_EXP in cell F16 has been replaced with B16..E16.

Table of Range Names

An alphabetical list of range names can be created by using the **R**ange **N**ame **T**able command. Decide on a location for the table before beginning the command. This area should be blank so that the table does not overwrite existing data.

Retrieve the BUDGET file and create range names for SALES, SALARIES, and TOTAL EXPENSES that include the values for QTR1 through QTR4 for each item. Then create an alphabetical list of the range names by using the following procedure:

Press /

Select Range

Select Name

Select Table

When prompted to enter the range for the table, place the cell pointer in the upper left corner of the output area.

Press Esc

Move the cell pointer to cell A35

Press ↵

The table should be placed below the worksheet assumptions and your screen should look like Figure 3-36.

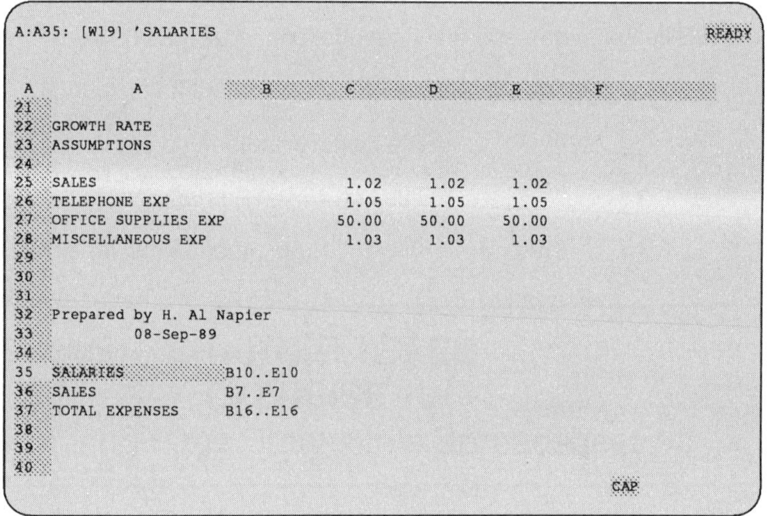

Figure 3-36

■ RECALCULATION OF A SPREADSHEET

Retrieve the file BUDGET2 for this exercise. To change the value of a cell on the worksheet:

Move the cell pointer to cell B7

Type 70000

Press ↵

The worksheet is recalculated with the new entry $70,000 for YEAR 1 of SALES. Your screen should look like Figure 3-37 Part 1. The initial settings for recalculation are Automatic and Natural; the worksheet recalculates automatically and in natural order every time any cell is changed. Sometimes when new data is input, it may take several seconds or even minutes for the worksheet to recalculate. If you have several changes to make, then time will be wasted while you wait for 1-2-3 to recalculate the worksheet as you make each change. A way to reduce the amount of time wasted is to set the Recalculation option to Manual.

To control the recalculation in a worksheet manually:

Press	/
Select	Worksheet
Select	Global
Select	Recalc
Select	Manual

The recalculation options are described below.

Natural:	first recalculates other formulas on which a particular formula depends.
Columnwise:	causes the worksheet to recalculate in columnwise order.
Rowwise:	causes the worksheet to recalculate in rowwise order.
Automatic:	causes the worksheet to recalculate every time the worksheet data is changed.
Manual:	causes the worksheet to recalculate only by pressing the F9 function key.
Iteration	causes the worksheet to recalculate a designated number of times, or iterations.

To change the SALES amount in cell B7 again:

Type	80000
Press	↵

Note that when the number 80000 was entered, the worksheet was not recalculated and the letters CALC appeared at the bottom right corner of the screen. Your screen should look like Figure 3-37 Part 2.

```
A:B7: (C0) 70000                                                    READY

A         A             B        C        D        E        F        G
1                                                           ABC COMPANY
2                                                             BUDGET
3
4
5                    YEAR 1   YEAR 2   YEAR 3   YEAR 4   YEAR 5   YEAR 6
6
7  SALES            $70,000  $71,400  $72,828  $74,285  $75,771  $77,286
8
9  EXPENSES
10   SALARIES        35,000   35,500   36,200   37,000   37,000   37,000
11   RENT             9,000    9,000    9,000    9,000    9,000    9,000
12   TELEPHONE        1,000    1,050    1,103    1,158    1,216    1,277
13   OFFICE SUPPLIES    750      800      850      900      950    1,000
14   MISCELLANEOUS    1,000    1,030    1,061    1,093    1,126    1,160
15                 ------------------------------------------------------
16     TOTAL EXPENSES 46,750   47,380   48,214   49,151   49,292   49,437
17                 ------------------------------------------------------
18 GROSS PROFIT     $23,250  $24,020  $24,614  $25,134  $26,479  $27,849
19                 ======================================================
20
                                                         CAP
```

Figure 3-37
Part 1

```
A:B7: (C0) 80000                                                    READY

A         A             B        C        D        E        F        G
1                                                           ABC COMPANY
2                                                             BUDGET
3
4
5                    YEAR 1   YEAR 2   YEAR 3   YEAR 4   YEAR 5   YEAR 6
6
7  SALES            $80,000  $71,400  $72,828  $74,285  $75,771  $77,286
8
9  EXPENSES
10   SALARIES        35,000   35,500   36,200   37,000   37,000   37,000
11   RENT             9,000    9,000    9,000    9,000    9,000    9,000
12   TELEPHONE        1,000    1,050    1,103    1,158    1,216    1,277
13   OFFICE SUPPLIES    750      800      850      900      950    1,000
14   MISCELLANEOUS    1,000    1,030    1,061    1,093    1,126    1,160
15                 ------------------------------------------------------
16     TOTAL EXPENSES 46,750   47,380   48,214   49,151   49,292   49,437
17                 ------------------------------------------------------
18 GROSS PROFIT     $23,250  $24,020  $24,614  $25,134  $26,479  $27,849
19                 ======================================================
20
                                             CALC        CAP
```

Figure 3-37
Part 2

To recalculate the worksheet:

Press F9

The F9 key is sometimes referred to as the CALC key.

Your worksheet is now recalculated. If another number is changed at this point, CALC will reappear on the screen. Multiple entries can be made without the worksheet recalculating after each new entry. The F9 key must be pressed again before the worksheet will be recalculated. Your screen should look like Figure 3-37, Part 3.

```
A:B7: (C0) 80000                                                        READY

A         A              B        C        D        E        F        G
1                                                            ABC COMPANY
2                                                              BUDGET
3
4
5                      YEAR 1   YEAR 2   YEAR 3   YEAR 4   YEAR 5   YEAR 6
6
7   SALES             $80,000  $81,600  $83,232  $84,897  $86,595  $88,327
8
9   EXPENSES
10    SALARIES         35,000   35,500   36,200   37,000   37,000   37,000
11    RENT              9,000    9,000    9,000    9,000    9,000    9,000
12    TELEPHONE         1,000    1,050    1,103    1,158    1,216    1,277
13    OFFICE SUPPLIES     750      800      850      900      950    1,000
14    MISCELLANEOUS     1,000    1,030    1,061    1,093    1,126    1,160
15                    ------------------------------------------------------
16      TOTAL EXPENSES 46,750   47,380   48,214   49,151   49,292   49,437
17                    ------------------------------------------------------
18  GROSS PROFIT      $33,250  $34,220  $35,018  $35,746  $37,303  $38,890
19                    ======================================================
20
                                                              CAP
```

Figure 3-37
Part 3

To cause the worksheet to recalculate automatically when the contents of a cell are changed or new data is entered:

Press /

Select Worksheet

Select Global

Select Recalc

Select Automatic

Your worksheet will now recalculate automatically whenever a change is made.

SEARCH AND REPLACE

The **R**ange **S**earch command finds a string of characters in a label, formula, or both and highlights the string. If you specify the command to replace the string, 1-2-3 finds the string and then replaces it with the string of characters you enter.

Uppercase and lowercase letters are treated without sensitivity. In the **F**ind option, you are given the choice of continuing the search or quitting.

The **R**eplace option highlights the matching cell. It provides the following four options:

Replace: inserts the replacement and moves to the next occurrence.

All: replaces each occurrence of the string.

Next: finds the next matching string without replacing it.

Quit: quits the search and replace procedure.

When there are no further matching strings, an error message is displayed. When this occurs, press ↵ or Esc to return to the READY mode.

Retrieve the BUDGET file and search for the word SALES.

Press /

Select Range

Select Search

When prompted to enter a range to be searched, highlight the entire worksheet.

Press ↵

When you are prompted for the search string:

Type SALES

Press ↵

Select Both

Select Find

Your screen should look like Figure 3-38.

```
A:A7: [W19] 'SALES                                                      MENU
Next  Quit
Find next matching string without replacing current string
 A          A              B        C        D        E        F
1                                      ABC COMPANY
2                                        BUDGET
3
4
5                           QTR1     QTR2     QTR3     QTR4   YR TOTAL
6
7   SALES                 $60,000  $61,200  $62,424  $63,672 $247,296
8
9   EXPENSES
10    SALARIES             35,000   35,500   36,200   37,000  143,700
11    RENT                  9,000    9,000    9,000    9,000   36,000
12    TELEPHONE             1,000    1,050    1,103    1,158    4,311
13    OFFICE SUPPLIES         750      800      850      900    3,300
14    MISCELLANEOUS         1,000    1,030    1,061    1,093    4,184
15                       ---------------------------------------------
16      TOTAL EXPENSES     46,750   47,380   48,214   49,151  191,495
17                       ---------------------------------------------
18  GROSS PROFIT          $13,250  $13,820  $14,210  $14,521  $55,801
19                       =============================================
20
                                                                  CAP
```

Figure 3-38

Select Next

until you hear a beep indicating there are no additional matches.

When there are no other matching strings, press ↵ or Esc to return to the READY mode.

To replace a string, choose **R**eplace and type in the replacement string at the prompt. You may then proceed in the same manner as the **F**ind option.

■ STATUS OF A WORKSHEET

Retrieve the BUDGET2 file.

To look at the Status (settings) of the worksheet:

Press /

Select Worksheet

Select Status

Various settings are displayed. The displayed settings indicate available memory as well as the default or global settings for recalculation, format, label prefixes, column widths, and protected cells for the current file (in this example, the BUDGET2 file). Additional information is provided such as whether a math coprocessor is used, how many iterations are used to recalculate the worksheet, whether circular references exist and whether zero suppression is being used. Your screen should look similar to Figure 3-39. The available memory, processor and math coprocessor settings depend upon the system being used.

```
                                                                    STAT

Available memory: 479436 of 479436 Bytes (100%)

Processor: 80286
Math coprocessor: 80287

Recalculation:
  Method........... Automatic
  Order............ Natural
  Iterations....... 1

Circular reference: (None)

Cell display:
  Format........... (G)
  Label prefix..... '
  Column width..... 9
  Zero setting..... No

Global protection: Off
```

Figure 3-39

To exit from the status screen:

Press Esc

The ↵ key can also be used to exit from the status screen.

■ SYSTEM COMMAND

You may exit Lotus 1-2-3 temporarily to issue operating system level commands by using the System command.

To access the System command:

Press /

Select System

Lotus is still in memory, but the cursor is blinking at the operating system prompt. At this point, you can issue operating system commands.

To return to Lotus 1-2-3:

Type EXIT

Your screen should look similar to Figure 3-40.

```
(Type EXIT and press [ENTER] to return to 1-2-3)


The IBM Personal Computer DOS
Version 3.00 (C)Copyright IBM Corp 1981, 1982, 1983, 1984

C:\123R3J>EXIT
```

Figure 3-40

Press 

The cell pointer will appear in the same worksheet position as it was before you used the System command.

TITLES

When working on a large spreadsheet and moving the cell pointer to a distant row or column, headings and row labels may "scroll" off the screen. When this happens, it is difficult to see exactly where data is to be input. The following example demonstrates how such a problem may occur, and how to solve the problem by "freezing" titles on the screen.

Retrieve the file BUDGET2 for use in the following exercise:

To move to a "distant" cell location:

Move the cell pointer to cell H25

(In this example, use the pointer movement keys and **not** the F5 (GOTO) key to move to H25).

Note that it is difficult to tell what the numbers represent because neither the column titles nor the labels in column A are displayed on the screen as guides. Your screen should look like Figure 3-41.

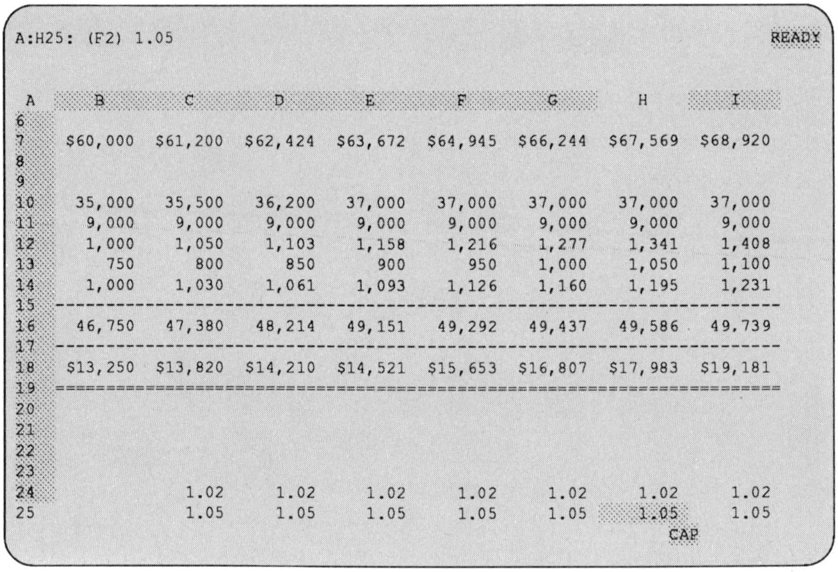

A:H25: (F2) 1.05 READY

A	B	C	D	E	F	G	H	I
6								
7	$60,000	$61,200	$62,424	$63,672	$64,945	$66,244	$67,569	$68,920
8								
9								
10	35,000	35,500	36,200	37,000	37,000	37,000	37,000	37,000
11	9,000	9,000	9,000	9,000	9,000	9,000	9,000	9,000
12	1,000	1,050	1,103	1,158	1,216	1,277	1,341	1,408
13	750	800	850	900	950	1,000	1,050	1,100
14	1,000	1,030	1,061	1,093	1,126	1,160	1,195	1,231
15	----------	----------	----------	----------	----------	----------	----------	----------
16	46,750	47,380	48,214	49,151	49,292	49,437	49,586	49,739
17	----------	----------	----------	----------	----------	----------	----------	----------
18	$13,250	$13,820	$14,210	$14,521	$15,653	$16,807	$17,983	$19,181
19	==========	==========	==========	==========	==========	==========	==========	==========
20								
21								
22								
23								
24		1.02	1.02	1.02	1.02	1.02	1.02	1.02
25		1.05	1.05	1.05	1.05	1.05	1.05	1.05

CAP

Figure 3-41

To position the cell pointer so that the appropriate headings and descriptive labels are visible on the screen:

Press (Home)

Move the cell pointer to cell B6

Before using the menu to freeze the title, the cell pointer must already be in the correct position as described below:

> The column(s) you wish to keep displayed on the screen must be to the left of the cell pointer (in this example, column A will remain on the screen because the cell pointer is in column B).
>
> The row(s) you desire to keep displayed on the screen must be above the cell pointer (in this example, rows 1 through 5 will remain on the screen, because the cell pointer is in row 6).

To access the menu commands to freeze the titles and descriptive labels:

Press /

Select Worksheet

Select Titles

Move the cell pointer to the Vertical menu option

(Do NOT press **V** for **V**ertical)

The description "Freeze all columns to the left of the cell pointer" under the **V**ertical option explains how to freeze vertical titles. A similar description is displayed when the **H**orizontal option is highlighted. See Figure 3-42.

```
A:B6:                                                              MENU
Both  Horizontal  Vertical  Clear
Freeze all columns to the left of the cell pointer
 A          A             B        C        D        E        F        G
1                                                            ABC COMPANY
2                                                              BUDGET
3
4
5                      YEAR 1   YEAR 2   YEAR 3   YEAR 4   YEAR 5   YEAR 6
6
7  SALES               $60,000  $61,200  $62,424  $63,672  $64,945  $66,244
8
9  EXPENSES
10   SALARIES           35,000   35,500   36,200   37,000   37,000   37,000
11   RENT                9,000    9,000    9,000    9,000    9,000    9,000
12   TELEPHONE           1,000    1,050    1,103    1,158    1,216    1,277
13   OFFICE SUPPLIES       750      800      850      900      950    1,000
14   MISCELLANEOUS       1,000    1,030    1,061    1,093    1,126    1,160
15                     ------------------------------------------------------
16     TOTAL EXPENSES   46,750   47,380   48,214   49,151   49,292   49,437
17                     ------------------------------------------------------
18 GROSS PROFIT        $13,250  $13,820  $14,210  $14,521  $15,653  $16,807
19                     ======================================================
20
                                                                 CAP
```

Figure 3-42

Select Both (for both columns and rows)

Note that you can choose to freeze only the columns or only the rows or both rows and columns as mentioned above.

To see the results of freezing the screen:

Move the cell pointer to cell H25 (use the right and down arrow keys to move to this position)

Note that even though the cell pointer has been moved to a "distant" area of the spreadsheet, rows 1 through 5 and column A remain frozen on the screen. By using this option, it is possible to see the column and row descriptions and understand the content of the spreadsheet. For example, H18 contains the contents of GROSS PROFIT for YEAR 7. Your screen should look like Figure 3-43.

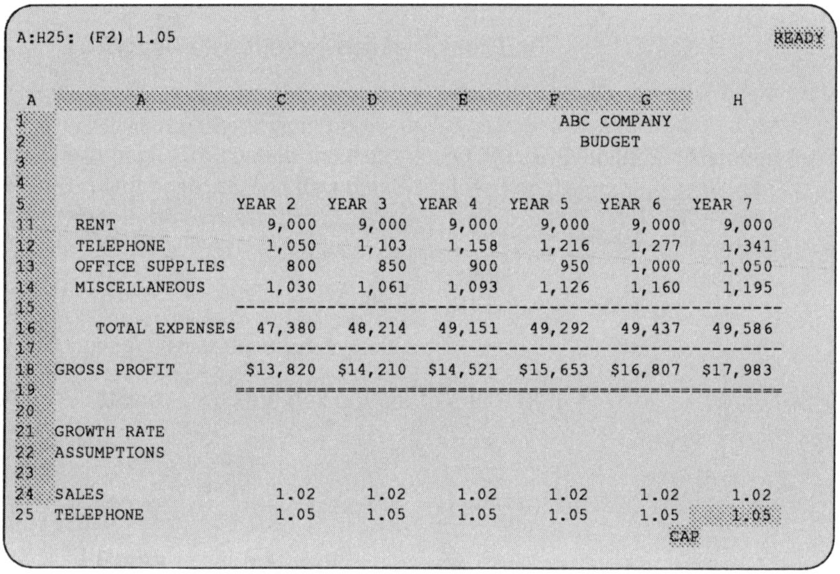

```
A:H25: (F2) 1.05                                                      READY

A        A                C        D        E        F        G        H
1                                                  ABC COMPANY
2                                                    BUDGET
3
4
5                      YEAR 2   YEAR 3   YEAR 4   YEAR 5   YEAR 6   YEAR 7
11   RENT               9,000    9,000    9,000    9,000    9,000    9,000
12   TELEPHONE          1,050    1,103    1,158    1,216    1,277    1,341
13   OFFICE SUPPLIES      800      850      900      950    1,000    1,050
14   MISCELLANEOUS      1,030    1,061    1,093    1,126    1,160    1,195
15                     -----------------------------------------------------
16     TOTAL EXPENSES  47,380   48,214   49,151   49,292   49,437   49,586
17                     -----------------------------------------------------
18  GROSS PROFIT      $13,820  $14,210  $14,521  $15,653  $16,807  $17,983
19                     =====================================================
20
21  GROWTH RATE
22  ASSUMPTIONS
23
24  SALES                1.02     1.02     1.02     1.02     1.02     1.02
25  TELEPHONE            1.05     1.05     1.05     1.05     1.05     1.05
                                                              CAP
```

Figure 3-43

Press Home

Note that the cell pointer cannot move to cell A1 since the titles are frozen, but rather moves only to cell B6.

To cancel the title settings:

Press /

Select Worksheet

Select Titles

Select Clear

Press Home

Notice the cell pointer is now in cell A1.

■ UNDO

The Undo feature creates a temporary copy of both the data and settings. 1-2-3 makes it possible to restore work to its original condition. The Alt-F4 keys operate Undo. However, it does not work like a toggle switch. Canceled changes are not restored.

At times when only a small amount of memory is available, 1-2-3 will display a menu to turn **Undo** off with three possible choices. These choices are:

Disable: turns off Undo; completes procedure.

Proceed: turns off Undo; completes procedure; turns on Undo.

Quit: quits procedure; saves changes made; Undo stays on.

Using [Ctrl-Break] or [Esc] produces the same results as **Quit**.

The primary purpose of **Undo** is to save time in having to redo procedures. However, it does not work with all commands. These commands do not respond:

File Admin (Reservation and Seal)
File (Erase, Save, and Xtract)
Graph Save
Print (Align, Go, Line, Page)
Worksheet Global Default

To turn on the **Undo** feature:

Press	/
Select	Worksheet
Select	Global
Select	Default
Select	Other
Select	Undo
Select	Enable
Select	Quit

Retrieve the BUDGET file.

Move	cell pointer to B10
Type	50000
Press	↵

Your worksheet now appears like Figure 3-44.

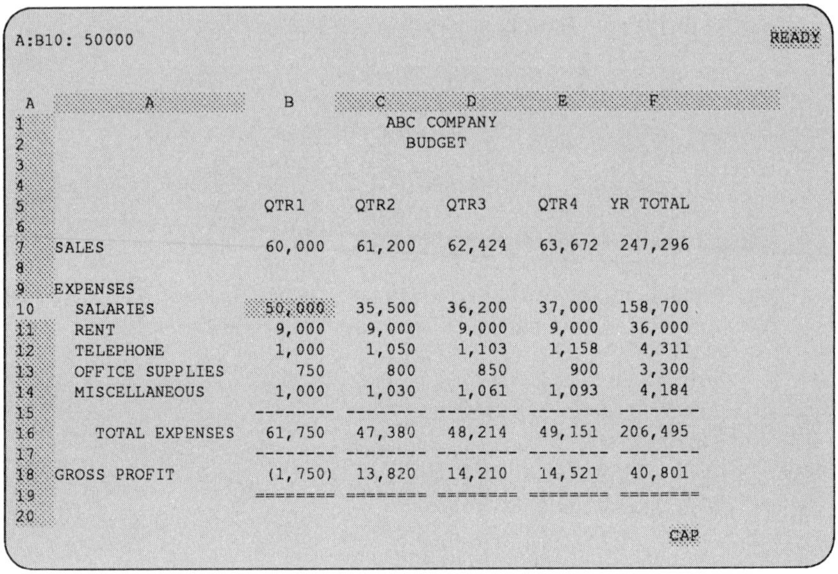

```
A:B10: 50000                                                    READY

A         A              B        C        D        E        F
1                                      ABC COMPANY
2                                        BUDGET
3
4
5                           QTR1     QTR2     QTR3     QTR4  YR TOTAL
6
7  SALES                  60,000   61,200   62,424   63,672  247,296
8
9  EXPENSES
10   SALARIES             50,000   35,500   36,200   37,000  158,700
11   RENT                  9,000    9,000    9,000    9,000   36,000
12   TELEPHONE             1,000    1,050    1,103    1,158    4,311
13   OFFICE SUPPLIES         750      800      850      900    3,300
14   MISCELLANEOUS         1,000    1,030    1,061    1,093    4,184
15                      -------- -------- -------- -------- --------
16     TOTAL EXPENSES     61,750   47,380   48,214   49,151  206,495
17                      -------- -------- -------- -------- --------
18 GROSS PROFIT          (1,750)   13,820   14,210   14,521   40,801
19                      ======== ======== ======== ======== ========
20
                                                                 CAP
```

Figure 3-44

To restore the figure in cell B10 to its original amount:

Press Alt-F4

Your screen now appears like Figure 3-45.

```
A:B10: (,0) 50000                                                         MENU
No  Yes
Do not undo any modifications to the worksheet
 A        A              B       C       D       E       F       G
1                                                     ABC COMPANY
2                                                       BUDGET
3
4
5                      YEAR 1   YEAR 2   YEAR 3   YEAR 4   YEAR 5   YEAR 6
6
7   SALES              $60,000  $61,200  $62,424  $63,672  $64,945  $66,244
8
9   EXPENSES
10    SALARIES          50,000   35,500   36,200   37,000   37,000   37,000
11    RENT               9,000    9,000    9,000    9,000    9,000    9,000
12    TELEPHONE          1,000    1,050    1,103    1,158    1,216    1,277
13    OFFICE SUPPLIES      750      800      850      900      950    1,000
14    MISCELLANEOUS      1,000    1,030    1,061    1,093    1,126    1,160
15                     ----------------------------------------------------
16      TOTAL EXPENSES  61,750   47,380   48,214   49,151   49,292   49,437
17                     ----------------------------------------------------
18  GROSS PROFIT       ($1,750) $13,820  $14,210  $14,521  $15,653  $16,807
19                     ====================================================
20
                                                              CAP
```

Figure 3-45

When queried about changes to the worksheet:

Select	Yes

Now the figure in cell B10 is restored to its original amount of $35,000.

To disable the Undo feature for the present example:

Press	/
Select	Worksheet
Select	Global
Select	Default
Select	Other
Select	Undo
Select	Disable
Select	Quit

■ WIDENING MULTIPLE COLUMNS IN ONE WORKSHEET

When you plan on placing data in cells that require more space than allowed by the default, you need to widen the columns. Otherwise, the cells will display asterisks each time the data exceeds the column width. When a cell contains asterisks, the contents of the cell are no longer visible. This situation may occur in several contiguous columns. By using a worksheet global command, all of the columns can be widened at one time. However, this global command does not change any columns set with a column-range command illustrated in this section.

Retrieve the BUDGET file. To widen columns B through E to 11 spaces:

Move	the cell pointer to cell B1
Press	/
Select	Worksheet
Select	Column
Select	Column-Range
Select	Set-Width
Move	the cell pointer to cell E1
Press	↵
Type	11
Press	↵

Now the columns B through E have widths of 11. Your screen should look like Figure 3-46.

```
A:B1: [W11]                                                          READY

A            A              B          C          D          E          F
1                                     ABC COMPANY
2                                       BUDGET
3
4
5                        QTR1       QTR2       QTR3       QTR4    YR TOTAL
6
7  SALES              $60,000    $61,200    $62,424    $63,672 $247,296
8
9  EXPENSES
10   SALARIES           35,000     35,500     36,200     37,000  143,700
11   RENT                9,000      9,000      9,000      9,000   36,000
12   TELEPHONE           1,000      1,050      1,103      1,158    4,311
13   OFFICE SUPPLIES       750        800        850        900    3,300
14   MISCELLANEOUS       1,000      1,030      1,061      1,093    4,184
15                 ---------------------------------------------------
16     TOTAL EXPENSES   46,750     47,380     48,214     49,151  191,495
17                 ---------------------------------------------------
18 GROSS PROFIT       $13,250    $13,820    $14,210    $14,521  $55,801
19                 ===================================================
20
                                                             CAP
```

Figure 3-46

■ WINDOWS

Lotus 1-2-3 allows you to view two different areas of the spreadsheet on the screen at the same time by using the **W**indows command. Retrieve the BUDGET2 file for use in the following exercise.

When creating windows, the cell pointer must be in the desired position before the menus are accessed. To position the cell pointer so that the windows will be divided at column D:

Move the cell pointer to cell D7

To access the menu commands to create the window:

Press /

Select Worksheet

Select Window

Select Vertical

Two windows are visible on the screen. Note that Lotus 1-2-3 allows you to make either horizontal or vertical windows. Your screen should look like Figure 3-47.

```
A:C7: (C0) @ROUND(B7*1.02,0)                                                READY

A           A             B         C      A    D        E        F        G
1                                          1                          ABC COMPANY
2                                          2                             BUDGET
3                                          3
4                                          4
5                       YEAR 1    YEAR 2   5  YEAR 3   YEAR 4   YEAR 5   YEAR 6
6                                          6
7   SALES              $60,000   $61,200   7  $62,424  $63,672  $64,945  $66,244
8                                          8
9   EXPENSES                               9
10    SALARIES          35,000    35,500  10   36,200   37,000   37,000   37,000
11    RENT               9,000     9,000  11    9,000    9,000    9,000    9,000
12    TELEPHONE          1,000     1,050  12    1,103    1,158    1,216    1,277
13    OFFICE SUPPLIES      750       800  13      850      900      950    1,000
14    MISCELLANEOUS      1,000     1,030  14    1,061    1,093    1,126    1,160
15                     ------------------15  -----------------------------------
16      TOTAL EXPENSES  46,750    47,380  16   48,214   49,151   49,292   49,437
17                     ------------------17  -----------------------------------
18  GROSS PROFIT       $13,250   $13,820  18  $14,210  $14,521  $15,653  $16,807
19                     ==================19  ===================================
20                                        20
                                                                  CAP
```

Figure 3-47

To move around in the left window:

Move the cell pointer to cell B7

Notice that the cell pointer can be moved anywhere in the spreadsheet.

To move to the right window:

Press [F6]

Move the cell pointer to cell L7 (YEAR TOTAL for SALES)

The [F6] key is sometimes referred to as the **window** key.

To return back to the left window:

Press [F6]

Move the cell pointer to cell B7

Type 65000

Press ↵

By using windows, you are able to see the effect of changing SALES on another area of the worksheet. In this example, you can see the updated amount for the YR TOTAL for SALES when the value for SALES in YEAR 1 is changed.

Your worksheet should look like Figure 3-48.

```
A:B7: (C0) 65000                                                                  READY

A      B        C        D        E      A      I        J        K        L
1                                        1
2                                        2
3                                        3
4                                        4
5   YEAR 1   YEAR 2   YEAR 3   YEAR 4    5   YEAR 8   YEAR 9   YEAR 10  YR TOTAL
6                                        6
7  $65,000  $66,300  $67,626  $68,979    7  $74,665  $76,158  $77,681  $711,735
8                                        8
9                                        9
10  35,000   35,500   36,200   37,000   10   37,000   37,000   37,000   365,700
11   9,000    9,000    9,000    9,000   11    9,000    9,000    9,000    90,000
12   1,000    1,050    1,103    1,158   12    1,408    1,478    1,552    12,583
13     750      800      850      900   13    1,100    1,150    1,200     9,750
14   1,000    1,030    1,061    1,093   14    1,231    1,268    1,306    11,470
15 ------------------------------------15 ------------------------------------
16  46,750   47,380   48,214   49,151   16   49,739   49,896   50,058   489,503
17 ------------------------------------17 ------------------------------------
18 $18,250  $18,920  $19,412  $19,828   18  $24,926  $26,262  $27,623  $222,232
19 ====================================19 ====================================
20                                      20
                                                              CAP
```

Figure 3-48

To clear the window setting:

Press	/
Select	Worksheet
Select	Windows
Select	Clear

The windows are now deleted from your screen.

■ WORKSHEET INSERTIONS AND DELETIONS

Columns and rows can be inserted into worksheets after the worksheet has been created. They can be deleted whenever necessary. Worksheets also can be added or deleted when you are working with multiple worksheets. They are referred to as sheets in the menu choices.

Inserting and Deleting Columns

To complete this exercise, create the worksheet in Figure 3-49 Part 1 and save the worksheet in a file named BOATSALE.

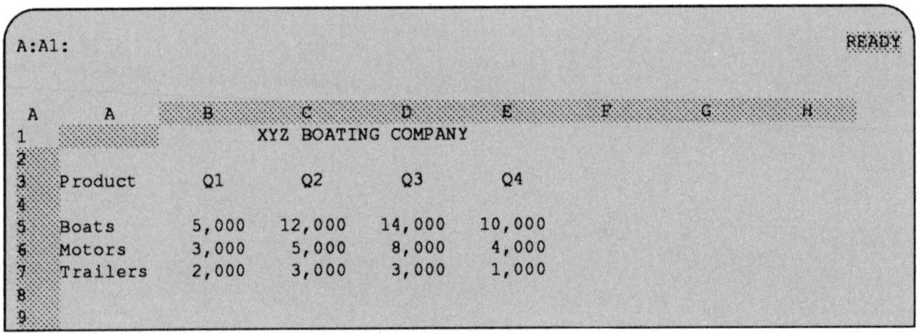

```
A:A1:                                                              READY

A    A        B          C          D          E          F          G          H
1                       XYZ BOATING COMPANY
2
3    Product      Q1         Q2         Q3         Q4
4
5    Boats        5,000     12,000     14,000     10,000
6    Motors       3,000      5,000      8,000      4,000
7    Trailers     2,000      3,000      3,000      1,000
8
9
```

Figure 3-49
Part 1

To insert a column between the columns for Q3 and Q4:

Move	the cell pointer to cell E3
Press	/
Select	Worksheet
Select	Insert
Select	Column
Press	↵

Your screen now should look like Figure 3-49 Part 2.

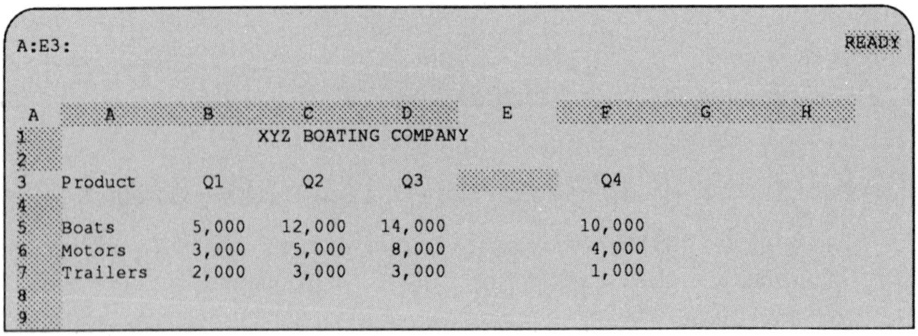

```
A:E3:                                                              READY

A    A        B          C          D          E          F          G          H
1                       XYZ BOATING COMPANY
2
3    Product      Q1         Q2         Q3                    Q4
4
5    Boats        5,000     12,000     14,000                10,000
6    Motors       3,000      5,000      8,000                 4,000
7    Trailers     2,000      3,000      3,000                 1,000
8
9
```

Figure 3-49
Part 2

To remove column E from the worksheet:

Move	the cell pointer to E3
Press	/
Select	Worksheet
Select	Delete
Select	Column
Press	↵

Your screen should look like Figure 3-49 Part 3. If you want to delete more than one column, you can highlight the columns to be deleted with the cell pointer whenever they are adjacent to one another.

```
A:E3: '     Q4                                                            READY

 A      A          B          C          D          E          F          G          H
 1                         XYZ BOATING COMPANY
 2
 3  Product       Q1         Q2         Q3         Q4
 4
 5  Boats       5,000     12,000     14,000     10,000
 6  Motors      3,000      5,000      8,000      4,000
 7  Trailers    2,000      3,000      3,000      1,000
 8
 9
```

Figure 3-49
Part 3

Inserting and Deleting Rows

Retrieve the BOATSALE file if necessary. To insert a blank row in a worksheet:

Move	the cell pointer to cell A3
Press	/
Select	Worksheet
Select	Insert
Select	Row
Press	↵

Your screen should look like Figure 3-50. If more than one row is to be inserted, move the cell pointer down an additional time for each row. Rows can be deleted in a similar manner by using **delete** instead of **insert.**

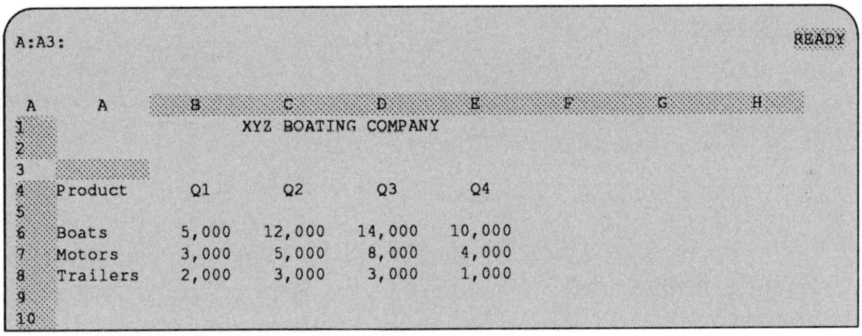

```
A:A3:                                                              READY

A    A          B         C         D         E         F         G         H
1                     XYZ BOATING COMPANY
2
3
4   Product       Q1        Q2        Q3        Q4
5
6   Boats      5,000    12,000    14,000    10,000
7   Motors     3,000     5,000     8,000     4,000
8   Trailers   2,000     3,000     3,000     1,000
9
10
```

Figure 3-50

Inserting and Deleting Worksheets

Sheet is a choice on the **W**orksheet **I**nsert and **W**orksheet **D**elete menus. Sheets can be added or deleted when working with multiple worksheets. The procedure for adding sheets is discussed in detail in Chapter 6.

■ ZERO-VALUE SUPPRESSION

The zero-value suppression command in Lotus 1-2-3 allows you to eliminate the display of all zeros in a worksheet. This command places a blank in place of a cell entry of zero whether the cell entry consists of the number zero or a cell formula that currently evaluates to zero.

Retrieve the original file BUDGET2 for use in this exercise.

For the purposes of this example, a zero will be placed in YEAR1 of SALES. All of the projections for SALES in the following years are based upon this number and, therefore, will also display zeros.

Move	the cell pointer to cell B7
Type	0
Press	↵

The row displaying the SALES data now contains zeros. Your screen should look like Figure 3-51.

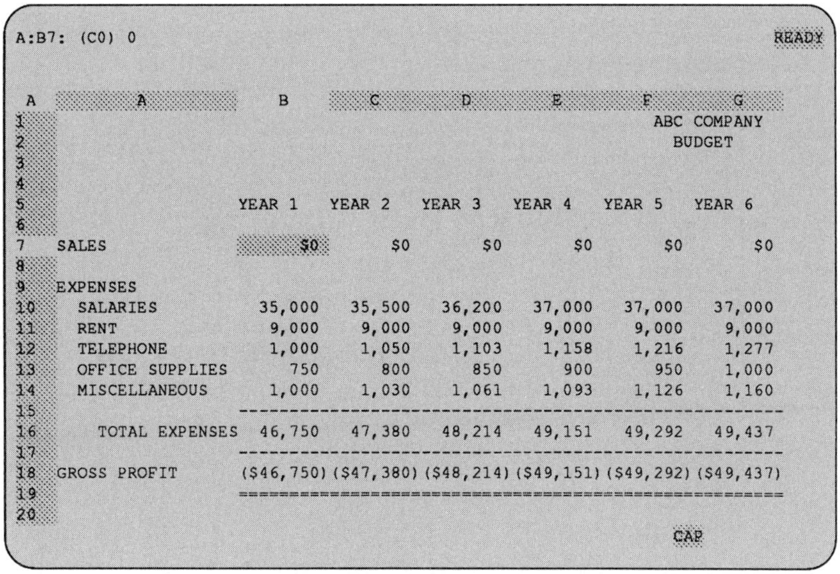

```
A:B7: (C0) 0                                                                    READY

A        A                B        C        D        E        F        G
1                                                              ABC COMPANY
2                                                                BUDGET
3
4
5                      YEAR 1   YEAR 2   YEAR 3   YEAR 4   YEAR 5   YEAR 6
6
7   SALES                 $0       $0       $0       $0       $0       $0
8
9   EXPENSES
10    SALARIES        35,000   35,500   36,200   37,000   37,000   37,000
11    RENT             9,000    9,000    9,000    9,000    9,000    9,000
12    TELEPHONE        1,000    1,050    1,103    1,158    1,216    1,277
13    OFFICE SUPPLIES    750      800      850      900      950    1,000
14    MISCELLANEOUS    1,000    1,030    1,061    1,093    1,126    1,160
15                     ------------------------------------------------------
16      TOTAL EXPENSES 46,750   47,380   48,214   49,151   49,292   49,437
17                     ------------------------------------------------------
18  GROSS PROFIT      ($46,750)($47,380)($48,214)($49,151)($49,292)($49,437)
19                     ======================================================
20
                                                                  CAP
```

Figure 3-51

The **W**orksheet **G**lobal **Z**ero menu option allows you to suppress zeros from your screen. To suppress the zeros:

Press	/
Select	Worksheet
Select	Global
Select	Zero
Select	Y (for Yes)
Move	the cell pointer to cell C7

The zeros are now suppressed. Notice that even though the zero value is suppressed, the formula for cell C7 still appears in the control panel. Your screen should look like Figure 3-52.

```
A:C7: (C0) @ROUND(B7*B24,0)                                              READY

A         A                B         C         D         E         F         G
1                                                                  ABC COMPANY
2                                                                    BUDGET
3
4
5                       YEAR 1    YEAR 2    YEAR 3    YEAR 4    YEAR 5    YEAR 6
6
7   SALES
8
9   EXPENSES
10    SALARIES           35,000    35,500    36,200    37,000    37,000    37,000
11    RENT                9,000     9,000     9,000     9,000     9,000     9,000
12    TELEPHONE           1,000     1,050     1,103     1,158     1,216     1,277
13    OFFICE SUPPLIES       750       800       850       900       950     1,000
14    MISCELLANEOUS       1,000     1,030     1,061     1,093     1,126     1,160
15                      -------------------------------------------------------
16      TOTAL EXPENSES   46,750    47,380    48,214    49,151    49,292    49,437
17                      -------------------------------------------------------
18  GROSS PROFIT       ($46,750) ($47,380) ($48,214) ($49,151) ($49,292) ($49,437)
19                      =======================================================
20
```

Figure 3-52

To allow the zeros to be visible on the screen again:

Press	/
Select	Worksheet
Select	Global
Select	Zero
Select	No

The zeros should now be visible again. Your screen should look like Figure 3-53.

```
A:C7: (C0) @ROUND(B7*1.02,0)                                          READY

 A        A               B        C        D        E        F        G
 1                                                          ABC COMPANY
 2                                                            BUDGET
 3
 4
 5                      YEAR 1   YEAR 2   YEAR 3   YEAR 4   YEAR 5   YEAR 6
 6
 7  SALES                   $0       $0       $0       $0       $0       $0
 8
 9  EXPENSES
10    SALARIES          35,000   35,500   36,200   37,000   37,000   37,000
11    RENT               9,000    9,000    9,000    9,000    9,000    9,000
12    TELEPHONE          1,000    1,050    1,103    1,158    1,216    1,277
13    OFFICE SUPPLIES      750      800      850      900      950    1,000
14    MISCELLANEOUS      1,000    1,030    1,061    1,093    1,126    1,160
15                      ------------------------------------------------------
16      TOTAL EXPENSES  46,750   47,380   48,214   49,151   49,292   49,437
17                      ------------------------------------------------------
18  GROSS PROFIT       ($46,750)($47,380)($48,214)($49,151)($49,292)($49,437)
19                      ======================================================
20
```

Figure 3-53

SUMMARY

Lotus 1-2-3 has various menu options and features that allow you to control how data is entered and viewed. These 1-2-3 commands allow you to work more effectively and efficiently when you are creating, editing or analyzing spreadsheets.

KEY CONCEPTS

Absolute cell reference
Annotating a formula
Annotating a range
Automatic formatting
Background printing
Borders
Cell protection
Error correction
File Admin Seal
File Admin Reservation-Settings
File Admin Tables
File Directory
File Erase
File List
File Password
File Save Backup
Footers
Headers
Hiding columns
Label Prefix
Landscape
Mapping a spreadsheet
Move
Page Break
Portrait
Range Erase
Range Format Percent
Range Name
Range Name Table
Recalculation
Relative cell reference
Search and Replace
Status
System
Undo
Widening multiple columns
Windows
Worksheet Column Hide
Worksheet Delete Column
Worksheet Delete Row
Worksheet Global Recalc Automatic
Worksheet Global Recalc Manual
Worksheet Global Zero No
Worksheet Global Zero Yes
Worksheet Insert Column
Worksheet Insert Row
Worksheet Insert Sheet
Worksheet Page
Worksheet Status
Worksheet Titles
Worksheet Window
Zero-value suppression

CHAPTER THREE
EXERCISE 1

INSTRUCTIONS: Circle T if the statement is true and F if the statement is false.

T F 1. An absolute cell reference means that the reference is kept constant, even when copied.

T F 2. The F2 key allows you to correct a cell entry without having to retype the entire entry.

T F 3. **W**orksheet **T**itles allows you to center titles on a spreadsheet.

T F 4. **W**orksheet **W**indow allows you to view two different areas of a spreadsheet at the same time.

T F 5. **W**orksheet **P**age creates a page break in a spreadsheet.

T F 6. If column D is hidden on a worksheet using **W**orksheet **C**olumn **H**ide, column D will not appear if the worksheet is printed.

T F 7. **W**orksheet **G**lobal **R**ecalculation **M**anual is activated so that data can be entered without the worksheet recalculating after each new entry.

T F 8. Changing the **F**ile **D**irectory changes the drive designation or path to which 1-2-3 saves and retrieves files.

T F 9. **F**ile **E**rase erases a file from memory.

T F 10. The **S**ystem command permanently returns you to the operating system.

T F 11. Formulas and data in cells can be annotated.

T F 12. After initiating a printing activity, you must wait until the printing is completed before issuing any command.

T F 13. Only one cell at a time can be erased.

T F 14. Automatic formatting of cells is permitted.

T F 15. The width for multiple columns that are contiguous to each other can be changed to the same width at the same time.

CHAPTER THREE
EXERCISE 2

INSTRUCTIONS: Explain a typical situation when the following keystrokes or Lotus 1-2-3 commands are used.

Problem 1: / **W**orksheet **W**indow **M**ap **E**nable

Problem 2: F4

Problem 3: / **R**ange **F**ormat **P**ercent

Problem 4: / **W**orksheet **T**itles

Problem 5: / **W**orksheet **W**indows

Problem 6: F6

Problem 7: / **W**orksheet **I**nsert **R**ow

Problem 8: / **W**orksheet **D**elete **C**olumn

Problem 9: / **W**orksheet **C**olumn **H**ide

Problem 10: / **W**orksheet **P**age

Problem 11: / **W**orksheet **G**lobal **R**ecalc **M**anual

Problem 12: F9

Problem 13: / **W**orksheet **G**lobal **Z**ero **Y**es

Problem 14: / **R**ange **E**rase

Problem 15: / **F**ile **L**ist

Problem 16: / **F**ile **E**rase

Problem 17: / **F**ile **D**irectory

Problem 18: / **S**ystem

Problem 19: F2

Problem 20: Ins in EDIT mode

Problem 21: / **W**orksheet **C**olumn **C**olumn-Range **S**et-Width

Problem 22: / **W**orksheet **I**nsert **S**heet

Problem 23: / **W**orksheet **G**lobal **D**efault **O**ther **U**ndo **E**nable

Problem 24: / **W**orksheet **G**lobal **F**ormat **O**ther **A**utomatic

Problem 25: / **R**ange **S**earch

Problem 26: / **P**rint **P**rinter **O**ptions **H**eader

Problem 27: / **P**rint **P**rinter **O**ptions **F**ooter

CHAPTER THREE
EXERCISE 3
Making a Cell Entry Absolute

INSTRUCTIONS: The following example illustrates a common error. Follow the instructions to create the error and solve the problem below.

Clear the screen.
In cell A1, type REVENUE and press ↵.
In cell A2, type ASSUMED REV RATE and press ↵.
Widen column A to 16 characters.
In cell B1, type 10000 and press ↵.
In cell B2, type .15 and press ↵.
In cell C1, type +B1*(1+B2) and press ↵.
Copy the formula in cell C1 to cells D1 and E1.

The screen should look like Figure 3-54.

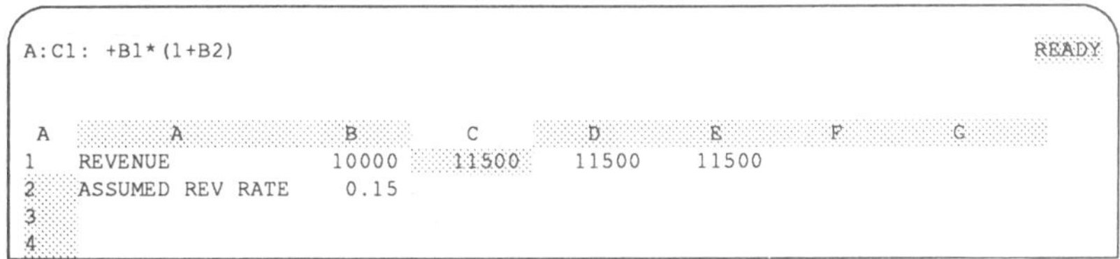

Figure 3-54

Change the formula in cell C1 and recopy it so that the formulas in cells D1 and E1 also refer to cell B2 for the projected revenue rate.

Print the worksheet.

CHAPTER THREE
EXERCISE 4
Annotating a Spreadsheet

INSTRUCTIONS: Retrieve the file SALES that was created as an exercise in Chapter 2.

Annotate the cell that contains TOTAL SALES for all sales persons.

Create the range name PERSONNEL that contains the cells with the salespersons' names as its range. Annotate the range name.

Create a range name note table for the SALES worksheet in cell A17.

Print the worksheet.

Create a "map" of the SALES worksheet. Indicate what each of the types of symbols means. Note: you cannot print the map.

CHAPTER THREE
EXERCISE 5
Protecting Cells in a Worksheet

INSTRUCTIONS: Retrieve the file PRACTICE you created as an exercise in Chapter 2.

Protect all cells in the worksheet.

Try to change the value of any cell on the worksheet. What happens?

Unprotect the cells containing the revenue growth rates.

Change the revenue growth rates to 8%, 5%, 10%, and 7% respectively for YEAR 2 through YEAR 5.

Print the worksheet after changing the growth rates.

CHAPTER THREE
EXERCISE 6
Erasing Cells

INSTRUCTIONS: Retrieve the file PRACTICE.

Erase the title line "PROJECTED PROFITS."

Print the worksheet after you erase the title line.

CHAPTER THREE
EXERCISE 7
Automatic Formatting

INSTRUCTIONS: Clear the Screen.

Activate the automatic formatting capability of Lotus 1-2-3.

Enter 12,000 in cell A1.

Place $9,700.00 in cell A2.

Widen column A so asterisks are removed from your screen.

Enter 28.5% in cell A3.

Print the worksheet.

CHAPTER THREE
EXERCISE 8
Hiding and Displaying a Column

INSTRUCTIONS: Follow the instructions below.

Retrieve the file BUDGET that was created in Chapter 2.

Hide columns B and F.

Print the worksheet.

Display columns B and F on the screen.

Print the worksheet.

CHAPTER THREE
EXERCISE 9
Label Prefixes

INSTRUCTIONS: Follow the instructions below:

Clear your screen.

Enter the value 123 in cell B1.

Enter 123 as a label and left-justify the characters in cell B3.

Right-justify the characters ABC in cell B5.

Repeat the characters XYZ in cell B7.

Center the characters ABC in cell B9.

Print the worksheet.

CHAPTER THREE
EXERCISE 10
Entering Page Breaks in a Spreadsheet

INSTRUCTIONS: Retrieve the file BUDGET that was created in Chapter 2.

Create a page break after the subtotal line for TOTAL EXPENSES.

Print the worksheet.

CHAPTER THREE
EXERCISE 11
Printing Headers and Footers

INSTRUCTIONS: Retrieve the file SALES.

Create the following Header and Footer:

Header:

SALES RESULTS

Footer:

ANNUAL SALES—CURRENT YEAR

Center the Header and Footer. Include the current date to the right of the text information of the Footer.

Print the worksheet.

CHAPTER THREE
EXERCISE 12
Printing Using the Landscape Mode

INSTRUCTIONS: Retrieve the file PRACTICE.

Print the PRACTICE worksheet so it appears sideways on the printout.

CHAPTER THREE
EXERCISE 13
Range Names

INSTRUCTIONS: Retrieve the file BUDGET2 that was created as an exercise in Chapter 2.

Create the range name SALES and include the cells containing the sales amounts for the 10 years as its range.

Create the range name TOTAL_EXPENSES and include the cells containing the TOTAL EXPENSES values for the 10 years as its range.

Create the range name GROSS_PROFIT and include the cells containing the GROSS PROFIT amounts for the 10 years as its range.

Place a table of the range names beginning in cell A38 at the bottom of the worksheet and print the table containing the range names and cells contained in the named ranges.

Print the worksheet.

CHAPTER THREE
EXERCISE 14
Search and Replace

INSTRUCTIONS: Retrieve the file BUDGET.

Use the Search and Replace command to change the name ABC COMPANY to ABC, Inc.

Change the word SALES to REVENUES using the Search and Replace command.

Print the worksheet.

CHAPTER THREE
EXERCISE 15
Widening Multiple Columns in One Worksheet

INSTRUCTIONS: Retrieve the file BUDGET.

Change the column width of columns B through E to 11 using the multiple column width option.

Print the worksheet.

CHAPTER THREE
EXERCISE 16
Inserting and Deleting Rows and Columns

INSTRUCTIONS: Retrieve the file SALES.

Insert a column at column C.

Insert two rows at row 12.

Print the worksheet.

Delete the column you inserted.

Delete the rows you inserted.

Print the worksheet.

CHAPTER THREE
EXERCISE 17
Suppressing Zero Values

INSTRUCTIONS:

Retrieve the file PRACTICE.

Enter the value 0 for the revenue value in YEAR 1.

Suppress the zero values in the worksheet so that no zeros appear.

Print the worksheet.

CHAPTER FOUR

CREATING AND PRINTING GRAPHS

OBJECTIVES:

In this chapter, you will learn to:

- Create a Graph
- Print a Graph
- Create Graphs Automatically
- Create Various Types of Graphs
- Display a Graph in a Window
- Use Additional Graph Commands

■ CHAPTER OVERVIEW

If a spreadsheet contains a large amount of data, it can be very difficult to detect trends and see relationships among various numbers. A graph depicting key elements of a spreadsheet can facilitate a more accurate analysis. Graphs can be easily created in Lotus 1-2-3 by using data that is entered on a spreadsheet. The graphic image can be viewed on the screen and may also be printed.

■ CREATING A GRAPH

The first graph that will be created in this chapter is based upon data in the file BUDGET that was created in Chapter 2. Retrieve the file BUDGET:

Press /

Select File

Select Retrieve

When prompted for the file name:

Press F3

Select BUDGET

Press ↵

The file BUDGET now should be visible on the screen (Figure 4-1).

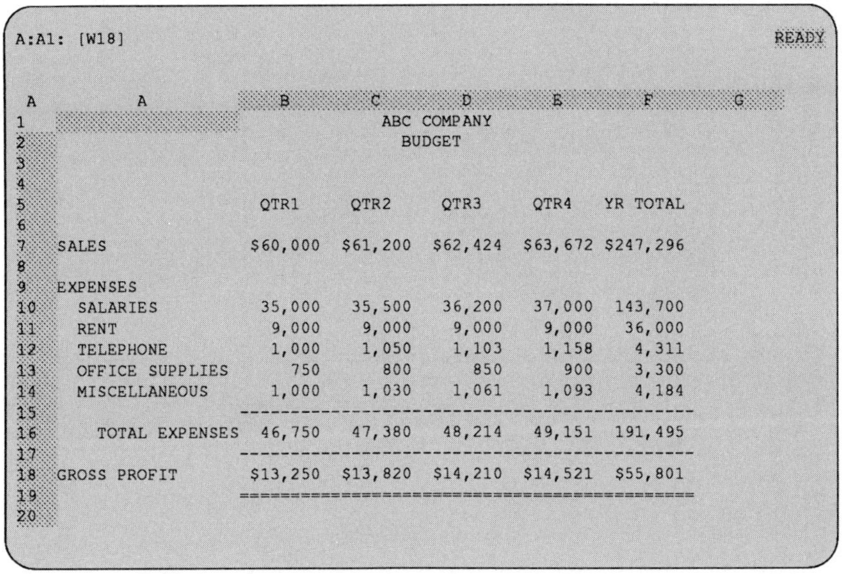

```
A:A1: [W18]                                                          READY

A          A              B        C        D        E        F        G
1                                  ABC COMPANY
2                                    BUDGET
3
4
5                         QTR1     QTR2     QTR3     QTR4   YR TOTAL
6
7  SALES               $60,000  $61,200  $62,424  $63,672 $247,296
8
9  EXPENSES
10   SALARIES           35,000   35,500   36,200   37,000  143,700
11   RENT                9,000    9,000    9,000    9,000   36,000
12   TELEPHONE           1,000    1,050    1,103    1,158    4,311
13   OFFICE SUPPLIES       750      800      850      900    3,300
14   MISCELLANEOUS       1,000    1,030    1,061    1,093    4,184
15                    ---------------------------------------------
16     TOTAL EXPENSES   46,750   47,380   48,214   49,151  191,495
17                    ---------------------------------------------
18 GROSS PROFIT        $13,250  $13,820  $14,210  $14,521  $55,801
19                    =============================================
20
```

Figure 4-1

You will first create a bar graph. The bars will represent the SALES, TOTAL EXPENSES, and GROSS PROFIT variables for the four quarters in BUDGET. When the graph is completed, it will look like Figure 4-2.

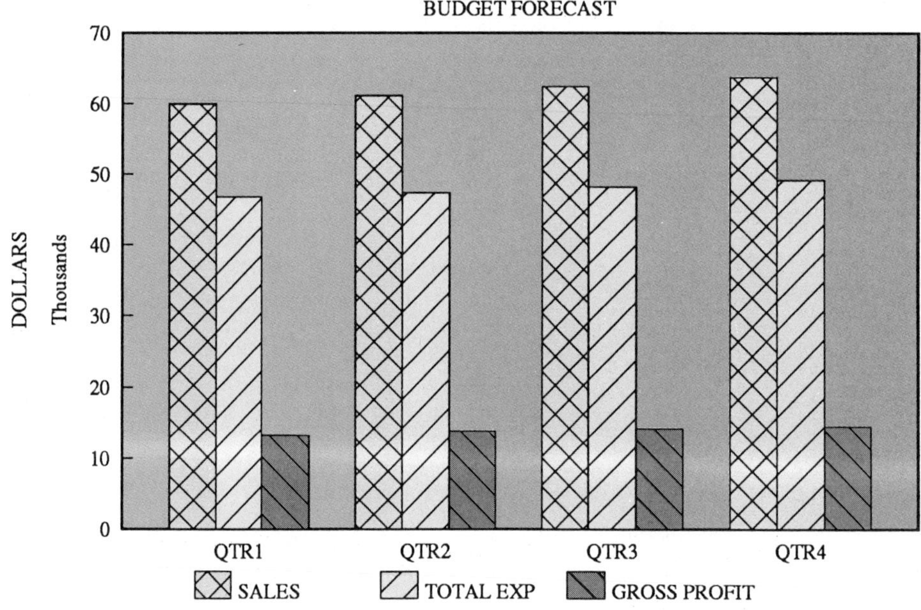

Figure 4-2

Specifying the Type of Graph

To specify the type of graph to create:

Press	/
Select	Graph
Select	Type
Select	Bar

The main graph menu appears again. The other types of graphs available are illustrated in exercises later in this chapter.

Specifying the X-axis and Data Ranges

To specify the labels that will be on the X-axis:

Select X

When prompted for the X-axis range:

Move the cell pointer to cell B5

Type .

Move the cell pointer to cell E5

Press ↵

Do not include the YR TOTAL label. If this label were accidentally highlighted, choose **X** again from the menu to reset the range. Press the Esc key to cancel the previous setting. Cells B5 through E5 contain the labels QTR1 through QTR4. QTR1 through QTR4 are the labels that will be used for the X-axis of the graph. See Figure 4-3, Part 1.

To indicate the data to display, use the menu options A through F. In this exercise, you use the menu options A through C to specify the data for SALES, TOTAL EXPENSES, and GROSS PROFIT. To specify the first data range:

Select A

When prompted to enter the first data range:

Move the cell pointer to cell B7

Type .

Move the cell pointer to cell E7

Press 

Cells B7 through E7 contain the data for SALES. The data for SALES for all four quarters will be the first data range displayed on the graph. See Figure 4-3, Part 2.

To specify the second data range:

Select B

When prompted to enter the second data range:

Move the cell pointer to cell B16

Type .

Move the cell pointer to cell E16

Press 

Cells B16 through E16 contain the data for TOTAL EXPENSES. The data for TOTAL EXPENSES will be the second data range displayed on the graph.

To specify the third data range:

Select C

When prompted to enter the third data range:

Move the cell pointer to cell B18

Type .

Move the cell pointer to cell E18

Press 

The data for GROSS PROFIT for all four quarters will be the third data range displayed on the graph.

Viewing the Graph

To view the graph:

Select View

The graph should look similar to Figure 4-3, Part 3. If you are using a color monitor, you may see solid colors rather than hatching patterns. If the screen does not display a graph, it may be because the computer being used does not have a graphics card. If this is the case, a graph cannot be seen on the screen, but it can still be created and printed. The hatch patterns on your screen may not appear exactly like those in the text. The patterns of graphs in the text were chosen because they present a clear illustration.

The X range highlights the data used for the X-axis labels in bar graphs.

```
A:E5: ^QTR4                                                          POINT
Enter x-axis range: A:B5..A:E5

 A          A              B         C         D         E         F
 1                                     ABC COMPANY
 2                                       BUDGET
 3
 4
 5                           QTR1      QTR2      QTR3      QTR4   YR TOTAL
 6
 7  SALES                  $60,000   $61,200   $62,424   $63,672 $247,296
 8
 9  EXPENSES
10    SALARIES              35,000    35,500    36,200    37,000  143,700
11    RENT                   9,000     9,000     9,000     9,000   36,000
12    TELEPHONE              1,000     1,050     1,103     1,158    4,311
13    OFFICE SUPPLIES          750       800       850       900    3,300
14    MISCELLANEOUS          1,000     1,030     1,061     1,093    4,184
15                         ---------------------------------------------
16      TOTAL EXPENSES      46,750    47,380    48,214    49,151  191,495
17                         ---------------------------------------------
18  GROSS PROFIT           $13,250   $13,820   $14,210   $14,521  $55,801
19                         =============================================
20
```

Figure 4-3
Part 1

The A range highlights the data used for the first data range in the graph.

```
A:E7: (C0) @ROUND(D7*E25,0)                                          POINT
Enter first data range: A:B7..A:E7

 A          A              B         C         D         E         F
 1                                     ABC COMPANY
 2                                       BUDGET
 3
 4
 5                           QTR1      QTR2      QTR3      QTR4   YR TOTAL
 6
 7  SALES                  $60,000   $61,200   $62,424   $63,672 $247,296
 8
 9  EXPENSES
10    SALARIES              35,000    35,500    36,200    37,000  143,700
11    RENT                   9,000     9,000     9,000     9,000   36,000
12    TELEPHONE              1,000     1,050     1,103     1,158    4,311
13    OFFICE SUPPLIES          750       800       850       900    3,300
14    MISCELLANEOUS          1,000     1,030     1,061     1,093    4,184
15                         ---------------------------------------------
16      TOTAL EXPENSES      46,750    47,380    48,214    49,151  191,495
17                         ---------------------------------------------
18  GROSS PROFIT           $13,250   $13,820   $14,210   $14,521  $55,801
19                         =============================================
20
```

Figure 4-3
Part 2

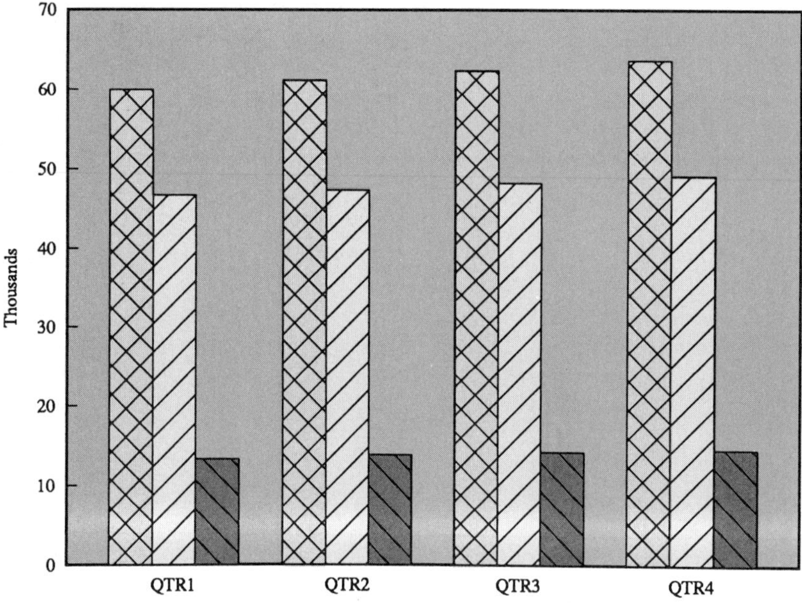

Figure 4-3
Part 3

To return to the worksheet after viewing the graph:

Press the ↵ key or the Esc key

Actually, any key on the keyboard can be used.

The basic settings for the graph have been specified. Now you will add the titles, legends, and other features necessary to complete the graph.

If you are using a color monitor, you can display the graph in color. To display a color graph:

Select Options

Select Color

Select Quit

To view the color graph:

Select View

The graph is displayed in solid color bars. If the monitor is not a color monitor, the graph will be displayed as solid bars in varying shades of the monitor's primary color (e.g., green or amber). Note that the color graph is not an appropriate setting if the graph is to be printed on a one-color printer because all bars will appear in just one color. The colors on the screen are *not* indicative of the color the graph will be when it is printed with a color printer or plotter. The colors on the printed graph depend upon the *printer's* available ink or pen colors.

To return to the worksheet after viewing the color graph:

Press ↵

To set the graph to print on a printer with only black ink (i.e., not a color plotter):

Select Options

Select B&W (Black and White)

Select Quit

If the graph remained set as a color graph, a printer with only a black ribbon would have printed out a graph with solid black bars. The B&W setting sets cross-hatch patterns to distinguish the bars from each other. If you want to continue using the color option as you complete this chapter, repeat the **G**raph **O**ptions **C**olor command sequence.

Entering the Titles for the Graph

Using the main graph menu, enter the first title:

Select Options

Select Titles

Select First

When prompted to enter the top line of the graph title:

Type ABC COMPANY

Press ↵

To enter the second title:

Select Titles

Select Second

When prompted to enter the second line of the graph title:

Type BUDGET FORECAST

Press ↵

To enter a title for the Y-axis:

Select Titles

Select Y-Axis

When prompted to enter the Y-axis title:

Type DOLLARS

Press ↵

To view the graph with titles on it:

Press F10

The graph should look like Figure 4-4.

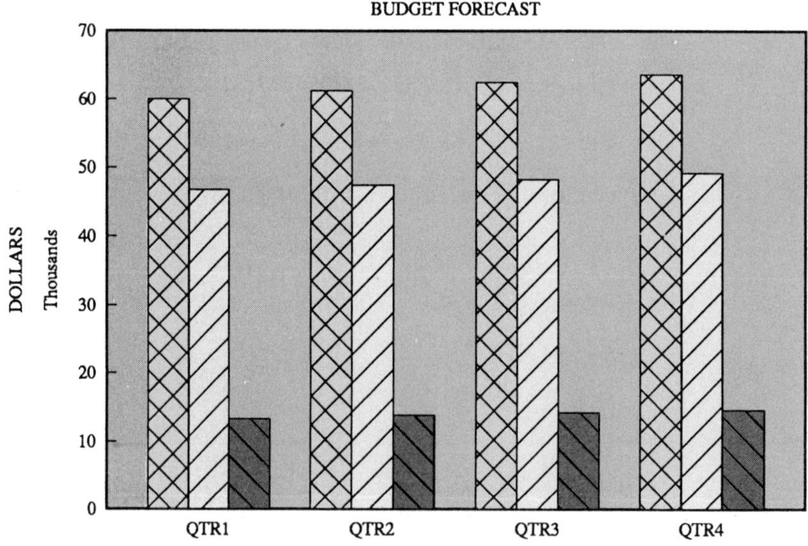

Figure 4-4

Note that you can press the F10 key instead of moving to the main graph menu to use the view option.

To return to the graph menu after viewing the graph:

Press ↵

Specifying the Legends

To enter the legend for the first data range (highlighted as data range A earlier in this exercise):

Select Legend

Select A

When prompted to enter the legend for data range A:

Type SALES

Press ↵

To enter the legend for the second data range (placed in data range B earlier in this exercise):

Select Legend

Select B

When prompted for the legend for data range B:

Type TOTAL EXP

Press ↵

To enter the legend for the third data range (placed in data range C earlier in this exercise):

Select Legend

Type C

When prompted for the legend for data range C:

Type GROSS PROFIT

Press ↵

To view the graph with titles and legends:

Press F10

Your screen should look like Figure 4-5.

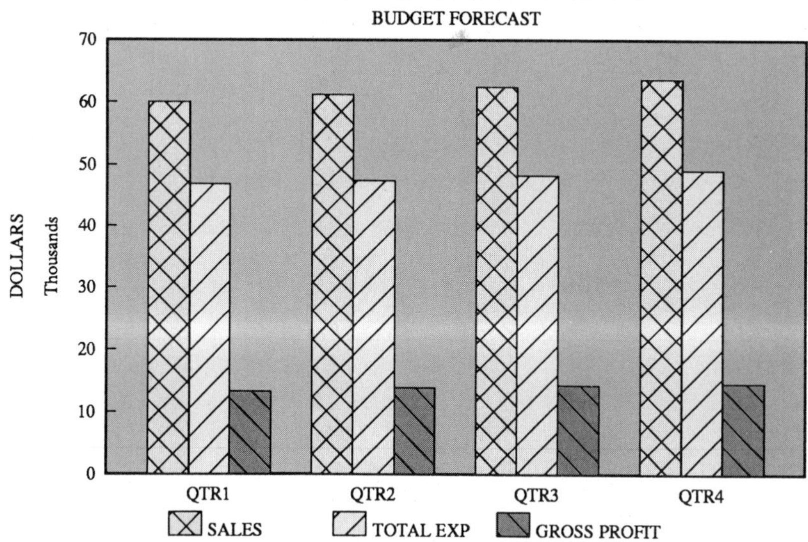

Figure 4-5

To return to the worksheet:

Press ↵

To return to the main graph menu:

Select Quit

Naming and Saving the Graph

To name the graph:

Select Name

Select Create

When prompted for the graph name:

Type BUDBAR

Press ↵

Naming a graph in a worksheet is especially important if more than one graph will be created from the data in a worksheet. When a particular graph setting is needed, the **G**raph **N**ame **U**se command sequence displays all graph names so that the desired graph can be selected and viewed.

To save the graph as a file on the disk:

Select Save

When prompted for the graph file name:

Type BUDBAR

Press ↵

A file titled BUDBAR is now saved. This file contains only a *picture* of the graph that can be used to print the graph. The file BUDBAR does not end with the extension .WK3 because it is not a worksheet file. BUDBAR is listed on the disk as BUDBAR.CGM (it is possible to see the file listing for graph files using the **F**ile **L**ist **G**raph command sequence).

The **G**raph **N**ame **C**reate command assigned the name BUDBAR to the graph settings *in the worksheet*. The file BUDBAR created with the **S**ave command in the Graph menu is a separate file containing only the picture of the graph, *not* the graph settings. The graph settings are a part of the worksheet BUDGET. The settings sheet and the .CGM file do not have to have the same name. If BUDBAR.CGM does not print the desired graph, you must retrieve the worksheet file BUDGET and correct the settings sheet; if the settings sheet has the same name as the graph file, it will be easier to find and edit. The file BUDBAR.CGM would have to be saved again and replaced so that it would show the changes made the next time it was printed. Your screen should look like Figure 4-6, Parts 1 and 2.

Graph **N**ame **C**reate assigns a name to the graph settings for a graph. (**F**ile **S**ave will permanently save the graph settings as a part of the worksheet file.)

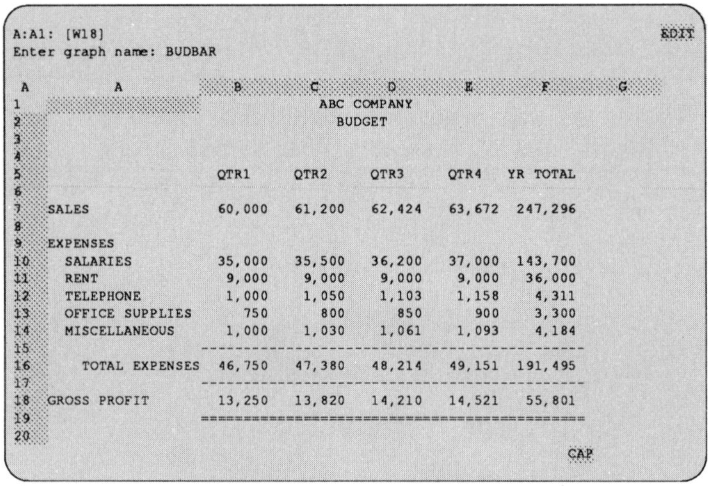

```
A:A1: [W18]                                                              EDIT
Enter graph name: BUDBAR

 A          A          B         C         D         E         F         G
1                                    ABC COMPANY
2                                      BUDGET
3
4
5                        QTR1      QTR2      QTR3      QTR4   YR TOTAL
6
7  SALES                60,000    61,200    62,424    63,672  247,296
8
9  EXPENSES
10   SALARIES           35,000    35,500    36,200    37,000  143,700
11   RENT                9,000     9,000     9,000     9,000   36,000
12   TELEPHONE           1,000     1,050     1,103     1,158    4,311
13   OFFICE SUPPLIES       750       800       850       900    3,300
14   MISCELLANEOUS       1,000     1,030     1,061     1,093    4,184
15                   ---------------------------------------------
16     TOTAL EXPENSES   46,750    47,380    48,214    49,151  191,495
17                   ---------------------------------------------
18 GROSS PROFIT         13,250    13,820    14,210    14,521   55,801
19                   =============================================
20
                                                              CAP
```

Figure 4-6
Part 1

Graph **S**ave saves the graph in a .CGM file for later printing.

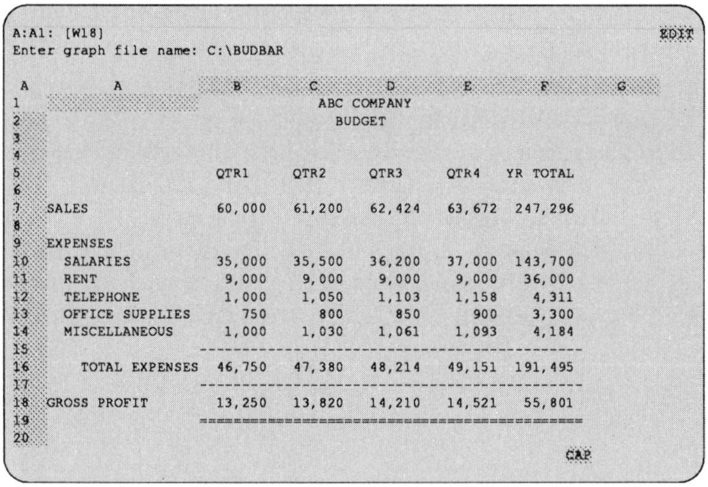

```
A:A1: [W18]                                                              EDIT
Enter graph file name: C:\BUDBAR

 A          A          B         C         D         E         F         G
1                                    ABC COMPANY
2                                      BUDGET
3
4
5                        QTR1      QTR2      QTR3      QTR4   YR TOTAL
6
7  SALES                60,000    61,200    62,424    63,672  247,296
8
9  EXPENSES
10   SALARIES           35,000    35,500    36,200    37,000  143,700
11   RENT                9,000     9,000     9,000     9,000   36,000
12   TELEPHONE           1,000     1,050     1,103     1,158    4,311
13   OFFICE SUPPLIES       750       800       850       900    3,300
14   MISCELLANEOUS       1,000     1,030     1,061     1,093    4,184
15                   ---------------------------------------------
16     TOTAL EXPENSES   46,750    47,380    48,214    49,151  191,495
17                   ---------------------------------------------
18 GROSS PROFIT         13,250    13,820    14,210    14,521   55,801
19                   =============================================
20
                                                              CAP
```

Figure 4-6
Part 2

The settings used to make the graph should be saved with the worksheet file BUDGET.WK3 in the event that changes will be made later. For this reason, the next step is to save and replace the BUDGET.WK3 file so that the file will include the graph settings.

To exit the graph menu:

Select Quit

To save the graph settings with the spreadsheet BUDGET:

Press /

Select File

Select Save

When prompted for the file name:

Press ↵

In response to the prompt to either Cancel the command or Replace the file:

Select Replace

The graph specifications and name are now saved on the BUDGET worksheet file.

■ CREATING VARIOUS TYPES OF GRAPHS

In the previous exercise, a bar graph was created. Lotus has six other types of graphs that can be created: Line, XY, Stacked-Bar, High-Low-Close-Open, Mixed and Pie graphs. The BUDGET worksheet is used to create some of the graphs. If necessary, you need to retrieve BUDGET:

Press /

Select File

Select Retrieve

When prompted for the file name:

Move the cell pointer to the word BUDGET

Press ↵

Creating a Bar Graph

The directions for creating the bar graph are covered in the previous section titled "Creating a Graph" so they will not be duplicated here.

Creating a Line Graph

The graph settings saved on the file BUDGET contain the graph data range specifications for SALES, TOTAL EXPENSES and GROSS PROFIT. Because the graph settings are already designated, they can be used to display the same data as a line graph. Only the graph type must be changed. The newly designated graph then can be given a graph name.

To create a line graph:

Press /

Select Graph

Select Type

Select Line

To view the graph:

Press F10 or

Select View

The lines on the screen appear more jagged than they will when they are printed. Your screen should look similar to Figure 4-7.

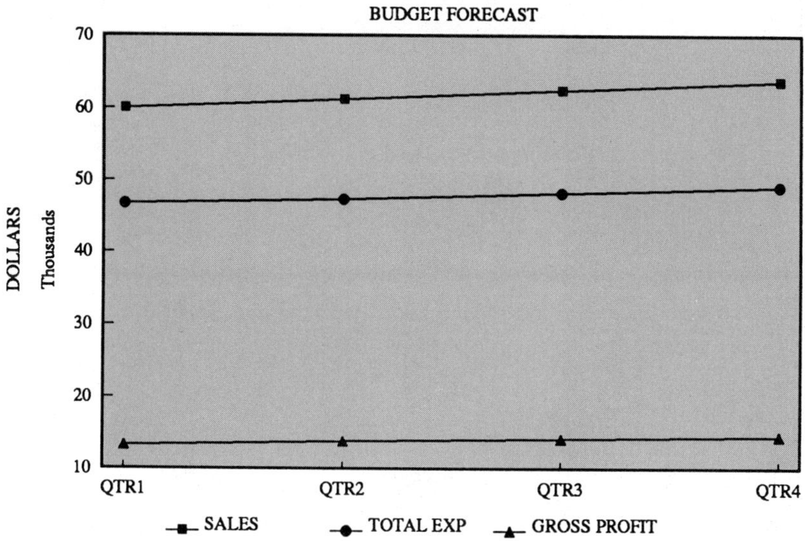

Figure 4-7

To return to the worksheet:

Press ↵

Notice that since the graph settings were set in an earlier exercise, specifications such as data ranges, titles, and legends do not have to be specified again.

To name the graph:

Select Name

Select Create

When prompted for the graph name:

Type BUDLINE

Press ↵

To save the graph image in a file:

Select Save

When prompted for the graph file name:

Type BUDLINE

Press ↵

The graph has now been saved to a graph file.

To leave the graph menu:

Select Quit

To save the line graph specifications with the worksheet BUDGET:

Press /

Select File

Select Save

The word BUDGET should appear. To replace the current version of BUDGET:

Press ↵

When prompted to either Cancel or **R**eplace:

Select Replace

The graph specifications and name for the line graph are now saved on the BUDGET worksheet file.

Creating a Mixed (Combined Bar and Line) Graph

In some situations, you may desire to have a bar for one variable and a line for another variable on a graph. You can use the mixed graph type to create such a graph.

Suppose you want to graph the TOTAL EXPENSES data using a bar and the SALES data as a line for the BUDGET spreadsheet. In creating a mixed graph, you use the A, B and C data ranges for the items that you want to graph using a bar. Data ranges D, E and F are used for the data that is depicted using a line. When you finish this section, you will have a graph like Figure 4-8 on your screen.

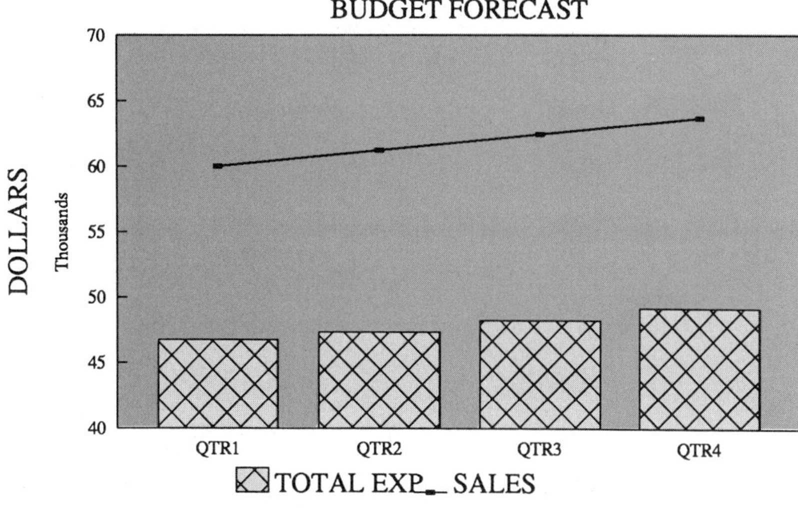

Figure 4-8

Make sure the BUDGET worksheet appears on your screen. Before creating the mixed graph, you need to delete the previous data ranges using the **G**raph **R**eset command sequence.

To delete the ranges:

Press	/
Select	Graph
Select	Reset
Select	Ranges

To return to the main graph menu:

Select	Quit

To specify that a mixed graph is desired:

Select Type

Select Mixed

To indicate the X-axis data range:

Select X

Move the cell pointer to cell B5

Type .

Move the cell pointer to cell E5

Press ↵

To specify TOTAL EXPENSES as the data to display with a bar:

Select A

Move the cell pointer to cell B16

Type .

Move the cell pointer to cell E16

Press ↵

To designate the legend for TOTAL EXPENSES:

Select Options

Select Legend

Select A

To erase the current legend:

Press Esc

Type TOTAL EXP

Press ↵

Select Quit

To specify SALES as the data to illustrate with a line:

Select D

Move the cell pointer to cell B7

Type .

Move the cell pointer to cell E7

Press ↵

To designate the legend for SALES:

Select Options

Select Legend

Select D

Type SALES

Select Quit

To display graphs on your screen:

Press F10

Your screen now should look like Figure 4-9.

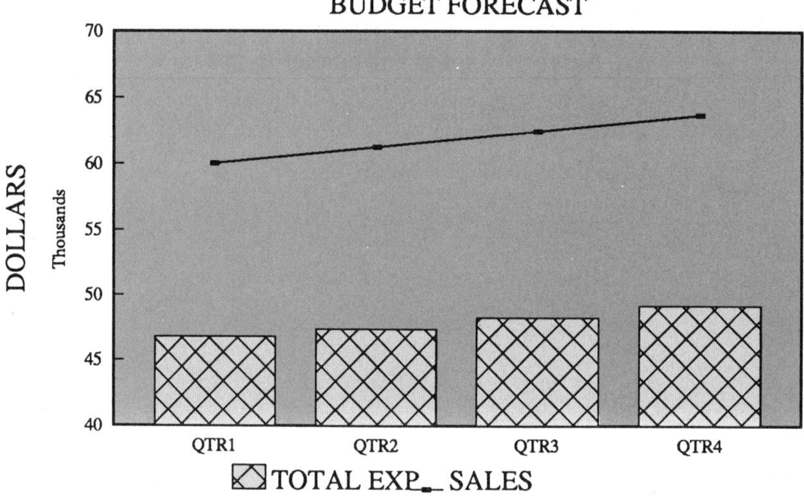

Figure 4-9

To return to the worksheet:

Press ↵

To name the graph:

Select Name

Select Create

When prompted for the graph name:

Type BUDMIXED

Press ↵

To save the graph:

Select Save

When prompted for the graph file name:

Type BUDMIXED

Press ↵

The graph now has been saved on a graph file.

To exit the graph menu:

Select Quit

To save the mixed graph specifications with the worksheet BUDGET:

Press /

Select File

Select Save

The word BUDGET should appear on your screen. To replace the current version of BUDGET.

Press ↵

When prompted to either Cancel or **R**eplace:

Select Replace

The graph specifications and the name for the mixed graph are now saved on the BUDGET worksheet file.

Creating a Stacked-Bar Graph

The file BUDGET worksheet is again used in this exercise. The graph settings saved on the graph file under BUDBAR contain the graph range specifications for SALES, TOTAL EXPENSES, and GROSS PROFIT. Because the graph settings are already set, they can be used to display the same data as a stacked-bar graph. Only the graph type has to be changed. The newly designated graph will be given a graph name. To create a stacked-bar graph, first retrieve file BUDGET, and issue the **G**raph **N**ame **U**se command sequence and select BUDBAR. Then,

Press /

Select Graph

Select Type

Select Stack-Bar

To view the graph:

Press (F10)

Your screen should look like Figure 4-10.

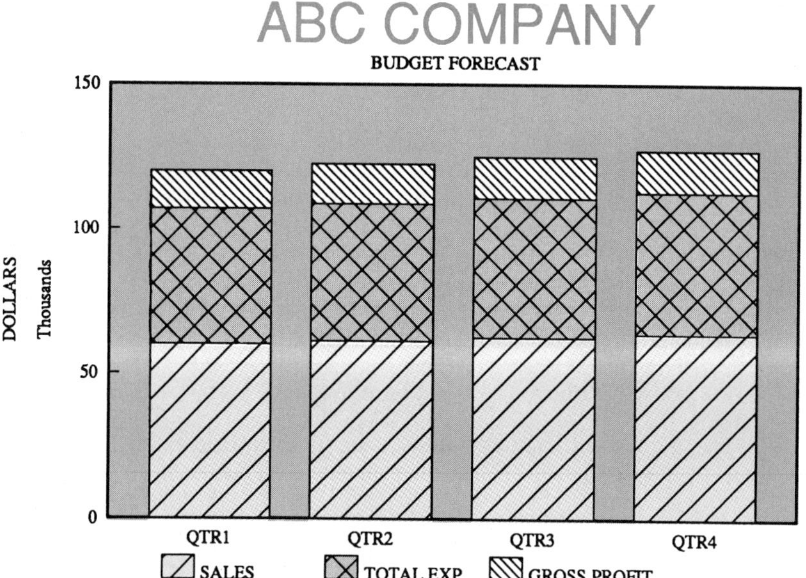

Figure 4-10

To return to the worksheet:

Press ↵

The graph settings were completed in an earlier exercise; therefore, specifications such as data ranges, titles, and legends are already set. The settings are not appropriate, however, for a stacked-bar graph. The data options and legends need to be altered so the stacked-bar graph more accurately depicts the data on the BUDGET worksheet.

To reset data ranges:

Select Reset

When prompted for the ranges to reset:

Select A

Select C

To leave the Reset menu:

Select Quit

To reset range A:

Select A

When prompted for the first data range:

Move the cell pointer to cell B18

Type .

Move the cell pointer to cell E18

Press ↵

Variable A now contains the data for GROSS PROFIT.

Before the changes were made, data ranges A, B, and C represented SALES, TOTAL EXPENSES, and GROSS PROFIT, respectively. The three data ranges added together were not appropriate on a stacked-bar graph. The data was rearranged as follows: data range A was changed to the data for GROSS PROFIT, data range B was left as TOTAL EXPENSES, data range C was cancelled. In this manner the stacked-bar stacks ranges A and B (GROSS PROFIT and TOTAL EXPENSES) add up to total SALES.

To change the legends:

Select Options

Select Legend

Select A

The current legend is SALES. To replace the legend for range A:

Press Esc

Type GROSS PROFIT

Press ↵

To reset the legend for range C:

Select	Legend
Select	C
Press	the [Esc] key
Press	[↵]

The [Esc] key was pressed to cancel the legend for the C range.

To return to the main graph menu:

Select	Quit

To view the graph:

Press	[F10]

Note that the data ranges are now appropriate. Data range A (GROSS PROFIT) and data range B (TOTAL EXPENSES) are stacked and result in a pictorial addition and representation of SALES. A third data range is not needed. Your screen should look like Figure 4-11.

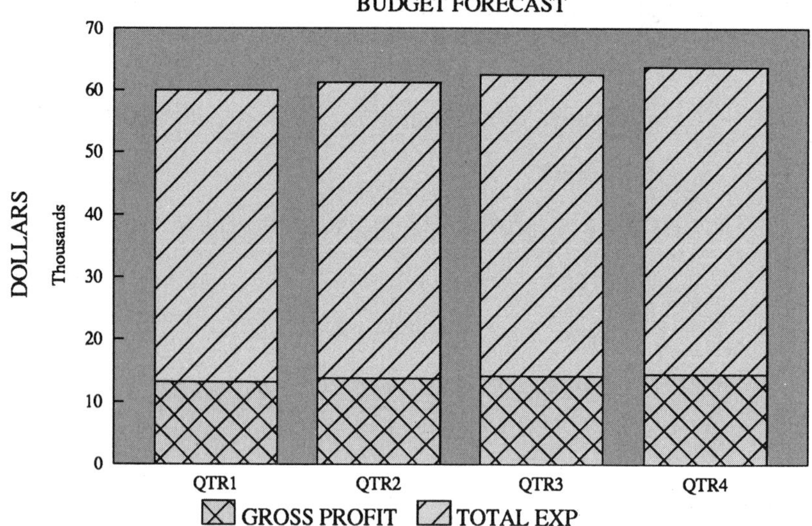

Figure 4-11

When you finish viewing the graph:

Press ↵

To name the graph:

Select Name

Select Create

When prompted for the graph name:

Type BUDSTBAR

Press ↵

To save the graph:

Select Save

When prompted for the graph file name:

Type BUDSTBAR

Press ↵

The graph now has been saved on a graph file.

To leave the graph menu:

Select Quit

To save the stacked-bar graph specifications with the worksheet BUDGET:

Press /

Select File

Select Save

The word BUDGET should appear. To replace the current version of BUDGET:

Press ↵

When prompted to either Cancel or Replace:

Select Replace

The graph specifications and name for the stacked-bar graph are now saved on the BUDGET worksheet file.

Creating a Pie Graph

The BUDGET worksheet is used in this exercise. You will create a pie graph, name the pie graph and save it for later use.

Before creating the pie graph, you need to reset all of the previously defined graph data and option ranges.

Press /

Select Graph

Select Reset

To reset all previously defined graph settings:

Select Graph

You will create a pie graph to show the breakdown of expenses for QTR1.

To create the pie graph:

Select Type

Select Pie

To specify the labels for the pie segments:

Select X

Move the cell pointer to cell A10

Type .

Move the cell pointer to cell A14

Press ↵

To indicate QTR1 expense data to graph:

Select A

Move the cell pointer to cell B10

Type .

Move the cell pointer to cell B14

Press ↵

To add titles to the graph:

Select Options

Select Titles

Select First

Type ABC COMPANY

Press ↵

Select Titles

Select Second

Type EXPENSE ANALYSIS

Press ↵

To view the graph:

Press F10

Your screen should look like Figure 4-12.

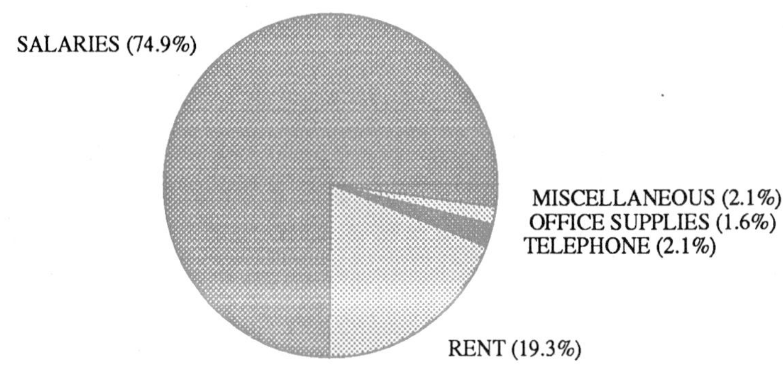

Figure 4-12

When you finish viewing the graph:

Press ↵

Select Quit

To name the graph:

Select Name

Select Create

When prompted for the graph name:

Type BUDPIE

Press ↵

To save the graph:

Select Save

When prompted for the graph file name:

Type BUDPIE

Press ↵

The graph now has been saved on a graph file.

To leave the graph menu:

Select Quit

To save the pie graph specifications with the worksheet BUDGET:

Press /

Select File

Select Save

The word BUDGET should now appear. To replace the current version of BUDGET:

Press ↵

When prompted to either Cancel of Replace:

Select Replace

The graph specifications and name for the pie graph are now saved on the BUDGET worksheet file.

Creating an XY Graph

XY graphs are basically line graphs that use numeric values for both the X-axis and the Y-axis. Retrieve the file UNITPROD (Unit Production) for use in this exercise. The file UNITPROD was created in an exercise you completed in Chapter 2. Since the file has no graph settings, you will need to create all of the graph settings.

To designate the graph type:

Press /

Select Graph

Select Type

When prompted for the graph type:

Select XY

This graph will represent the number of UNITS PRODUCED on the X-axis and the number of UNITS SOLD on the Y-axis.

To designate the data for the X-axis:

Select X

When prompted for the X-axis range:

Move the cell pointer to cell C7

Type .

Move the cell pointer to cell C12

Press ↵

To indicate the data for the Y-axis:

Select A

When prompted to enter the A range:

Move the cell pointer to cell D7

Type .

Move the cell pointer to cell D12

Press ↵

An option that would clarify the data points is **D**ata-Labels, which you can use to place data labels above each data point:

Select Options

Select Data-Labels

Select A

Move the cell pointer to cell B7

Type .

Move the cell pointer to cell B12

Press ↵

Select Left

To exit the current menu:

Select Quit

To enter the first title:

Select Titles

Select First

When prompted to enter the top line of the graph title:

Type ABC COMPANY

Press ↵

To enter an X-axis title:

Select Titles

Select X-Axis

When prompted for the title:

Type UNITS PRODUCED

Press ↵

To enter a Y-axis title:

Select Titles

Select Y-Axis

When prompted for the title:

Type UNITS SOLD

Press ↵

To exit the current menu:

Select Quit

To view the graph:

Press (F10)

The graph should look like Figure 4-13. Note that the graph on the screen and the printed graph may look slightly different since the scale on the printout may vary from the scale on the screen display. For example, the screen's Y-axis scale is in increments of 100 (300...400...800) while the printout's X-axis scale is in increments of 50 (350...400...800). The X-axis also has different increments in the screen display and the printed display.

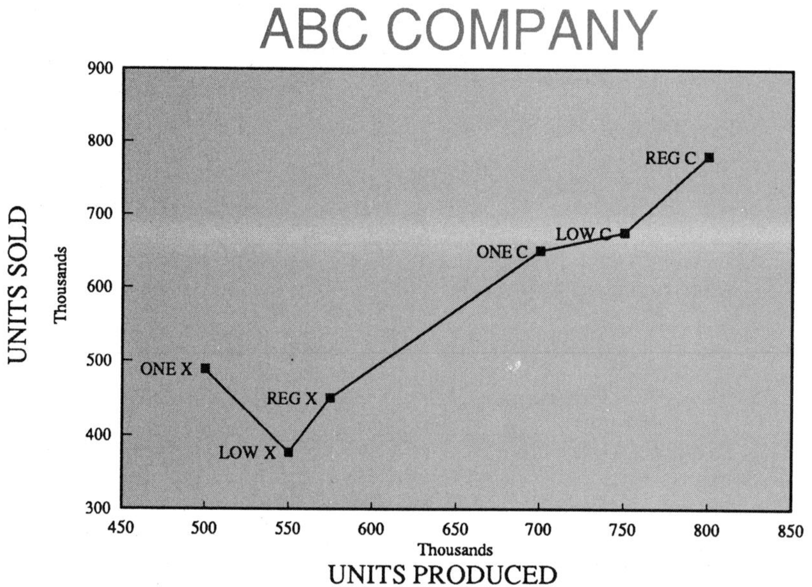

Figure 4-13

To return to the worksheet after viewing the graph:

Press ↵

To exit the current menu:

Select Quit

You do not need to save the graph settings.

Creating a High-Low-Close-Open Graph

Many individuals who use 1-2-3 may have investments in stocks and bonds. The High-Low-Close-Open (HLCO) graph provides a convenient way to track prices and sales volumes for stocks and bonds.

Suppose you are given the information in Figure 4-14.

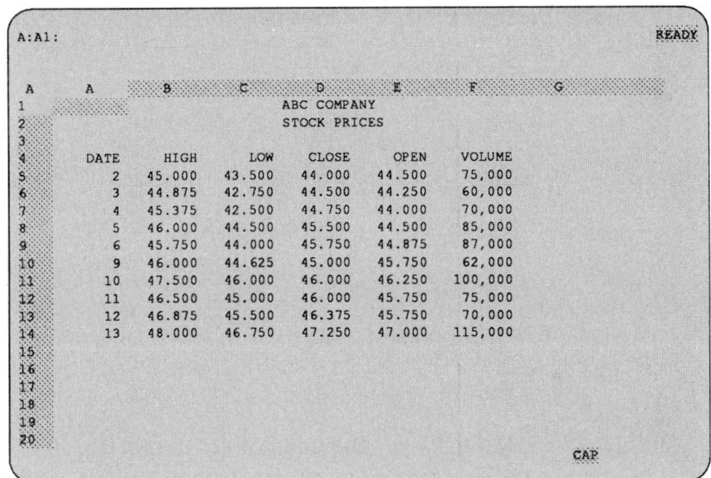

A:A1: READY

ABC COMPANY
STOCK PRICES

DATE	HIGH	LOW	CLOSE	OPEN	VOLUME
2	45.000	43.500	44.000	44.500	75,000
3	44.875	42.750	44.500	44.250	60,000
4	45.375	42.500	44.750	44.000	70,000
5	46.000	44.500	45.500	44.500	85,000
6	45.750	44.000	45.750	44.875	87,000
9	46.000	44.625	45.000	45.750	62,000
10	47.500	46.000	46.000	46.250	100,000
11	46.500	45.000	46.000	45.750	75,000
12	46.875	45.500	46.375	45.750	70,000
13	48.000	46.750	47.250	47.000	115,000

CAP

Figure 4-14

Assume that you have purchased some ABC Company stock and desire to follow the price of the stock using a HLCO graph.

Before creating the graph, you will need to construct a worksheet like the one in Figure 4-14. After you finish the worksheet, save the worksheet on file ABCHLCO.

To create the HLCO graph:

Press /

Select Graph

Select Type

Select HLCO

The following table indicates what information to place in the various data ranges:

Data Range	Item
X	Date
A	High price for the date
B	Low price for the date
C	Closing price for the date
D	Opening price for the date
E	Volume of stock traded for the date

To enter the DATES in the X data range:

Select X

Move the cell pointer to cell A5

Type .

Move the cell pointer to cell A14

Press ↵

To enter the HIGH prices for the dates in the A data range:

Select A

Move the cell pointer to cell B5

Type .

Move the cell pointer to cell B14

Press ↵

To place the LOW prices for the dates in the B data range:

Select B

Move the cell pointer to cell C5

Type .

Move the cell pointer to cell C14

Press ↵

To specify the CLOSE prices for the dates in the C data range:

Select C

Move the cell pointer to cell D5

Type .

Move the cell pointer to cell D14

Press ↵

To enter the OPEN prices for the dates in the D data range:

Select D

Move the cell pointer to cell E5

Type .

Move the cell pointer to cell E14

Press ↵

To indicate VOLUME for the dates in the E data range:

Select E

Move the cell pointer to cell F5

Type .

Move the cell pointer to cell F14

Press ↵

To view the HLCO graph:

Press F10

Notice that the Y-axis represents the stock prices and a vertical line is drawn for each date. The highest point on the line is the high price for the date. Likewise, the lowest point on the line is the lowest price. The left tick mark on each line represents the opening price. The right tick mark indicates the closing price. At the bottom of the graph the volume data is drawn. The second Y-axis is used to indicate the scale for volume.

To return to the worksheet:

Press ↵

To specify the graph titles:

Select Options
Select Titles
Select First
Type ABC COMPANY
Press ↵
Select Titles
Select Second
Type STOCK PRICES
Press ↵

To specify DATE as the X-axis title:

Select Titles
Select X-Axis
Type DATE
Press ↵

To indicate that PRICE is the Y-axis title:

Select Titles
Select Y-Axis
Type PRICE
Press ↵

To denote that VOLUME is the title for the second Y-axis:

Select Titles
Select 2Y-Axis

Type VOLUME

Press ↵

To place a footnote on the graph:

Select Titles

Select Note

Type Prepared on February 14

Press ↵

Select Titles

Select Other-Note

Type YOUR NAME (insert your name here)

Press ↵

To view the HLCO graph at this point:

Press F10

Your screen should look like Figure 4-15.

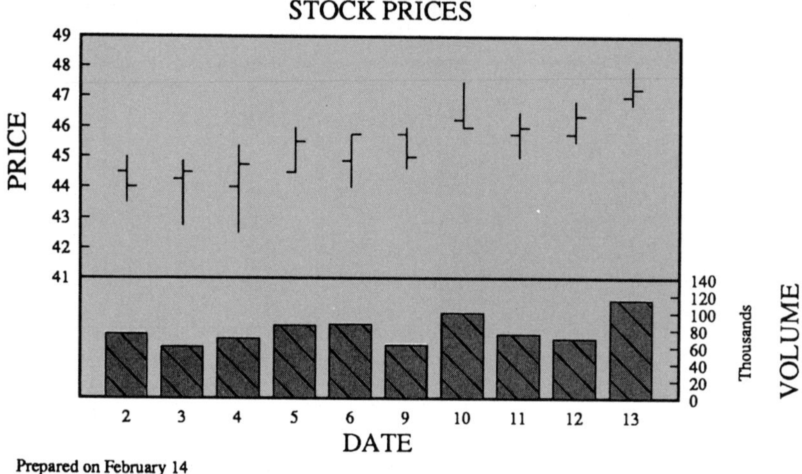

Figure 4-15

To return to the worksheet:

Press ↵

To format the Y-axis to include a $ sign by each price:

Select Scale

Select Y-Scale

Select Format

Select Currency

When prompted for the number of decimal places:

Type 0

Press ↵

To view the completed graph:

Press (F10)

Your screen should look like Figure 4-16.

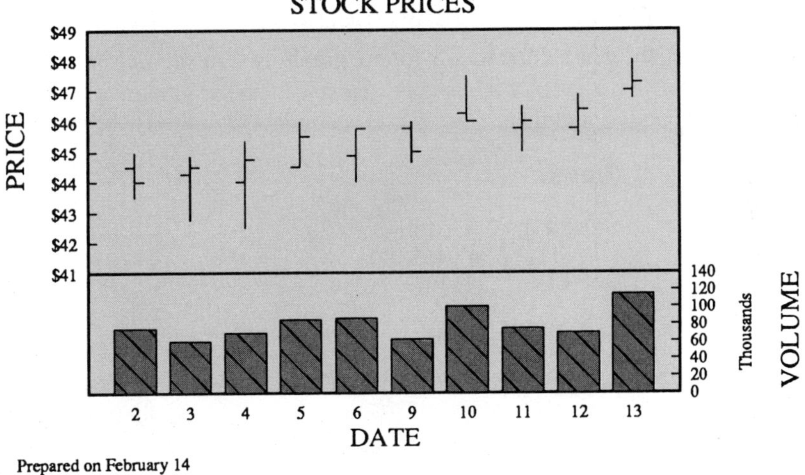

Figure 4-16

To return to the worksheet:

Press ↵

To exit the graph menus:

Select Quit three times

■ USING SPECIAL FEATURES WITH VARIOUS TYPES OF GRAPHS

There are several features that can be used with the various types of graphs available in 1-2-3. For example, you can draw a graph upright or sideways. You can also stack the data ranges and graph each data range as a percentage of the total for all ranges. Two Y-axes can be used on a graph. In this section, these features are discussed and illustrated.

Specifying a Horizontal Orientation

In 1-2-3, the default orientation for bar graphs is vertical. In some situations, you may want to display a bar graph horizontally. To select the bar graph you saved earlier, first retrieve file BUDGET, and then:

Press	/
Select	Graph
Select	Name
Select	Use
Press	
Move	the pointer to BUDBAR
Press	

The bar graph you created earlier now should be on the screen. Your screen should look like Figure 4-17.

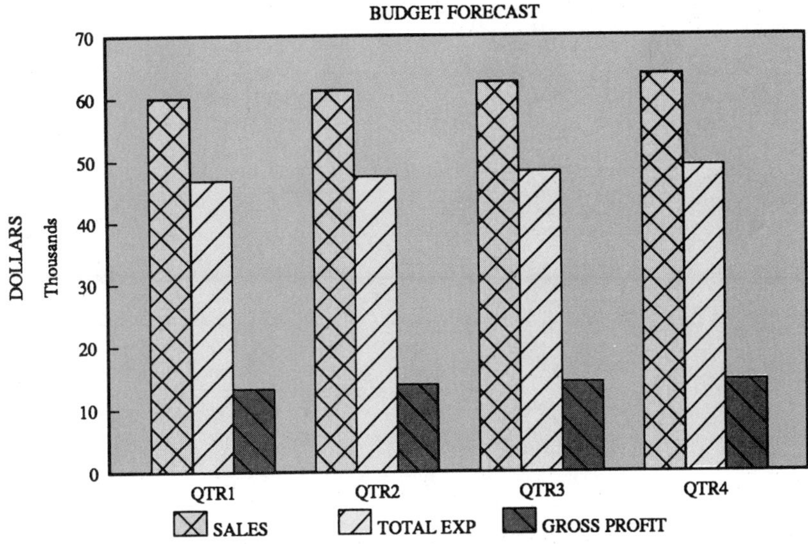

Figure 4-17

To return to the worksheet:

Press ↵

To use a horizontal or sideways display orientation:

Select Type

Select Features

Select Horizontal

To view the graph:

Press F10

Notice the change from vertical to horizontal orientation. Your screen should look like Figure 4-18.

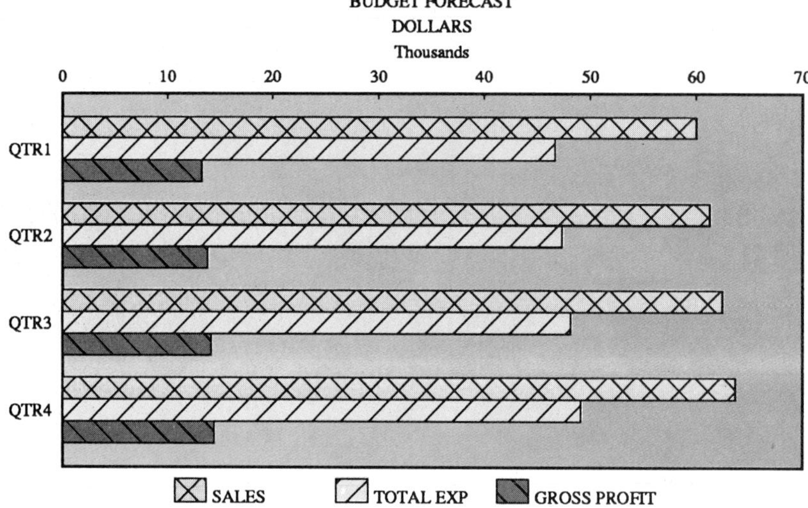

Figure 4-18

To return to the worksheet and exit the graph menus:

Press ↵

Select Quit twice

Specifying a Vertical Orientation

If you are in a situation where the current graph has a horizontal orientation, you can switch to a vertical orientation.

Assuming that you have just completed the example in the last section, you can change to a vertical orientation by completing the following steps:

Press /

Select Graph

Select Type

Select Features

Select Vertical

To view the graph:

Press (F10)

The graph now has a vertical orientation and your screen should look like Figure 4-19.

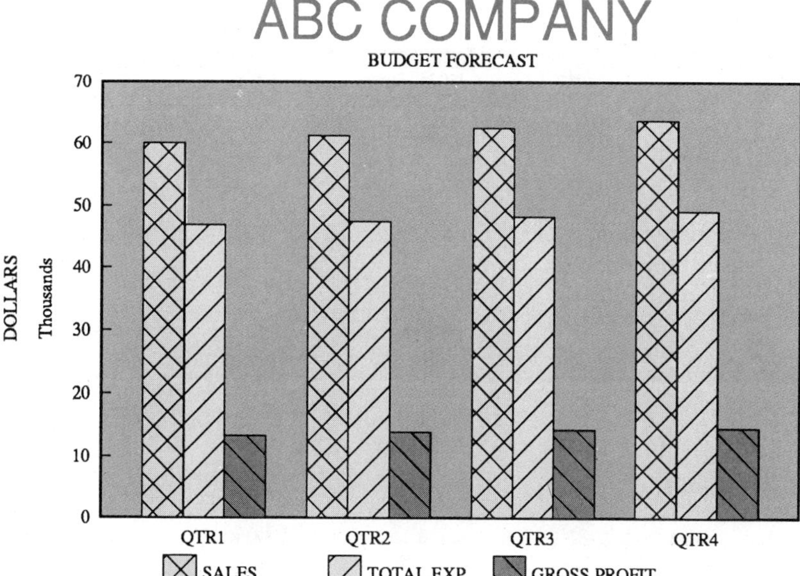

Figure 4-19

To return to the worksheet and exit the graph menus:

Press (↵)

Select Quit twice

Stacking the Data Ranges

There may be some circumstances in which you desire to stack the data ranges on top of each other. For example, suppose for the BUDGET worksheet you want to stack the data ranges for Sales, Total Expenses and Gross Profit.

Make sure that the BUDGET worksheet is on your screen and that a vertical orientation for the graph has been selected. To stack the data ranges:

Press	/
Select	Graph
Select	Type
Select	Features
Select	Stacked
Select	Yes

To view the data ranges for SALES, TOTAL EXPENSES and GROSS PROFIT after they have been stacked:

Press	F10

You now should have a graph on your screen that stacks the data ranges and looks like Figure 4-20.

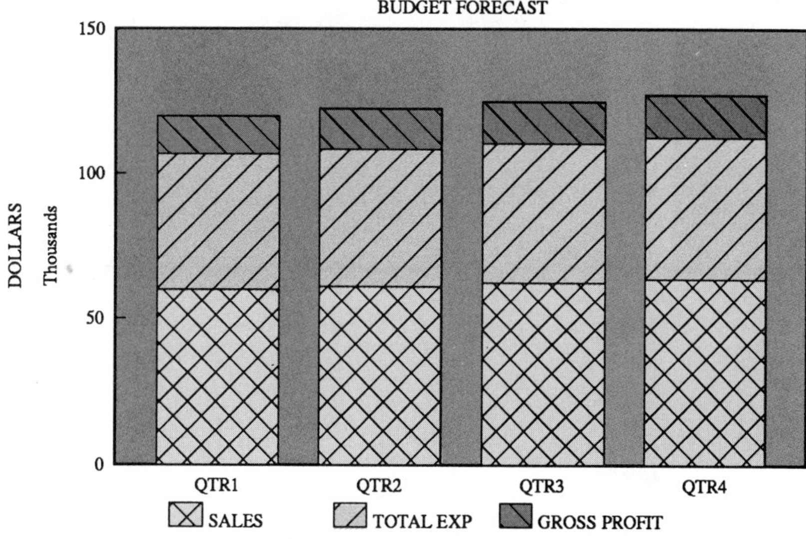

Figure 4-20

To return to the worksheet and exit the graph menus:

Press	↵
Select	Quit twice

Graphing Each Data Range as a Percentage of the Total for All Ranges

Retrieve the file BOATSALE which you created in Chapter 3. Your screen should look like Figure 4-21.

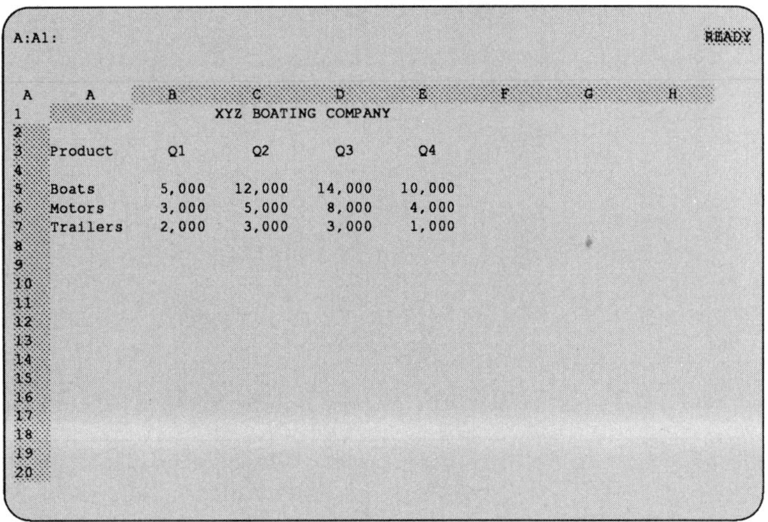

Figure 4-21

Your supervisor would like you to construct a graph that shows the sales of each product as a percentage of total sales for each quarter. The graph you need to create appears in Figure 4-22.

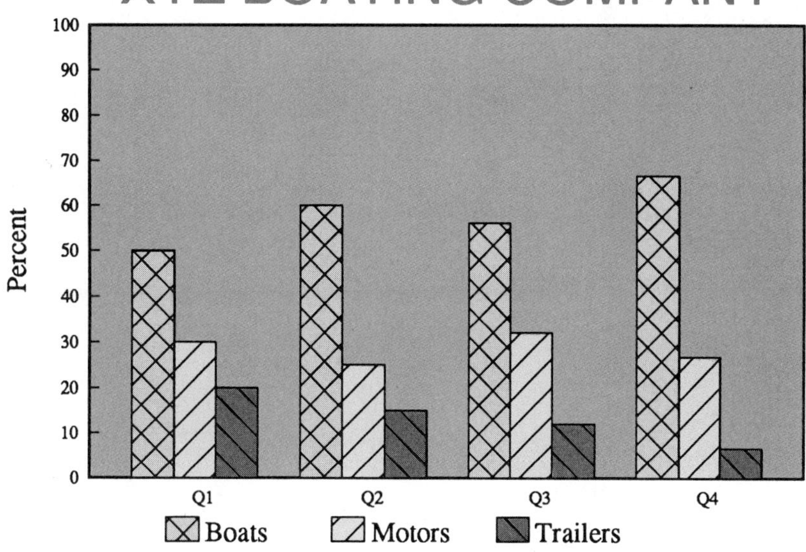

Figure 4-22

To specify the type of graph:

Press	/
Select	Graph
Select	Type
Select	Bar

To indicate the data ranges:

Select	X
Move	the cell pointer to cell B3
Type	.

Move	the cell pointer to cell E3
Press	↵
Select	A
Move	the cell pointer to cell B5
Type	.
Move	the cell pointer to cell E5
Press	↵
Select	B
Move	the cell pointer to cell B6
Type	.
Move	the cell pointer to cell E6
Press	↵
Select	C
Move	the cell pointer to cell B7
Type	.
Move	the cell pointer to cell E7
Press	↵

To view the graph:

Press	F10

A bar graph should appear on your screen and look like Figure 4-23.

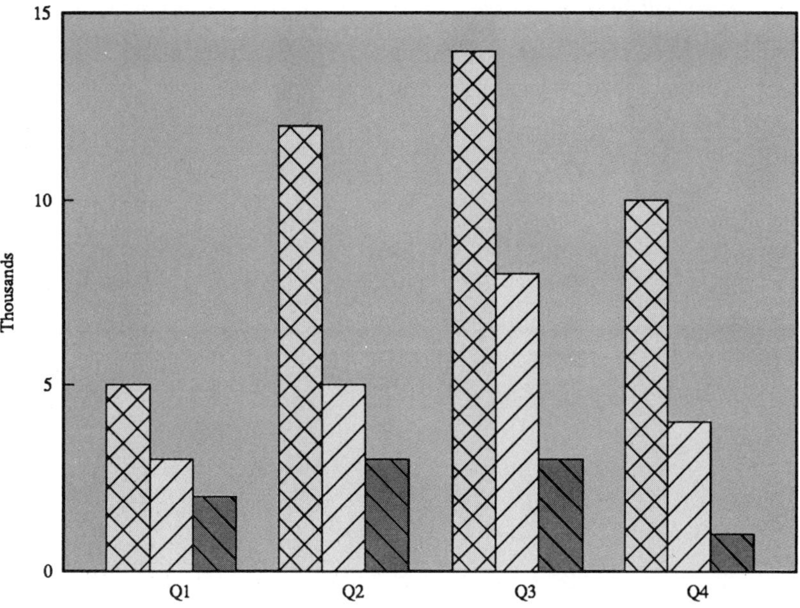

Figure 4-23

To return to the worksheet and the main graph menu:

Press ↵

To select the option to show each product as a percentage of total sales for each quarter:

Select Type

Select Features

Select 100%

Select Yes

To see the new graph:

Press F10

Notice that the Y-axis now represents percent and the corresponding data-range values have been converted to percentages of their total value For example, the boat sales in Quarter 1 represent 50% of total sales while motors and trailers account for 30% and 20% respectively during the quarter.

To return to the worksheet and the main graph menu:

Press ↵

Select Quit

Select Options

To complete the graph by placing titles and legends on it:

Select Titles

Select First

Type XYZ BOATING COMPANY

Press ↵

Select Titles

Select Y-Axis

Type Percent

Press ↵

To place the legends on the graph:

Select Legend

Select A

Type Boats

Press ↵

Select Legend

Select B

Type Motors

Press ↵

Select Legend

Select C

Type Trailers

Press ↵

To view the completed graph:

Press F10

Your screen should look like Figure 4-24.

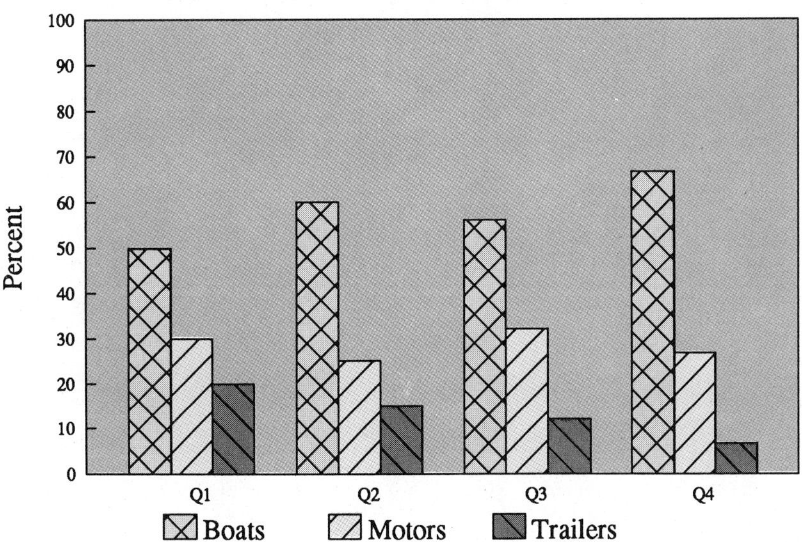

Figure 4-24

To return to the worksheet and exit the graph menus:

Press ↵

Select Quit twice

Using a Second Y-axis and the Area Graph Format

In some situations, you may need to use the second Y-axis available in 1-2-3. One additional option available that can be very useful is the capability to fill the area between the items included in a line graph.

When you finish this exercise, you will have completed a graph that looks like the one in Figure 4-25.

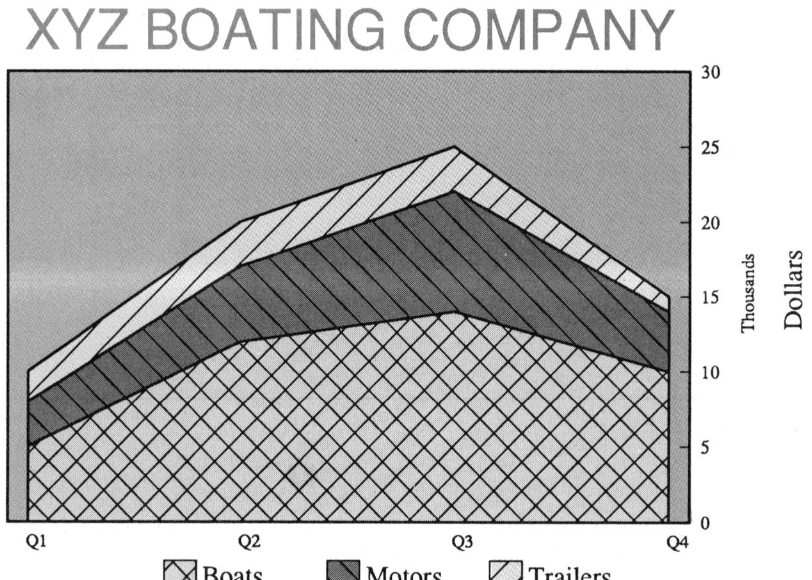

Figure 4-25

You will use the BOATSALE spreadsheet; so please retrieve the file BOATSALE.

To reset all of the graph settings:

Press	/
Select	Graph

Select	Reset
Select	Graph

To specify the type of graph:

Select	Type
Select	Line

To indicate the data ranges:

Select	X
Move	the cell pointer to cell B3
Type	.
Move	the cell pointer to cell E3
Press	↵
Select	A
Move	the cell pointer to cell B5
Type	.
Move	the cell pointer to cell E5
Press	↵
Select	B
Move	the cell pointer to cell B6
Type	.
Move	the cell pointer to cell E6
Press	↵
Select	C
Move	the cell pointer to cell B7
Type	.

Move the cell pointer to cell E7

Press ↵

To view the graph:

Press F10

A line graph should appear on your screen and look like Figure 4-26.

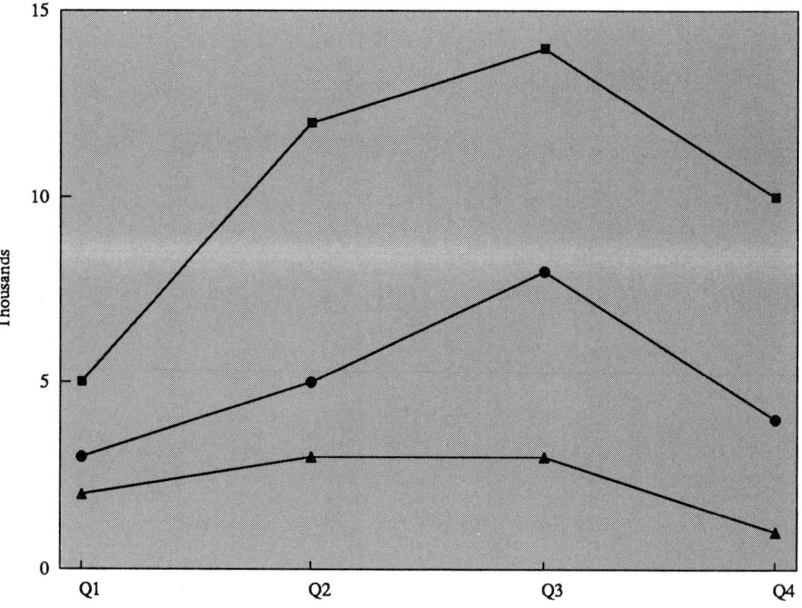

Figure 4-26

To return to the worksheet and the main graph menu:

Press ↵

To indicate that the second Y-axis is to be used and the data ranges are to be assigned to the second Y-axis:

Select Type

Select Features

Select 2Y-Ranges

Select Graph

The last option assigns all data ranges to the second Y-axis.

To view the graph in which the second Y-axis is now used:

Press F10

Notice that the data ranges set previously are now graphed and the Y-axis values appear on the second Y-axis. Your screen should look like Figure 4-27.

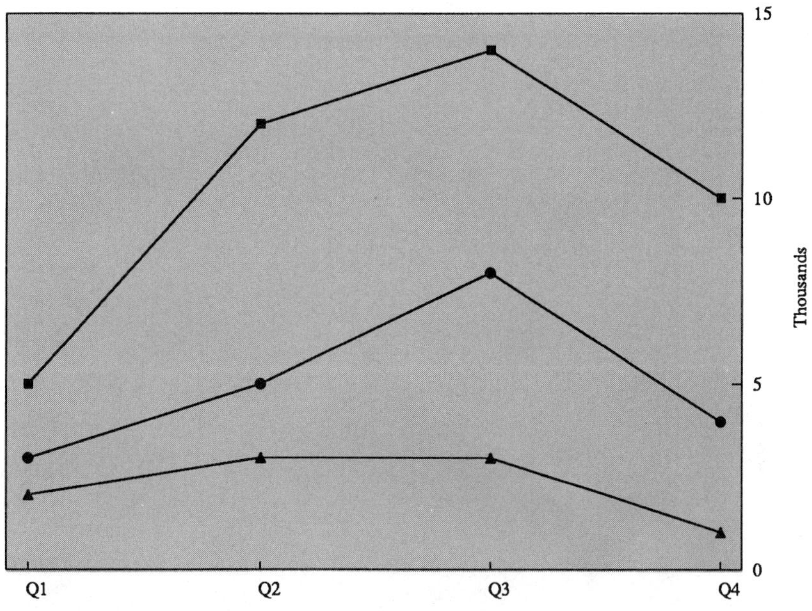

Figure 4-27

To return to the worksheet and exit to the main graph menu:

Press ↵

Select Quit twice

To delineate the data that is being graphed more effectively by filling the areas between the lines:

Select	Options
Select	Format
Select	Graph
Select	Area

To view the line graph with the areas filled:

Press	F10

Your screen now should look like Figure 4-28.

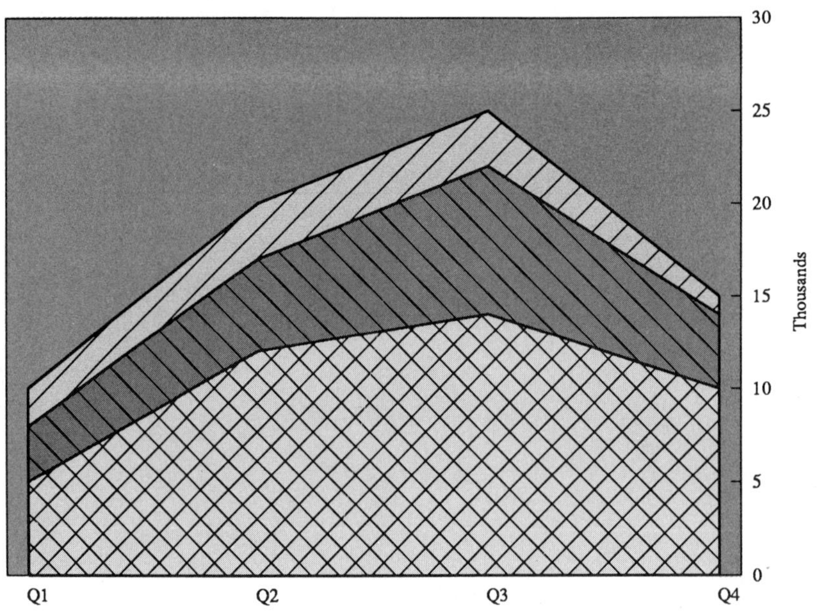

Figure 4-28

To return to the worksheet and the graph options menu:

Press	↵
Select	Quit twice

Select	Options

To complete the graph by placing titles and legends on it:

Select	Titles
Select	First
Type	XYZ BOATING COMPANY
Press	↵
Select	Titles
Select	2Y-Axis
Type	Dollars
Press	↵

To place the legends on the graph:

Select	Legend
Select	A
Type	Boats
Press	↵
Select	Legend
Select	B
Type	Motors
Press	↵
Select	Legend
Select	C
Type	Trailers
Press	↵

To view the completed graph:

Press F10

Your screen should look like Figure 4-29.

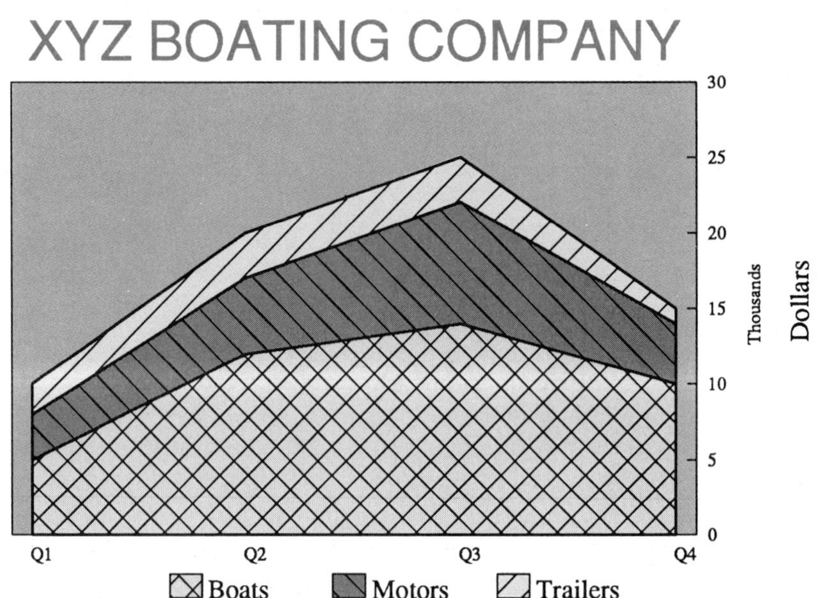

Figure 4-29

To return to the worksheet and exit the graph menus:

Press ↵

Select Quit twice

■ AUTOMATIC GRAPHING

In the previous sections, you created a graph by specifying the type of graph and the individual data ranges to include on the graph. 1-2-3 also permits the automatic drawing of a graph based on the location of the cell pointer.

Assume that you are given a worksheet that looks like Figure 4-30 and you want to create a line graph automatically based on where you place the cell pointer.

```
A:A1: [W17]                                                                READY

 A          A              B         C         D         E         F         G
 1                                  ABC COMPANY
 2
 3
 4                            QTR1      QTR2      QTR3      QTR4
 5   SALES                  60,000    61,200    62,424    63,672
 6   TOTAL EXPENSES         46,750    47,380    48,214    49,151
 7   GROSS PROFIT           13,250    13,820    14,210    14,521
 8
 9
10
11
12
13
14
15
16
17
18
19
20
```

Figure 4-30

When you finish this exercise, your screen will look like Figure 4-31.

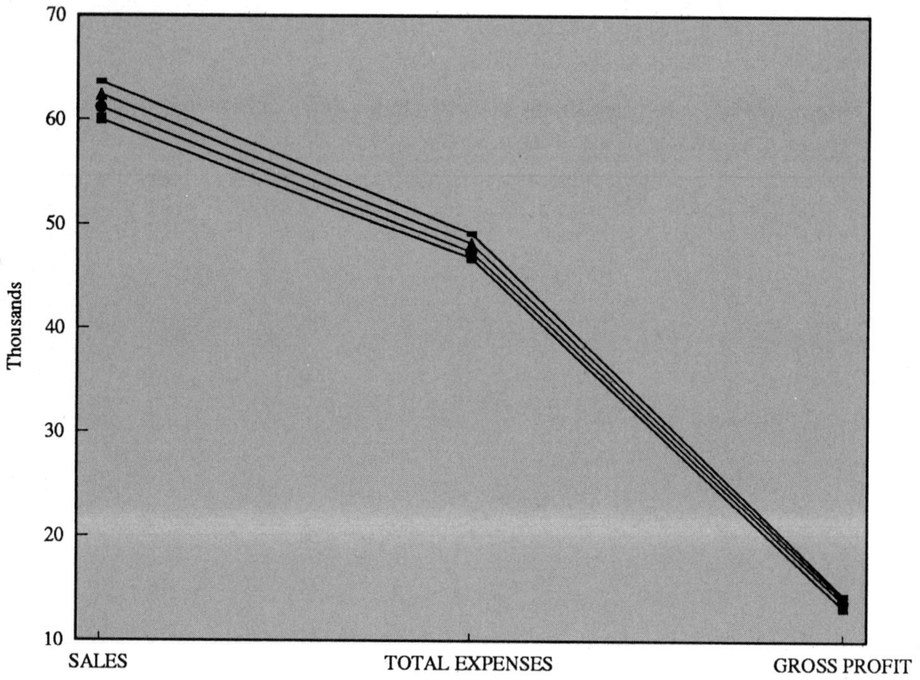

Figure 4-31

There are specific rules for using the automatic graphic option that follow:

1. The graph range must be a single worksheet range.
2. The columns must be contiguous.
3. The X data range must be in the first column (the column in which the cell pointer is located) followed by the A, B, C, D, E and F data ranges in consecutive columns.
4. The cells immediately above or to the left of the automatic graph range must be labels, otherwise the range must be separated from the rest of the data on the worksheet by at least two blank rows or columns.

First, create a worksheet like the one appearing in Figure 4-30 and save it using the file name AUTOMATI.

To obtain a graph automatically:

Move	the cell pointer to A4
Press	F10

A line graph will appear on your screen, because you have not yet specified the type of graph you want. Your screen should look like Figure 4-32.

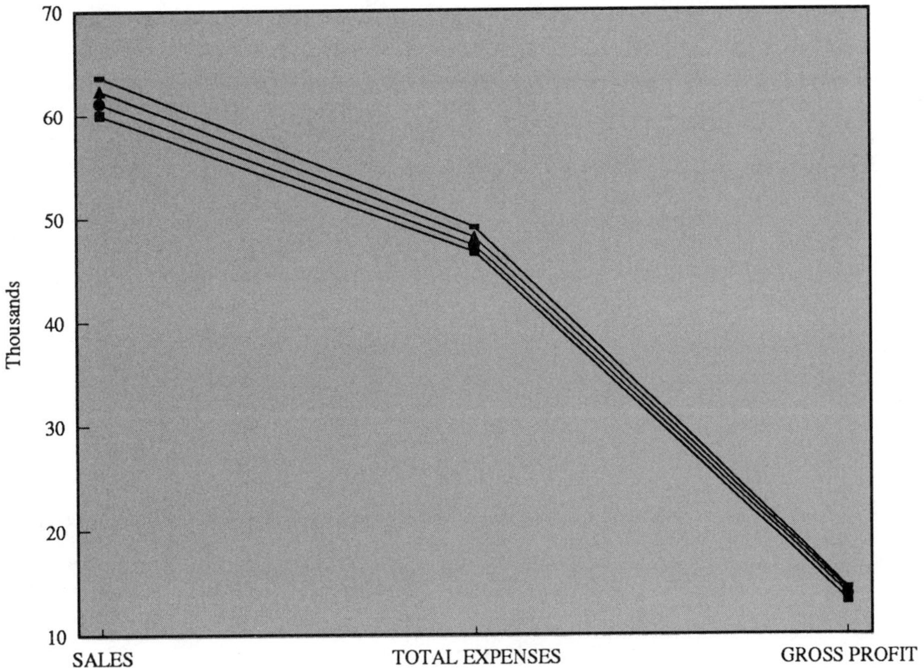

Figure 4-32

To return to the worksheet:

Press ↵

To obtain a bar graph automatically, first select Bar as the type of graph:

Press /

Select Graph

Select Type

Select Bar

To exit the menus:

Select Quit

To automatically create the bar graph:

Press F10

A bar graph should now appear on your screen and look like Figure 4-33.

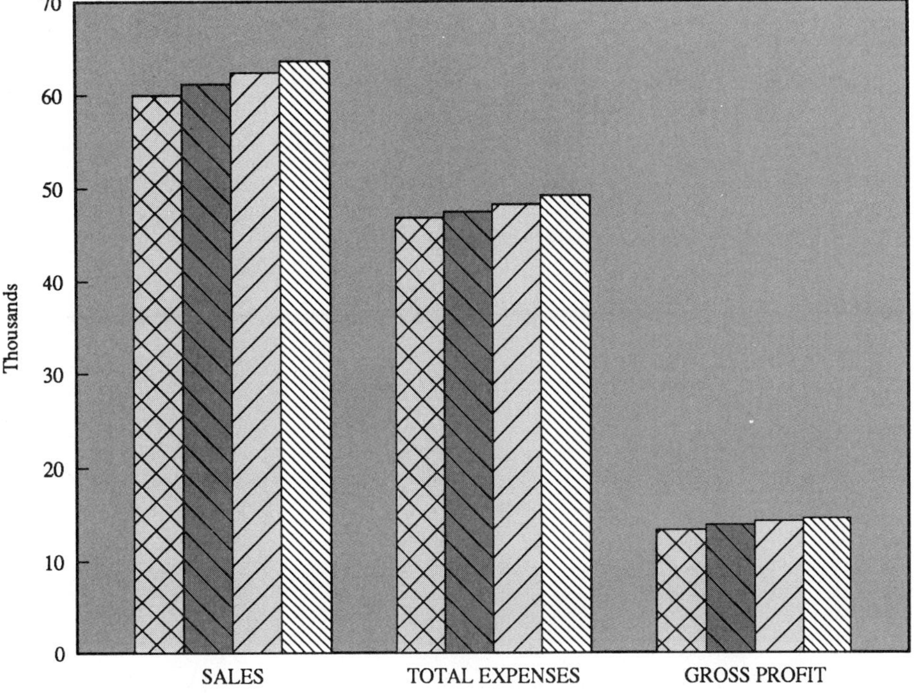

Figure 4-33

To return to the worksheet:

Press 

GROUP GRAPHING

In the previous section, you created a graph using the automatic graphing capability. This graphing capability placed all of the data for SALES, TOTAL EXPENSES and GROSS PROFIT together when the graph was drawn.

Another way to quickly create a graph is through the **Graph Group** command sequence. If you use this option, the data ranges X and A through F are specified simultaneously. The X and A through F ranges must be in consecutive rows or columns in a range. When you finish this section, a graph like the one in Figure 4-34 will be displayed on your screen.

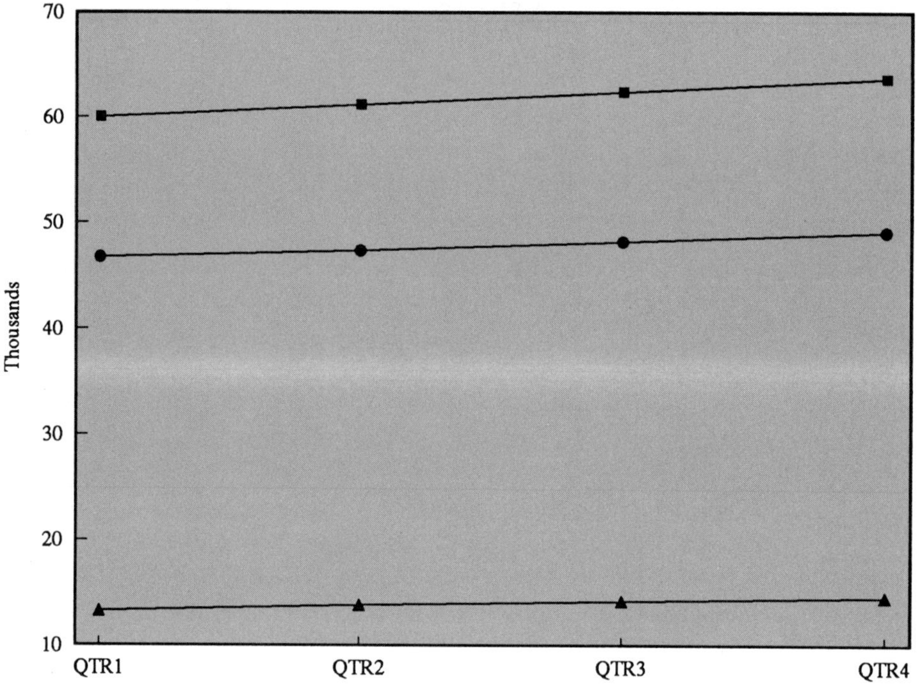

Figure 4-34

You will need to use the worksheet that you saved on file AUTOMATI which you used in the last section. If the worksheet is not on your screen, please retrieve it. Before you use the group graphing option, you need to reset the previous graph settings.

Press	/
Select	Graph
Select	Reset
Select	Graph

You should now be on the main graph menu. To create a graph using the group graphing option:

Select Group

To enter the group range of cells:

Move the cell pointer to cell B4

Type .

Move the cell pointer to cell E7

Press ↵

To specify that rows are to be used as the data ranges:

Select Rowwise

You have indicated that the X data range consists of cells B4 through E4 (QTR1 through QTR4). You also have specified that the A, B and C data ranges include the data for SALES, TOTAL EXPENSES and GROSS PROFIT respectively.

To view the graph you have created:

Press F10

Your screen should look like Figure 4-34.

Notice that since you did not indicate the type of graph to draw, 1-2-3 defaults to the line graph option.

To return to the worksheet:

Press ↵

To exit the graph menu:

Select Quit

■ DISPLAYING A GRAPH IN A WINDOW

You can display a graph on the screen along with a worksheet if you are using a high resolution monitor or a monochrome monitor with a graphics card. To include the current graph on the BUDGET spreadsheet, first retrieve the file BUDGET. Then you need to complete the following steps:

Move	the cell pointer to cell D1
Press	/
Select	Worksheet
Select	Window
Select	Graph

You should now see the current graph in a graph window on your screen. This capability can only be seen on your screen if you have a high resolution monitor or graphics card. If you cannot see a graph, move on to the next section.

One advantage this capability provides is that you can see the change in the graph when you change a number on the worksheet. To illustrate this point, change the SALES value for the first quarter to 100,000:

Move	the cell pointer to cell B7
Type	100000
Press	↵

Notice that the graph changed instantaneously when the worksheet was recalculated based on the new SALES value.

The size of the graph window depends on where you place the cell pointer. If you place it in a cell on the right side of the screen, the graph window will be smaller than if you place the cell pointer on the left side of the screen.

To remove the graph window from your screen:

Press	/
Select	Worksheet
Select	Window
Select	Clear

PRINTING A GRAPH

After creating a graph, you will most likely want to print the graph. In some instances, you may want to print a graph that you created in an earlier 1-2-3 work session. Furthermore, you may want to print a graph in conjunction with data from a worksheet. In this section, you will learn how to print graphs for each of these situations and examine some advanced printing options.

Printing the Current Graph

Before printing a graph, make sure the BUDGET worksheet appears on your screen. If it does not, retrieve the file BUDGET.

To select the BUDBAR graph you created:

Press /

Select Graph

Select Name

Select Use

Move the pointer to BUDBAR

Press ↵

The graph will appear on your screen. To leave the graph menu:

Press ↵

Select Quit

To print the current graph associated with the BUDGET worksheet:

Press /

Select Print

Select Printer

Select Image

Select Current

Select Align

Select Go

Select Page

The graph will now be printed. Assuming you are using the BUDBAR graph, your output will look like Figure 4-35.

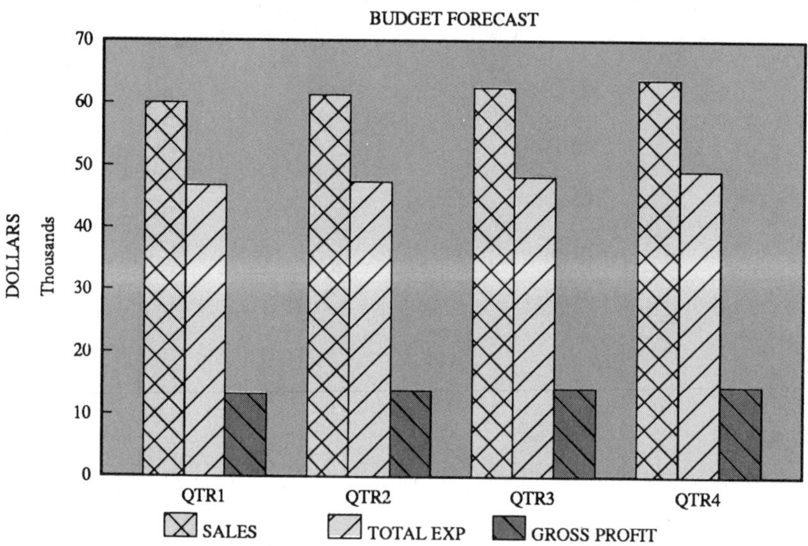

Figure 4-35

To exit the graph menus:

Select Quit

Printing a Named Graph

Assuming that you still have the BUDGET worksheet on the screen that was used when you created, named and saved the various types of graphs in an earlier section of this chapter, the steps necessary to print the pie graph are:

Press /

Select Print

Select	Printer
Select	Image
Select	Named-Graph
Press	F3
Move	the pointer to BUDPIE
Press	↵
Select	Align
Select	Go
Select	Page
Select	Quit

Printing a Graph with Worksheet Data

Suppose that you want to print a graph immediately after you print a worksheet. First you need to print the worksheet data, then you need to print the graph. As an example, you will print a portion of the BUDGET worksheet and then the bar chart that is associated with the worksheet.

Make sure the BUDGET worksheet is on your screen. If it is not on your screen, retrieve the file BUDGET.

To print the worksheet and a named graph on the same page, you specify the range to print followed by a comma, then the graph name preceded by an asterisk. First specify the print range.

Press	Home
Press	/
Select	Print
Select	Printer
Select	Range

Highlight cells A1..F19.

To specify that the graph named BUDBAR is to be printed following A1..F19:

Type ,

Type *BUDBAR

Your screen now should look like Figure 4-36.

```
A:A1: [W19]                                                          EDIT
Enter print range: A:A1..A:F19,*BUDBAR

A          A              B        C        D        E        F
1                                  ABC COMPANY
2                                    BUDGET
3
4
5                         QTR1     QTR2     QTR3     QTR4   YR TOTAL
6
7  SALES                 $60,000  $61,200  $62,424  $63,672 $247,296
8
9  EXPENSES
10   SALARIES             35,000   35,500   36,200   37,000  143,700
11   RENT                  9,000    9,000    9,000    9,000   36,000
12   TELEPHONE             1,000    1,050    1,103    1,158    4,311
13   OFFICE SUPPLIES         750      800      850      900    3,300
14   MISCELLANEOUS         1,000    1,030    1,061    1,093    4,184
15                       ---------------------------------------------
16     TOTAL EXPENSES     46,750   47,380   48,214   49,151  191,495
17                       ---------------------------------------------
18 GROSS PROFIT          $13,250  $13,820  $14,210  $14,521  $55,801
19                       =============================================
20
                                                                   CAP
```

Figure 4-36

To complete the print process for the worksheet and the graph:

Press ↵

Select Align

Select Go

Select Page

Select Quit

The printout should look like Figure 4-37.

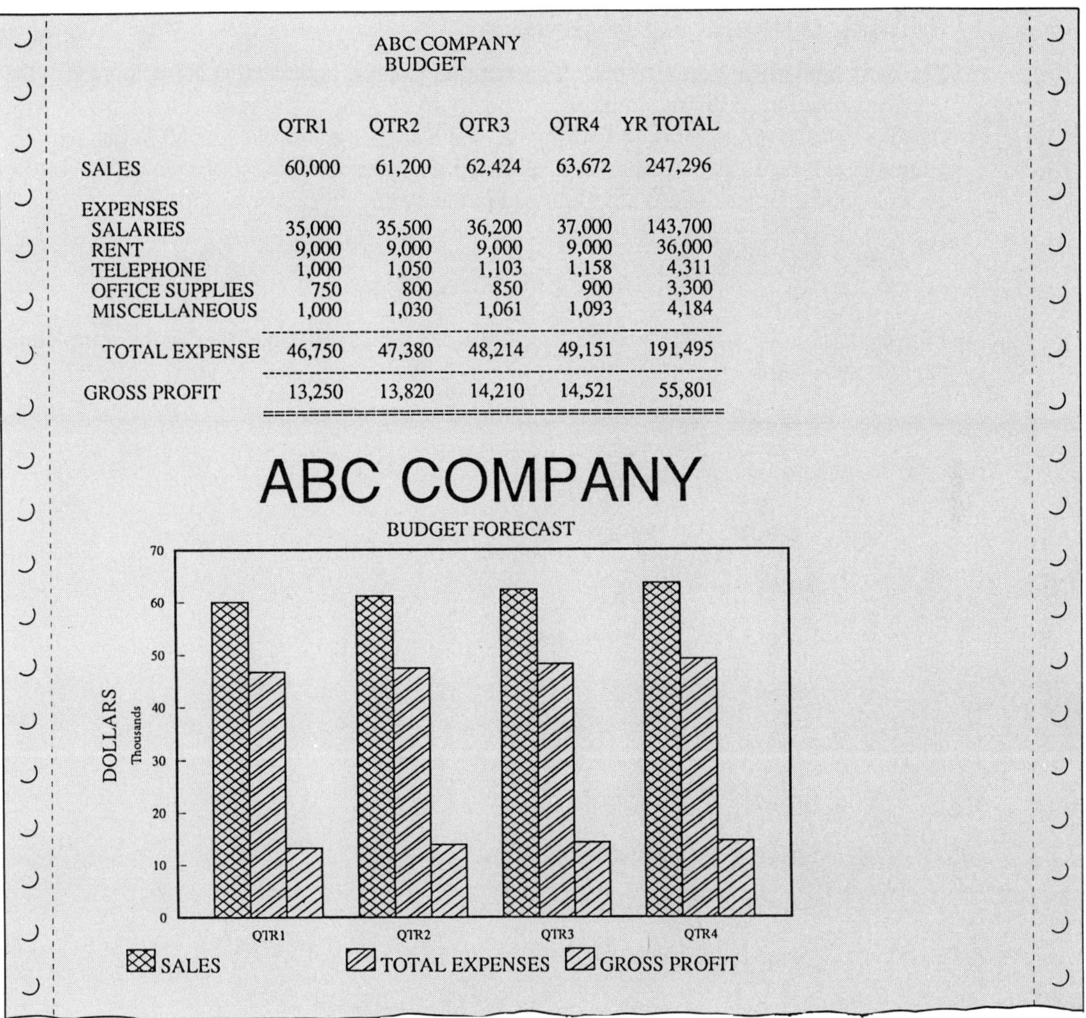

ABC COMPANY
BUDGET

	QTR1	QTR2	QTR3	QTR4	YR TOTAL
SALES	60,000	61,200	62,424	63,672	247,296
EXPENSES					
SALARIES	35,000	35,500	36,200	37,000	143,700
RENT	9,000	9,000	9,000	9,000	36,000
TELEPHONE	1,000	1,050	1,103	1,158	4,311
OFFICE SUPPLIES	750	800	850	900	3,300
MISCELLANEOUS	1,000	1,030	1,061	1,093	4,184
TOTAL EXPENSE	46,750	47,380	48,214	49,151	191,495
GROSS PROFIT	13,250	13,820	14,210	14,521	55,801

Figure 4-37

Printing Different Sized Graphs

You can print various sized graphs. For example, you can indicate that a graph is to fill the page from the left to the right margin or specify the length of the graph on the page. You can also reshape the graph by specifying the width and length for the graph. In this section, you will print a full page graph. It is assumed that you are using a printer with 8 1/2 by 11-inch paper. Other options are discussed in the command reference appendix.

Make sure you have the BUDGET worksheet on the screen. Select the BUDBAR named-graph using the **G**raph **N**ame **U**se command sequence.

With the BUDGET worksheet on the screen, you can print a full page bar graph by completing the following steps:

Press /

Select Print

Select Printer

Select Image

Select Named-Graph

Move the pointer to BUDBAR

Press ↵

Select Options

Select Advanced

Select Image

Select Image-Sz

Select Length-Fill

Press ↵

You have indicated that your printer has 66 available lines for printing. If your printer has a different number of lines that can be printed on a 8 1/2 by 11-inch sheet of paper or your paper length is not 11 inches, you will need to type a different number after you select the Length-Fill option.

To complete the printing process:

Select Quit three times

Select Align

Select Go

Select Page

Select Quit

Your printout should look similar to Figure 4-38.

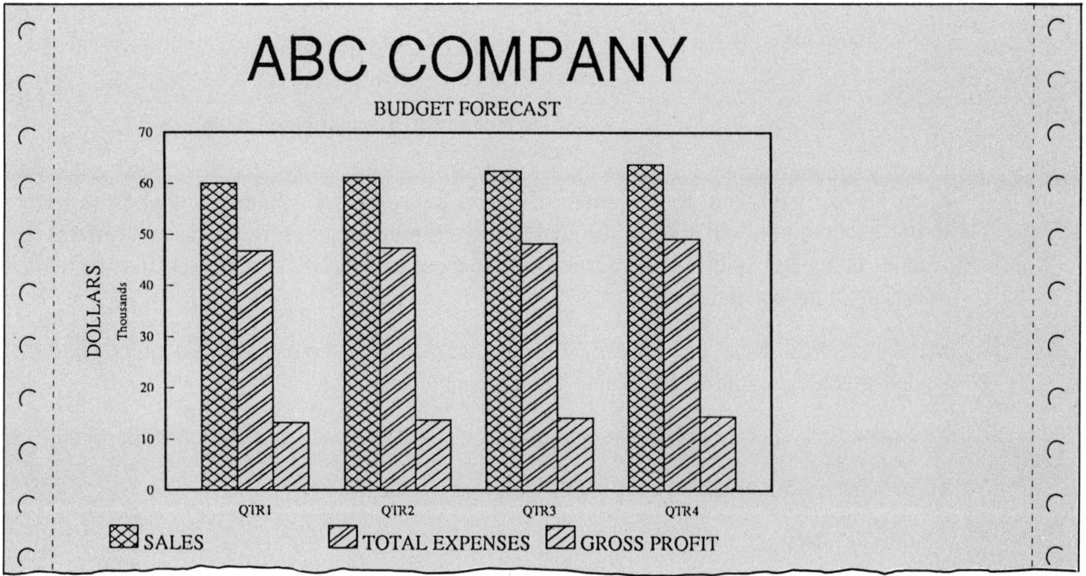

Figure 4-38

Printing a Graph with Advanced Options (Colors, Fonts, Sizes and Hatches)

If desired, you can use advanced options to specify colors, fonts and sizes for various groups of items on a graph when it is printed. There are three groups of graph parameters.

Graph-text Group	Items Included
1	First line of the graph title
2	Second line of the graph title, axes titles and legend text
3	Scale indicators, axes labels, data labels and footnotes

There are many possible combinations of colors, fonts, sizes and hatches that you can select. In this section, you will specify the fonts for the three groups using the default options for your printer. For additional information on these advanced options, see the command reference in the appendix.

Make sure you have the BUDGET worksheet on the screen. Select the BUDBAR named-graph using the **G**raph **N**ame **U**se command sequence.

You must first specify the fonts desired using the graph menus and then print the graph.

To indicate the font desired for the first graph-text group:

Press	/
Select	Graph
Select	Options
Select	Advanced
Select	Text
Select	First
Select	Font
Select	Default
Select	Quit

Note that you can select one of the numbers 1 through 8 instead of the default if you know the fonts that have been assigned to those numbers for your printer.

To specify the font to use with the second graph-text group:

Select	Second
Select	Font
Select	Default
Select	Quit

To define the font to use with the third graph-text group:

Select	Third
Select	Font
Select	Default
Select	Quit

To exit the graph menus:

Select	Quit four times

To print the graph with the specified fonts for the graph-text groups:

Press	/
Select	Print
Select	Printer
Select	Image
Select	Named-Graph
Press	F3
Move	the pointer to BUDBAR
Press	↵
Select	Align
Select	Go
Select	Page

Your printout should be similar to Figure 4-39. The fonts may be different because your set of fonts may be different from those used in preparing this example.

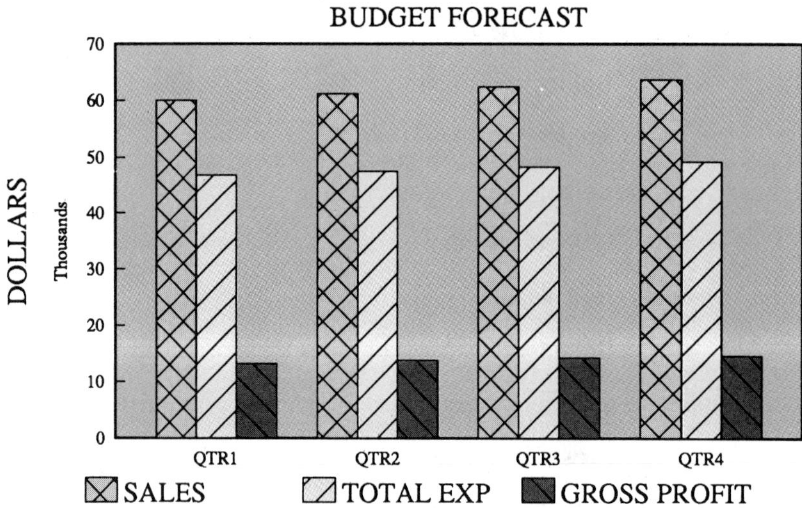

Figure 4-39

■ OTHER GRAPH COMMANDS

A summary of other commonly used graph commands is included for your reference. Tasks such as viewing a particular graph, deleting graph settings, erasing all graphs in a worksheet, erasing graph files, and removing the scale indicator from a graph are discussed.

Viewing the Current Graph

Retrieve the file BUDGET for this exercise. It is assumed that the previous exercises on graphs have been completed. As seen in an earlier exercise, there are two ways to view the current graph in a worksheet.

Press F10 or

Press /

Select Graph

Select View

The current graph appears on your screen. To return to the worksheet after viewing the graph:

Press ↵

To exit the current menu:

Select Quit

Selecting a Graph to View

In order to assign two or more graphs to a worksheet, each graph must be named and saved with the worksheet, just as BUDBAR and BUDLINE were two of the graphs named in the BUDGET file. As an example, earlier you named the bar graph BUDBAR and line graph BUDLINE. Then you saved the graph specifications and names on the BUDGET file.

To choose the graph to view:

Press /

Select Graph

Select Name

Select Use

Press F3 (graphs names are listed)

Move the pointer to the graph to view

In this example, highlight the name BUDBAR. When BUDBAR is highlighted:

Press ↵

The graph will appear on the screen and looks like Figure 4-40.

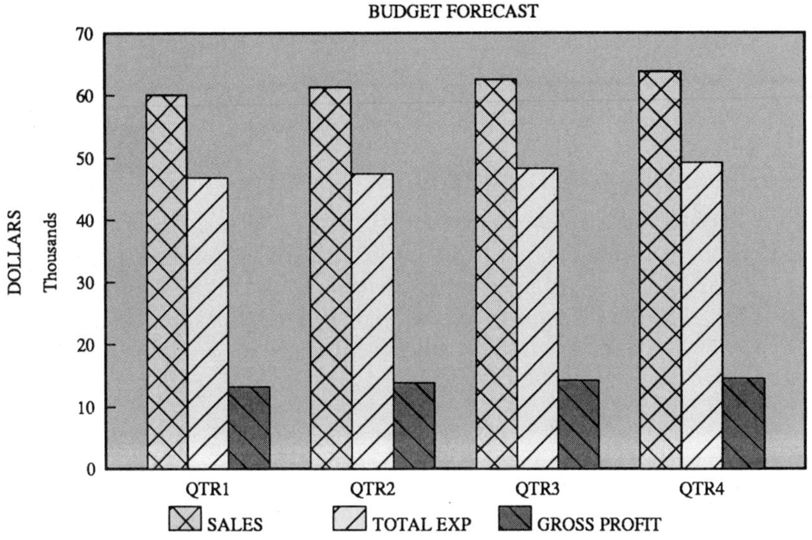

Figure 4-40

To return to the worksheet after viewing the graph:

Press ↵

To exit the current menu:

Select Quit

Note: The following steps give further information about graphs and are not a part of the exercise. If the exercises are completed, graphs that were created earlier will be erased. This will not cause a problem because the graphs are not used again in this book.

Deleting a Named Graph

To delete a named graph that was saved on a worksheet:

Press /

Select Graph

Select Name

Select	Delete
Move	the cursor to the name of the graph to erase (in this case, BUDLINE)
Press	↵

To exit the menu:

Select	Quit

To delete the graph specifications for BUDLINE from the BUDGET file, you need to complete the **F**ile **S**ave **R**eplace command sequence for the BUDGET file.

Erasing the Settings for a Graph

You can erase some or all of the settings associated with the current or named graph.

To erase the various settings for a specific graph, you first need to specify a named graph to use. In this example you will use BUDBAR.

Press	/
Select	Graph
Select	Name
Select	Use
Press	F3
Move	the pointer to BUDBAR
Press	↵

To return to the main graph menu:

Press	↵

To illustrate the process of erasing some or all of the graph settings:

Select	Reset

The **R**eset menu now appears on your screen which looks like Figure 4-41.

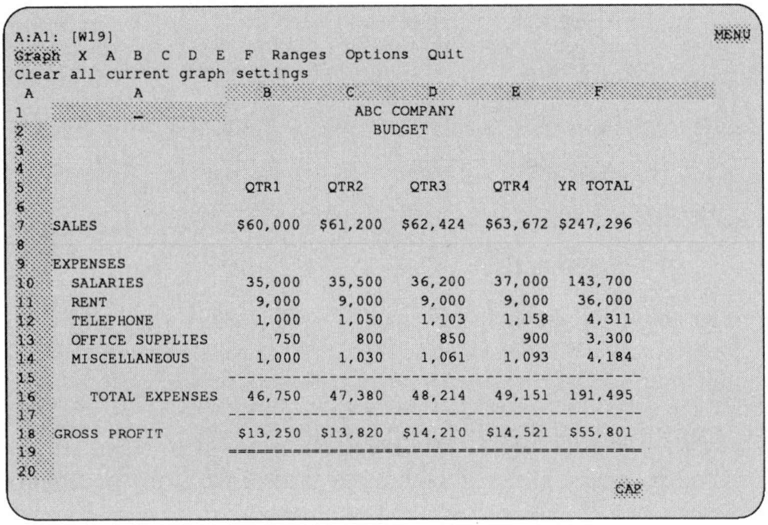

```
A:A1: [W19]                                                                MENU
Graph  X  A  B  C  D  E  F  Ranges  Options  Quit
Clear all current graph settings
 A          A              B          C          D          E          F
1                                    ABC COMPANY
2                                      BUDGET
3
4
5                          QTR1       QTR2       QTR3       QTR4    YR TOTAL
6
7   SALES                $60,000    $61,200    $62,424    $63,672  $247,296
8
9   EXPENSES
10    SALARIES             35,000     35,500     36,200     37,000   143,700
11    RENT                  9,000      9,000      9,000      9,000    36,000
12    TELEPHONE             1,000      1,050      1,103      1,158     4,311
13    OFFICE SUPPLIES         750        800        850        900     3,300
14    MISCELLANEOUS         1,000      1,030      1,061      1,093     4,184
15                       ------------------------------------------------
16      TOTAL EXPENSES     46,750     47,380     48,214     49,151   191,495
17                       ------------------------------------------------
18  GROSS PROFIT         $13,250    $13,820    $14,210    $14,521   $55,801
19                       ================================================
20
                                                                   CAP
```

Figure 4-41

If you select **G**raph, all graph settings will be deleted. When you select **R**anges, the X and A-F ranges **will be** eliminated. If the letter **X**, **A**, **B**, **C**, **D**, **E** or **F** is selected, then only the data associated with the item chosen will be deleted. When **O**ptions is selected, all settings related to the **G**raph **O**ptions menu are deleted. For example the titles and legend settings are deleted.

To exit from the graph menus:

Select Quit twice

To permanently change the graph settings on the BUDGET file, you will need to complete the **F**ile **S**ave **R**eplace command sequence for the BUDGET file. Do not issue this command sequence because you will use the graph in a later chapter.

Erasing Graph Files from the Disk

Even if the BUDGET worksheet file is erased from the disk, any files saved as graph files will remain on the disk. To list the graph files on the disk for the current directory:

Press /

Select File

Select List

Select Graph

If there are any graph files in the directory, the graph file names will appear on your screen. If there are none saved, no name will appear on the screen and you will need to press the Esc key several times to exit the menu structure. Your screen will look similar to Figure 4-42.

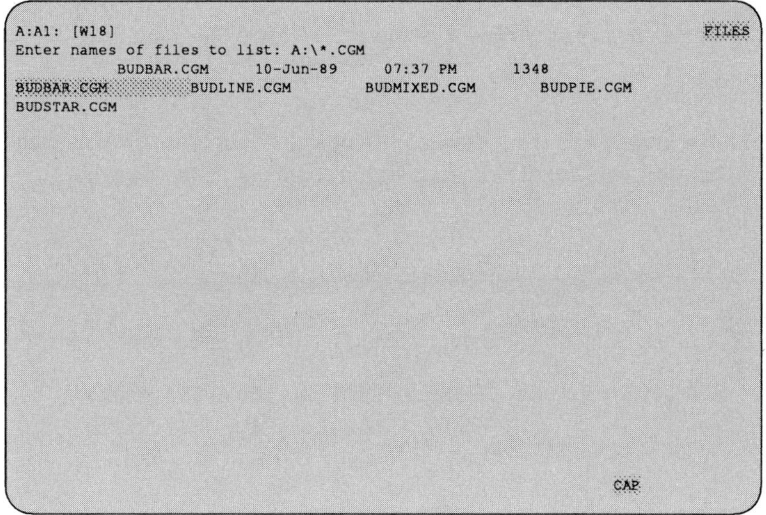

Figure 4-42

To return to the worksheet screen:

Press ↵

To erase a graph file:

Press /

Select File

Select Erase

Select Graph

Press F3

A list of the graph files appears.

Move the cell pointer to the graph file to erase (BUDLINE in this case)

Press ↵

Menu choices of **N**o and **Y**es appear. To erase the graph file:

Select Yes

The graph file has been erased from the disk. In order for you to check if the file has been erased, complete the **F**ile **L**ist **G**raph command sequence again.

Removing the Scale Indicator from a Graph or Changing the Scale Indicator

In some situations, you may want to remove or insert your own scaling indicator.

If necessary, retrieve the file BUDGET for use in this exercise.

To pick a graph for use:

Press /

Select Graph

Select Name

Select Use

When prompted for the graph to use:

Press F3

Move the pointer to BUDBAR

Press ↵

On the Y-scale the word **Thousands** is displayed as the scale indicator as shown in Figure 4-43.

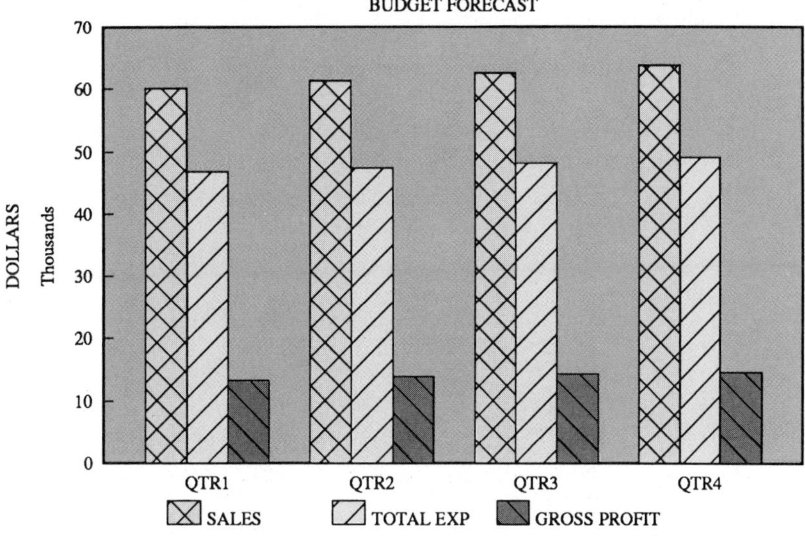

Figure 4-43

To return to the worksheet:

Press ↵

To remove the indicator from the Y-scale, select the following menu options:

Select Options

Select Scale

Select Y-Scale

Select Indicator

Select None

To view the graph:

Press (F10)

The Y-scale indicator no longer appears on your screen. Your screen should now look like Figure 4-44.

To return to the worksheet after viewing the graph:

Press ↵

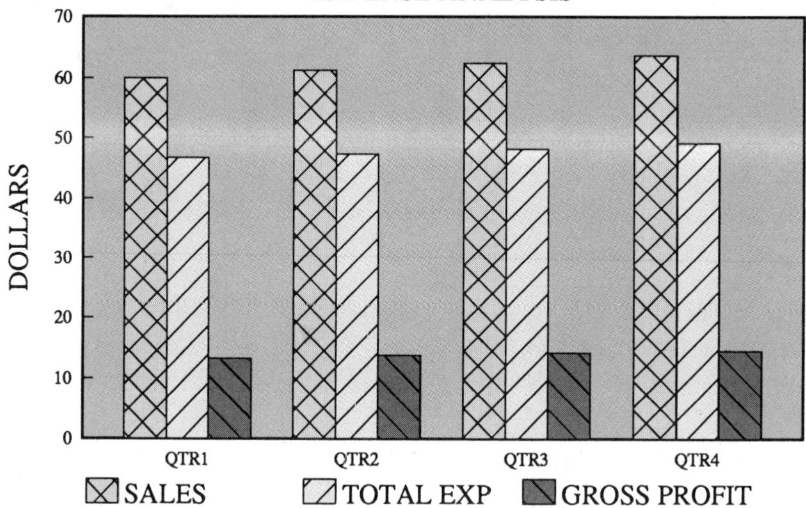

Figure 4-44

To return to the main graph menu:

Select Quit twice

Assume that the numbers in the BUDGET worksheet should represent millions of dollars rather than thousands of dollars. Then a Y-scale indicator of $000,000 is needed.

To place the new Y-scale indicator on the Y-axis:

Select Options

Select	Scale
Select	Y-Scale
Select	Indicator
Select	Manual
Type	($000,000)
Press	↵

To view the new Y-scale indicator:

Press	F10

Your screen should look like Figure 4-45.

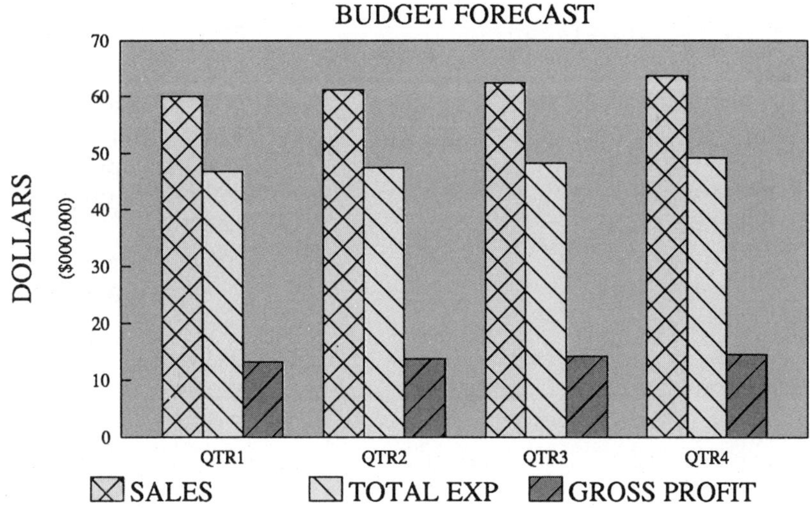

Figure 4-45

The X-scale and 2Y-scale (second Y-axis scale) can be removed or modified in a similar manner.

To return to the worksheet and exit the graph menus:

Press ↵

Select Quit three times

SUMMARY

Lotus 1-2-3 allows you to integrate graphics with spreadsheets. Creating graphics using spreadsheet data is easy to do, because the data to be graphed does not have to be entered a second time. In fact, if the data on a spreadsheet is changed and the spreadsheet is recalculated, the graph reflects the changes in the data the next time the graph is viewed. Graphic representations of data on a spreadsheet allow you to use graphs as an aid not only in analyzing spreadsheet data, but in presenting the data to others.

KEY CONCEPTS

A-Range
B-Range
Bar graph
C-Range
D-Range
E-Range
Erasing graphs
F-Range
Graph
High-Low-Close-Open graph
Image-Select
Legends
Line graph
Mixed graph
Naming a graph
Pie graph
Printing a graph
Saving a graph
Scale Indicator
Stacked-Bar graph
Titles
Type of graph
Viewing a graph
X-axis
X-Range
X-Scale
XY graph
Y-axis
Y-scale
2Y-axis
2Y-scale

CHAPTER FOUR
EXERCISE 1

INSTRUCTIONS: Circle T if the statement is true and F if the statement is false.

T F 1. A Lotus 1-2-3 graph can contain up to six different data ranges.

T F 2. To change a bar graph into a line graph, change the **G**raph **T**ype from **B**ar to **L**ine.

T F 3. If numbers are changed on the spreadsheet, the graph will reflect the changes when the graph is viewed again on the screen.

T F 4. If numbers are changed on the spreadsheet, the changes will be automatically reflected on any graph file that was previously created from the worksheet.

T F 5. It is possible to create three completely different graphs with data from one worksheet.

T F 6. If **F**ile **S**ave is not executed after a graph is made, the graph settings will not be saved.

T F 7. If a computer is not configured to show graphics on the screen, it is not possible to create and print a Lotus 1-2-3 graph.

T F 8. A color graph on the screen displays the colors in which the graph will be printed on a color printer or plotter.

T F 9. A pie graph displays the data in data range A.

T F 10. An XY graph is different from other Lotus graphs because it graphs data for variable X.

T F 11. High-Low-Close-Open graphs cannot be created using 1-2-3.

T	F	12.	Only one Y-axis can be used in 1-2-3.
T	F	13.	The scale indicator can be changed or deleted.
T	F	14.	Bar and line graphs cannot be combined on one chart.
T	T	15.	Data ranges can be graphed as a percentage of the total.

CHAPTER FOUR
EXERCISE 2

INSTRUCTIONS: Explain a typical situation when the following keystrokes or Lotus 1-2-3 commands are used.

Problem 1: / **G**raph **A**

Problem 2: / **G**raph **N**ame **U**se

Problem 3: / **G**raph **V**iew

Problem 4: / **G**raph **N**ame **C**reate

Problem 5: / **G**raph **O**ptions **L**egends

Problem 6: / **G**raph **O**ptions **T**itles

Problem 7: / **G**raph **O**ptions **D**ata-Labels

Problem 8: / **G**raph **T**ype **P**ie

Problem 9: / **P**rint **P**rinter **I**mage

Problem 10: / **G**raph **T**ype **M**ixed

CHAPTER FOUR
EXERCISE 3
Creating a Bar Graph

INSTRUCTIONS: Retrieve file PRACTICE.

Create a bar graph that includes Revenue, Expenses and Profit before Tax with 5 years as the graph ranges.

Include the Year 1 through Year 5 captions on the X-axis.

Place legend and titles information on the graph.

Save the graph on a file using the name PROFIT.

Print the graph.

CHAPTER FOUR
EXERCISE 4
Creating a Stacked-Bar Graph

INSTRUCTIONS: Retrieve file PRACTICE.

Create a stacked-bar graph for the Revenue, Profit before Tax, and Profit after Tax data for the five-year period.

Include appropriate information for the X-axis range, legends and graph titles.

Name and save the graph using the name PROFSTBR.

Print the graph.

CHAPTER FOUR
EXERCISE 5
Creating a Pie Graph

INSTRUCTIONS: Retrieve file SALES.

Create a pie graph using the data for the individual salespersons.

Place appropriate titles on the graph.

Save the graph using the name SALESPCT.

Print the graph.

CHAPTER FOUR
EXERCISE 6
Creating a Mixed Graph

INSTRUCTIONS: Retrieve file PRACTICE.

Create a mixed graph using Profit before Tax and Profit after Tax values for the five-year period.

The Profit after Tax values should appear as bars and the Profit before Tax amounts should appear as a line.

Place appropriate titles, legend, and X-axis range information on the graph.

Save the graph using the name MIXED.

Print the graph.

CHAPTER FOUR
EXERCISE 7
Creating an XY Graph

INSTRUCTIONS: Create the worksheet shown in Figure 4-46.

```
A:A1: [W16]                                                        READY

A        A             B           C              D          E         F
1                             ABC COMPANY
2
3                                  NO. OF        NO. OF
4        UNITS         CODE   UNITS PRODUCED  UNITS SOLD
5
6   FISHING BOAT       FISH              800          780
7   SKI BOAT           SKI               750          675
8   SAIL BOAT          SAIL              700          650
9   CANOE              CANOE             575          450
10  HOUSE BOAT         HOUSE             550          375
11  RAFT               RAFT              500          490
12
13
14
15
16
17
18
19
20
                                                           CAP
```

Figure 4-46

Create an XY graph using the number of units produced as the X item and the number of units sold as the Y item.

Include the code information on the graph to the right of each point to identify the points.

Place appropriate title, X-axis, and Y-axis information on the graph.

Print the graph.

CHAPTER FOUR
EXERCISE 8
Creating a High-Low-Close-Open Graph

INSTRUCTIONS: **Create the worksheet in Figure 4-47.**

```
A:A1: [W9]                                                    READY

A    A       B        C        D        E        F        G        H
1                            XYZ, INC.
2                          STOCK PRICES
3
4    DATE     HIGH      LOW     CLOSE     OPEN    VOLUME
5       5   25.000   24.500   24.750   24.500   15,000
6       6   25.875   25.000   25.000   25.000   10,000
7       7   25.000   24.000   24.250   25.000   12,500
8       8   24.500   23.500   24.250   24.000   10,000
9       9   24.500   23.000   23.750   24.500   12,000
10     12   23.875   22.500   23.000   23.500   14,000
11     13   23.500   22.000   22.250   23.250   15,000
12     14   22.500   21.000   21.750   22.500   10,000
13     15   23.500   21.750   22.875   21.750   17,000
14     16   23.750   22.875   23.000   23.000   15,000
15     19   25.000   24.000   24.250   24.000   20,000
16     20   25.875   24.250   25.250   24.250   19,000
17     21   25.750   25.250   25.250   25.250   15,000
18     22   27.000   25.000   26.750   25.750   20,000
19     23   28.000   26.000   28.000   26.000   22,000
20
```

Figure 4-47

Create a High-Low-Close-Open graph for the stock price data of XYZ, Inc.

Include appropriate documentation on the graph.

Print the graph.

CHAPTER FOUR
EXERCISE 9
Displaying a Graph in a Window

Instructions: Retrieve the file PRACTICE that has the graph file PROFIT associated with it. You created the graph file in Exercise 1 of this chapter.

Display the current GRAPH4 graph stored with file PRACTICE on the screen so the data for the first two years also appears on the screen.

Change the revenue value in Year 1 to 75,000.

Note: You cannot work this problem if you do not have a high-resolution monitor.

CHAPTER FIVE

CREATING AND USING A TEMPLATE

OBJECTIVES

In this chapter, you will learn to:

- Create and use a template

■ CHAPTER OVERVIEW

In Lotus 1-2-3, a **template** is a term used to describe a worksheet that can be used to create a series of other worksheets. A template usually consists of the general format (headings, labels, numeric format) and formulas that will be common to all of the worksheets. When data is entered in the template, the worksheet formulas calculate accordingly. The new data is then saved under a different file name. The use of a template can save you hours of time and effort in creating worksheets.

The template you will create computes the total salaries for employees in various divisions of the ABC Company example used earlier. Since the salaries for each division will be on a separate worksheet, you will build a template that can be used to create the worksheets for the various divisions of ABC Company. When you complete the template, your screen will look like Figure 5-1.

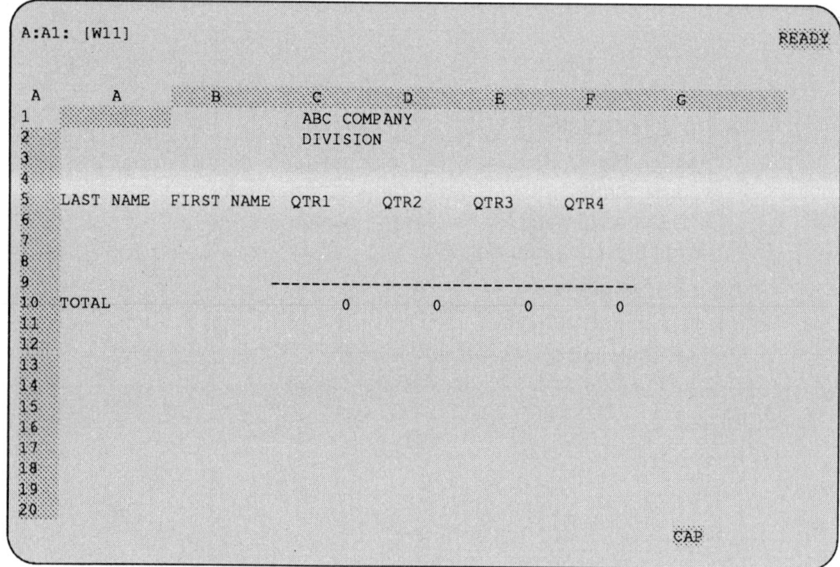

Figure 5-1

■ CREATING A TEMPLATE

There are three steps for creating the template:

1. Create the worksheet title, column headings, and labels.

2. Enter subtotal lines, total lines, and formulas.

3. Set the numeric format for the worksheet.

It is also useful to name areas of the spreadsheet with range names where appropriate. The use of range names was introduced in Chapter 3.

Creating the Worksheet Title, Column Headings, and Labels

If necessary, clear your screen.

To enter the titles for the template:

Press	the (CapsLock) key (if the CAP indicator does not appear on the screen)
Move	the cell pointer to cell C1
Press	the space bar three times
Type	ABC COMPANY
Press	↓
Press	the space bar three times
Type	DIVISION
Press	↵
Move	the cell pointer to cell A5
Type	LAST NAME[1]
Press	↵

To widen column A:

Press	/
Select	Worksheet
Select	Column
Select	Set-Width

When prompted for the column width:

Enter	11

To enter the next heading:

Move	the cell pointer to cell B5

[1] By this point you should be thoroughly familiar with entering labels and data. Therefore, the remainder of the text uses the shortcut instruction Enter label or data. It is assumed that you will type the label or data and press the ↵ key when asked to enter the information.

Enter FIRST NAME

To widen column B:

Press /

Select Worksheet

Select Column

Select Set-Width

When prompted for the column width:

Enter 10

To place the column headings in cells C5 through F5, respectively:

Enter ^QTR1 in cell C5

Enter ^QTR2 in cell D5

Enter ^QTR3 in cell E5

Enter ^QTR4 in cell F5

To enter the label TOTAL:

Move the cell pointer to cell A10

Enter TOTAL

Your screen should look like Figure 5-2.

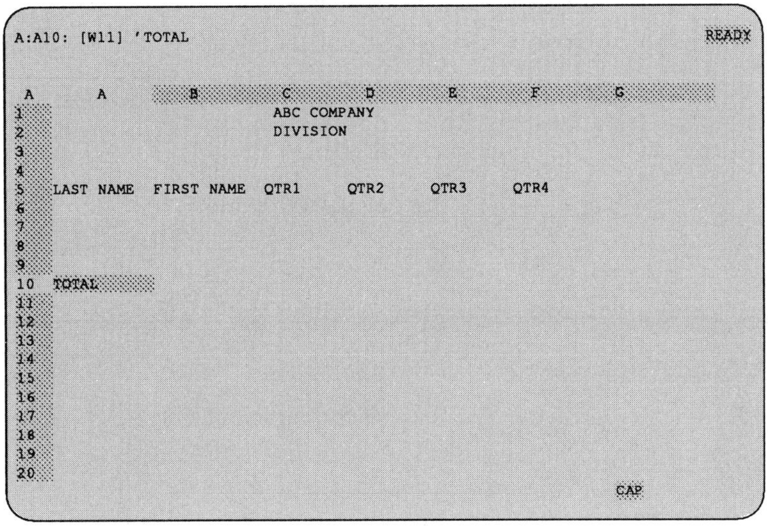

```
A:A10: [W11] 'TOTAL                                                    READY

 A      A          B          C          D          E          F          G
 1                            ABC COMPANY
 2                            DIVISION
 3
 4
 5  LAST NAME  FIRST NAME  QTR1       QTR2       QTR3       QTR4
 6
 7
 8
 9
10  TOTAL
11
12
13
14
15
16
17
18
19
20
                                                              CAP
```

Figure 5-2

Entering Subtotal Lines, Total Lines, and Formulas

To enter subtotal lines:

Move	the cell pointer to cell C9
Type	\ (for repeat)
Type	-
Press	↵

To copy the subtotal line to the rest of the row:

Press	/
Select	Copy

When prompted for the range to copy FROM:

Press	↵

Cell C9 (the cell containing the subtotal line) is the selection for the range to copy. When prompted for the range to copy TO:

Move	the cell pointer to cell D9
Type	.

Move the cell pointer to cell F9

Press ↵

To enter the formula to sum the salaries:

Move the cell pointer to cell C10

Type @SUM(

Move the cell pointer to cell C5

Type .

Move the cell pointer to cell C9

Type)

Press ↵

A zero (0) should appear in the cell, because the template does not contain any numbers to add. By including the rows above and below where data will be input, the @SUM formula allows the @SUM command to adjust correctly in the event rows of data are inserted or deleted. Since the cells in the fifth and ninth rows contain labels, their **values** are assumed to be zero and therefore will not cause the results of using the @SUM formula to be incorrect.

To copy the formula to the rest of the row:

Press /

Select Copy

When prompted for the range to copy FROM:

Press ↵

Cell C10 (the @SUM formula) is the selection for the cell to copy. When prompted for the range to copy TO:

Move the cell pointer to cell D10

Type .

Move the cell pointer to cell F10

Press ↵

Setting the Numeric Format for the Worksheet

To set the global format:

Press /

Select Worksheet

Select Global

Select Format

Select , (comma)

Select 0

Press ↵

When numbers are entered, they will be formatted with commas and no decimal places. The template worksheet is now complete. Your screen should look like Figure 5-3.

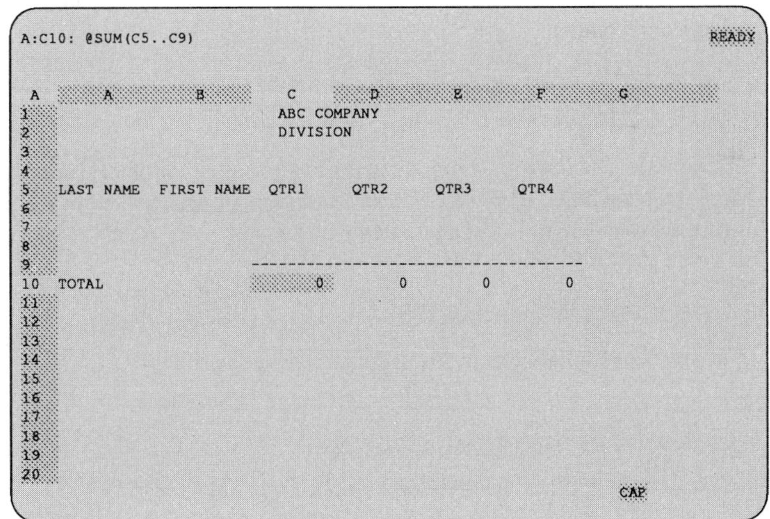

Figure 5-3

Saving the Template on a File

To save the file:

Press [Home]

Press /

Select File

Select Save

When prompted for the file name:

Type DIVTEMP

Press ↵

Your worksheet now has been saved and can be used as a template for the various division worksheets.

An alternative way to create the template is to first create a worksheet for a division. After creating the file and making sure that all of the formulas and other elements of the worksheet are correct, save the file. Then erase the data for all cells that will be different for the other division worksheets and save the **shell** as the template. In this example, the names and division number would be erased. This method may be preferable in some cases because it would be easier to check the appearance and accuracy of the worksheet, especially if it is large and complex.

USING A TEMPLATE

The purpose of having a template is to use it as a shell for other spreadsheets. In this exercise, the template DIVTEMP (Division Template) that was created in the previous exercise will be used to create the file DIV1 (Division 1).

Retrieve the Template

To use the template for inserting data, retrieve the file DIVTEMP.

Enter Data into the Template

To enter the appropriate division number in the title:

Move the cell pointer to cell C2

Press F2

Press the space bar

Type 1

Press ↵

To enter the data for Division 1:

Move the cell pointer to cell A6

Using the data in Figure 5-4 as a reference, type the names and the quarterly salary information in rows 6 and 7 of columns A through F. The formulas in the TOTAL row will compute the totals as the data for each quarter is input. Notice that the appropriate numeric format is also used for the values.

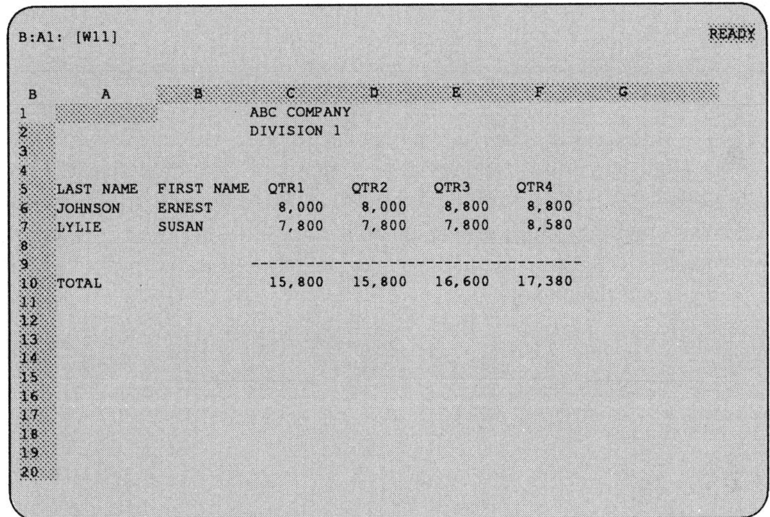

Figure 5-4

Save the Worksheet Under Another Name

Use the File Save command sequence to save the salary data for DIVISION 1 as DIV1.

Press /

Select File

Select Save

Type DIV1

Press ↵

Two files exist. DIVTEMP is the template, which can be used for creating worksheets of additional divisions. DIV1 contains the data for DIVISION 1. When DIVTEMP is in **memory**, it can be altered and saved under a different file name; the file DIVTEMP on the **disk** is not altered *unless* a **F**ile **S**ave command is executed and the original file DIVTEMP is **R**eplaced. Since it is very easy to accidentally save over a template, it is wise to keep a copy of the template file handy as a backup.

SUMMARY

A template is a shell document that can be used to create multiple worksheets that have the same basic format. The template contains the features that will be common to all other worksheets having a similar appearance. For example, titles, descriptions, formulas, range names and even print settings may be created in a template. When data is entered into the template, the results should be saved under a separate name so the template may be used to create additional worksheets.

KEY CONCEPTS

Template
Shell
Worksheet in memory
Worksheet on disk

CHAPTER FIVE
EXERCISE 1

INSTRUCTIONS: Circle T if the statement is true and F if the statement is false.

T F 1. In Lotus 1-2-3, a template file must be combined with another file containing data to generate a new spreadsheet.

T F 2. A template is a good way to keep spreadsheets standardized.

T F 3. When data is added to a template in memory, it is automatically added to the template file on the disk.

T F 4. A template can be used to create multiple worksheets.

T F 5. After adding data to a template in order to create a new spreadsheet, the worksheet should be saved using a name other than the template file name.

CHAPTER FIVE
EXERCISE 2
Creating a Template from an Existing Worksheet

INSTRUCTIONS: Retrieve the file DIV1. Erase the number 1 from the title DIVISION 1. Erase the data for LAST NAME, FIRST NAME, and all four quarters for Ernest Johnson and Susan Lylie.

Save the file as DIVTEMP2. The file DIVTEMP2 should be identical to the file DIVTEMP that was created in this chapter. The screen should look like Figure 5-5.

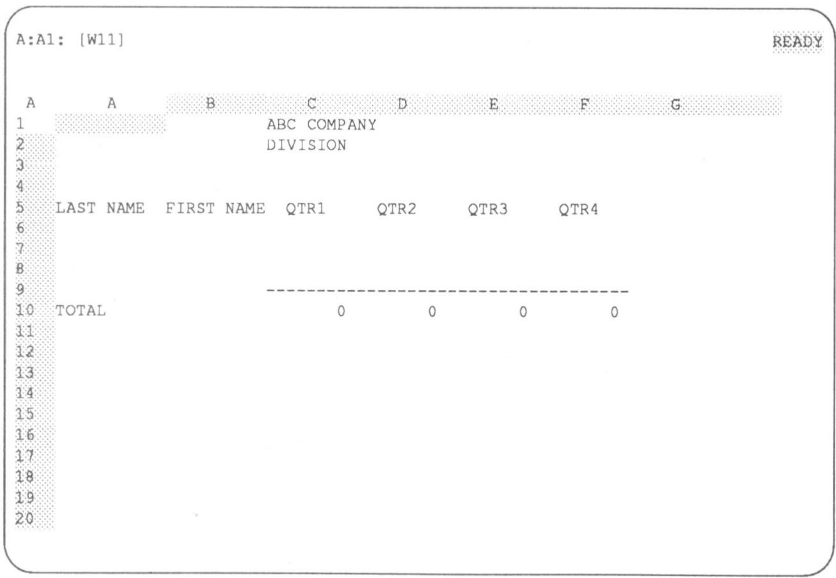

Figure 5-5

CHAPTER FIVE
EXERCISE 3
Creating a Template

INSTRUCTIONS: Create the template in Figure 5-6.

```
A:A1: [W21]                                                      READY

A          A              B         C         D         E         F
1                                 XYZ, INC.
2                              PROFIT FORECAST
3
4                            JAN       FEB       MAR      QTR1
5
6    SALES                    $0        $0        $0        $0
7    EXPENSES                 $0        $0        $0        $0
8                        ------------------------------------
9    PROFIT AFTER TAX         $0        $0        $0        $0
10                       ====================================
11
12   ASSUMPTIONS:
13   INITIAL SALES AMOUNT
14   SALES GROWTH RATE
15   EXPENSE RATE
16
17
18
19
20
                                                         CAP
```

Figure 5-6

Sales for the month of January are determined from the amount entered in cell B13 by placing the formula +B13 in cell B6. The values for SALES in February and March are computed by multiplying the SALES amount for the previous month times the growth rate for the current month.

EXPENSES are calculated by multiplying the expense rate for each month times the sales amount for the month.

Save the template using the file name PROFTEMP.

After placing the values in the appropriate assumption cells, the screen should look like Figure 5-7.

```
A:E9: (C0) +E6-E7                                                     READY

A          A              B         C         D         E          F
1                                 XYZ, INC.
2                              PROFIT FORECAST
3
4                        JAN       FEB       MAR      QTR1
5
6   SALES              $50,000   $52,750   $56,970 $159,720
7   EXPENSES           $35,500   $36,925   $39,594 $112,019
8                      ------------------------------------
9   PROFIT AFTER TAX   $14,500   $15,825   $17,376  $47,701
10                     ====================================
11
12  ASSUMPTIONS:
13  INITIAL SALES AMOUNT $50,000
14  SALES GROWTH RATE                 5.5%      8.0%
15  EXPENSE RATE            71.0%    70.0%     69.5%
16
17
18
19
20
```

Figure 5-7

CHAPTER SIX

CREATING AND USING MULTIPLE WORKSHEETS AND FILES

OBJECTIVES

In this chapter, you will learn to:

- Create multiple worksheets in a file
- Add worksheets to a file
- Move between multiple worksheets
- Enter data and formulas into multiple worksheets
- Copy data and formulas from one worksheet to other worksheets
- Print data from multiple worksheets
- Open and use more than one worksheet file

CHAPTER OVERVIEW

In the previous chapters, you worked with files that contained only one worksheet. The worksheets had only two dimensions. You are introduced to the concept of multiple worksheets and files in this chapter. Essentially, a third dimension is added. Instead of having only one worksheet with a set of rows and columns, you may have multiple worksheets in a file. Another option available is to open several files and place them in your computer's memory.

The ability to have multiple worksheets or multiple files in memory at one time provides you with additional flexibility in organizing and using the data available to you. Multiple worksheets and files are particularly useful when you want to summarize and consolidate information from several worksheets.

A maximum of 256 worksheets can be in one file. Likewise, 256 files are the maximum that can be in memory at one time. The actual number of worksheets and files that you can use depends upon the memory size of your computer and the number and the size of the worksheets.

EXAMPLE PROBLEM

Suppose ABC Company has three operating divisions and sells two products in each of the divisions. Data for projected sales in the three divisions are as follows.

Division 1:	Q1	Q2	Q3	Q4
Mowers	5,000	12,000	14,000	10,000
Edgers	3,000	5,000	8,000	4,000
Division 2:	**Q1**	**Q2**	**Q3**	**Q4**
Mowers	7,000	14,000	16,000	11,000
Edgers	2,000	4,000	7,000	5,000
Division 3:	**Q1**	**Q2**	**Q3**	**Q4**
Mowers	6,000	12,000	15,000	8,000
Edgers	1,000	7,000	8,000	3,000

You need to create a file that includes the data for the divisions on individual worksheets. Company-wide totals for each quarter and for annual sales also need to be computed.

CREATING THE INITIAL WORKSHEET

Since you completed many worksheets as you progressed through the earlier chapters, the instructions for creating the worksheet for DIVISION 1 are abbreviated and do not include all of the steps.

Figure 6-1 includes the spreadsheet for DIVISION 1. Create the worksheet and enter all of the data for sales of the two products for each of the quarters. Use the @SUM function to compute the quarterly and annual totals. Do **not** format the data.

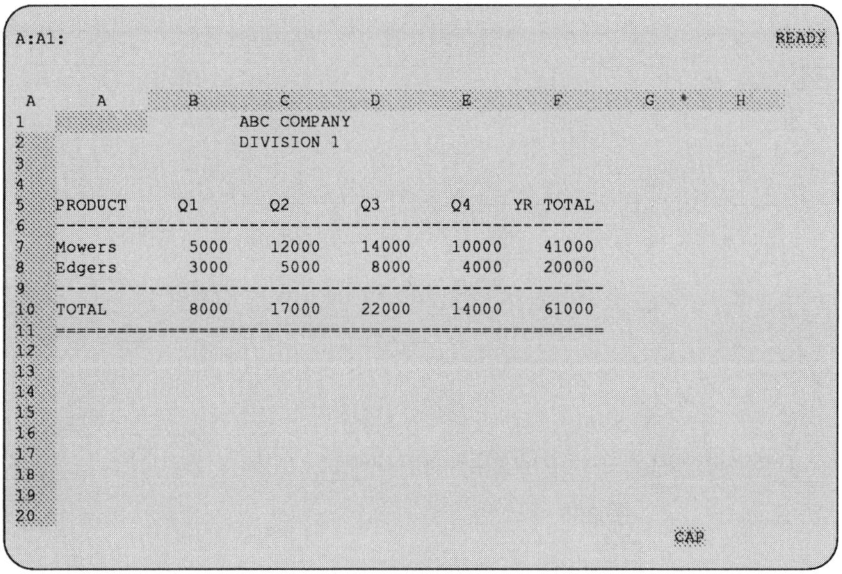

```
A:A1:                                                          READY

 A    A         B         C         D         E         F          G  *  H
 1                   ABC COMPANY
 2                   DIVISION 1
 3
 4
 5  PRODUCT     Q1        Q2        Q3        Q4    YR TOTAL
 6  ------------------------------------------------------
 7  Mowers      5000     12000     14000     10000     41000
 8  Edgers      3000      5000      8000      4000     20000
 9  ------------------------------------------------------
10  TOTAL       8000     17000     22000     14000     61000
11  ======================================================
12
13
14
15
16
17
18
19
20
                                                         CAP
```

Figure 6-1

Save the worksheet as file DIVSALES using the **F**ile **S**ave command sequence.

ADDING WORKSHEETS TO A FILE

Before inserting a worksheet, you need to have the ability to see more than one spreadsheet on your screen.

To see multiple worksheets on your screen:

Press	/
Select	Worksheet
Select	Window
Select	Perspective

Three worksheets now appear on your screen, but the last two do not have a worksheet letter, column letters or row numbers. Your screen should look like Figure 6-2.

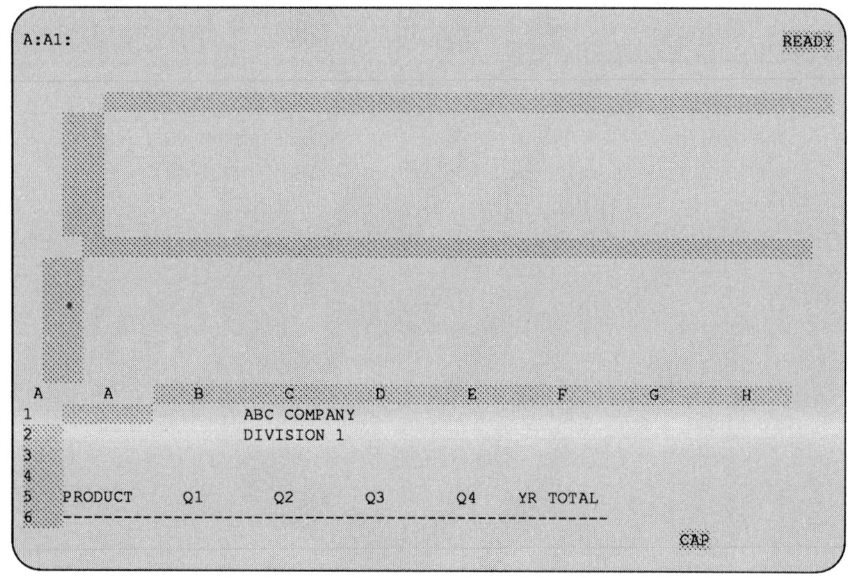

Figure 6-2

To add worksheets for DIVISIONS 2 and 3:

Press /

Select Worksheet

Select Insert

Select Sheet

Select After

You are then asked to "Enter the number of worksheets to insert."

Type 2 (to indicate two worksheets are to be added)

Press ↵

You now can see worksheet B and worksheet C. The worksheets (sometimes referred to as sheets) are added after the DIVISION 1 worksheet. Your screen should look like Figure 6-3.

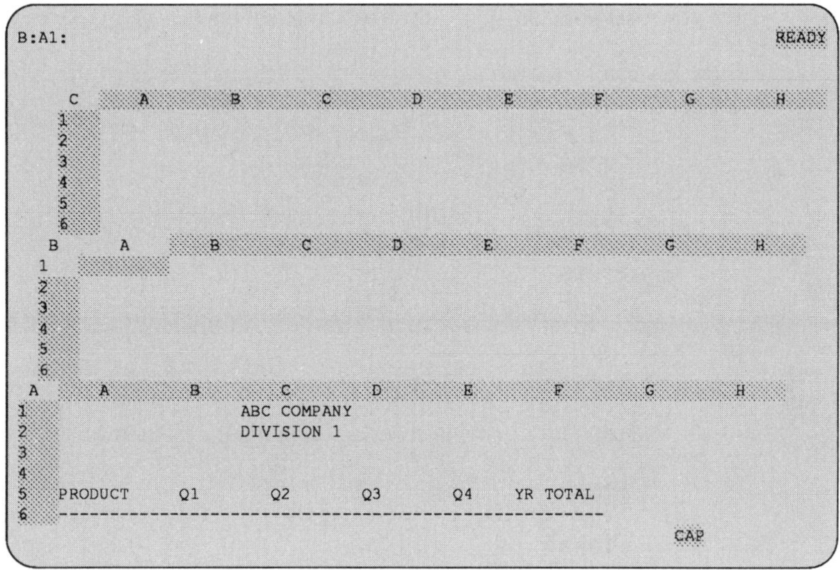

Figure 6-3

■ MOVING AROUND MULTIPLE WORKSHEETS

To move the cell pointer between worksheets, you use combinations of the (Ctrl) key and the (PgUp), (PgDn) and (End) keys. The (F5) ((GoTo)) key can also be used.

For example, to move the cell pointer from B:A1 (cell A1 in worksheet B) to C:A1:

Press (Ctrl-PgUp)

You must hold the (Ctrl) key down and then press the (PgUp) key once.

The pointer-movement keys can now be used to move around worksheet C. Move the cell pointer to cell C:C10. Notice the rows and columns in the other worksheets move in a synchronous manner and the same segments of all of the worksheets appear on the screen. If you want to only scroll through worksheet C and not have the rows and columns in the other worksheets move, you can execute the **W**orksheet **W**indow **U**nsync command sequence. To return to the synchronous movement process, you will need to execute the **W**orksheet **W**indow **S**ync command sequence.

To return to cell A:A1:

Make sure the cell pointer is in cell C:A1

Press (Ctrl-PgDn) twice

Again, you must hold the Ctrl key down and then tap the PgDn key two times.

The F5 key can be used to move between worksheets. For example, to move to cell B5 in worksheet C:

Press F5

Type C:B5

Press ↵

To move quickly to the "home" cell in worksheet A from any other worksheet:

Press Ctrl-Home

Similarly, you can move to the last worksheet in the file as follows:

Press End

Press Ctrl-PgUp

When the perspective option is not used, you can still move between the worksheets with the combination of the Ctrl key with the PgUp and PgDn keys.

■ COPYING INFORMATION BETWEEN WORKSHEETS

To copy the worksheet titles and column headings from worksheet A to worksheets B and C:

Press Ctrl-Home to move to cell A:A1

Press /

Select Copy

When prompted for the Range to copy FROM:

Move the cell pointer to cell A:F6

Cells A1 through F6 on worksheet A are now highlighted as the cells to be copied. On the control panel, the characters A:A1..A:F6 appear to indicate the desired range of cells to copy. Your screen should look like Figure 6-4 Part 1.

```
A:F6: \-                                                          POINT
Enter range to copy FROM: A:A1..A:F6

    C    A       B       C       D       E       F       G       H
    1
    2
    3
    4
    5
    6
  B    A       B       C       D       E       F       G       H
  1
  2
  3
  4
  5
  6
A    A       B       C       D       E       F       G
1                    ABC COMPANY
2                    DIVISION
3
4
5  PRODUCT    QTR1    QTR2    QTR3    QTR4   YR TOTAL
6  ------------------------------------------------------
                                                        CAP
```

Figure 6-4
Part 1

Press ↵

When prompted for the Range to copy TO:

Press [Ctrl-PgUp]

Cell A1 in worksheet B is now highlighted.

Type .

The period key anchors the cell pointer in B:A1.

Press [Ctrl-PgUp]

By pressing the [Ctrl-PgUp] keys, the cell pointer is moved to cell A1 in worksheet C. You have now indicated the range to copy TO. Notice in the control panel the range is identified as B:A1..C:A1. Your screen should look like Figure 6-4 Part 2.

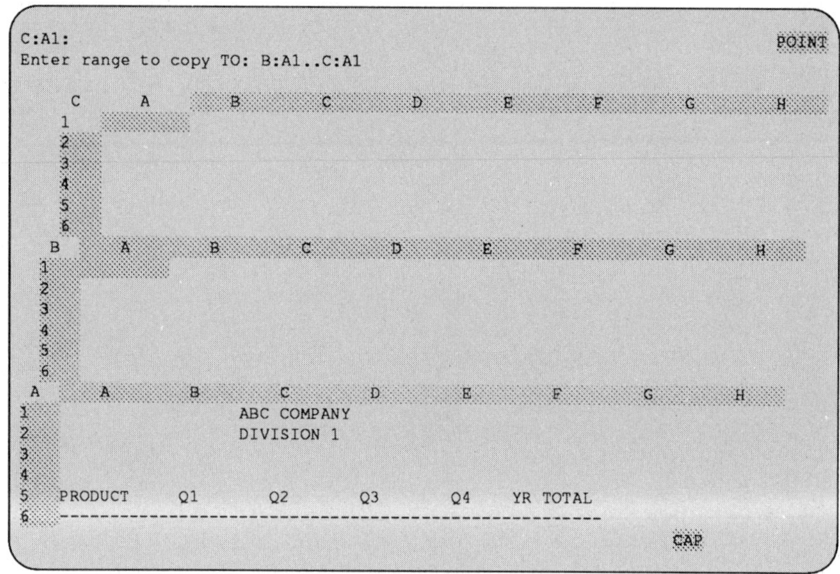

Figure 6-4
Part 2

Press ↵

The spreadsheet title lines and column headings now have been copied to worksheets B and C and your screen should look like Figure 6-4 Part 3.

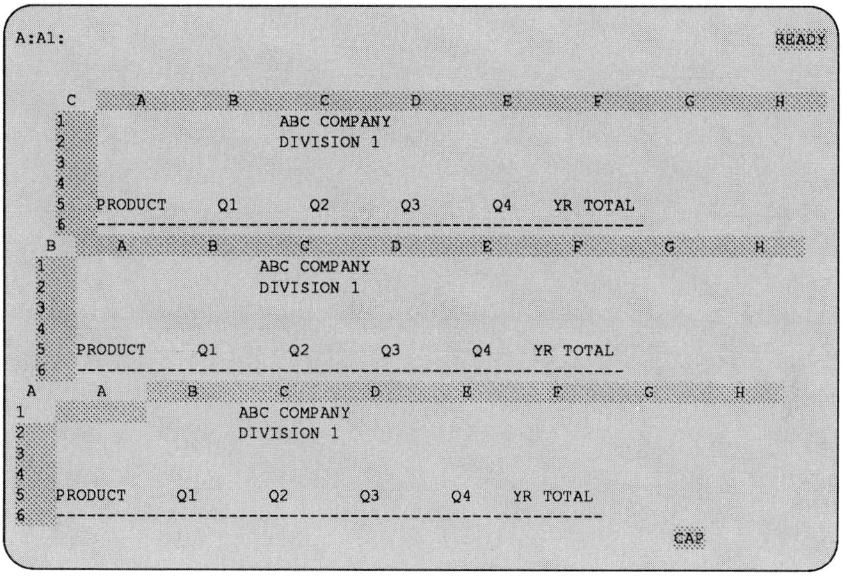

```
A:A1:                                                               READY

      C    A        B        C        D        E        F        G        H
      1                    ABC COMPANY
      2                    DIVISION 1
      3
      4
      5   PRODUCT      Q1       Q2       Q3       Q4    YR TOTAL
      6   ----------------------------------------------------------
    B    A        B        C        D        E        F        G        H
    1                    ABC COMPANY
    2                    DIVISION 1
    3
    4
    5   PRODUCT      Q1       Q2       Q3       Q4    YR TOTAL
    6   ----------------------------------------------------------
  A      A        B        C        D        E        F        G        H
  1                    ABC COMPANY
  2                    DIVISION 1
  3
  4
  5   PRODUCT      Q1       Q2       Q3       Q4    YR TOTAL
  6   ----------------------------------------------------------
                                                            CAP
```

Figure 6-4
Part 3

ENTERING NUMBERS AND FORMULAS IN MULTIPLE WORKSHEETS

Enter the labels Mowers, Edgers and TOTAL in cells A7, A8 and A10 respectively in worksheets B and C. Place the underline character in cells A6 through F6 and A9 through F9 in worksheets B and C. Enter double underline characters in cells A11 through F11 in worksheets B and C. Edit the division titles so that DIVISION 2 appears in worksheet B and DIVISION 3 appears in worksheet C. You may copy the labels to further practice the process of copying information from one worksheet to other worksheets.

In worksheets B and C, enter the quarterly sales data for DIVISIONS 2 and 3 respectively. Your screen should look like Figure 6-5.

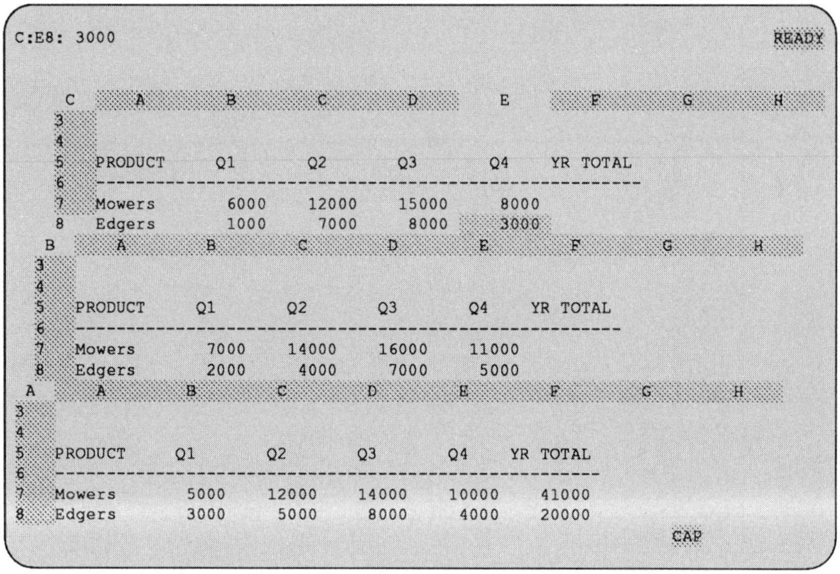

```
C:E8: 3000                                                    READY

   C   A         B          C          D          E          F         G         H
   3
   4
   5  PRODUCT      Q1         Q2         Q3         Q4     YR TOTAL
   6  -----------------------------------------------------------
   7  Mowers       6000      12000      15000      8000
   8  Edgers       1000       7000       8000      3000
  B    A         B          C          D          E          F         G         H
  3
  4
  5  PRODUCT      Q1         Q2         Q3         Q4     YR TOTAL
  6  -----------------------------------------------------------
  7  Mowers       7000      14000      16000     11000
  8  Edgers       2000       4000       7000      5000
 A     A         B          C          D          E          F         G         H
 3
 4
 5  PRODUCT      Q1         Q2         Q3         Q4     YR TOTAL
 6  -----------------------------------------------------------
 7  Mowers       5000      12000      14000     10000      41000
 8  Edgers       3000       5000       8000      4000      20000
                                                                CAP
```

Figure 6-5

To examine the formulas for determining annual sales for each of the products.

Press Ctrl-Home

Your cell pointer now appears in cell A1 of worksheet A.

Move the cell pointer to cell F7

The formula for computing the annual total for the Mower sales @SUM(B7..E7) appears in the control panel. A similar formula for Edgers appears in cell F8.

Press the ↓ key so row 8 appears on the screen for each worksheet

To copy the formulas for computing the annual sales for the products from worksheet A to worksheets B and C:

Move the cell pointer to cell F7

Press /

Select Copy

Press ↓

The cells F7 through F8 are now highlighted as the range of cells to copy FROM.

Press ↵

When prompted for the range of cells to copy TO:

Press Ctrl-PgUp

Type .

Press Ctrl-PgUp

The range B:F7..C:F7 appearing in the control panel indicates the formulas will be copied to worksheets B and C.

Press ↵

The formulas for computing annual sales have been copied and the appropriate values now appear in all of the worksheets. Your screen should look like Figure 6-6.

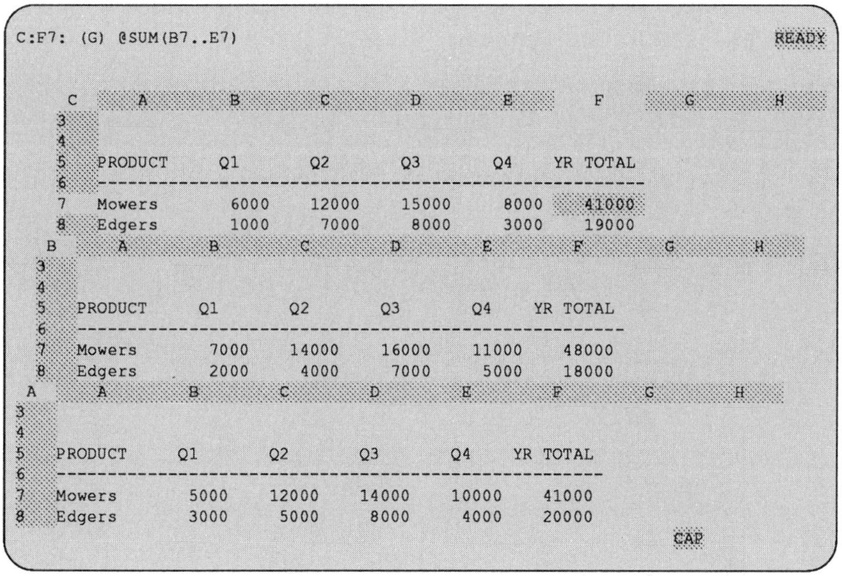

```
C:F7: (G) @SUM(B7..E7)                                                READY

      C    A          B          C          D          E          F          G          H
      3
      4
      5    PRODUCT        Q1         Q2         Q3         Q4     YR TOTAL
      6    -------------------------------------------------------
      7    Mowers       6000      12000      15000       8000      41000
      8    Edgers       1000       7000       8000       3000      19000
    B    A          B          C          D          E          F          G          H
    3
    4
    5    PRODUCT        Q1         Q2         Q3         Q4     YR TOTAL
    6    -------------------------------------------------------
    7    Mowers       7000      14000      16000      11000      48000
    8    Edgers       2000       4000       7000       5000      18000
  A    A          B          C          D          E          F          G          H
  3
  4
  5    PRODUCT        Q1         Q2         Q3         Q4     YR TOTAL
  6    -------------------------------------------------------
  7    Mowers       5000      12000      14000      10000      41000
  8    Edgers       3000       5000       8000       4000      20000
                                                                  CAP
```

Figure 6-6

To enter the formulas for determining the total sales for each quarter in worksheets B and C:

Move the cell pointer to cell B10 in worksheet A

Press /

Select Copy

Move the cell pointer to F10

Press 

The cells B10 through F10 have been designated as the cells to be copied FROM.

When prompted for the range to copy TO:

Press Ctrl-PgUp

Type .

Press Ctrl-PgUp

The range to copy TO is now highlighted.

Press 

The formulas for quarterly product totals have been copied and the appropriate values now appear in each of the worksheets. Refer to Figure 6-7.

```
A:B10: @SUM(B7..B8)                                                        READY

        C    A          B          C          D          E          F          G          H
        5    PRODUCT    QTR1       QTR2       QTR3       QTR4       YR TOTAL
        6    -----------------------------------------------------------
        7    Mowers         6000      12000      15000       8000      41000
        8    Edgers         1000       7000       8000       3000      19000
        9    -----------------------------------------------------------
        10   TOTAL          7000      19000      23000      11000      60000
      B      A          B          C          D          E          F          G          H
      5    PRODUCT    QTR1       QTR2       QTR3       QTR4       YR TOTAL
      6    -----------------------------------------------------------
      7    Mowers         7000      14000      16000      11000      48000
      8    Edgers         2000       4000       7000       5000      18000
      9    -----------------------------------------------------------
      10   TOTAL          9000      18000      23000      16000      66000
    A      A          B          C          D          E          F          G
    5    PRODUCT    QTR1       QTR2       QTR3       QTR4       YR TOTAL
    6    -----------------------------------------------------------
    7    Mowers         5000      12000      14000      10000      41000
    8    Edgers         3000       5000       8000       4000      20000
    9    -----------------------------------------------------------
    10   TOTAL          8000      17000      22000      14000      61000
                                                                    CAP
```

Figure 6-7

■ FORMATTING MULTIPLE WORKSHEETS

For this example, the format specifications need to be the same for all of the worksheets. Rather than format each worksheet individually, you can use the GROUP mode capability in 1-2-3. When this option is on, you can format multiple worksheets at the same time.

Prior to using GROUP, make sure you are in the proper worksheet since 1-2-3 changes the format for all worksheets in the file based on the format change made to the current worksheet.

You must first turn on the GROUP mode and then format worksheet A. When the formatting process is completed, worksheets B and C will be formatted automatically using the format specification selected for worksheet A.

First, position the cell pointer so rows 5 through 10 appear on the screen for each worksheet.

Move	the cell pointer to cell B7 in worksheet A
Press	/
Select	Worksheet
Select	Global
Select	Group
Select	Enable

The GROUP mode has now been initiated. Notice the GROUP indicator at the bottom of the screen. Your screen should look like Figure 6-8.

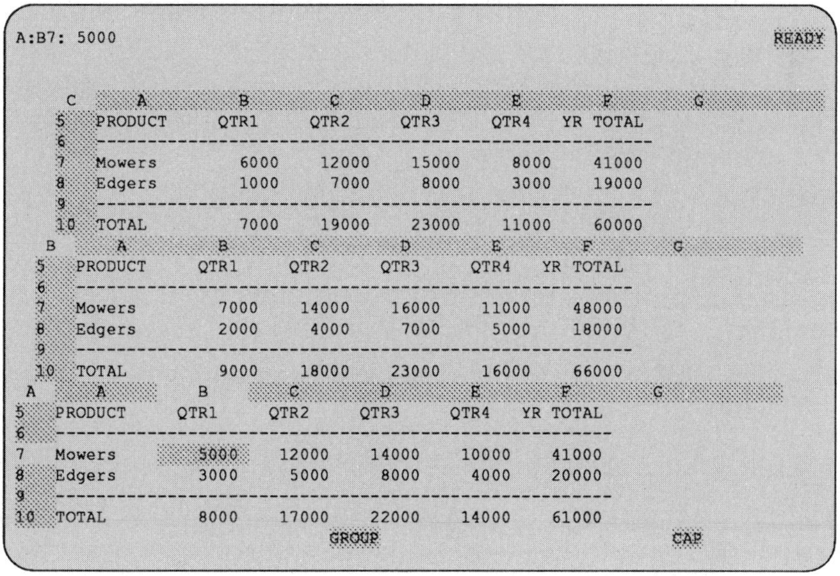

```
A:B7: 5000                                                              READY

      C    A          B          C          D          E          F          G
      5  PRODUCT     QTR1       QTR2       QTR3       QTR4    YR TOTAL
      6  ---------------------------------------------------------------
      7  Mowers        6000      12000      15000       8000      41000
      8  Edgers        1000       7000       8000       3000      19000
      9  ---------------------------------------------------------------
      10 TOTAL         7000      19000      23000      11000      60000
    B    A          B          C          D          E          F          G
    5  PRODUCT     QTR1       QTR2       QTR3       QTR4    YR TOTAL
    6  ---------------------------------------------------------------
    7  Mowers        7000      14000      16000      11000      48000
    8  Edgers        2000       4000       7000       5000      18000
    9  ---------------------------------------------------------------
    10 TOTAL         9000      18000      23000      16000      66000
  A    A          B          C          D          E          F          G
  5  PRODUCT     QTR1       QTR2       QTR3       QTR4    YR TOTAL
  6  ---------------------------------------------------------------
  7  Mowers        5000      12000      14000      10000      41000
  8  Edgers        3000       5000       8000       4000      20000
  9  ---------------------------------------------------------------
  10 TOTAL         8000      17000      22000      14000      61000
                                   GROUP                            CAP
```

Figure 6-8

To specify the format:

Make	sure the cell pointer is in cell B7 in worksheet A
Press	/
Select	Range
Select	Format
Type	, (comma)

When prompted for the number of decimal places:

Type	0
Press	↵
Move	the cell pointer to cell F10

The highlighted range specifies the range of cells to be formatted.

Press	↵

Notice that all of the worksheets have been formatted using the same format specification.

To stop using the GROUP mode:

Press	/
Select	Worksheet
Select	Global
Select	Group
Select	Disable

The GROUP indicator no longer appears on the screen. Your screen should look like Figure 6-9.

```
A:B7: (,0) 5000                                                         READY

      C    A          B          C          D          E          F          G
      5  PRODUCT      QTR1       QTR2       QTR3       QTR4    YR TOTAL
      6  -------------------------------------------------------------
      7  Mowers       6,000     12,000     15,000      8,000     41,000
      8  Edgers       1,000      7,000      8,000      3,000     19,000
      9  -------------------------------------------------------------
      10 TOTAL        7,000     19,000     23,000     11,000     60,000
    B    A          B          C          D          E          F          G
    5  PRODUCT      QTR1       QTR2       QTR3       QTR4    YR TOTAL
    6  -------------------------------------------------------------
    7  Mowers       7,000     14,000     16,000     11,000     48,000
    8  Edgers       2,000      4,000      7,000      5,000     18,000
    9  -------------------------------------------------------------
    10 TOTAL        9,000     18,000     23,000     16,000     66,000
  A    A          B          C          D          E          F          G
  5  PRODUCT      QTR1       QTR2       QTR3       QTR4    YR TOTAL
  6  -------------------------------------------------------------
  7  Mowers       5,000     12,000     14,000     10,000     41,000
  8  Edgers       3,000      5,000      8,000      4,000     20,000
  9  -------------------------------------------------------------
  10 TOTAL        8,000     17,000     22,000     14,000     61,000
                                                                    CAP
```

Figure 6-9

PRINTING MULTIPLE WORKSHEET DATA

Just as it was convenient to format all worksheets at one time, you may want to print ranges of cells from several worksheets at one time. To print the worksheets A, B and C:

Make sure the cell pointer is in cell A1 of worksheet A

Press /

Select Print

Select Printer

Select Range

Type .

The cell pointer is now anchored in cell A1.

Move the cell pointer to F11

The print range for worksheet A is now highlighted and contains cells A1 through F11.

To extend the specified print range to worksheets B and C:

Press Ctrl-PgUp two times

The print range is now extended to include worksheets B and C.

Press ↵

To complete the printing of the worksheets:

Select Align

Select Go

Select Page

Select Quit

Your printout should look like Figure 6-10.

Save the worksheets on file DIVSALES using the **F**ile **S**ave **R**eplace command sequence.

ABC COMPANY
DIVISION 1

PRODUCT	Q1	Q2	Q3	Q4	YR TOTAL
Mowers	5,000	12,000	14,000	10,000	41,000
Edgers	3,000	5,000	8,000	4,000	20,000
Total	8,000	17,000	22,000	14,000	61,000

ABC COMPANY
DIVISION 2

PRODUCT	Q1	Q2	Q3	Q4	YR TOTAL
Mowers	7,000	14,000	16,000	11,000	48,000
Edgers	2,000	4,000	7,000	5,000	18,000
	9,000	18,000	23,000	16,000	66,000

ABC COMPANY
DIVISION 3

PRODUCT	Q1	Q2	Q3	Q4	YR TOTAL
Mowers	6,000	12,000	15,000	8,000	41,000
Edgers	1,000	7,000	8,000	3,000	19,000
	7,000	19,000	23,000	11,000	60,000

Figure 6-10

In some situations, you may want to print only selected ranges from each worksheet. To print a group of print ranges, you name all of the ranges you want to print separated by commas and with no spaces.

For the example problem, suppose you want to print only the total sales values by quarter and the annual sales total for each of the divisions. To accomplish this objective, complete the following steps.

Move	the cell pointer to cell C1 in worksheet A
Press	/
Select	Print
Select	Printer
Select	Range

If necessary, press the Esc key to unanchor the range; then move the cell pointer to cell C1 in worksheet A.

Type	.
Move	the cell pointer to D1 in worksheet A
Type	,
Move	the cell pointer to cell A5 in worksheet A
Type	.
Move	the cell pointer to cell F5
Type	,
Move	the cell pointer to cell A10 in worksheet A
Type	.
Move	the cell pointer to cell A:F10
Type	,
Press	Ctrl-PgUp
Move	the cell pointer to cell B:A10
Type	.
Move	the cell pointer to cell B:F10

Type ,

Press Ctrl-PgUp twice to reach worksheet C

Move the cell pointer to cell C:A10

Type .

Move the cell pointer C:F10

Your screen should look like Figure 6-11.

```
C:F10: (,0) [W10] @SUM(F7..F8)                                        POINT
Enter print range: A:C1..A:D1,A:A5..A:F5,A:A10..A:F10,B:A10..B:F10,C:A10..C:F10

    C    A          B          C          D          E          F          G
    5  PRODUCT      Q1         Q2         Q3         Q4      YR TOTAL
    6  ----------------------------------------------------------------
    7  Mowers       6,000     12,000     15,000      8,000     41,000
    8  Edgers       1,000      7,000      8,000      3,000     19,000
    9  ----------------------------------------------------------------
    10 Total        7,000     19,000     23,000     11,000     60,000
  B    A          B          C          D          E          F          G
  5  PRODUCT      Q1         Q2         Q3         Q4      YR TOTAL
  6  ----------------------------------------------------------------
  7  Mowers       7,000     14,000     16,000     11,000     48,000
  8  Edgers       2,000      4,000      7,000      5,000     18,000
  9  ----------------------------------------------------------------
  10 Total        9,000     18,000     23,000     16,000     66,000
A    A          B          C          D          E          F          G
5  PRODUCT      Q1         Q2         Q3         Q4      YR TOTAL
6  ----------------------------------------------------------------
7  Mowers       5,000     12,000     14,000     10,000     41,000
8  Edgers       3,000      5,000      8,000      4,000     20,000
9  ----------------------------------------------------------------
10 Total        8,000     17,000     22,000     14,000     61,000
```

Figure 6-11

Press ↵

The ranges of cells to print are now identified. To complete the printing process:

Select Align

Select Go

Select Page

Select Quit

Your printout should look like Figure 6-12.

ABC COMPANY					
PRODUCT	Q1	Q2	Q3	Q4	YR TOTAL
Total	8,000	17,000	22,000	14,000	61,000
Total	9,000	18,000	23,000	16,000	66,000
Total	7,000	19,000	23,000	11,000	60,000

Figure 6-12

■ USING MULTIPLE FILES

In Lotus 1-2-3 you can have multiple files open at the same time. When more than one file is open in memory, you can also copy data between the open files. However, you cannot format files using the GROUP mode and you cannot print multiple files at one time.

To illustrate the process of using multiple files, complete the following steps:

Press /

Select File

Select Retrieve

Press F3

Press the pointer-movement keys until the file SALES is highlighted

Press ↵

The file SALES now appears on your screen. To open the existing file UNITPROD and place it after the file SALES:

Press /

Select File

Select Open

Select After

Press F3

Press the pointer-movement keys until the file UNITPROD is highlighted

Press ↵

To see portions of both files on your screen:

Press /

Select Worksheet

Select Window

Select Perspective

The screen now contains the first six rows of the files SALES and UNITPROD. Your screen should look like Figure 6-13. Notice that each worksheet on the screen is worksheet A of the respective files.

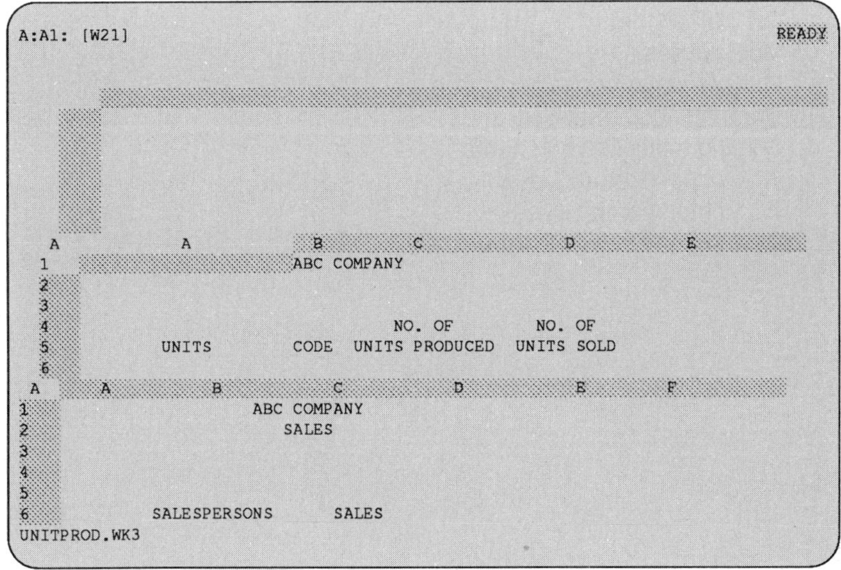

Figure 6-13

To move between files, you can use the combinations of Ctrl-PgUp and Ctrl-PgDn keys. The contents of cells can be copied from one file to another. Notice the file indicator changes when you move to a different file.

One of the advantages of having multiple files open is the capability to link files together. This concept is illustrated in the next chapter.

SUMMARY

Using multiple worksheets provide flexibility to individuals creating spreadsheet applications that have similar structure and formats. The capability to have multiple files open in memory at the same time also provides you with more options for spreadsheet applications.

KEY CONCEPTS

Adding a worksheet to a file
Copying data between files
Copying data between worksheets
File Open
Formatting multiple worksheets
GROUP mode
Multiple files
Multiple worksheets
Opening additional files
Printing multiple worksheets
Worksheet Global Group
Worksheet Insert Sheet
Worksheet Window Perspective

CHAPTER SIX
EXERCISE 1

INSTRUCTIONS: Circle T if the statement is true and F if the statement is false.

T F 1. At most three worksheets can be placed in a file in Lotus 1-2-3.

T F 2. One or more worksheets can be inserted before or after a worksheet existing in the memory of a computer.

T F 3. The F5 key can be used to move between multiple worksheets in a file.

T F 4. Cells can be copied from one worksheet to another.

T F 5. Cells cannot be copied from one file to another.

T F 6. When multiple worksheets exist in a file, only one worksheet at a time can be viewed on the screen.

T F 7. More than one file can be open at one time.

T F 8. The GROUP mode option available in 1-2-3 allows you to format more than one worksheet or file at one time.

CHAPTER SIX
EXERCISE 2

INSTRUCTIONS: Explain a typical situation when the following keystrokes or Lotus 1-2-3 commands are used.

Problem 1: / **F**ile **O**pen

Problem 2: / **W**orksheet **I**nsert **S**heet

Problem 3: / **W**orksheet **W**indow **P**erspective

Problem 4: / **W**orksheet **W**indow **P**erspective **C**lear

Problem 5: / **W**orksheet **G**lobal **G**roup

Problem 6: Ctrl-PgUp

Problem 7: Ctrl-PgDn

Problem 8: Ctrl-Home

CHAPTER SIX
EXERCISE 3

INSTRUCTIONS: XYZ Consulting Company provides computer training, computer consulting and system documentation services. The company has offices in New York, Chicago, Houston and Los Angeles. Data on sales for the months of June, July and August for each of the locations follows:

New York:	June	July	August
Training	15,000	19,000	17,000
Consulting	9,000	8,000	10,000
Documentation	5,000	7,000	9,000

Chicago:	June	July	August
Training	12,000	15,000	14,000
Consulting	12,000	18,000	11,000
Documentation	3,000	5,000	7,000

Houston:	June	July	August
Training	20,000	15,000	22,000
Consulting	17,000	18,000	19,000
Documentation	8,000	6,000	4,000

Los Angeles:	June	July	August
Training	13,000	12,000	15,000
Consulting	11,000	9,000	14,000
Documentation	10,000	10,000	12,000

Create a file that has the data for each of the locations on a separate worksheet.

Calculate the total sales by month and type of service for each of the locations.

Format the cells appropriately and include subtotal lines as well as double underlines to indicate the end of each worksheet.

Save the worksheets on a file using the name XYZSALES. Print the four worksheets.

CHAPTER SIX
EXERCISE 4
Adding a Worksheet to an Existing File

INSTRUCTIONS: Retrieve the file DIVSALES.

ABC Company forgot to reveal that it has acquired another company that sells Mowers and Edgers. The newly acquired organization has been designated as Division 4. The data on sales for the new division follows:

Division 4:	**Q1**	**Q2**	**Q3**	**Q4**
Mowers	3,000	2,000	9,000	2,000
Edgers	2,000	3,000	6,000	1,000

Add a worksheet to the file DIVSALES, and include the data for Division 4. The format of the worksheet for Division 4 should be the same as for the other three divisions.

CHAPTER SIX
EXERCISE 5
Create a File with Multiple Worksheets

INSTRUCTIONS: Create a file with multiple worksheets that will be helpful to you in some way.

Print the worksheets.

CHAPTER SEVEN

CONSOLIDATING WORKSHEETS AND LINKING FILES

OBJECTIVES

In this chapter, you will learn to:

- Create several worksheets quickly with a template
- Combine the data from several worksheets into a summary worksheet
- Move information between files by linking them together
- Open a new file

CHAPTER OVERVIEW

Sometimes it is necessary to combine information from several worksheets into one summary worksheet. An example of such a situation occurs when organizations need to consolidate worksheets for several operating divisions during the budgeting process. In some situations, it is desirable to link worksheets together to facilitate the movement of data between worksheets. When using the linking feature, a change made in one worksheet will automatically update the appropriate cells in the linked worksheets.

In this chapter, you will use the template you constructed for salaries in Chapter 5 to create a worksheet for each of the three divisions in ABC Company. Then you will create a summary worksheet and combine the total salaries data from the three worksheets into the summary worksheet. At this point you will have the total salaries for ABC Company. You will then link the total salary cells in the summary worksheet to the cells associated with salaries on the worksheet in the file BUDGET to copy the salary totals.

■ USE OF A TEMPLATE TO CREATE SEVERAL WORKSHEETS

In the following exercise, you will use the template DIVTEMP you constructed in Chapter 5 to create worksheets for computing total salaries in ABC Company's three operating divisions. Then you will construct a summary worksheet that includes the total salaries for each of the divisions. Finally, the sum of the total salaries for the three divisions will be calculated.

To retrieve the file DIVTEMP:

Press	/
Select	File
Select	Retrieve
Press	F3
Press	the pointer-movement keys until the file DIVTEMP is highlighted
Press	↵

Make sure your screen looks like Figure 7-1.

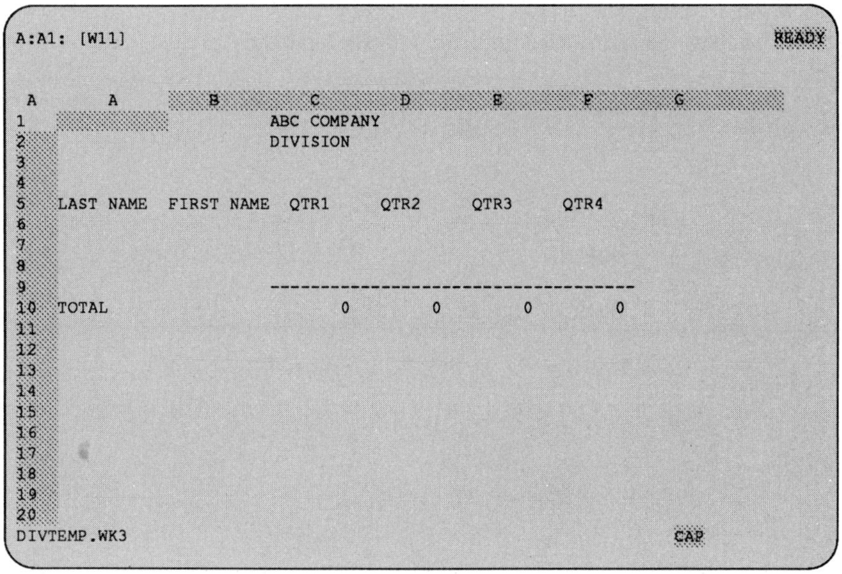

```
A:A1: [W11]                                                        READY

 A      A          B          C         D         E         F         G
1                            ABC COMPANY
2                            DIVISION
3
4
5   LAST NAME  FIRST NAME  QTR1      QTR2      QTR3      QTR4
6
7
8
9                            ------------------------------------
10  TOTAL                           0         0         0         0
11
12
13
14
15
16
17
18
19
20
DIVTEMP.WK3                                                   CAP
```

Figure 7-1

Save the worksheet using the file name DIVISION so you do not take the risk of possibly replacing the template file after you enter data.

Press	/
Select	File
Select	Save
Type	DIVISION
Press	↵

You now need to add two worksheets after the current worksheet.

Press	/
Select	Worksheet
Select	Insert
Select	Sheet
Select	After
Type	2
Press	↵

You have inserted two additional worksheets in the file.

To see the three worksheets on your screen:

Press /

Select Worksheet

Select Window

Select Perspective

The three worksheets now should be on your screen. Refer to Figure 7-2.

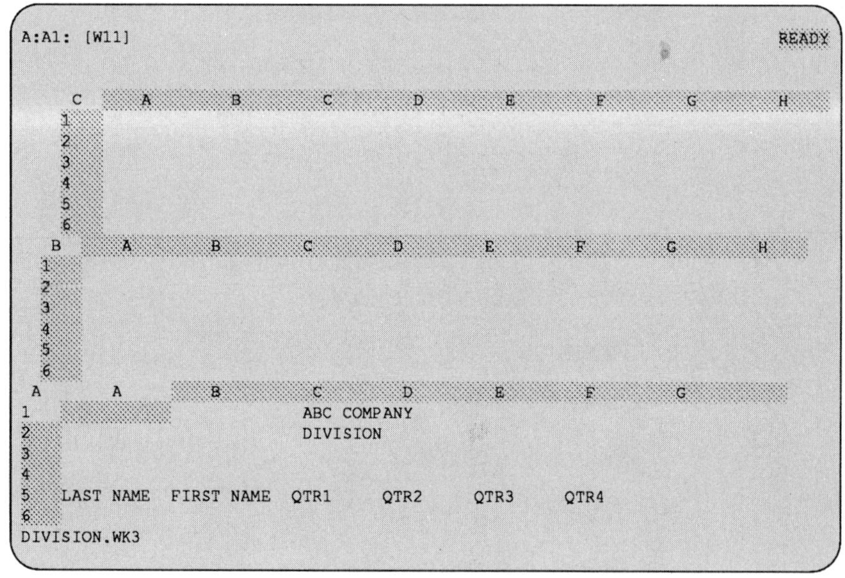

Figure 7-2

Be sure you are in GROUP mode so that when you copy the contents of worksheet A to worksheets B and C, you will also copy the formats.

Press Ctrl-Home

You are now in cell A1 in worksheet A. You must be in the worksheet that has the desired formats if you want the formats to be correct after the data is copied to the other worksheets.

Press /

Select Worksheet

Select Global

Select Group

Select Enable

Notice the GROUP indicator at the bottom of your screen is now on.

Copy the information in worksheet A to worksheets B and C:

Press /

Select Copy

Move the cell pointer to F10

The range of cell to copy is now highlighted.

Press 

To finish copying the information and formats:

Press Ctrl-PgUp

Type .

Press Ctrl-PgUp

The range to copy TO in the control panel is B:A1..C:A1 indicating that the appropriate range has been specified.

Press 

To disable the GROUP mode:

Press /

Select Worksheet

Select Global

Select Group

Select Disable

The GROUP indicator no longer appears on your screen. Your screen should look like Figure 7-3.

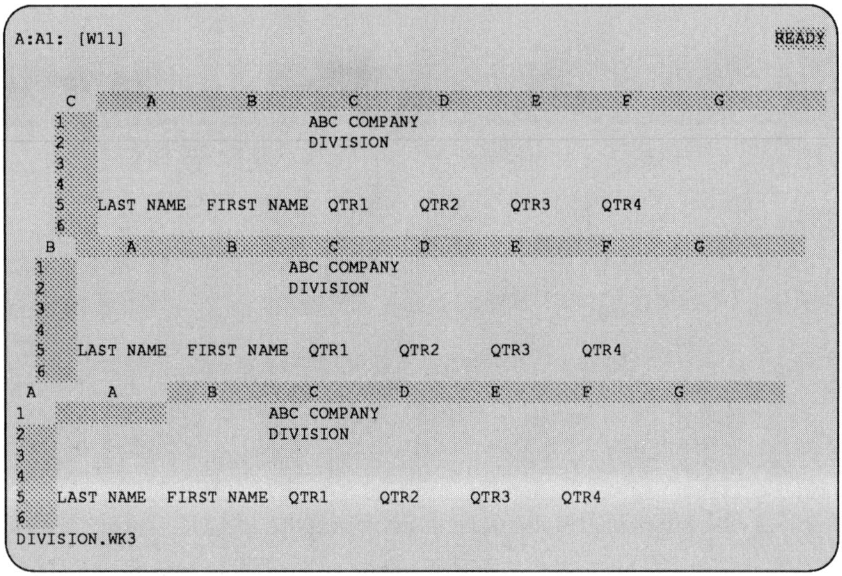

```
A:A1: [W11]                                                        READY

     C     A          B          C          D          E          F          G
     1                       ABC COMPANY
     2                       DIVISION
     3
     4
     5  LAST NAME  FIRST NAME  QTR1       QTR2       QTR3       QTR4
     6
    B     A          B          C          D          E          F          G
    1                       ABC COMPANY
    2                       DIVISION
    3
    4
    5  LAST NAME  FIRST NAME  QTR1       QTR2       QTR3       QTR4
    6
  A      A          B          C          D          E          F          G
  1                       ABC COMPANY
  2                       DIVISION
  3
  4
  5  LAST NAME  FIRST NAME  QTR1       QTR2       QTR3       QTR4
  6
DIVISION.WK3
```

Figure 7-3

At this point, enter the data for salaries for the three divisions in worksheets A, B and C. Parts 1 through 3 of Figure 7-4 include the data for the three divisions. Enter the data into the appropriate worksheets. Note the screens illustrate the ability to examine the worksheets in a file when the **Worksheet Window Clear** command is used to eliminate the 3-D perspective.

When the perspective option is not used, you can still move between the worksheets using the combination of the [Ctrl] key with the [PgUp] and [PgDn] keys.

```
A:A1: [W11]                                                           READY

 A      A          B          C        D        E        F        G
1                          ABC COMPANY
2                          DIVISION 1
3
4
5   LAST NAME  FIRST NAME  QTR1     QTR2     QTR3     QTR4
6   JOHNSON    ERNEST        8,000    8,000    8,800    8,800
7   LYLIE      SUSAN         7,800    7,800    7,800    8,580
8
9                          ------------------------------------
10  TOTAL                   15,800   15,800   16,600   17,380
11
12
13
14
15
16
17
18
19
20
DIVISION.WK3                                                 CAP
```

Figure 7-4
Part 1

```
B:A1: [W11]                                                           READY

 B      A          B          C        D        E        F        G
1                          ABC COMPANY
2                          DIVISION 2
3
4
5   LAST NAME  FIRST NAME  QTR1     QTR2     QTR3     QTR4
6   ARMOUR     CYNTHIA       5,200    5,200    5,400    5,400
7   CHIN       TOMMY         5,000    5,000    5,200    5,200
8
9                          ------------------------------------
10  TOTAL                   10,200   10,200   10,600   10,600
11
12
13
14
15
16
17
18
19
20
DIVISION.WK3                                                 CAP
```

Figure 7-4
Part 2

```
C:A1: [W11]                                                           READY

C     A          B          C         D         E         F         G
1                          ABC COMPANY
2                          DIVISION 3
3
4
5   LAST NAME  FIRST NAME  QTR1      QTR2      QTR3      QTR4
6   JONES      NINA          6,750     6,750     6,750     7,450
7   SPROUT     AL            5,950     5,950     6,450     6,450
8   VALETTI    GEORGE        5,900     5,900     6,300     6,300
9                          ------------------------------------
10  TOTAL                   18,600    18,600    19,500    20,200
11
12
13
14
15
16
17
18
19
20
DIVISION.WK3                                               CAP
```

Figure 7-4
Part 3

Please enter the data in the appropriate worksheets. Notice that a total salary value is computed for each quarter for each of the divisions. After entering the data and making sure you are using the perspective option, your screen should look like Figure 7-5.

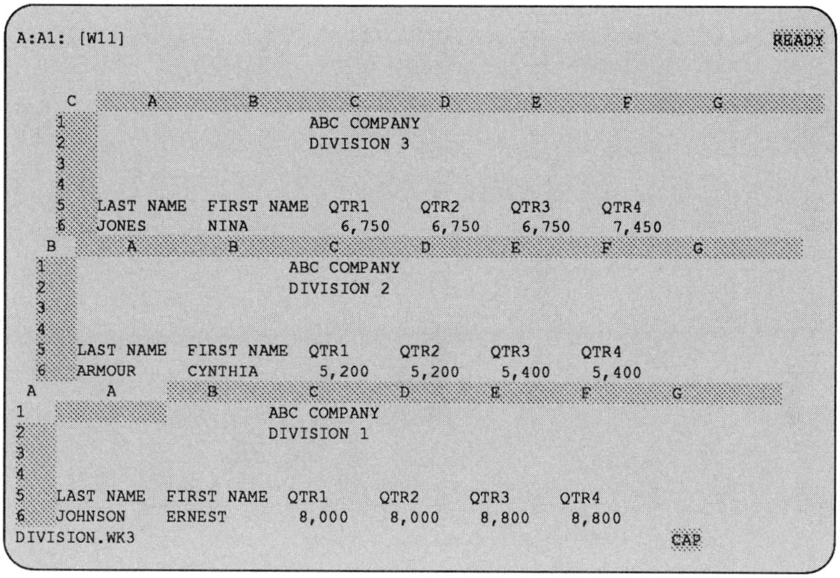

```
A:A1: [W11]                                                              READY

       C      A          B          C          D          E          F          G
       1                       ABC COMPANY
       2                       DIVISION 3
       3
       4
       5  LAST NAME  FIRST NAME  QTR1       QTR2       QTR3       QTR4
       6  JONES      NINA          6,750      6,750      6,750      7,450
     B      A          B          C          D          E          F          G
     1                       ABC COMPANY
     2                       DIVISION 2
     3
     4
     5  LAST NAME  FIRST NAME  QTR1       QTR2       QTR3       QTR4
     6  ARMOUR     CYNTHIA       5,200      5,200      5,400      5,400
   A        A          B          C          D          E          F          G
   1                       ABC COMPANY
   2                       DIVISION 1
   3
   4
   5  LAST NAME  FIRST NAME  QTR1       QTR2       QTR3       QTR4
   6  JOHNSON    ERNEST        8,000      8,000      8,800      8,800
DIVISION.WK3                                                        CAP
```

Figure 7-5

CONSOLIDATING SEVERAL WORKSHEETS INTO A SUMMARY WORKSHEET

Suppose the management of ABC Company wants a summary worksheet that includes the salary totals, by quarter, for each of the divisions and the total salaries for the company. When this exercise is completed, your screen will look like Figure 7-6.

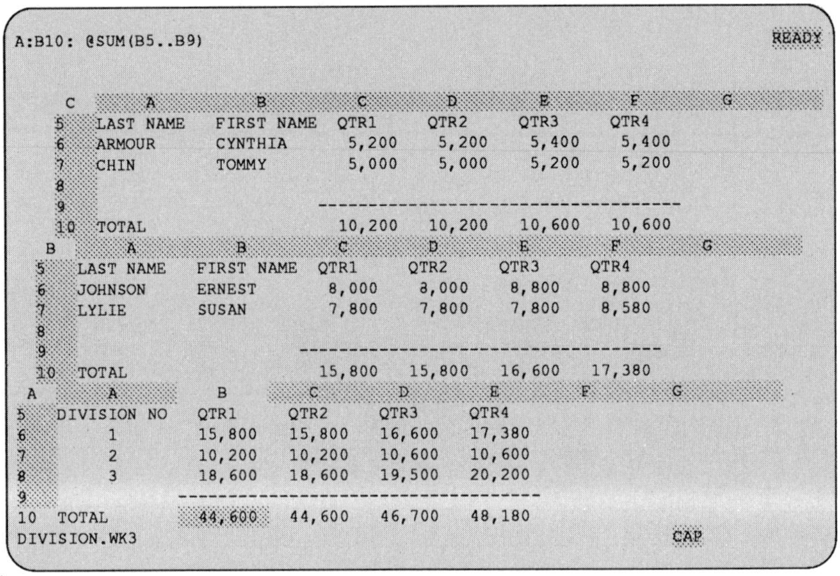

```
A:B10: @SUM(B5..B9)                                                    READY

    C     A          B           C          D          E          F          G
    5  LAST NAME  FIRST NAME  QTR1       QTR2       QTR3       QTR4
    6  ARMOUR     CYNTHIA       5,200      5,200      5,400      5,400
    7  CHIN       TOMMY         5,000      5,000      5,200      5,200
    8
    9                        ------------------------------------
    10 TOTAL                   10,200     10,200     10,600     10,600
   B      A          B           C          D          E          F          G
   5  LAST NAME  FIRST NAME  QTR1       QTR2       QTR3       QTR4
   6  JOHNSON    ERNEST        8,000      8,000      8,800      8,800
   7  LYLIE      SUSAN         7,800      7,800      7,800      8,580
   8
   9                        ------------------------------------
   10 TOTAL                   15,800     15,800     16,600     17,380
  A       A          B          C          D          E          F          G
  5  DIVISION NO  QTR1       QTR2       QTR3       QTR4
  6       1       15,800     15,800     16,600     17,380
  7       2       10,200     10,200     10,600     10,600
  8       3       18,600     18,600     19,500     20,200
  9             ------------------------------------
  10 TOTAL        44,600     44,600     46,700     48,180
  DIVISION.WK3                                                   CAP
```

Figure 7-6

The first step is to add a **summary** worksheet before the present worksheet A.

Press	Ctrl-Home keys to move the cell pointer to cell A1 in worksheet A
Press	/
Select	Worksheet
Select	Insert
Select	Sheet
Select	Before
Type	1
Press	↵

Notice that a blank worksheet now appears as worksheet A. The information for the three divisions has moved to the next worksheet. That is, the salary data for DIVISIONS 1, 2, and 3 are now in worksheets B, C, and D respectively. Since a maximum of three worksheets can appear on the screen at once you cannot see worksheet D. Your screen should look like Figure 7 7.

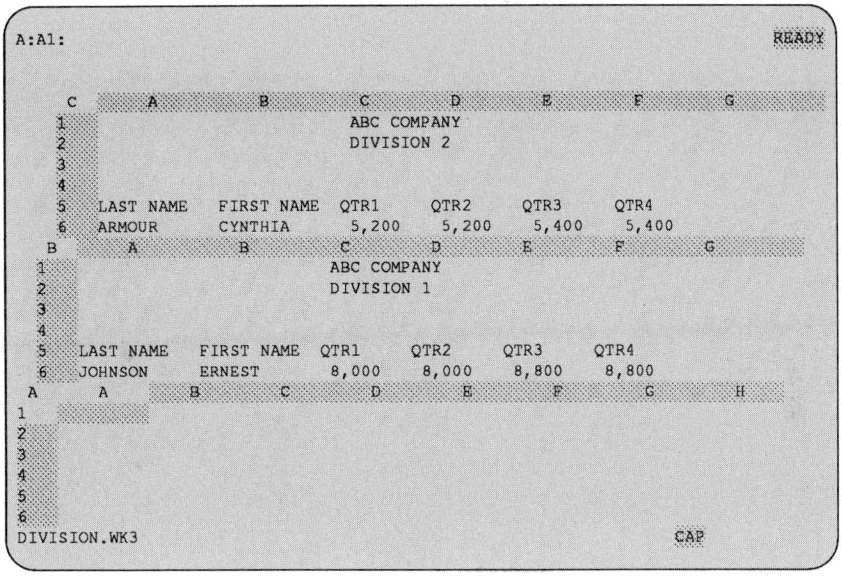

```
A:A1:                                                                   READY

     C       A          B          C          D          E          F          G
     1                              ABC COMPANY
     2                              DIVISION 2
     3
     4
     5   LAST NAME   FIRST NAME  QTR1       QTR2       QTR3       QTR4
     6   ARMOUR      CYNTHIA       5,200      5,200      5,400      5,400
   B       A          B          C          D          E          F          G
   1                              ABC COMPANY
   2                              DIVISION 1
   3
   4
   5   LAST NAME   FIRST NAME  QTR1       QTR2       QTR3       QTR4
   6   JOHNSON     ERNEST        8,000      8,000      8,800      8,800
 A       A          B          C          D          E          F          G          H
 1
 2
 3
 4
 5
 6
DIVISION.WK3                                                  CAP
```

Figure 7-7

Prior to summarizing the information, you need to enter the titles, column headings, labels and underlines in worksheet A. When you are finished placing this information on worksheet A, your screen should look like Figure 7-8 after pressing the Alt-F6 keys. This key combination lets you "zoom" on to one worksheet.

```
A:A1:                                                                    READY

A     A        B        C        D        E        F        G        H
1                       ABC COMPANY
2                   SALARY INFORMATION
3
4
5  DIVISION QTR1     QTR2     QTR3     QTR4
6        1
7        2
8        3
9           ------------------------------------
10 TOTAL
11
12
13
14
15
16
17
18
19
20
DIVISION.WK3                                                   CAP
```

Figure 7-8

After comparing your screen to Figure 7-8, return to the perspective mode by pressing the [Alt-F6] keys again.

At this point, you need to combine the total salary information by quarter from each of the divisions into the summary worksheet as it appears in worksheet A.

Press [Ctrl-Home] keys to make sure you are in cell A1 of worksheet A

Move the cell pointer to cell B6

Type +

Press [Ctrl-PgUp] keys to move the cell pointer to worksheet B

Move the cell pointer to cell B:C10

Press [↵]

Use the **W**orksheet **W**indow **C**lear command sequence and your screen should now look like Figure 7-9. Notice that the formula +B:C10 is stored in cell A:B6 indicating that the total salary for DIVISION 1 in QTR 1 appears in the cell.

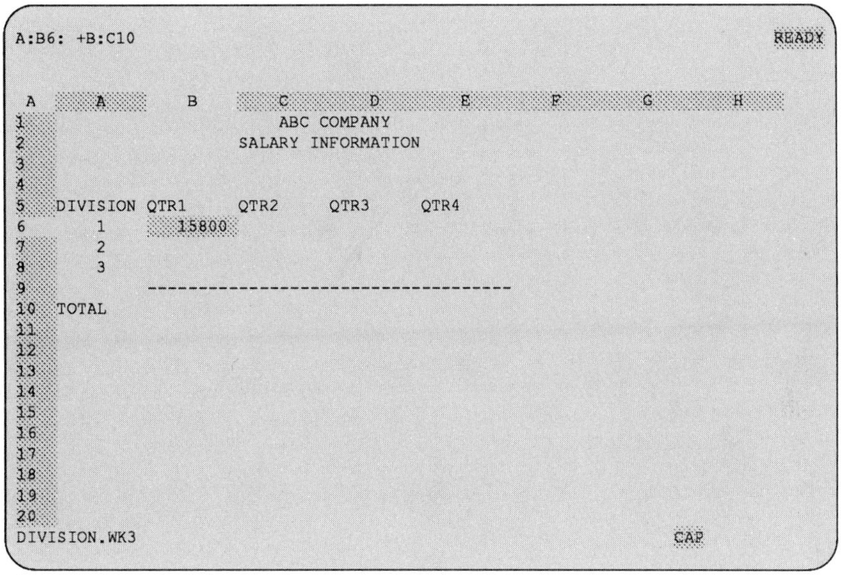

```
A:B6: +B:C10                                                        READY

A      A         B         C         D         E         F         G         H
1                          ABC COMPANY
2                       SALARY INFORMATION
3
4
5    DIVISION  QTR1      QTR2      QTR3      QTR4
6        1        15800
7        2
8        3
9              ------------------------------------
10   TOTAL
11
12
13
14
15
16
17
18
19
20
DIVISION.WK3                                                   CAP
```

Figure 7-9

Now copy the formula in cell A:B6 to the other cells in row 6 of the summary worksheet.

Press	/
Select	Copy
Press	↵
Move	the cell pointer to cell C6
Type	.
Move	the cell pointer to cell E6
Press	↵

Your screen now should look like Figure 7-10.

```
A:B6: +B:C10                                                        READY

 A      A        B        C        D        E        F        G        H
1                             ABC COMPANY
2                         SALARY INFORMATION
3
4
5  DIVISION QTR1      QTR2     QTR3     QTR4
6        1      15800    15800    16600    17380
7        2
8        3
9          ----------------------------------
10 TOTAL
11
12
13
14
15
16
17
18
19
20
DIVISION.WK3                                                  CAP
```

Figure 7-10

To place the total salary values for DIVISIONS 2 and 3 in the summary worksheet:

Move the cell pointer to cell B7 in worksheet A

Type +

Press Ctrl-PgUp keys twice to move the cell pointer to worksheet C

Move the cell pointer to cell C:C10

Press ↵

To copy the formula to cells C7 through E7 in the summary worksheet:

Press /

Select Copy

Press ↵

Move the cell pointer to cell C7

Type .

Move the cell pointer to cell E7

Press ↵

Move the cell pointer to cell B8 in worksheet A

Type +

Press Ctrl-PgUp keys three times to move the cell pointer to worksheet D

Move the cell pointer to cell D:C10

Press ↵

To copy the formula to cell C8 through E8 in the summary worksheet:

Press /

Select Copy

Press ↵

Move the cell pointer to cell C8

Type .

Move the cell pointer to cell E8

Press ↵

The total salary, by quarter, for each division now appears and your screen should look like Figure 7-11.

```
A:B8: +D:C10                                                          READY

 A     A        B        C        D        E        F        G        H
 1                         ABC COMPANY
 2                     SALARY INFORMATION
 3
 4
 5  DIVISION QTR1     QTR2     QTR3     QTR4
 6       1      15800    15800    16600    17380
 7       2      10200    10200    10600    10600
 8       3      18600    18600    19500    20200
 9           ------------------------------------
10  TOTAL
11
12
13
14
15
16
17
18
19
20
DIVISION.WK3                                                   CAP
```

Figure 7-11

To compute the total salary value for each quarter and format the summary worksheet you need to complete the following steps:

Move	the cell pointer to cell B10 in the summary worksheet
Type	@SUM(
Move	the cell pointer to cell B5
Type	.
Move	the cell pointer to cell B9
Type	)
Press	↵

To copy the sum formula to cells C10 through E10:

Press	/
Select	Copy
Press	↵

Move	the cell pointer to cell C10
Type	.
Move	the cell pointer to cell E10
Press	↵

To format the summary worksheet properly:

Press	/
Select	Worksheet
Select	Global
Select	Format
Select	,
Type	0
Press	↵

The summary worksheet is now completed. Your screen should look like Figure 7-12.

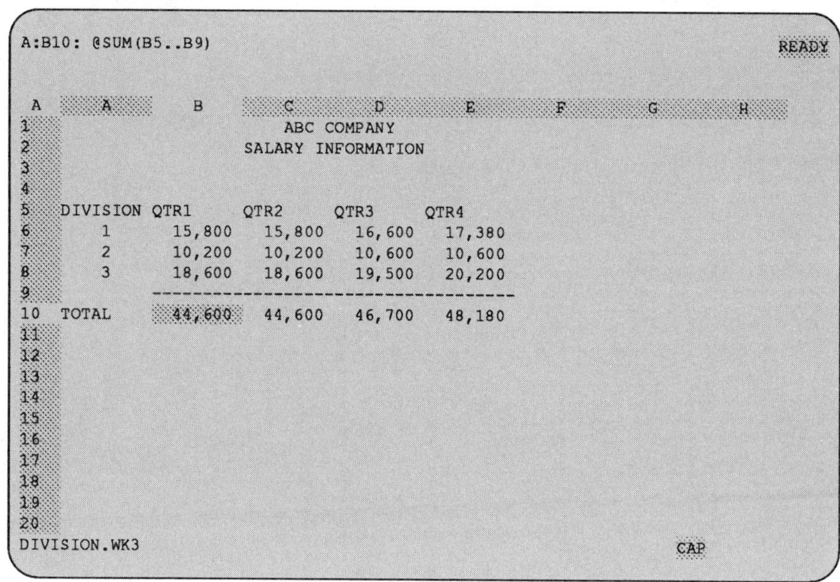

Figure 7-12

You essentially linked the worksheets in the file by using formulas. The advantage of such a process is that if you change the salary for an individual, then the summary worksheet will automatically be updated. Before illustrating this capability, use the **W**orksheet **W**indow **P**erspective command so you can see three worksheets. To demonstrate the updating process:

Press Ctrl-PgUp keys to move the cell pointer to worksheet B

Move the cell pointer to cell C6

Type 10000

Press ↵

Notice that the total salary value for QTR 1 in the summary worksheet increased by the same amount that you increased the salary for ERNEST JOHNSON.

Your screen now should look like Figure 7-13. Change the value back to 8,000 and move the cell pointer to cell A1 in worksheet A by pressing the Ctrl-Home keys.

```
B:C6: 10000                                                          READY

    C    A          B           C         D         E         F         G
    5  LAST NAME  FIRST NAME  QTR1      QTR2      QTR3      QTR4
    6  ARMOUR     CYNTHIA      5,200     5,200     5,400     5,400
    7  CHIN       TOMMY        5,000     5,000     5,200     5,200
    8
    9                         ------------------------------------
    10 TOTAL                  10,200    10,200    10,600    10,600
   B    A          B           C         D         E         F         G
   5  LAST NAME  FIRST NAME  QTR1      QTR2      QTR3      QTR4
   6  JOHNSON    ERNEST      10,000     8,000     8,800     8,800
   7  LYLIE      SUSAN        7,800     7,800     7,800     8,580
   8
   9                         ------------------------------------
   10 TOTAL                  17,800    15,800    16,600    17,380
  A    A          B         C         D         E         F         G
  5  DIVISION NO  QTR1      QTR2      QTR3      QTR4
  6       1       17,800    15,800    16,600    17,380
  7       2       10,200    10,200    10,600    10,600
  8       3       18,600    18,600    19,500    20,200
  9            ------------------------------------
  10 TOTAL        46,600    44,600    46,700    48,180
DIVISION.WK3                                               CAP
```

Figure 7-13

Save file DIVISION using the **F**ile **S**ave **R**eplace command sequence.

■ LINKING FILES TO MOVE INFORMATION BETWEEN FILES

In the previous section, three worksheets were created and some data from the worksheets were consolidated into a summary worksheet by linking the cells in the worksheets of the file together using formulas. Now you will learn how to link files together.

First, you will need to open the file BUDGET and place it before the file DIVISION. Then you will erase the salary values that appear on worksheet A in file BUDGET. Finally, you will link the two files together and the total salary values will appear on worksheet A in file BUDGET.

Press Ctrl-Home keys to make sure the cell pointer is in worksheet A

Press /

Select File

Select Open

Select Before

Press F3

Move the cell pointer to the file name BUDGET

Press ↵

The worksheet you created in Chapter 2 is shown on your screen. You now have two active files: BUDGET and DIVISION. To get a 3-D look at the files:

Press /

Select Worksheet

Select Window

Select Perspective

Your screen now should look like Figure 7-14. Notice that the worksheet stored in file BUDGET appears before the multiple worksheets in file DIVISION.

```
A:A1: [W18]                                                          READY

     B      A          B          C         D         E         F         G
     1                            ABC COMPANY
     2                            DIVISION 1
     3
     4
     5  LAST NAME   FIRST NAME  QTR1      QTR2      QTR3      QTR4
     6  JOHNSON     ERNEST        8,000     8,000     8,800     8,800
   A     A          B          C         D         E         F         G
   1                            ABC COMPANY
   2                       SALARY INFORMATION
   3
   4
   5  DIVISION NO   QTR1      QTR2      QTR3      QTR4
   6       1        15,800    15,800    16,600    17,380
 A        A          B          C         D         E         F         G
 1                                 ABC COMPANY
 2                                   BUDGET
 3
 4
 5                      QTR1      QTR2      QTR3      QTR4    YR TOTAL
 6
BUDGET.WK3                                                 CAP
```

Figure 7-14

To erase the salary values in file BUDGET:

Move	the cell pointer to cell B10 in worksheet A of file BUDGET
Press	/
Select	Range
Select	Erase
Move	the cell pointer to cell E10
Press	↵

Your screen now should look like Figure 7-15.

```
A:B10:                                                                  READY

     B     A           B           C          D          E          F         G
     5  LAST NAME   FIRST NAME  QTR1       QTR2       QTR3       QTR4
     6  JOHNSON     ERNEST        8,000      8,000      8,800      8,800
     7  LYLIE       SUSAN         7,800      7,800      7,800      8,580
     8
     9                          ------------------------------------
     10 TOTAL                    15,800     15,800     16,600     17,380
   A     A            B         C          D          E          F         G
   5  DIVISION NO   QTR1      QTR2       QTR3       QTR4
   6       1        15,800    15,800     16,600     17,380
   7       2        10,200    10,200     10,600     10,600
   8       3        18,600    18,600     19,500     20,200
   9                -------------------------------------
   10 TOTAL         44,600    44,600     46,700     48,180
 A         A               B          C          D          E          F         G
 5                       QTR1       QTR2       QTR3       QTR4     YR TOTAL
 6
 7  SALES              $60,000    $61,200    $62,424    $63,672   $247,296
 8
 9  EXPENSES
 10    SALARIES                                                       0
 BUDGET.WK3                                                         CAP
```

Figure 7-15

To link the salary values in worksheet A of file DIVISION to the SALARIES cells in file BUDGET:

Make sure the cell pointer is in cell B10 in worksheet A of file BUDGET

Type +

Press Ctrl-PgUp keys to move to cell B10 in worksheet A of file DIVISION

Press ↵

Notice by the cell address in Figure 7-16 the information that appears denotes the directory, file name and cell that are linked to the cell.

To copy the link for the formula appearing in cell B10 to cells C10 through E10:

Press /

Select Copy

Press ↵

Move the cell pointer to cell C10

Type .

Move	the cell pointer to cell E10
Press	↵

The cells of the two files are now properly linked and your screen should look like Figure 7-16.

```
A:B10: +<<C:\DIVISION.WK3>>A:B10..A:B10                                      READY

     B      A          B          C          D          E          F          G
     5  LAST NAME  FIRST NAME  QTR1       QTR2       QTR3       QTR4
     6  JOHNSON    ERNEST         8,000      8,000      8,800      8,800
     7  LYLIE      SUSAN          7,800      7,800      7,800      8,580
     8
     9                        ------------------------------------
    10  TOTAL                    15,800     15,800     16,600     17,380
   A      A          B          C          D          E          F          G
   5  DIVISION NO   QTR1       QTR2       QTR3       QTR4
   6        1       15,800     15,800     16,600     17,380
   7        2       10,200     10,200     10,600     10,600
   8        3       18,600     18,600     19,500     20,200
   9             ------------------------------------
  10  TOTAL         44,600     44,600     46,700     48,180
 A            A             B          C          D          E          F          G
 5                         QTR1       QTR2       QTR3       QTR4    YR TOTAL
 6
 7  SALES                 60,000     61,200     62,424     63,672   247,296
 8
 9  EXPENSES
10    SALARIES            44,600     44,600     46,700     48,180   184,080
BUDGET.WK3                                                          CAP
```

Figure 7-16

You can also link to files that are not currently in memory, but reside on a disk. For example, suppose only the BUDGET file is open. To link to the DIVISION file, you can type the formula +<<C:\DIVISION.WK3>>A:B10..A:B10 in cell B10 of the BUDGET worksheet. This formula then can be copied to cells C10 through E10.

■ OPENING A NEW FILE

In the last section you opened an additional file that already existed. In some situations, you may need to have a new file in memory along with another file that is currently in memory.

Before illustrating the process for inserting a new file in memory, retrieve file SALES.

To place a new file in memory after file SALES:

Press	/
Select	File
Select	New

Select After

To specify the name for the new file:

Type EXAMPLE

Press ↵

The file EXAMPLE appears on your screen. Use the **W**orksheet **W**indow **P**erspective command sequence so you can see portions of both files. Your screen should look like Figure 7-17.

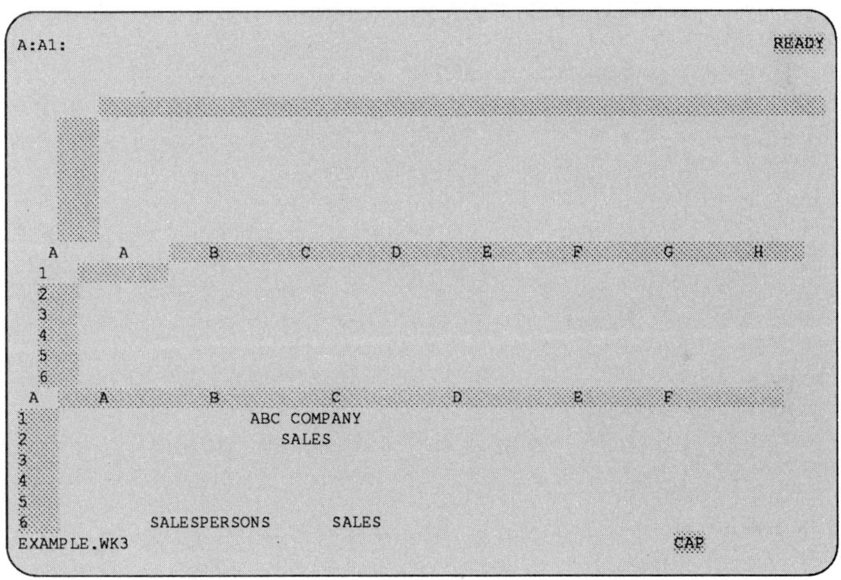

Figure 7-17

Note that file SALES appears before file EXAMPLE.

■ CLOSING AN ACTIVE FILE

In some situations you may need to close a file that is presently active. Suppose you need to close the file EXAMPLE that you opened in the last section.

To delete the file from your computer's memory:

Press /

Select Worksheet

Select Delete

Select File

To specify you want to delete EXAMPLE:

Type F3

Select the pointer-movement keys until the file EXAMPLE is highlighted

Press ↵

The file EXAMPLE has been removed from your computer's memory, and your screen should look like Figure 7-18.

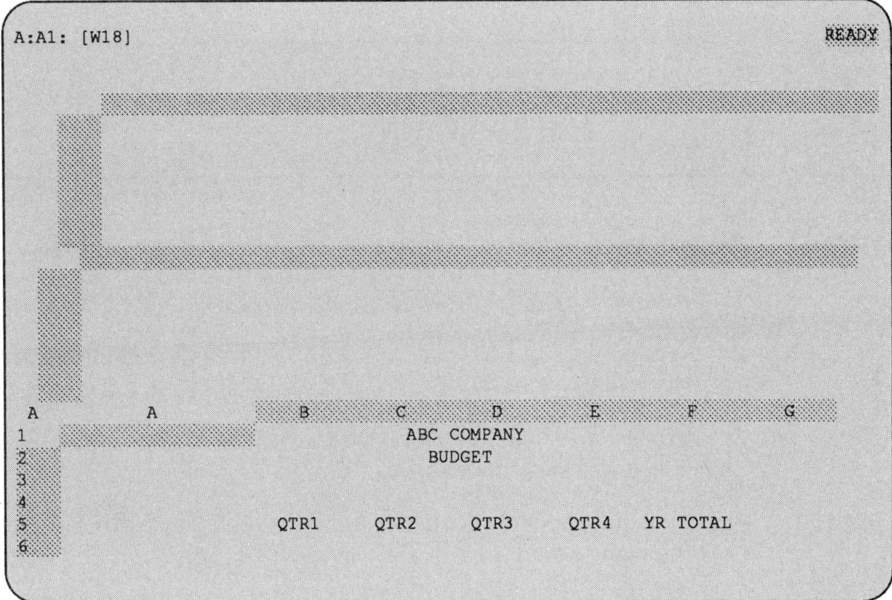

Figure 7-18

SUMMARY

You can use a template to create several identical worksheets in a file. Appropriate data can then be entered into the worksheets. A summary worksheet can be used to summarize the data in the individual worksheets in the file. Lotus 1-2-3 also provides the capability to link files to each other through the use of formulas that link cells.

KEY CONCEPTS

Consolidating information between worksheets
File New
File Open
Linking files
Worksheet Delete File

CHAPTER SEVEN
EXERCISE 1

INSTRUCTIONS: Circle T if the statement is true and F if the statement is false.

T F 1. A template can be used to create several worksheets very rapidly.

T F 2. Worksheets in a file can be linked together through the use of formulas.

T F 3. While worksheets can be linked by formulas, files cannot be linked in the same manner.

T F 4. Multiple worksheets make it easy to combine information between the worksheets.

T F 5. Only two files can be open at one time, but many worksheets can be open within one file.

CHAPTER SEVEN
EXERCISE 2

INSTRUCTIONS: Explain a typical situation when the following keystrokes or Lotus 1-2-3 commands are used.

Problem 1: / **F**ile **O**pen **B**efore

Problem 2: / **W**orksheet **I**nsert **S**heet

Problem 3: / **W**orksheet **G**lobal **G**roup **E**nable

Problem 4: Ctrl-Home

Problem 5: Ctrl-PgUp

Problem 6: Ctrl-PgDn

CHAPTER SEVEN
EXERCISE 3
Consolidating Worksheets

INSTRUCTIONS: Retrieve the file XYZSALES that was created as an exercise in Chapter 6.

Add a summary worksheet that contains the total revenues for the New York, Chicago, Houston and Los Angeles locations.

Include a total line on the summary sheet that computes the total revenues for XYZ Consulting Company.

Print the summary worksheet.

CHAPTER SEVEN
EXERCISE 4
Linking Files

INSTRUCTIONS: Retrieve the file DIVSALES that was completed as an exercise in Chapter 6.

Rather than include an additional worksheet in the file DIVSALES, open a new file named ABCSUMRY in front of file DIVSALES.

Create a summary worksheet in file ABCSUMRY that includes cells for the quarterly sales of each division and calculates the total revenue by quarter and for the year of ABC Company.

Link the appropriate cells containing the data from the worksheets in file DIVSALES to the proper cells in file ABCSUMRY to complete the exercise.

Print the ABCSUMRY worksheet.

CHAPTER SEVEN
EXERCISE 5
Consolidate Multiple Worksheets in a File

INSTRUCTIONS: Create a file with multiple worksheets and include a summary worksheet that will be helpful to you in some way. Link some of the data in the worksheets to the summary.

Print your worksheets.

CHAPTER SEVEN
EXERCISE 6
Linking Files

INSTRUCTIONS: Create an application of 1-2-3 which uses the concept of linking files that will be helpful to you in some way.

Print worksheets associated with the files.

CHAPTER EIGHT

INTRODUCTION TO DATABASE CAPABILITIES

OBJECTIVES

In this chapter, you will learn to:

- Identify basic database terms
- Sort data in a spreadsheet
- Query for desired data on a spreadsheet
- Create a computed column in a query operation
- Use additional data query options

CHAPTER OVERVIEW

Lotus 1-2-3 can perform **database** capabilities such as sorting data and querying on data in a worksheet. Suppose some of the personal information for all employees of an organization is entered into a single worksheet. To sort the names by division within the organization, you can use the **D**ata **S**ort command sequence. To generate a report listing all employees who have been employed by the company for over 10 years, you can use the **D**ata **Q**uery command sequence. However, 1-2-3 cannot perform database capabilities as extensively as a database management system like dBASE III PLUS or IV,[1] R:BASE System V,[2] or Paradox Release 3.0.[3] This chapter discusses the basic database capabilities of 1-2-3. Chapter 9 contains additional database features available in 1-2-3.

[1] dBASE III PLUS and dBASE IV are registered trademarks of Ashton-Tate; Culver City, California.

[2] R:BASE System V is a registered trademark of Microrim, Inc.; Bellevue, Washington.

[3] Paradox Release 3.0 is a registered trademark of Ansa Software, a Borland Company; Belmont, California.

■ BASIC DEFINITIONS

Some of the basic terms used in database management are **field**, **record**, **file**, and **key**.

A **field** is a collection of characters that are grouped together. In 1-2-3, each field is contained in a separate column within the database, or file. An example would be a person's last name. A **field name** is the term used to describe each field. For example, the title LAST NAME might be the field name for the field in which a person's last name is listed. In 1-2-3, each field name is listed in the column containing the field and is located in the cell *immediately* above the first listed field.

A **record** is a group of data fields that are combined in some logical pattern. For example, the personnel record for individuals in a company might include the individual's social security number, last name, first name, middle initial, department in which the individual works and so forth. In 1-2-3, each record is listed as a separate row.

A **file** is a group of records that are combined together. For example, the personnel file would include all of the personnel records. In 1-2-3, a group of records that are placed together on a worksheet in a logical manner is referred to as a **database table.**

A **key** is a specific field that can be used for distinguishing between records. For example, an identification number or the social security number for an employee can be used as a key for a personnel file.

■ SORTING

Sometimes you may need to sort data in order. For example, it may be necessary to sort transactions in order by type of transaction. The following exercises demonstrate how to sort information in 1-2-3.

Sorting by a Primary Key

Create the worksheet appearing in Figure 8-1 and save it using the file name ABCSAL.

A:A1: [W7] READY

A	A	B	C	D	E	F	G	H	I
1					ABC COMPANY				
2					SALARY BUDGET				
3									
4									
5	EMP NO	LAST NAME	FIRST NAME	DIV	QTR1	QTR2	QTR3	QTR4	TOTAL
6	568	SPROUT	AL	3	5,950	5,950	6,450	6,450	24,800
7	123	LYLIE	SUSAN	1	7,800	7,800	7,800	8,580	31,980
8	390	CHIN	TOMMY	2	5,000	5,000	5,200	5,200	20,400
9	972	JOHNSON	SANDRA	1	8,200	8,200	9,000	9,000	34,400
10	898	VALETTI	GEORGE	3	5,900	5,900	6,300	6,300	24,400
11	239	ARMOUR	CYNTHIA	2	5,200	5,200	5,400	5,400	21,200
12	576	JOHNSON	ERNEST	1	8,000	8,000	8,800	8,800	33,600
13	833	JONES	NINA	3	6,750	6,750	6,750	7,450	27,700
14					----------	----------	----------	----------	----------
15		TOTAL			52,800	52,800	55,700	57,180	218,480
16									
17									
18									
19									
20									

Figure 8-1

Suppose you need to sort the data in the ABCSAL worksheet in order by Division number.

Specifying the Data Range

Before sorting the spreadsheet, you need to specify the data range. The **data range** indicates where the database records you want to sort are located on the worksheet. To specify the data range:

Press	/
Select	Data
Select	Sort
Select	Data-Range

When prompted for the data range:

Move	the cell pointer to cell A6
Type	.
Move	the cell pointer to cell I13
Press	↵

All of the records in cells A6 through I13 comprise the data range. Note that only the records and *not* the field titles (EMP NO, LAST NAME, FIRST NAME, ...) are included in the data range. If the field titles are included, they will also be sorted. Another common error is to highlight only the column that needs to be sorted when indicating the data range. If this error occurs, only the column specified in the data range will be sorted; none of the data in the adjacent columns (e.g., EMP NO, LAST NAME, FIRST NAME) will be sorted with the appropriate division. Note that the underline and TOTAL rows should not be included in the data range.

Specifying the Primary Key

To specify the primary key:

Select	Primary-Key
Move	the cell pointer to cell D5 (or any other cell in column D)
Press	↵

The **primary key** indicates the column containing the field by which the database should sort the records. Since column D contains the data to sort by (in this example, by division), any cell in the column containing the division numbers can be used to specify the primary key. When prompted for the desired sort order:

Type	A (for Ascending)
Press	↵

The two options for sorting are Ascending and Descending. **Ascending** order can refer to alphabetical order (from A to Z) or numerical order (from the smallest number to the largest number). **Descending** order can refer to reverse alphabetical order (from Z to A) or numerical order (from the largest number to the smallest number).

Sorting the Data

To begin the sort procedure:

Select	Go

The records should be sorted in order by division number. Your screen should look like the final illustration in Figure 8-2. Figure 8-2, Parts 1 through 3 display the entire sort procedure.

Step 1 of the Sort Procedure: Specify the Data-Range.

```
A:I13: @SUM(E13..H13)                                                    POINT
Enter data range: A:A6..A:I13

 A     A       B         C        D      E        F        G        H        I
 1                                         ABC COMPANY
 2                                         SALARY BUDGET
 3
 4
 5   EMP NO LAST NAME FIRST NAME DIV    QTR1     QTR2     QTR3     QTR4    TOTAL
 6      568 SPROUT     AL           3   5,950    5,950    6,450    6,450   24,800
 7      123 LYLIE      SUSAN        1   7,800    7,800    7,800    8,580   31,980
 8      390 CHIN       TOMMY        2   5,000    5,000    5,200    5,200   20,400
 9      972 JOHNSON    SANDRA       1   8,200    8,200    9,000    9,000   34,400
10      898 VALETTI    GEORGE       3   5,900    5,900    6,300    6,300   24,400
11      239 ARMOUR     CYNTHIA      2   5,200    5,200    5,400    5,400   21,200
12      576 JOHNSON    ERNEST       1   8,000    8,000    8,800    8,800   33,600
13      833 JONES      NINA         3   6,750    6,750    6,750    7,450   27,700
14                                   ------------------------------------------
15          TOTAL                      52,800   52,800   55,700   57,180  218,480
16
17
18
19
20
```

Figure 8-2
Part 1

Step 2 of the Sort Procedure: Specify the Sort Column and the Sort Order.

```
A:A1: [W7]                                                                EDIT
Primary sort key: A:D5                        Sort order (A or D): A

 A     A       B         C        D      E        F        G        H        I
 1                                         ABC COMPANY
 2                                         SALARY BUDGET
 3
 4
 5   EMP NO LAST NAME FIRST NAME DIV    QTR1     QTR2     QTR3     QTR4    TOTAL
 6      568 SPROUT     AL           3   5,950    5,950    6,450    6,450   24,800
 7      123 LYLIE      SUSAN        1   7,800    7,800    7,800    8,580   31,980
 8      390 CHIN       TOMMY        2   5,000    5,000    5,200    5,200   20,400
 9      972 JOHNSON    SANDRA       1   8,200    8,200    9,000    9,000   34,400
10      898 VALETTI    GEORGE       3   5,900    5,900    6,300    6,300   24,400
11      239 ARMOUR     CYNTHIA      2   5,200    5,200    5,400    5,400   21,200
12      576 JOHNSON    ERNEST       1   8,000    8,000    8,800    8,800   33,600
13      833 JONES      NINA         3   6,750    6,750    6,750    7,450   27,700
14                                   ------------------------------------------
15          TOTAL                      52,800   52,800   55,700   57,180  218,480
16
17
18
19
20
```

Figure 8-2
Part 2

Step 3 of the Sort Procedure: Select **Go** from the Sort Menu to Sort the Database.

A:A1: [W7] READY

A	A	B	C	D	E	F	G	H	I
1					ABC COMPANY				
2					SALARY BUDGET				
3									
4									
5	EMP NO	LAST NAME	FIRST NAME	DIV	QTR1	QTR2	QTR3	QTR4	TOTAL
6	123	LYLIE	SUSAN	1	7,800	7,800	7,800	8,580	31,980
7	972	JOHNSON	SANDRA	1	8,200	8,200	9,000	9,000	34,400
8	576	JOHNSON	ERNEST	1	8,000	8,000	8,800	8,800	33,600
9	390	CHIN	TOMMY	2	5,000	5,000	5,200	5,200	20,400
10	239	ARMOUR	CYNTHIA	2	5,200	5,200	5,400	5,400	21,200
11	568	SPROUT	AL	3	5,950	5,950	6,450	6,450	24,800
12	898	VALETTI	GEORGE	3	5,900	5,900	6,300	6,300	24,400
13	833	JONES	NINA	3	6,750	6,750	6,750	7,450	27,700
14					----------	----------	----------	----------	----------
15		TOTAL			52,800	52,800	55,700	57,180	218,480
16									
17									
18									
19									
20									

Figure 8-2
Part 3

Sorting by Primary and Secondary Keys

In this exercise, the records in the file ABCSAL are sorted so that the names appear in alphabetical order within each division. It has been written with the assumption that the exercise in the previous section has just been completed and that the sorted records are currently displayed on your screen.

Specifying the Primary Key

A common error at this point is to indicate that the LAST NAME column is the **primary** key. This would not be correct. In this case, when the database is sorted, the last names would be sorted correctly, but the divisions would be out of order. The Division column will be the primary key so that the database is sorted *primarily* by division. The LAST NAME column will be specified as the **secondary** key so that the database is sorted *secondarily* by last name. This will cause the last names to appear in alphabetical order within each division. To specify the primary key:

Press /

Select Data

Select Sort

Select Primary-Key

Cell D5 should be highlighted as a result of the previous exercise. If it is not, highlight cell D5 by moving the cell pointer to cell D5 or any other cell in column D at this time. With cell D5 highlighted:

Press ↵

When prompted for the sort order, make sure that the letter A (for Ascending order) appears. The A should appear as a result of being selected in the previous exercise. If it does not, type A at this time. With A specified as the sort order:

Press ↵

Specifying the Secondary Key

To specify the secondary key:

Select Secondary-Key

Move the cell pointer to cell B5 (or any other cell in column B)

Press ↵

Since column B contains the data to sort by (in this example, by LAST NAME), any cell in column B can be specified as the Secondary Key.

When prompted for the desired sort order:

Type A

Press ↵

Sorting the Data

To begin the sort procedure:

Select Go

The database should now be sorted so that the last names are in alphabetical order by division. Your screen should look like Figure 8-3.

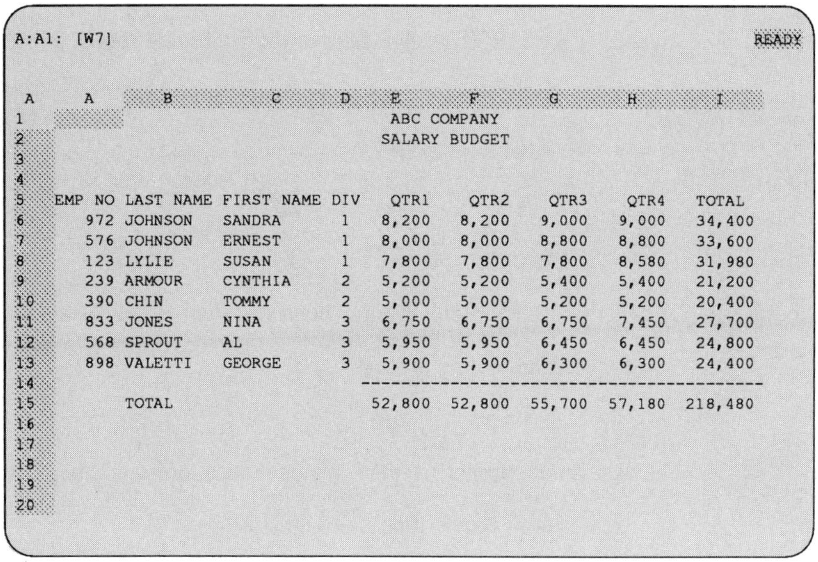

```
A:A1: [W7]                                                          READY

A    A       B          C        D     E        F        G        H        I
1                                        ABC COMPANY
2                                       SALARY BUDGET
3
4
5  EMP NO LAST NAME FIRST NAME DIV    QTR1     QTR2     QTR3     QTR4     TOTAL
6     972 JOHNSON   SANDRA       1   8,200    8,200    9,000    9,000    34,400
7     576 JOHNSON   ERNEST       1   8,000    8,000    8,800    8,800    33,600
8     123 LYLIE     SUSAN        1   7,800    7,800    7,800    8,580    31,980
9     239 ARMOUR    CYNTHIA      2   5,200    5,200    5,400    5,400    21,200
10    390 CHIN      TOMMY        2   5,000    5,000    5,200    5,200    20,400
11    833 JONES     NINA         3   6,750    6,750    6,750    7,450    27,700
12    568 SPROUT    AL           3   5,950    5,950    6,450    6,450    24,800
13    898 VALETTI   GEORGE       3   5,900    5,900    6,300    6,300    24,400
14                                  ------------------------------------------
15        TOTAL                     52,800   52,800   55,700   57,180   218,480
16
17
18
19
20
```

Figure 8-3

Sorting by More than Two Keys

The example in the previous section sorted the last names in alphabetical order within each division. Notice that the records are not in alphabetical order. Sandra Johnson appears before Ernest Johnson in the list of employees. Fortunately, 1-2-3 allows you to add extra sort keys. You can use a maximum of 256 sort keys.

Continuing with the example from the previous section, you need to include the FIRST NAME as an extra sort key to sort the employee name in alphabetical order within each division. Since the settings for the Data-Range, Primary-Key and Secondary-Key have already been specified, you only need to complete the commands for the extra key.

Press /

Select Data

Select Sort

Select Extra-Key (or type in 1)

To accept Extra Key 1:

Press ↵

To specify the FIRST NAME field as the additional sort key:

Move	the cell pointer to cell C5 (or any cell in column C)
Press	↵
Type	A
Press	↵

The FIRST NAME field has now been specified as the extra sort key.

To complete the sorting process:

Select	Go

The data is now properly sorted in alphabetical order within each division.

Your screen now should look like Figure 8-4.

A:A1: [W7] READY

A	A	B	C	D	E	F	G	H	I
1					ABC COMPANY				
2					SALARY BUDGET				
3									
4									
5	EMP NO	LAST NAME	FIRST NAME	DIV	QTR1	QTR2	QTR3	QTR4	TOTAL
6	576	JOHNSON	ERNEST	1	8,000	8,000	8,800	8,800	33,600
7	972	JOHNSON	SANDRA	1	8,200	8,200	9,000	9,000	34,400
8	123	LYLIE	SUSAN	1	7,800	7,800	7,800	8,580	31,980
9	239	ARMOUR	CYNTHIA	2	5,200	5,200	5,400	5,400	21,200
10	390	CHIN	TOMMY	2	5,000	5,000	5,200	5,200	20,400
11	833	JONES	NINA	3	6,750	6,750	6,750	7,450	27,700
12	568	SPROUT	AL	3	5,950	5,950	6,450	6,450	24,800
13	898	VALETTI	GEORGE	3	5,900	5,900	6,300	6,300	24,400
14					----------	----------	----------	----------	----------
15		TOTAL			52,800	52,800	55,700	57,180	218,480
16									
17									
18									
19									
20									

Figure 8-4

■ QUERYING

At times, you may need to perform a **query**, which is the process of searching through a file and selecting items based upon specific criteria. For example, you may wish to select all stores in a database file that have revenues in excess of $75,000 a year. The following exercises demonstrate how to perform queries in 1-2-3.

Querying with a Simple Criteria

In this exercise, the data in the database table ABCSAL will be queried to find individuals in the file that have a total salary greater than $25,000.

Retrieve the original file ABCSAL for use in this exercise.

Placing the Criteria on a Separate Worksheet

Since you have the capability to have multiple worksheets in an individual file, it is useful to place the criteria on a separate worksheet in the file and leave the database table in another worksheet. By using this approach, you do not take as much of a risk of altering the data.

To add the worksheet for the criteria:

Press /

Select Worksheet

Select Insert

Select Sheet

Select Before

To indicate that one worksheet is to be placed before the database table:

Press ↵

You should now have a blank worksheet on your screen.

To view the database table along with the new worksheet:

Press /

Select Worksheet

Select Window

Select Perspective

Your screen should look like Figure 8-5.

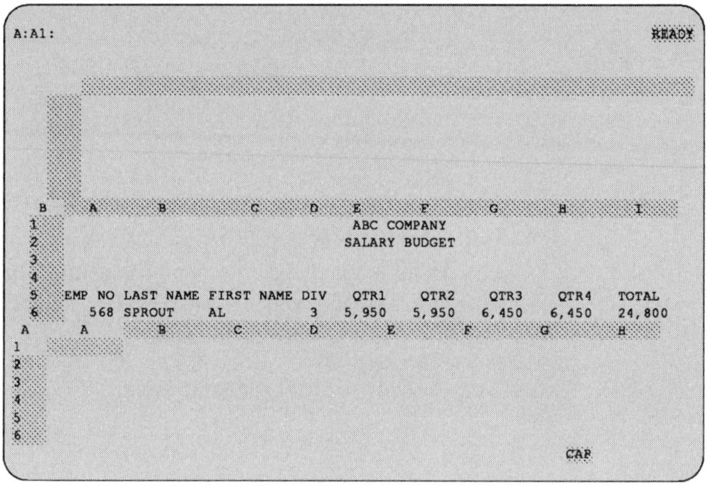

```
A:A1:                                                                  READY

 B     A         B          C       D     E         F        G        H        I
 1                                        ABC COMPANY
 2                                       SALARY BUDGET
 3
 4
 5   EMP NO  LAST NAME  FIRST NAME  DIV   QTR1      QTR2     QTR3     QTR4    TOTAL
 6      568  SPROUT     AL            3   5,950     5,950    6,450    6,450   24,800
A      A         B          C       D         E         F        G        H
1
2
3
4
5
6
                                                                   CAP
```

Figure 8-5

At this point, you need to place the criteria on the worksheet. When you finish placing the criteria on the worksheet, your screen will look like Figure 8-6.

To place the descriptive information on the worksheet A:

Move	the cell pointer to cell A:A4
Type	CRITERIA RANGES
Press	↵

The criteria must consist of at least two cells. The first cell specifies the field name that contains the data relevant to the query (in this case, the relevant data field name is TOTAL). The second line of the criteria must consist of a formula or data that specifies the actual query. The name in the first cell of the criteria must match the field name in the database table exactly. Therefore, you will copy the field name TOTAL from the database table to the criteria range on worksheet A. To specify the criteria for the query:

Move	the cell pointer to cell A:B6
Press	/
Select	Copy

When prompted for the range to copy FROM:

Press	Esc

Move the cell pointer to cell B:I5 using the Ctrl-PgUp and → keys

Press ↵

When prompted for the range to copy TO, the cell pointer will be in cell A:B6.

Press ↵

As indicated earlier, the word TOTAL in the criteria must be listed exactly the way it is specified in the worksheet. It does not matter if the label is listed in lowercase or uppercase letters or which label prefix (^, " or ') is used. However, TOTAL must match the field name TOTAL character for character. For example, TOTALS would not render the correct results because the S in TOTALS is not present in the field name in the database table (cell B:I5).

To define the second line of the criteria:

Move the cell pointer to cell A:B7

Type +TOTAL>25000

Press ↵

The two cells required for the criteria—the field name TOTAL and the condition (+TOTAL>25000) have been entered. In this example, the criteria indicates that the query will be for cells under the field name TOTAL that contain data greater than 25,000.

ERR appears in cell B7 because 1-2-3 assumes that TOTAL is a named range. However, in this case you are referring to the field name TOTAL in the input range. It is not necessary to create a range name to complete the query; therefore, the ERR is valid.

To format cell B7 so that the formula for the criteria is displayed rather than ERR:

Press /

Select Range

Select Format

Select Text

When prompted for the range to format:

Press ↵

Cell B7 now displays +TOTAL>2, which is not the complete formula. In order to show the complete criteria, widen column B so its width is set to 13 characters.

The formula +TOTAL>25000 is now fully displayed in cell B7. Your screen should look like Figure 8-6.

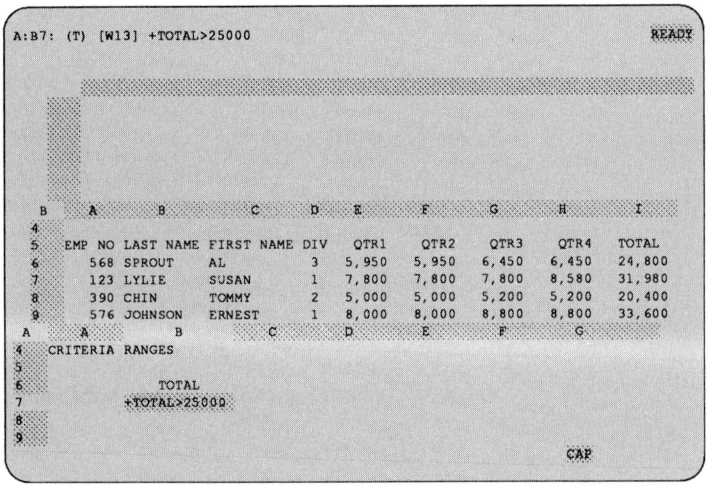

```
A:B7: (T) [W13] +TOTAL>25000                                              READY

 B    A       B          C          D     E        F        G        H        I
 4
 5  EMP NO LAST NAME FIRST NAME DIV   QTR1     QTR2     QTR3     QTR4     TOTAL
 6     568 SPROUT    AL           3   5,950    5,950    6,450    6,450    24,800
 7     123 LYLIE     SUSAN        1   7,800    7,800    7,800    8,580    31,980
 8     390 CHIN      TOMMY        2   5,000    5,000    5,200    5,200    20,400
 9     576 JOHNSON   ERNEST       1   8,000    8,000    8,800    8,800    33,600
A      A          B          C        D        E        F        G
4  CRITERIA RANGES
5
6             TOTAL
7         +TOTAL>25000
8
9                                                               CAP
```

Figure 8-6

Placing the Output Range on the Worksheet

Once the records matching the criteria have been located, it is possible to copy these records to another part of the worksheet called an output range. By specifying an output range, the desired records can be analyzed and manipulated without disturbing the database in which the records are contained. You will place the output range on worksheet A.

In this exercise, the fields for the LAST NAME, FIRST NAME, and TOTAL for each record that satisfies the criteria will be copied to the specified output range on worksheet A. The field names define the **output range.** The records that match the criteria are copied or **output** to the cells immediately beneath the field names in the output range. As illustrated by this example, the field names can be specified so that the entire record does not have to be output. In this case, only the LAST NAME, FIRST NAME, and TOTAL will be output. The information for the employee number, division, and the salaries in the four quarters will not be output.

To specify the output range on worksheet A, the appropriate field names must be copied from worksheet B. The field titles in the output range must match the names in the input range character for character. For this reason, you will use the copy command.

To copy the LAST NAME and FIRST NAME field names as two of the fields to output:

Move the cell pointer to cell A:C10

Press /

Select Copy

When prompted for the range to copy FROM:

Press Esc

Move the cell pointer to cell B:B5

Type .

Move the cell pointer to cell B:C5

Press ↵

When prompted for the range to copy TO:

Press ↵

Widen columns C and D so that they are wide enough to display 12 characters.

To specify the TOTAL field as another field to output:

Move the cell pointer to cell A:E10

Press /

Select Copy

When prompted for the range to copy FROM:

Press Esc

Move the cell pointer to cell B:I5

Press ↵

When prompted for the range to copy TO:

Press 

To document where the output ranges are located (an optional step):

Move the cell pointer to cell A:A9

Type OUTPUT RANGE

Press ↵

Your screen should look like Figure 8-7.

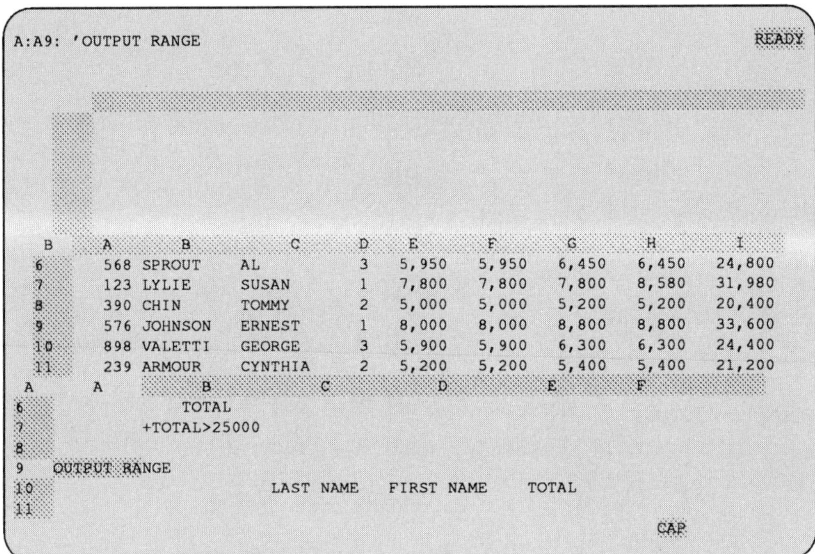

Figure 8-7

Specifying the Input Range

Now that the criteria and the headings for the output have been entered on the worksheet, you will indicate through the Lotus 1-2-3 menu where the records, criteria, and output range are located. After these steps are finished, you will complete the actual query operations.

First, indicate the input range. The **input range** is the term for the field names and data records located in the database table on worksheet B.

To specify the input range:

Press /

Select Data

Select Query

Select Input

When prompted to indicate the Input range:

Move the cell pointer to cell B:A5

Type .

Move the cell pointer to cell I13

Your screen should look like Figure 8-8.

Press ⏎

Note that the input range includes the field names (EMP NO, LAST NAME, FIRST NAME, . . .). If there are two lines of field titles, include only the bottom row in the input range and use only the words in the bottom line as the field names in your criteria and output ranges. Remember that the first database record must be in the row immediately under the field names without any rows separating the field name from the first record.

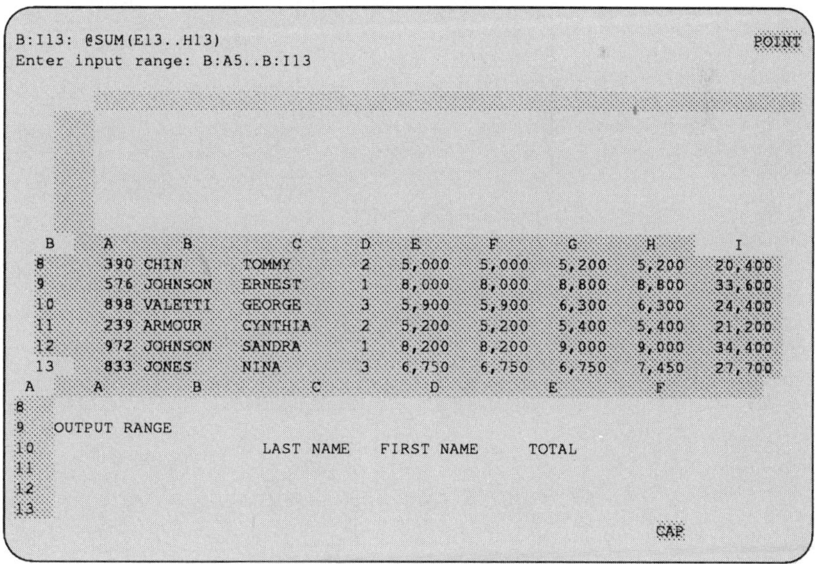

Figure 8-8

Specifying the Criteria Range

To specify where the criteria are located:

Select	Criteria

When prompted for the Criteria range:

Move	the cell pointer to cell A:B6
Type	.
Move	the cell pointer to cell B7

Your screen should now look like Figure 8-9.

Press	↵

```
A:B7: (T) [W13] +TOTAL>25000                                              POINT
Enter criteria range: A:B6..A:B7

 B     A      B          C         D    E       F       G       H       I
 6    568 SPROUT     AL          3   5,950   5,950   6,450   6,450   24,800
 7    123 LYLIE      SUSAN       1   7,800   7,800   7,800   8,580   31,980
 8    390 CHIN       TOMMY       2   5,000   5,000   5,200   5,200   20,400
 9    576 JOHNSON    ERNEST      1   8,000   8,000   8,800   8,800   33,600
10    898 VALETTI    GEORGE      3   5,900   5,900   6,300   6,300   24,400
11    239 ARMOUR     CYNTHIA     2   5,200   5,200   5,400   5,400   21,200
A    A         B             C           D           E          F
6           TOTAL
7           +TOTAL>25000
8
9   OUTPUT RANGE
10                      LAST NAME   FIRST NAME    TOTAL
11
                                                             CAP
```

Figure 8-9

Cells B6 and B7 define the criteria.

Performing a Find

The **Find** command highlights each record that satisfies the criteria. To determine whether the criteria has been specified correctly, you can use the following steps to perform a "Find" that will locate and highlight the records in the database that match the criteria.

To perform the **F**ind procedure:

Select Find

The first record that should be highlighted is that of SUSAN LYLIE on row 7. Since her salary total is $31,980, the criteria is satisfied.

To move to the next record that matches the criteria:

Press ↓

The record of SANDRA JOHNSON should be highlighted because the salary total is $34,400 and this amount matches the criteria.

To move to the next record that matches the criteria:

Press ↓

The record for ERNEST JOHNSON is highlighted.

Press ↓

The record for NINA JONES is highlighted.

Press ↓

Lotus 1-2-3 "beeps" when no more records that satisfy the criteria are in the database (not because Nina Jones is the last record in this database table).

To exit from "FIND" mode:

Press ↵

The Data Query menu should be visible at the top of the screen.

Specifying the Output Range

To specify the Output range:

Select Output

Move the cell pointer to cell A:C10

Type .

Move the cell pointer to cell E10

When the output range is highlighted, your screen should look like Figure 8-10.

Press ⏎

```
A:E10: ^TOTAL                                                          POINT
Enter output range: A:C10..A:E10

  B     A     B          C         D    E       F       G       H       I
  6    568 SPROUT     AL           3  5,950   5,950   6,450   6,450   24,800
  7    123 LYLIE      SUSAN        1  7,800   7,800   7,800   8,580   31,980
  8    390 CHIN       TOMMY        2  5,000   5,000   5,200   5,200   20,400
  9    576 JOHNSON    ERNEST       1  8,000   8,000   8,800   8,800   33,600
 10    898 VALETTI    GEORGE       3  5,900   5,900   6,300   6,300   24,400
 11    239 ARMOUR     CYNTHIA      2  5,200   5,200   5,400   5,400   21,200
 A       A        B          C          D          E          F
 6             TOTAL
 7         +TOTAL>25000
 8
 9   OUTPUT RANGE
10                         LAST NAME   FIRST NAME   TOTAL
11
                                                          CAP
```

Figure 8-10

Extracting (Copying) the Desired Data Fields to the Output Range

After the **I**nput range, the **C**riteria range, and the **O**utput range were specified in the **D**ata **Q**uery menu, the **F**ind option verified that the **C**riteria was set correctly. 1-2-3 located only the records in the database (**I**nput range) that matched the criteria. The records that match the criteria can be copied to the area below the specified **O**utput range using the **E**xtract menu option. Only the fields specified in the **O**utput range will be copied. Note that although the menu option you will use is **E**xtract, the records are not really **extracted**—they are **copied**; in other words, the records are **not** omitted from the original database table.

To copy the records that satisfy the criteria to the output range:

Select Extract

To view the extracted data:

Select Quit

Move the cell pointer to cell A:A15

The last name, first name, and total are now listed for the specified records. Your worksheet should look like Figure 8-11.

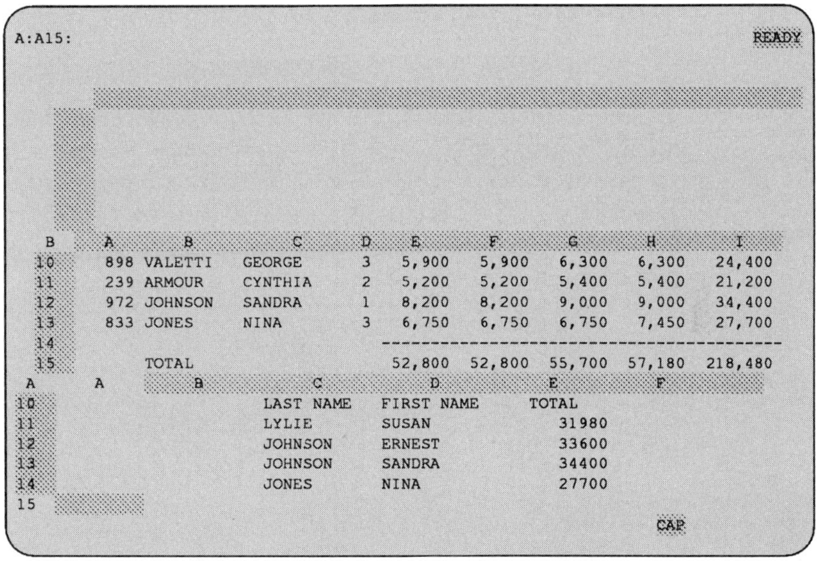

```
A:A15:                                                              READY

    B    A      B          C          D    E        F        G        H        I
   10   898 VALETTI    GEORGE         3   5,900    5,900    6,300    6,300   24,400
   11   239 ARMOUR     CYNTHIA        2   5,200    5,200    5,400    5,400   21,200
   12   972 JOHNSON    SANDRA         1   8,200    8,200    9,000    9,000   34,400
   13   833 JONES      NINA           3   6,750    6,750    6,750    7,450   27,700
   14                                     ----------------------------------------
   15       TOTAL                         52,800   52,800   55,700   57,180  218,480
  A       A        B          C              D              E          F
  10                       LAST NAME     FIRST NAME       TOTAL
  11                       LYLIE         SUSAN               31980
  12                       JOHNSON       ERNEST              33600
  13                       JOHNSON       SANDRA              34400
  14                       JONES         NINA                27700
  15
                                                          CAP
```

Figure 8-11

Querying with Multiple Conditions Using #AND#

In this exercise, you will modify the criteria used in the previous exercise so that the criteria contain multiple conditions. The database table in File ABCSAL will be queried to find records for individuals who have a total salary between $20,000 and $22,000, including any salaries that are exactly $20,000 or $22,000. To perform this query, the logical operator #AND# will be used to combine two conditions.

Assuming you have just completed the previous exercise and the results are still visible on your screen, complete the following problem.

Changing the Current Criteria to the Desired Criteria

In this exercise you will change the current criteria from +TOTAL>25000 to +TOTAL>=20000#AND#TOTAL<=22000. To change the criteria:

Move the cell pointer to cell A:B7

Type +TOTAL>=20000#AND#TOTAL<=22000

Press ↵

(The **first** line of the criteria (in cell B6—TOTAL) should remain the same.)

To make sure TOTAL still appears in cell B6:

Move	the cell pointer to cell B6.

To see the entire formula, column B could be widened using the **W**orksheet **C**olumn **S**et-Width command sequence. This step is optional. The entire formula in the criteria does not have to be visible on the screen in order to perform a query. The entire formula can be viewed by placing the cell pointer in cell B7 and looking at the control panel, which shows the contents of a highlighted cell. Assuming that the cell pointer is in cell B7, your screen should look like Figure 8-12.

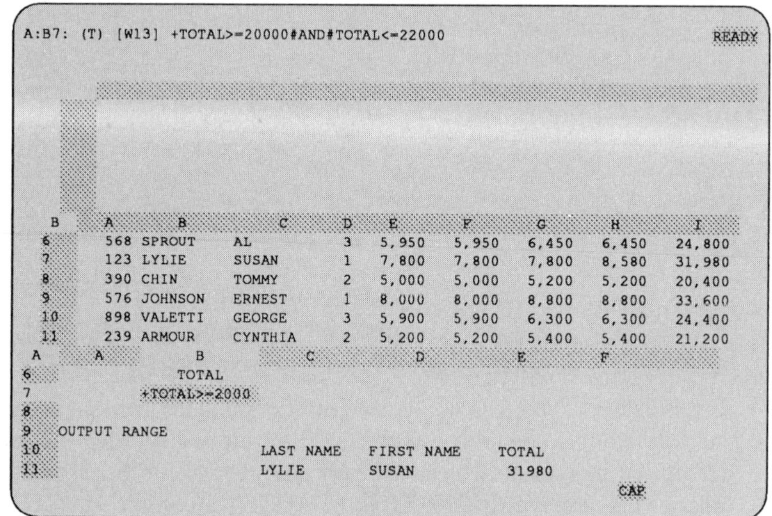

Figure 8-12

The output range, input range, and criteria range were set and remain the same. Although the criteria now being used are different, the **range** where the criteria are located is the same. To perform the query extract with the new criteria:

Press	/
Select	Data
Select	Query
Select	Extract

To view the data that has been extracted:

Select	Quit
Move	the cell pointer to cell A:A15

The desired data is now listed. Note that the data in the output range from the previous exercise using **D**ata **Q**uery **E**xtract was deleted completely and replaced with the data for the current **D**ata **Q**uery **E**xtract.

Your screen should look like Figure 8-13.

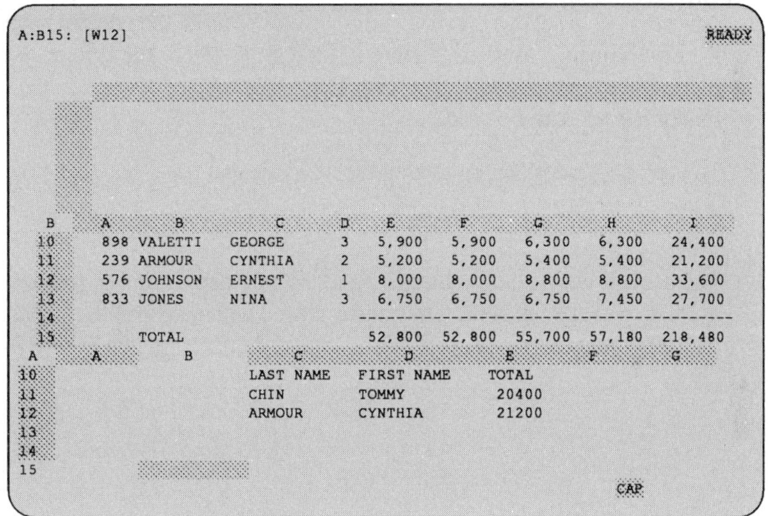

Figure 8-13

Querying with Multiple Conditions Using #OR# and Using the Query F7 Key

In this exercise, the database table ABCSAL will be queried to find individuals that have a salary less than $22,000 or greater than $30,000 using the logical operator #OR#. You will use the QUERY key (the F7 function key) rather than the **D**ata **Q**uery **E**xtract command sequence.

Changing the Current Criteria to the Desired Criteria

In this exercise, the current criteria will be changed from +TOTAL>=20000#AND#TOTAL<=22000 to +TOTAL<22000#OR#TOTAL>30000.

To change the criteria:

Move the cell pointer to cell A:B7

Type +TOTAL<22000#OR#TOTAL>30000

Press ↵

(The **first** line of the criteria (in cell B6—TOTAL) will remain the same.) Column B can be widened to see the entire formula using the **W**orksheet **C**olumn **S**et-Width command sequence. This step is optional. Because the same **O**utput range, **I**nput range, and **C**riteria range that were set in a previous exercise will be used, they do not have to be reset. Although the criteria being used are different, the **range** where the criteria are located is the same. Instead of executing the **D**ata **Q**uery **E**xtract command sequence, the QUERY key (the F7 function key), can be used.

To perform a query extract using the new criteria:

Press F7

The desired data are now listed. Note that the data from the previous **D**ata **Q**uery **E**xtract exercise was deleted completely and replaced with data for the current query. Assuming that the cell pointer is in cell A15. Your screen should look like Figure 8-14.

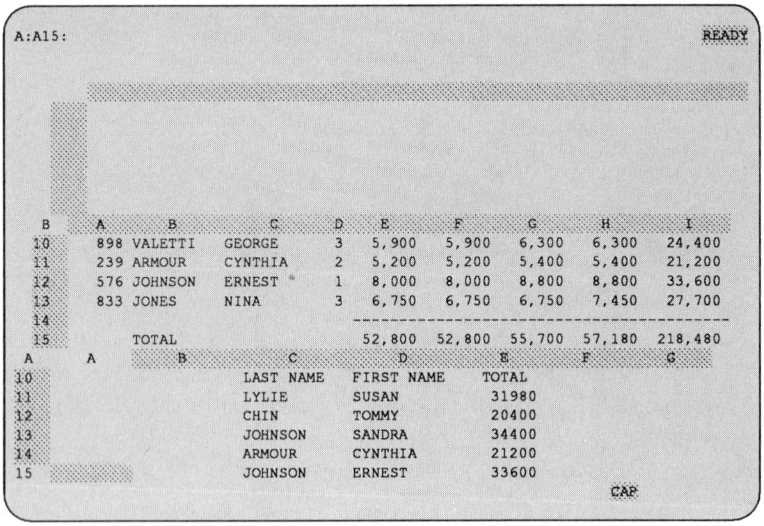

```
A:A15:                                                                 READY

 B      A    B         C         D    E       F       G       H       I
 10   898 VALETTI   GEORGE       3   5,900   5,900   6,300   6,300   24,400
 11   239 ARMOUR    CYNTHIA      2   5,200   5,200   5,400   5,400   21,200
 12   576 JOHNSON   ERNEST       1   8,000   8,000   8,800   8,800   33,600
 13   833 JONES     NINA         3   6,750   6,750   6,750   7,450   27,700
 14                                  --------------------------------------
 15       TOTAL                     52,800  52,800  55,700  57,180  218,480
A     A        B          C               D           E          F        G
10                     LAST NAME    FIRST NAME     TOTAL
11                     LYLIE        SUSAN          31980
12                     CHIN         TOMMY          20400
13                     JOHNSON      SANDRA         34400
14                     ARMOUR       CYNTHIA        21200
15                     JOHNSON      ERNEST         33600
                                                               CAP
```

Figure 8-14

Querying with Multiple Criteria

In this exercise, you will query the ABCSAL database table to find the records for individuals who have a salary less than $25,000 and who are also in DIVISION 3. It is assumed that the results of the previous exercise are still displayed on your screen.

Changing the Current Criteria to the Desired Criteria

In this exercise, the current criteria +TOTAL<22000#OR#TOTAL>30000 will be changed to +TOTAL<25000 and will serve as the **first** criteria. A **second** criteria (DIV equal 3) will appear in cells C6 and C7, respectively.

To change the criteria under TOTAL:

Move the cell pointer to cell A:B7

Type +TOTAL<25000

Press ↵

(The **first** line of the criteria (in cell A:B6—TOTAL) will remain the same.)

To place the new criteria on worksheet A:

Move the cell pointer to cell A:C6

Press /

Select Copy

When prompted for the range to copy FROM:

Press Esc

Move the cell pointer to cell B:D5

Press ↵

When prompted for the range to copy TO:

Press ↵

The field name for division (DIV) now appears in cell A:C6. To enter the specific value to be used:

Move the cell pointer to cell A:C7

Type 3

Press ↵

To specify the proper criteria for the query:

Press /

Select Data

Select Query

Select Criteria

Notice that only the criteria in column B (cells B6 and B7) are highlighted from a previous exercise. Since you placed new criteria in cells C6 and C7, these cells need to be highlighted before performing the extract.

To include the new criteria in the **C**riteria **R**ange setting:

Press →

Cells B6, B7, C6, and C7 should be highlighted. These cells contain the criteria displayed in Figure 8-15. The results of the previous **D**ata **Q**uery **E**xtract are still visible on the screen.

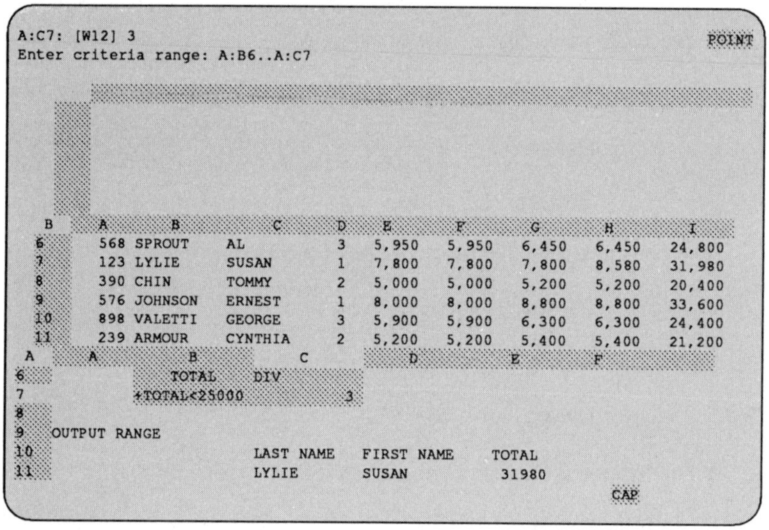

```
A:C7: [W12] 3                                                          POINT
Enter criteria range: A:B6..A:C7

  B     A    B           C          D    E       F       G       H       I
  6    568 SPROUT      AL           3   5,950   5,950   6,450   6,450   24,800
  7    123 LYLIE       SUSAN        1   7,800   7,800   7,800   8,580   31,980
  8    390 CHIN        TOMMY        2   5,000   5,000   5,200   5,200   20,400
  9    576 JOHNSON     ERNEST       1   8,000   8,000   8,800   8,800   33,600
 10    898 VALETTI     GEORGE       3   5,900   5,900   6,300   6,300   24,400
 11    239 ARMOUR      CYNTHIA      2   5,200   5,200   5,400   5,400   21,200
 A      A          B          C            D             E         F
 6               TOTAL      DIV
 7               +TOTAL<25000           3
 8
 9   OUTPUT RANGE
10                          LAST NAME   FIRST NAME    TOTAL
11                          LYLIE       SUSAN          31980
                                                              CAP
```

Figure 8-15

To accept cells B6..C7 as the **C**riteria range:

Press ↵

To perform the query extract:

Select Extract

Select Quit

The data for the designated criteria now should be listed. Assuming you place the cell pointer in cell A:C13, your screen should look like Figure 8-16.

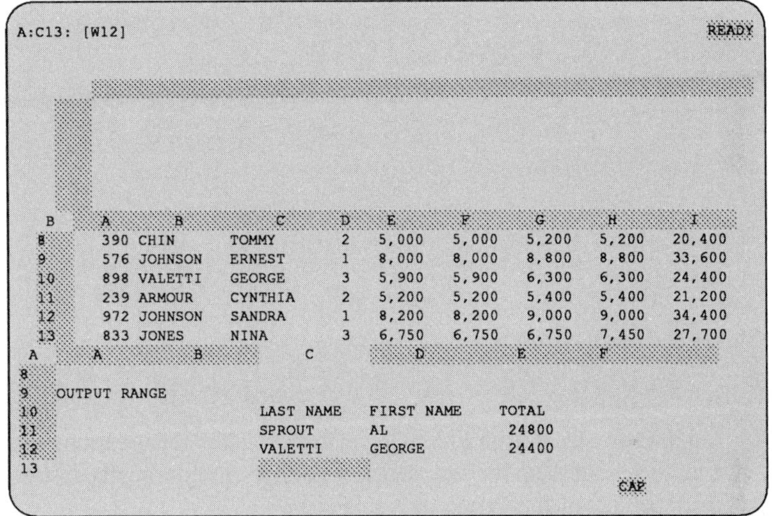

Figure 8-16

■ CREATING A COMPUTED COLUMN IN THE OUTPUT RANGE

In some situations, you may need to complete a computation on extracted data. You can accomplish such a task using the capability provided by 1-2-3 for placing a computed column in the output range.

Before completing this exercise, you need to erase cells C11 through E12 and modify the output range so your screen looks like Figure 8-17. Change the criteria in cell B7 to +TOTAL>25000.

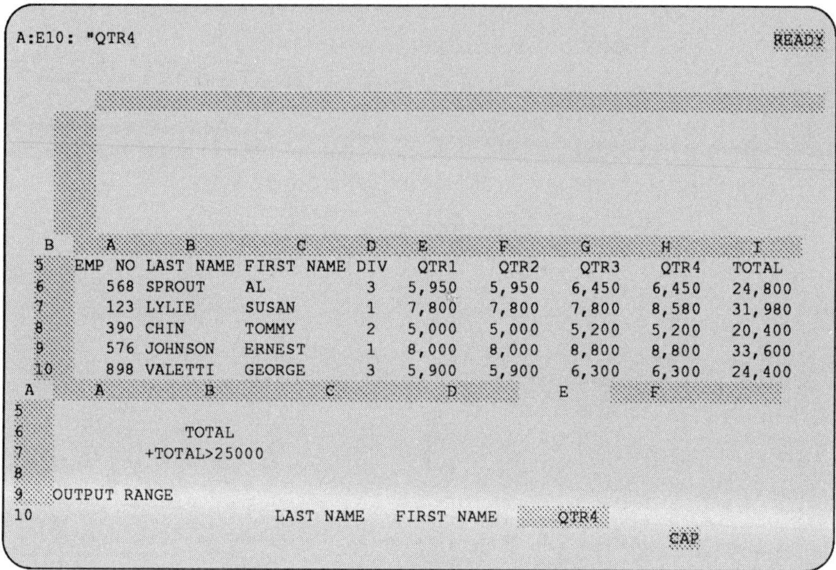

Figure 8-17

Suppose you want to provide a bonus to those individuals earning more than $25,000 for the year to reward them for their superior performance during the last year. The bonus is equal to 10 percent of fourth quarter's salary.

To add a column that will calculate the amount of the bonus for those employees:

Move the cell pointer to cell A:F10

Type +QTR4*.1

Press ↵

The characters ERR appear in cell F10, because a range name does not exist for QTR4. This is acceptable in the criteria range because QTR4 is a field name in the input range. Use the **R**ange **F**ormat **T**ext command sequence so you can see the expression on your screen rather than ERR. You will also need to set the column width for column F to 10.

Your screen should look like Figure 8-18.

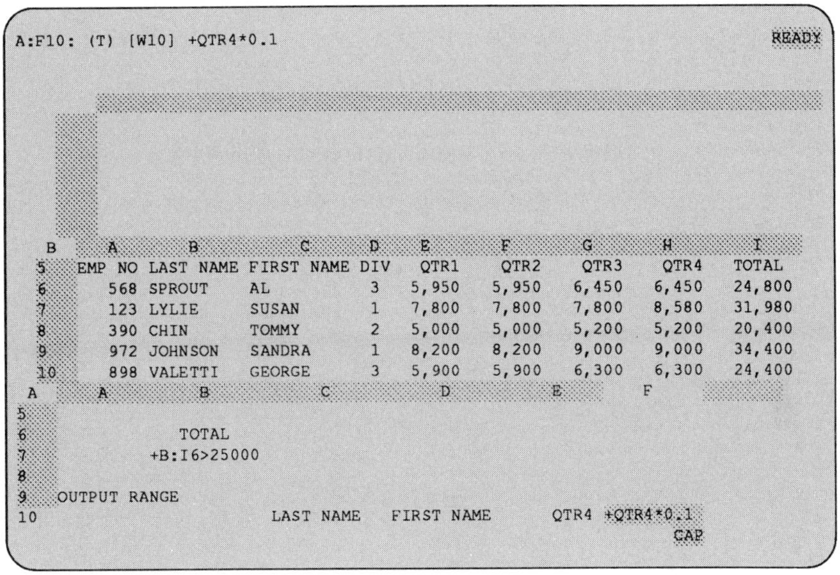

```
A:F10: (T) [W10] +QTR4*0.1                                                  READY

 B      A       B         C        D     E       F       G       H        I
 5  EMP NO LAST NAME FIRST NAME DIV   QTR1    QTR2    QTR3    QTR4    TOTAL
 6     568 SPROUT    AL           3  5,950   5,950   6,450   6,450   24,800
 7     123 LYLIE     SUSAN        1  7,800   7,800   7,800   8,580   31,980
 8     390 CHIN      TOMMY        2  5,000   5,000   5,200   5,200   20,400
 9     972 JOHNSON   SANDRA       1  8,200   8,200   9,000   9,000   34,400
10     898 VALETTI   GEORGE       3  5,900   5,900   6,300   6,300   24,400
 A       A         B          C          D          E         F
 5
 6              TOTAL
 7           +B:I6>25000
 8
 9  OUTPUT RANGE
10                        LAST NAME   FIRST NAME       QTR4 +QTR4*0.1
                                                                  CAP
```

Figure 8-18

To complete the query using the computed column:

Press	/
Select	Data
Select	Query

Define the Input range as cells B:A5 through B:I13 and the Criteria range as cells A:B6 through A:B7.

To include the computed column in the output range:

Select	Output
Move	the cell pointer to cell A:C10
Type	.
Move	the cell pointer to cell A:F10
Press	↵

To calculate the information for the computed column:

Select	Extract

To see the results:

Select Quit

Move the cell pointer to cell A:F15

Notice that the 745 appearing in cell A:F14 is 10 percent of Nina Jones' fourth quarter salary. Your screen should look like Figure 8-19.

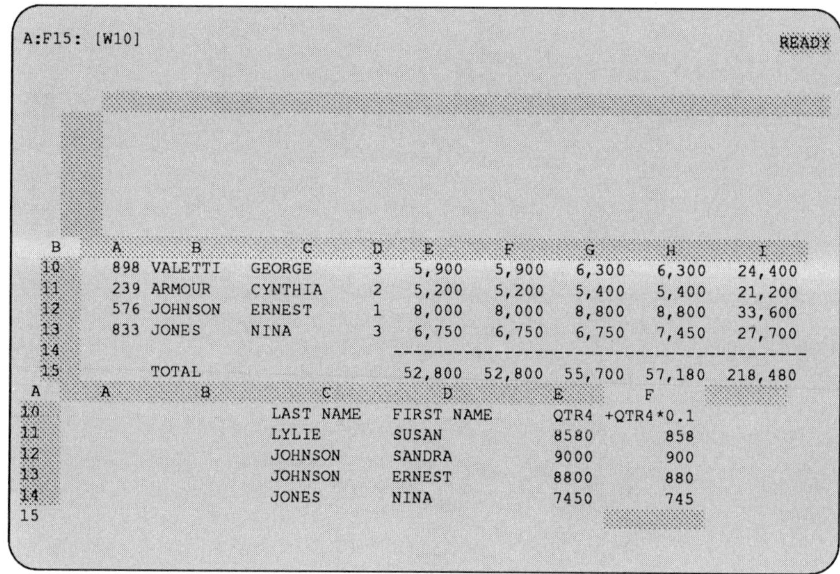

Figure 8-19

■ USEFUL DATA QUERY OPTIONS

In this section, you will use the **Data Query Unique** and the **Data Query Delete** command sequences.

Using the Query Unique Command

You will continue to use the database table in the file ABCSAL with the results of the previous exercise. For the purposes of this exercise, use these instructions to alter the file so that it has a duplicate record.

Move the cell pointer to cell B:A9

To insert a row:

Press /

Select Worksheet

Select Insert

Select Row

Press ↵

To copy Al Sprout's record from row 6 to row 9:

Move the cell pointer to cell B:A6

Press /

Select Copy

When prompted for the range to copy FROM:

Move the cell pointer to cell B:I6

Cells A6 through I6 should be highlighted.

Press ↵

When prompted for the range to copy TO:

Move the cell pointer to cell B:A9

Press ↵

To modify the current criteria so Sprout will be selected:

Move the cell pointer to cell A:B7

Type +TOTAL<25000

Press ↵

To execute a query:

Move to cell A:B15

Press F7

Your screen should look like Figure 8-20.

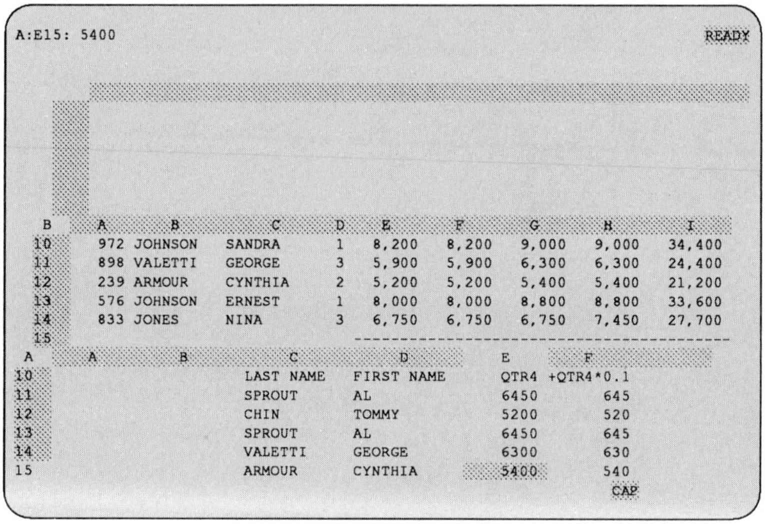

```
A:E15: 5400                                                                    READY

 B      A         B              C         D     E        F        G        H        I
 10    972 JOHNSON    SANDRA        1    8,200    8,200    9,000    9,000    34,400
 11    898 VALETTI    GEORGE        3    5,900    5,900    6,300    6,300    24,400
 12    239 ARMOUR     CYNTHIA       2    5,200    5,200    5,400    5,400    21,200
 13    576 JOHNSON    ERNEST        1    8,000    8,000    8,800    8,800    33,600
 14    833 JONES      NINA          3    6,750    6,750    6,750    7,450    27,700
 15                                     -----------------------------------------
A       A          B           C              D                 E          F
10                        LAST NAME    FIRST NAME         QTR4  +QTR4*0.1
11                        SPROUT       AL                 6450          645
12                        CHIN         TOMMY              5200          520
13                        SPROUT       AL                 6450          645
14                        VALETTI      GEORGE             6300          630
15                        ARMOUR       CYNTHIA            5400          540
                                                                       CAP
```

Figure 8-20

Because the record for Al Sprout was duplicated in the database, the name Al Sprout appears twice in the output range. By using the following command one of the duplicate records will be deleted from the output range.

Press /

Select Data

Select Query

Select Unique

To leave the Data menu:

Select Quit

Al Sprout appears in the output range only once. Your screen should look like Figure 8-21.

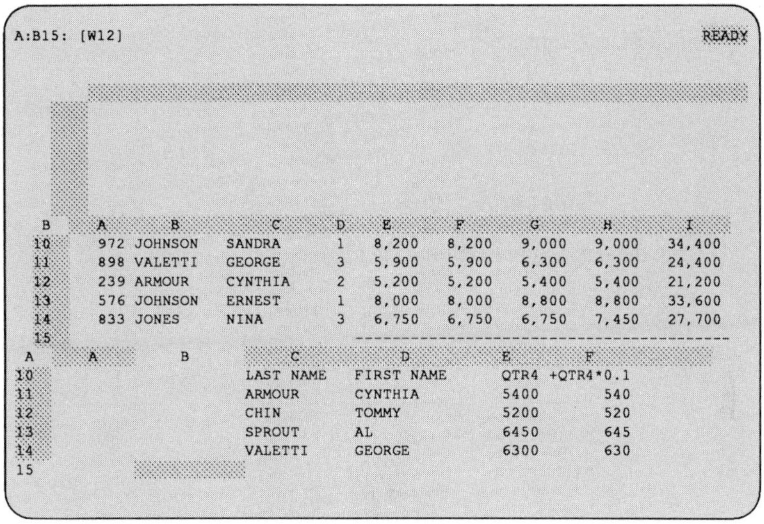

```
A:B15: [W12]                                                                  READY

 B    A       B            C          D    E        F        G        H        I
 10     972 JOHNSON    SANDRA        1    8,200    8,200    9,000    9,000   34,400
 11     898 VALETTI    GEORGE        3    5,900    5,900    6,300    6,300   24,400
 12     239 ARMOUR     CYNTHIA       2    5,200    5,200    5,400    5,400   21,200
 13     576 JOHNSON    ERNEST        1    8,000    8,000    8,800    8,800   33,600
 14     833 JONES      NINA          3    6,750    6,750    6,750    7,450   27,700
 15                                  ---------------------------------------------
A     A          B           C            D                E          F
10                           LAST NAME    FIRST NAME       QTR4  +QTR4*0.1
11                           ARMOUR       CYNTHIA          5400        540
12                           CHIN         TOMMY            5200        520
13                           SPROUT       AL               6450        645
14                           VALETTI      GEORGE           6300        630
15
```

Figure 8-21

Note that this option does **not** delete duplicate records in the database itself, only in the output range. Al Sprout's record still appears twice in the database.

Using the Query Delete Command

In this exercise you will use the **D**ata **Q**uery **D**elete command. This command is **extremely powerful**, because it **deletes all records in the database that MATCH the criteria.** To make this change permanent on the ABCSAL file, you would perform a **F**ile **S**ave. However, in this case, you will not save the file. In this example, all individuals in the file ABCSAL that earn less than $25,000 will be deleted from the database. It is assumed that you have just completed the previous exercise:

To delete the records that satisfy the criteria:

Press	/
Select	Data
Select	Query
Select	Delete

The **C**ancel **D**elete menu appears so that you are given a chance to cancel this command or go ahead and delete the records.

To complete the process:

Select Delete

To leave the current menu:

Select Quit

To see the database table after the records for individuals with salaries less than $25,000:

Move the cell pointer to cell B:A5

Your screen should look like Figure 8-22.

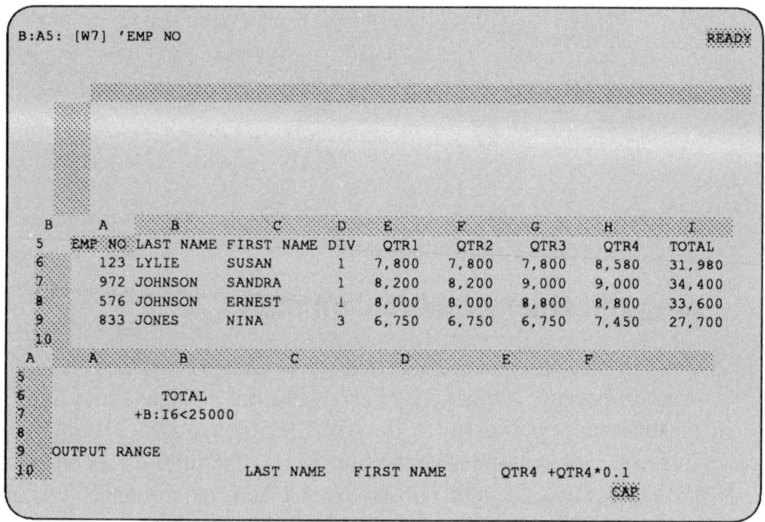

Figure 8-22

SUMMARY

In Lotus 1-2-3, a spreadsheet may be set up as a database, or a collection of related records. The **Data Sort** command sequence can sort records in a database with up to 256 sort keys chosen by the user. The **Data Query** can perform a query upon a database according to the criteria you specify. You must specify the database range, indicate the criteria, and may even specify an output range for the desired data. You can create a computed column based on specific criteria. Additional **Data Query** options allow you to delete duplicate records in an output range and also to delete specified records in a database (**Unique** and **Delete**).

KEY CONCEPTS

#AND#
#OR#
Criteria
Data Query Delete
Data Query Extract
Data Query Find
Data Query Unique
Data Range
Data Sort
Database
Database table
Extra-Key
Field
Field title
File
Input range
Key
Output range
Primary Key
Query
QUERY key (the F7 key)
Record
Secondary Key

CHAPTER EIGHT
EXERCISE 1

INSTRUCTIONS: Circle T if the statement is true and F if the statement is false.

T F 1. When sorting a database in Lotus 1-2-3, the data-range must include the field titles.

T F 2. The field titles must be located in the line directly above the first record of the database for the **D**ata **Q**uery command sequence to work properly.

T F 3. It is appropriate to have more than one line consisting of field titles designated in the input range.

T F 4. Each criteria consists of two cells (a field title and the actual criteria).

T F 5. The input range, criteria, and output range must be manually set up on the worksheet and then identified through the menu options.

T F 6. The output range allows you to copy the desired fields that match the criteria to another area on the worksheet.

T F 7. When designating the output range, you may highlight only the field names that are desired; the records will appear directly below the field names on the worksheet in the output range when the **Q**uery **F**ind is executed.

T F 8. The QUERY key allows you to perform a query based upon previously set ranges.

T F 9. The criteria for a worksheet can be set by setting the bin range.

T F 10. The **Q**uery **U**nique command deletes multiple records in a database.

CHAPTER EIGHT
EXERCISE 2
Sorting Records Using the Primary Key

INSTRUCTIONS: Create the file PERSON. Use Figure 8-23 as a guide.

Column A is 18 characters wide.

Column B is 11 characters wide.

Column C is 14 characters wide.

Column D is 5 characters wide.

```
A:A1: [W18]                                                    READY

A          A               B          C           D     E       F
1                      ABC COMPANY
2
3
4
5      LAST NAME       FIRST NAME       CITY      STATE
6   ADAMS              JOSEPH      NEW YORK       NY
7   AARON              SANDRA      SAN ANTONIO    TX
8   ADAMS              JENNIFER    NEW YORK       NY
9   FERNANDEZ          JOE         MIAMI          FL
10  NGUYEN             ALFRED      SAN ANTONIO    TX
11  ADAMS              CHARLES     SAN ANTONIO    TX
12  CERNOSKY           ELENA       MIAMI          FL
13  NOLAN              RYAN        NEW YORK       NY
14
15
```

Figure 8-23

Sort the data in the file PERSON in alphabetical order by city.

Print the worksheet with the properly sorted data.

CHAPTER EIGHT
EXERCISE 3
Sorting Records Using Primary and Secondary Keys

INSTRUCTIONS: Sort the last names in the file PERSON in alphabetical order by city. (Exercise 4 will place Joseph and Jennifer Adams in the proper order by first name).

Print the worksheet with the properly sorted data.

CHAPTER EIGHT
EXERCISE 4
Sorting Records Using an Extra Sort Key

INSTRUCTIONS: Assuming that Exercise 3 has just been completed, notice that Joseph Adams and Jennifer Adams from the city of New York are not in the proper order. To place these names in order:

Sort the data using an extra sort key so the names are in proper order.

Print the worksheet with the properly sorted data.

CHAPTER EIGHT
EXERCISE 5
Querying Records Using One Criteria

INSTRUCTIONS: Retrieve the original file PERSON for use in this exercise.

Create the appropriate criteria to extract only individuals living in Miami, FL.

For the output range, extract the person's last name and first name.

Place the criteria and output range on a separate worksheet. Extract the data for the city of Miami.

Print the worksheet with the database table and the worksheet containing the extracted data.

CHAPTER EIGHT
EXERCISE 6
Querying Records Using Two Criteria

INSTRUCTIONS: Retrieve the original file PERSON for use in this exercise.

Create the appropriate criteria to extract only those individuals living in New York, NY or San Antonio, TX.

For the output range, extract the person's last name, first name, city and state.

Place the criteria and output range on a separate worksheet. Extract the data for those individuals living in New York or San Antonio.

Print the worksheet with the database table and the worksheet containing the extracted data.

CHAPTER EIGHT
EXERCISE 7
Querying with Multiple Criteria

INSTRUCTIONS: Retrieve the original file PERSON for use in this exercise.

Create the appropriate criteria to extract only those individuals having a last name of Adams who live in New York, NY.

For the output range, extract the person's last name and first name.

Place the criteria and the output range on a separate worksheet. Extract the data for the persons with the last name Adams who live in New York.

Print the worksheet with the database table and the worksheet containing the extracted data.

CHAPTER EIGHT
EXERCISE 8
Using a Computed Column

INSTRUCTIONS: Retrieve the file SALES you created in Chapter 2.

Suppose you want to provide a bonus to those individuals who sold more than $4,000. The bonus is equal to 2% of the sales amount.

Create a "computed column" to calculate the bonus.

For those individuals having sales greater than $4,000, output their name, sales amount and the computed bonus.

Place the criteria, output range and computed bonus on a separate worksheet.

Print the worksheet with the database table. Also, print the worksheet containing the extracted data and computed column.

CHAPTER NINE

ADVANCED DATABASE CAPABILITIES

OBJECTIVES

In this chapter, you will learn to:

- Fill cells with sequences of data
- Create data tables
- Query an External Database
- Create a Frequency Distribution
- Graph a Frequency Distribution

CHAPTER OVERVIEW

In the last chapter, you learned some of the basic database features available in 1-2-3. You will expand your knowledge of the database capabilities in this chapter. You will learn to fill cells with specific sequences of data, create data tables for use in decision-making situations, use data created by an external database management system, combine information using multiple database tables and create and graph a frequency distribution.

FILLING CELLS WITH DATA

In many situations, you may need to enter a sequence of numbers, dates or times on a worksheet. 1-2-3 facilitates the input of such data using the **Data Fill** command sequence to enter data into various cells on a worksheet as well as multiple worksheets.

Entering Sequences of Numbers on a Worksheet

Suppose that you want to enter a sequence of numbers 1 through 10 into cells B6 through B15 of a worksheet. Make sure you have a blank worksheet on your screen.

To enter the sequence of numbers:

Press	/
Select	Data
Select	Fill

When you are prompted for the "fill" range:

Move	the cell pointer to cell B6
Type	.
Move	the cell pointer to cell B15

Press ↵

You have designated the set of cells B6 through B15 as the cells in which the sequence of numbers is to be placed.

When prompted for the "start" number:

Type 1

Press ↵

To indicate that the "step" value between each number in the sequence is to be the default value of 1:

Press ↵

When you are prompted for the "stop" number:

Press ↵

You accept the stop number of 8191 because the capacity of the range to be filled will limit the maximum value to less than 8191.

Your screen now should have the sequence of numbers 1 through 10 in cells B6 through B15 and look like Figure 9-1.

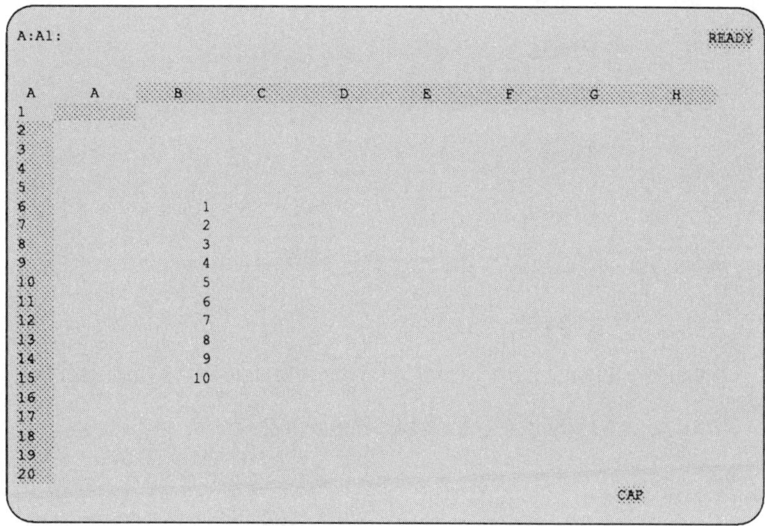

Figure 9-1

Now, suppose you are asked to enter a sequence of even numbers beginning in cell A3 and ending in cell H3.

To enter this sequence of numbers:

Press /

Select Data

Select Fill

Note that the fill range from the previous exercise is highlighted. To escape from the previously defined range:

Press [Esc]

To indicate the fill range for the present problem:

Move the cell pointer to cell A3

Type .

Move the cell pointer to cell H3

Press ↵

When prompted for the starting value:

Type 2

Press ↵

To specify that the step value is 2:

Type 2

Press ↵

When you are asked for the stopping point,

Press ↵

because you have already indicated the fill range is A3 through H3.

Your screen should now look like Figure 9-2.

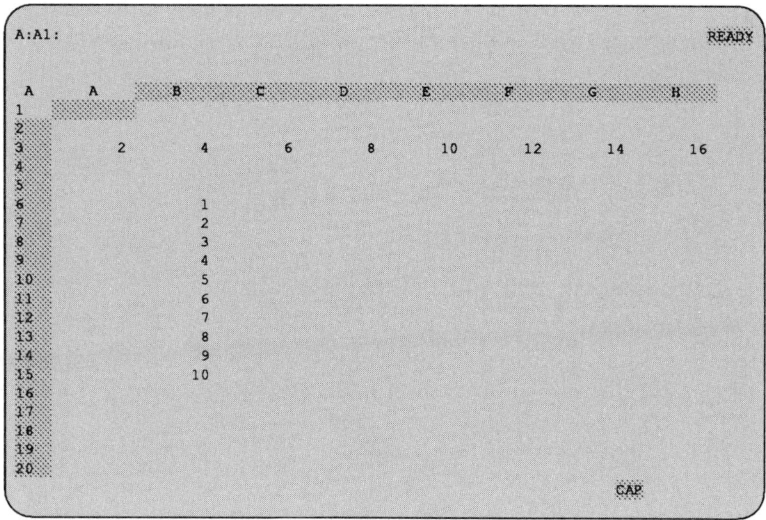

Figure 9-2

Entering a Sequence of Dates

At times, you may desire to place a series of dates on a worksheet. For example, it may be necessary to place the dates for 10 days in a column, or you may want to enter a series of dates that are a specified amount of time apart such as a week, month, or quarter.

To illustrate the process of placing a sequence of 10 days on a worksheet, first make sure that you have a blank worksheet on your screen. Then,

Press /

Select Data

Select Fill

To specify the fill range:

Move the cell pointer to cell B3

Type .

Move the cell pointer to cell B12

Press ↵

When you are asked for the starting value, you can indicate that the initial date is July 1, 1989 as follows:

Type 7/1/89

Press ↵

You could have also used 1-JUL-89.

To indicate that step value between dates is one:

Press ↵

To specify the ending date:

Type 7/10/89

Press ↵

You must enter a stop date and not use the default value of 8191.

Your screen should look like Figure 9-3.

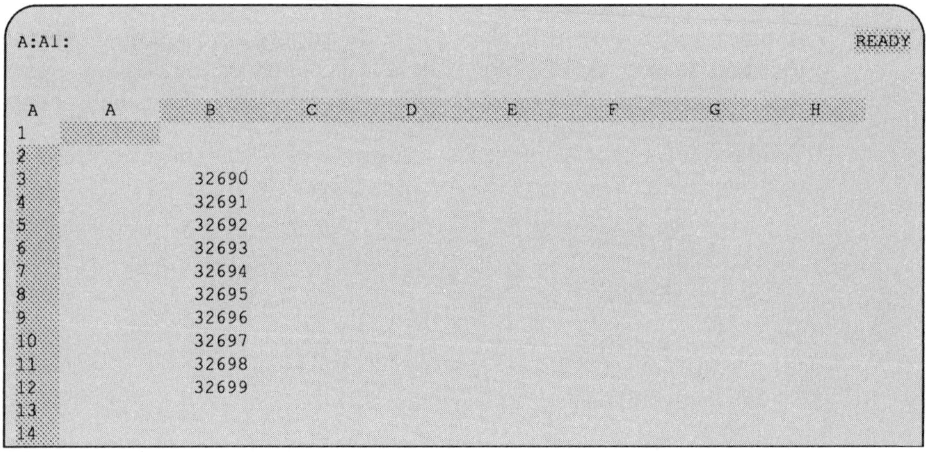

```
A:A1:                                                         READY

A      A       B       C       D       E       F       G       H
1
2
3            32690
4            32691
5            32692
6            32693
7            32694
8            32695
9            32696
10           32697
11           32698
12           32699
13
14
```

Figure 9-3

The numbers in cells B3 through B12 are called date serial numbers. Each number represents the number of days that have elapsed since December 31, 1899.

To properly format the dates:

Move the cell pointer to cell B3

Press /

Select Range

Select Format

Select Date

Select 4 (to indicate the long international format is to be used.)

Move the cell pointer to cell B12

Press ↵

The dates should now be properly formatted and your screen should look like Figure 9-4.

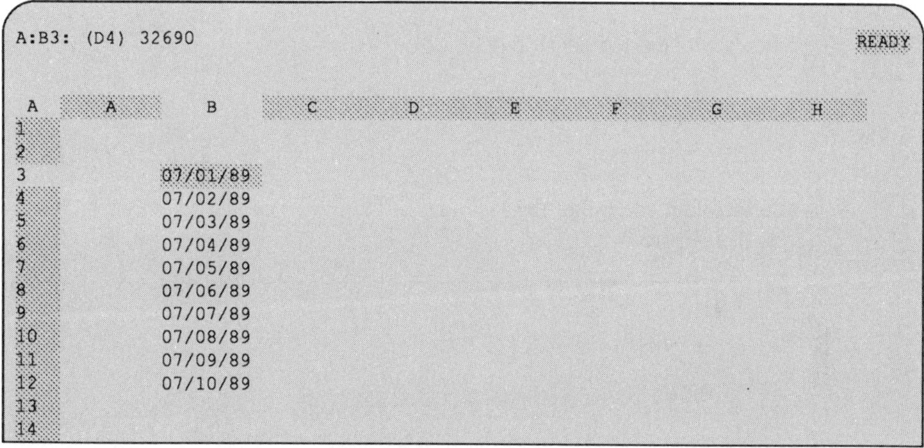

Figure 9-4

Suppose you are asked to create a worksheet in which the column headings are a series of six dates, each a week apart with the initial date being August 2 and the last date being September 6 appearing in cells B2 through G2. To place this series of dates on a worksheet, first make sure that you have a blank worksheet on your screen. Then,

Press /

Select Data

Select Fill

Press Esc

Move the cell pointer to cell B2

Type .

Move the cell pointer to cell G2

Press ↵

To indicate that August 2, 1989 is the start date:

Type 8/2/89

Press ↵

To specify that the step value is 1 week:

Type 1W

Press ↵

When prompted for the stop date,

Type 9/6/89

Press ↵

You have indicated that the last date in the sequence is September 6. Your screen should look like Figure 9-5.

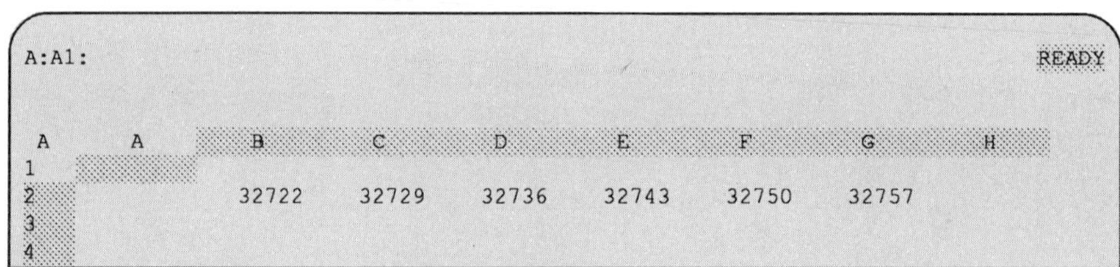

Figure 9-5

To format the data so only the month and day appear on your screen:

Move the cell pointer to cell B2

Press /

Select Range

Select Format

Select Date

Select 5

Move the cell pointer to cell G2

Press ↵

Your screen now should be properly formatted and look like Figure 9-6.

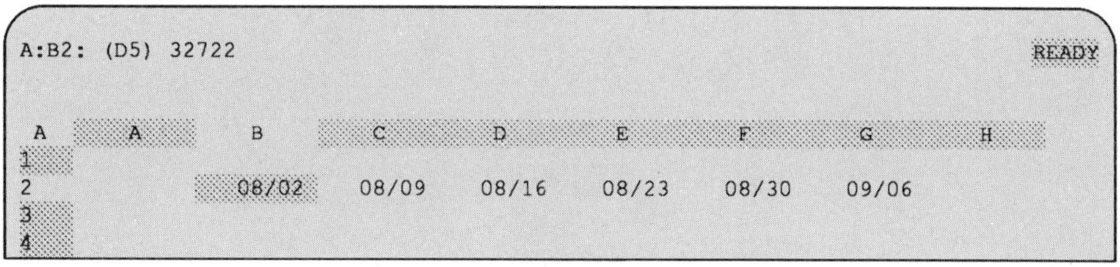

```
A:B2: (D5) 32722                                                    READY

 A      A        B        C        D        E        F        G        H
1
2             08/02    08/09    08/16    08/23    08/30    09/06
3
4
```

Figure 9-6

The various step values that you can use for dates are summarized in the following table:

Desired Increment	Step Value
Days	Integer followed by the letter D
Weeks	Integer followed by the letter W
Months	Integer followed by the letter M
Quarters	Integer followed by the letter Q
Years	Integer followed by the letter Y

Entering Sequences of Times

In the last section, you placed sequences of dates on a worksheet. Sometimes you may want to enter specific sequences of times. For example, it might be necessary to prepare a schedule with times separated by a specific time increment.

Suppose you need to prepare a daily calendar that has the sequence of times from 8:00 a.m. to 5:00 p.m. with one hour intervals between each specified time. Before creating this sequence of times, make sure that you have a blank worksheet on your screen.

To place the time sequence in cells A4 through A12:

Press /

Select Data

Select Fill

To indicate the fill range:

Move the cell pointer to cell A4

Type .

Move the cell pointer to cell A12

Press ↵

To specify the starting time:

Type 8:00 AM

Press ↵

To define the step increment as one hour:

Type 1H

Press ↵

Since you have already specified the fill range, you can:

Press ↵ when you are prompted for the stop point

A series of decimal equivalent times should appear on your screen like those in Figure 9-7.

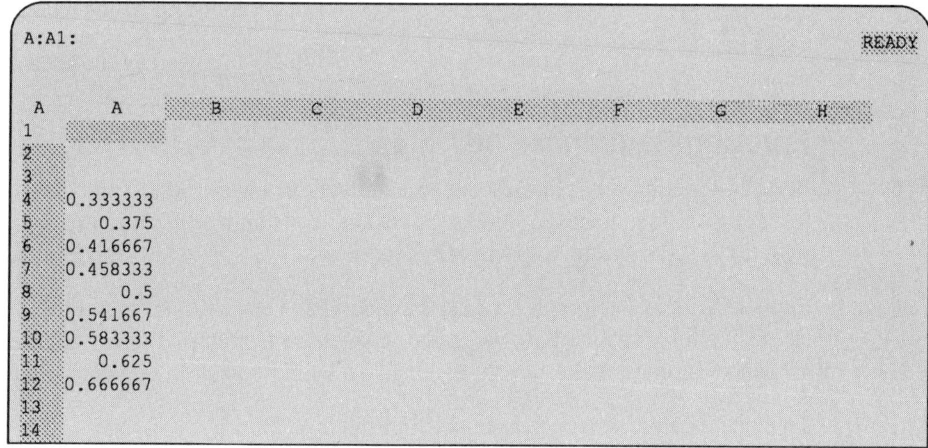

Figure 9-7

To properly format the times:

Make sure the cell pointer is in cell A4

Press /

Select Range

Select Format

Select Date

Select Time

To select the HH:MM AM/PM format option and identify the range of cells to format:

Select 2

Move the cell pointer to cell A12

Press ↵

Your screen now should look like Figure 9-8.

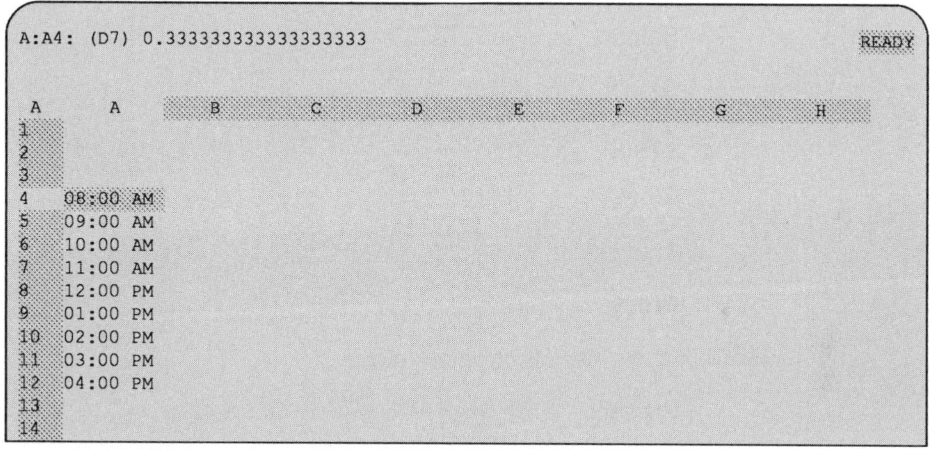

Figure 9-8

The various step values that you can use for times are summarized in the following table:

Desired Increment	Step Value
Seconds	Integer followed by the letter S
Minutes	Integer followed by the letters MIN
Hours	Integer followed by the letter H

Placing a Sequence of Data on Multiple Worksheets

In some situations, you may need to enter a sequence of data in multiple worksheets. For example, you may want to enter the month and year in a series of worksheets.

Suppose you are working on a budget and desire to use separate worksheets for individual months and want to have the month and year appear in cell A1 of a series of worksheets. Before you create the series of worksheets, make sure you have a blank worksheet on your screen.

To place information for January, 1990 through March, 1990 in worksheets A through C, you need to add two worksheets after worksheet A and display the three worksheets using the Worksheet Window Perspective command sequence.

To insert the two worksheets:

Press /

Select Worksheet

Select Insert

Select Sheet

Select After

Type 2

Press ↵

To see the three worksheets on your screen:

Press /

Select Worksheet

Select Window

Select Perspective

Your screen now should look like Figure 9-9.

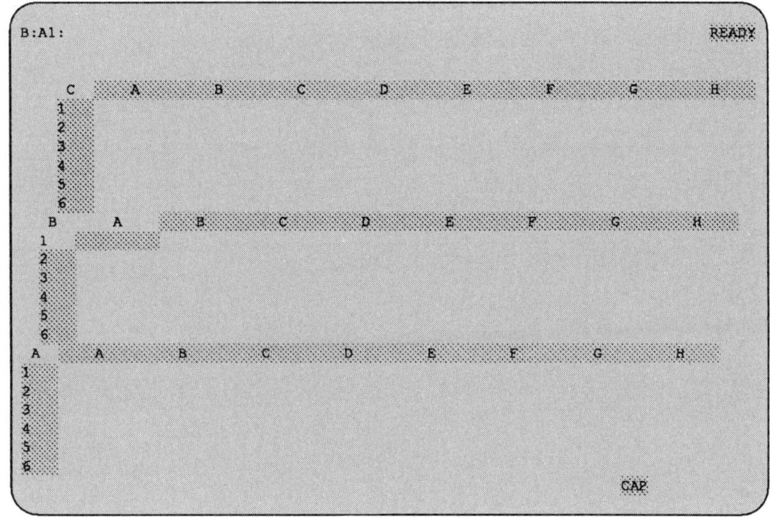

Figure 9-9

To place the monthly series of data in cell A1 of the worksheets A through C:

Move	the cell pointer to cell A:A1
Press	/
Select	Data
Select	Fill

To specify the fill range:

Type	.
Move	the cell pointer to cell C:A1 using the Ctrl-PgUp key combination
Press	↵

To indicate that the start date is January, 1990:

Type	1/1/90
Press	↵

You can define the step amount to be one month as follows:

Type	1M

To indicate that you want to stop in March, 1990:

Type 3/1/90

Press ↵

Your screen should like Figure 9-10.

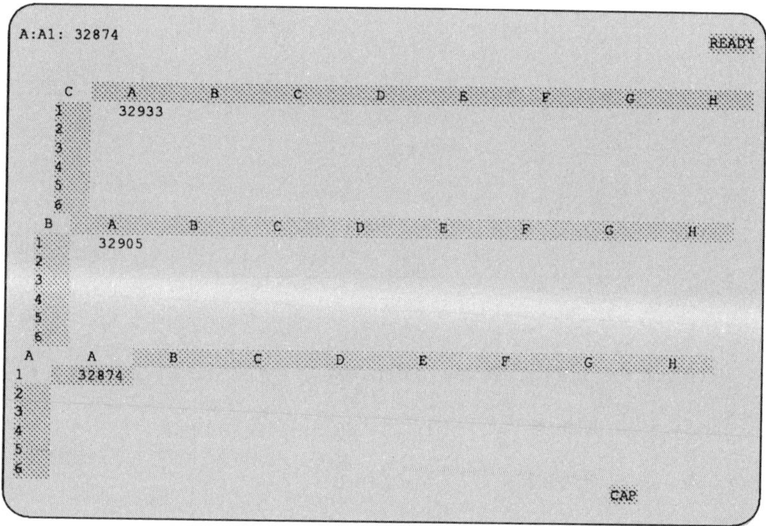

Figure 9-10

Note that the numbers appearing in the worksheets represent January 1, February 1 and March 1 of 1990.

You can then format the dates:

Press /

Select Range

Select Format

Select Date

Select 3 (for the MMM-YY format option)

When prompted to enter the range to format:

Move cell pointer to C:A1 using the Ctrl-PgUp key combination

Press ↵

The dates now are properly formatted and your screen should look like Figure 9-11.

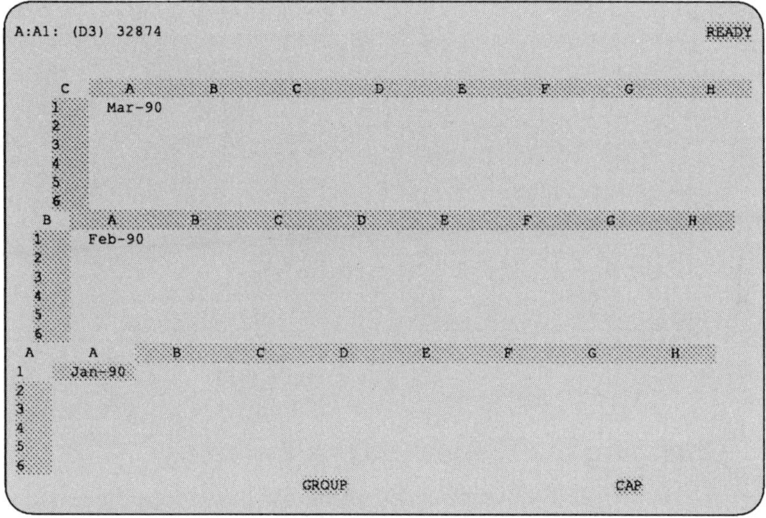

Figure 9-11

■ USING DATA TABLES

Data tables are used to illustrate the impact of changing values of variables on the results obtained when formulas are used. A classic example of the need for using a data table occurs when a person tries to evaluate the monthly payment on a loan for various principal amounts, interest rates and time periods. Another example occurs when a sales manager desires to evaluate the impact on an employee's compensation of proposed changes in quotas and commission rates.

Suppose you are considering the purchase of a new luxury automobile by borrowing the money from a bank. The variables that can change include the principal amount, interest rate and number of time periods to repay the loan. In this section, you will use the **D**ata **T**able command sequence available in 1-2-3 to evaluate the impact of changes in these loan variables.

Before using the data table options, you need to have a blank worksheet on your screen and then create a worksheet that looks like Figure 9-12.

The payment amount is computed by using the payment function, @PMT, that is available in 1-2-3. Cell A7 should have the formula +A5/12 and represents the monthly interest rate. Cell A8 should contain the formula @PMT(A4,A7,A6). Notice that since you want a monthly payment value, the annual interest rate must be converted to a monthly rate by dividing by 12. Each of the entries in the @PMT function is referred to as an argument. The three arguments, A4, A7 and A6, refer to the values used for the principal amount, interest rate and time period.

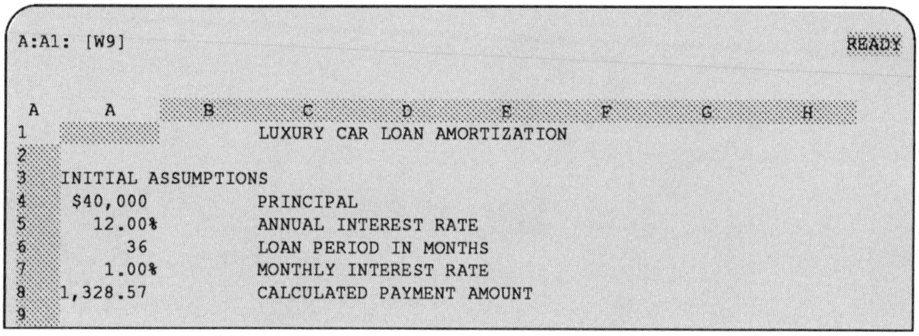

```
A:A1: [W9]                                                          READY

A       A        B        C        D        E        F        G        H
1                         LUXURY CAR LOAN AMORTIZATION
2
3   INITIAL ASSUMPTIONS
4     $40,000             PRINCIPAL
5       12.00%            ANNUAL INTEREST RATE
6          36             LOAN PERIOD IN MONTHS
7        1.00%            MONTHLY INTEREST RATE
8   1,328.57              CALCULATED PAYMENT AMOUNT
9
```

Figure 9-12

Changing the Values of One Variable

The **D**ata **T**able **1** sequence of commands can be used to change one of the variables used in computing the payment amount. Suppose you want to see the impact of changing the loan period while holding the principal amount and interest rate constant.

To construct a data table for varying the loan period:

Enter LOAN in cell A11 and PERIOD in cell A12

Enter the numbers 36, 48, 60, 72 and 84 in cells A15 through A19

You may use the **D**ata **F**ill command sequence illustrated earlier in this chapter to expedite the process for entering the loan period values that represent 3 through 7 year loan periods.

Enter PAYMENT in cell B11 and AMOUNT in cell B12

Data **T**able operations require the use of input cells. In this case the input cell will be A6 which is the loan period value. To complete the data table:

Move the cell pointer to cell B14

Type +A8

Press ↵

The payment amount for a loan period of three years appears in cell B14. This indicates to 1-2-3 that you are using the @PMT function computation that appears in cell A8. Your screen now should look like Figure 9-13.

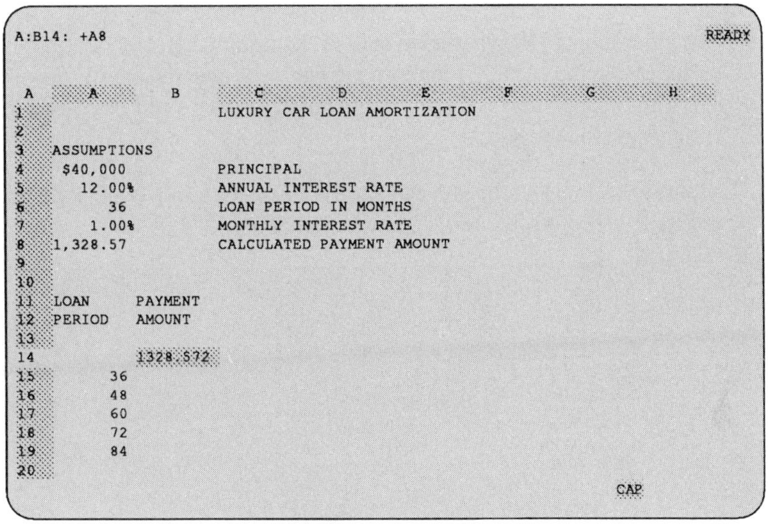

```
A:B14: +A8                                                    READY

A      A          B        C        D        E        F        G        H
1                          LUXURY CAR LOAN AMORTIZATION
2
3    ASSUMPTIONS
4     $40,000              PRINCIPAL
5       12.00%             ANNUAL INTEREST RATE
6           36             LOAN PERIOD IN MONTHS
7        1.00%             MONTHLY INTEREST RATE
8    1,328.57              CALCULATED PAYMENT AMOUNT
9
10
11   LOAN       PAYMENT
12   PERIOD     AMOUNT
13
14             1328.572
15          36
16          48
17          60
18          72
19          84
20
                                                       CAP
```

Figure 9-13

To initiate the **D**ata **T**able command sequence for varying one input variable:

Press	/
Select	Data
Select	Table
Select	1

To specify the data table range:

Move	the cell pointer to cell A14
Type	.
Move	the cell pointer to cell B19
Press	↵

When prompted for the input cell:

Move	the cell pointer to cell A6
Press	↵

The values for the loan period in cells A15 through A19 will be substituted for the loan period parameter in the @PMT function one at a time and a value for the payment amount will be determined. In a few seconds, the payment amounts will be placed in column B next to the loan period numbers.

You now can format the values in cell B14 through B19 using the **R**ange **F**ormat, command sequence so your screen looks like Figure 9-14.

```
A:B14: (,2) +A8                                                    READY

A       A         B       C        D        E        F        G        H
1                         LUXURY CAR LOAN AMORTIZATION
2
3   ASSUMPTIONS
4    $40,000              PRINCIPAL
5      12.00%             ANNUAL INTEREST RATE
6          36             LOAN PERIOD IN MONTHS
7       1.00%             MONTHLY INTEREST RATE
8   1,328.57              CALCULATED PAYMENT AMOUNT
9
10
11  LOAN        PAYMENT
12  PERIOD      AMOUNT
13
14             1,328.57
15          36 1,328.57
16          48 1,053.35
17          60   889.78
18          72   782.01
19          84   706.11
20
                                                              CAP
```

Figure 9-14

As expected, the payment amount decreases as the loan period increases.

Using the Data Table 1 Command Sequence with Several Formulas

1-2-3 permits you to substitute the value of the input cell in more than one formula. For example, you may want to set up a table that lets you examine simultaneously a change in the principal amount and interest rate for the various loan periods.

Suppose you need to evaluate the following sensitivity cases for the car purchase decision discussed in the last section.

1. What is the payment amount for the various loan period options if the principal is $45,000 instead of $40,000?

2. What is the payment amount for the various loan period options if the interest rate is 10% instead of 12%?

Before starting this exercise, make sure that your screen looks like Figure 9-14. Prior to issuing the **Data Table 1** sequence of commands, complete the following instructions:

To enter the additional @PMT function formulas:

Enter the labels CASE 1 in cell C10, LOAN in cell C11 and PAYMENT in cell C12

Enter the labels CASE 2 in cell D10, LOAN in cell D11 and PAYMENT in cell D12

Move the cell pointer to cell C14

Type @PMT (45000,A7,A6)

Press ↵

Move the cell pointer to cell D14

Type @PMT (A4,0.1/12,A6)

Press ↵

Notice that A6 (the loan period) is used in both formulas, because it is the input cell that will be used in the **D**ata **T**able 1 command sequence. To see the text form of these formulas, first widen columns C and D so each can display 20 characters using the **W**orksheet Column Column-Range Set-Width command sequence. Then,

Move the cell pointer to cell C14

Press /

Select Range

Select Format

Select Text

Move the cell pointer to cell D14

Press ↵

When you are finished, your screen should look like Figure 9-15.

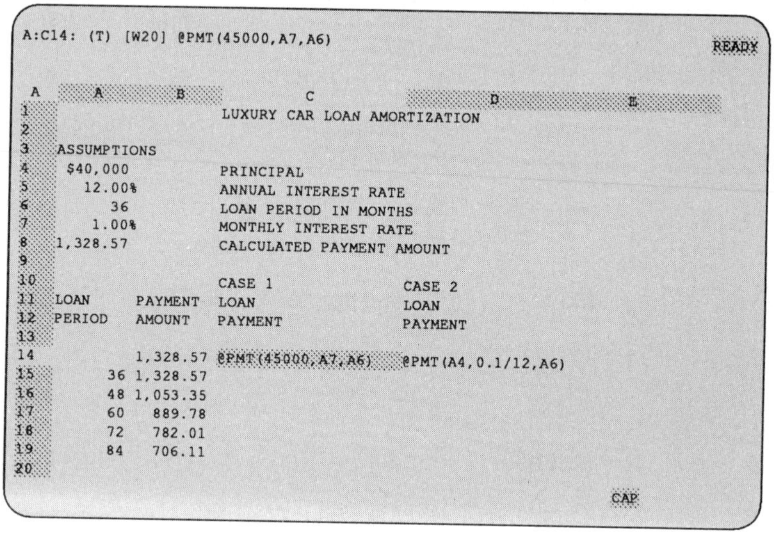

```
A:C14: (T) [W20] @PMT(45000,A7,A6)                                        READY

 A     A         B                C                     D                E
 1                       LUXURY CAR LOAN AMORTIZATION
 2
 3  ASSUMPTIONS
 4   $40,000             PRINCIPAL
 5     12.00%            ANNUAL INTEREST RATE
 6         36            LOAN PERIOD IN MONTHS
 7      1.00%            MONTHLY INTEREST RATE
 8  1,328.57             CALCULATED PAYMENT AMOUNT
 9
10                       CASE 1                 CASE 2
11  LOAN      PAYMENT    LOAN                   LOAN
12  PERIOD    AMOUNT     PAYMENT                PAYMENT
13
14            1,328.57   @PMT(45000,A7,A6)      @PMT(A4,0.1/12,A6)
15         36 1,328.57
16         48 1,053.35
17         60   889.78
18         72   782.01
19         84   706.11
20
                                                                   CAP
```

Figure 9-15

To initiate the **D**ata **T**able **1** command sequence:

Press	/
Select	Data
Select	Table
Select	1

To expand the data table range to include the additional formulas:

Move	the cell pointer to column D
Press	↵

To accept A6 as the input cell:

Press	↵

The values for the loan period will then be substituted into the original formula as well as the new formulas one at a time and a value for the payment amounts will be determined. These payment amounts will appear in columns B through D next to the loan period values.

You now can format the payment amount data using the **R**ange **F**ormat command sequence and right-justify the labels in cells C10 through D12.

Move	the cell pointer to cell C10

Press /

Select Range

Select Label

Select Right

To highlight all cells that need to be right justified:

Move the cell pointer to cell D12

Press ↵

Your screen should look like Figure 9-16.

```
A:C10: [W20] "CASE 1                                                    READY

A    A        B              C                      D                E
1            LOAN AMORTIZATION
2
3   ASSUMPTIONS
4    $40,000             PRINCIPAL
5      12.00%            ANNUAL INTEREST RATE
6         36             LOAN PERIOD IN MONTHS
7       1.00%            MONTHLY INTEREST RATE
8   1,328.57             CALCULATED PAYMENT AMOUNT
9
10                                      CASE 1               CASE 2
11  LOAN     PAYMENT                      LOAN                 LOAN
12  PERIOD   AMOUNT                    PAYMENT              PAYMENT
13
14           1,328.57 @PMT(45000,A7,A6)    @PMT(A4,0.1/12,A6)
15        36 1,328.57               1,494.64             1,290.69
16        48 1,053.35               1,185.02             1,014.50
17        60   889.78               1,001.00               849.88
18        72   782.01                 879.76               741.03
19        84   706.11                 794.37               664.05
20
                                                                CAP
```

Figure 9-16

Changing the Values of Two Variables

At times, you may want to change two of the variables in a formula. 1-2-3 permits you to simultaneously modify two such input cells using the **D**ata **T**able **2** command sequence.

Suppose for the luxury car loan decision introduced in the previous section, you want to vary the loan period and interest rates in the loan payment calculation. You specifically want to determine the loan payment amount for 36, 48, 60, 72 and 84 months using 9%, 10%, 11%, 12%, 13% and 14% interest rates.

Before initiating the **D**ata **T**able command sequence, create the worksheet in Figure 9-17. Cell A8 contains the function @PMT (A4,A7,A6).

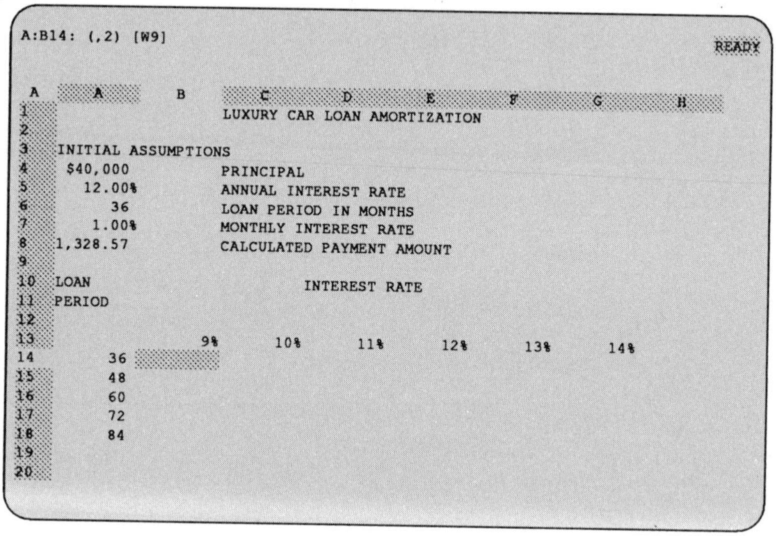

```
A:B14: (,2) [W9]                                                   READY

A     A        B      C       D       E       F       G       H
1                     LUXURY CAR LOAN AMORTIZATION
2
3  INITIAL ASSUMPTIONS
4   $40,000           PRINCIPAL
5     12.00%          ANNUAL INTEREST RATE
6         36          LOAN PERIOD IN MONTHS
7      1.00%          MONTHLY INTEREST RATE
8  1,328.57           CALCULATED PAYMENT AMOUNT
9
10 LOAN                          INTEREST RATE
11 PERIOD
12
13                  9%      10%      11%      12%      13%      14%
14        36
15        48
16        60
17        72
18        84
19
20
```

Figure 9-17

When you create a data table that allows you to modify the values of two input cells, the formula that uses the input cells must be placed in the top left corner cell of the data table. In this case you need to place the payment function formula in cell A13.

Move	the cell pointer to cell A13
Type	+A8
Press	↵

The payment amount using the initial assumptions now appears in cell A13. If you so desire, you can format the loan payment amount to two decimal places using the **R**ange **F**ormat **,** (comma) command sequence.

To start the **D**ata **T**able command sequence for varying two input cells:

Press	/
Select	Data
Select	Table
Select	2

When prompted for the data table range:

Move	the cell pointer to cell A13

Type .

Move the cell pointer to cell G18

Press ↵

To specify loan period as the first input cell:

Move the cell pointer to cell A6

Press ↵

To indicate interest rate is the second input cell:

Move the cell pointer to cell A5

Press ↵

The values for loan period and interest rate will then be substituted into the loan payment calculation formula and in a few seconds the values for the various combinations of loan periods and interest rates will appear on the worksheet. The values in the left column of the data table (column A) were substituted into input cell 1 (loan period). The values in the top row of the data table (row 13) were substituted into input cell 2 (interest rate). Format the results using the **R**ange **F**ormat, command sequence so your screen will look like Figure 9-18.

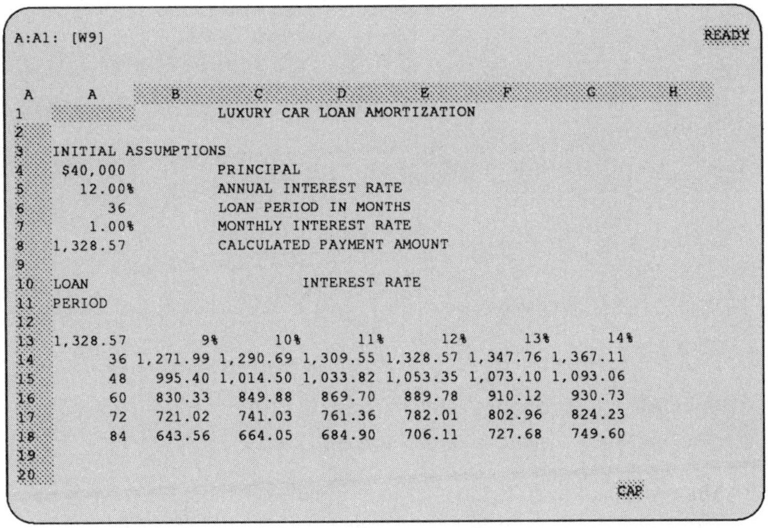

```
A:A1: [W9]                                                              READY

A      A       B        C        D        E        F        G        H
1                       LUXURY CAR LOAN AMORTIZATION
2
3   INITIAL ASSUMPTIONS
4    $40,000            PRINCIPAL
5      12.00%           ANNUAL INTEREST RATE
6          36           LOAN PERIOD IN MONTHS
7       1.00%           MONTHLY INTEREST RATE
8   1,328.57            CALCULATED PAYMENT AMOUNT
9
10  LOAN                          INTEREST RATE
11  PERIOD
12
13  1,328.57         9%      10%      11%      12%      13%      14%
14        36 1,271.99 1,290.69 1,309.55 1,328.57 1,347.76 1,367.11
15        48   995.40 1,014.50 1,033.82 1,053.35 1,073.10 1,093.06
16        60   830.33   849.88   869.70   889.78   910.12   930.73
17        72   721.02   741.03   761.36   782.01   802.96   824.23
18        84   643.56   664.05   684.90   706.11   727.68   749.60
19
20                                                          CAP
```

Figure 9-18

Changing the Values of Three Variables

In the last section, you used the **Data Table 2** command sequence to simultaneously vary the values for loan period and interest rates for the luxury car loan decision. Now you will create a series of data tables that will let you modify the values of all three of the loan variables at one time.

Suppose you want to vary the values for loan period, interest rate and principal simultaneously. You also desire to have an individual worksheet for each principal amount that includes the payment amounts for the various loan periods and interest rates that are considered. In this instance, you need to create worksheets for the possible principal amounts of $40,000, $45,000 and $50,000. On each of the worksheets you want to use 36, 48, 60, 72 and 84 for the loan period values and 9%, 10%, 11%, 12%, 13% and 14% for the interest rates.

Before initiating the **Data Table 3** command sequence, you need to create a worksheet like the one in Figure 9-19.

```
A:A1:                                                                    READY

A     A          B         C         D         E         F         G         H
1               LUXURY CAR LOAN AMORTIZATION
2
3    ASSUMPTIONS
4     $40,000             PRINCIPAL
5       12.00%            ANNUAL INTEREST RATE
6           36            LOAN PERIOD IN MONTHS
7        1.00%            MONTHLY INTEREST RATE
8    1,328.57             CALCULATED PAYMENT AMOUNT
9
10   LOAN                           INTEREST RATE
11   PERIOD
12
13                   9%       10%        11%        12%        13%        14%
14          36
15          48
16          60
17          72
18          84
19
20                                                                   CAP
```

Figure 9-19

If you have just completed the exercise in the last section, you can prepare the worksheet by erasing cells A13 and cells B14 through G18.

Since you will need to have an individual worksheet for each of the principal amounts, you need to insert two additional worksheets after worksheet A.

To insert the two additional worksheets:

Press /

Select	Worksheet
Select	Insert
Select	Sheet
Select	After
Type	2
Press	↵

Use the **W**orksheet **W**indow **P**erspective command sequence so you can see portions of the three worksheets on your screen. At this point, copy the contents of worksheet A to worksheets B and C using the **C**opy command sequence.

To complete the preparation of the data tables, enter $45,000 and $50,000 in cells B:A4 and C:A4 respectively. Your screen now should look like Figure 9-20.

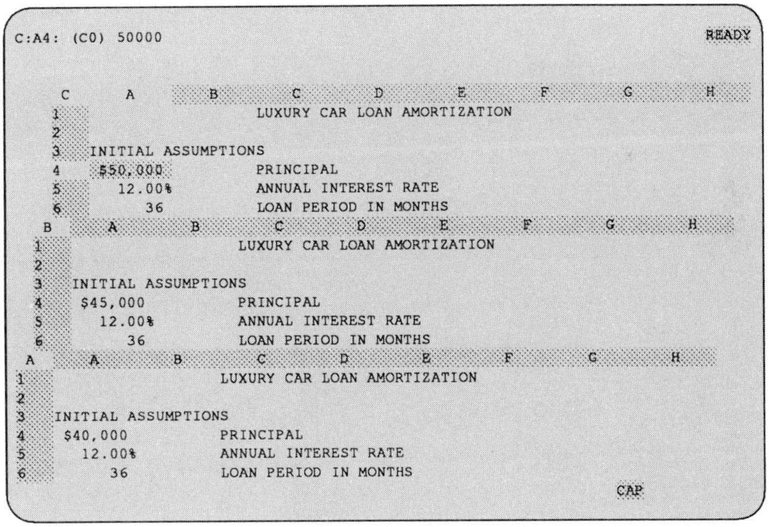

```
C:A4: (C0) 50000                                                        READY

      C     A         B         C         D         E         F         G         H
      1                    LUXURY CAR LOAN AMORTIZATION
      2
      3  INITIAL ASSUMPTIONS
      4    $50,000             PRINCIPAL
      5       12.00%           ANNUAL INTEREST RATE
      6          36            LOAN PERIOD IN MONTHS
    B     A         B         C         D         E         F         G         H
    1                    LUXURY CAR LOAN AMORTIZATION
    2
    3  INITIAL ASSUMPTIONS
    4    $45,000             PRINCIPAL
    5       12.00%           ANNUAL INTEREST RATE
    6          36            LOAN PERIOD IN MONTHS
  A     A         B         C         D         E         F         G         H
  1                    LUXURY CAR LOAN AMORTIZATION
  2
  3  INITIAL ASSUMPTIONS
  4    $40,000             PRINCIPAL
  5       12.00%           ANNUAL INTEREST RATE
  6          36            LOAN PERIOD IN MONTHS
                                                              CAP
```

Figure 9-20

To use the **D**ata **T**able **3** command sequence properly, you must place the value for the third input cell in the top left corner of the data table. To enter the principal amount in the appropriate cells:

Move	the cell pointer to cell A:A13
Type	+A4
Press	↵

Format cell A:A13 so that no decimal places are displayed. If necessary, widen the columns so that the numbers are displayed.

You need to copy this formula to cells B:A13 and C:A13 using the Copy command sequence. So that you will be able to see the entire set of loan payment values for all three tables on your screen, move the cell pointer down until row 13 is the first row appearing in each worksheet. Your screen should now look like Figure 9-21.

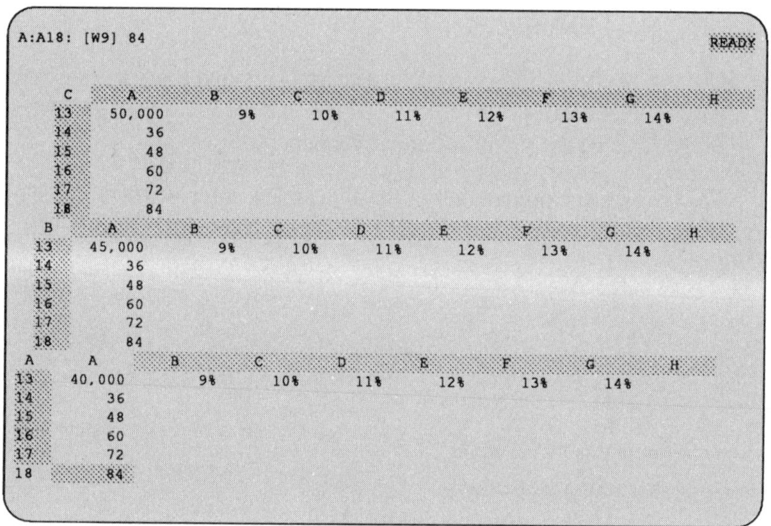

Figure 9-21

To initiate the **Data Table 3** command sequence:

Make	sure the cell pointer is in cell A:A13
Press	/
Select	Data
Select	Table
Select	3

To define the table range A:A13 through C:G18:

Type	.
Move	the cell pointer to cell A:G18
Press	the Ctrl-PgUp keys until the cell pointer is in cell C:G18

Press ↵

When prompted for the formula cell, indicate that it is in cell A:A8.

Move the cell pointer to cell A:A8

Press ↵

To indicate loan period is the first input cell:

Move the cell pointer to cell A:A6

Press ↵

To specify annual interest rate as the second input cell:

Move the cell pointer to cell A:A5

Press ↵

To define principal as the third input cell:

Move the cell pointer to cell A:A4

Press ↵

The various combinations of values for loan period, interest rate and principal will then be substituted into the @PMT function calculation cell and in a few seconds, the computed loan payment values will appear in the appropriate data tables. After moving the cell pointer to cell A:A18, your screen should look like Figure 9-22.

A:A18: 84 READY

C	A	B	C	D	E	F	G	H
13	50,000	9%	10%	11%	12%	13%	14%	
14	36	1,589.99	1,613.36	1,636.94	1,660.72	1,684.70	1,708.88	
15	48	1,244.25	1,268.13	1,292.28	1,316.69	1,341.37	1,366.32	
16	60	1,037.92	1,062.35	1,087.12	1,112.22	1,137.65	1,163.41	
17	72	901.28	926.29	951.70	977.51	1,003.71	1,030.29	
18	84	804.45	830.06	856.12	882.64	909.60	937.00	

B	A	B	C	D	E	F	G	H
13	45,000	9%	10%	11%	12%	13%	14%	
14	36	1,430.99	1,452.02	1,473.24	1,494.64	1,516.23	1,537.99	
15	48	1,119.83	1,141.32	1,163.05	1,185.02	1,207.24	1,229.69	
16	60	934.13	956.12	978.41	1,001.00	1,023.89	1,047.07	
17	72	811.15	833.66	856.53	879.76	903.33	927.26	
18	84	724.01	747.05	770.51	794.37	818.64	843.30	

A	A	B	C	D	E	F	G	H
13	40,000	9%	10%	11%	12%	13%	14%	
14	36	1,271.99	1,290.69	1,309.55	1,328.57	1,347.76	1,367.11	
15	48	995.40	1,014.50	1,033.82	1,053.35	1,073.10	1,093.06	
16	60	830.33	849.88	869.70	889.78	910.12	930.73	
17	72	721.02	741.03	761.36	782.01	802.96	824.23	
18	84	643.56	664.05	684.90	706.11	727.68	749.60	

CAP

Figure 9-22

USING AN EXTERNAL DATABASE

Lotus 1-2-3 provides you with the ability of accessing databases that are created using database management system software. Regardless of what database management software is used, these databases are referred to as external databases. The database tables contained in an external database are called external database tables.

1-2-3 provides the capability to connect to external database tables that have been created by dBASE III. As more database connections are developed, it will be possible to connect to database tables created by other database management software.

In this section you will learn to connect to an external database table, to copy data from an external database table to a 1-2-3 worksheet, to query an external database and combine information between an external database table and a 1-2-3 database table.

Connecting to an External Database

Earlier in this chapter you used the file ABCSAL that included the employee number, last name, first name, salaries for four quarters and annual salary total for each employee of ABC COMPANY. Assume that the data represented information for individuals currently employed by the company. The data for the current employees appears in Figure 9-23.

A:A1: [W7] READY

A	A	B	C	D	E	F	G	H	I
1					ABC COMPANY				
2					SALARY BUDGET				
3									
4									
5	EMP NO	LAST NAME	FIRST NAME	DIV	QTR1	QTR2	QTR3	QTR4	TOTAL
6	568	SPROUT	AL	3	5,950	5,950	6,450	6,450	24,800
7	123	LYLIE	SUSAN	1	7,800	7,800	7,800	8,580	31,980
8	390	CHIN	TOMMY	2	5,000	5,000	5,200	5,200	20,400
9	972	JOHNSON	SANDRA	1	8,200	8,200	9,000	9,000	34,400
10	898	VALETTI	GEORGE	3	5,900	5,900	6,300	6,300	24,400
11	239	ARMOUR	CYNTHIA	2	5,200	5,200	5,400	5,400	21,200
12	576	JOHNSON	ERNEST	1	8,000	8,000	8,800	8,800	33,600
13	833	JONES	NINA	3	6,750	6,750	6,750	7,450	27,700
14					--------	--------	--------	--------	--------
15		TOTAL			52,800	52,800	55,700	57,180	218,480
16									
17									
18									
19									
20									

Figure 9-23

During the year, some employees resigned or were terminated. A listing of all personnel employed during the year and their addresses is available in an external database table developed using dBASE III. A listing of the records in the external database table appear in Figure 9-24. It is placed in Lotus 1-2-3 screen format.

A:A1: [W6] 'EMPNO READY

A	A	B	C	D	E	F	G
1	EMPNO	LNAME	FNAME	ADDRESS	CITY	STATE	ZIP
2	109	GONZALES	CARLOS	98 E. MAIN	KATY	TX	77123
3	123	LYLIE	SUSAN	2800 FOUNDREN	HOUSTON	TX	77063
4	239	ARMOUR	CYNTHIA	6450 CLARA	HOUSTON	TX	77041
5	256	MARTINEZ	MARIA	765 TEXAS AVE.	HOUSTON	TX	77063
6	390	CHIN	TOMMY	7110 BRITTMORE RD	HOUSTON	TX	77041
7	487	SMITH	JAMES	4198 E. 29TH ST.	DALLAS	TX	75225
8	568	SPROUT	AL	8333 DOUGLAS AVE	DALLAS	TX	75225
9	576	JOHNSON	ERNEST	7102 VILLAGE LAKE	CYPRESS	TX	77433
10	753	POWERS	DAVID	90 PEARL AVE.	HOUSTON	TX	77026
11	833	JONES	NINA	654 GESSNER	HOUSTON	TX	77024
12	898	VALETTI	GEORGE	109 MOUNTAIN DALE	HOUSTON	TX	77024
13	900	KENT	MARY	7640 AVE. D	KATY	TX	77035
14	972	JOHNSON	SANDRA	11467 POST OAK	HOUSTON	TX	77098
15							
16							
17							
18							
19							
20							

CAP

Figure 9-24

Suppose you need to connect to the external database table illustrated in Figure 9-24 and have available a dBASE III file named ABCEMADD (employee addresses for ABC Company). If you have dBASE III, you can create the file very quickly using the following information on the database structure:

Field Name	Data Type	Field Width
EMPNO	Numeric	(3,0)
LNAME	Character	10
FNAME	Character	10
ADDRESS	Character	20
CITY	Character	10
STATE	Character	2
ZIP	Numeric	5

The remaining portion of this section assumes you have the database file ABCMADD available. Make sure you have a blank worksheet on your screen.

To access the external database table:

Press /

Select Data

Select External

At this point a menu appears that contains the options available for working with external databases.

To connect to the ABCEMADD database so you can use it:

Select Use

The table name Sample appears in the control table. This table contains the driver that allows you to access a dBASE III file. Your screen should look like Figure 9-25.

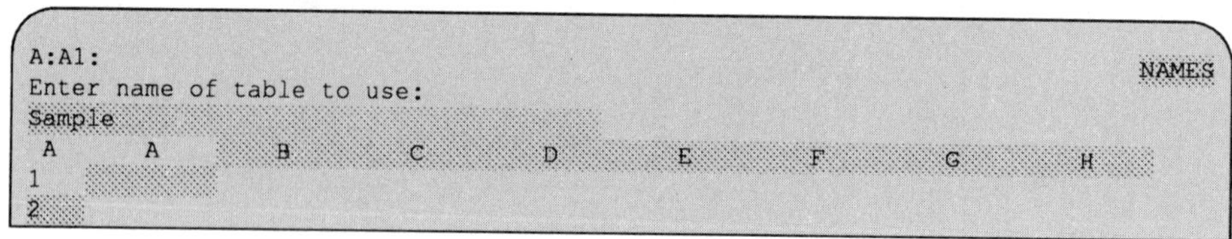

Figure 9-25

To indicate you want to use this file:

Press ⏎

The next entry on the control panel requests the directory path for the Sample file. Make sure that you have the proper directory path for your computer. Note that the file containing your external database table must also be in this directory. For this example, it is assumed that the default path that was created when 1-2-3 Release 3 was installed appears in the control panel.

To select this path:

Press ⏎

You are then asked to enter the name of the table to use. Your screen should look like Figure 9-26.

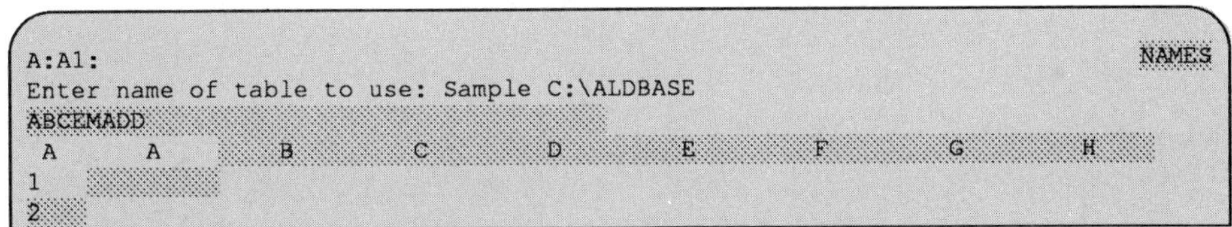

Figure 9-26

To specify your desire to access ABCEMADD:

Press F3

Move the pointer to ABCEMADD

Press ⏎

At the next prompt, you are requested to enter the range name in 1-2-3 you want to use to refer to the external database. 1-2-3 assumes that you want to use the name of the external database table so ABCEMADD appears in the control panel as a suggested range name. You can indicate a different name if you desire. Your screen should look like Figure 9-27.

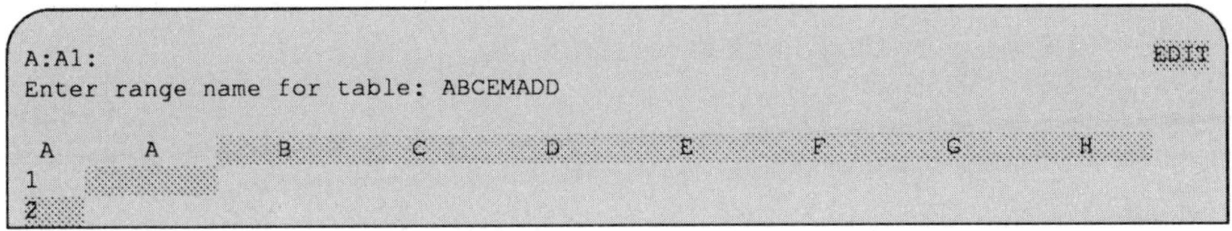

Figure 9-27

To specify ABCEMADD is appropriate as the range name:

Press ↵

You are now connected to the external database table.

To exit the external database menu:

Select Quit

Listing the Fields in an External Database Table

Suppose you want to see a listing of the field names for the external database table.

To create a list of the field names on your screen:

Press /

Select Data

Select External

Select List

Select Fields

When you are prompted for the range name whose fields are to be listed,

Press F3

Move the pointer to ABCEMADD

Press ↵

You are then asked to specify where you want the field names to be copied.

To indicate you want the field names placed beginning in cell A1:

Press ↵

Your screen should look like Figure 9-28.

```
A:A1: 'EMPNO                                                                 READY

A    A        B           C        D         E         F         G         H
1    EMPNO    Numeric    3,0       NA        NA        NA
2    LNAME    Character   10       NA        NA        NA
3    FNAME    Character   10       NA        NA        NA
4    ADDRESS  Character   20       NA        NA        NA
5    CITY     Character   10       NA        NA        NA
6    STATE    Character    2       NA        NA        NA
7    ZIP      Character    5       NA        NA        NA
8
9
```

Figure 9-28

NA indicates data is not available at this time.

To exit the current menu:

Select Quit

Copying the External Database Table into a 1-2-3 Worksheet

Since you have access to the external database table, you can copy it into a 1-2-3 worksheet. Before copying the external database table, you need to enter the field names horizontally on your worksheet. You can accomplish the task by transposing the field names in column A to a row below the information appearing on your screen. Make sure the cell pointer is in cell A1, and then,

Press /

Select Range

Select Trans

Move the cell pointer to cell A7

Press ↵

When you are prompted to enter the TO range for transpose:

Move the cell pointer to cell A10

Press ↵

The field names appear in cell A10 through F10. You no longer need the data field information above the field name. Delete nine rows from your worksheet using the **W**orksheet **D**elete **R**ow command sequence so the horizontal listing of the field names is in row 1. Your screen should look like Figure 9-29.

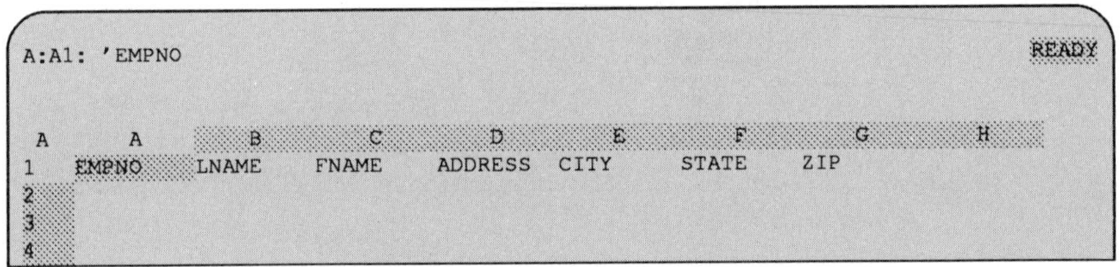

Figure 9-29

Prior to copying the external database to your 1-2-3 worksheet:

Copy cells A1 through G1 to A5 through G5

To copy the external database you must complete a data query using the external database.

Press /

Select Data

Select Query

To specify the input range:

Select Input

Type ABCEMADD

Press ↵

Exit the current menu:

Select Quit

To place a criteria on your worksheet that will include all employee records:

Move the cell pointer to cell A6

Type >0

Press ↵

To specify the criteria to use in the query:

Press	/
Select	Data
Select	Query
Select	Criteria
Move	the cell pointer to cell A5
Type	.
Move	the cell pointer to cell A6
Press	↵

To designate the proper field names as the output range:

Select	Output
Move	the cell pointer to cell A1
Type	.
Move	the cell pointer to cell G1
Press	↵

To complete the copying of the external database to your worksheet:

Select	Extract

To exit the current menu:

Select	Quit

The external database table appears on your screen. Your screen should look like Figure 9-30.

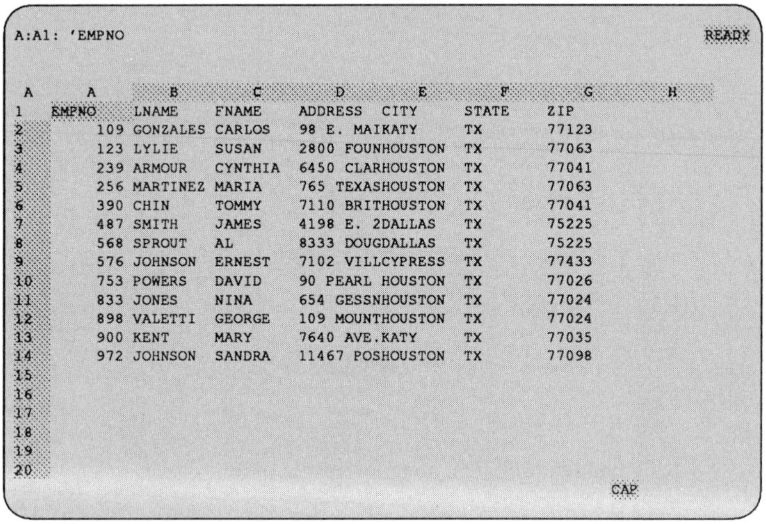

```
A:A1: 'EMPNO                                                                    READY

A    A     B          C          D           E          F         G          H
1  EMPNO   LNAME      FNAME      ADDRESS  CITY          STATE     ZIP
2      109 GONZALES   CARLOS     98 E. MAIKATY          TX        77123
3      123 LYLIE      SUSAN      2800 FOUNHOUSTON       TX        77063
4      239 ARMOUR     CYNTHIA    6450 CLARHOUSTON       TX        77041
5      256 MARTINEZ   MARIA      765 TEXASHOUSTON       TX        77063
6      390 CHIN       TOMMY      7110 BRITHOUSTON       TX        77041
7      487 SMITH      JAMES      4198 E. 2DALLAS        TX        75225
8      568 SPROUT     AL         8333 DOUGDALLAS        TX        75225
9      576 JOHNSON    ERNEST     7102 VILLCYPRESS       TX        77433
10     753 POWERS     DAVID      90 PEARL HOUSTON       TX        77026
11     833 JONES      NINA       654 GESSNHOUSTON       TX        77024
12     898 VALETTI    GEORGE     109 MOUNTHOUSTON       TX        77024
13     900 KENT       MARY       7640 AVE.KATY          TX        77035
14     972 JOHNSON    SANDRA     11467 POSHOUSTON       TX        77098
15
16
17
18
19
20
                                                                          CAP
```

Figure 9-30

Set up the column widths as follows so you can see the entire external database table that you copied to your worksheet.

Column	Width
A	6
B	10
C	10
D	20
E	10
F	6
G	5

You set columns A, F and G wider than the actual database field for screen readability purposes only. Your screen should look like Figure 9-31. Save the worksheet using the name EMPADDRS.

A:G1: [W5] 'ZIP READY

A	A	B	C	D	E	F	G
1	EMPNO	LNAME	FNAME	ADDRESS	CITY	STATE	ZIP
2	109	GONZALES	CARLOS	98 E. MAIN	KATY	TX	77123
3	123	LYLIE	SUSAN	2800 FOUNDREN	HOUSTON	TX	77063
4	239	ARMOUR	CYNTHIA	6450 CLARA	HOUSTON	TX	77041
5	256	MARTINEZ	MARIA	765 TEXAS AVE.	HOUSTON	TX	77063
6	390	CHIN	TOMMY	7110 BRITTMORE RD	HOUSTON	TX	77041
7	487	SMITH	JAMES	4198 E. 29TH ST.	DALLAS	TX	75225
8	568	SPROUT	AL	8333 DOUGLAS AVE	DALLAS	TX	75225
9	576	JOHNSON	ERNEST	7102 VILLAGE LAKE	CYPRESS	TX	77433
10	753	POWERS	DAVID	90 PEARL AVE.	HOUSTON	TX	77026
11	833	JONES	NINA	654 GESSNER	HOUSTON	TX	77024
12	898	VALETTI	GEORGE	109 MOUNTAIN DALE	HOUSTON	TX	77024
13	900	KENT	MARY	7640 AVE. D	KATY	TX	77035
14	972	JOHNSON	SANDRA	11467 POST OAK	HOUSTON	TX	77098
15							
16							
17							
18							
19							
20							

CAP

Figure 9-31

■ COMBINING INFORMATION FROM MULTIPLE DATABASE TABLES

In some situations, you may need to combine information between database tables based on a specific criteria. The process of combining such information is called joining database tables.

To illustrate the joining of information from two database tables into one table, suppose you need a list of the addresses for the current employees at ABC Company. Recall that file ABCSAL has only the individuals presently employed by the company along with salary information. The file EMPADDRS that you saved earlier in this chapter has the addresses for both current and previous employees.

Each of the files has an employee number field that identifies the record. These fields are called key fields or sometimes just keys. A key field contains unique information that is common across one or more database tables.

To prepare for creating the current employee address data table you need to retrieve file ABCSAL, and then open file EMPADDRS after file ABCSAL. Insert a new file named JOIN before the ABCSAL file by using the **F**ile **N**ew **B**efore command sequence. After completing these steps, and using the **W**orksheet **W**indow **P**erspective command sequence to place portions of all the worksheet files on the screen. Your screen should look like Figure 9-32.

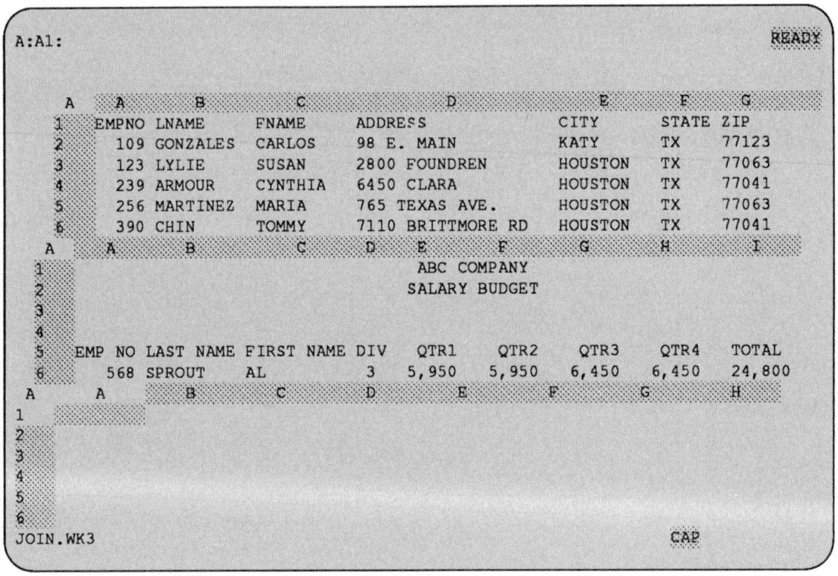

```
A:A1:                                                                 READY

   A    A      B          C           D                  E         F     G
   1  EMPNO LNAME      FNAME      ADDRESS              CITY      STATE ZIP
   2    109 GONZALES   CARLOS     98 E. MAIN           KATY      TX    77123
   3    123 LYLIE      SUSAN      2800 FOUNDREN        HOUSTON   TX    77063
   4    239 ARMOUR     CYNTHIA    6450 CLARA           HOUSTON   TX    77041
   5    256 MARTINEZ   MARIA      765 TEXAS AVE.       HOUSTON   TX    77063
   6    390 CHIN       TOMMY      7110 BRITTMORE RD    HOUSTON   TX    77041
  A    A       B          C       D      E        F        G        H        I
  1                                      ABC COMPANY
  2                                     SALARY BUDGET
  3
  4
  5  EMP NO LAST NAME FIRST NAME DIV    QTR1     QTR2     QTR3     QTR4    TOTAL
  6     568 SPROUT    AL           3   5,950    5,950    6,450    6,450   24,800
 A       A        B         C         D         E         F         G         H
 1
 2
 3
 4
 5
 6
JOIN.WK3                                                          CAP
```

Figure 9-32

Define the range name ADDRESS that contains cells A:A1 through A:G14 in file EMPADDRS as its range. Define another range name CURRENT that has cells A:A5 through A:I13 of file ABCSAL as its range.

Entering the JOIN Formula for the Criteria

To combine information from the two database tables, you need to place a criteria range in file JOIN that contains a formula that **joins** the database tables in files ABCSAL and EMPADDRS. For this exercise:

Move	the cell pointer to cell A:B1 in file JOIN
Type	CRITERIA
Press	↵
Move	the cell pointer to cell A:B2
Type	+EMP NO=EMPNO
Press	↵

The characters ERR appear in cell A:B2 because you do not have the range names for EMP NO or EMPNO defined. These are the key fields that include the employee number that is common to salary records in file ABCSAL and the address records in file EMPADDRS. The formula indicates that information will be extracted from the database tables when the employee numbers are equal.

To see the text form of the JOIN formula in cell A:B2, format the cell using the **R**ange **F**ormat **T**ext command sequence. You will need to set the column width for column B to 14 to see the entire JOIN formula.

The output range specifies the field names you want to include in the new database table that is formed by joining the database tables in files ABCSAL and EMPADDR. Use the field names that you want in the new database table in file JOIN as the output range. Use cells A4 through G4 of file JOIN in Figure 9-33 as a guide to enter the output range field names.

```
A:G4: 'ZIP                                                              READY

     A   A        B         C          D                  E         F     G
     1   EMPNO LNAME     FNAME      ADDRESS            CITY      STATE ZIP
     2     109 GONZALES  CARLOS     98 E. MAIN         KATY      TX    77123
     3     123 LYLIE     SUSAN      2800 FOUNDREN      HOUSTON   TX    77063
     4     239 ARMOUR    CYNTHIA    6450 CLARA         HOUSTON   TX    77041
     5     256 MARTINEZ  MARIA      765 TEXAS AVE.     HOUSTON   TX    77063
     6     390 CHIN      TOMMY      7110 BRITTMORE RD  HOUSTON   TX    77041
   A   A        B          C     D     E      F        G        H       I
   1                                ABC COMPANY
   2                               SALARY BUDGET
   3
   4
   5 EMP NO LAST NAME FIRST NAME DIV   QTR1    QTR2    QTR3    QTR4    TOTAL
   6    568 SPROUT     AL          3   5,950   5,950   6,450   6,450   24,800
 A   A         B            C          D            E          F       G
 1           CRITERIA
 2           +EMP NO=EMPNO
 3
 4 EMP NO    LAST NAME     FIRST NAMADDRESS    CITY       STATE      ZIP
 5
 6
JOIN.WK3                                                      CAP
```

Figure 9-33

To see the entire field names and eventually the extracted data, set the column width for column A to 6, column C to 11, column D to 20, column E to 10, column F to 6 and column G to 5. Note that the first three field names in the output range are from the ABCSAL database table and the remaining field names are from the EMPADDRS database table.

Extracting the Data for the New Database Table

To create the new "joined" database table:

Press /

Select Data

Select Query

To indicate the input range, you must include the ABCSAL and EMPADDRS database tables.

Select Input

When prompted for the input range:

Type <<ABCSAL.WK3>>CURRENT,
<<EMPADDRS.WK3>>ADDRESS

Press ↵

To define the criteria range:

Select Criteria

Move the cell pointer to cell A:B1 in file JOIN

Type .

Move the cell pointer to cell A:B2

Press ↵

To specify the output range:

Select Output

Move the cell pointer to cell A:A4

Type .

Move the cell pointer to cell A:G4

Press ↵

To extract from the database tables in file ABCSAL and EMPADDRS and create the database table as a result of using the JOIN formula:

Select Extract

Your screen should look like Figure 9-34.

To quit the current menu:

Select Quit

```
A:A5: [W6] 123                                                       MENU
Input  Criteria  Output  Find  Extract  Unique  Del  Modify  Reset  Quit
Copy to output range all records that match criteria
    A   A    B        C         D                   E        F      G
    1  EMPNO LNAME    FNAME    ADDRESS             CITY     STATE ZIP
    2    109 GONZALES CARLOS   98 E. MAIN          KATY     TX    77123
    3    123 LYLIE    SUSAN    2800 FOUNDREN       HOUSTON  TX    77063
    4    239 ARMOUR   CYNTHIA  6450 CLARA          HOUSTON  TX    77041
    5    256 MARTINEZ MARIA    765 TEXAS AVE.      HOUSTON  TX    77063
    6    390 CHIN     TOMMY    7110 BRITTMORE RD   HOUSTON  TX    77041
   A   A     B         C       D    E        F        G       H       I
   1                                ABC COMPANY
   2                               SALARY BUDGET
   3
   4
   5 EMP NO LAST NAME FIRST NAME DIV   QTR1    QTR2    QTR3    QTR4   TOTAL
   6    568 SPROUT    AL           3  5,950   5,950   6,450   6,450  24,800
  A   A      B         C         D                     E       F
  1      CRITERIA
  2      +EMP NO=EMPNO
  3
  4 EMP NOLAST NAME    FIRST NAME ADDRESS              CITY     STATE
  5    123 LYLIE       SUSAN      2800 FOUNDREN        HOUSTON  TX
  6    239 ARMOUR      CYNTHIA    6450 CLARA           HOUSTON  TX
JOIN.WK3                                                        CAP
```

Figure 9-34

Note the current employee address database table is in order by employee number, because the process of finding the matches is quicker if both the ABCSAL and EMPADDRS files are sorted in order by the employee number key before the search and matching process begins.

■ CREATING A FREQUENCY DISTRIBUTION

The **D**ata **D**istribution menu option allows you to determine the frequency distribution of any column or row of numbers. A frequency distribution counts the number of values that fall within specified intervals. Retrieve the original file ABCSAL for use in this exercise.

In this example, you will determine the frequency distribution of salaries based on a bin range set up in cells B17 through B20. The **bin range** is a column containing numbers or formulas that specify the intervals for the frequency distribution. The intervals in the bin range are determined by the user and must always be in ascending order. A blank column should exist to the right of this column (with an additional blank row below the last value in the interval range) where the results will be placed after the **D**ata **D**istribution procedure is invoked through the menu. First, set up the bin range. Use Figure 9-35 as a guide to enter this information in cells B17 through B20, C17 and D21.

```
A:D21: [W3] '(INDICATES NUMBERS ABOVE MAXIMUM RANGE)                         READY

A      A      B           C        D    E       F       G       H       I
2                                       SALARY BUDGET
3
4
5   EMP NO LAST NAME FIRST NAME DIV   QTR1    QTR2    QTR3    QTR4    TOTAL
6      568 SPROUT    AL           3  5,950   5,950   6,450   6,450   24,800
7      123 LYLIE     SUSAN        1  7,800   7,800   7,800   8,580   31,980
8      390 CHIN      TOMMY        2  5,000   5,000   5,200   5,200   20,400
9      576 JOHNSON   ERNEST       1  8,000   8,000   8,800   8,800   33,600
10     898 VALETTI   GEORGE       3  5,900   5,900   6,300   6,300   24,400
11     239 ARMOUR    CYNTHIA      2  5,200   5,200   5,400   5,400   21,200
12     972 JOHNSON   SANDRA       1  8,200   8,200   9,000   9,000   34,400
13     833 JONES     NINA         3  6,750   6,750   6,750   7,450   27,700
14                                  -----------------------------------------
15         TOTAL                    52,800  52,800  55,700  57,180  218,480
16
17         BIN RANGE FREQUENCY
18            23,000
19            28,000
20            33,000
21                               (INDICATES NUMBERS ABOVE MAXIMUM RANGE)
                                                                   CAP
```

Figure 9-35

To find the data distribution for the salaries:

Press /

Select Data

Select Distribution

The prompt "Enter Values range:" appears. Since the distribution for this example is for salaries, highlight the total salary amounts:

Move the cell cursor to cell I6

Type .

Move the cell cursor to cell I13

Press ↵

The prompt "Enter Bin range:" appears. The bin range chosen for this example is from 23,000 through 33,000.

Move the cell cursor to cell B18

Type .

Move the cell cursor to cell B20

Press ↵

The frequency of the salary amounts appears in cells C18 through C21. Note that the number 2, which is listed in cell C21, indicates that two numbers in the values range were above 33,000.

The 2 in cell C18 indicates the number of salaries that are less than or equal to $23,000. The 3 in cell C19 indicates the number of salaries between $23,000 and $28,000, including $28,000.

The 1 in cell C20 indicates the number of salaries between $28,000 and $33,000, including $33,000. The 2 in cell C21 indicates the number of salaries greater than $33,000.

Your screen should look like the final illustration in Figure 9-36. Parts 1 through 3 of Figure 9-36 display the entire **D**ata **D**istribution command sequence.

Step One of the Data Distribution Procedure: Specify the Desired Values through the Menu.

```
A:I13: @SUM(E13..H13)                                                   POINT
Enter values range: A:I6..A:I13

A    A        B          C        D     E        F        G        H        I
2                                       SALARY  BUDGET
3
4
5  EMP NO LAST NAME FIRST NAME DIV    QTR1     QTR2     QTR3     QTR4     TOTAL
6     568 SPROUT     AL          3   5,950    5,950    6,450    6,450    24,800
7     123 LYLIE      SUSAN       1   7,800    7,800    7,800    8,580    31,980
8     390 CHIN       TOMMY       2   5,000    5,000    5,200    5,200    20,400
9     576 JOHNSON    ERNEST      1   8,000    8,000    8,800    8,800    33,600
10    898 VALETTI    GEORGE      3   5,900    5,900    6,300    6,300    24,400
11    239 ARMOUR     CYNTHIA     2   5,200    5,200    5,400    5,400    21,200
12    972 JOHNSON    SANDRA      1   8,200    8,200    9,000    9,000    34,400
13    833 JONES      NINA        3   6,750    6,750    6,750    7,450    27,700
14                                  ------------------------------------------
15        TOTAL                     52,800   52,800   55,700   57,180   218,480
16
17        BIN RANGE FREQUENCY
18           23,000
19           28,000
20           33,000
21                          (INDICATES NUMBERS ABOVE MAXIMUM RANGE)
                                                                    CAP
```

Figure 9-36
Part 1

Step Two of the Data Distribution Procedure: Specify the Desired Bin Range through the Menu.

```
A:B20: [W10] 33000                                                       POINT
Enter values range: A:I6..A:I13         Enter bin range: A:B18..A:B20

 A    A       B          C       D    E        F        G        H        I
 2                                       SALARY BUDGET
 3
 4
 5  EMP NO LAST NAME FIRST NAME DIV   QTR1     QTR2     QTR3     QTR4    TOTAL
 6     568 SPROUT    AL          3   5,950    5,950    6,450    6,450   24,800
 7     123 LYLIE     SUSAN       1   7,800    7,800    7,800    8,580   31,980
 8     390 CHIN      TOMMY       2   5,000    5,000    5,200    5,200   20,400
 9     576 JOHNSON   ERNEST      1   8,000    8,000    8,800    8,800   33,600
10     898 VALETTI   GEORGE      3   5,900    5,900    6,300    6,300   24,400
11     239 ARMOUR    CYNTHIA     2   5,200    5,200    5,400    5,400   21,200
12     972 JOHNSON   SANDRA      1   8,200    8,200    9,000    9,000   34,400
13     833 JONES     NINA        3   6,750    6,750    6,750    7,450   27,700
14                                  -----------------------------------------
15         TOTAL                    52,800   52,800   55,700   57,180  218,480
16
17         BIN RANGE FREQUENCY
18            23,000
19            28,000
20            33,000
21                                 (INDICATES NUMBERS ABOVE MAXIMUM RANGE)
                                                                      CAP
```

Figure 9-36
Part 2

Step Three of the Data Distribution Procedure: After pressing ⏎ , the Frequency Distribution is displayed next to the Specified Bin Range.

```
A:D21: [W3] '(INDICATES NUMBERS ABOVE MAXIMUM RANGE)                     READY

 A    A       B          C       D    E        F        G        H        I
 2                                       SALARY BUDGET
 3
 4
 5  EMP NO LAST NAME FIRST NAME DIV   QTR1     QTR2     QTR3     QTR4    TOTAL
 6     568 SPROUT    AL          3   5,950    5,950    6,450    6,450   24,800
 7     123 LYLIE     SUSAN       1   7,800    7,800    7,800    8,580   31,980
 8     390 CHIN      TOMMY       2   5,000    5,000    5,200    5,200   20,400
 9     576 JOHNSON   ERNEST      1   8,000    8,000    8,800    8,800   33,600
10     898 VALETTI   GEORGE      3   5,900    5,900    6,300    6,300   24,400
11     239 ARMOUR    CYNTHIA     2   5,200    5,200    5,400    5,400   21,200
12     972 JOHNSON   SANDRA      1   8,200    8,200    9,000    9,000   34,400
13     833 JONES     NINA        3   6,750    6,750    6,750    7,450   27,700
14                                  -----------------------------------------
15         TOTAL                    52,800   52,800   55,700   57,180  218,480
16
17         BIN RANGE FREQUENCY
18            23,000           2
19            28,000           3
20            33,000           1
21                             2 (INDICATES NUMBERS ABOVE MAXIMUM RANGE)
                                                                      CAP
```

Figure 9-36
Part 3

■ GRAPHING A FREQUENCY DISTRIBUTION

Assuming that the previous exercise has just been completed and the data distribution worksheet is on your screen, you will now complete the exercise by graphing the distribution of salaries. For the X-axis on the graph you will use the bin range. To document the cell indicating the numbers above the maximum range:

Move the pointer to cell B21

Type ">33,000

Press ↵

By performing this step, >33,000 will appear on the graph to indicate those numbers beyond the bin range. (The double quote right-justifies this label in cell B21.)

To create a graph depicting the results of the frequency distribution in the previous exercise:

Press /

Select Graph

Select Type

Select Pie

For the X-axis on the graph, select the numbers in the bin range:

Select X-Axis

For the X-axis:

Type B18.B21

Press ↵

To choose the first data range for the frequency value data:

Select A

Type C18.C21

Press ↵

To enter a title for the graph:

Select Options

Select Titles

Select First

For the graph title:

Type FREQUENCY DISTRIBUTION OF SALARIES

Press ↵

To exit the current menu:

Select Quit

To view the graph:

Select View

The graph should look like Figure 9-37.

FREQUENCY DISTRIBUTION OF SALARIES

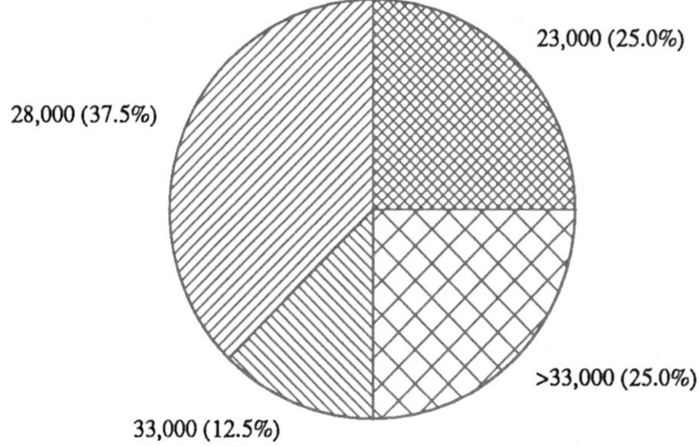

Figure 9-37

After viewing the graph:

Press ↵

To leave the current menu:

Select Quit

You do not need to save or print the graph.

SUMMARY

The **Data Fill** option provides an easy way to place sequences of dates and times on one or more worksheets. The **Data Table** capability in 1-2-3 allows you to create tables that illustrate the impact of changing values for a variable in a decision-making situation. External database tables created using database management software can be accessed, queried and copied to a 1-2-3 worksheet. Lotus 1-2-3 also contains a **Data Distribution** command that you can use to determine the frequency distribution of data in a specified range.

KEY CONCEPTS

Bin range
Criteria
Data Distribution
Data External
Data Fill
Data Table
External database
External database table
Frequency distribution

CHAPTER NINE
EXERCISE 1

INSTRUCTIONS: Circle T if the statement is true and F if the statement is false.

T F 1. Database tables created by database management software packages can be accessed using Lotus 1-2-3.

T F 2. Sequences of numbers or times cannot be placed on multiple worksheets at one time.

T F 3. The **D**ata **T**able option makes it possible to analyze changes in variables that impact decision-making situations.

T F 4. A frequency distribution can be created using the **D**ata **D**istribution command sequence.

T F 5. A graph of a frequency distribution can be prepared by using the **G**raph **D**istribution command sequence.

CHAPTER NINE
EXERCISE 2
Filling Cells with Numbers

INSTRUCTIONS: Make sure you have a blank worksheet on your screen.

Using the **D**ata **F**ill command sequence, place the sequence of numbers 1, 4, 7, 10, 13, 16 and 19 in cells A2 through G2.

Using the **D**ata **F**ill command sequence, place the sequence of numbers .1, .2, .3, .4, .5 and .6 in cells A6 through A11.

Print the completed worksheet.

CHAPTER NINE
EXERCISE 3
Filling Cells with Dates

INSTRUCTIONS: Make sure you have a blank worksheet on your screen.

Using the **D**ata **F**ill command sequence, place the sequence of dates May 3, May 7, May 11 and May 15 for the year 1991 in cells B2 through E2.

Using the **D**ata **F**ill command sequence, place the dates July 1, August 1, September 1, October 1, November 1 and December 1 for the year 1992 in cells B6 through G6.

Using the **D**ata **F**ill command sequence, place the dates January 15, April 15, July 15 and October 15 for the year 1995 in cells B10 through E10.

Using the **D**ata **F**ill command sequence, place the sequence of dates for January 1 of the years 1990, 1992, 1994, 1996, 1998 and 2000 in cells B15 through G15.

As required, format the date serial numbers so that an appropriate form of the date appears. Print the worksheet after entering the indicated data.

CHAPTER NINE
EXERCISE 4
Filling Cells with Times

INSTRUCTIONS: Make sure you have a blank worksheet on your screen.

Using the **D**ata **F**ill command sequence, place the times 9:00 a.m., 9:02 a.m., 9:04 a.m., 9:06 a.m. and 9:08 a.m. in cells A1 through A5.

Using the **D**ata **F**ill command sequence, enter the times 8:00 a.m. through 8:00 p.m. where the interval between each time on the worksheet is 2 hours. Place the time 8:00 a.m. in cell A7 and the remaining times should appear in column A below cell A7.

Format the time numbers so they appear properly.

Print the worksheet after placing the times on the worksheet.

CHAPTER NINE
EXERCISE 5
Placing a Sequence of Data on Multiple Worksheets

INSTRUCTIONS: Make sure you have a blank worksheet on your screen.

Using the **D**ata **F**ill command sequence, place the dates for the years January 1 of the years 1990, 1991, and 1992 in cell B2 of the worksheets A, B and C of a file.

Format the date numbers so that they appear properly.

Print the worksheets after entering and formatting the dates.

CHAPTER NINE
EXERCISE 6
Changing the Values of One Variable in a Data Table

INSTRUCTIONS: Suppose you are considering the purchase of a house. The current interest rate is 11% for a 20-year fixed-rate loan. Create a data table that contains the monthly payment for a house if the price is $75,000, $80,000, $85,000, $90,000 or $95,000 using the interest rate of 11% and assuming a 20-year loan period.

Print the data table after it is prepared.

CHAPTER NINE
EXERCISE 7
Changing the Values of Two Variables in a Data Table

INSTRUCTIONS: Suppose you are considering the purchase of some property that is priced in the $50,000 to $70,000 price range. Assume that you can obtain a 30-year fixed-rate loan from several financial institutions with an interest rate varying between 9% and 11%.

Create a data table that contains the monthly payment amount after varying the purchase price form $50,000 to $70,000 in increments of $5,000. You also need to use an initial interest rate of 9% and increase it to a maximum of 11% using one-half percent increments.

Use a 30-year loan period for all calculations.

Print the data table after the monthly payment values have been determined.

CHAPTER NINE
EXERCISE 8
Changing the Values of Three Variables in a Data Table

INSTRUCTIONS: Use the worksheet completed in Exercise 14 for this exercise.

Assume that you can finance the purchase of the property for either 20, 25 or 30 years.

Determine the monthly payments for the various loan periods using the purchase price and interest rate assumptions specified in Exercise 14.

Print the worksheets containing the calculated monthly payment values.

CHAPTER NINE
EXERCISE 9
Combining Information from Multiple Database Tables

INSTRUCTIONS: Use the files ABCSAL and EMPADDRS created earlier in this chapter for this exercise.

Create a database table that contains the addresses of all present employees of ABC Company that live in Houston.

Print the worksheet containing the database table of the addresses of former employees.

CHAPTER NINE
EXERCISE 10
Creating a Frequency Disribution

INSTRUCTIONS: Retrieve the original file ABCSAL for use in this exercise.

Use the **D**ata **D**istribution menu option to determine the number of people in each division in the ABCSAL data table.

The bin range should encompass the division numbers in the database and be placed on a separate worksheet. Print the worksheet after calculating the number of people there are in each division.

CHAPTER NINE
EXERCISE 11
Graphing a Frequency Distribution

INSTRUCTIONS: Use the results of Exercise 17 in this exercise.

Create a pie graph using the data for the distribution of people for the three divisions in ABC Company.

Print the pie graph depicting the data distribution.

CHAPTER TEN

SPECIAL FUNCTIONS IN LOTUS 1-2-3

OBJECTIVES

In this chapter, you will learn to use and apply the following types of special functions available in Lotus 1-2-3:

- Statistical Analysis
- Financial Analysis
- Date and Time
- Logical
- Database
- Mathematical
- Special
- String

CHAPTER OVERVIEW

Lotus 1-2-3 has 103 special functions. Suppose you want to compute the monthly payment for a 30-year, $100,000 bank loan with an 11% interest rate. 1-2-3 has the `@PMT` function that allows you to compute the payment amount. In earlier exercises, you have used some of the other special functions such as `@SUM` and `@ROUND`. In this chapter, you will learn to apply many of the special functions used for the following categories: statistical analysis, financial analysis, date and time, logical, database, mathematical, special, and string. Each of the special functions has a specific structure that you must use. The general format of a special function is:

```
@function name(argument1,argument2,...argumentn)
```

You must enter the function on your worksheet using the correct syntax or errors will occur. In some cases, an argument may be optional. If an argument is optional, brackets will appear in the text, but are not required when the function is used. Press the ↵ key after entering the function.

Since each function requires various types of data to utilize, you will need to erase your screen each time you work through the example for a new function. You do not need to save the results of any of the example problems covered in this chapter.

STATISTICAL ANALYSIS FUNCTIONS

Lotus 1-2-3 has 10 statistical analysis functions. They include:

`@SUM`	Computes the sum of a list of cell values
`@COUNT`	Computes the number of items in a list of cell values
`@AVG`	Computes the arithmetic mean for a list of cell values
`@MIN`	Identifies the minimum value for a list of cell values
`@MAX`	Identifies the maximum value for a list of cell values
`@VAR`	Computes the population variance for a list of cell values
`@STD`	Computes the population standard deviation for a list of cell values
`@VARS`	Computes the sample variance for a list of cell values
`@SUMPRODUCT`	Computes the sum of the products of corresponding items in multiple ranges
`@STDS`	Computes the sample standard deviation for a list of cell values

The general format for the statistical analysis functions is as follows:

```
@function name(first cell..last cell)
```

For example, to compute the sum of the numbers in cells A1 through G1 in a worksheet, the formula `@SUM(A1..G1)` is used. The function name should be used exactly as it is listed above (e.g., the function name for averaging numbers is written as AVG).

Using the Statistical Analysis Functions

In this section you will learn to use each of the statistical functions. First, create a worksheet like Figure 10-1.

```
A:A1: [W31] 'STATISTICAL ANALYSIS FUNCTIONS                                    READY

 A                 A                      B        C        D        E
 1  STATISTICAL ANALYSIS FUNCTIONS
 2
 3
 4                                          58
 5                                          50
 6                                          67
 7                                          89
 8
 9  SUM
10  COUNT
11  AVERAGE
12  MINIMUM
13  MAXIMUM
14  POPULATION VARIANCE
15  POPULATION STANDARD DEVIATION
16  SAMPLE VARIANCE
17  SAMPLE STANDARD DEVIATION
18  SUM OF PRODUCTS
19
20
                                                                 CAP
```

Figure 10-1

@SUM

To compute the sum of the four numbers in cells B4 through B7 using the `@SUM` function:

Move	the cell pointer to cell B9
Type	`@SUM(`
Move	the cell pointer to cell B4
Type	.
Move	the cell pointer to cell B7
Type	)

The formula `@SUM(B4..B7)` now should appear in the control panel.

Press	↵

The formula was entered into cell B9; the result is 264.

When using the @SUM formula in worksheets, you may wish to include the cell immediately above and below the range of numbers actually being added. For example, the formula @SUM(B3..B8) could be used instead of @SUM(B4..B7) to total the numbers in this exercise. If a row is inserted (or deleted) at the top or bottom of the range to add (or delete) a number, the @SUM command will adjust correctly to the change. If a label such as a subtotal line is included in the range, it will not be a problem because Lotus 1-2-3 considers labels to have a value of 0. For the purposes of this example, this technique was not used.

Rather than moving the cell pointer to the cells to be used in computation, you can type the formula @SUM(B4.B7) directly in cell B9 and press ⏎ to obtain the same result. The advantage of highlighting the numbers to be used in the formula is that you will be less likely to make errors and enter the wrong cells. When entering the remaining statistical analysis functions, the formula will be typed directly into the cell to save you some time.

@COUNT

To count the items in cells B4 through B7 using the @COUNT function:

Move	the cell pointer to cell B10
Enter	@COUNT(B4.B7)

Note that only one period can be typed within the formula. Typing @COUNT(B4.B7) produces the same result as typing @COUNT(B4..B7). The formula @COUNT(B4..B7) appears in the control panel. The number 4 appears in cell B10.

@AVG

To compute the average of the numbers in cells B4 through B7 using the @AVG function:

Move	the cell pointer to cell B11
Enter	@AVG(B4.B7)

The formula @AVG(B4..B7) appears in the control panel. The number 66 appears in cell B11.

@MIN

To determine the smallest value of the items in cells B4 through B7 using the @MIN function:

Move	the cell pointer to cell B12
Enter	@MIN(B4.B7)

The formula @MIN(B4..B7) appears in the control panel. The number 50 appears in cell B12.

@MAX

To determine the largest value of the items in cells B4 through B7 using the @MAX function:

Move the cell pointer to cell B13

Enter `@MAX(B4.B7)`

The formula `@MAX(B4..B7)` appears in the control panel. The number 89 appears in cell B13.

@VAR for a Population

To determine the population variance of the numbers in cells B4 through B7 using the @VAR function:

Move the cell pointer to cell B14

Enter `@VAR(B4.B7)`

The formula `@VAR(B4..B7)` appears in the control panel. The number 212.5 appears in cell B14. It is assumed you have all the values that need to be considered and the data is not a sample of values from a larger set of data.

@STD for a Population

To determine the standard deviation of the numbers in cells B4 through B7 using the @STD function:

Move the cell pointer to cell B15

Enter `@STD(B4.B7)`

The formula `@STD(B4..B7)` appears in the control panel. The number 14.57738 appears in cell B15. It is assumed you have all the values that need to be considered and the data is not a sample of values from a larger set of data.

@VARS

When you computed the population variance, you assumed that you had all of the data that you were considering. If instead, the data is only a sample of all the data that you want to consider, then the formula for computing the variance is:

$$\sum_{i=1}^{n} (x_i - \bar{x})^2/(n-1) \text{ rather than } \sum_{i=1}^{n} (x_i - \mu)^2/n .$$

Assuming the data in B4 through B7 is a sample, calculate the sample variance.

Move the cell pointer to cell B16

Enter `@VARS(B4.B7)`

@STDS

When you computed the population standard deviation, you assumed that you had all of the data that you want to examine. If instead, the data is only a sample, then the formula for computing the standard deviations is:

$$\sqrt{\frac{\sum_{i=1}^{n}(x_i-\bar{x})^2}{n-1}} \text{ rather than } \sqrt{\frac{\sum_{i-1}^{n}(x_i-\mu)^2}{n}}.$$

If the data in cells B4 through B7 is a sample, then you can compute the sample standard deviation as follows.

Move the cell pointer to cell B17

Enter `@STDS(B4.B7)`

Your screen should look like Figure 10-2.

```
A:B18:                                                      READY

A              A                     B          C       D       E
1  STATISTICAL ANALYSIS FUNCTIONS
2
3
4                                        58
5                                        50
6                                        67
7                                        89
8
9  SUM                                  264
10 COUNT                                  4
11 AVERAGE                               66
12 MINIMUM                               50
13 MAXIMUM                               89
14 POPULATION VARIANCE                212.5
15 POPULATION STANDARD DEVIATION   14.57738
16 SAMPLE VARIANCE                 283.3333
17 SAMPLE STANDARD DEVIATION       16.83251
18 SUM OF PRODUCTS
19
20                                                    CAP
```

Figure 10-2

@SUMPRODUCT

In some situations, you may need to multiply one set of numbers by another set of numbers and then sum the results. Refer to Figure 10-3 and notice that two additional sets of values have been placed on the worksheet in cells D9..D11 and E9..E11. Suppose you want to multiply the corresponding values in column D by the values in column E and place the results in cell B18. Enter the values appearing in cells D9 through E11 in Figure 9-3.

Move	the cell pointer to cell B18
Enter	`@SUMPRODUCT(D9.D11,E9.E11)`

The result is 275 which is computed by summing the product of the corresponding elements in columns D and E. The products that are included in the sum are 50, 120 and 105.

When you finish the statistical functions exercise, your screen should look like Figure 10-3.

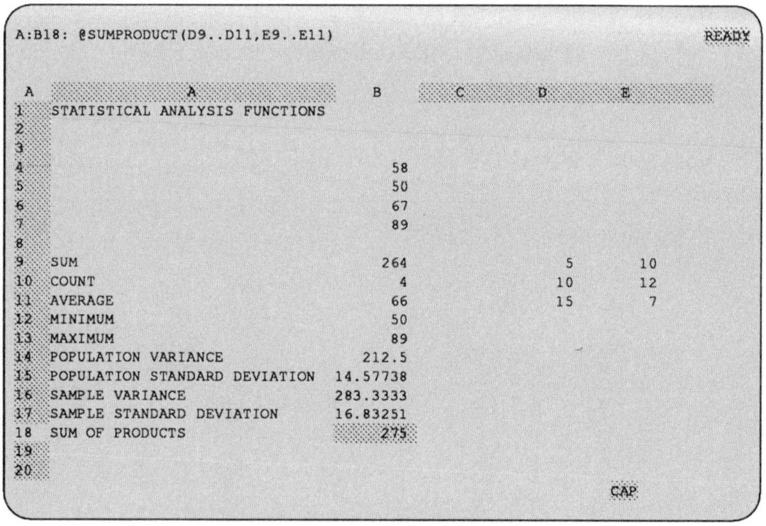

```
A:B18: @SUMPRODUCT(D9..D11,E9..E11)                                   READY

A              A                      B         C         D         E
1   STATISTICAL ANALYSIS FUNCTIONS
2
3
4                                          58
5                                          50
6                                          67
7                                          89
8
9   SUM                                   264                 5        10
10  COUNT                                   4                10        12
11  AVERAGE                                66                15         7
12  MINIMUM                                50
13  MAXIMUM                                89
14  POPULATION VARIANCE                 212.5
15  POPULATION STANDARD DEVIATION    14.57738
16  SAMPLE VARIANCE                  283.3333
17  SAMPLE STANDARD DEVIATION        16.83251
18  SUM OF PRODUCTS                       275
19
20
                                                                  CAP
```

Figure 10-3

When using the statistical analysis functions, it is important to note that labels have a value of zero and can distort the desired computations. In the following exercise, you will erase one of the numbers in the range B4..B7 by pressing the space bar. The results are then discussed.

Move	the cell pointer to cell B6
Press	the space bar
Press	↵

Although cell B6 appears to be blank, it actually contains a label. In the control panel, an apostrophe appears. Whenever a label is typed, the default label prefix is the apostrophe. The cell is not really blank; it contains a space. A space is treated as a label and therefore is given a value of 0 when used in a computation. For example, the minimum value computed by the `@MIN` function is now zero. The count computed by the `@COUNT` function still shows four items since the `@COUNT` function counts both numeric and nonnumeric items. Refer to Figure 10-4 to see how the label distorts the results of the computations.

A label counts as the value 0 in computations.

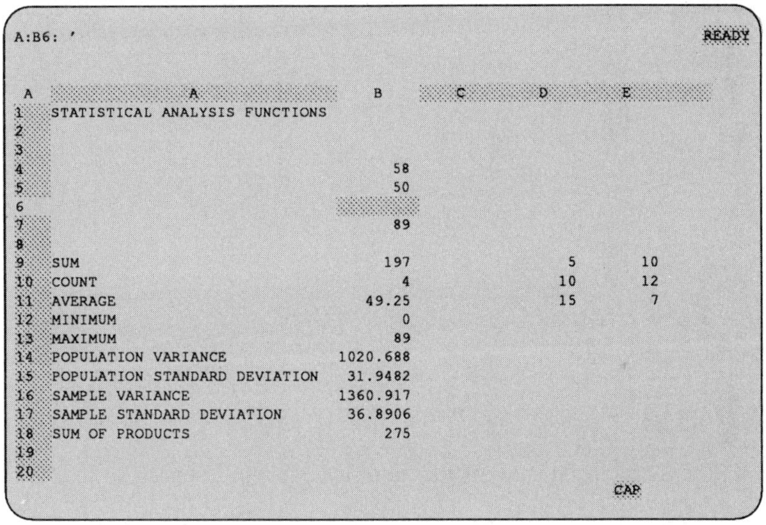

A:B6: ' READY

A	A	B	C	D	E
1	STATISTICAL ANALYSIS FUNCTIONS				
2					
3					
4		58			
5		50			
6					
7		89			
8					
9	SUM	197		5	10
10	COUNT	4		10	12
11	AVERAGE	49.25		15	7
12	MINIMUM	0			
13	MAXIMUM	89			
14	POPULATION VARIANCE	1020.688			
15	POPULATION STANDARD DEVIATION	31.9482			
16	SAMPLE VARIANCE	1360.917			
17	SAMPLE STANDARD DEVIATION	36.8906			
18	SUM OF PRODUCTS	275			
19					
20					

CAP

Figure 10-4

You can correct this problem by erasing the contents of cell B6. To truly erase cell B6, use the **R**ange **E**rase command sequence. Notice that the formulas have accurately calculated the desired results. Your screen should look like Figure 10-5.

A blank cell will not be used as a value in computations.

```
A:B6:                                                        READY

A   A                              B        C    D    E
1   STATISTICAL ANALYSIS FUNCTIONS
2
3
4                                        58
5                                        50
6
7                                        89
8
9   SUM                                 197        5   10
10  COUNT                                 3       10   12
11  AVERAGE                        65.66667       15    7
12  MINIMUM                              50
13  MAXIMUM                              89
14  POPULATION VARIANCE            282.8889
15  POPULATION STANDARD DEVIATION   16.8193
16  SAMPLE VARIANCE                424.3333
17  SAMPLE STANDARD DEVIATION      20.59935
18  SUM OF PRODUCTS                     275
19
20
                                                   CAP
```

Figure 10-5

FINANCIAL ANALYSIS FUNCTIONS

The 12 financial analysis functions available in Lotus 1-2-3 include:

CAPITAL BUDGETING:

@IRR	Internal rate of return
@NPV	Net present value

ANNUITIES:

@FV	Future value
@PV	Present value
@TERM	Number of time periods needed in the term of an ordinary annuity to accumulate a future value earning a specific periodic interest rate
@PMT	Payment amount

DEPRECIATION:

@SLN	Straight-line depreciation
@DDB	Double-declining balance depreciation
@SYD	Sum-of-the-years'-digits depreciation
@VDB	Variable declining balance depreciation

COMPOUNDING:

@CTERM	Number of time periods necessary for the value of an investment to increase to a specific value in the future
@RATE	Periodic interest rate necessary for the value of an investment to grow to a specific future value

Capital Budgeting

The two financial functions that can be used in capital budgeting and project evaluation activities are @IRR and @NPV.

@IRR

The @IRR function computes the internal rate of return for a series of cash flows that occur at regular periodic intervals. The user must supply the cash flows and a guess rate for the internal rate of return. The format of the @IRR function is as follows:

```
@IRR(rate,range of cash flows)
```

Two sets of information are needed in the formula—the guess rate and the cash flows. Sets of information needed for a function to compute accurately are referred to as **arguments**. Arguments must be entered in the correct order and must be separated by a comma. Note that no space should be entered after the comma that separates the two arguments in the @IRR function.

In this exercise, suppose that an investment is being considered that requires a cash investment of $2,100 the first year and the anticipated cash flows in years 2 through 5 are respectively $1,300, $700, $500 and $300.

If necessary, erase your screen. Create a worksheet like Figure 10-6.

```
A:A8: 0.18                                                        READY

A      A      B      C      D      E      F      G      H
1    -2100
2     1300
3      700
4      500
5      300
6
7
8     0.18
9
10
```

Figure 10-6

The initial investment, actually a cash outflow, is in cell A1. The negative number indicates the initial cash investment made by the investor. The range of anticipated cash flows from the investment appear in cells A2 through A5. The guess at the internal rate of return of 18 percent appears in cell A8.

To find the internal rate of return for the investment on which you entered data:

Move the cell pointer to cell A11

Type `@IRR(A8,A1.A5)`

The first argument in the `@IRR` formula identifies A8 as the cell with the guess rate of 18 percent. The second argument identifies A1..A5 as the cash flows beginning with the initial investment of $2,100 and ending with the cash flow in YEAR 5 of $300.

To enter the function in cell A11:

Press 

The function appears in the control panel. The result .168349 or about 16.83 percent is displayed. Your screen should look like Figure 10-7.

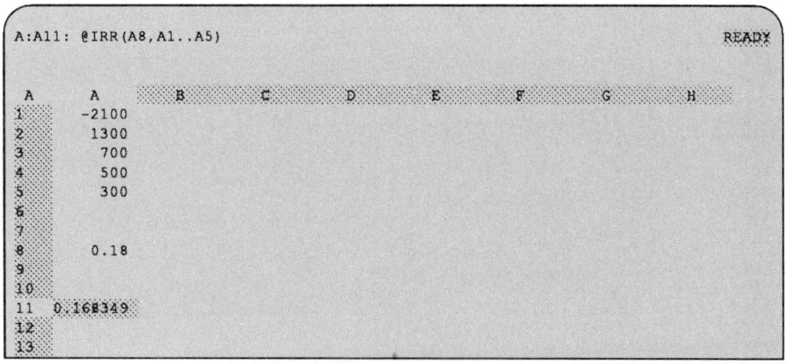

```
A:A11: @IRR(A8,A1..A5)                                              READY

 A     A       B       C       D       E       F       G       H
 1   -2100
 2    1300
 3     700
 4     500
 5     300
 6
 7
 8    0.18
 9
10
11  0.168349
12
13
```

Figure 10-7

Note that the guess rate could have been entered directly into the function as `@IRR(.18,A1..A5)`. The advantage of the guess rate being entered outside of the function is that it can be changed more readily. The cash flows must be entered as a range that is located elsewhere on the worksheet. A single-cell item, however, either can be entered directly into the formula or referenced with a cell address (e.g., .18 or A8 is acceptable in the `@IRR` function in the previous exercise).

ERR may appear as a result of using the `@IRR` function if convergence to within .0000001 does not occur within 30 iterations. Change the guess rate to a higher or lower value until a value appears for the internal rate of return.

@NPV

The net present value computes the present value for a set of cash flows using a specified discount rate. All cash flows are assumed to occur at the end of each year. The format of the `@NPV` function is:

```
@NPV(rate,range of cells)
```

In this exercise, consider an investment project that requires you to invest $2,000 initially and you receive payments of $900, $850, $600, $350, $200, and $50 at the end of the first through the sixth years. Assume that 10 percent is an appropriate discount rate.

To solve this problem, create the worksheet in Figure 10-8.

```
A:B6: 50                                                        READY

A      A         B         C       D       E       F       G       H
1        0.1       900
2                  850
3      -2000       600
4                  350
5                  200
6                   50
7
8
```

Figure 10-8

The discount rate is 10 percent and appears in cell A1. The initial investment is in cell A3. The cash flow payments are in cells B1 through B6.

To compute the net present value of the cash flows and add it to the initial investment of $2,000 (in cell A3):

Move the cell pointer to cell C1

Type `@NPV(A1,B1.B6)+A3`

The first argument identifies A1 as the discount rate of 10 percent. The second argument identifies B1..B6 as the cash flows beginning with the first year of $900 and ending with the last year at $50. Note that A3 (the initial investment) must be added to the net present value of the cash flows because, if it is included in the formula, it will be discounted.

To enter the function in cell C1:

Press ↵

The formula appears in the control panel. The result 362.9127 or $362.91 is displayed. Your screen should look like Figure 10-9.

```
A:C1: @NPV(A1,B1..B6)+A3                                        READY

A      A         B         C       D       E       F       G       H
1        0.1       900  362.9127
2                  850
3      -2000       600
4                  350
5                  200
6                   50
7
8
```

Figure 10-9

If desired, you can format with a dollar sign and two decimal places by using the **Range Format Currency** command sequence.

Annuities

The four functions that are available in 1-2-3 that are related to ordinary annuities include: `@FV, @PV, @TERM` and `@PMT`.

@FV

The future value function computes the future value of an annuity given the payment per period, an interest rate per period, and the number of periods. The general format of the `@FV` function is as follows:

```
@FV(payment, interest rate, term)
```

Assume you want to compute the future value of an annuity when the payment amount is $1,500, the interest rate is 13 percent, and the term is 10 years.

In the previous exercises in this chapter, single-cell items used in the financial analysis functions were not placed directly into the function, but were referenced by cell address. In this example, all three arguments are single-cell items. Instead of entering a formula in a format such as the following —`@FV(C1,C2,C3)`—all of the arguments in this formula can be placed directly into the formula—`@FV(1500,.13,10)`.

To find the future value of the given data:

Press [Home] (if necessary)

Type `@FV(1500,.13,10)`

The first argument specifies the payment per year as $1,500. The second argument specifies the interest rate as 13 percent. The third argument specifies the term as 10 years. To enter the function:

Press ↵

The function appears in the control panel. The result, 27629.62 or $27,629.62, is displayed on the worksheet. Your screen should look like Figure 10-10.

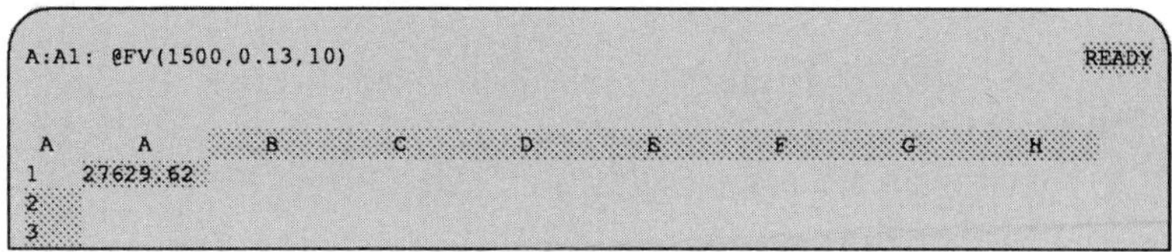

Figure 10-10

@PV

The present value function computes the present value of an annuity given a payment per period, interest rate per period, and the number of time periods. The general format of the `@PV` function is as follows:

```
@PV(payment, rate, number of periods)
```

In this exercise, you will determine the present value of an annuity where payments are $1,500 per year, the interest rate is 13 percent, and the term is 10 years.

To find the present value of the given data:

Press [Home] (if necessary)

Type `@PV(1500,.13,10)`

The first argument identifies the payment amount of $1,500. The second argument identifies the interest rate of 13 percent. The third argument identifies the term as 10 years.

To enter the function:

Press ↵

The function appears in the control panel. The result is 8139.365 or $8,139.37. Your screen should look like Figure 10-11.

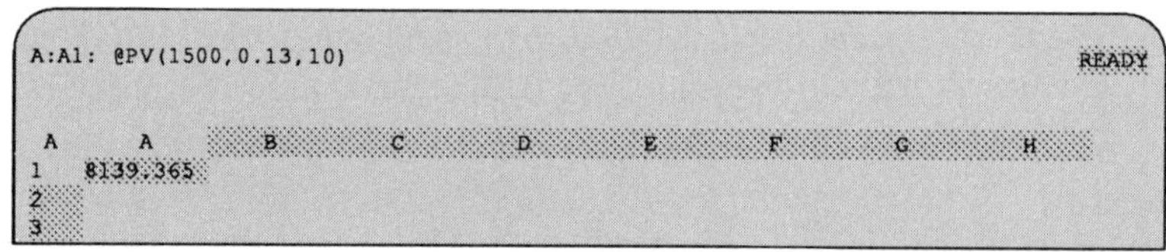

Figure 10-11

@TERM

`@TERM` calculates the number of payment periods in a term of an ordinary annuity necessary to accumulate a future value earning a periodic interest rate. Each payment is equal to the given payment amount in the formula. The general format for the `@TERM` function is as follows:

```
@TERM(payment,periodic interest rate,future value)
```

In this exercise, assume that $4,500 has been deposited each year on the same date into an account that pays an interest rate of 6 percent, compounded annually. The `@TERM` function will be used to determine how long it will take for you to have $20,000 in the account.

Using the given data:

Press [Home] (if necessary)

Type `@TERM(4500,.06,20000)`

The first argument identifies $4,500 as the payment amount. The second argument identifies .06 as the periodic interest rate. The third argument represents $20,000 as the future value.

To enter the function:

Press ↵

The answer is 4.05686, or about 4 years. Your screen should look like Figure 10-12.

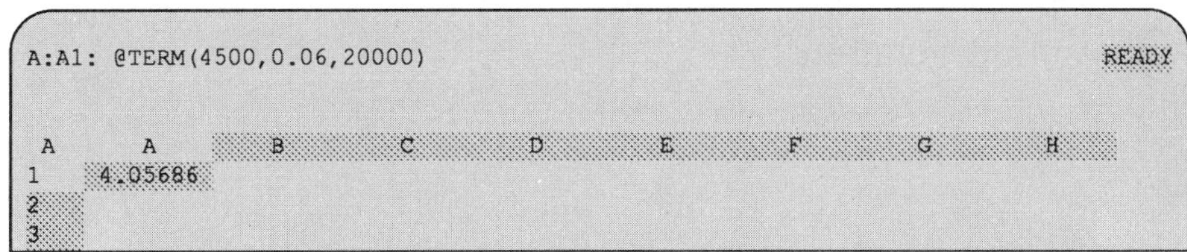

Figure 10-12

@PMT

You can compute the payment per period if you are given the principal amount, the interest rate per period and the number of periods. The general format for the `@PMT` function is as follows:

```
@PMT(principal, interest rate, term)
```

Suppose the principal of a loan is $1,200, the interest rate is 15 percent and the number of time periods is 10 years.

To determine the payment per year of the given data:

Press [Home] (if necessary)

Type `@PMT(1200,.15,10)`

The first argument identifies the principal of $1,200. The second argument identifies the interest rate of 15 percent. The third argument identifies the term as 10 years.

To enter the function:

Press ↵

The function appears in the control panel. The result is 239.1025 or $239.10 per year. Your screen should look like Figure 10-13.

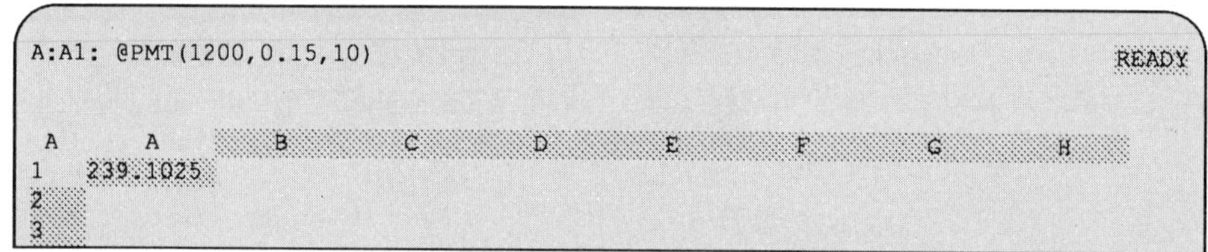

Figure 10-13

Depreciation

The four depreciation functions included in 1-2-3 are: `@SLN`, `@DDB`, `@SYD` and `@VDB`.

@SLN

The straight-line depreciation of an asset can be computed for one period given the cost, salvage value and estimated useful life of the asset. The general format for the `@SLN` function is as follows:

```
@SLN(cost,salvage value,estimated useful life)
```

In this exercise, you will determine the straight-line depreciation for equipment that is purchased for $13,000. The estimated useful life of the equipment is 6 years and the salvage value is estimated at $1,000.

To complete the next four exercises, create the worksheet in Figure 10-14, but do not include the function for computing the straight line depreciation.

To determine the straight-line depreciation for the equipment data:

Move the cell pointer to cell B5

Type `@SLN(B1,B2,B3)`

The first argument identifies B1 as the cell containing the cost of $13,000. The second argument identifies B2 as the cell containing the salvage value of $1,000. The third argument identifies B3 as the cell containing the useful life of 6 years. The formula `@SLN(13000,1000,6)` could have been entered as an alternative to using cell addresses for the various arguments.

To enter the function:

Press ↵

The function appears in the control panel. The result 2000 or $2,000 is displayed on the worksheet. Your screen should look like Figure 10-14.

```
A:B5: @SLN(B1,B2,B3)                                                    READY

A                A                         B        C        D        E        F
1  COST                                13000
2  SALVAGE VALUE                        1000
3  USEFUL LIFE                             6
4
5  STRAIGHT LINE                        2000
6  DOUBLE DECLINING BALANCE
7  SUM-OF-THE-YEARS DIGITS
8  VARIABLE DECLINING BALANCE
9
10
```

Figure 10-14

If you desire, you can format the results with a dollar sign and two decimal places.

@DDB

This exercise assumes you have just finished the previous exercise and the results are still displayed on the screen.

The depreciation of an asset using the double-declining balance method can be computed for a specified period given the cost, salvage value, estimated useful life, and the desired time period. The general format for the `@DDB` function is as follows:

```
@DDB(cost,salvage value,estimated useful life,period)
```

In this exercise, you will use the data given in the previous exercise to compute the depreciation for the equipment for the first year using the double-declining balance method.

To document that the depreciation will be computed only for YEAR 1 in this example (an optional step):

Move the cell pointer to cell C6

Enter YEAR 1

To compute the depreciation using the double-declining balance method:

Move the cell pointer to cell B6

Type `@DDB(B1,B2,B3,1)`

The first argument identifies B1 as the cell containing the cost at $13,000. The second argument identifies B2 as the cell containing the salvage value at $1,000. The third argument identifies B3 as the cell containing the useful life of the equipment at 6 years. The fourth argument indicates that this computation represents the depreciation for YEAR 1.

To enter the function:

Press ↵

The function appears in the control panel. The result 4333.333 or $4,333.33 is displayed. Your screen should look like Figure 10-15.

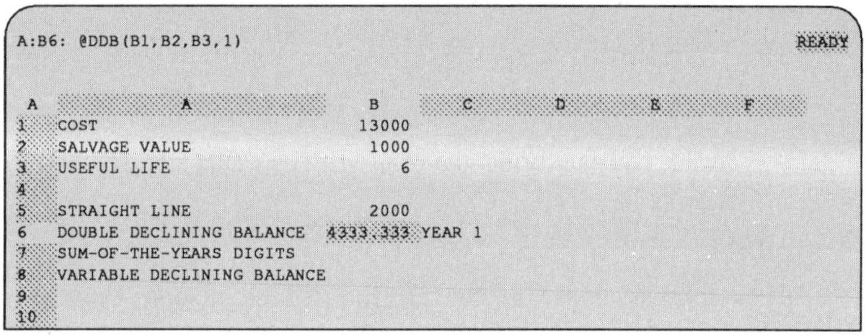

```
A:B6: @DDB(B1,B2,B3,1)                                              READY

A          A                      B         C       D       E       F
1  COST                         13000
2  SALVAGE VALUE                 1000
3  USEFUL LIFE                      6
4
5  STRAIGHT LINE                 2000
6  DOUBLE DECLINING BALANCE  4333.333 YEAR 1
7  SUM-OF-THE-YEARS DIGITS
8  VARIABLE DECLINING BALANCE
9
10
```

Figure 10-15

To compute the depreciation for the other time periods, you would have to enter the function again for each of the desired time periods.

@SYD

This exercise assumes you have just finished the previous exercise and the results are still displayed on the screen.

The depreciation of an asset using the sum-of-the-years'-digits method can be computed for a specified period given the cost, salvage value, estimated useful life, and the desired time period. The general format for the @SYD function is as follows:

```
@SYD(cost,salvage value,estimated useful life,period)
```

In this exercise, you will use the data given in the previous exercise to calculate the depreciation for the equipment for the third year using the sum-of-the-years'-digits method.

To indicate that the depreciation will be computed only for YEAR 3 in this example:

Move the cell pointer to cell C7

Type YEAR 3

To compute the depreciation using the sum-of-the-years'-digits method:

Move the cell pointer to cell B7

Type `@SYD(B1,B2,B3,3)`

The first argument identifies B1 as the cell containing the cost at $13,000. The second argument identifies B2 as the cell containing the salvage value of $1,000. The third argument identifies B3 as the cell containing the useful life of 6 years. The fourth argument indicates that this computation is for YEAR 3.

To enter the function:

Press ↵

The function appears in the control panel. The result 2285.714 or $2,285.71 is displayed on the worksheet. Your screen should look like Figure 10-16.

```
A:B7: @SYD(B1,B2,B3,3)                                                    READY

 A                A                    B        C        D        E        F
 1  COST                           13000
 2  SALVAGE VALUE                   1000
 3  USEFUL LIFE                        6
 4
 5  STRAIGHT LINE                   2000
 6  DOUBLE DECLINING BALANCE    4333.333 YEAR 1
 7  SUM-OF-THE-YEARS DIGITS     2285.714 YEAR 3
 8  VARIABLE DECLINING BALANCE
 9
10
```

Figure 10-16

To compute the depreciation values for the other time periods, you would have to enter the function again for each of the desired time periods.

@VDB

This exercise assumes that you have just completed the exercise in the previous section and the results are still displayed on your screen. The general formula for the `@VDB` function is:

```
@VDB(cost,salvage,life,start-period,end-period,
[depreciation-factor],[switch])
```

This function calculates the depreciation allowance of an asset for a length of time specified by the start-period and the end-period using the double-declining balance method. You can use the optional depreciation-factor to allow the percentage of straight-line depreciation to vary so you calculate depreciation values other than those determined using the double-declining balance method. The optional switch allows you to change the depreciation values in periods when the straight-line depreciation value is greater than that determined using the double-declining balance calculation.

The depreciation-factor can be any value greater than 0. If you do not specify a value for depreciation-factor, the `@VDB` function will compute depreciation using the double-declining balance method.

You should only include a value for the switch option, if you do not want `@VDB` to automatically switch from declining balance to straight-line when the straight-line depreciation is greater than declining-balance. The values that can be used for the switch are 0 and 1. If the value for the switch is 0, which is the default value, `@VDB` automatically changes from declining-balance to straight-line when straight-line values are greater. If the value assigned to the switch is 1, then `@VDB` never switches from the declining-balance method.

In this exercise you will use the data given in the previous exercise to compute the depreciation for YEAR 1 using 150 percent instead of 200 percent for the depreciation factor. You will also assume that you want to automatically switch to straight-line depreciation when the values for straight-line depreciation are greater than the values for 150 percent declining balance.

To document that the depreciation value will be computed only for YEAR 1 (an optional step):

Move	the cell pointer to cell C8
Enter	YEAR 1

To calculate the depreciation for the first year, assuming you purchased the equipment on the first day of the year, using the variable-rate depreciation function:

Move	the cell pointer to cell B8
Type	`@VDB(B1,B2,B3,0,1,1.5,0)`

The first three arguments indicate the cost is $13,000, the salvage value is $1,000 and the estimated useful life is 6 years. The fourth and fifth arguments specify that the depreciation is to be computed for the first year. The sixth argument designates the depreciation factor is 150 percent. The seventh argument indicates that the `@VDB` function is to automatically switch to straight-line depreciation when it is greater than the declining-balance depreciation.

Note: The 0 value did not actually need to be included, because switch is optional and the default value is 0.

To enter the function:

Press ↵

The function appears in the control panel. The result 3250 or $3,250.00 is displayed in cell B8. Your screen should look like Figure 10-17.

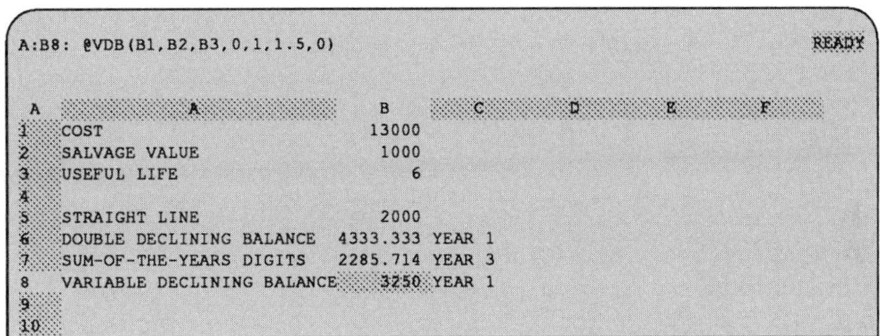

Figure 10-17

To compute the depreciation values for the other time periods, you would have to enter the function again for each of the desired time periods.

Single-Sum Compounding

The two single-sum compounding functions available in 1-2-3 are @CTERM and @RATE.

@CTERM

The @CTERM function calculates the number of compounding periods for an investment with a specified initial value to increase to a future value. A fixed interest rate per compounding period is used. The general format for the @CTERM function is as follows:

```
@CTERM(periodic interest rate, future value, present value)
```

In this exercise, assume that $4,500 was deposited in an account that pays an annual interest rate of 6 percent, compounded monthly. The @CTERM function can be used to determine how long it will be before you have $20,000 in the account.

Using the given data:

Press Home

Type @CTERM(.06/12,20000,4500)

The first argument identifies the periodic interest rate compounded monthly as .06/12. The second argument specifies the future value at $20,000. The third argument indicates the present value of $4,500.

To enter the function:

Press ↵

The answer is 299.0761 (represented in months), or about 25 years. Your screen should look like Figure 10-18.

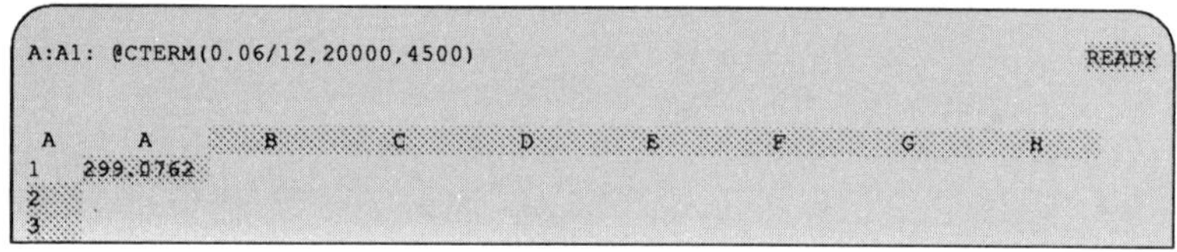

Figure 10-18

If you desire, you can format the number 299.0761 to 2 decimal places and place MONTHS in cell B1.

@RATE

`@RATE` calculates the periodic interest rate necessary for a specific initial value to increase to a particular future value over the number of compounding periods in the term. If the investment is compounded monthly, you must multiply the `@RATE` by 12 to determine the annual rate. The general format for the `@RATE` function is as follows:

```
@RATE(future value,present value,term)
```

Suppose $4,500 has been invested in a bond which matures in 14 years to $20,000. Interest is compounded monthly. You must use the `@RATE` function to determine the periodic interest rate.

Using the given data:

Press Home

Type `@RATE(20000,4500,14*12)`

The first argument identifies $20,000 is the future value. The second argument identifies $4,500 as the present value. The third argument specifies the terms in 168 months (14 years times 12 months).

To enter the function:

Press ↵

The answer is 0.008918 per month. You must multiply the value in cell A1 by 12 and place the results in A2 to calculate an annual rate. Your screen should look like Figure 10-19.

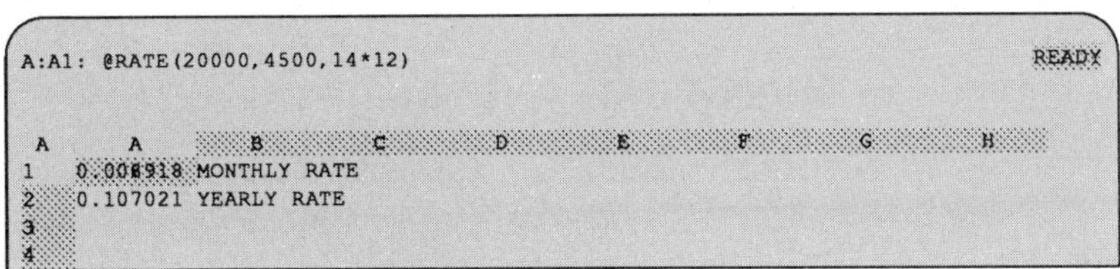

Figure 10-19

If you desire, you can format the rates as you deem appropriate and place the MONTH RATE and YEARLY RATE tables on your worksheet.

■ DATE AND TIME FUNCTIONS

There are 13 date and time functions available in 1-2-3. They can be grouped as follows:

DATE:

`@DATE`	Determines date number for a specified date
`@DATEVALUE`	Changes a string of characters that looks like a date into a date number
`@DAY`	Calculates the day of the month from a date number
`@MONTH`	Computes the month from a date number
`@YEAR`	Determines the year from a date number
`@D360`	Calculates the number of days between two dates assuming there are 360 days in a year

TIME:

`@TIME`	Computes a time number for a specific time consisting of an hour, minute and second
`@TIMEVALUE`	Changes a string of characters that looks like a time into a time number

@HOUR	Calculates the hour from a time number
@MINUTE	Computes the minute from a time number
@SECOND	Determines the second from a time number

CURRENT DATE AND TIME:

@TODAY	Computes the date number for the current date
@NOW	Calculates a value that corresponds to the current date and time

Date

The six date functions available in 1-2-3 include @DATE, @DATEVALUE, @DAY, @MONTH, @YEAR and @D360.

@DATE

The format of the @DATE function is:

```
@DATE(year,month,day)
```

where year is any two-digit number between 00 and 99, month is any integer between 1 and 12 and day is any integer between 1 and 31.

To enter the date June 24, 1990 with the @DATE function in cell A1:

Move	the cell pointer to cell A1
Type	@DATE(90,6,24)
Press	↵

The number 33048 appears in cell A1. This number indicates that 33,048 days have passed since December 31, 1899.

To format the date appropriately:

Press	/
Select	Range
Select	Format
Select	Date

Five different options for ways to display the date appear on the menu. The sixth option for displaying the time is discussed later in this chapter. Your screen should look like Figure 9-20.

```
A:A1: @DATE(90,6,24)                                                    MENU
1 (DD-MMM-YY)  2 (DD-MMM)  3 (MMM-YY)  4 (Long Intn'l)  5 (Short Intn'l)  Time
Lotus standard long form
 A      A       B       C       D       E       F       G       H
1     33048
2
3
```

Figure 10-20

Depending upon which option is chosen, the date in cell A1 can be displayed in one of the following five formats:

24-Jun-90

24-Jun

Jun-90

06/24/90

06/24

There are other formats for options 4 and 5 that can be accessed through the **W**orksheet **G**lobal **D**efault **O**ther **I**nternational **D**ate command sequence.

To choose option 4 from the Data Format menu:

Type 4

When prompted for the range to format:

Press ↵

The date format 06/24/90 is now displayed. Your screen should look like Figure 10-21.

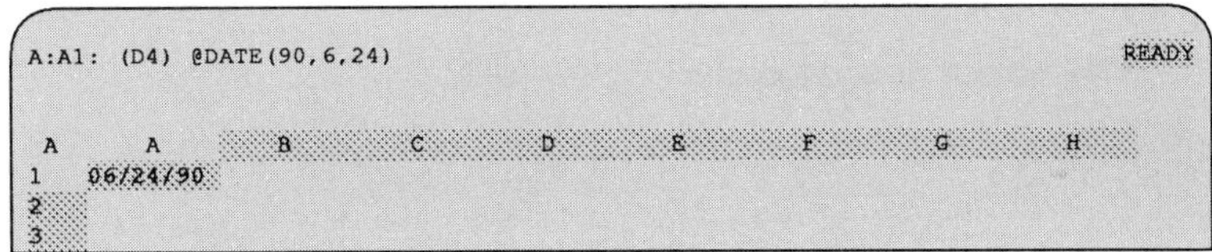

Figure 10-21

@DATEVALUE

This function returns the number of days that have elapsed since December 31, 1899 just as the `@DATE` function does. However, a single string of characters can be entered for the argument in the parentheses. The date string used in the `@DATEVALUE` function must be one of the acceptable Lotus 1-2-3 date formats. The format of the `@DATEVALUE` function is:

```
@DATEVALUE(string of characters)
```

Suppose you want to use the `@DATEVALUE` function to place June 24, 1990 on your worksheet.

Move the cell pointer to cell A1 (if necessary)

Type `@DATEVALUE("24-Jun-90")`

Press ↵

Then you decide to determine the number of days between December 31, 1990 and June 24, 1990. To calculate the number of days between the two dates:

Move the cell pointer to cell A2

Type `@DATEVALUE("31-Dec-90")`
`-@DATEVALUE("24-Jun-90")`

Press ↵

An alternative way to determine the number of days between June 24, 1990 and December 31, 1990 is:

Move the cell pointer to cell A3

Type `@DATEVALUE("31-Dec-90")-A1`

Press ↵

Your screen should look like Figure 10-22.

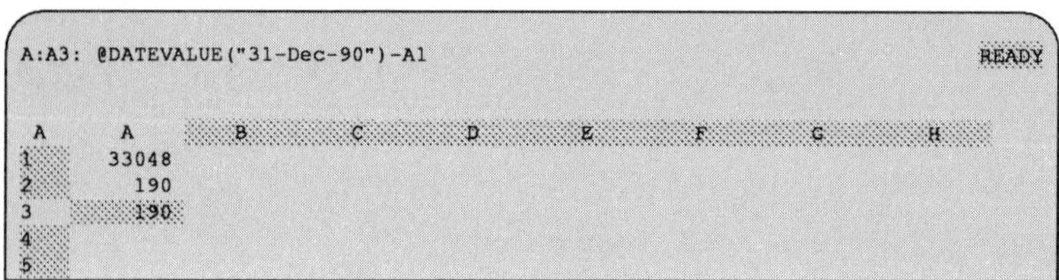

Figure 10-22

Note the values in cells A2 and A3 are the same, because you used two different approaches for entering the formulas.

@MONTH

At times, you may be given a date number for which you need to determine the month, day or year corresponding to the date number. For example, suppose you need to determine the month, day and year represented by the date number 33048.

The `@MONTH` function determines the month in which a particular date number occurs. The value computed using the `@MONTH` function will be an integer between 1 and 12 for the months January through December respectively. The format of the `@MONTH` function is:

```
@MONTH(date number)
```

To determine the month in which the date number 33048 occurs:

Move	the cell pointer to cell A1
Enter	Month
Move	the cell pointer cell B1
Type	`@MONTH(33048)`
Press	↵

Your screen should look like Figure 10-23. The value of 6 appearing in cell B1 indicates the date number occurs in the month of June.

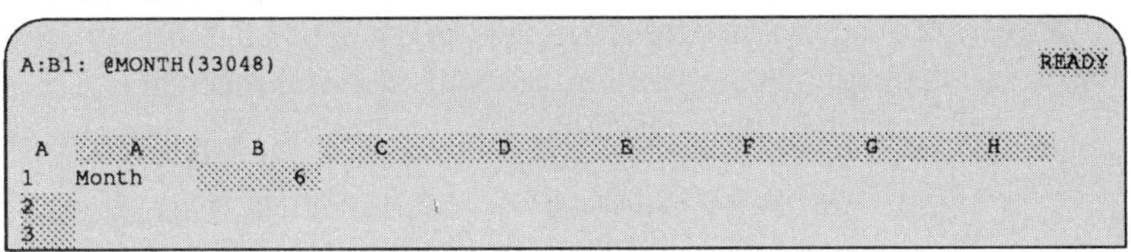

Figure 10-23

@DAY

The `@DAY` function determines on what day of the month a date occurs for a date number. An integer between 1 and 31 is entered into the cell in which the `@DAY` function is used. The format of the @DAY function is:

```
@DAY(date number)
```

For example, suppose you want to know the day of the month on which the date number 33048 occurred. To calculate the day of the month while leaving the results of the previous example in your worksheet:

Move	the cell pointer to cell A2
Enter	Day
Move	the cell pointer to cell B2
Type	`@DAY(33048)`
Press	↵

Your screen should look like Figure 10-24.

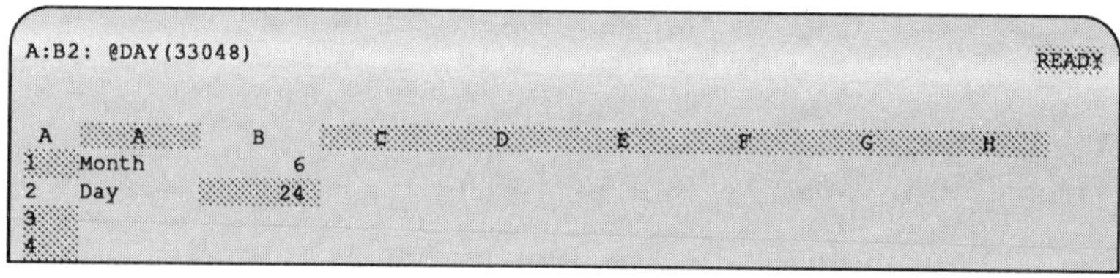

Figure 10-24

@YEAR

The `@YEAR` function determines the year in which a date number occurs. The value that appears in a cell in which the function is used will be a number between 0 and 99 representing the last two digits in the year for the remainder of this century. The number sequence 100, 101 and so on indicates years 2000, 2001 and so on. The format of the `@YEAR` function is:

```
@YEAR(date number)
```

Keep the results of the previous example in your worksheet. To determine the year in which the date number 33048 occurs:

Move	the cell pointer to cell A3
Enter	Year
Move	the cell pointer to cell B3
Type	`@YEAR(33048)`
Press	↵

Your screen should look like Figure 10-25.

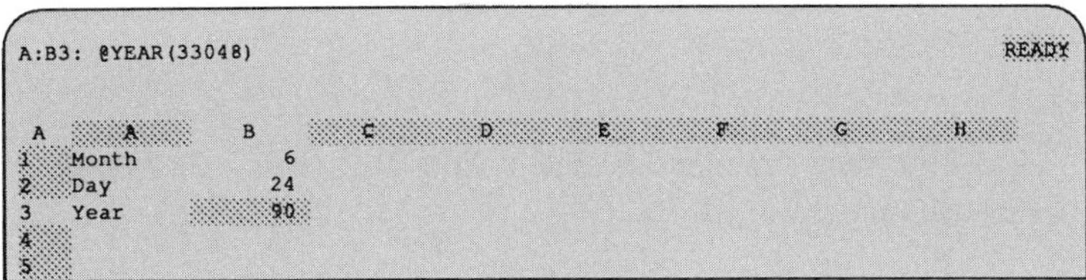

Figure 10-25

The value of 90 in cell B3 indicates the date number 33048 occurs in the year 1990. Combining the information appearing in Figure 10-25, the date number represents June 24, 1990. This result is consistent with the date number you computed using the `@DATE` function for June 24, 1990 earlier in this chapter.

@D360

The `@D360` function computes the number of days between two dates. This function uses a 360-day year and assumes there are 30 days in each month. The format of the `@D360` function is:

```
@D360(start-date,end-date)
```

Suppose you want to determine the number of days between July 1, 1990 and January 1, 1990. Begin this example with a blank worksheet. To calculate the number of days:

Move the cell pointer to cell A1

Type `@D360(@DATE(90,1,1),@DATE(90,7,1))`

Press ↵

Your screen should look like Figure 10-26.

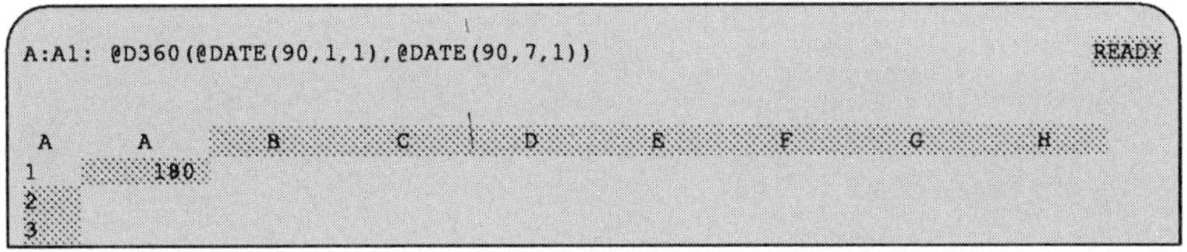

Figure 10-26

Notice that the time period represents six months and the calculated number of days is 180 indicating that the function in fact does assume there are 30 days per month.

Time

The five time functions available in 1-2-3 include @TIME, @HOUR, @TIMEVALUE, @MINUTE and @SECOND.

@TIME

This function is used to calculate a time serial number that represents the percentage of the day for the time specified by you. The function returns a value between 0 and .99999. For example, the number 0 represents 12:00 midnight. The format of the @TIME function is:

```
@TIME(hour,minute,second)
```

Suppose you want to know the serial time number for the time 7:10:59 p.m. To obtain the time serial number:

Move the cell pointer to cell A1

Type @TIME(19,10,59)

Press ↵

The number .799294 now appears in cell A1. This time serial number indicates that 7:10:59 is about 80 percent through the day.

Your screen should look like Figure 10-27.

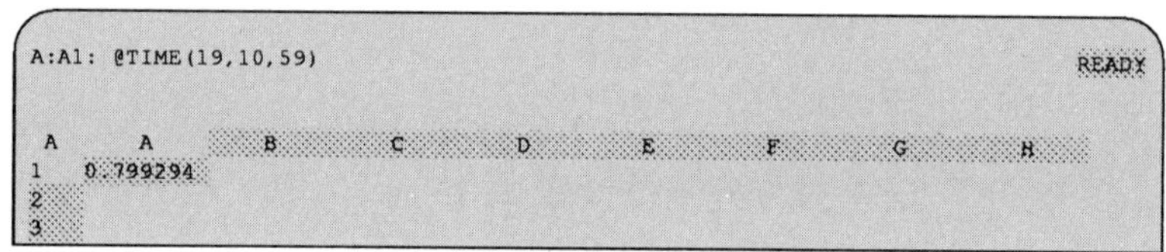

Figure 10-27

@TIMEVALUE

This function returns the time serial number just as the @TIME function does. However, a single string of characters can be entered for the arguments instead of the hour, time and minute. The time string used in the @TIMEVALUE function must be one of the acceptable time formats available in Lotus 1-2-3. The format of the @TIMEVALUE function is:

```
@TIMEVALUE(string of characters)
```

Suppose you want to determine the time serial number for the time 7:10:59 p.m.

Move the cell pointer to cell A1

Type @TIMEVALUE("7:10:59 p.m.")

Press ↵

Your screen should look like Figure 10-28.

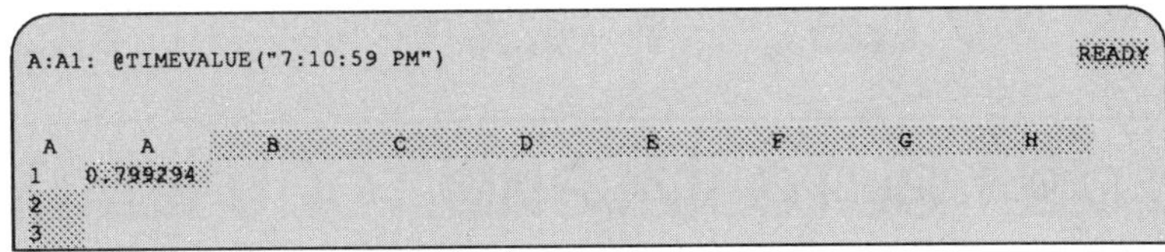
A:A1: @TIMEVALUE("7:10:59 PM") READY

A	A	B	C	D	E	F	G	H
1	0.799294							
2								
3								

Figure 10-28

Notice that the time serial number 0.799924 is the same value that you obtained when you used the @TIME function.

To format your screen so you can see the time:

Press /

Select Range

Select Format

Select Date

Select Time

Select 1

Press ↵

You will need to widen column A to 12 characters using the **W**orksheet **C**olumn **S**et-Width command sequence.

@HOUR

In some situations, you may be given a time serial number for which you need to determine the hour, minute and second corresponding to the time serial number. The @HOUR function determines the hour associated with a given time serial number. The format for the @HOUR function is:

```
@HOUR(time serial number)
```

Suppose you are given the time serial number 0.799294. To determine the hour of the day represented by this time serial number:

Move the cell pointer to cell A1

Enter	Hour
Move	the cell pointer to cell B1
Type	`@HOUR(0.799294)`
Press	↵

Your screen should look like Figure 10-29.

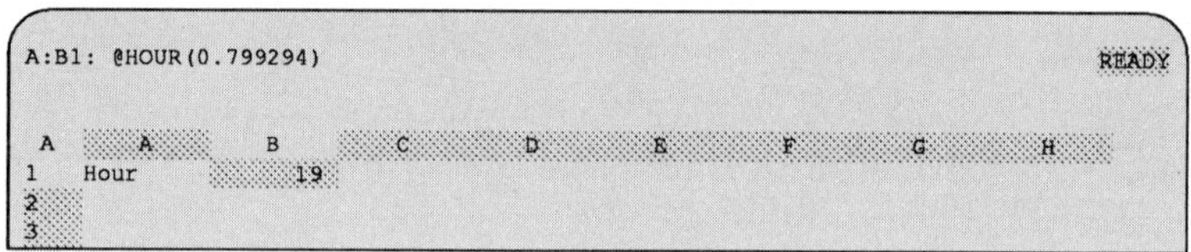

Figure 10-29

The value 19 appearing in cell B1 indicates that the time serial number represents a time between 7:00 p.m. and 8:00 p.m.

@MINUTE

The `@MINUTE` function calculates the minute of the hour represented by a time serial number. The format of the `@MINUTE` function is:

```
@MINUTE(time serial number)
```

Using the example time serial number 0.799294 again, you can compute the minute indicated by the time serial number using this function.

To compute the minute number while leaving the results of the previous example in your worksheet:

Move	the cell pointer to cell A2
Enter	Minute
Move	the cell pointer to cell B2
Type	`@MINUTE(0.799294)`
Press	↵

Your screen should look like Figure 10-30.

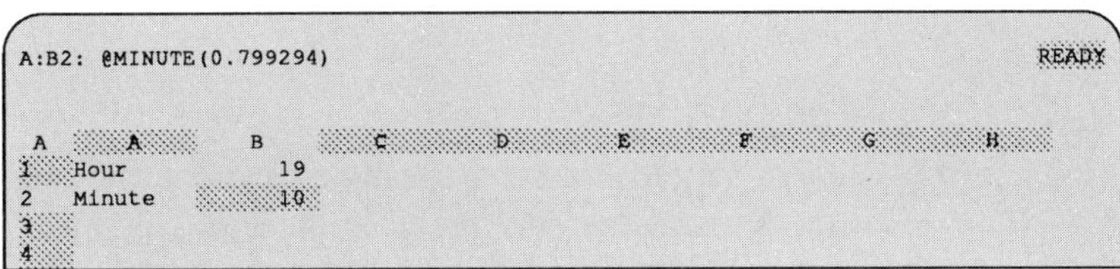

Figure 10-30

The value of 10 appearing in cell B2 specifies that the tenth minute is represented by the time serial number.

@SECOND

This function computes the second associated with a specific time serial number. The format for the `@SECOND` function is:

```
@SECOND(time serial number)
```

To determine the second associated with the time serial number 0.799294 that was used in the last two examples:

Move	the cell pointer to cell A3
Enter	Second
Move	the cell pointer to cell B3
Type	`@SECOND(0.799294)`
Press	↵

Your screen should look like Figure 10-31.

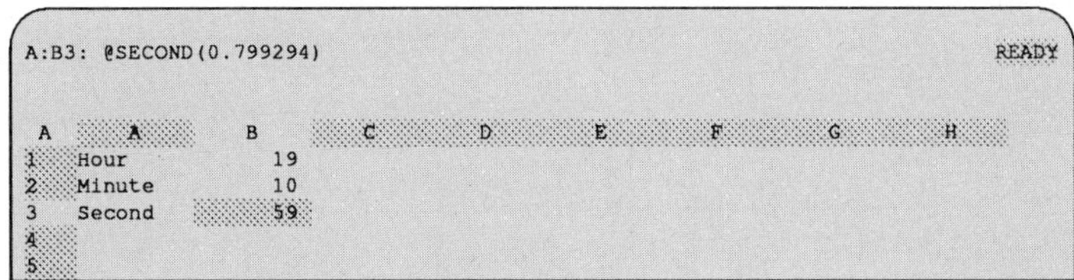

Figure 10-31

The value of 59 in cell B3 indicates the second represented by the time serial number is 59. Combining the information appearing in Figure 10-31, the time serial number 0.799294 represents the time 7:10:59 p.m. This result is consistent with the time serial number you calculated using the `@TIME` function for 7:10:59 p.m.

Current Date and Time

The two functions available in 1-2-3 to specify the current date and time are @TODAY and @NOW. These functions are very useful in documenting when a worksheet was last calculated. It is a good idea to use one of these functions on all of your worksheets.

@TODAY

The @TODAY function determines the date based on the current system date used by your computer. The format for the @TODAY function is:

@TODAY

To illustrate the use of the @TODAY function:

Move	the cell pointer to cell A1
Enter	Today
Move	the cell pointer to cell B1
Type	@TODAY
Press	↵

The date number for the current date now appears in cell B1. To format the date so you can determine the date, use the **R**ange **F**ormat **D**ate command sequence and select the first format option. You will need to set the column width to at least 10 using the **W**orksheet **C**olumn **S**et-Width command sequence.

Your screen should look similar to Figure 10-32.

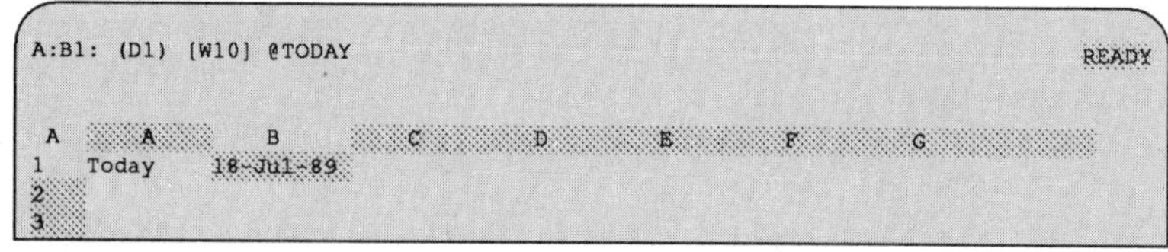

Figure 10-32

You should use this function when you only need to place the current date on your worksheet.

@NOW

The @NOW function returns the current date and time. You can format the resulting value using any of the date or time formats available in 1-2-3. The format for the @NOW function is:

```
@NOW
```

Suppose you want to place the current time on your worksheet with today's date from the last example.

Move	the cell pointer to cell A2
Enter	Now
Move	the cell pointer to cell B2
Type	@NOW
Press	↵

The value on your screen includes the current date number and the time serial number. The integer portion of the value is the date number and the decimal portion is the time serial number.

Use the **R**ange **F**ormat **D**ate **T**ime command sequence and select the second format option to format cell B2 so you can see a time.

Your screen should look similar to Figure 10-33.

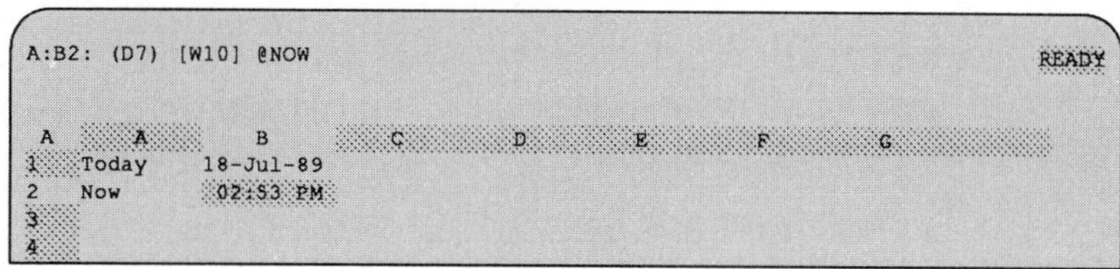

Figure 10-33

The current time now should appear on your screen. Note that if you enter anything in the worksheet, the time also will be updated on the screen. The @NOW function is particularly useful if you make changes to a worksheet several times in one day for "what-if" analysis purposes.

LOGICAL FUNCTIONS

There are eight logical special functions available in 1-2-3. The logical functions are:

`@IF`	Used to test a condition to determine if it is true or false
`@FALSE`	Returns a value of 0 (false)
`@TRUE`	Returns a value of 1 (true)
`@ISERR`	Returns a value of 1 (true) if the cell contains an error (ERR); otherwise the value returned is 0
`@ISNA`	Returns a value of 1 if not available (NA) appears in a cell; otherwise the value is 0
`@ISNUMBER`	Returns a value of 1 if a value or blank cell is present; otherwise the value is 0
`@ISRANGE`	Returns the value of 1 if a range is defined; otherwise the value is 0
`@ISSTRING`	Returns a value of 1 if a string of characters is present; otherwise the value is 0

@IF

The `@IF` function allows you to test a condition and select one of two options depending on the results of the test. The general format of the `@IF` function is:

```
@IF(condition,result if condition is true,result if
condition is false)
```

To illustrate the use of the `@IF` function, suppose the income before taxes for a company is $250,000 and the tax rate is 40 percent. Assume you enter 250000 in cell A1 of a worksheet and .40 in A2. To compute the taxes due, you could create the formula +A1*A2 and place it in cell A3.

However, in some situations, an organization may lose money. Therefore, the formula will not work properly, because the company cannot pay a negative amount of taxes. In fact, the tax amount should be zero.

The @IF function can be used so that the formula can work properly. To illustrate the use of the @IF function:

Move	the cell pointer to cell A1
Enter	250000
Move	the cell pointer to cell A2
Enter	.40
Move	the cell pointer to cell A3
Type	`@IF(A1>0,A1*A2,0)`

The first argument, A1>0, is the condition. This condition is used to determine if the value in A1 is greater than 0. The second argument, A1*A2, is the formula that will be used to place a value in cell A3 if the condition is true. The third argument, 0, indicates that a 0 will be entered in cell A3 if the condition is false.

To enter the @IF function in cell A3:

Press	↵

The formula appears in the control panel, and the number 100000 is in cell A3. Since the condition, A1>0, is true, the formula A1*A2 is calculated and the value of 100000 is placed in the cell.

Your screen should look like Figure 10-34.

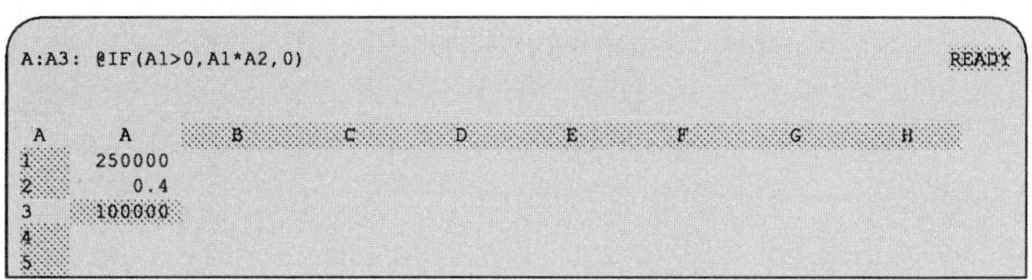

Figure 10-34

To test the **false** argument in the @IF function:

Move	the cell pointer to cell A1
Enter	-250000

Notice that the value in cell A3 changes to 0.

The remaining portion of the @IF function section includes illustrations of logical operators that can be used in an @IF function and nested @IF functions.

Logical Operators

Logical operators combine the numbers within conditional statements or formulas. The logical operators for simple logical statements are as follows:

Operator	Definition
=	equal
<	less than
<=	less than or equal
>	greater than
>=	greater than or equal
< >	not equal

Logical Operators for Compound Statements

Logical operators can be used to combine multiple conditions. The #AND#, #OR# and #NOT# logical operators for Lotus 1-2-3 are now discussed.

#AND#

#AND# can be used to combine multiple statements. For example, `@IF(A5=0#AND#B5=0,Z5,C5)` tests two conditions. More than one #AND# may be used in a formula. When the #AND# statement is used to link multiple conditions, *all* conditions must be true before the true result (Z5) can be executed.

#OR#

#OR# can be used to test if one argument *or* the other is true. For example, `@IF(A5=0#OR#B5=0,Z5,C5)` would result in the *true* result (Z5) if *either* A5=0 or B5=0. When the #OR# statement is used to link multiple conditions, *all* conditions must be false for the false result (C5) to be executed.

#NOT#

#NOT# can be used to indicate that a condition is not true. For example, `@IF(#NOT#A5=0#OR#B5=0,Z5,C5)` tests whether A5 is *not* equal to zero or if B5=0. Unlike the logical operators #OR# and #AND#, the #NOT# logical operator is used *before* a condition.

Nested IF

One @IF function may be nested inside another, as illustrated by the following example:

```
@IF(B1=25,B2*B1,@IF(B1=35,B3*B1,@IF(B1=45,B4*B1,0)))
```

The @IF function is read from left to right. The first two @IF functions have @IF functions for the false response. The parentheses used to end the @IF functions are at the end of the formula.

@FALSE

When the @FALSE function is used, it returns a value of 0. The format of the @FALSE function is:

```
@FALSE
```

Suppose you want to pay someone a commission of 10 percent of the sales amount if their sales are at least $1,000 and nothing if their sales are less than $1,000.

To illustrate the use of the @FALSE function to solve this problem:

Move	the cell pointer to cell A1
Enter	Sales
Move	the cell pointer to cell A2
Enter	Commission
Move	the cell pointer to cell C1
Enter	900
Move	the cell pointer to cell C2
Type	`@IF(C1>=1000,C1*.10,@FALSE)`

In this @IF function, the @FALSE function will place a value of 0 in cell C2 whenever the sales amount is less than $1,000. To enter the @IF function in cell C2:

Press	↵

Your screen should look like Figure 10-35.

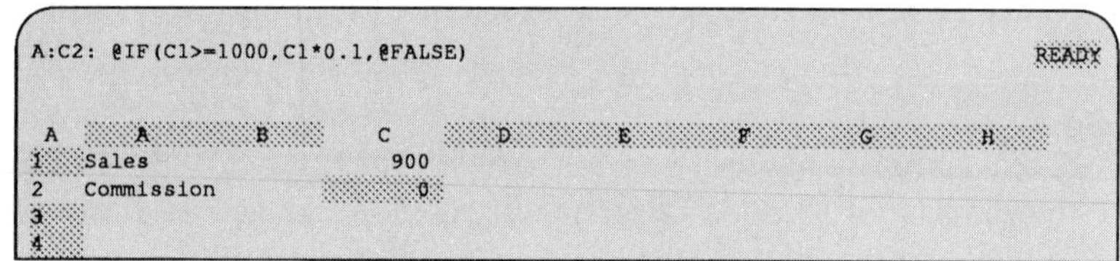

Figure 10-35

Notice that since the sales amount is less than $1,000, a value of 0 appears in cell C2. Change the value of sales to $1,000 and then $1,500 to make sure the `@FALSE` function works properly.

@TRUE

The `@TRUE` function returns a value of 1 when it is used. The format of the `@TRUE` function is:

```
@TRUE
```

Assume that you need to determine whether the value in a cell is less than 500. You can use the `@TRUE` and `@FALSE` functions together with an `@IF` function to indicate whether the value is less than 500.

To illustrate the use of the `@TRUE` function:

Move	the cell pointer to cell A1
Enter	450
Move	the cell pointer to cell A2
Type	`@IF(A1<500,@TRUE,@FALSE)`
Press	↵

Your screen should look like Figure 10-36.

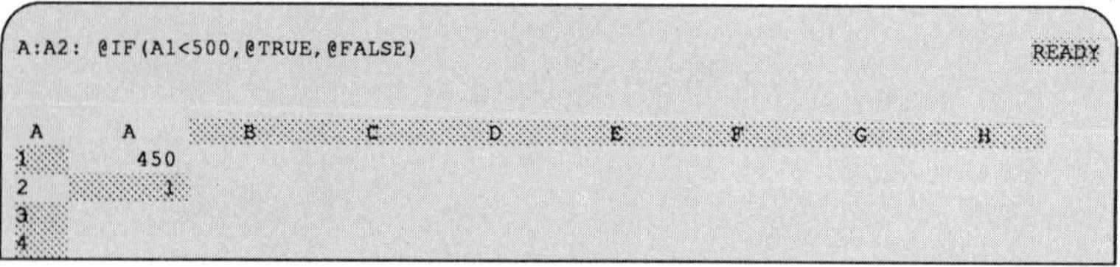

Figure 10-36

The value of 1 in cell A2 indicates that the @TRUE function was used. Change the value in cell A1 to 500 and then 750 to make sure the functions work properly.

@ISERR

The @ISERR function determines whether the contents of a cell contains ERR. For example, the characters are placed in a cell by 1-2-3 whenever you try to divide by zero. If ERR is present when the @ISERR function is used, the value of 1 (true) is returned, otherwise a value of 0 (false) is returned.

The format of the @ISERR function is:

```
@ISERR(x)
```

where *x* can be a cell location, string of characters, condition or value.

Suppose that you need to divide the value in one cell by the value in another cell. In some cases the denominator may be zero, but you do not want ERR to appear in the cell where the division occurs. The @ISERR function can be used in such a situation.

To illustrate the use of the @ISERR:

Move the cell pointer to cell B1

Enter 50

Move the cell pointer to cell B2

Enter 0

Move the cell pointer to cell B3

Enter +B1/B2

You now have the characters ERR in cell B3. Suppose you want the number 0 to appear in cell B3 if an attempt to divide by 0 occurs.

Type `@IF(@ISERR(B1/B2),0,B1/B2)`

If division by 0 is attempted, then a 0 is placed in cell B3, otherwise the cell B1 is divided by B2.

To enter the function in cell B3:

Press ↵

Your screen should look like Figure 10-37.

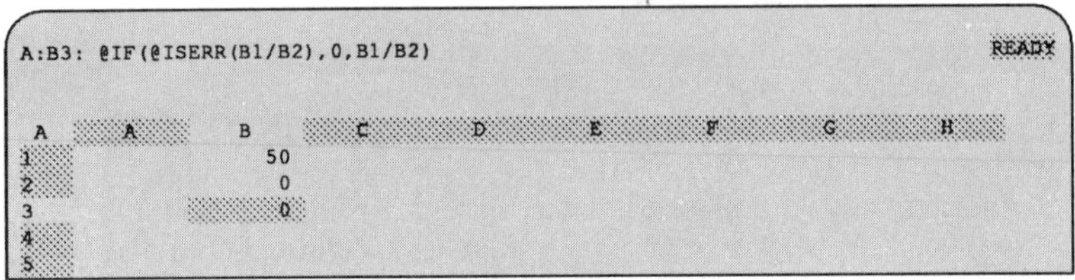

Figure 10-37

The value of 0 appearing in cell B3 indicates division by 0 was attempted. Change the value in B2 to 10 to verify the `@ISERR` function works properly.

@ISNA

The `@ISNA` function is used to verify whether NA appears in a cell. The format of the `@ISNA` function is :

`@ISNA(x)`

where *x* can be a cell location, string of characters, condition or value.

To illustrate the use of the `@ISNA` function:

Move	the cell pointer to cell A1
Enter	`@NA`

Note the characters NA, meaning not available, appear in cell A1.

Assume that you would like to place a 1 in cell B1 if NA is present and a 0 if NA does not appear.

Move	the cell pointer to cell B1
Type	`@IF(@ISNA(A1),1,0)`
Press	↵

Your screen should now look like Figure 10-38.

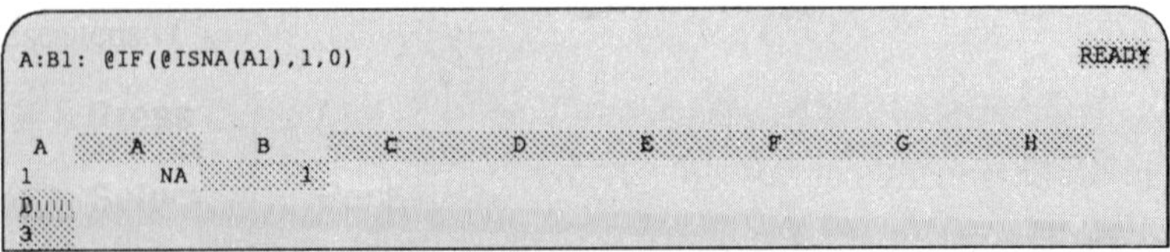

Figure 10-38

The value 1 in cell indicates NA appears in cell A1. To illustrate another approach to the problem enter `@IF(ISNA(A1), @TRUE, @FALSE)` in cell B1. The value of 1 should also appear in cell B1. Change the contents of cell A1 to 100 and verify the `@ISNA` function works properly when A1 does not contain NA.

@ISNUMBER

The `@ISNUMBER` function determines if a value or a blank is present. The format of the `@ISNUMBER` function is:

```
@ISNUMBER(x)
```

where *x* can be any cell location, string of characters, condition or value.

If a value or a blank cell is present, a 1 is returned, otherwise a 0 is returned.

Suppose you need to check a cell to determine what type of data is included in the cell. To ascertain whether a value or blank cell is present:

Move	the cell pointer to cell B1
Enter	100
Move	the cell pointer to cell A3
Type	`@ISNUMBER(B1)`
Press	↵

Your screen should look like Figure 10-39.

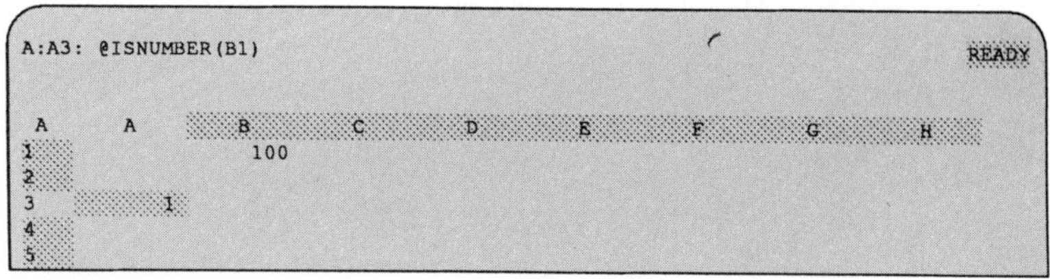

Figure 10-39

The number 1 appears in cell A3 indicating that a value appears in cell B1. Use the **R**ange **E**rase command sequence to erase cell B1. The value 1 remains in cell A3, because the B1 is now a blank cell. If you press the space bar and press the ↵ key, a 0 will appear in cell A3 specifying that B1 does not contain a value or it is not a blank cell.

@ISRANGE

The @ISRANGE function is used to determine whether a string of characters is a range name that has been defined for the worksheet. The format of the @ISRANGE function is:

```
@ISRANGE(string of characters)
```

Before you use the @ISRANGE function, you need to create the worksheet appearing in Figure 10-40.

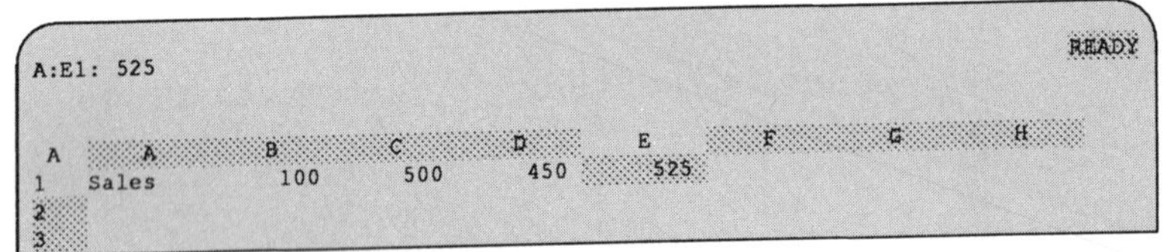

Figure 10-40

Use the **R**ange **N**ame **C**reate command sequence to create the name SALES for the range of cells that includes the sales values in cells B1 through E1.

To illustrate the use of the @ISRANGE function:

Move the cell pointer to cell A3

Type @ISRANGE(SALES)

Press ↵

Your screen should now look like Figure 10-41.

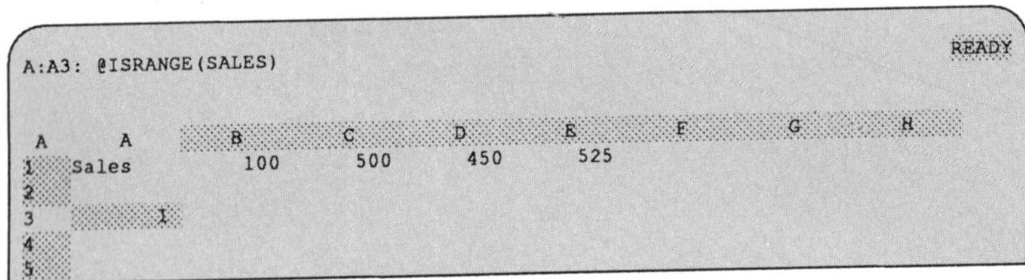

Figure 10-41

The value of 1 appearing in cell A3 indicates the range name SALES has been defined for the worksheet. If the range name had not been defined, a 0 would have appeared in cell A3.

@ISSTRING

The `@ISSTRING` function is used to determine whether a string of characters is present. The format for the `@ISSTRING` function is:

```
@ISSTRING(x)
```

where *x* can be a cell location, string of characters, condition or value. If a string of characters is present, a 1 is returned. When a value or a blank cell is present, a value of 0 is returned.

Suppose you have a set of characters in a cell and you need to determine whether the cell contains a set of alphanumeric characters.

To illustrate how you can use the `@ISSTRING` function to determine what type of characters are present in the cell:

Move the cell pointer to cell C1

Enter Lotus 1-2-3

Move the cell pointer to cell C3

Type `@ISSTRING(C1)`

Press ↵

Your screen should look like Figure 10-42.

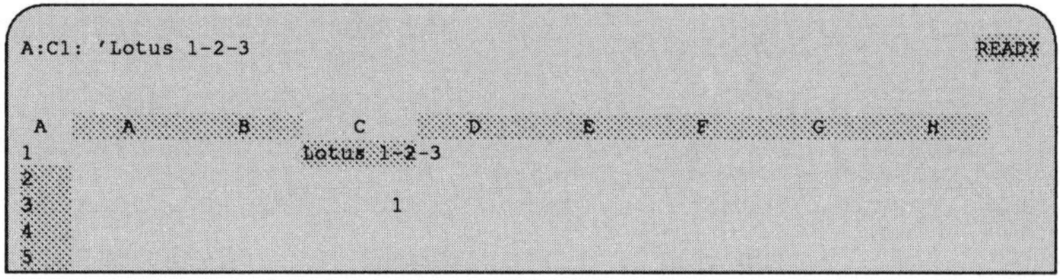

Figure 10-42

The value 1 appears in cell C3 indicating that the contents of C1 are a string of alphanumeric characters or a space. Use the **R**ange **E**rase command sequence to erase cell C1. A zero then appears in cell C3 indicating C1 is a blank cell. Enter the value 200 in cell C1. The zero value remains in cell C3, because a value is present in cell C1.

■ DATABASE FUNCTIONS

There are 11 database functions available in 1-2-3. They can be grouped into two categories:

DATABASE STATISTICAL FUNCTIONS:

`@DSUM`	Calculates the sum of values for a field in a database table satisfying a criteria range
`@DCOUNT`	Determines the number of nonblank cells for a field in a database table satisfying a criteria range
`@DAVG`	Computes the arithmetic mean of values for a field in a database table satisfying a criteria range
`@DMIN`	Determines the minimum value for a field in a database table satisfying a criteria range
`@DMAX`	Determines the maximum value for a field in a database table satisfying a criteria range
`@DVAR`	Calculates the population variance for a field in a database table satisfying a criteria range
`@DSTD`	Computes the population standard deviation for a field in a database table satisfying a criteria range
`@DVARS`	Calculates the sample variance for a field in a database table satisfying a criteria range
`@DSTDS`	Computes the sample standard deviation for a field in a database table satisfying a criteria range

DATABASE QUERY FUNCTIONS:

`@DGET`	Finds a value in a database table or field satisfying a criteria range
`@DQUERY`	Sends a command to an external database management software package

Database Statistical Functions

The nine database statistical functions available in 1-2-3 are: @DSUM, @DCOUNT, @DAVG, @DMIN, @DMAX, @DVAR, @DSTD, @DVARS, and @DSTDS. These functions are very similar to the statistical analysis functions discussed earlier in this chapter. As mentioned in Chapter 8, a **database** is a collection of related data or records. With the database statistical functions, you can complete statistical analysis on a set of cells that satisfy a particular criteria.

For example, you may have a database of all employees located in California, but you only want to know how many of the people live in Los Angeles. @COUNT can determine how many employees are in the database. @DCOUNT can be used to obtain a count for only those individuals living in Los Angeles. The database statistical functions are designed for use on database tables. The D in front of each function indicates that it is a database statistical function.

The format for all of the database statistical functions is:

```
@function name(input range,field location,criteria)
```

The **input range** is the database area that includes the field names and records in the database. The **field location** is used to indicate which column should be used for the calculations. When specifying the column in the database, start counting with the number zero. Therefore, if the third column in a database is the desired field location, it is referred to as field number two in the function. The **criteria** range specifies the criteria that must be satisfied.

Before you use the database statistical functions, you need to create the database table in Figure 10-43.

A:A1: 'NAME READY

A	A	B		C	D	E	F	G
1	NAME	SALARY	ST					
2	BROWN	32000	TX					
3	CHIN	28000	CA					
4	JONES	45000	TX					
5	MARTINEZ	31000	TX					
6	SMITH	27000	CA					
7	WHITE	35000	NY					
8								
9								

Figure 10-43

The database table includes the last name, salary and state location of employees working for an organization. Save the worksheet on a file using the name SALS.

Assume that you want to apply the database statistical functions to those individuals earning more than $30,000. The individuals satisfying this criteria are Brown, Jones, Martinez and White.

To place the criteria on your worksheet:

Move	the cell pointer to cell D2
Enter	SALARY
Move	the cell pointer to cell D3
Enter	+SALARY>30000

ERR should appear in cell D2. Use the **R**ange **F**ormat **T**ext command sequence to place the text version of the criteria on your screen. You will need to set the column width to 14 characters so you can see the entire formula.

Create the range name CRITERIA and include the cells D2 through D3 as the range. Place the word CRITERIA in cell D1 and names of the database statistical functions in cells D6 through D14. Your screen should look like Figure 10-44.

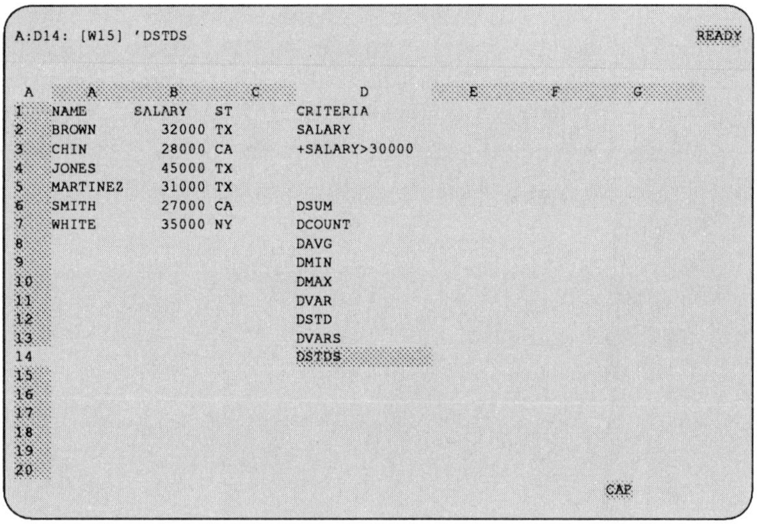

```
A:D14: [W15] 'DSTDS                                              READY

 A       A          B       C          D               E       F       G
 1   NAME       SALARY   ST      CRITERIA
 2   BROWN       32000  TX      SALARY
 3   CHIN        28000  CA      +SALARY>30000
 4   JONES       45000  TX
 5   MARTINEZ    31000  TX
 6   SMITH       27000  CA      DSUM
 7   WHITE       35000  NY      DCOUNT
 8                               DAVG
 9                               DMIN
10                               DMAX
11                               DVAR
12                               DSTD
13                               DVARS
14                               DSTDS
15
16
17
18
19
20
                                                            CAP
```

Figure 10-44

Create the range name DATABASE and include cells A1 through C7 as the range.

@DSUM

The `@DSUM` function computes the sum of values for a field that satisfies a criteria.

To compute the sum for the cells satisfying the criteria in the SALS worksheet:

Move the cell pointer to cell E6

Type `@DSUM(DATABASE,1,CRITERIA)`

Press ↵

DATABASE identifies cells A1 through C7 as the input range, the 1 indicates SALARY is the field location, and CRITERIA specifies D2 through D3 as the criteria range. The value 143000 appears in cell E6. This is the sum of the salaries for Brown, Chin, Martinez and White who each earn more than $30,000.

@DCOUNT

This function counts the number of nonblank cells for a field in a database table that satisfy a specified criteria.

To illustrate the use of the `@DCOUNT` function for the SALS worksheet:

Move the cell pointer to cell E7

Type `@DCOUNT(DATABASE,1,CRITERIA)`

Press ↵

The value 4 appears in cell E7 indicating there are four individuals in the database that have a salary greater than $30,000.

@DAVG

The `@DAVG` function calculates the arithmetic mean of the values for a field in a database table that satisfy a criteria.

To demonstrate the use of the `@DAVG` function for the SALS worksheet:

Move the cell pointer to cell E8

Type `@DAVG(DATABASE,1,CRITERIA)`

Press ↵

The value 35,750 appearing is the average salary of the four individuals that have a salary greater than $30,000.

@DMIN

The @DMIN function determines the minimum value for a field in a database table that satisfies a criteria.

To illustrate the use of the @DMIN function for the SALS worksheet:

Move the cell pointer to cell E9

Type `@DMIN(DATABASE,1,CRITERIA)`

Press ↵

The value 31,000 that appears in cell E9 indicates that the lowest salary among the individuals having a salary greater than $30,000 is $31,000.

@DMAX

The @DMAX function determines the maximum value for a field in a database table that satisfies a criteria.

To demonstrate the use of the @DMAX function for the SALS worksheet:

Move the cell pointer to cell E10

Type `@DMAX(DATABASE,1,CRITERIA)`

Press ↵

The value 45,000 that appears in cell E9 specifies that the highest salary among the employees having a salary greater than $30,000 is $45,000.

@DVAR

The @DVAR function computes the population variance for the values in a field of a database table that satisfy a criteria. It is assumed that the database table represents all of the data that can be considered.

To illustrate the use of the @DVAR function for the SALS worksheet:

Move the cell pointer to cell E11

Type `@DVAR(DATABASE,1,CRITERIA)`

Press ↵

The value 30,687,500 that appears in cell E10 is the population variance for the salaries for the persons having a salary greater than $30,000.

@DSTD

The @DSTD function computes the population standard deviation for the values in a field of a database table that satisfy a criteria.

To demonstrate the use of the @DSTD function for the SALS worksheet:

Move the cell pointer to cell E12

Type `@DSTD(DATABASE,1,CRITERIA)`

Press ↵

The value 5,539.63 is the population standard deviation for the salaries of the employees that have a salary greater than $30,000.

@DVARS

The @DVARS function computes the population sample variance for the values in a field of a database table that satisfy a criteria. It is assumed that the database table includes only a sample or portion of the data that can be considered.

To illustrate the use of the @DVARS function for the SALS worksheet:

Move the cell pointer to cell E13

Type `@DVARS(DATABASE,1,CRITERIA)`

Press ↵

The value 40,916,667 appearing in cell E13 is the sample variance for the salaries of the personnel earning more than $30,000.

@DSTDS

The @DSTDS function calculates the sample standard deviation for the values in a field of a database table that satisfy a criteria. It is assumed that the database table includes only a sample or a portion of the data that can be considered.

To demonstrate the use of the @DSTDS function for the SALS worksheet:

Move the cell pointer to cell E14

Type `@DSTDS(DATABASE,1,CRITERIA)`

Press ↵

The value 6,396.614 appearing in cell E14 is the sample standard deviation for the salaries of the employees having a salary greater than $30,000. After entering all of the database statistical functions, your screen should look like Figure 10-45.

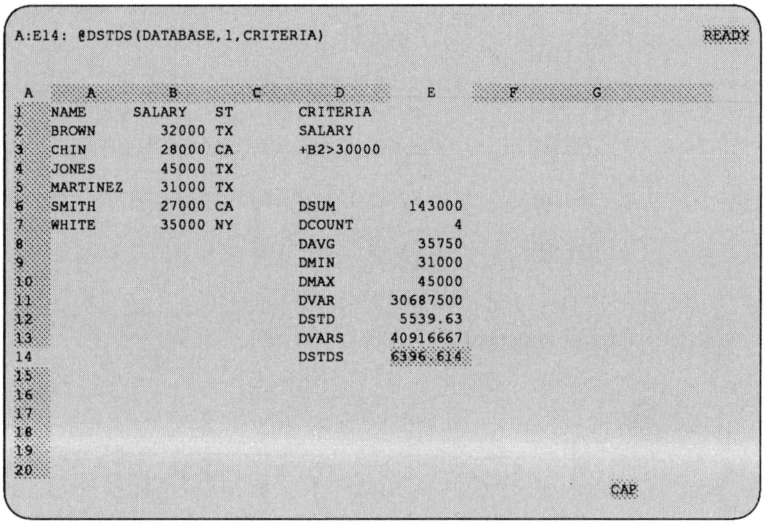

```
A:E14: @DSTDS(DATABASE,1,CRITERIA)                                READY

A     A          B        C        D            E        F        G
1   NAME       SALARY   ST       CRITERIA
2   BROWN       32000   TX       SALARY
3   CHIN        28000   CA       +B2>30000
4   JONES       45000   TX
5   MARTINEZ    31000   TX
6   SMITH       27000   CA       DSUM         143000
7   WHITE       35000   NY       DCOUNT            4
8                                DAVG          35750
9                                DMIN          31000
10                               DMAX          45000
11                               DVAR       30687500
12                               DSTD        5539.63
13                               DVARS      40916667
14                               DSTDS      6396.614
15
16
17
18
19
20
                                                           CAP
```

Figure 10-45

Database Query Functions

The two database Query functions available in 1-2-3 are `@DGET` and `@DQUERY`.

@DGET

The `@DGET` function allows you to search a database table and find a value or a label. The format of the `@DGET` function is:

```
@DGET(input,field,criteria)
```

where input is the range of fields to search, field is the name of the field within the input range to be searched, and criteria is the criteria range. Before illustrating the use of the `@DGET` function, you need to retrieve the file ABCSAL you created in Chapter 8 and define the range name DATABASE that has cells A5 through I13 as its range.

Suppose you would like to know the total salary for the employee with the last name ARMOUR. The `@DGET` function can be used to search the TOTAL column in the ABCSAL datatable to find the salary.

Move	the cell pointer to cell B17
Enter	CRITERIA
Move	the cell pointer to cell B18

Enter	LAST NAME
Move	the cell pointer to cell B19
Enter	ARMOUR

Define the range name CRITERIA that has cells B18 and B19 as its range.

To use the `@DGET` function to determine ARMOUR's total salary:

Move	the cell pointer to cell E19
Type	`@DGET(DATABASE,"TOTAL",CRITERIA)`
Press	↵

Your screen should look like Figure 10-46.

```
A:E19: [W8] 21200                                                          READY

A    A       B          C          D     E        F        G        H        I
1                                        ABC COMPANY
2                                      SALARY BUDGET
3
4
5  EMP NO LAST NAME  FIRST NAME DIV    QTR1     QTR2     QTR3     QTR4     TOTAL
6     568 SPROUT     AL           3   5,950    5,950    6,450    6,450    24,800
7     123 LYLIE      SUSAN        1   7,800    7,800    7,800    8,580    31,980
8     390 CHIN       TOMMY        2   5,000    5,000    5,200    5,200    20,400
9     576 JOHNSON    ERNEST       1   8,000    8,000    8,800    8,800    33,600
10    898 VALETTI    GEORGE       3   5,900    5,900    6,300    6,300    24,400
11    239 ARMOUR     CYNTHIA      2   5,200    5,200    5,400    5,400    21,200
12    972 JOHNSON    SANDRA       1   8,200    8,200    9,000    9,000    34,400
13    833 JONES      NINA         3   6,750    6,750    6,750    7,450    27,700
14                                   ----------------------------------------------
15        TOTAL                      52,800   52,800   55,700   57,180   218,480
16
17        CRITERIA
18        LAST NAME
19        ARMOUR                     21,200
20
                                                                     CAP
```

Figure 10-46

@DQUERY

The `@DQUERY` allows you to send a command to an external database management software program. The general format of the `@DQUERY` function is:

```
@DQUERY(function,external-argument)
```

where function is the name of a command available in the database management program and external-argument is the series of arguments the external command requires. See the 1-2-3 reference manual for more information on this function.

■ MATHEMATICAL FUNCTIONS

The 17 mathematical functions available in Lotus 1-2-3 include:

GENERAL:

@ABS	Computes the absolute value of a number in a cell
@EXP	Computes the number *e* raised to a specific power
@INT	Determines the integer portion of a value
@LN	Computes the natural logarithm (base *e*) of a value
@LOG	Computes the common logarithm (base 10) of a value
@MOD	Computes the remainder (modulus) of two values
@RAND	Generates a random number value between 0 and 1
@ROUND	Rounds a value to a specific number of decimal places
@SQRT	Computes the positive square root of a number

TRIGONOMETRIC:

@COS	Computes the cosine of an angle
@ACOS	Computes the arc cosine of a value
@SIN	Computes the sine of an angle
@ASIN	Computes the arc sine of a value
@TAN	Computes the tangent of an angle
@ATAN	Computes the arc tangent of a value

@ATAN2	Computes the four-quadrant arc tangent of two values
@PI	Returns the value for π (calculated at 3.14159265358979324)

General Functions

There are nine general mathematical functions. The general mathematical functions are @ABS, @EXP, @INT, @LN, @LOG, @MOD, @RAND, @ROUND and @SQRT.

@ABS

The @ABS function determines the absolute value. The number returned will always be positive.

The format of the @ABS function is:

```
@ABS(x)
```

where ***x*** is any value.

To illustrate the use of the @ABS function:

Move	the cell pointer to cell A1
Enter	25
Move	the cell pointer to cell A2
Enter	-50
Move	the cell pointer to cell B1
Type	@ABS(A1)
Press	↵
Move	the cell pointer to cell B2
Type	@ABS(A2)
Press	↵

Your screen should look like Figure 10-47.

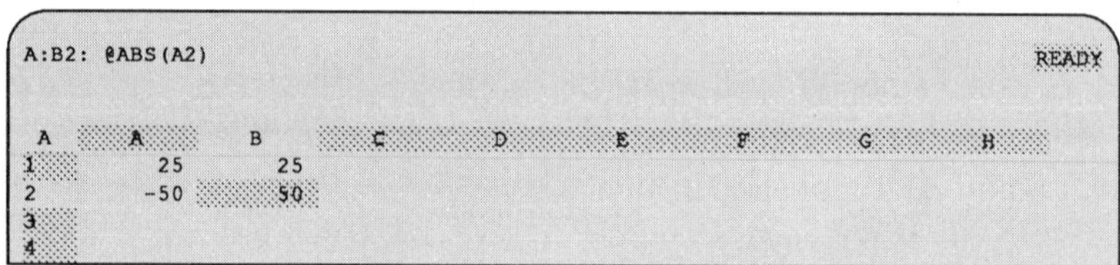

Figure 10-47

Notice that the absolute value of a positive number is the same positive number while the absolute value of a negative number is a positive number.

@EXP

The `@EXP` function computes the value of the number ***e*** raised to a specific power. The number ***e*** used in 1-2-3 has the approximate value of 2.718282.

The format of the `@EXP` function is:

```
@EXP(x)
```

where ***x*** is any value within the limits specified by the Lotus 1-2-3 reference manual. These limits are approximately from -11356 to 11356.

To demonstrate the use of the `@EXP` function:

Move	the cell pointer to cell A1
Type	`@EXP(3)`
Press	↵

Your screen should look like Figure 10-48.

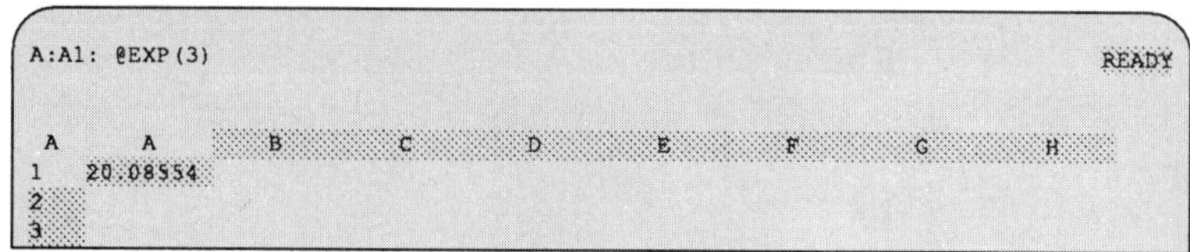

Figure 10-48

The value 20.08554 appearing in cell A1 is ***e*** (2.718282) raised to the power of 3.

@INT

The @INT function determines the integer portion of a value in a cell. The format for the @INT function is:

```
@INT(x)
```

where *x* is any value.

To demonstrate the use of the @INT function:

Move	the cell pointer to cell B1
Enter	33.1
Move	the cell pointer to cell B2
Type	@INT(B1)
Press	↵

Your screen should look like Figure 10-49.

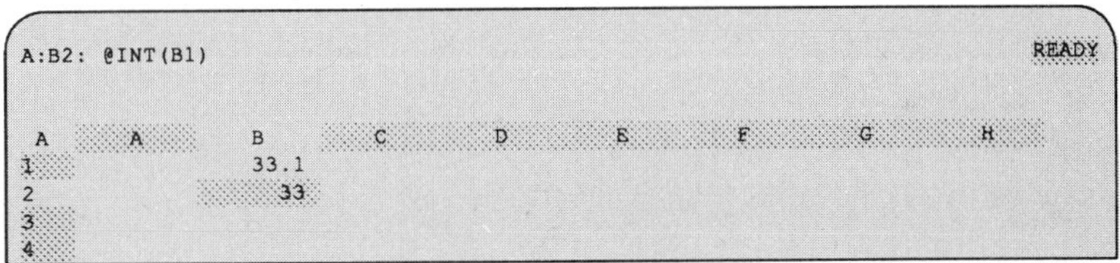

Figure 10-49

Notice that the value in cell B2 is 33 and the decimal portion of the number appearing in B1 has been omitted.

@LN

This function calculates the natural logarithm (base *e*) of a value. The format of the @LN function is:

```
@LN(x)
```

where *x* is any value greater than 0.

To illustrate the use of the @LN function:

Move	the cell pointer to cell A1
Enter	2
Move	the cell pointer to cell A2

Type `@LN(A1)`

Press ↵

Your screen should look like Figure 10-50.

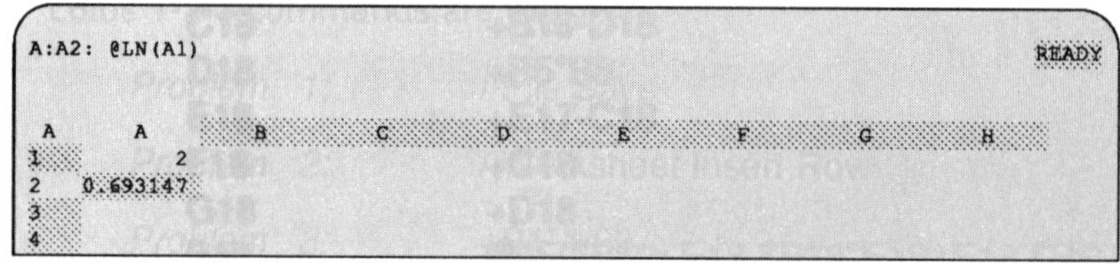

Figure 10-50

The value 0.693147 in A2 is the natural logarithm of the number 2.

@LOG

The `@LOG` function computes the common logarithm (base 10) for a value. The format for the `@LOG` function is:

```
@LOG(x)
```

where *x* is any value greater than 0.

To demonstrate the use of the `@LOG` function:

Move the cell pointer to cell B1

Enter 20

Move the cell pointer to cell B2

Type `@LOG(B1)`

Press ↵

Your screen should look like Figure 10-51.

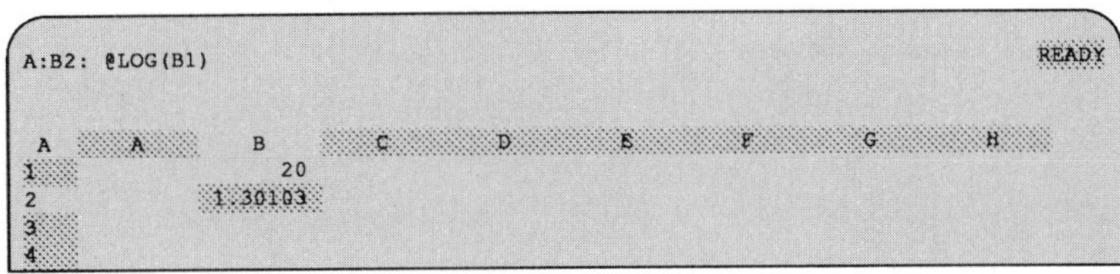

Figure 10-51

The value 1.30103 in cell B2 is the common logarithm for the number 20.

@MOD

The @MOD function computes the remainder (modulus) when you divide one number by another. The format for the @MOD function is:

```
@MOD(x,y)
```

where ***x*** is any value and ***y*** is any value other than 0. The sign (+ or -) of the value ***x*** specifies the sign of the result.

To illustrate the use of the @MOD function:

Move	the cell pointer to cell A1
Enter	X
Move	the cell pointer to cell B1
Enter	15
Move	the cell pointer to cell A2
Enter	Y
Move	the cell pointer to cell B2
Enter	6
Move	the cell pointer to cell C1
Type	@MOD(B1,B2)

Your screen should look like Figure 10-52.

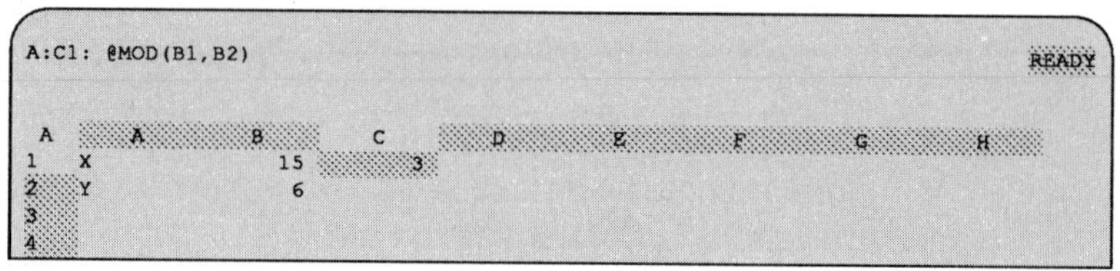

Figure 10-52

The value 3 is computed by dividing 15 by 6 and determining that the answer is 2 plus a remainder (modulus) of 3.

@RAND

The @RAND function calculates a random number between 0 and 1. The format of the @RAND function is:

```
@RAND
```

If you need to have a random number within a particular interval you must multiply the @RAND function by an appropriate value.

To illustrate the use of the @RAND function:

Move the cell pointer to cell A1

Type `@RAND`

Press ↵

Move the cell pointer to cell A2

Type `100*@RAND`

Press ↵

Your screen should look similar to Figure 10-53.

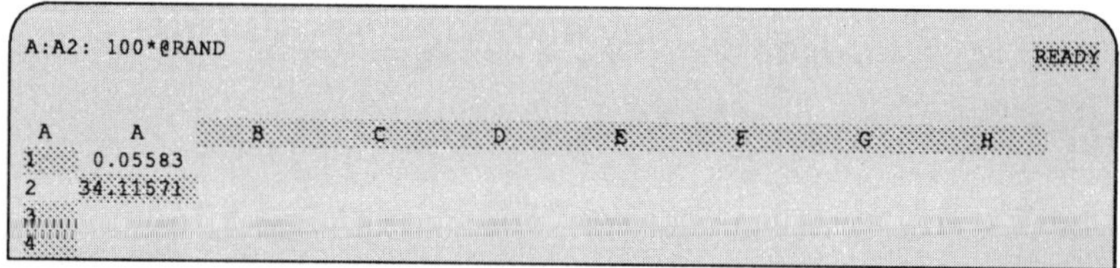

Figure 10-53

The value appearing in cell A1 is a random number between 0 and 1. The value in cell A2 is a random number between the interval 0 and 100. It was computed by multiplying a value determined using the @RAND function by 100.

@ROUND

The @ROUND function is use to round a value to a specific number of decimal places. The format for the @ROUND function is:

```
@ROUND(x,y)
```

where *x* is any value or formula and *y* is the number of decimal places you desire to the right of the decimal place. Chapter 2 includes an extensive discussion of the @ROUND function and several illustrations of its use.

@SQRT

The @SQRT function determines the positive square root for a value. The format of the @SQRT function is:

```
@SQRT(x)
```

where *x* is any positive value or formula that results in a positive number.

To demonstrate the use of the @SQRT function:

Move	the cell pointer to cell A1
Enter	25
Move	the cell pointer to cell A2
Type	@SQRT(A1)
Press	↵

Your screen should look like Figure 10-54.

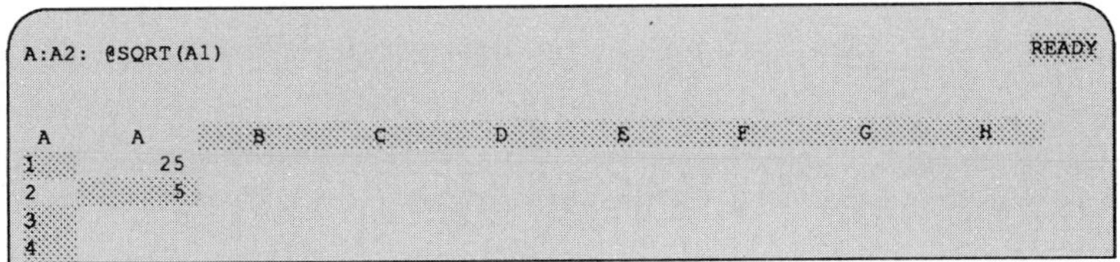

Figure 10-54

The value 5 appearing in cell A2 is the square root of 25. If you attempt to compute the square root of a negative value, the characters ERR will appear on your screen.

Trigonometric Functions

The trigonometric related functions available in 1-2-3 are @COS, @ACOS, @SIN, @ASIN, @TAN, @ATAN, @ATAN2 and @PI. These functions are used primarily by engineers and scientists. If you need to use these functions, please see the Lotus 1-2-3 reference manual.

■ SPECIAL FUNCTIONS

There are 14 special functions available in 1-2-3. They can be categorized as follows:

CELL AND RANGE INFORMATION:

@@	Returns the contents of the cell whose name or address another cell contains
@CELL	Returns information about a cell or its contents
@CELLPOINTER	Returns information about the current cell or its contents
@COLS	Determines the number of columns that are in a range
@COORD	Creates an absolute, mixed or relative cell address from values specified as arguments
@ROWS	Determines the number of rows in a range
@SHEETS	Determines the number of worksheets in a range

ERROR TRAPPING:

@ERR	Returns the characters ERR for error
@NA	Returns the characters NA for not available

LOOKUP CALCULATIONS:

@CHOOSE	Finds a specific value or string in a list
@HLOOKUP	Finds the contents of a cell in a specified row in a horizontal lookup table

@VLOOKUP	Finds the contents of a cell in a specified column of a vertical lookup table
@INDEX	Finds the contents of the cell in a specified row and column in a range

SYSTEM AND SESSION INFORMATION:

@INFO	Provides information on the current session

Cell and Range Information

The seven cell and range information functions available in 1-2-3 are @@, @CELL, @CELLPOINTER, @COLS, @COORD, @ROWS and @SHEETS.

@@

The @@ function returns the contents of the cell whose name or address another cell contains. The format of the @@ function is:

```
@@(location)
```

where location is the name or address of a single-cell range.

To illustrate the use of the @@ function:

Move	the cell pointer to cell A1
Enter	15
Move	the cell pointer to cell C1
Enter	A1
Move	the cell pointer to cell C3
Type	@@(C1)
Press	↵

C1 has as it contents, the label A1. The @@ function directs 1-2-3 to go to the cell referenced in cell A1, and place the contents of cell A1 in C3.

Your screen should look like Figure 10-55.

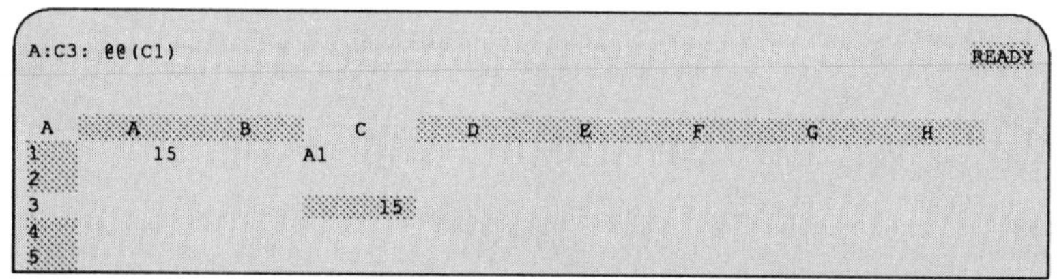

Figure 10-55

If the location you use refers to more than one cell, ERR will be returned.

@CELL

The `@CELL` function returns information about a cell or its contents. The format of the `@CELL` function is:

```
@CELL(attribute,location)
```

The attribute can be any of 12 strings allowed by 1-2-3. The location can be any cell address or range name. The 1-2-3 reference manual contains a list of the 12 strings that can be used for the attribute argument and the value returned for each of the possible attributes.

@CELLPOINTER

The `@CELLPOINTER` function returns information about the current cell. The format of the `@CELLPOINTER` function is:

```
@CELLPOINTER(attribute)
```

The attribute can be any of 12 strings allowed by 1-2-3 for the `@CELL` function. Refer to the 1-2-3 reference manual for the possible attributes and the value returned for each of the possible attributes.

@COLS

The `@COLS` function counts the number of columns in a specified range. The format of the `@COLS` function is:

```
@COLS(range)
```

where the range can be specified or a range name can be used.

To demonstrate the use of the @COLS function:

Move	the cell pointer to cell A1
Type	@COLS(B1.M1)
Press	↵

Your screen should look like Figure 10-56.

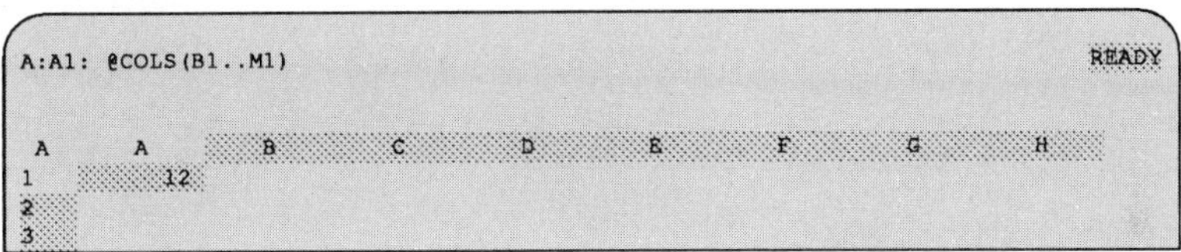

Figure 10-56

The value 12 appearing in cell A1 indicates there are 12 columns in the specified range B1 through M1.

@COORD

The @COORD function creates an absolute, mixed or relative cell address from values you provide as arguments. The format of the @COORD function is:

```
@COORD(worksheet,column,row,absolute)
```

where worksheet and column can be any integer between 1 and 256. Row can be any value between 1 and 8,192. Absolute can be an integer between 1 and 8. This function uses the value for absolute to determine the reference type as relative, absolute or mixed. The following table, taken from the 1-2-3 reference manual, includes the possible values of absolute and the effect on the cell address that is created.

Value	Worksheet	Column	Row	Example
1	Absolute	Absolute	Absolute	$A:$A$1
2	Absolute	Relative	Absolute	$A:A$1
3	Absolute	Absolute	Relative	$A:$A1
4	Absolute	Relative	Relative	$A:A1
5	Relative	Absolute	Absolute	A:$A$1
6	Relative	Relative	Absolute	A:A$1
7	Relative	Absolute	Relative	A:$A1
8	Relative	Relative	Relative	A:A1

To illustrate the use of the @COORD function:

Move	the cell pointer to cell A1

Type @COORD(2,3,5,7)

Press ⏎

Your screen should look like Figure 10-57.

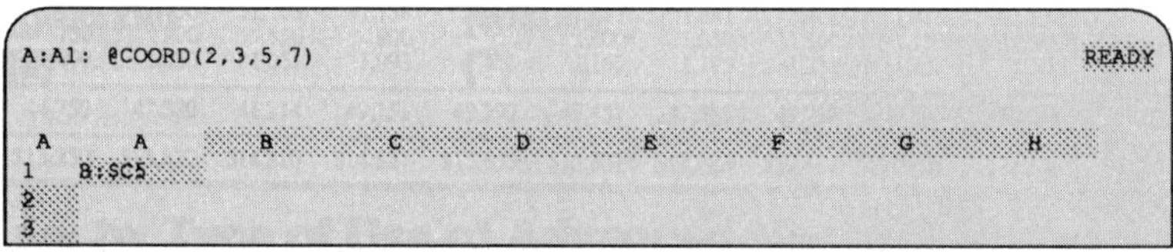

Figure 10-57

The cell address B:$C5, created by the @COORD function, appears in cell A1.

@ROWS

The @ROWS function counts the number of rows in a range. The format of the @ROWS function is:

```
@ROWS(range)
```

where range can be a specified range or a range name.

To illustrate the use of the @ROWS function:

Move the cell pointer to cell A1

Type @ROWS(B32.B297)

Press ⏎

Your screen should look like Figure 10-58.

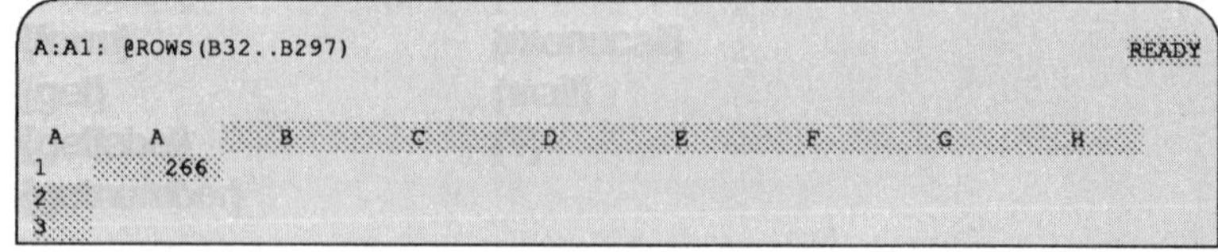

Figure 10-58

The value 266 appearing in cell A1 indicates that there are 266 rows in the range B32 through B297.

@SHEETS

The @SHEETS function determines how many worksheets there are in a specified range. The format of the @SHEETS function is:

```
@SHEETS(range)
```

where range can be a specified range or a range name.

To demonstrate the use of the @SHEETS function, erase your screen and insert 5 worksheets after worksheet A, then:

Move the cell pointer to cell A:B1

Type @SHEETS(B:A1.F:A1)

Press ↵

Your screen should look like Figure 10-59.

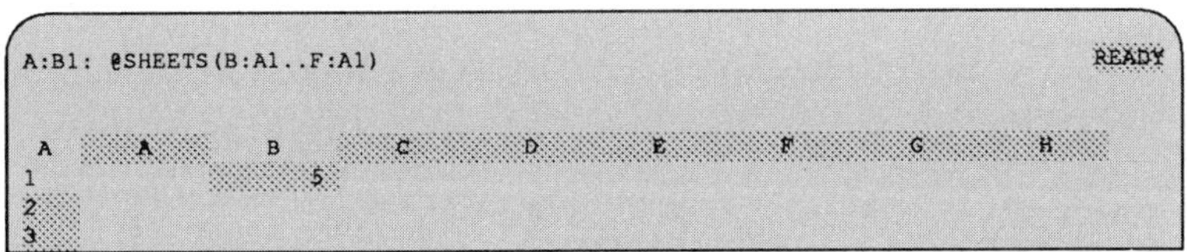

Figure 10-59

The number 5 in cell B1 indicates there are five worksheets in the indicated range.

Error Trapping

The two error trapping functions available in 1-2-3 are @ERR and @NA.

@ERR

The @ERR function returns the characters ERR (Error). The format for the @ERR is:

```
@ERR
```

To illustrate the use of the @ERR function:

Move the cell pointer to cell A1

Enter 25

Move the cell pointer to cell A2

Enter 5

Suppose you want to place a formula in cell A3 that will divide the value in cell A1 by the value in cell A2 only if the value in A2 is greater than 10. If the value is less than or equal to 10 you want to place the ERR characters in cell A3. To accomplish this task:

Move	the cell pointer to cell A3
Type	`@IF(A2>10,A1/A2,@ERR)`
Press	↵

Your screen should look like Figure 10-60.

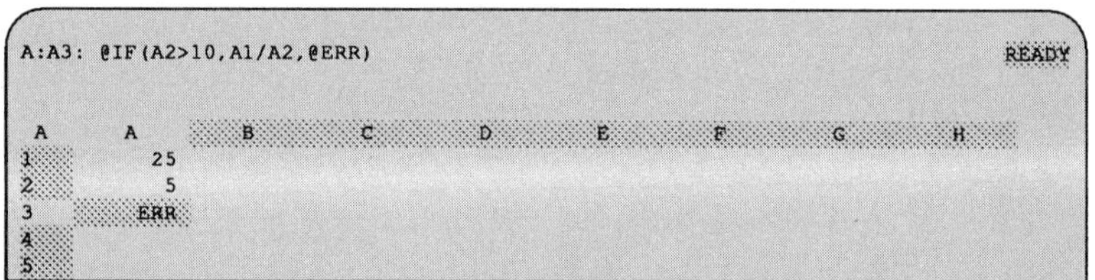

Figure 10-60

The characters ERR appcar in cell A3, because the value in cell A2 is not greater than 10. Change the value in A2 to a value greater than 10 to verify that the function works properly.

@NA

The `@NA` function returns the characters NA (not available). The format for the `@NA` function is:

```
@NA
```

To demonstrate the use of the `@NA` function:

Move	the cell pointer to cell B1
Enter	0

Suppose you want to place the characters NA in cell A4 if the value in cell B1 is 0 meaning the data is not available yet. Otherwise you want to place the value appearing in cell B1 in cell A4.

Move	the cell pointer to cell A4
Type	`@IF(B1=0,@NA,B1)`
Press	↵

Your screen should look like Figure 10-61.

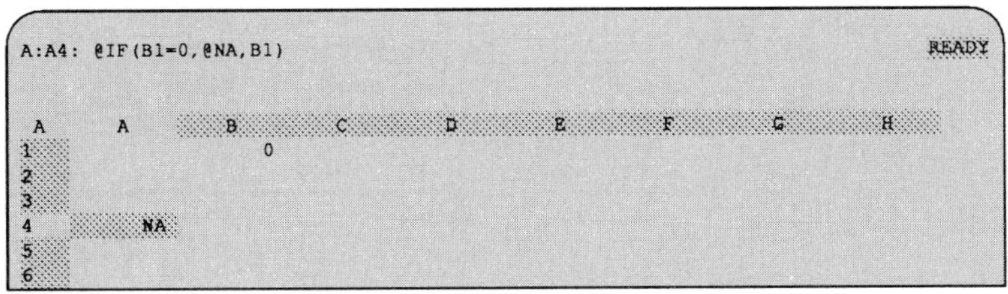

Figure 10-61

The NA appearing in cell A4 indicates that the value in cell B1 is a 0 and NA therefore should appear in cell A4. Change the value in cell B1 to some other number and the value will appear in cells B1 and A4.

Lookup Calculations

The four lookup calculation functions available in 1-2-3 include: `@CHOOSE`, `@HLOOKUP`, `@VLOOKUP` and `@INDEX`.

@CHOOSE

The `@CHOOSE` function finds a value or a string in a specified list. The format of the `@CHOOSE` function is:

```
@CHOOSE(offset number,list)
```

The offset number is the position of an item in a list. The initial item in the list has an offset number of 0. The second item has an offset number of 1 and so on. The final offset number is the total number of items minus 1. The offset number must be a positive integer and have a value less than or equal to 49. The list can contain any set of values, strings and range references, or any combination of them. Before using the `@CHOOSE` function, you need to create the worksheet appearing in Figure 10-62.

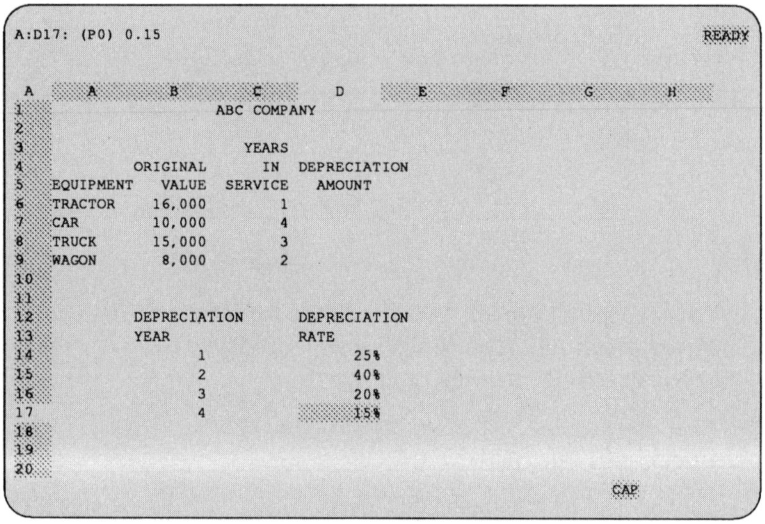

```
A:D17: (P0) 0.15                                                      READY

A      A          B          C          D           E     F     G     H
1                        ABC COMPANY
2
3                                 YEARS
4            ORIGINAL                IN   DEPRECIATION
5    EQUIPMENT  VALUE    SERVICE     AMOUNT
6    TRACTOR     16,000          1
7    CAR         10,000          4
8    TRUCK       15,000          3
9    WAGON        8,000          2
10
11
12           DEPRECIATION          DEPRECIATION
13           YEAR                  RATE
14                      1                  25%
15                      2                  40%
16                      3                  20%
17                      4                  15%
18
19
20
                                                                 CAP
```

Figure 10-62

You need to compute the annual depreciation for the three pieces of equipment in cells A5 through A7. Suppose that each of the properties has an economic useful life of four years. The depreciation rate used for the properties depends on how long the property has been in service. For example, the depreciation rate for the tractor is 25 percent, because it has been in service for only one year. The depreciation amount for the tractor is $4,000 (.25 times 16,000).

To demonstrate the use of the `@CHOOSE` function to compute the depreciation amount for the tractor:

Move the cell pointer to cell D6

Type `+B6*@CHOOSE(C6,@ERR,$D$14,$D$15,`
`$D$16,$D$17,@ERR)`

Press ↵

The value 4,000 appearing in cell D6 is the depreciation amount based on the depreciation rate of 25 percent. Cell C6 is the cell having the offset number and has the value 1 in it. Since the YEARS IN SERVICE value in cell C6 is 1, the second item in the list is used. Note that `@ERR` is used for the items in the list if the offset number is 0 and greater than 4. In this manner, if YEARS IN SERVICE is entered incorrectly, then ERR will appear for the depreciation amount.

Verify that the `@CHOOSE` function works for the other equipment by copying the formula in cell D6 to cells D7 through D9.

Your screen should look like Figure 10-63.

```
A:D6: +B6*@CHOOSE(C6,@ERR,A:$D$14,A:$D$15,A:$D$16,A:$D$17,@ERR)          READY

A      A          B          C          D          E     F     G     H
1                     ABC COMPANY
2
3                            YEARS
4            ORIGINAL         IN     DEPRECIATION
5    EQUIPMENT  VALUE      SERVICE     AMOUNT
6    TRACTOR    16,000         1        4000
7    CAR        10,000         4        1500
8    TRUCK      15,000         3        3000
9    WAGON       8,000         2        3200
10
11
12           DEPRECIATION            DEPRECIATION
13           YEAR                    RATE
14                     1                25%
15                     2                40%
16                     3                20%
17                     4                15%
18
19
20                                                          CAP
```

Figure 10-63

Change the value for the YEARS OF SERVICE to 0 and 5 for one of the equipment types. ERR will appear in the cell in both cases.

@HLOOKUP

The `@HLOOKUP` function determines the contents of a cell for a specified row in a horizontal lookup table. A horizontal lookup table is a range of cells that has value or label information in ascending order in the first row. The format of the `@HLOOKUP` function is:

```
@HLOOKUP(x,range,row-offset)
```

where *x* is a value or label and range is the set of cells contained in the horizontal lookup table. Row-offset is the number of rows down a column to the cell whose contents are to be returned.

The column that is searched is determined by comparing *x* with the cells in the first row beginning with the leftmost cell in the row. 1-2-3 locates the cell in the first row having a label that matches *x* or a value that is greater than or equal to *x* and less than the value in the cell to the immediate right of the cell being compared. It then moves down the column based on the row-offset number and returns the contents of the cell. If labels appear in the first row instead of values, 1-2-3 checks for exact matches.

The row-offset number is the position a row occupies in the range. The first row has an offset number of zero, the second row has an offset number of 1 and so on. The row-offset number can be 0 or any positive integer between 1 and 19. The maximum value that row-offset can have is 19.

Before illustrating the use of the @HLOOKUP function, you need to create the worksheet in Figure 10-64.

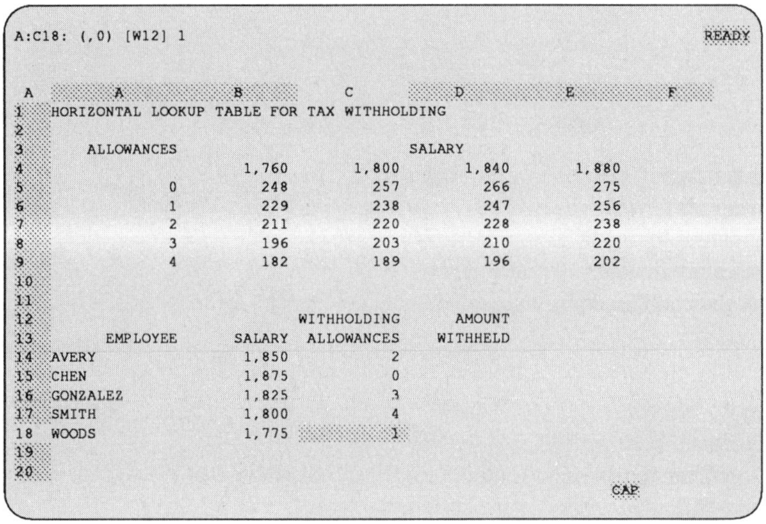

```
A:C18: (,0) [W12] 1                                                    READY

A        A              B            C            D            E           F
1  HORIZONTAL LOOKUP TABLE FOR TAX WITHHOLDING
2
3      ALLOWANCES                               SALARY
4                     1,760        1,800        1,840        1,880
5               0       248          257          266          275
6               1       229          238          247          256
7               2       211          220          228          238
8               3       196          203          210          220
9               4       182          189          196          202
10
11
12                             WITHHOLDING       AMOUNT
13          EMPLOYEE    SALARY  ALLOWANCES      WITHHELD
14 AVERY                1,850            2
15 CHEN                 1,875            0
16 GONZALEZ             1,825            3
17 SMITH                1,800            4
18 WOODS                1,775            1
19
20                                                          CAP
```

Figure 10-64

The horizontal lookup table contains the cells B4 through E9. The information in cells A5 through A9 is for documentation purposes only. The table is used to determine the amount of withholding tax an employee must pay depending on the salary and number of exemptions declared. For example, an individual earning more than $1,840 and less than or equal to $1,880 who has 2 exemptions must have $228 withheld from his paycheck.

To demonstrate the use of the @HLOOKUP function for this situation:

Move	the cell pointer to cell D14
Type	`@HLOOKUP(B14,$B$4.$E$9,C14+1)`
Press	↵

Make sure you include the $ signs to specify the absolute references. The value 228 appearing in cell D14 is the amount of withholding for an individual who has 2 withholding allowances, earning more than $1,840 and less than $1,880. Note that the value 1,850 is greater than or equal to 1,840 and less than 1,880. Therefore, the third column in the horizontal lookup table is used. The offset number is the value of cell C14 plus one because the row offset is one more than the corresponding number of allowances.

To verify the @HLOOKUP function works properly for the remaining employees, copy the formula in cell D14 to cells D15 through D18. When you are finished, your screen should look like Figure 10-65.

```
A:D14: (,0) [W12] @HLOOKUP(B14,$B$4..$E$9,C14+1)                              READY
```

	A	B	C	D	E
1	HORIZONTAL LOOKUP TABLE FOR TAX WITHHOLDING				
2					
3	ALLOWANCES			SALARY	
4		1,760	1,800	1,840	1,880
5	0	248	257	266	275
6	1	229	238	247	256
7	2	211	220	228	238
8	3	196	203	210	220
9	4	182	189	196	202
10					
11					
12			WITHHOLDING	AMOUNT	
13	EMPLOYEE	SALARY	ALLOWANCES	WITHHELD	
14	AVERY	1,850	2	228	
15	CHEN	1,875	0	266	
16	GONZALEZ	1,825	3	203	
17	SMITH	1,800	4	189	
18	WOODS	1,775	1	229	
19					
20					

Figure 10-65

@VLOOKUP

The @VLOOKUP function determines the contents of a cell for a specified column in a vertical lookup table. A vertical lookup table is a range of cells that has label or value information in ascending order in the first column. The format of the @VLOOKUP function is:

```
@VLOOKUP(x,range,column-offset)
```

where *x* is a label or value and range is the set of cells contained in the vertical lookup table. Column-offset is the number of columns across a row to the cell whose contents are to be returned.

The row that is searched is determined by comparing *x* with the values in the first column of the range beginning with the top cell in the column. 1-2-3 locates the cell in the first column having a label that matches *x* or a value that is greater than or equal to *x* and less than the value in the cell immediately below the cell being compared. It then moves across the row based on the column-offset number and returns the contents of the cell. If labels are used in the first column instead of values, 1-2-3 checks for exact matches.

The column-offset number is the position a column occupies in the range. The first column can have a value of 0; the second column has an offset number of 1 and so on. The column-offset number can be 0 or any positive integer between 1 and 19. The maximum value that the column-offset can have is 19.

Before illustrating the use of the `@VLOOKUP` function, you need to create the worksheet in Figure 10-66. The AMOUNT cells are calculated by multiplying QUANTITY times PRICE, and the total AMOUNT is determined by summing the individual item sales amounts.

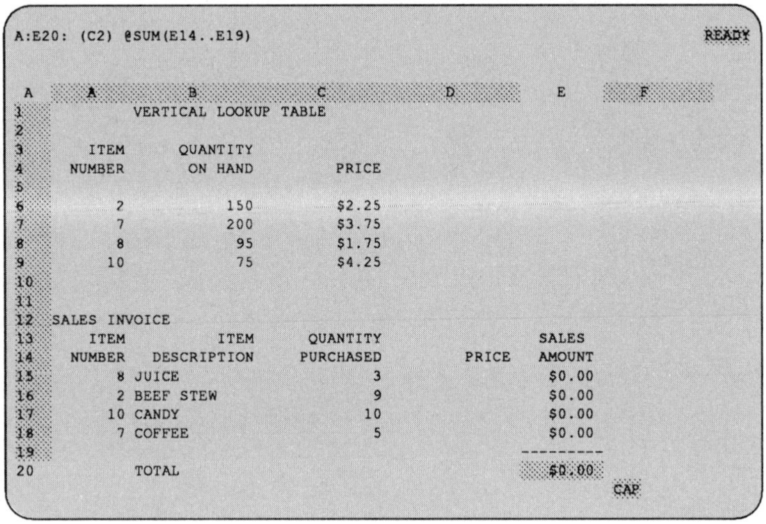

```
A:E20: (C2) @SUM(E14..E19)                                              READY

A     A          B            C            D         E          F
1              VERTICAL LOOKUP TABLE
2
3      ITEM      QUANTITY
4     NUMBER      ON HAND        PRICE
5
6          2          150        $2.25
7          7          200        $3.75
8          8           95        $1.75
9         10           75        $4.25
10
11
12  SALES INVOICE
13     ITEM            ITEM      QUANTITY                  SALES
14    NUMBER    DESCRIPTION     PURCHASED        PRICE    AMOUNT
15         8 JUICE                      3                  $0.00
16         2 BEEF STEW                  9                  $0.00
17        10 CANDY                     10                  $0.00
18         7 COFFEE                     5                  $0.00
19                                                       ---------
20           TOTAL                                         $0.00
                                                                   CAP
```

Figure 10-66

The vertical lookup table is in cells A6 through C9. This table includes information on the prices for four items sold by a distributor. The table is used to specify the proper sales price for items on a sales invoice.

To demonstrate the use of the `@VLOOKUP` function for this situation:

Move	the cell pointer to cell D15
Type	`@VLOOKUP(A15,$A$6.$C$9,2)`
Press	↵

Make sure you include the $ signs to specify the absolute references. The value of $1.75 in cell D15 is the price for juice (ITEM NUMBER 8). Note that the column-offset number is 2, because the prices for the items are in the third column of the vertical lookup table.

To verify that the `@VLOOKUP` function works properly for the other sales items, copy the contents of cell D15 to cells D16 through D18.

When you are finished, your screen should look like Figure 10-67.

```
A:D15: (C2) [W14] @VLOOKUP(A15,$A$6..$C$9,2)                                READY

A        A           B              C              D             E          F
1              VERTICAL LOOKUP TABLE
2
3       ITEM        QUANTITY
4      NUMBER        ON HAND            PRICE
5
6           2            150            $2.25
7           7            200            $3.75
8           8             95            $1.75
9          10             75            $4.25
10
11
12 SALES INVOICE
13      ITEM            ITEM          QUANTITY                   SALES
14     NUMBER      DESCRIPTION       PURCHASED          PRICE    AMOUNT
15          8 JUICE                          3          $1.75     $5.25
16          2 BEEF STEW                      9          $2.25    $20.25
17         10 CANDY                         10          $4.25    $42.50
18          7 COFFEE                         5          $3.75    $18.75
19                                                               ---------
20             TOTAL                                             $86.75
```

Figure 10-67

@INDEX

The `@INDEX` function determines the contents of a cell in a range of cells for a specific set of column-offset, row-offset and worksheet-offset numbers. The worksheet-offset number is optional. The format of the `@INDEX` function is:

```
@INDEX(range,column-offset,row-offset,
[worksheet-offset])
```

The range can be any specified range of cells or range name.

Column-offset, row-offset and worksheet-offset are offset numbers. These numbers correspond to the column, row or worksheet position of the desired cell in the range. The first column, row and worksheet in the range has an offset of 0. Subsequent columns, rows and worksheets are numbered as positive integers to a maximum value of 19.

Before illustrating the use of the `@INDEX` function, you need to create the worksheet in Figure 10-68.

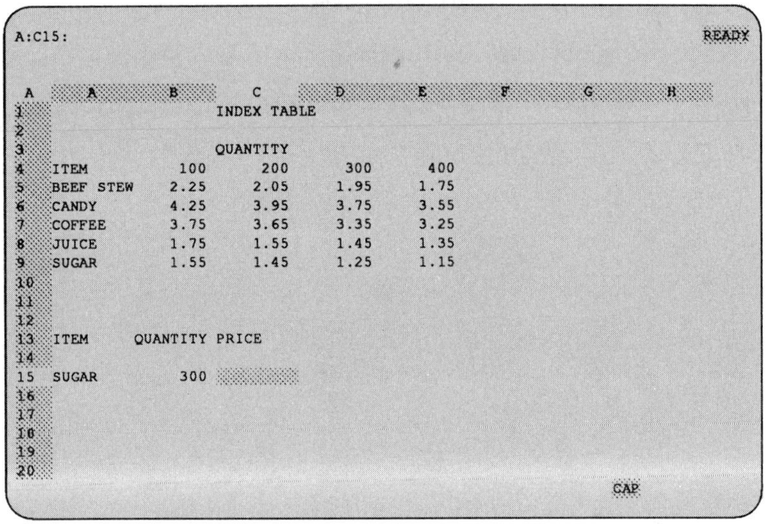

```
A:C15:                                                          READY

A     A          B          C          D          E        F    G    H
1                          INDEX TABLE
2
3                          QUANTITY
4    ITEM          100        200        300        400
5    BEEF STEW    2.25       2.05       1.95       1.75
6    CANDY        4.25       3.95       3.75       3.55
7    COFFEE       3.75       3.65       3.35       3.25
8    JUICE        1.75       1.55       1.45       1.35
9    SUGAR        1.55       1.45       1.25       1.15
10
11
12
13   ITEM      QUANTITY PRICE
14
15   SUGAR          300
16
17
18
19
20
                                                          CAP
```

Figure 10-68

This worksheet includes an index table containing the price for some items based on the quantity purchased.

To demonstrate the use of the `@INDEX` function:

Move the cell pointer to cell C15

Type `@INDEX($B$5.$E$9,2,4)`

Press ↵

Your screen should look like Figure 10-69.

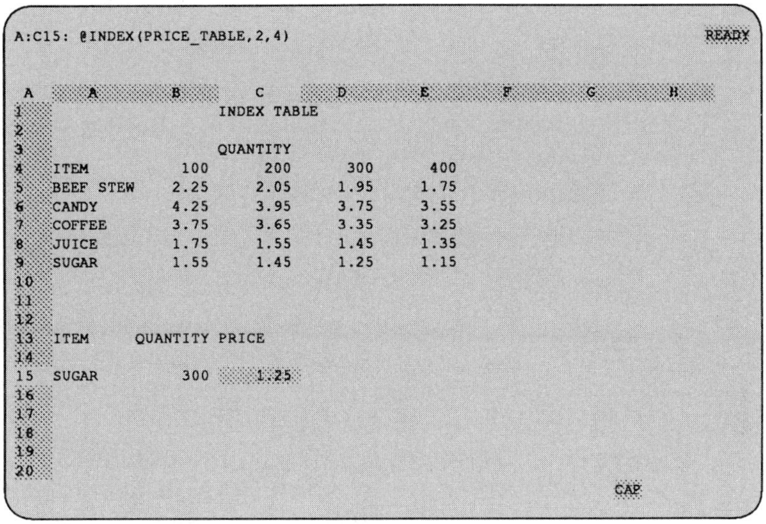

```
A:C15: @INDEX(PRICE_TABLE,2,4)                                      READY

A      A          B          C          D          E          F     G     H
1                      INDEX TABLE
2
3                      QUANTITY
4  ITEM             100        200        300        400
5  BEEF STEW       2.25       2.05       1.95       1.75
6  CANDY           4.25       3.95       3.75       3.55
7  COFFEE          3.75       3.65       3.35       3.25
8  JUICE           1.75       1.55       1.45       1.35
9  SUGAR           1.55       1.45       1.25       1.15
10
11
12
13 ITEM       QUANTITY PRICE
14
15 SUGAR            300       1.25
16
17
18
19
20
                                                             CAP
```

Figure 10-69

The value 1.25 appears in cell C15 indicating the price for SUGAR when the purchase QUANTITY is 300 units.

System and Session Information

The `@INFO` function is the only system and session information function.

@INFO

The `@INFO` function returns information on various attributes for the current session. The format of the `@INFO` function is:

```
@INFO(attribute)
```

There are 11 attributes that can be used. The Lotus 1-2-3 reference manual contains a list of these attributes and the information returned.

■ STRING FUNCTIONS

There are 18 string functions available in 1-2-3. The term string refers to any set of characters. The string functions can be categorized as follows:

SPECIAL CHARACTERS AND CREATING CHARACTERS:

@CHAR	Returns the character which the Lotus Multibyte Character Set (LMBCS) code produces
@CODE	Returns the LMBCS code corresponding to the first character in a string
@REPEAT	Duplicates a string of characters a specified number of times

EXTRACTING PORTIONS OF A STRING FROM A LABEL:

@FIND	Determines the position of the first character of a string within another string
@LEFT	Returns a specified number of characters beginning with the first character in the string
@LENGTH	Determines the number of characters in a string
@MID	Returns an indicated number of characters beginning with a specific character
@REPLACE	Replaces the characters in one string with another specified string of characters
@RIGHT	Returns a specified number of characters at the end of a string

CHANGING THE CASE OF A STRING:

@LOWER	Changes all letters in a string to lowercase
@PROPER	Changes the first letter of each word in a string to uppercase; all other letters in the string are lowercase

`@UPPER`	Changes all letters in a string to uppercase

CONVERTING VALUES TO STRINGS AND STRINGS TO VALUES:

`@STRING`	Changes a value into a label with a specified number of decimal places
`@TRIM`	Deletes all leading, trailing and consecutive spaces from a string
`@VALUE`	Changes a string of characters from a label to a number

DETERMINING THE CHARACTERISTICS OF A STRING:

`@EXACT`	Determines whether two strings of characters are the same
`@N`	Returns the value (number) in the first cell in a range if it contains a number; otherwise a zero is returned
`@S`	Returns the label in the first cell in a range if it contains a label; otherwise a blank cell is returned

Special Characters and Creating Characters

The three functions for manipulating special characters in 1-2-3 are `@CHAR`, `@CODE` and `@REPEAT`.

The `@CHAR` returns the character that the Lotus Multibyte Character Set (LMBCS) code provides. The format of the `@CHAR` function is:

```
@CHAR(x)
```

where *x* is an integer. See the Lotus 1-2-3 reference manual for further information.

@CODE

The `@CODE` function returns the Lotus Multibyte Character Set (LMBCS) code for the first character in a string. The format of the `@CODE` function is:

```
@CODE(x)
```

where *x* is a string. See the Lotus 1-2-3 reference manual for further information.

@REPEAT

The @REPEAT function is used to duplicate a string of characters a specific number of times. The format of the @REPEAT function is:

```
@REPEAT(string,n)
```

where string is a set of characters and ***n*** is the number of times the string is to be repeated. The value of ***n*** can be any positive integer.

To illustrate the use of the @REPEAT function:

Move	the cell pointer to cell A1
Enter	@REPEAT("Worksheet ",3)
Press	↵

Your screen should look like Figure 10-70.

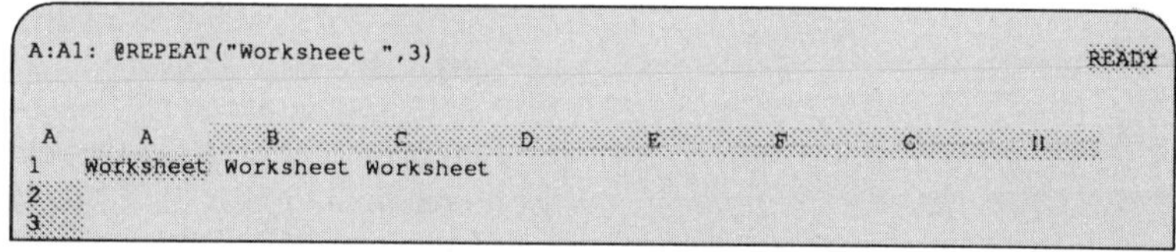

Figure 10-70

The set of characters "Worksheet " is repeated three times in cell A1. Note that a space occurs between the words because you placed a space before the second " in the string definition.

Extracting Portions of a String from a Label

The six string functions in 1-2-3 used to extract portions of a string from a label are @FIND, @LEFT, @LENGTH, @MID, @REPLACE and @RIGHT.

@FIND

The @FIND function determines the position within a string where another string starts. The format of the @FIND function is:

```
@FIND(search-string,string,start-number)
```

where search-string is the set of characters being sought in the string. The search-string and string can be any string of characters, a reference to a cell or a formula that evaluates to a string. Start-number is an offset number of a character in a string. It can have a value of 0 or any positive integer. The first character in string is the number zero, the second is number one and so on.

To illustrate the use of the `@FIND` function:

Move	the cell pointer to cell A1
Enter	Spreadsheet Analysis
Move	the cell pointer to cell A3
Type	`@FIND("sheet",A1,0)`
Press	↵

Your screen should look like Figure 10-71.

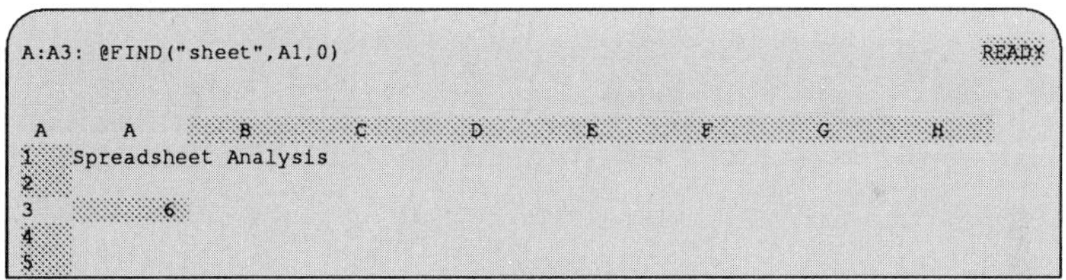

Figure 10-71

The number 6 is the position of the first character of search-string within the string being searched. If the `@FIND` function cannot locate the search string in the string, ERR is returned and will appear in cell A3. `@FIND` is case sensitive. For example, if "Sheet" had been specified in the example, ERR would have appeared in cell A3 because sheet is not capitalized in the string.

@LEFT

The `@LEFT` function returns a specified number of characters from a string beginning with the first character in the string. The format of the `@LEFT` function is:

```
@LEFT(string,n)
```

String can be any string of characters, a reference to a cell or a formula that evaluates to a label. The ***n*** is the number of characters to be returned from the string.

To demonstrate the use of the `@LEFT` function:

Move the cell pointer to cell B1

Enter Mastering and Using Lotus 1-2-3 Release 3

Suppose you want to return the characters *Mastering* and place them in cell B3.

Move the cell pointer to cell B3

Type `@LEFT(B1,9)`

Press ↵

Your screen should look like Figure 10-72.

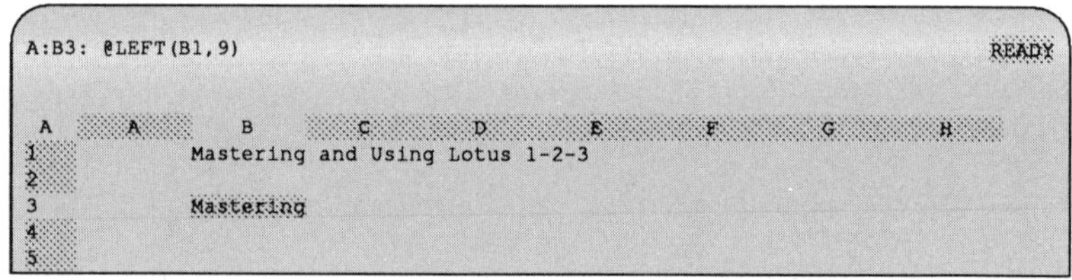

Figure 10-72

The string of characters *Mastering* now appears in cell B3.

@LENGTH

The `@LENGTH` function counts the number of characters in a string. The format of the `@LENGTH` function is:

```
@LENGTH(string)
```

where a string is any string of characters, a reference to a cell or a formula that evaluates to a string.

To illustrate the use of the `@LENGTH` function:

Move the cell pointer to cell A1

Enter Boyd & Fraser Publishing Company

Move the cell pointer to cell A4

Type `@LENGTH(A1)`

Press ↵

Your screen should look like Figure 10-73.

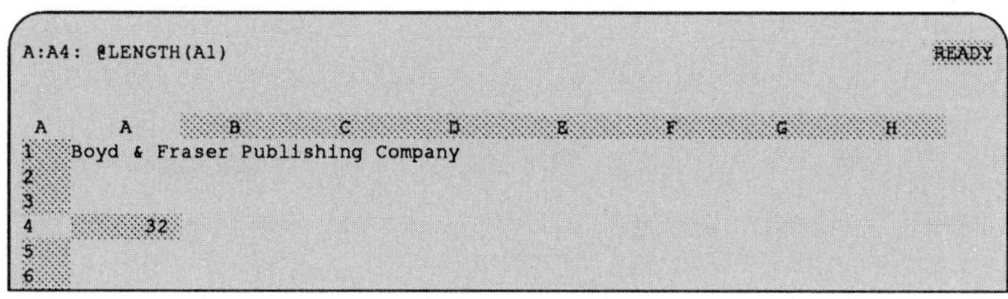

Figure 10-73

The number 32 appears in cell A4 indicating there are 32 characters in the string that is contained in cell A1.

@MID

The `@MID` function is used to return a specific number of characters beginning at a particular point in a string. The format of the `@MID` function is:

```
@MID(string,start-number,n)
```

where string is any string of characters, reference to a cell or a formula that evaluates to a string, and ***n*** is the number of characters to return. Start-number can be zero or any positive integer.

To demonstrate the use of the `@MID` function:

Move	the cell pointer to cell B1
Enter	Mastering and Using Lotus 1-2-3 Release 3
Move	the cell pointer to cell B3
Type	`@MID(B1,20,11)`
Press	↵

Your screen should look like Figure 10-74.

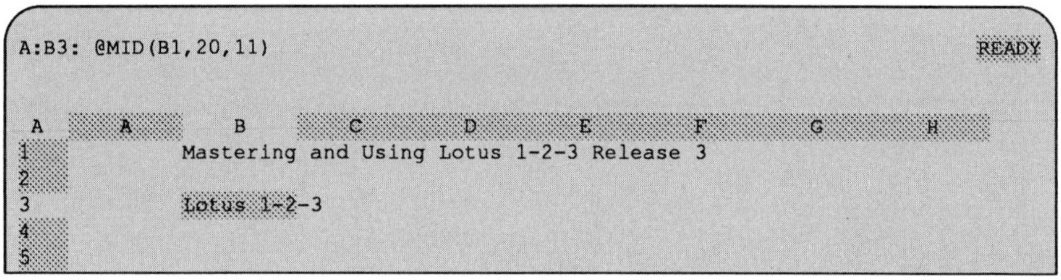

```
A:B3: @MID(B1,20,11)                                                  READY

A    A        B        C        D        E        F        G        H
1             Mastering and Using Lotus 1-2-3 Release 3
2
3             Lotus 1-2-3
4
5
```

Figure 10-74

The set of characters Lotus 1-2-3 appears in cell B3 as a result of using the `@MID` function.

@REPLACE

The `@REPLACE` function finds a set of characters in a string and replaces the characters with another set of characters. The format of the `@REPLACE` function is:

```
@REPLACE(original-string,start-number,n,new-string)
```

where original-string and new-string can be any string of characters, a reference to a cell or a formula that evaluates to a string. *N* is the number of characters to be replaced and start-number is an offset-number identifying where to start replacing characters in the original-string. Start-number and *n* can have a value of zero or any positive integer.

To illustrate the use of the `@REPLACE` function:

Move the cell pointer to cell A1

Enter Softball and Feetball are popular sports

To replace the *ee* in Feetball with *oo*:

Move the cell pointer to cell A3

Type `@REPLACE(A1,14,2,"oo")`

Press ↵

Your screen should look like Figure 10-75.

```
A:A3: @REPLACE(A1,14,2,"oo")                                    READY

A     A        B       C       D       E       F       G       H
1  Softball and Feetball are popular sports
2
3  Softball and Football are popular sports
4
5
```

Figure 10-75

The spelling error appearing in cell A1 is now corrected in cell A3.

@RIGHT

The `@RIGHT` function returns characters from the end of a string. The format of the `@RIGHT` function is:

`@RIGHT(string,n)`

where string is any string of characters, a reference to a cell or a formula that evaluates to a string. The ***n*** is the number of characters to return and can be any positive integer.

To demonstrate the use of the `@RIGHT` function:

Move	the cell pointer to cell B1
Enter	Software Package
Move	the cell pointer to cell B3
Type	`@RIGHT(B1,7)`
Press	↵

Your screen should look like Figure 10-76.

Figure 10-76

The word Package now appears in cell B3 because it represents the last seven characters of the string in B1.

Changing the Case of a String

The three functions available in 1-2-3 to change the case of a string are @LOWER, @PROPER and @UPPER.

@LOWER

The @LOWER function changes all letters in a string to lowercase. The format of the @LOWER function is:

```
@LOWER(string)
```

where string is any string of characters, a reference to a cell or a formula that evaluates to a string.

To illustrate the use of the @LOWER function:

Move	the cell pointer to cell A1
Enter	SOUTHWEST
Move	the cell pointer to cell A3
Type	@LOWER(A1)
Press	↵

Your screen should look like Figure 10-77.

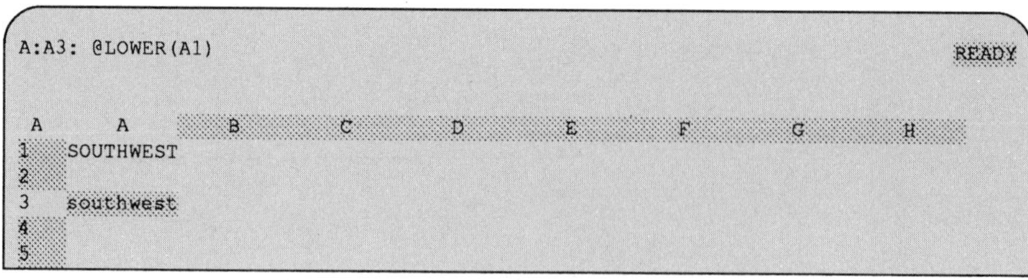

Figure 10-77

The letters appearing in cell A3 are all lowercase.

@PROPER

The `@PROPER` function makes the first letter of each word in a string uppercase. The remaining letters are lowercase. The format of the `@PROPER` function is:

```
@PROPER(string)
```

where string is any string of characters, a reference to a cell or a formula that evaluates to a string.

To demonstrate the use of the `@PROPER` function:

Move	the cell pointer to cell B1
Enter	mastering and using lotus 1-2-3 release 3
Move	the cell pointer to cell B3
Type	`@PROPER(B1)`
Press	↵

Your screen should look like Figure 10-78.

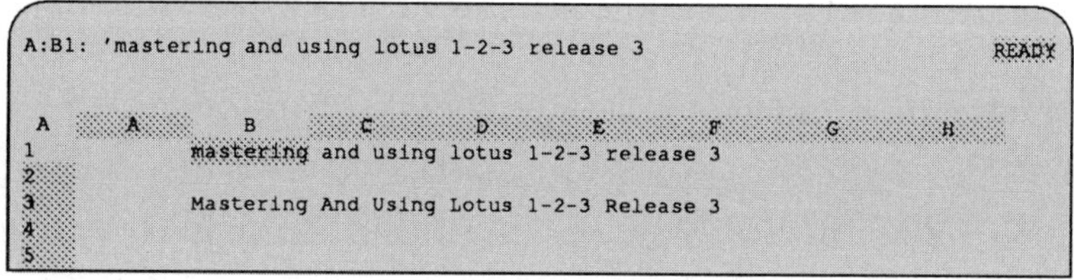

Figure 10-78

The first letter of each word in row 3 is uppercase and the other letters are lowercase.

@UPPER

The `@UPPER` function converts all lowercase letters in a string to uppercase letters. The format of the `@UPPER` function is:

```
@UPPER(string)
```

where string is any string of characters, a reference to a cell or a formula that evaluates to a string.

To illustrate the use of the @UPPER function:

Move	the cell pointer to cell A1
Enter	California
Move	the cell pointer to cell A3
Type	@UPPER(A1)
Press	↵

Your screen should look like Figure 10-79.

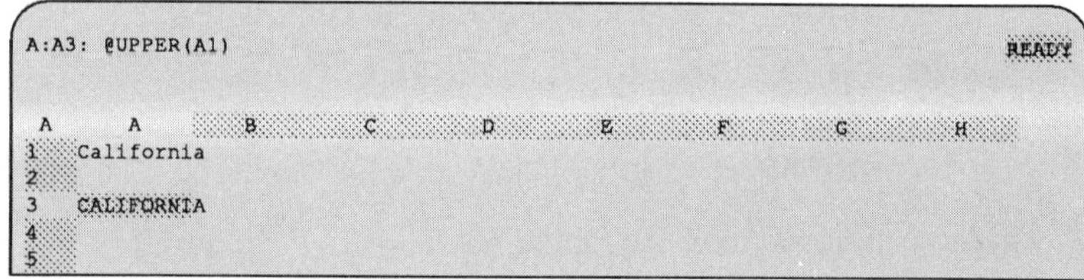

Figure 10-79

All letters in California are now uppercase in cell A3.

Converting Values to Strings and Strings to Values

The three functions available in 1-2-3 related to converting values to strings and strings to values are: @STRING, @TRIM and @VALUE.

@STRING

The @STRING function changes a value into a label with a specified number of decimal places. The format of the @STRING function is:

```
@STRING(x,n)
```

where *x* can be a value, a reference to a cell or a formula that evaluates to a string. The *n* can be 0 or any positive integer between 1 and 15.

To demonstrate the use of the `@STRING` function:

Move the cell pointer to cell B1

Enter 123.45

Move the cell pointer to cell B3

Type `@STRING(B1,0)`

Press ↵

Your screen should look like Figure 10-80.

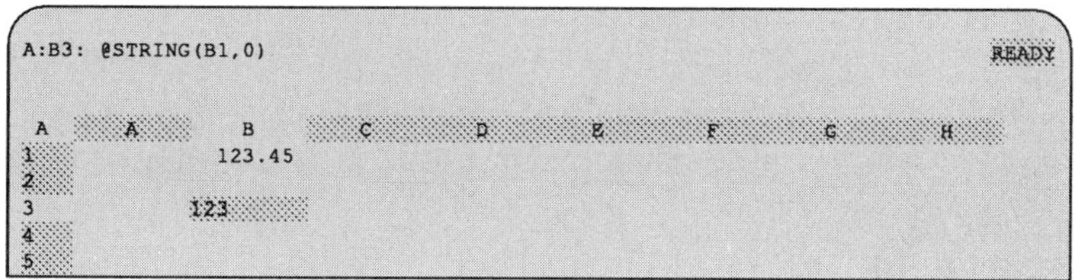

Figure 10-80

The value in cell B1 has been converted to the string 123 that appears in cell B3. Note the characters in cell B3 are left-justified indicating that the data is considered as a label and not a value.

@TRIM

The `@TRIM` function deletes all leading, trailing and consecutive spaces from a string. Single spaces in the string are preserved. The format of the `@TRIM` function is:

```
@TRIM(string)
```

where string is any string of characters, a reference to a cell or a formula that evaluates to a string.

To illustrate the use of the `@TRIM` function:

Move the cell pointer to cell A1

Enter   Worksheets are fun to create

Note that there are two spaces before Worksheets and between the words Worksheets, are, fun and to.

Move the cell pointer to cell A3

Type `@TRIM(A1)`

Press ↵

Your screen should look like Figure 10-81.

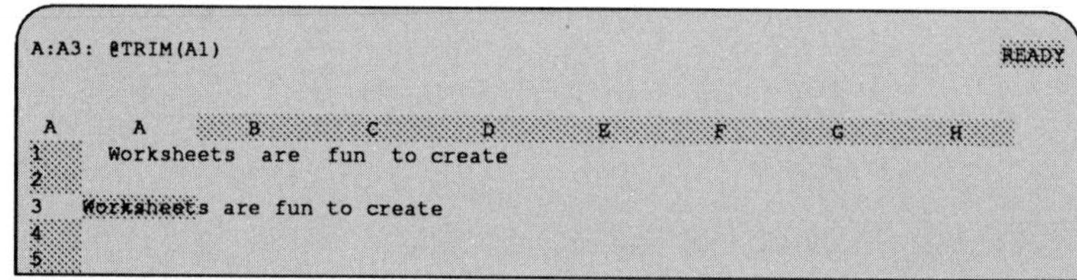

Figure 10-81

The leading spaces and extra spaces in the string have been deleted. Note that the space between to and create remains because there was only one space originally.

@VALUE

The `@VALUE` function changes a string of characters that looks like a number into a value. The format of the `@VALUE` function is:

```
@VALUE(string)
```

where string can only include numbers or numeric symbols.

To demonstrate the use of the `@VALUE` function:

Move the cell pointer to cell B1

Enter '97.5%

Move the cell pointer to cell B3

Type `@VALUE(B1)`

Press ↵

Your screen should look like Figure 10-82.

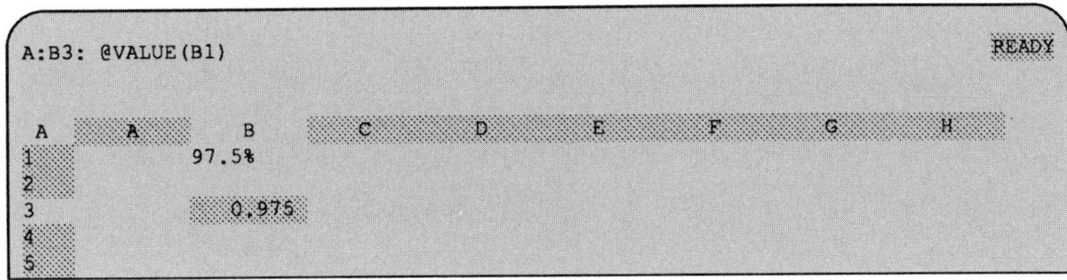

Figure 10-82

The string in cell B1 has been converted into the numeric value appearing in cell B3.

Determining the Characteristics of a String

The three functions available in 1-2-3 for determining the characteristics of a string are: `@EXACT`, `@N` and `@S`.

@EXACT

The `@EXACT` function determines whether two strings of characters are the same. The format of the `@EXACT` function is:

```
@EXACT(string1,string2)
```

where string1 and string2 can be any string of characters, a reference to a cell or a formula that evaluates to a string.

If string1 and string2 are exactly the same, a value of one is returned; otherwise a zero is returned.

To illustrate the use of the `@EXACT` function:

Move	the cell pointer to cell A1
Enter	Southwestern states
Copy	cell A1 to cell A3
Move	the cell pointer to A5
Type	`@EXACT(A1,A3)`
Press	↵

Your screen should look like Figure 10-83.

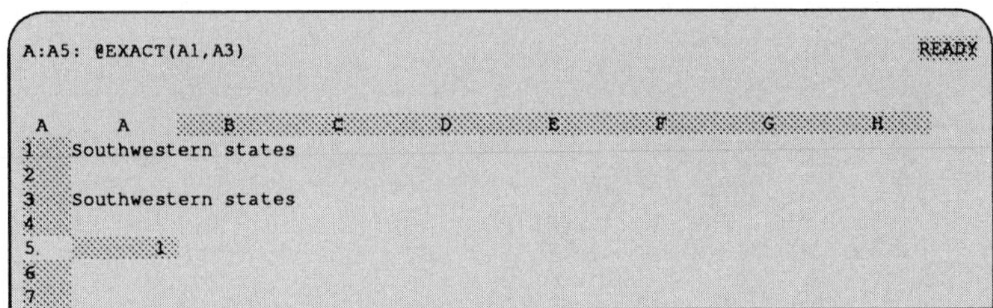

Figure 10-83

The number 1 appears in cell A5 indicating that the strings in cells A1 and A3 are the same. Edit cell A3 so the string ends with a space.

Move	the cell pointer to cell A3
Press	F2
Press	the spacebar
Press	↵

The number 0 appears in cell A5 because the strings in cells A1 and A3 are not exactly alike. Any differences in case between the two strings would also result in a 0 in cell A5.

@N

The `@N` function returns the value appearing in the first cell of a range if the content of the cell is a numeric value, otherwise a zero is returned. The format of the `@N` function is:

```
@N(range)
```

where range is any specified set of cells, or a range name.

To demonstrate the use of the `@N` function:

Move	the cell pointer to cell B1
Enter	125
Move	the cell pointer to cell C1
Enter	150

Create the range name NUM_TEST that has cells B1 and C1 as its range.

Move	the cell pointer to cell B3

Type	`@N(NUM_TEST)`
Press	⏎

Your screen should look like Figure 10-84.

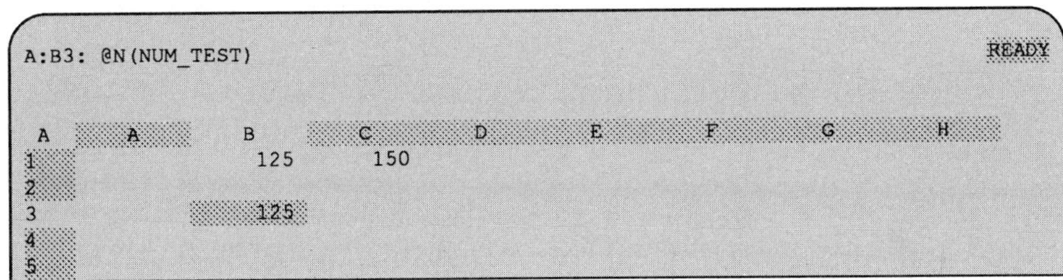

Figure 10-84

The number 125 appearing in cell B3 indicates that the first cell in the range NUM_TEST is a value. Change the contents of B1 to a label and a value of zero will appear in cell B3, indicating that the content of the first cell of the range NUM_TEST is not a number.

@S

The format of the `@S` function is:

```
@S(range)
```

where range is any specified set of cells or a range name.

To illustrate the use of the `@S` function:

Move	the cell pointer to cell A1
Enter	June
Move	the cell pointer to cell B1
Enter	July

Create the range name LABEL_TEST that has cells A1 and B1 as its range.

Move	the cell pointer to cell A3
Type	`@S(LABEL_TEST)`
Press	⏎

Your screen should look like Figure 10-85.

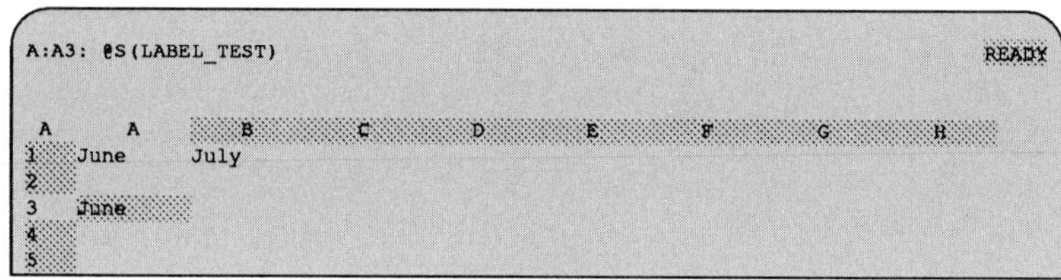

Figure 10-85

The month June appears in cell A3 indicating that the first cell in the range LABEL_TEST has a label as its contents. Enter a number in cell A1, and cell A3 will appear as a blank cell. If you erase cell A1, cell A3 will also appear as a blank cell.

SUMMARY

Lotus 1-2-3 has many functions that can perform standard calculations. There are eight different categories of functions: statistical analysis, financial analysis, date and time, logical, database, mathematical, special and string.

KEY CONCEPTS

Database Functions
Date and Time Functions
Financial Analysis Functions
Logical Functions
Mathematical Functions
Special Functions
Statistical Analysis Functions
String Functions

CHAPTER TEN
EXERCISE 1

INSTRUCTIONS: Circle T if the statement is true and F if the statement is false.

T F 1. @MIN determines the minute for a given serial number.

T F 2. Multiple items in a range may be listed individually (e.g., the syntax in the formula @COUNT(B1,B3,B4) is correct).

T F 3. Arguments within an @ function may be placed in any order desired by the user.

T F 4. Extra spaces are not acceptable within @ functions.

T F 5. A label has a value of 0 and will be counted as such if included in a range for an @ function.

T F 6. It is possible to alter an @ function with arithmetic operations to get the desired result (e.g., the formula @PMT(B1,B2/12,B3*12) is syntactically correct).

T F 7. If a worksheet file containing the @NOW function (formatted to show the date) is retrieved from a file and actively recalculates, the @NOW function will display the *current* system date.

T F 8. A single-cell item in an argument may not be entered directly into the formula (e.g., the formula @NPV(A1,B1..B6) cannot be entered as @NPV(.1,B1..B6).

T F 9. More than one @ function may be used in a formula.

T F 10. The @IF statement allows you to test one or more conditions in a worksheet and provide appropriate responses for either a true result or a false result.

T F 11. Date and time special functions are available in 1-2-3.

T F 12. XLOOKUP allows you to look up values in a row or a table.

T F 13. You can modify the appearance of a series of characters using the string functions.

T F 14. Data queries cannot be accomplished using special functions.

CHAPTER TEN
EXERCISE 2
Using the Statistical Analysis Functions

INSTRUCTIONS: Using the data 111, 125, 116, 130 and 127, apply the statistical analysis functions available in Lotus 1-2-3 to:

1. Determine the sum of the numbers.
2. Count the number of values.
3. Compute the arithmetic mean of the values.
4. Determine the minimum value.
5. Calculate the maximum value.
6. Compute the population variance.
7. Determine the population standard deviation.
8. Compute the sample variance.
9. Calculate the sample standard deviation.

Print the worksheet after completing the calculations.

CHAPTER TEN
EXERCISE 3
Using the SUMPRODUCT Function

INSTRUCTIONS: Make sure you have a blank worksheet on your screen.

Place the numbers 10, 25 and 15 in cells A3 through A5. Enter the numbers 5, 10 and 20 in cells D3 through D5.

Compute the sum of the products of the numbers and place the answer in cell A10.

Print the worksheet.

CHAPTER TEN
EXERCISE 4
Using the Financial Analysis Functions

INSTRUCTIONS: Use the Financial Analysis Functions available in Lotus 1-2-3 to solve the following exercises.

1. Compute the internal rate of return for the following cash flow stream using .15 as the guess rate:

   -1000, -500, 900, 800, 700, 600, 400, 200, 100

2. Compute the net present value for the following cash flow stream using .10 as the discount rate:

   -1500, 900, 800, 700, 600, 400, 200, 100

3. Compute the future value if the payment per period is 500, the interest rate is 10%, and the term is 15 years.

4. Compute the present value using the arguments previously given in problem 3.

5. Compute the payment amount for a $100,000 loan that has an interest rate of 10 percent and is to be paid on an annual basis for a period of 12 years.

6. Compute the *monthly* payment amount assuming all arguments in problem 5 stay the same except the time period is 30 years.

7. Compute the straight-line depreciation for an office machine having an initial cost of $13,000, an estimated useful life of 8 years and a salvage value of $200.

8. Using the data given in problem 7, compute the depreciation of the office machine for the sixth year using the double-declining balance method.

9. Using the data given in problem 7, compute the depreciation of the office machine for the sixth year using the sum-of-the-years'-digits method.

10. Using the data given in problem 7, compute the depreciation of the office machine for the fourth year using the variable declining balance method. You should use 150% as the depreciation factor.

11. Suppose $10,000 has been invested in an account that pays an annual interest rate of 10%, compounded monthly. Determine how long it will take to get $30,000 in the account.

12. Suppose that $5,000 is deposited at the end of each year into a bank account. If 8% interest is earned per year, compute how long it will take to earn $20,000.

13. Suppose $15,000 has been invested in a bond which matures in 9 years to $25,000. Interest is compounded monthly. Determine the monthly interest rate.

Print the worksheet(s) showing your answers.

CHAPTER TEN
EXERCISE 5
Using the Date and Time Functions

INSTRUCTIONS:

1. Using the @DATE function, enter the date January 19, 1989 into cell A1. Format the date using option 1 from the Date format menu. Notice that the cell fills with asterisks; widen column A appropriately.
2. Using the @TIME function, enter the time 9:49 PM in cell A2.
3. Calculate the number of days between January 3, 1991, and June 27, 1989.
4. Determine the number of days between January 3, 1991, and June 27, 1989, assuming there are 360 days in a year.
5. Use the @NOW function to place the current date on your screen.
6. For the time 8:14:10 a.m., place the hour in cell B1, the minute in cell B2 and the second in cell B3.
7. Determine the time of day represented by the time serial number .481234.

Print the worksheet after completing all parts of the exercise.

CHAPTER TEN
EXERCISE 6
Using the Logical Functions

INSTRUCTIONS: Make sure you have a blank worksheet on your screen. Then enter the following data on the worksheet.

Cell	Data
A1	20
A2	30
A3	50
A10	@NA
A11	10
A12	Worksheet

1. In cell B1, determine whether the value in A1 is within the range from 30 to 40. If the value is in the range, place the word **True** in cell B1; otherwise, place the word **False** in cell B1.

2. In cell B2, determine whether the value in A2 is greater than 25. If the value in cell A2 is greater than 25, use the @TRUE function to enter a value of 1 in cell B2. If the value is less than or equal to 25, use the @FALSE function to place the value 0 in cell B2.

3. In cell B3, determine whether the value in A3 is greater than 60. If the value in cell A3 is greater than 60, use the @TRUE function to enter a value of 1 in cell B3. If the value is less than or equal to 60, use the @FALSE function to place the value 0 in cell B3.

Print the worksheet with the results of the first three questions.

4. Change the values entered in cells A1, A2, A3 to:

Cell	Data
A1	35
A2	10
A3	75

Print the worksheet with the results after entering the new values. Print a list of the cell formulas for cells A1 through B3.

Define the range name ABC and include cells A10 through A12 as its range.

5. In cell B10, determine if the content of cell A10 contains @NA; if so, place a 1 in cell B10; otherwise place a 0 in cell B10.

6. In cell B11, determine if the content of cell A11 is a value. If cell A11 contains a value, place a 1 in cell B11; otherwise enter a 0 in cell B11.

7. In cell B12, determine if cell A12 contains a string of characters. If a string of characters appears in cell A12, place a 1 in cell B12; otherwise, place a 0 in cell B12.

8. In cell B14, determine if the range ABC is defined for the worksheet. If the range is present, place a 1 in cell B14; otherwise, enter a 0 in cell B14.

Print the results for questions 5 through 8. Include a list of cell formulas for cells A10 through B14.

CHAPTER TEN
EXERCISE 7
Using the Database Statistical Functions

INSTRUCTIONS: Create the database table in Figure 10-86.

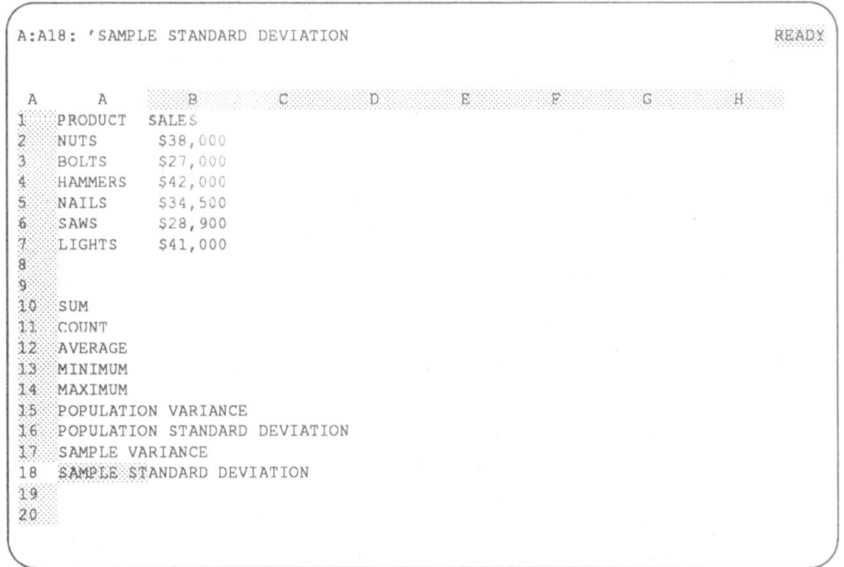

Figure 10-86

1. Construct a criteria that will determine if a product included in the database table has sales of more than $35,000.

2. Place the appropriate database statistical functions in cells E10 through E18 to compute the indicated items.

Print the worksheet after answering questions 1 and 2.

CHAPTER TEN
EXERCISE 8
Using the Mathematical Functions

INSTRUCTIONS: Make sure you have a blank worksheet on your screen. Then enter the following data on the worksheet.

Cell	Data
B1	-45
B2	45
B3	2
B4	52.9876
B5	1.5
B6	10
B7	20
B8	12
B9	67.3468
B10	225

1. In cell C1, compute the absolute value of the contents of cell B1. Calculate the absolute value of the contents of cell B2 and place the results in cell C2.

2. In cell C3, determine the value for ***e*** raised to the power of the number included in cell B3.

3. In cell C4, calculate the integer portion of the value appearing in cell B4.

4. In cell C5, compute the natural logarithm for the value in cell B5.

5. In cell B6, specify the common logarithm for the value in cell B6.

6. In cell C7, determine the remainder (modulus) for the values in cells B7 and B8. In computing the remainder, divide the value in cell B7 by the value in cell B8.

7. In cell C8, enter a random number between 0 and 1.

8. In cell C9, round the value appearing in cell B9 to three decimal places.

9. In cell C10, compute the square root of the value in cell B10.

Print the worksheet with the answers to questions 1 through 9. Also print the cell formulas.

CHAPTER TEN
EXERCISE 9
Using the Cell, Range and Error Trapping Functions

INSTRUCTIONS: Make sure you have a blank worksheet on your screen.

1. Enter the number 25 in cell A2. Place A2 in cell D1. Use the @@ function to place 25 in cell B3.

2. Define the range name COLUMNS that includes cells A1 through K1. In cell A5, specify the number of columns in the range named COLUMNS.

3. In cell A7, specify the worksheet coordinate C:$D$1 using the @COORD function.

4. Define the range named ROWS that includes cells B2 through B233. In cell A9, specify the number of rows in the range named ROWS.

5. Insert 5 worksheets after the current worksheet. Define the range name SHTS that includes cells B:A1 through F:A1 as its range. In cell A:A11 specify the number of sheets in the range SHTS.

6. Enter a 10 in cell B14 and a 0 in cell C14. In cell A14, place a formula that enters ERR in cell A14 when the value in cell C14 is zero; otherwise, compute the product of the values in cells B14 and C14.

7. Enter the number 100 in cell B16. Place the characters @NA (meaning not available) in cell A16 if the value in cell B16 is less than 500; otherwise, place the contents of cell B16 in cell A16.

Print the worksheet after solving questions 1 through 7. Also print the cell formulas.

CHAPTER TEN
EXERCISE 10
Using the Lookup Functions

INSTRUCTIONS: 1. Create the worksheet appearing in Figure 10-87.

A:A1: READY

A	A	B	C	D	E	F	G
1			Sales Tax	Sales			
2	Product	Price	Rate Code	Tax			
3	Beans	0.79	1				
4	Hammer	2.59	2				
5	Nail	0.25	2				
6	Cake	1.25	1				
7							
8							
9			Sales Tax				
10			Rate Code	Tax Rate			
11			1	0%			
12			2	8%			
13							
14							

Figure 10-87

You need to compute the Sales Tax amount for the four products based on the Sales Tax Rate Code. Use the @CHOOSE function to assist you in computing the proper sales tax amount for the four items.

Print the worksheet after completing the calculation of the sales tax amounts. Also print the cell formulas.

2. Create the worksheet appearing in Figure 10-88.

```
A:D9: [W12] ^AMOUNT                                                          READY

A       A              B             C              D            E         F
1
2   COMMISSION                   SALES AMOUNT
3      CODE          $2,000        $3,000         $4,000       $5,000
4            1          200           300            400          500
5            2          100           150            200          250
6            3           40            60             80          100
7
8                     SALES     COMMISSION     COMMISSION
9   EMPLOYEE         AMOUNT        CODE          AMOUNT
10  ABRAMS           $2,500            3
11  CHEN             $3,500            1
12  MARTINEZ         $3,100            1
13  SMITH            $4,900            2
14  ZACHARY          $3,000            3
15
16
```

Figure 10-88

You need to calculate the commission owed each of the salespersons. The amount of commission is based on a commission code assigned to each individual and the sales amount for the individuals. For example, a person that has a sales amount of $2,800 and a commission code of 2 is owed a commission of $100. Use the @HLOOKUP function to help calculate the proper commission amounts.

Print the worksheet after computing the commission amounts. Also print the cell formulas.

3. Create the worksheet appearing in Figure 10-89.

```
A:D9: "TAXES                                                        READY

A    A          B         C          D        E        F        G        H
1
2                 TAX
3    SALARY      RATE
4   $25,000        2%
5   $50,000        7%
6   $75,000       15%
7
8
9   EMPLOYEE    SALARY TAX RATE    TAXES
10  ABBOTT     $78,000
11  GARCIA     $52,000
12  MONTEGUET  $60,000
13  SMITH      $48,000
14
15
```

Figure 10-89

You must compute the state income taxes owed by the individuals. The tax amount owed by each employee is computed by multiplying the salary amount times the appropriate tax rate. For example, if a person has a salary equal to $50,000, then the amount of state income tax due is $3,500. Use the @VLOOKUP function to determine the proper tax rate for each employee.

Print the worksheet after calculating the tax amount due for each of the employees. Also print the cell formulas.

CHAPTER TEN
EXERCISE 11
Using the String Functions

INSTRUCTIONS: Make sure you have a blank worksheet on your screen.

1. Repeat the string of characters "Graph" six times in cell A1. Do not include the quotes.
2. Enter the label: "Lotus 1-2-3 is a great software package" in cell A3. Do not include the quotes. Find the position of the word *great* in the label and place the answer in cell B4.
3. Using the label in cell A3, place the characters *Lotus 1-2-3* in cell D4.
4. Using the label in cell A3, determine the number of characters in the label and place the answer in cell F4.
5. Using the label in cell A3, place the word *software* in cell B6.
6. Copy the label in cell A3 to cell A8. Using the label in cell A8, replace the word *great* with *wonderful.*
7. Using the label in cell A8, place the words *software package* in cell B9.
8. Enter the words "Fall is a beautiful time of year" in cell A11. Do not include the quotes.
9. Using the label in cell A11, change all of the letters to lowercase and place the results in cell A12.
10. Using the label in cell A11, change all of the letters to uppercase and place the results in cell A13.
11. Using the label in cell A11, capitalize the first letter in each word and make all other letters lowercase and place the results in cell A14.

Print the worksheet with the answers to questions 1 through 11. Also print the cell formulas.

CHAPTER TEN
EXERCISE 12
Using the String Functions

INSTRUCTIONS: Make sure you have a blank worksheet on your screen.

1. Enter the number 592.783 in cell A1. Using the value in cell A1, change the value to a label with three decimal places and place the results in cell B1.

2. Enter the label "Lotus 1-2-3 is fun to use" in cell A3. Do not include the quotes. Remove the leading spaces and extra spaces between the words. Place the results in cell A4.

3. Enter 123.456 as a label in cell A6. Change the label in cell A6 to a number and place the results in cell B6.

4. Enter the string of characters "Northeast" in cell A8. Do not include the quotes. Place the same characters in cell A9 except omit the letter ***s***. In cell A10, determine whether the contents of cells A8 and A9 are exactly the same. If they are not exactly the same, place a 0 in cell A10; otherwise, a 1 should appear in cell A10.

5. Place the values 1, 2 and 3 in cells A12, B12 and C12 respectively, and create the range name NUM that includes these cells as the range. In cell A13, place the contents of the first cell in the range if the first cell in the range is a value.

Print the worksheet after completing questions 1 through 5.

CHAPTER ELEVEN

INTRODUCTION TO MACROS

OBJECTIVES

In this chapter, you will learn to:

- Use a standard procedure for creating a macro
- Define range names for use in macros
- Place macros in a suitable location on a worksheet
- Create and execute a macro
- Create a print macro
- Create a macro using the record feature
- Create and use a macro library

CHAPTER OVERVIEW

A **macro** is a set of written instructions representing keystrokes in Lotus 1-2-3. The macro keystrokes represent the keystrokes exactly as they are typed when you select them from various worksheet menus, enter data or move the cell pointer.

Macros are especially useful when performing detailed, repetitive routines. You can write macros that consolidate worksheets, perform special edit routines or print reports and graphs. Advanced uses of macros can involve using macro commands that allow you to perform loops, subroutines, *IF* statements and many other features common to programming languages. A macro enables users of 1-2-3 to do intricate spreadsheet analysis. In this chapter, you will learn the basics of macros. The next chapter contains more advanced topics related to macros.

DEFINING RANGE NAMES

A **range name** is a name that is assigned to a specific cell or group of cells. Range names are used to specify the location of a macro. They are also used to identify ranges of cells within macros. By using range names, you can create macro programs that are more self-sufficient and require less editing and maintenance.

To illustrate the use of a range name, retrieve the BUDGET file you created in Chapter 2. Your screen should now look like Figure 11-1.

A:A1: [W18] READY

A	A	B	C	D	E	F	G
1			ABC COMPANY				
2			BUDGET				
3							
4							
5		QTR1	QTR2	QTR3	QTR4	YR TOTAL	
6							
7	SALES	$60,000	$61,200	$62,424	$63,672	$247,296	
8							
9	EXPENSES						
10	SALARIES	35,000	35,500	36,000	37,200	143,700	
11	RENT	9,000	9,000	9,000	9,000	36,000	
12	TELEPHONE	1,000	1,050	1,103	1,158	4,311	
13	OFFICE SUPPLIES	750	800	850	900	3,300	
14	MISCELLANEOUS	1,000	1,030	1,061	1,093	4,184	
15		----------	----------	----------	----------	----------	
16	TOTAL EXPENSES	46,750	47,380	48,014	49,351	191,495	
17		----------	----------	----------	----------	----------	
18	GROSS PROFIT	$13,250	$13,820	$14,410	$14,321	$55,801	
19		==========	==========	==========	==========	==========	
20							

Figure 11-1

Suppose you want to use a range name to represent the SALES values in cells B7 through E7.

To specify the range name SALES for these cells:

Move the cell pointer to cell B7

Press /

Select Range

Select Name

Select Create

When prompted for a range name:

Type SALES

Press ↵

To define the range of cells to include:

Move the cell pointer to cell E7

After highlighting the cells B7 through E7,

Press ↵

The range of cells associated with the named range SALES was substituted in the @SUM formula for the word SALES and the proper total was computed. Your screen should look like Figure 11-1. Move the cell pointer to cell F7 and note that the @SUM formula now has SALES in it rather than B7..E7.

You can use the F5 key to go to the first cell in a range on a worksheet. For example:

Press F5

When prompted for the address to go TO:

Type SALES

Press ↵

The cell pointer should now be in cell B7.

■ PROCESS FOR CREATING A MACRO

The steps you can use to create a macro are:

1. Create a macro by first *practicing the procedure* that the macro is to perform; manually press the keystrokes necessary to execute the macro.

2. While going through the macro steps, *record every keystroke* exactly as it is typed.

3. After practicing the macro manually, *record the keystrokes on a separate worksheet or a separate file.*

   The macro instructions must be in the proper order and must appear as labels contained in one column. Begin each of the macro instructions with an apostrophe (the ' symbol is located on the double quote key). This procedure will prevent the macro from executing some commands as they are being entered (for example, typing / to bring up the command menu). Using the apostrophe will also allow 1-2-3 to accept all macro instructions when they contain a combination of numeric and alphabetical characters.

4. After entering the complete macro, *name the macro as a named range.* There are two ways to name a macro. You can use a \ and a single letter, or a range name that consists of any other combination of 15 allowable characters, such as PRINT_MACRO. Only the first cell in the macro is needed for the range name; however, the entire macro can be specified in the range. The macro will stop executing when it attempts to process a blank in the column containing the macro.

5. Before running and testing the macro, *save the file containing the macro and the worksheet* on which the macro is applicable. Then, if the macro does not work properly, you can retrieve the worksheet and the macro as it was before any changes were made by the macro.

6. *Execute the macro.* If you named your macro using the \ key and a single letter, you can run the macro by holding down the [Alt] key and then pressing the letter. If the macro name consists of any other combination of characters, hold down the [Alt] key and press the [F3] key. Then move the pointer to the proper macro name and press the [↵] key or type the name of the macro and press the [↵] key.

7. The macro should perform automatically. If it does not, the macro instructions are incorrect and you will have to *edit and revise the macro.* You may need to press the [Esc] key to exit a macro that has stopped because it encountered an error. Another way to stop a macro once it has begun execution is to hold down the [Ctrl] key and to press the [Break] key. The [Break] key is located on the [Pause] key on most keyboards.

   After determining the error, **retrieve** the file with the macro. Edit the macro on the retrieved worksheet, then **save** and **replace** it before testing the macro again. If the original worksheet and macro are not retrieved from the disk after it has incorrectly run, the worksheet may contain unwanted changes that were made to the worksheet during execution.

8. After a macro has executed correctly, you should *document (write an explanation of what the macro instructions do)* the macro in a column to the right of the macro steps and then write the macro's name either above or to the left of the macro steps. The documentation process is optional. However, a written explanation of a macro's purpose will prove valuable to a user who did not create the macro but needs to know what the macro does without spending extra time to analyze it. Documentation is also useful for the macro's author, saving time from having to decipher the macro at a later date when the macro may need to be altered or used in another application.

LOCATION OF A MACRO

Macros can be placed on separate files, separate worksheets or on the same worksheet on which the macro is to be used. It is recommended that the macro be saved on a separate file or on a separate worksheet. By using either of these approaches to storing your macro, you are less likely to modify by accident the cells containing the macro keystrokes when you are working on the worksheet file.

If you must place the macro on the worksheet on which it will be used, place it to the right and below the data on the worksheet. For example, suppose you are using cells A1 through F35 on your worksheet, then your macros should be below row 35 and to the right of column F. By using this approach, you are less likely to accidentally delete or modify one of the macro instructions.

■ CREATING AND EXECUTING A MACRO

In Chapter 7, you consolidated salary information for three divisions of ABC Company into a summary worksheet. You then linked the total salary data appearing in the DIVISION file to the SALARIES row in the BUDGET file. 1-2-3 also allows you to combine information between files rather than linking them. In this section, you will build a macro to combine the total salary data from the summary worksheet in the DIVISION file into the BUDGET file.

In this example, you will place the macro instructions on worksheet B of the BUDGET file. By placing the macro instructions on a separate worksheet from the BUDGET worksheet, you are less likely to accidentally modify the macro keystrokes.

First retrieve the BUDGET file, then add a worksheet after the BUDGET worksheet and place both worksheets on your screen. After you have completed these steps, your screen should look like Figure 11-2.

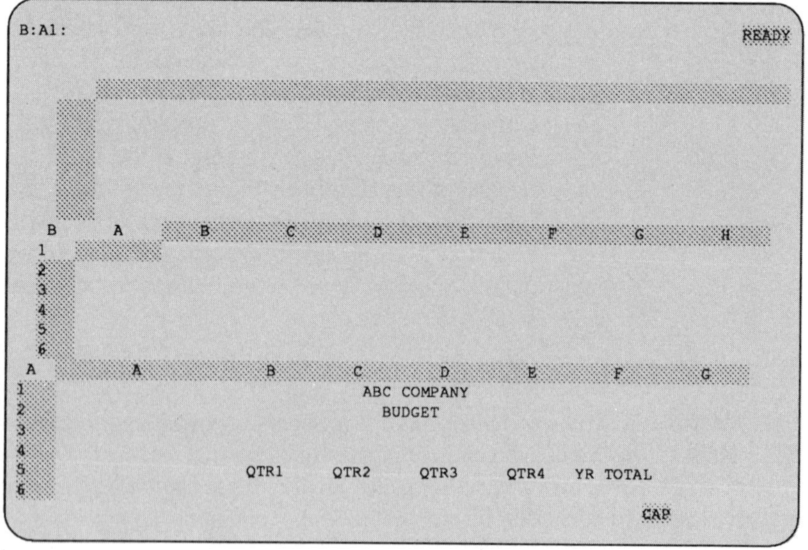

Figure 11-2

Manually Practicing the Macro Keystrokes and Recording Every Keystroke on Paper

For the purposes of this exercise, it is assumed that you have gone through the process for combining files and written the required keystrokes on a sheet of paper.

Entering the Keystrokes on the Appropriate Worksheet

Begin entering the macro by placing the name of the macro as a title on worksheet B.

Move the cell pointer to cell B:A1

Type Macro \C

Press ↵

Move the cell pointer to cell B:B1

Type Macro for combining data from the DIVISION file into the BUDGET file

Press ↵

When you name the macro later using the **R**ange **N**ame command sequence, you will give it the name \C.

You will place the macro instructions as labels beginning in cell B:B3. To enter the first macro instruction:

Move the cell pointer to cell B:B3

Type '/reSALARIES~

Press ↵

SALARIES is a range name for the cells A:B10 through A:E10. You will create the range name prior to executing the macro.

The macro instruction records the keystrokes for pressing the / key, selecting the **R**ange **E**rase command from the menu structure, using the SALARIES range name to specify the range of cells to erase and pressing the ↵ key to complete the procedure. The entry must begin with an apostrophe to enter the keystrokes as a label. The ~ character represents the ↵ key in a macro instruction. Notice that the command letters for **R**ange **E**rase are lowercase letters and that the range name SALARIES is in uppercase letters. This procedure is optional. Many macro authors use this convention so that the macro can be read more easily; the uppercase characters represent what you input, such as range names, cell addresses or file names.

To enter the second macro instruction:

Move the cell pointer to cell B:B4

Type '{goto}SALARIES~

Press ⏎

This instruction records pressing the F5 key, typing the named range SALARIES and pressing the ⏎ key. As a result of executing this macro instruction, the cell pointer is moved to the initial cell in the range name SALARIES which is cell A:B10 in this example.

To enter the third macro instruction:

Move the cell pointer to cell B:B5

Type '/fcanTOTAL~

Press ⏎

In this macro instruction, you have indicated that you want to execute the **F**ile **C**ombine **A**dd **N**amed/Specified-Range command sequence. TOTAL is the range name for the total salary cells in the DIVISION file that will be added to the SALARIES cells in the BUDGET file.

To specify the fourth macro instruction:

Move the cell pointer to cell B:B6

Type 'DIVISION~

Press ⏎

This instruction indicates that the range name TOTAL is in file DIVISION. Before executing the macro, you will need to define TOTAL as the range name for cells B10 through E10 in file DIVISION that contains the total of the salaries for the three divisions. When this macro instruction is executed, the values from the range name TOTAL in the DIVISION file are added to the respective cells of the range name SALARIES in the BUDGET file.

To enter the final macro instruction:

Move the cell pointer to cell B:B7

Type '{goto}A1~

Press ⏎

This instruction is optional. It was included so that the cell pointer will be moved to cell A1 after the macro is executed. If the cell pointer is not in cell A1 after the macro is executed, you will know that the macro has not executed correctly. When all of the macro instructions are entered, your screen should look like Figure 11-3.

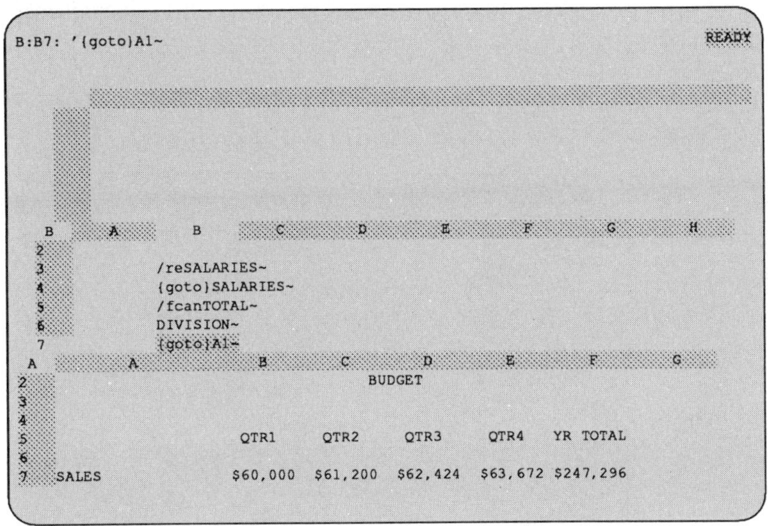

Figure 11-3

To create the range name SALARIES:

Move	the cell pointer to cell A:B10
Press	/
Select	Range
Select	Name
Select	Create

To specify the range name to create:

Type	SALARIES
Press	↵

When you are prompted to enter the range of cells:

Move	the cell pointer to cell A:E10
Press	↵

To save the range name permanently and the macro worksheet with the BUDGET file worksheet, save the file with the name BUDGET3 using the **F**ile **S**ave command sequence.

Before you can define the range name TOTAL, you must open the DIVISION file and place it after the BUDGET file. Use the **F**ile **O**pen **A**fter command sequence to open the DIVISION file.

Move the cell pointer to cell A:A10 in file BUDGET. Your screen should look like Figure 11-4.

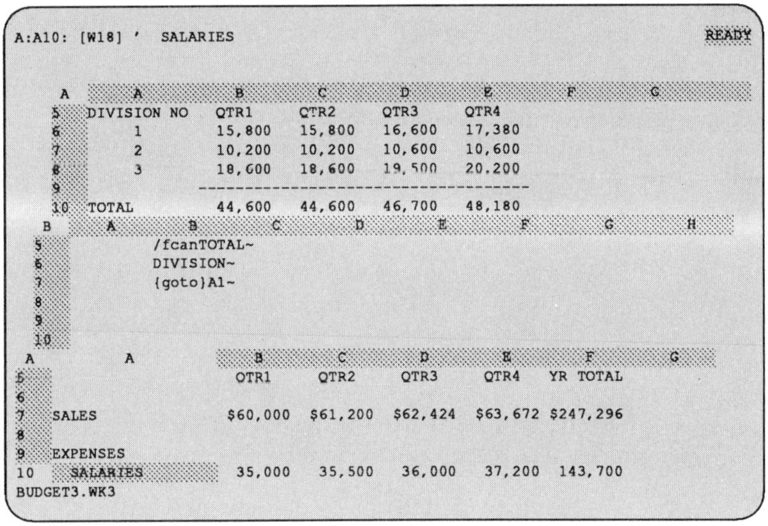

```
A:A10: [W18] '  SALARIES                                                READY

   A    A             B         C         D         E        F        G
   5  DIVISION NO   QTR1      QTR2      QTR3      QTR4
   6           1    15,800    15,800    16,600    17,380
   7           2    10,200    10,200    10,600    10,600
   8           3    18,600    18,600    19,500    20,200
   9                ----------------------------------
   10 TOTAL         44,600    44,600    46,700    48,180
  B    A        B         C         D         E         F        G        H
  5             /fcanTOTAL~
  6             DIVISION~
  7             {goto}A1~
  8
  9
  10
 A          A              B         C         D         E        F          G
 5                        QTR1      QTR2      QTR3      QTR4     YR TOTAL
 6
 7  SALES                $60,000   $61,200   $62,424   $63,672  $247,296
 8
 9  EXPENSES
 10   SALARIES            35,000    35,500    36,000    37,200   143,700
BUDGET3.WK3
```

Figure 11-4

To define the range name TOTAL:

Move	the cell pointer to cell A:B10 in the DIVISION file
Press	/
Select	Range
Select	Name
Select	Create

To specify the range name to create:

Type	TOTAL
Press	↵

When prompted for the cell range:

Move the cell pointer to cell A:E10

Press ↵

Save the range name with the DIVISION file by using the **F**ile **S**ave **R**eplace command sequence.

Naming the Macro

To define \C as the name for the macro:

Move the cell pointer to cell B:B3 in the BUDGET file

Note that B3 is the first cell that contains a macro instruction.

Press /

Select Range

Select Name

Select Create

When prompted enter the name:

Type \C

Press ↵

To indicate the first cell of the macro as the range:

Press 

The macro now is named \ C. The macro will execute the instructions in cell B3 and continue executing macro instructions in column B below cell B3 until it encounters a blank. When a blank is found, the macro will stop executing. If you so desire, you can include all macro instructions in the range name \ C.

Saving the File Containing the Macro Keystrokes

Before executing or testing the macro, you should save the file containing the macro and any worksheets that will be modified as a result of using the macro. In this case, you need to save the BUDGET3 file using the **F**ile **S**ave **R**eplace command sequence.

Executing the Macro

To execute the macro:

Press Alt

While holding down the Alt key:

Type C

Release both keys. The macro will now execute.

If the macro has executed properly, your screen should look like Figure 11-5.

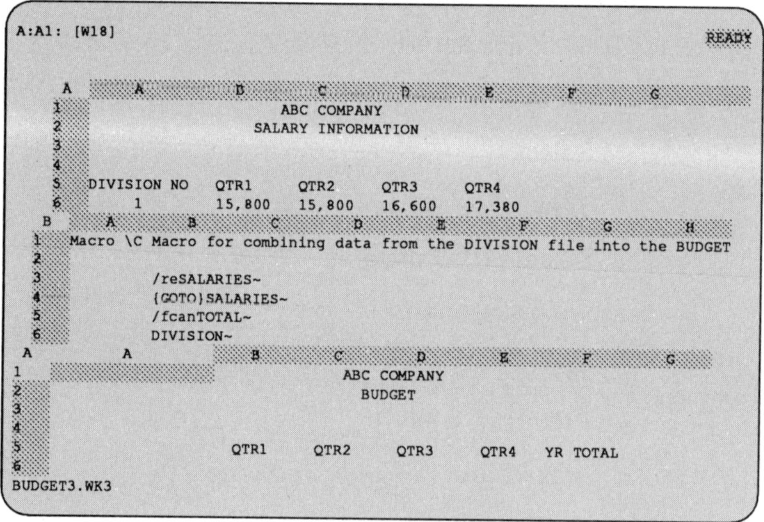

Figure 11-5

To see the results of the macro on the SALARIES row, move the cell pointer to cell A:A10. Notice that the cells in range name TOTAL (cells A:C10 through E10 in the DIVISION file) have been added to the cells in the range name SALARIES of the BUDGET3 file. Your screen should look like Figure 11-6.

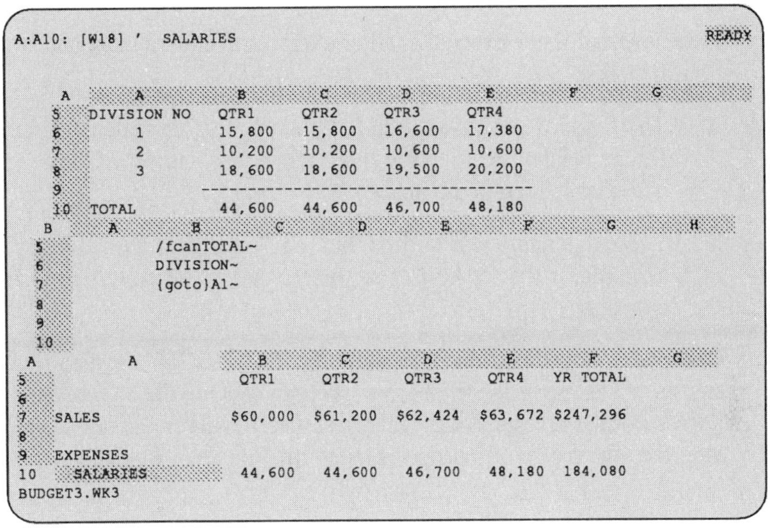

```
A:A10: [W18] '  SALARIES                                                      READY

     A       A          B          C          D          E          F          G
     5  DIVISION NO   QTR1       QTR2       QTR3       QTR4
     6          1     15,800     15,800     16,600     17,380
     7          2     10,200     10,200     10,600     10,600
     8          3     18,600     18,600     19,500     20,200
     9                -----------------------------------------
     10 TOTAL         44,600     44,600     46,700     48,180
   B       A          B          C          D          E          F          G          H
   5              /fcanTOTAL~
   6              DIVISION~
   7              {goto}A1~
   8
   9
   10
 A             A              B          C          D          E          F          G
 5                          QTR1       QTR2       QTR3       QTR4     YR TOTAL
 6
 7  SALES                   $60,000    $61,200    $62,424    $63,672  $247,296
 8
 9  EXPENSES
 10   SALARIES              44,600     44,600     46,700     48,180   184,080
BUDGET3.WK3
```

Figure 11-6

Editing and Correcting a Macro

If the macro stops and "beeps," look carefully at the screen to determine at what point the macro seemed to have trouble executing. To exit the macro error, press the Ctrl and Break keys simultaneously. Depending on the macro, the Esc key may need to be pressed after pressing Ctrl-Break. (The Break key is located on the Pause key.) Move to the area where the macro instructions are written to see if the error can be determined. Compare keystrokes with the macro keystrokes in Figure 11-3. Typical errors include:

- Macro steps were preceded with the incorrect apostrophe (use the apostrophe on the double quote key).
- Another character was entered instead of the tilde or a tilde was omitted in an instruction.
- Parentheses (the ( ) symbols) or brackets (the [ ] symbols) were entered instead of braces (the { } symbols).
- The backward slash (the \ symbol) was used instead of the slash (the / symbol) (Recall that the backward slash is a repeating prefix that repeats any characters following it.)
- A space was inserted in an inappropriate place.
- The uppercase letter O was typed instead of a zero; the lowercase letter l was typed instead of the number one.

If the macro doesn't execute at all or attempts to enter a label and stops, consider these two typical errors:

- The forward slash was used for the range name instead of the backward slash (use **R**ange **N**ame **C**reate to see if the range was named / C instead of \ C), or no range name was given to the macro.

- The range name was correct, but the first line of the macro is not a macro step (for example, if the top cell of the macro is a blank cell, the macro will never complete executing).

Once the error is determined, **retrieve** the file BUDGET3 and correct the appropriate macro steps(s). Then **save** the file before trying to execute the macro again. If the original file is not retrieved, the results of the incorrect macro will remain on the spreadsheet. Save the file after the macro executes properly using the **F**ile **S**ave **R**eplace command sequence.

Documenting the Macro

Documenting a macro is optional, but you can save valuable time later when you are trying to edit or execute the macro. The documentation in this example explains every cell of the macro. Sometimes it is more appropriate to document a macro by writing a paragraph to explain a macro's overall purpose and then write additional paragraphs to explain sections. Refer to Chapter 13 for instructions on how to write a paragraph on a worksheet.

To enter the corresponding explanations of the macro commands in column C to document what the macro does, retrieve the file BUDGET3 using the **F**ile **R**etrieve command sequence.

To create a title for the macro (an optional step):

Move	the cell pointer to cell B:A3
Type	'\ C
Press	↵

Recall that you placed Macro \ C in cell B:A1.

Creating a title is optional because it is not required to make the macro execute; however, the macro title is useful as documentation. A common convention is to put the macro name in the column to the left of the macro keystrokes. In this way, if several macros are on a single worksheet, the names will be clearly visible in the column to the left of the multiple macros.

To document the macro steps:

Move	the cell pointer to cell B:D3

Refer to Figure 11-7 to enter the documentation for the macro in cells B:D3 through B:D7.

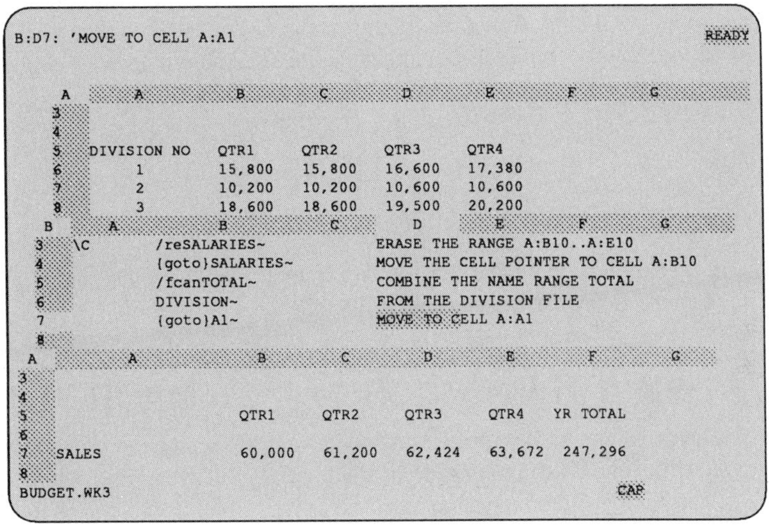

```
B:D7: 'MOVE TO CELL A:A1                                                READY

    A      A          B          C          D          E          F          G
    3
    4
    5  DIVISION NO    QTR1       QTR2       QTR3       QTR4
    6       1         15,800     15,800     16,600     17,380
    7       2         10,200     10,200     10,600     10,600
    8       3         18,600     18,600     19,500     20,200
   B      A          B          C          D          E          F          G
   3  \C        /reSALARIES~              ERASE THE RANGE A:B10..A:E10
   4            {goto}SALARIES~           MOVE THE CELL POINTER TO CELL A:B10
   5            /fcanTOTAL~               COMBINE THE NAME RANGE TOTAL
   6            DIVISION~                 FROM THE DIVISION FILE
   7            {goto}A1~                 MOVE TO CELL A:A1
   8
  A      A          B          C          D          E          F          G
  3
  4
  5                  QTR1       QTR2       QTR3       QTR4    YR TOTAL
  6
  7  SALES           60,000     61,200     62,424     63,672   247,296
  8
BUDGET.WK3                                                         CAP
```

Figure 11-7

After entering the documentation:

Press [Home]

Save the BUDGET3 file using the **F**ile **S**ave **R**eplace command sequence.

■ PROCESS FOR DEBUGGING A MACRO

Whenever a macro contains many instructions, it may be difficult to determine which macro entry may be causing an error. Fortunately, Lotus 1-2-3 has a feature that allows you to execute the macro one macro keystroke at a time. This process can be used to help eliminate errors, sometimes referred to as "bugs," and is therefore sometimes called "debugging."

To use the single-step mode of execution:

Press [Alt-F2]

Select Step

The word STEP now appears at the bottom of your screen. When you execute the macro you are examining, it will be executed one keystroke at a time by pressing the ↵ key each time you want to move to the next keystroke in the macro. As you start executing the macro, the characters SST replace the word STEP to indicate that you are stepping through the macro one keystroke at a time.

When an error is determined, the (Esc) key can be pressed one or more times to end the process. Another alternative is to press the (Ctrl-Break) combination of keys. You can then edit the appropriate cell contents in the macro so it will execute properly.

To leave the STEP mode:

Press (Alt-F2)

Select Step

If execution of the macro has not been completed, then the remaining macro steps will be executed as soon as you leave STEP mode.

CREATING A PRINT MACRO AND A MACRO LIBRARY

Macros can be used to print worksheets. In the last section you wrote a macro to combine data from one file to another file. In this section, you will write a macro to print the BUDGET3 worksheet, and then create a macro library.

You developed the macro \C to combine some information from the DIVISION file into the BUDGET3 file. It is logical to include such a macro on a separate worksheet in the BUDGET3 file because you are not very likely to use it for other files.

However, when you do need to use the same macro in more than one file, it is a good idea to save it on a separate file. The macro file can then be opened when necessary and used with a specific worksheet in another file. When you have several such macros, you may want to combine them on one file and create a **macro library**. A macro library is a convenient way to organize macros that can be used with many worksheet files.

An example of a macro that might be included in a macro library is one that can be used to print worksheets. To illustrate the process of creating a macro library, you will first create a macro to print the BUDGET3 worksheet, and then save it in a file you will use as a macro library.

Before creating the print macro, erase whatever you presently have on your screen and retrieve the BUDGET3 file.

The first step in creating the print macro and a macro library is to add a new file after the BUDGET3 file.

Press /

Select File

Select New

Select After

When you are prompted for the name of the file:

Type MACROLIB

Press ↵

You have indicated that the file MACROLIB is to be placed after the BUDGET3 file.

To give the macro a title:

Move the cell pointer to cell A:A1 in the new file

Type 'PRINT_MACRO

Press ↵

The macro will be named later. Widen column A to 12 so it contains the macro title.

To enter the first instruction of the macro:

Move the cell pointer to cell B1

Type '/wtc

Press ↵

This instruction clears any title settings that may have been specified using the **W**orksheet **T**itle command sequence.

To place the second instruction of the macro on the worksheet:

Move the cell pointer to cell B2

Type '/ppr{home}.{end}{home}~

Press ↵

This instruction specifies that the range of cells A1 through the last cell in the worksheet is to be printed on the printer.

To place the third instruction of the macro on the worksheet:

Move the cell pointer to cell B3

Type 'agppq

Press ↵

This instruction directs 1-2-3 to accept the present alignment of the paper in the printer, print the worksheet range, eject to the top of the next page, eject another page to make it easy to remove the paper from the printer and quit the print menu.

Your screen should now look like Figure 11-8.

```
A:B3: 'agppq                                                          READY

     A        A           B         C         D         E         F         G
     1   PRINT_MACRO /wtc
     2               /ppr{home}.{end}{home}~
     3               agppq
     4
     5
     6
    B       A         B         C         D         E         F         G         H
    1   Macro\C   Macro for combining data from the DIVISION file into the BUDGET
    2
    3   \C        /reSALARIES~      ERASE THE RANGE A:B10..A:E10
    4             {goto}SALARIES~   MOVE THE CELL POINTER TO CELL A:B10
    5             fcanTOTAL~        COMBINE THE NAME RANGE TOTAL
    6             DIVISION~         FROM THE DIVISION FILE
   A          A           B         C         D         E         F
   1                                 ABC COMPANY
   2                                   BUDGET
   3
   4
   5                     QTR1      QTR2      QTR3      QTR4    YR TOTAL
   6
MACROLIB.WK3
```

Figure 11-8

To name the macro:

Move	the cell pointer to cell B1
Press	/
Select	Range
Select	Name
Select	Create

When you are prompted to enter the name to create:

Type	PRINT_MACRO
Press	↵

Notice that you used a different naming mechanism. This approach was taken so you can learn to execute a macro using a method other than the one used in the last section.

You can specify the initial cell of the macro as the range as follows:

Press	↵

To save the macro library file and include the print macro on it:

Press /

Select File

Select Save

When you are prompted for the file name:

Type MACROLIB

Press ↵

Select Replace

You have created a file on which you can keep a group of macros that are useful on a worksheet file. You can later place additional macros in the macro library file.

To save all modified files:

Press /

Select File

Select Save

When asked to specify the file name:

Press ↵

By pressing the ↵ key you indicated that all modified files are to be saved.

When prompted whether to Cancel, Replace or Backup:

Select Replace

You have saved the files prior to executing the macro.

To execute PRINT_MACRO:

Move the cell pointer to cell A:A1 in BUDGET3

Press Alt-F3 keys simultaneously

To select the PRINT_MACRO from the macro library file MACROLIB:

Press F3

Select <<MACROLIB.WK3>>

You have indicated that the macro you need to use is in the file MACROLIB.

To specify PRINT_MACRO is the appropriate macro to use:

Press F3

Select PRINT_MACRO

The BUDGET3 worksheet will then be printed. Document your print macro using the information in Figure 11-9.

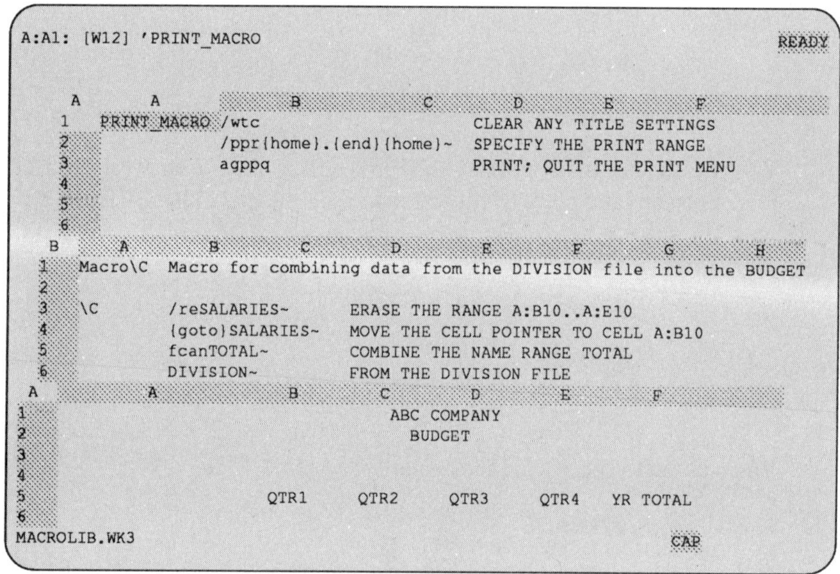

Figure 11-9

Save the MACROLIB file so the documentation will be permanently attached to the macro instructions.

■ CREATING A MACRO USING THE RECORD FEATURE

In the first part of this chapter, you created a macro by entering the macro keystrokes that comprise the macro instructions one keystroke at a time. As you work through the remaining portion of this chapter, you will learn an easier way to create a macro.

You will create the macro that appeared in the last section using the macro record capability of 1-2-3. Prior to recording the macro, make sure the file BUDGET is on your screen and that the range name SALARIES has been created and contains cells B10 through E10.

In this exercise, you will place the macro on a worksheet within file BUDGET. However, you can use a separate file or include the macro on the macro library file you created in the last section.

Retrieve file BUDGET, insert another worksheet after worksheet A in file BUDGET, and use the **W**orksheet **W**indow **P**erspective command sequence to display both worksheets.

To place a title for the macro on the new worksheet:

Move the cell pointer to cell B:A3

Type '\C

Press ↵

Rather than recording the macro keystrokes on paper as you go through the process of combining the data from the DIVISION file into the worksheet in the BUDGET file, you can have 1-2-3 record the keystrokes for you. There are four steps you need to complete:

1. Enter the record mode.
2. Erase the record buffer.
3. Complete the task you want to include in the macro.
4. Place the recorded keystrokes on the appropriate worksheet.

Recording the Macro Keystrokes

To enter the record mode:

Press Alt-F2

Select Copy

There already may be some characters in the record buffer that you do not want to include in your macro. To erase the characters:

Press Esc twice

Select Erase

Now you are ready to go through the process you used earlier in this chapter to combine the salary information from the file DIVISION into worksheet A of the BUDGET3 file. You need not be concerned about typing errors, because you can correct them at a later point.

The keystrokes are listed below:

Press F5

Type	A:A1
Press	↵
Press	/
Select	Range
Select	Erase
Type	SALARIES
Press	↵
Press	F5
Type	SALARIES
Press	↵
Press	/
Select	File
Select	Combine
Select	Add
Select	Named / Specified-Range
Type	TOTAL
Press	↵
Type	DIVISION
Press	↵
Press	Home

To see the recorded keystrokes:

Press	Alt-F2
Select	Copy

You can see the keystrokes that have been recorded at the top of the screen. Your screen should look similar to Figure 11-10. If you made typing errors while entering the keystrokes, your screen will not look exactly like Figure 11-10, but you can correct the errors shortly.

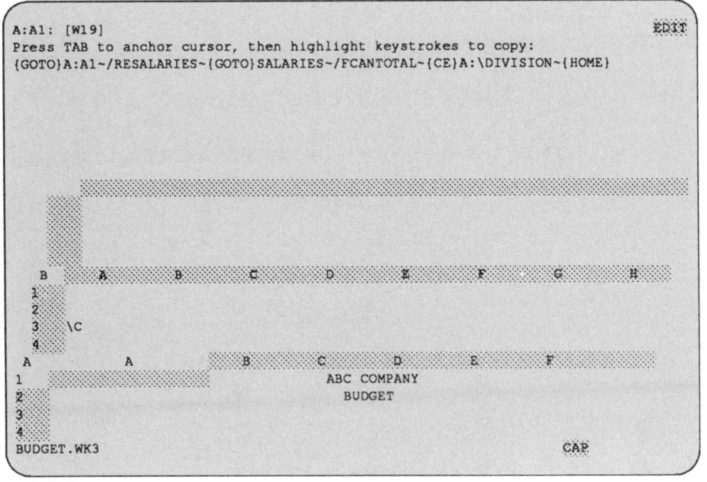

Figure 11-10

When you are finished comparing your screen with Figure 11-10,

Press Esc three times

Placing the Macro Keystrokes on the Appropriate Worksheet

To copy the macro keystrokes on worksheet B and place the keystrokes in cells based on logical break points in the macro:

Move the cell pointer to cell B:B3

Widen column B so it contains 15 characters

You need to widen column B so the longest macro instruction can fit in a cell. Otherwise, 1-2-3 will place some of the characters in the cell below.

To enter the first macro instruction in B:B3:

Press Alt-F2

Select Copy

To move to the initial character in the macro keystroke string:

Press Home

To specify the cells to copy:

Press ⇥ (Tab key)

The ⇥ key is used rather than the period to identify the initial character to highlight.

Press → (right arrow)

until the first ~ keystroke is highlighted. Your screen now should look like Figure 11-11.

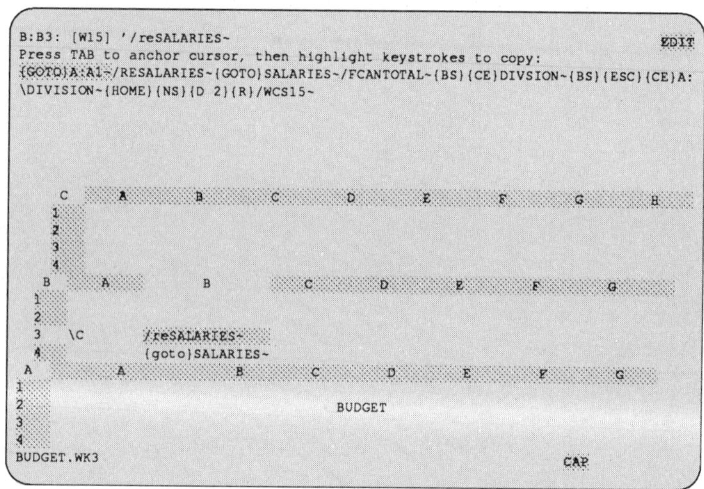

Figure 11-11

To place the highlighted keystrokes in cell B:B3:

Press ↵ twice

The first ↵ key indicates that the highlighted keystrokes are to be copied. The second ↵ key confirms that you want the keystrokes copied to cell B:B3. This set of keystrokes specifies the cell pointer is to be moved to cell A:A1.

To place the second macro instruction in cell B:B4:

Move the cell pointer to cell B:B4

Press Alt-F2

Select Copy

Move the pointer to the first /

Press ⇥

Press → until the ~ after the first occurrence of SALARIES is highlighted

Press ↵ twice

This set of keystrokes indicates that the cells in the range name SALARIES are to be erased.

To place the third macro instruction in cell B:B5:

Move the cell pointer to cell B:B5

Press Alt-F2

Select Copy

Move the pointer to the second {

Press ⇥

Move the pointer to the ~ key after {GOTO}SALARIES

Press ↵ twice

This set of keystrokes specifies that the cell pointer is to be moved to the initial cell in the range name SALARIES. In this example, the cell pointer will be moved to cell A:B10 when the macro is executed.

You can enter the fourth macro instruction in cell B:B6 at this point.

Move the cell pointer to cell B:B6

Press Alt-F2

Select Copy

Highlight / FCANTOTAL~

Press ↵ twice

With this macro instruction, you have specified that you want 1-2-3 to complete a File Combine Add command sequence using the cells in range name TOTAL.

You can enter the fifth macro instruction:

Move the cell pointer to cell B:B7

Press Alt-F2

Select Copy

Highlight DIVISION~

Press ↵ twice

This set of macro keystrokes indicates that the named range TOTAL is in the file DIVISION.

To enter the sixth and final macro instruction:

Move	the cell pointer to cell B:B8
Press	Alt-F2
Select	Copy
Highlight	{HOME}
Press	↵ twice

Your screen now should look like Figure 11-12.

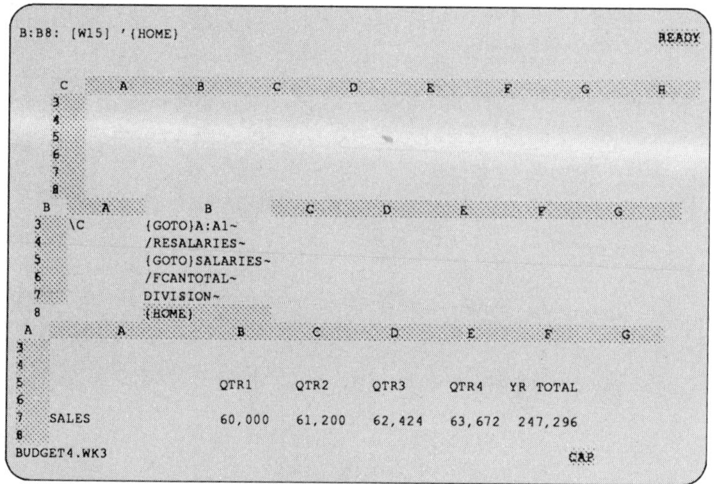

Figure 11-12

If you have errors in any of the cells, correct them using Figure 11-12 as a guide.

To name the macro:

Move	the cell pointer to cell B:B3
Press	/
Select	Range
Select	Name
Select	Create

When prompted for a range name:

Type	\ C
Press	↵

To specify the first cell in the macro as the range:

Press	↵

Executing the Macro

Before executing the macro, save the file on BUDGET4.

To execute the macro:

Press	Alt

While holding down the Alt key:

Type	C

The macro will then execute. Move the cell pointer to cell A:B10 to see that the macro did in fact execute properly. Your screen now should look like Figure 11-13.

```
A:B10: 44600                                                        READY

 B        A              B            C          D          E         F         G
 8                   {HOME}
 9
10
11
12
13
 A                A                 B          C          D          E          F
 8
 9  EXPENSES
10     SALARIES                  44,600     44,600     46,700     48,180   184,080
11     RENT                       9,000      9,000      9,000      9,000    36,000
12     TELEPHONE                  1,000      1,050      1,103      1,158     4,311
13     OFFICE SUPPLIES              750        800        850        900     3,300
BUDGET4.WK3                                                          CAP
```

Figure 11-13

Document your macro using the comments in Figure 11-14 to specify the macro title and what the individual instructions do.

```
B:B3: [W15] '{GOTO}A:A1~                                            READY

 B        A              B            C          D          E         F         G
 3   \C          {GOTO}A:A1~                  MOVE TO CELL A:A1
 4               /RESALARIES~                 ERASE THE SALARIES RANGE
 5               {GOTO}SALARIES~              MOVE THE CELL POINTER TO CELL A:B10
 6               /FCANTOTAL~                  COMBINE THE NAME RANGE TOTAL
 7               DIVISION~                    FROM THE DIVISION FILE
 8               {HOME}                       MOVE TO CELL A:A1
 A                A                 B          C          D          E          F
 3
 4
 5                                QTR1       QTR2       QTR3       QTR4   YR TOTAL
 6
 7  SALES                      $60,000    $61,200    $62,424    $63,672 $247,296
 8
BUDGET4.WK3                                                          CAP
```

Figure 11-14

USING A MACRO LIBRARY

In an earlier section in this chapter you created a macro library file and saved the macro PRINT_MACRO on the file. To illustrate the process of using a macro library, assume that you now want to print the BUDGET worksheet. Open the file MACROLIB after the BUDGET3 file. Your screen should look like Figure 11-15.

```
A:A1: [W19]                                                          READY

     A    A              B              C          D         E          F
     1  PRINT_MACRO /wtc                         MOVE THE CELL POINTER TO CELL A:A1
     2              /ppr{home}.{end}{home}~      SPECIFY THE PRINT RANGE
     3              agppq                        PRINT; QUIT THE PRINT MENU
     4
     5
     6
   B     A         B          C         D         E         F        G        H
   1  Macro\C  Macro for combining data from the DIVISION file into the BUDGET
   2
   3  \C       /reSALARIES~       ERASE THE RANGE A:B10..A:E10
   4           {goto}SALARIES~    MOVE THE CELL POINTER TO CELL A:B10
   5           fcanTOTAL~         COMBINE THE NAME RANGE TOTAL
   6           DIVISION~          FROM THE DIVISION FILE
 A          A              B          C          D          E          F
 1                                  ABC COMPANY
 2                                    BUDGET
 3
 4
 5                      QTR1       QTR2       QTR3       QTR4    YR TOTAL
 6
BUDGET3.WK3                                                       CAP
```

Figure 11-15

To execute the macro and print the worksheet:

Move	the cell pointer to any cell in worksheet A of the BUDGET file
Press	Alt-F3
Press	F3
Select	<<MACROLIB.WK3>>
Select	PRINT_MACRO

The macro will then execute and print the specified range.

SUMMARY

A macro is a way to automate Lotus 1-2-3 keystrokes. Macros are an efficient way to automate repetitive procedures. Macros allow people who are unfamiliar with 1-2-3 to use it to process spreadsheet operations such as printing a worksheet. It is important to define range names for specific cells and use the range names in macro instructions. Macros can be as simple or as complex as you desire to make them. The use of a macro library file to store frequently used macros can save you time.

KEY CONCEPTS

Alt-F2
Alt-F3
Ctrl-Break
Documentation
Location of a macro
Macro
Macro library
Macro name
Record
Tilde

CHAPTER ELEVEN
EXERCISE 1

INSTRUCTIONS: Circle T if the statement is true and F if the statement is false.

T F 1. The range name for a macro must be taken from a label already existing on the worksheet.

T F 2. The range name for a macro must begin with a forward slash and a letter of the alphabet.

T F 3. A macro is a way to automate a repetitive procedure.

T F 4. Certain keystrokes in a macro must be enclosed in braces (the { and } characters).

T F 5. In a macro, the tilde (the ~ symbol) represents pressing the forward slash (the command key /).

T F 6. To execute the macro named \ Z, you must hold down the Ctrl key and tap the letter Z.

T F 7. A named range for a macro must contain the first macro step as the first line in the range.

T F 8. When entering data on a worksheet manually, the tilde can be used instead of pressing ↵.

T F 9. Either apostrophe (the ' or the ') can be used to preface a macro step.

T F 10. Documentation must be included in a macro.

T F 11. You can automatically record macro keystrokes.

T F 12. Macro libraries can be used to store macros that are applicable to more than one worksheet.

T F 13. Macro instructions can be executed one step at a time by using Alt-F1.

T F 14. It does not matter where you place macros on a worksheet.

CHAPTER ELEVEN
EXERCISE 2
Creating a Macro

INSTRUCTIONS: Retrieve the file DIVSALES you created in Chapter 6. The file contained data on sales of mowers and edgers for the three divisions in ABC Company.

Write a macro that:

Inserts a new worksheet at the beginning of the file.

Creates a summary worksheet on the inserted worksheet that contains the total sales for each quarter of each division.

Computes the total annual sales for each division and the annual sales for the company.

For the purposes of this exercise, use the **F**ile **C**ombine **A**dd or **F**ile **C**ombine **C**opy command sequence to place the information on the summary worksheet.

The macro should be placed on a separate worksheet. The macro should be properly documented.

Print the summary worksheet, the sales worksheets and the worksheet on which the macro appears.

Save the worksheets, including the macro worksheet on a file named ABCMAC.

CHAPTER ELEVEN
EXERCISE 3
Creating a Print Macro

INSTRUCTIONS: Retrieve the file ABCMAC you created in the previous exercise.

Create a macro that prints the summary worksheet and the division sales worksheets.

Place the print macro on the worksheet on which the macro you completed in the previous exercise appears. Document the print macro properly.

Print the worksheet that has the print macro on it.

CHAPTER ELEVEN
EXERCISE 4
Using a Macro to Sort Data

INSTRUCTIONS: Retrieve the file PERSON you created as an exercise in Chapter 8.

Write a macro that sorts the database in order by state, last name and first name.

Place the macro on a separate worksheet after the worksheet containing the database table.

Create a macro that prints the sorted database table. Document both macros properly.

Print the sorted database table and the worksheet containing the macros for sorting and printing the database table.

CHAPTER ELEVEN
EXERCISE 5
Using Macros to Create and Print a Graph

INSTRUCTIONS:

Retrieve the file PRACTICE you created as an exercise in Chapter 2.

Reset all graph settings associated with the file and delete any graph files present.

Write a macro to create a bar graph that includes the data of the variables Revenue, Profit before Tax and Profit after Tax for the four quarters. Include appropriate graph title and legend information.

Create a macro that prints the bar graph.

Place the macros for creating and printing the bar graph on a separate worksheet.

Document both macros properly.

Print the worksheet that contains the macros.

CHAPTER TWELVE

ADVANCED MACRO COMMANDS AND EXAMPLES

OBJECTIVES

In this chapter, you will learn to:

- Create macros for various types of worksheet operations such as sorting data, restricting input to specific cells, and automatically executing a macro
- Use advanced macro commands to:
  Create interactive macros
  Change program flow and loop through a series of instructions
  Develop subroutines
  Create user-designed menus

CHAPTER OVERVIEW

In Chapter 11 the use of macros in Lotus 1-2-3 was introduced. The process for creating a macro was defined. In the first part of this chapter, some additional macro examples are illustrated. The command language available in Lotus 1-2-3 is then presented. Finally, you will learn to use the command language by creating several macros.

MACRO SYMBOLS

In the process of creating a macro, many symbols are used to represent operations that are available in Lotus 1-2-3. For example, the **down** pointer movement key is designated by the symbol {down} or {D}. A list of the symbols used to designate keystrokes including symbols for function keys and directional keys follows.

The symbols have been placed in alphabetical order. Symbols that incorporate special characters appear at the end of the list.

Keys	Macro Instruction
Abs [F4]	{abs}
Addin [Alt-F10]	{addin} or {app4}
App1 [Alt-F7]	{app1}
App2 [Alt-F8]	{app2}
App3 [Alt-F9]	{app3}
Backspace	{backspace} or {bs}
Bigleft	[Ctrl-Left]
Bigright	[Ctrl-Right]
Calc [F9]	{calc}
[Ctrl-Break] (in menu mode)	{break}
Del	{delete} or {del}
Down [↓]	{Down} or {D}
Edit [F2]	{edit}
End	{end}
Escape [Esc]	{esc}
File [Ctrl-End]	{file}
First Cell [Ctrl-Home]	{firstcell} or {fc}
First File [Ctrl-End] [Home]	{firstfile}, {ff} or {file} {home}
GoTo [F5]	{goto}
Graph [F10]	{graph}
Help [F1]	{help}
Home	{home}
Insert [Ins]	{ins}
Last Cell [End] [Ctrl-Home]	{lastcell} or {lc}
Last File [Ctrl-End] [End]	{lastfile}, {lf} or {file} {end}
Left [←]	{left} or {l}
Name [F3]	{name}
Next File [Ctrl-End] [Ctrl-PgUp]	{nextfile}, {nf} or {file} {ns}
Next Sheet [Ctrl-PgDn]	{nextsheet} or {ns}
PgDn [PgDn]	{pgdn}
PgUp [PgUp]	{pgup}
Prev File [Ctrl-End] [Ctrl-PgDn]	{prevfile}, {pf}, or {file} {ps}
Prev Sheet [Ctrl-PgDn]	{prevsheet} or {ps}
Query [F7]	{query}
Right [→]	{right} or {r}
Table [F8]	{table}
Up [↑]	{up} or {u}
Window [F6]	{window}
Zoom [Alt-F6]	{zoom}
/ (slash) or < (less than)	/, < or {menu}

~	↵
{~} to have tilde appear as	{~}
{{} and {}} to have braces appear	{{} and {}}

Sometimes you may want to specify two or more repetitions of the same key. This repeating can be accomplished by including a repetition factor within the braces. For example, to move the cell pointer down four cells you can use either of the following macro instructions:

{down 4} or {d 4}

■ SOME ADDITIONAL MACRO EXAMPLES

To help you learn more about using macros, you will create and execute additional macros in this section for sorting data, completing a data query, inputting values for a worksheet, restricting the entry of data to specific cells in a worksheet and automatically executing a macro.

Sorting Data

In Chapter 8 you created a worksheet that had salary information on the employees of ABC Company and saved it on a file named ABCSAL. To complete this example problem, you need to retrieve file ABCSAL. Suppose that you want to sort the data in ascending order by division and alphabetically within each division.

To display a worksheet on which the macro will be saved:

Insert an additional worksheet after the ABCSAL worksheet

After inserting the worksheet, use the Worksheet Window Perspective command sequence to display both worksheets. Your screen should look like Figure 12-1.

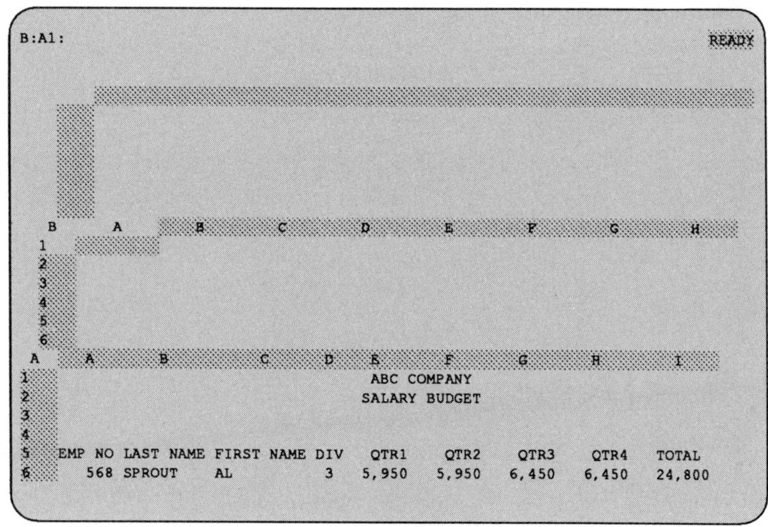

Figure 12-1

To accomplish the sort, you must:

1. Erase any previously set sort ranges.
2. Specify the data range to sort.
3. Define sort keys for the division number, last name and first name.
4. Indicate that the data is to be sorted.

To enter the macro title in cell B:A1:

Type	Macro Sort
Press	↵
Move	the cell pointer to cell C1
Type	Macro for Sorting Data
Press	↵

To enter the macro name:

Move	the cell pointer to A3
Type	SORT
Press	↵

To make sure no sort settings are on the file,

Move	the cell pointer to cell B3
Type	'/dsrq
Press	↵

To specify the data range to sort:

Move	the cell pointer to cell B4
Type	'/dsdSORT_DATA~
Press	↵

To indicate that DIV is the primary sort key and that it is to be sorted in ascending order:

Move	the cell pointer to cell B5
Type	'pA:D5~a~
Press	↵

To define LAST NAME as the secondary key and that the names are to be sorted in alphabetical order:

Move	the cell pointer to cell B6
Type	'sA:B5~a~
Press	↵

To include FIRST NAME as the third sort key, you need to add an extra sort key, specify the FIRST NAME as the proper field to sort and show that the names are to be sorted in alphabetical order.

Move	the cell pointer to cell B7
Type	'e~A:C5~a~
Press	↵

To indicate it is appropriate to execute the sort and then exit the data menu:

Move the cell pointer to cell B8

Type 'g

Except for the documentation that appears on the macro worksheet, your screen now should look like Figure 12-2.

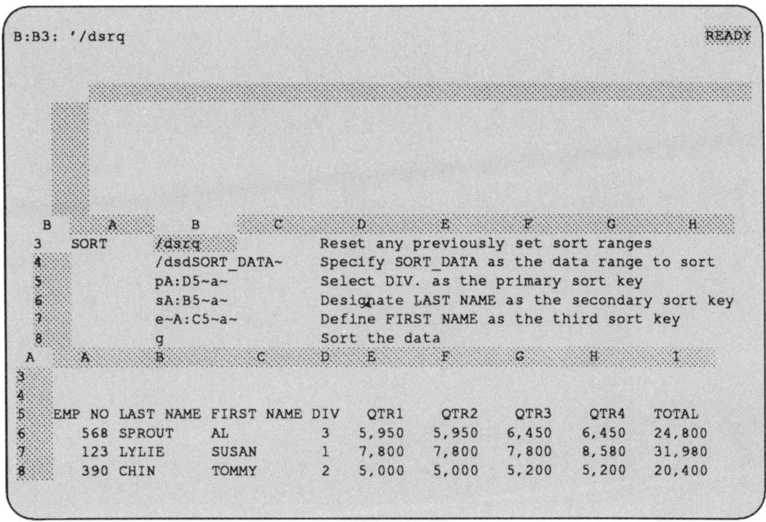

Figure 12-2

Before you can execute the macro, you need to define the named range SORT_DATA and name the macro.

Move the cell pointer to cell A:A6

Create the range name SORT_DATA including in it the range of cells A:A6..A:I13

Move the cell pointer to cell B:B3

Create the macro name SORT and indicate the macro instructions begin in cell B:B3

After checking your macro with the one in Figure 12-2 and making any necessary corrections, save the file on ABCSAL2.

Execute the macro SORT.

Press (Alt-F3)

Press (F3)

Select Sort

After the macro is executed and you use the **Worksheet Window Clear** to display the SALARY BUDGET worksheet, your screen should look like Figure 12-3. Notice that the data has been sorted in the proper order.

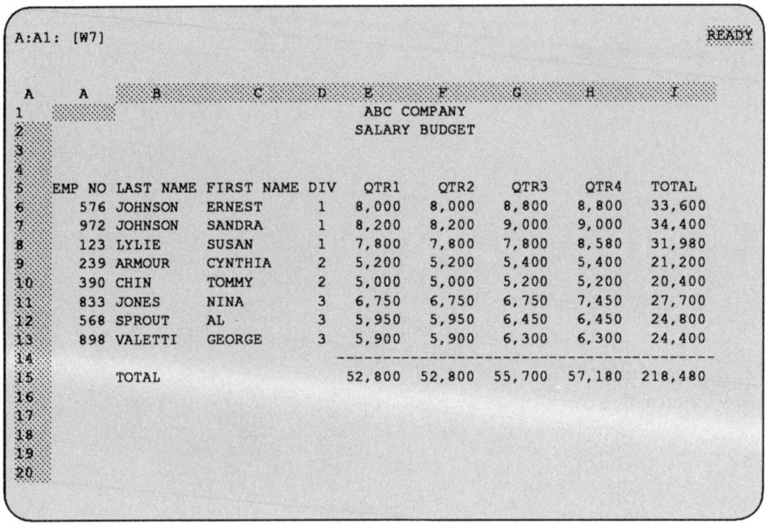

```
A:A1: [W7]                                                              READY

A    A        B         C         D      E        F        G        H        I
1                                       ABC COMPANY
2                                      SALARY BUDGET
3
4
5   EMP NO LAST NAME FIRST NAME DIV    QTR1     QTR2     QTR3     QTR4    TOTAL
6      576 JOHNSON   ERNEST       1   8,000    8,000    8,800    8,800   33,600
7      972 JOHNSON   SANDRA       1   8,200    8,200    9,000    9,000   34,400
8      123 LYLIE     SUSAN        1   7,800    7,800    7,800    8,580   31,980
9      239 ARMOUR    CYNTHIA      2   5,200    5,200    5,400    5,400   21,200
10     390 CHIN      TOMMY        2   5,000    5,000    5,200    5,200   20,400
11     833 JONES     NINA         3   6,750    6,750    6,750    7,450   27,700
12     568 SPROUT    AL           3   5,950    5,950    6,450    6,450   24,800
13     898 VALETTI   GEORGE       3   5,900    5,900    6,300    6,300   24,400
14                                  -----------------------------------------
15         TOTAL                     52,800   52,800   55,700   57,180  218,480
16
17
18
19
20
```

Figure 12-3

Move to sheet B and document your macro using the comments in Figure 12-2. After completing the documentation, save the worksheet on file ABCSAL2.

Restricting Data Entry to Specific Cells in a Worksheet

To complete this exercise, you will need to create a loan amortization worksheet. This loan amortization worksheet will also be used in later sections of this chapter. Enter the labels and values for the worksheet by referring to Figure 12-4 Part 1.

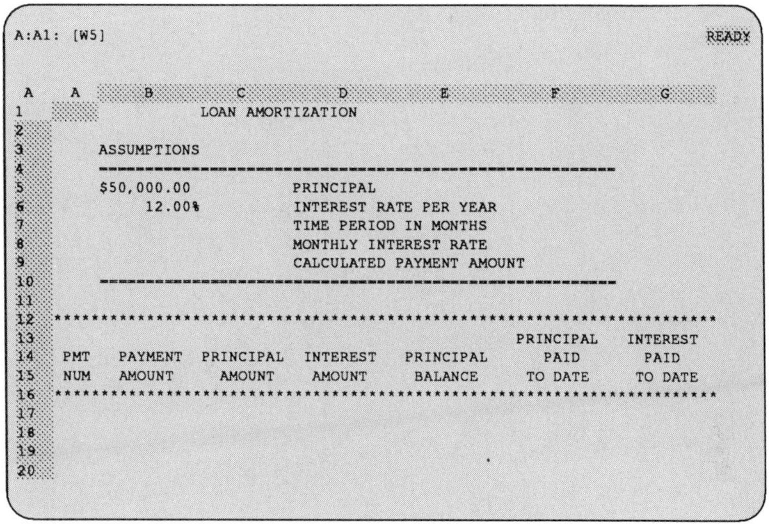

```
A:A1: [W5]                                                              READY

A   A       B          C          D           E            F           G
1                 LOAN AMORTIZATION
2
3        ASSUMPTIONS
4        -------------------------------------------------------------
5        $50,000.00             PRINCIPAL
6             12.00%            INTEREST RATE PER YEAR
7                               TIME PERIOD IN MONTHS
8                               MONTHLY INTEREST RATE
9                               CALCULATED PAYMENT AMOUNT
10       -------------------------------------------------------------
11
12 ********************************************************************************
13                                                   PRINCIPAL    INTEREST
14  PMT   PAYMENT  PRINCIPAL  INTEREST   PRINCIPAL      PAID         PAID
15  NUM   AMOUNT      AMOUNT    AMOUNT     BALANCE     TO DATE      TO DATE
16 ********************************************************************************
17
18
19
20
```

Figure 12-4
Part 1

To assist you in the preparation of the worksheet, the column widths are:

Column	Width
A	5
B	11
C	10
D	11
E	12
F	12
G	11

Use the **Data Fill** command sequence to enter the numbers 1 through 60 in cells A18 through A77.

Enter formulas into cells as described below.

Cell	Formula
B8	+B6/12
B9	@PMT(B5,B8,B7)
E17	+B5
B18	+B9
C18	+B18-D18
D18	+B5*B8
E18	+E17-C18
F18	+C18
G18	+D18
B19	@IF($B$9>E18,$B$8*E18+E18,$B$9)
C19	+B19-D19
D19	+$B$8*E18
E19	+E18-C19
F19	+F18+C19
G19	+G18+D19

After you have entered the formulas for cells B19..G19, copy these cell formulas to cells B20..G77. At present ERR appears in many cells. When you enter the time period, proper values will appear. You have created an amortization schedule worksheet that can be used for loan repayment periods from one to 60 months. Your screen should now look like Figure 12-4 Part 2. Save the worksheet using the file name AMORT.

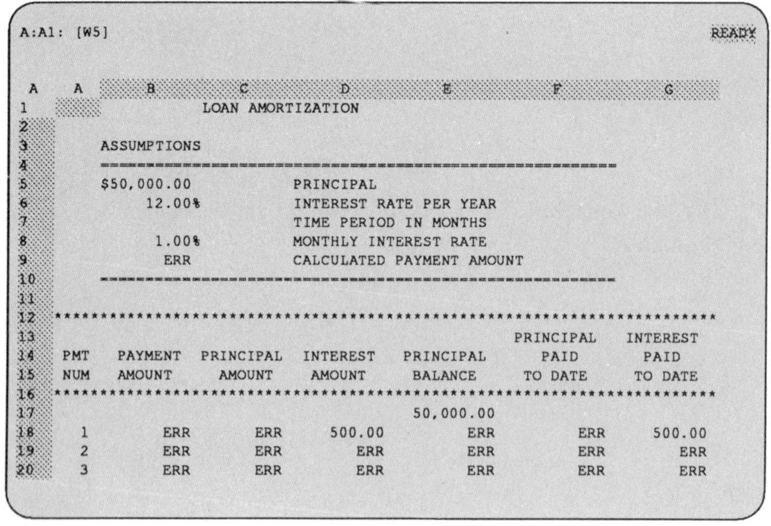

Figure 12-4
Part 2

Sometimes it may be useful to limit an individual's ability to enter data in only a certain set of cells. For example, in the loan amortization schedule worksheet, suppose you want an individual to be only allowed to change the principal, interest rate and time period. Such an approach prohibits users of the amortization worksheet from accidentally changing any of the formulas on the worksheet.

The steps that you need to have in a macro for restricting the data entry to the principal, interest rate and time period cells are as follows:

1. Change the calculation mode to manual so you will recalculate the worksheet after all data items have been entered.

2. Protect all of the cells in the worksheet.

3. Unprotect those cells that can be modified.

4. Calculate the worksheet after all data entry is completed.

Before you enter the macro instructions, insert a worksheet after the loan amortization schedule on which you will save the macro. Display both worksheets by executing the **W**orksheet **W**indow **P**erspective command sequence.

To place a title for the macro on the worksheet:

Move the cell pointer to cell B:A1

Enter Macro Data Entry

Move the cell pointer to cell C1

Enter Macro for Restricting Data Entry to the Cells

Move the cell pointer to cell C2

Enter for Principal, Interest Rate and Time Period

To place the name of the macro on the worksheet:

Move the cell pointer to cell A4

Enter '\D

To make sure the macro is used for worksheet A:

Move the cell pointer to cell B4

Enter '{goto}A:A1~

To specify that manual calculation mode is to be used:

Move the cell pointer to cell B5

Enter '/wgrm

You can protect all cells in the worksheet as follows:

Move the cell pointer to cell B6

Enter '/wgpe

To allow data entry for the principal, interest rate and time period, you must unprotect the range of cells A:B5 through A:B7:

Move the cell pointer to cell B7

Enter '/ruA:B5.A:B7~

The **R**ange **I**nput command in 1-2-3 is used to restrict the cells in which you can enter data on the worksheet. Since you have protected all cells on the worksheet and unprotected the cells in which data entry is allowed, you can specify the entire worksheet (cells A:A1 .. A:G77) in the **R**ange **I**nput command. So that you can see the cells for data entry more easily, enter the **R**ange **I**nput command so that only the cells A:A4 .. A:G77 are included in the range specification.

Move the cell pointer to cell B8

Enter '/riA:A4.A:G77~

To specify that the worksheet is to be recalculated after the data entry is completed and move the cell pointer to cell A:A1:

Move the cell pointer to cell B9

Enter '{calc}

Move the cell pointer to cell B10

Enter '{goto}A:A1~

Except for the documentation on the macro worksheet, your screen should look like Figure 12-5.

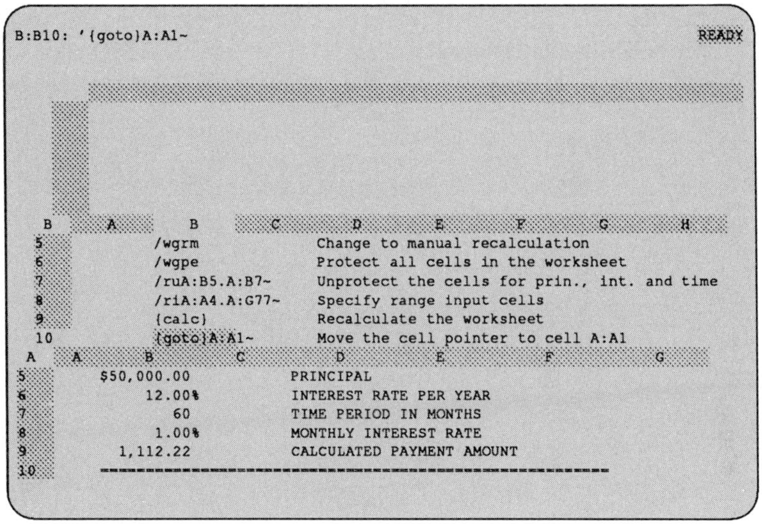

```
B:B10: '{goto}A:A1~                                              READY

 B    A        B          C       D       E        F         G        H
 5           /wgrm              Change to manual recalculation
 6           /wgpe              Protect all cells in the worksheet
 7           /ruA:B5.A:B7~      Unprotect the cells for prin., int. and time
 8           /riA:A4.A:G77~     Specify range input cells
 9           {calc}             Recalculate the worksheet
10           {goto}A:A1~        Move the cell pointer to cell A:A1
 A    A        B          C       D       E        F         G
 5      $50,000.00          PRINCIPAL
 6          12.00%          INTEREST RATE PER YEAR
 7              60          TIME PERIOD IN MONTHS
 8           1.00%          MONTHLY INTEREST RATE
 9        1,112.22          CALCULATED PAYMENT AMOUNT
10      ---------------------------------------------------------
```

Figure 12-5

Before you execute the macro, name it \D.

Move	the cell pointer to cell B4
Press	/
Select	Range
Select	Name
Select	Create
Type	\D
Press	↵ twice

After checking your macro with the one in Figure 12-5 and making any necessary changes, save the file on AMORTRI.

Suppose that you want to use the loan amortization schedule worksheet to determine the monthly payment if you borrow $15,000 at an interest rate of 10 percent and have 48 months to repay the loan. To determine the payment amount, execute the macro:

Press Alt-D

The macro pauses at cell A:B5 to wait for you to enter the data for the new principal, interest rate and time period. Notice that the cells for these items are a different color if you are using a color monitor. If you are using a monochrome monitor, the cells will appear to be brighter.

Press the →, ↓, ← and ↑ keys several times and note that you can only enter data in cells A:B5 through A:B7. The characters CMD appear at the bottom of the screen indicating that the macro is being executed and is waiting for you to enter the new data.

To enter the appropriate values:

Move	the cell pointer to A:B5
Type	15000
Press	↓
Type	.10
Press	↓
Type	48
Press	↵

To finish execution of the macro:

Press	↵

Use the **W**orksheet **W**indow **C**lear command sequence to display more of the loan amortization schedule on your screen. Your screen should look like Figure 12-6.

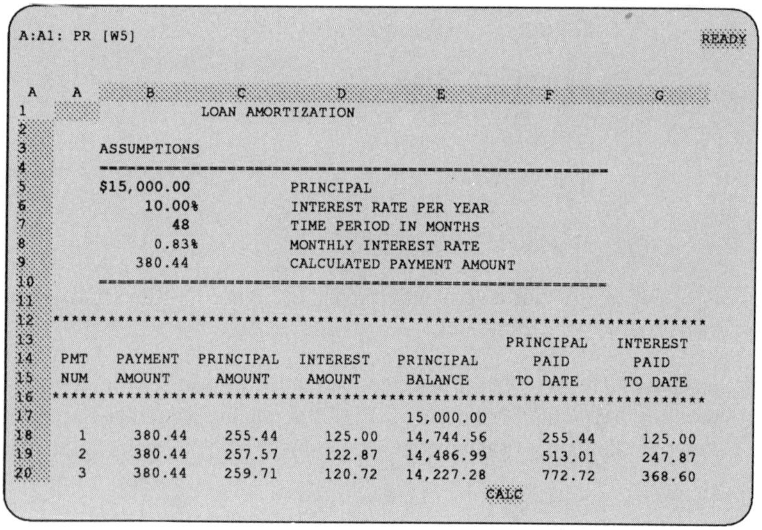

```
A:A1: PR [W5]                                                          READY

A   A      B          C          D          E          F          G
1                     LOAN AMORTIZATION
2
3       ASSUMPTIONS
4       ---------------------------------------------------------------
5       $15,000.00               PRINCIPAL
6            10.00%              INTEREST RATE PER YEAR
7                48              TIME PERIOD IN MONTHS
8             0.83%              MONTHLY INTEREST RATE
9            380.44              CALCULATED PAYMENT AMOUNT
10      ===============================================================
11
12 ***********************************************************************
13                                                PRINCIPAL   INTEREST
14   PMT   PAYMENT  PRINCIPAL  INTEREST  PRINCIPAL     PAID       PAID
15   NUM   AMOUNT     AMOUNT    AMOUNT    BALANCE    TO DATE    TO DATE
16 ***********************************************************************
17                                       15,000.00
18     1   380.44     255.44    125.00   14,744.56    255.44     125.00
19     2   380.44     257.57    122.87   14,486.99    513.01     247.87
20     3   380.44     259.71    120.72   14,227.28    772.72     368.60
                                             CALC
```

Figure 12-6

Retrieve the file AMORTRI and document your macro using the information in Figure 12-5. After placing the documentation on the macro worksheet, save the worksheet file on AMORTRI.

Executing a Macro Automatically

In some situations, you may want to execute a macro automatically when the file on which it is saved is retrieved. For example, you may want the macro on the file that contains the loan amortization schedule to execute immediately so the individual using the loan amortization schedule only has to enter the new values for the principal, interest rate and time period.

When a macro is named \ 0 (zero), it will be executed when the file on which it resides is retrieved or opened. Before you can execute the loan amortization schedule macro automatically, you must retrieve the file containing the macro, change the name of the macro to \ 0, and save the file.

To accomplish these steps:

Retrieve	the file AMORTRI
Move	the cell pointer to cell B:A4
Enter	'\0
Delete	the range name \D
Move	the cell pointer to cell B:B4
Create	the range name \0 that includes cell B:B4 as the range

Save the worksheet using the file name AUTOMAC. After moving the cell pointer to cell A:B5, your screen should look like Figure 12-7.

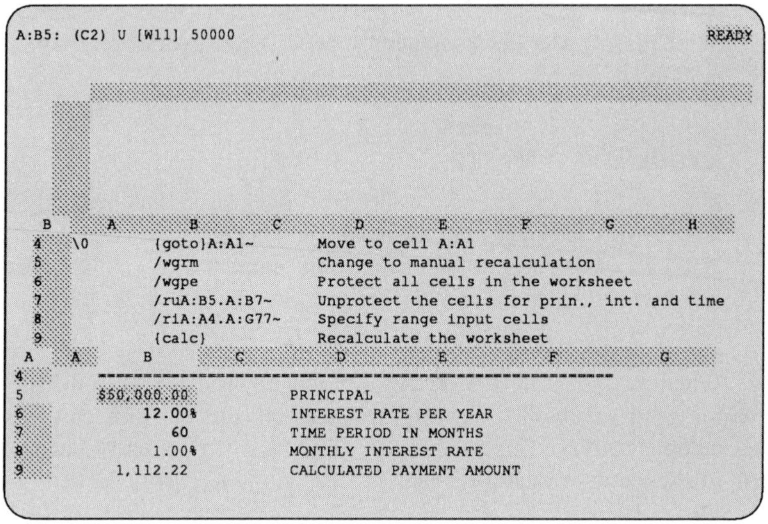

```
A:B5: (C2) U [W11] 50000                                              READY

 B      A          B              C          D          E          F          G          H
 4   \0         {goto}A:A1~          Move to cell A:A1
 5              /wgrm                Change to manual recalculation
 6              /wgpe                Protect all cells in the worksheet
 7              /ruA:B5.A:B7~        Unprotect the cells for prin., int. and time
 8              /riA:A4.A:G77~       Specify range input cells
 9              {calc}               Recalculate the worksheet
A    A          B             C          D          E          F          G
4      ----------------------------------------------------------------
5      $50,000.00               PRINCIPAL
6          12.00%               INTEREST RATE PER YEAR
7              60               TIME PERIOD IN MONTHS
8           1.00%               MONTHLY INTEREST RATE
9        1,112.22               CALCULATED PAYMENT AMOUNT
```

Figure 12-7

Suppose that you want to determine the monthly payment amount for a loan of $10,000 at an interest rate of 11 percent and time period of 36 months to pay the loan.

To illustrate the use of the automatic execution of a macro for this situation:

Erase	the worksheet from your screen
Retrieve	the file AUTOMAC

Notice that the macro has been initiated and the cell pointer is in cell A:B5. You now need to enter the data for the principal amount, interest rate and time period.

Enter	10000 in cell A:B5
Enter	.11 in cell A:B6
Enter	36 in cell A:B7
Press	↵

The macro has finished executing. After moving the cell pointer to cell A:A10 so you can see the payment amount, your screen should look like Figure 12-8. You do not need to save the new loan amortization schedule.

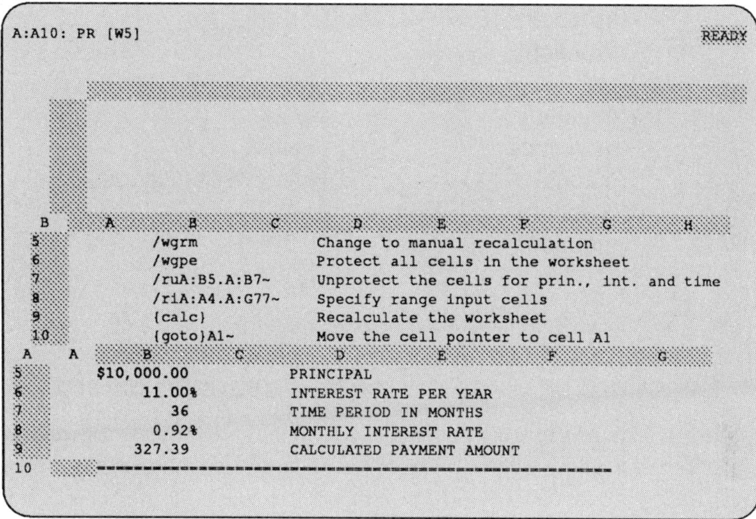

Figure 12-8

■ ADVANCED MACRO COMMANDS

Lotus 1-2-3 Release 3 has 51 advanced macro commands. In this section, a list of the commands is introduced, groupings of the commands by typical use are presented, and a brief explanation of each command is given.

Listing of Advanced Macro Commands

The advanced macro commands available in Release 3 are:

{appendbelow}	{indicate}
{appendright}	{let}
{beep}	{look}
{blank}	{menubranch}
{branch}	{menucall}
{break}	{onerror}
{breakoff}/{breakon}	{open}
{close}	{paneloff}/{panelon}
{contents}	{put}
{define}	{quit}
{dispatch}	{read}
{filesize}	{readln}
{for}	{recalc}
{forbreak}	{recalccol}
{form}	{restart}

{frameoff}	{return}
{frameon}	{setpos}
{get}	{subroutine}
{getlabel}	{system}
{getnumber}	{wait}
{getpos}	{windowsoff}/{windowson}
{graphon}	{write}
{graphoff}	{writeln}
{if}	{?}

Summary by Type of Use of Advanced Macro Commands

In this section, the advanced macro commands are grouped together by typical use. For ease of reference they are placed in alphabetical order within each grouping.

Controlling the Appearance of the Screen

In some situations, you may want to change the appearance of the screen. The following macro commands can be used to alter the appearance of the screen:

{beep}	{indicate}
{break}	{paneloff}
{frameoff}	{panelon}
{frameon}	{windowsoff}
{graphoff}	{windowson}
{graphon}	

Interaction between User and Keyboard

The following commands can be employed to create macros that provide interactive use:

{breakoff}	{look}
{breakon}	{menubranch}
{form}	{menucall}
{get}	{wait}
{getlabel}	{?}
{getnumber}	

Changing the Flow of Instructions in a Macro

In some cases, it may be desirable to modify the exact sequence of commands in a macro. The following commands permit you to control the sequence of command execution.

{branch}
{define}
{dispatch}
{for}
{forbreak}
{if}
{onerror}
{quit}
{restart}
{return}
{system}
{subroutine}

Manipulating the Format and Location of Data

The listed commands can be used to manipulate the format and location of data in a worksheet:

{appendbelow}
{appendright}
{blank}
{contents}
{let}
{put}
{recalc}
{recalccol}

File Operations

In some cases, it may be useful to execute tasks related to files. These commands permit users to manipulate files during the execution of a macro.

{close}
{filesize}
{getpos}
{open}
{read}
{readln}
{setpos}
{write}
{writeln}

Specific Advanced Macro Commands

Explanations of the various advanced macro commands are contained in this section. For additional details on the many commands, see the Lotus 1-2-3 reference manual that comes with the software package.

The following format is used in the descriptions of the commands:

```
{Keyword arg1,arg2,...,argn}
```

Arguments which are shown within angle brackets (<>) are optional.

{appendbelow}

The {appendbelow} command permits you to copy data in a worksheet from a source location to a target location and append the information immediately below the target location.

The {appendbelow} command has the following format:

```
{appendbelow target-location,source-location}
```

{appendright}

The {appendright} command allows you to copy data in a worksheet from a source location to a target location and append the data immediately to the right of the target location.

The {appendright} command has the following format:

```
{appendright target-location,source-location}
```

{beep}

The {beep} command causes the computer bell to sound. The number is optional. There are four tones to the "beep". Therefore, the number 1, 2, 3, or 4 can appear within the {beep} command. If no number is specified, the default is the first tone.

The {beep} command has the following format:

```
{beep <number>}
```

The {beep} command does not produce a tone if you turn off the bell by using the **W**orksheet **G**lobal **D**efault **O**ther **B**eep **N**o command sequence.

{blank}

The {blank} command erases the contents of the designated cell. The cell pointer does not move to the designated cell location.

The {blank} command has the following format:

```
{blank cell-location}
```

{branch}

The {branch} command directs control to the designated cell and continues the execution of the macro using the instructions in the designated cell.

The {branch} command has the following format:

```
{branch cell-location}
```

{break}

The {break} command clears the current data, menu or prompt from the control panel and returns Lotus 1-2-3 to READY mode.

The {break} command has the following format:

```
{break}
```

{breakoff} and {breakon}

The {breakoff} command disables the Ctrl-Break functionality that interrupts a macro. The {breakon} command reverses the {breakoff} command.

The {breakoff} and {breakon} commands have the following format:

```
{breakoff}
{breakon}
```

{close}

The {close} command closes a file that was previously opened using the {open} command.

The {close} command has the following format:

```
{close}
```

{contents}

The {contents} command stores the data from one cell in another cell as a label. The width of the label as well as the type of format desired can be specified for the target location. Refer to the 1-2-3 reference manual for the codes for the format numbers.

The {contents} command has the following format:

```
{contents target-location,source-location,
<width-number>,<format-number>}
```

{define}

The {define} command allocates where variables that are passed to a subroutine are stored. If used, it is the first command in the subroutine.

The {define} command has the following format:

```
{define cell-location1:type1,cell-location2:type 2...}
```

{dispatch}

The {dispatch} command directs control to another cell for instructions on where the macro should branch.

The {dispatch} command has the following format:

```
{dispatch cell-location}
```

{filesize}

The {filesize} command records the number of bytes in the currently open file. The number is recorded in the specified cell-location.

The {filesize} command has the following format:

```
{filesize cell-location}
```

{for}

The {for} command allows a set of commands to be repeated a specified number of times. The process of repeating a set of commands is often referred to as looping.

The {for} command has the following format:

```
{for counter-location,begin-number,end-number,step,
starting-location}
```

The counter-location is used to keep track of the number of times the loop of instructions is to be executed. The begin-number specifies the initial number with which the loop should begin its count, and the end-number specifies the number at which the loop should stop executing. The step tells what increment the loop count should use. The starting-location indicates the first cell or range name of the subroutine to be executed.

{forbreak}

The {forbreak} command breaks or interrupts the current {for} loop.

The {forbreak} command has the following format:

```
{forbreak}
```

{form}

The {form} command temporarily halts the execution of a macro to allow the entry and editing of data in the unprotected cells in the input-location.

The {form} command has the following format:

```
{form input-location,<call-table>,<include-list>,
<exclude-list>}
```

The call-table, include-list, and exclude-list are optional items.

{frameoff}

The {frameoff} command suppresses the display of the worksheet frame that includes the worksheet letter, column letters and row numbers.

The {frameoff} command has the following format:

```
{frameoff}
```

{frameon}

The {frameon} command restores the display of the worksheet frame that includes the worksheet letter, column letters and row numbers.

The {frameon} command has the following format:

```
{frameon}
```

{get}

The {get} command stops the macro and allows an individual to enter a single character in the designated cell-location.

The {get} command has the following format:

```
{get cell-location}
```

{getlabel}

The {getlabel} command stops the macro and prompts a person to enter a label that will be placed in the specified cell-location.

The {getlabel} command has the following format:

```
{getlabel prompt-string,cell-location}
```

{getnumber}

The {getnumber} command stops the macro and prompts an individual to enter a value that will be placed in the specified cell-location.

The {getnumber} command has the following format:

```
{getnumber prompt-string,cell-location}
```

{getpos}

The {getpos} command determines where the file pointer is in the open file and stores the position in the designated cell-location.

The {getpos} command has the following format:

```
{getpos cell-location}
```

{graphoff}

The {graphoff} command erases a graph displayed by the {graphon} command and displays the current worksheet on the screen.

The {graphoff command has the following format:

```
{graphoff}
```

{graphon}

The {graphon} command has the following format:

```
{graphon <named-graph>,<nodisplay>}
```

The named-graph and nodisplay arguments are optional.

Depending on the options selected, three things can happen when the {graphon} command is used. If {graphon} is used with no arguments, then a full-screen view of the current graph will be displayed on your screen as the macro continues to execute. If {graphon named-graph} is used, then the named-graph will appear on your screen while the macro continues to execute. If {graphon named-graph, nodisplay} is executed, the named-graph will become the current graph and there will be no graph displayed on your screen.

{if}

The {if} command tests the condition following the word ***if***. When the ***if*** condition is true, the commands that immediately follow the {if} command in the same cell are then executed. If the condition is false, the command in the cell immediately below the {if} command is executed.

The {if} command has the following format:

```
{if condition}
```

{indicate}

The {indicate} command allows you to change the mode indicator, located at the top right corner of the screen.

The {indicate} command has the following format:

```
{indicate <string>}
```

If this command is used, Lotus 1-2-3 replaces the mode indicator with the specified string of characters.

{let}

The {let} command stores the specified entry (a number or string) in the designated cell-location.

The {let} command has the following format:

```
{let cell-location,entry}
```

{look}

The {look} command keeps track of whether or not you typed a keystroke while a macro was running. The keystroke (if any) is stored in the designated cell-location.

The {look} command has the following format:

```
{look cell-location}
```

{menubranch}

The {menubranch} command allows you to select a menu item and then execute the corresponding macro commands for the menu item. Menu items begin in the designated cell-location.

The {menubranch} command has the following format:

```
{menubranch cell-location}
```

{menucall}

The {menucall} command allows a user to select a menu item and then execute the corresponding subroutine for the menu item. Menu items begin in the designated cell-location.

The {menucall} command has the following format:

```
{menucall cell-location}
```

{onerror}

If an error occurs during execution of a macro, then the macro will continue at the designated branch-location. If desired, an error message can be included in the cell designated for the message-location.

The {onerror} command has the following format:

```
{onerror branch-location,<message-location>}
```

{open}

The {open} command allows you to open a text file for the purposes of reading or writing.

The {open} command has the following format:

```
{open filename,access-mode}
```

The access-mode indicates R(Read), W(Write) or M(Modify) the file.

{paneloff} and {panelon} commands

The {paneloff} commands prevents the appearance of information in the control panel during macro execution. The {panelon} command reverses the {paneloff} command.

The {paneloff} and {panelon} commands have the following format:

```
{paneloff}
{panelon}
```

{put}

The {put} command places an entry (number or string of characters) at the designated column and row within the designated two-dimensional range.

The {put} command has the following format:

```
{put range,column-number,row-number,entry}
```

For example, if the range was A1..B3, the column number was 0 and the row number was 1, the number or string would be placed in cell A2.

{quit}

The {quit} command stops the execution of the macro.

The {quit} command has the following format:

```
{quit}
```

{read}

The {read} command reads a specified number of characters or bytes (0 to 511 characters can be used) from a file and places the characters at the designated cell-location.

The {read} command has the following format:

```
{read byte-number,cell-location}
```

{readln}

The {readln} command reads and copies one line of information from the open file to the designated cell location.

The {readln} command has the following format:

```
{readln cell-location}
```

{recalc}

The {recalc} command recalculates the cells in the designated cell-location row by row.

The {recalc} command has the following format:

```
{recalc cell-location,<condition>,<iterations>}
```

{recalccol}

The {recalccol} command recalculates the cells in designated cell-location column by column.

The {recalccol} command has the following format:

```
{recalccol cell-location,<condition>,<iterations>}
```

{restart}

The {restart} command clears the subroutine stack. When {restart} is encountered, 1-2-3 continues to the end of the current subroutine. Instead of returning to the original macro location, the macro then stops executing.

The {restart} command has the following format:

```
{restart}
```

{return}

The {return} command transfers control from a subroutine to the next instruction in the macro from which the subroutine was called.

The {return} command has the following format:

```
{return}
```

{setpos}

The {setpos} command sets the new position for the byte pointer in the currently open file to the indicated position.

The {setpos} command has the following format:

```
{setpos byte-position}
```

{subroutine}

The {subroutine} command calls a subroutine. The optional arguments can be utilized to pass information to a subroutine.

The {subroutine} command has the following format:

```
{subroutine <argument>,<argument>...}
```

{system}

The {system} command temporarily halts execution of 1-2-3 and the specified operating system command is processed.

The {system} command has the following format:

```
{system command}
```

The command is any legal operating system command that needs to be executed.

{wait}

The {wait} command suspends macro execution until the designated time.

The {wait} command has the following format:

```
{wait time-number}
```

{windowsoff} and {windowson}

The {windowsoff} command prevents redrawing the screen (except for the control panel) during macro execution. The {windowson} command reverses the {windowsoff} command.

The {windowsoff} and {windowson} commands have the following format:

```
{windowsoff}
{windowson}
```

{write}

The {write} command writes characters into the currently open file.

The {write} command has the following format:

```
{write string}
```

{writeln}

The {writeln} command writes the specified string of characters to the currently open file and adds a carriage-return line-feed sequence to the end of the string.

The {writeln} command has the following format:

```
{writeln string}
```

{?}

The {?} command halts the execution of a macro to allow you either to move the cell pointer to enter data in a cell or to move the menu pointer to complete part of a command. When you press the ↵ key, the macro continues execution.

The {?} has the following format:

```
{?}
```

■ SOME EXAMPLES OF USING ADVANCED MACRO COMMANDS

In this section, you will create several macros that illustrate some typical applications of advanced macro commands.

Interactive Macros

In many situations, you may want to allow users of a macro to enter data while a macro is executing. For example, you may want to prompt an individual to enter values or labels into some specific cells.

Entering a Sequence of Numbers

Sometimes you may need to enter rows or columns of numbers on a worksheet. Suppose you wanted to enter the set of numbers 10, 25, 15 and 32 in cells B2 through B5 in worksheet A of a worksheet file. You will create a macro that moves the cell pointer down one cell after entering each of the numbers to expedite the process of entering the data.

Before creating the macro, make sure you have a blank worksheet on your screen. Insert an additional worksheet and display both worksheets so that your screen looks like Figure 12-9.

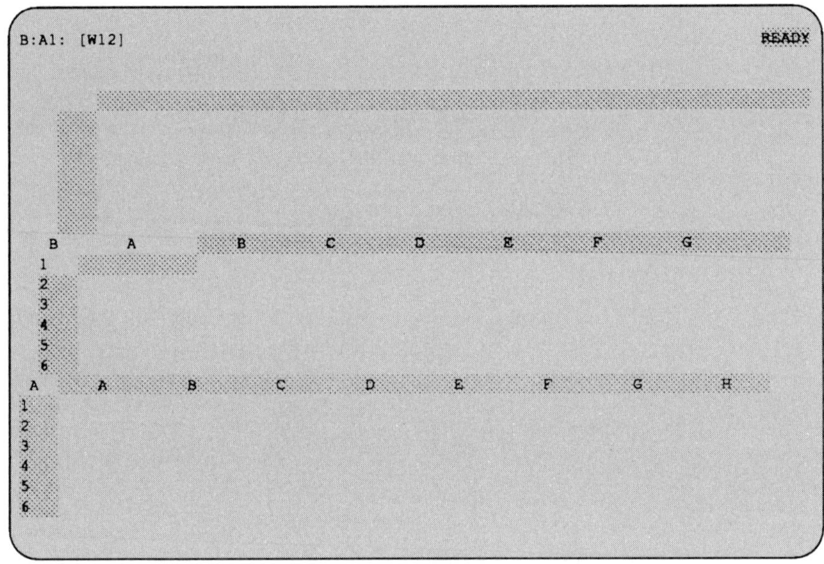

Figure 12-9

To place a title for the macro that will be used for entering the set of numbers:

Move the cell pointer to cell B:A1

Enter Macro Input

Move the cell pointer to cell B:C1

Enter Macro for entering numbers in a column

To place the name of the macro on the macro worksheet:

Move the cell pointer to cell B:A3

Enter COL_INPUT

Widen column A so it will display 12 characters.

To enter the first macro instruction:

Move the cell pointer to cell B:B3

Enter {?}

This instruction halts the execution of the macro until you input a value and press the ↵ key.

To indicate that you want to move the cell pointer down one cell after the value is entered.

Move the cell pointer to cell B:B4

Enter {down}

You also could have used {d}.

To specify that another number may need to be input:

Move the cell pointer to cell B:B5

Enter {branch COL_INPUT}

This instruction directs 1-2-3 to move to the first instruction in the macro so that you may enter another number if you desire.

Before you execute the macro:

Name the macro COL_INPUT and include cell B:B3 as the cell in the range

Enter the documentation in cells E3..E5, as shown in Figure 12-10

After moving the cell pointer to cell B:B3, except for the documentation, your screen should look like Figure 12-10.

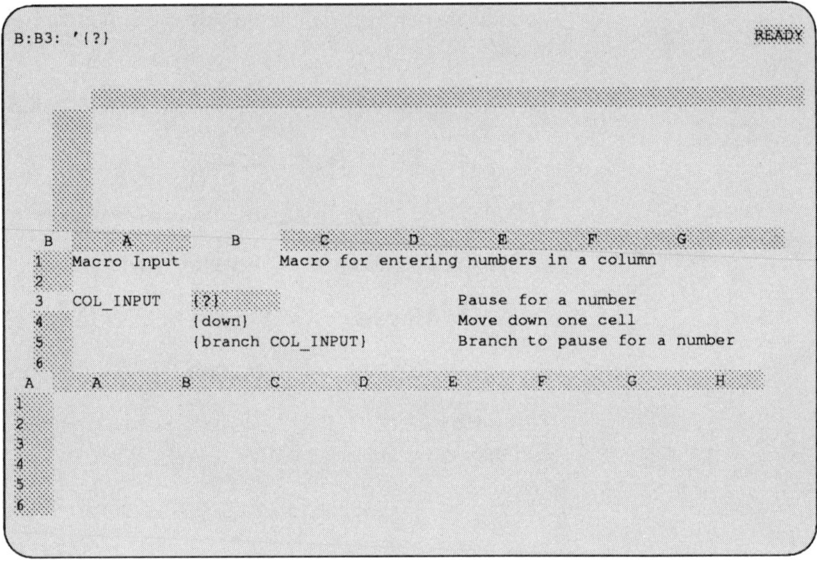

Figure 12-10

After comparing your macro with Figure 12-10 and making any necessary modifications, save the macro on file ENTRYMAC.

Before executing the macro, move the cell pointer to the cell in which you want to enter the first number.

Move the cell pointer to cell A:B2

Execute the macro. Note that as soon as you start executing the macro, CMD appears at the bottom of the screen indicating that the macro is executing and is waiting for you to enter a number.

Enter 10

After you press the ↵ key, the cell pointer will be moved down one cell and the macro will pause again for you to enter another number in cell A:B3. Continue to enter the numbers until 25, 15 and 32 appear in cells B3 through B5.

To terminate the execution of the macro:

Press Ctrl-Break

Press Esc

A beep will be sounded to indicate the macro has been terminated. Your screen should look like Figure 12-11. Do not save the results that appear on your screen.

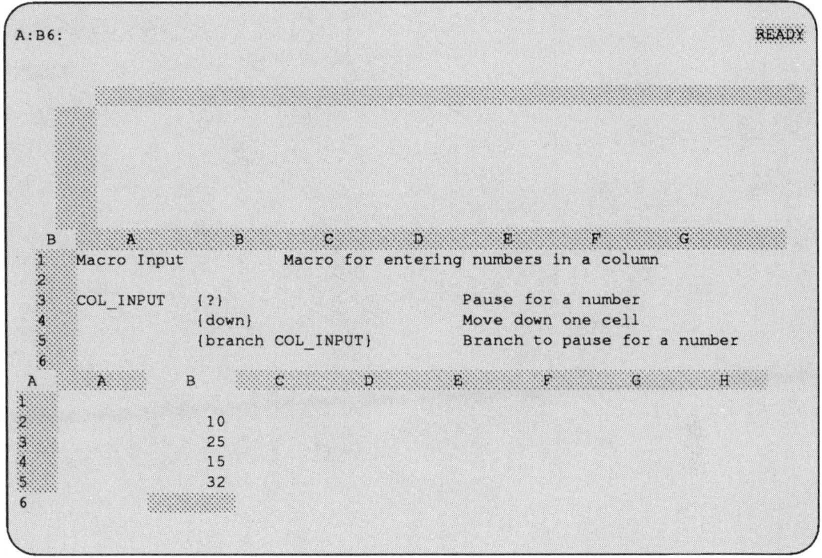

Figure 12-11

Prompting Users to Enter Labels and Numeric Data

At times it is helpful to place a message at the top of the screen to prompt a user to enter a specific label or a value. In this section, you will use the {getlabel} and {getnumber} commands to display prompts requesting the entry of labels and numbers.

Suppose that you want to create a macro that prompts a person using the loan amortization schedule worksheet to enter the purpose for obtaining the loan, the principal amount, interest rate and time period.

You will need to retrieve the file AMORT, insert worksheet B for the macro and display the two worksheets. Enter the macro title, description and name as it appears in Figure 12-12. When you are finished, your screen should look like Figure 12-12.

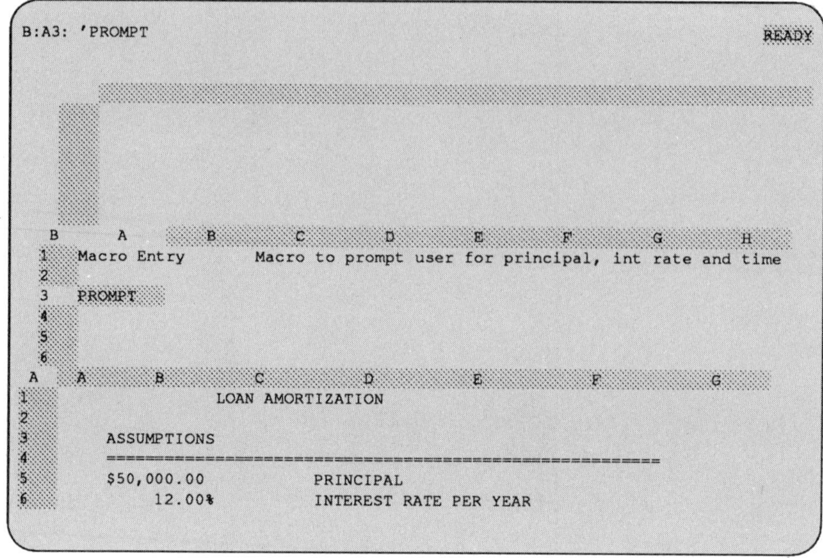
B:A3: 'PROMPT READY

B	A	B	C	D	E	F	G	H
1	Macro Entry	Macro to prompt user for principal, int rate and time						
2								
3	PROMPT							
4								
5								
6								

A	A	B	C	D	E	F	G
1			LOAN AMORTIZATION				
2							
3		ASSUMPTIONS					
4		===					
5		$50,000.00		PRINCIPAL			
6		12.00%		INTEREST RATE PER YEAR			

Figure 12-12

The set of steps that must be included in your macro are:

1. Erase the old values in cells A:B5 through A:B7.
2. Set the calculation mode to manual.
3. Use the {getlabel} and {getnumber} commands to prompt the user to enter the information for loan purpose, principal amount, interest rate and time period.
4. Calculate the monthly payment amount after all necessary information has been input.

Before creating the macro instructions, create the range name DATA_AREA and include cells A:B5..A:B7 as the range of cells.

To include an instruction in the macro that erases the current entries for principal amount, interest rate and time period:

Move the cell pointer to cell B:B3

Enter {blank DATA_AREA}

To specify that manual recalculation mode is to be used:

Move the cell pointer to cell B:B4

Enter '/wgrm

To include a macro instruction that displays a message requesting the user to input the purpose of the loan and place the entry in cell C2:

Move the cell pointer to cell B:B5

Enter {getlabel "Enter Purpose of the Loan: ",C2}~

The prompt string must be enclosed in quotation marks (") because it includes punctuation (a colon).

To include an instruction in the macro requesting the user to enter the principal amount:

Move the cell pointer to cell B:B6

Enter {getnumber "Enter Principal Amount: ",B5}~

To specify similar macro instructions for requesting the user to enter the interest rate and time period data:

Move the cell pointer to cell B:B7

Enter {getnumber "Enter Interest Rate in Decimal Form: ",B6}~

Move the cell pointer to cell B:B8

Enter {getnumber "Enter Time Period in Months: ",B7}~

To include an instruction that indicates the worksheet needs recalculation:

Move the cell pointer to cell B:B9

Enter {calc}

After entering the macro instructions, your screen should look like Figure 12-13.

```
B:B9: '{calc}                                                        READY

  B    A       B         C         D         E         F         G         H
  4            /wgrm
  5            {getlabel "Enter Purpose of the Loan:  ",C2}~
  6            {getnumber "Enter Principal Amount:  ",B5}~
  7            {getnumber "Enter Interest Rate in Decimal Form:  ",B6}~
  8            {getnumber "Enter Time Period in Months:  ",B7}~
  9            {calc}
A    A       B         C         D         E         F         G
4         ==========================================================
5      $50,000.00          PRINCIPAL
6          12.00%          INTEREST RATE PER YEAR
7              60          TIME PERIOD IN MONTHS
8           1.00%          MONTHLY INTEREST RATE
9        1,112.22          CALCULATED PAYMENT AMOUNT
```

Figure 12-13

Create the macro name PROMPT and include B:B3 as the cell in its range. If you have not already done so, create a range name called DATA_AREA for cells A:B5..A:B7. Before executing the macro PROMPT, save the current worksheets on file PROMPTMC.

So that you can see the use of the macro, use the **W**orksheet **W**indow **C**lear command sequence and display worksheet A on your screen. Make sure the cell pointer is in cell A:A1. Execute the macro. Notice that the cells B5 through B7 have been *blanked.* A message appears at the top of the screen requesting you to "Enter Purpose of the Loan:"

Enter Furniture Purchases

The label now appears in cell C2 and a new prompt requesting you to enter the principal amount of the loan appears at the top of the screen.

Enter 20000

The number $20,000 now appears in the worksheet in cell B5. A prompt indicating that you need to enter the interest rate in decimal form now appears at the top of the screen.

Enter .12

The interest rate 12 percent now appears in cell B6 and you are requested to enter the time period in months for repaying the loan.

Enter 60

The time period for 60 months now appears in cell B7. The macro completes the calculation of the monthly payment amount, and your screen should look like Figure 12-14. Do not save the results of this exercise.

```
A:A1: [W5]                                                              READY

A  A       B          C          D           E            F           G
1                  LOAN AMORTIZATION
2                  Furniture Purchases
3      ASSUMPTIONS
4      =======================================================
5      $20,000.00           PRINCIPAL
6           12.00%          INTEREST RATE PER YEAR
7              60           TIME PERIOD IN MONTHS
8            1.00%          MONTHLY INTEREST RATE
9          444.89           CALCULATED PAYMENT AMOUNT
10     =======================================================
11
12 ***********************************************************************
13                                                  PRINCIPAL    INTEREST
14  PMT   PAYMENT  PRINCIPAL  INTEREST   PRINCIPAL     PAID        PAID
15  NUM   AMOUNT    AMOUNT     AMOUNT     BALANCE     TO DATE     TO DATE
16 ***********************************************************************
17                                       20,000.00
18   1    444.89    244.89     200.00    19,755.11     244.89      200.00
19   2    444.89    247.34     197.55    19,507.77     492.23      397.55
20   3    444.89    249.81     195.08    19,257.96     742.04      592.63
```

Figure 12-14

Changing Program Flow and Looping

Sometimes you may want to change the flow of instructions when a macro is used. For example you may want to repeat a set of instructions a specific number of times or until a particular condition occurs. In this section, you will create macros that *loop* through a sequence of instructions when the number of iterations that needs to be completed is either known or unknown.

Executing a Loop of Instructions When the Number of Iterations Is Known

The macro you will create in this section illustrates the use of the {for} command to loop through a set of instructions a specific number of times. For this exercise, you need to have two blank worksheets on your screen in perspective windows. Enter the numbers on worksheet A so that your screen looks like Figure 12-15.

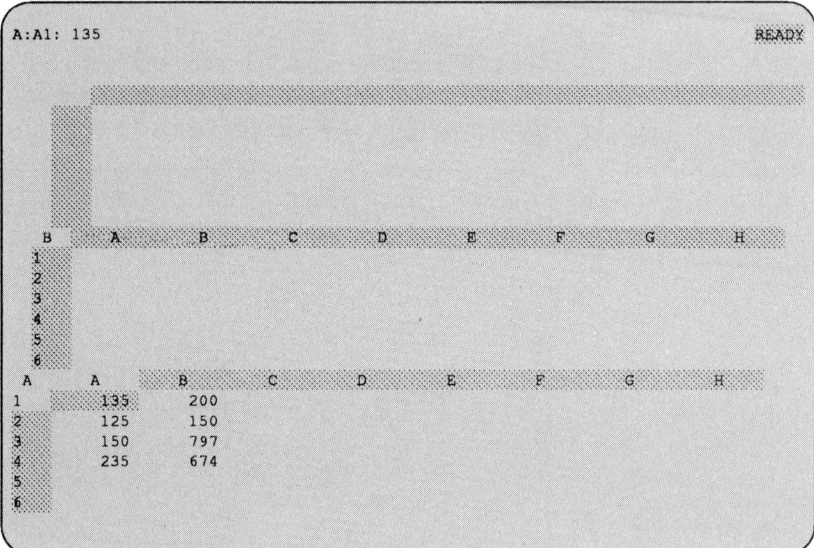

Figure 12-15

Suppose you want to add the numbers in column A and column B for each row and place the sum in column C. You will now create a macro to accomplish this objective. Before entering the macro, enter the title and macro name information that appear in Figure 12-16.

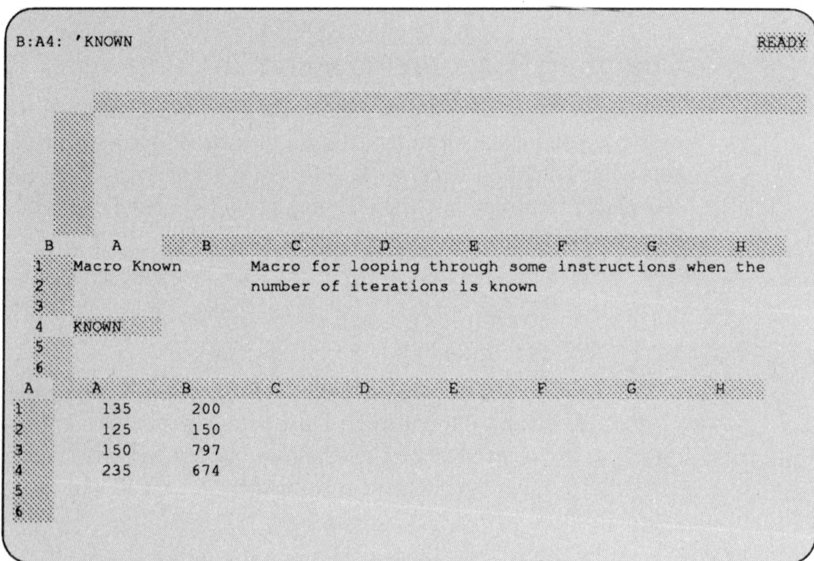

Figure 12-16

To place an instruction in the macro that will place the cell pointer in the proper starting cell position:

Move the cell pointer to cell B:B4

Enter {goto}A:C1~

To solve this problem, you need a macro command that will process a loop of instructions that adds the numbers in columns A and B for each row and places the cell pointer in the proper starting cell position for the next summation operation:

Move the cell pointer to cell B:B5

Enter {for COUNT,1,4,1,LOOP}

This macro command indicates that the set of macro instructions which starts with the initial cell in the range name LOOP is to be executed four times. The cell which has the range name COUNT is initialized with a value of 1 and incremented by 1 each time the LOOP routine is executed. The first number after COUNT is the initialization value, the second number is the termination value and the third number is the value by which COUNT is to be incremented each time the set of instructions is executed. When the value of COUNT exceeds the termination value, the looping process is ended.

To specify that the cell pointer is to be moved to cell A:A1 after the macro is executed:

Move the cell pointer to cell B:B6

Enter {goto}A:A1~

To place the name of the LOOP routine on the worksheet:

Move the cell pointer to cell B:A8

Enter LOOP

To include a macro instruction that adds the numbers in column A and B for a row and enters the sum in column C for the row.

Move the cell pointer to cell B:B8

Enter '+{left} {left}+{left}~

Assuming that the cell pointer is in A:C1 when the macro is executed, this macro instruction specifies that a formula is used that sums the value two columns to the left of C1 and the value one column to the left of C1. The ~ symbol represents the ⏎ key. When the macro processes this keystroke, the formula (+A1+B1) is placed in C1.

To indicate that the cell pointer needs to be moved down one cell in column C before the routine is executed again:

Move	the cell pointer to cell B:B9
Enter	{down}

To include the COUNT variable name on your screen:

Move	the cell pointer to cell B:A12
Enter	COUNT

You must create a range name for LOOP and COUNT. The range name LOOP should only include cell B:B8 and the range name COUNT should only include cell B:B12.

After creating the range names LOOP and COUNT and using the **W**orksheet **W**indow **C**lear command sequence to display only worksheet B, your screen should look like Figure 12-17.

```
B:A1: 'Macro Known                                                        READY

B       A        B          C          D         E        F        G        H
1   Macro Known           Macro for looping through some instructions when the
2                         number of iterations is known
3
4   KNOWN      {goto}A:C1~
5              {for COUNT,1,4,1,LOOP}
6              {goto}A:A1~
7
8   LOOP       +{left}{left}+{left}~
9              {down}
10
11
12  COUNT
13
14
```

Figure 12-17

After comparing your macro instructions with those in Figure 12-17 and making any necessary modifications, create the range name KNOWN for the macro name and include cell B:B4 as its range. Save the worksheet file using the name KNOWNMAC.

After you execute the macro and issue the **W**orksheet **W**indow **P**erspective command sequence, your screen should look like Figure 12-18. Notice that the values for columns A and B for each row have been added and the resulting total placed in column C.

```
A:A1: 135                                                        READY

B    A         B         C         D         E         F         G         H
1    Macro Known        Macro for looping through some instructions when the
2                       number of iterations is known
3
4    KNOWN     {goto}A:C1~
5              {for COUNT,1,4,1,LOOP}
6              {goto}A:A1~
A    A         B         C         D         E         F         G         H
1       135       200       335
2       125       150       275
3       150       797       947
4       235       674       909
5
6
```

Figure 12-18

To see what happened on the macro worksheet, display only worksheet B on your screen. Refer to Figure 12-19.

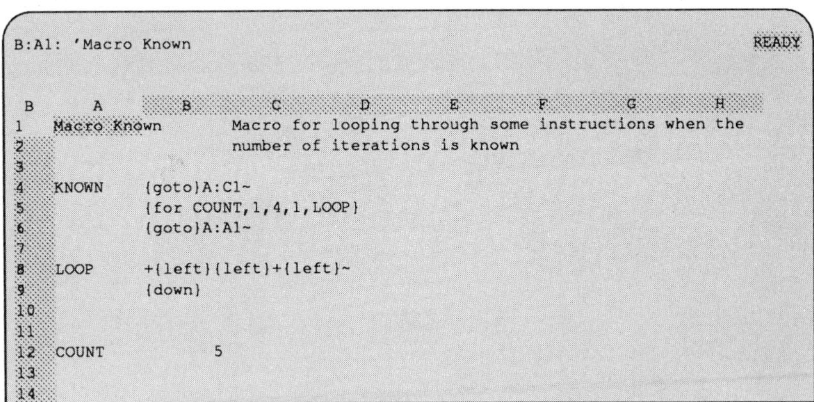

```
B:A1: 'Macro Known                                               READY

B    A         B         C         D         E         F         G         H
1    Macro Known        Macro for looping through some instructions when the
2                       number of iterations is known
3
4    KNOWN     {goto}A:C1~
5              {for COUNT,1,4,1,LOOP}
6              {goto}A:A1~
7
8    LOOP      +{left}{left}+{left}~
9              {down}
10
11
12   COUNT           5
13
14
```

Figure 12-19

Notice that the number 5 appears in cell B12. The number 5 indicates that as the set of macro instructions associated with the range name LOOP were executed, the value of COUNT was incremented from an initial value of 1 by 1 each time the set of instructions were executed. The value of COUNT was compared to the termination value of 4. When the value of COUNT was less than or equal to 4, the set of instructions associated with the range name LOOP was again executed. When the value of COUNT became 5, it was greater than the termination value and the macro stopped executing.

Executing a Loop of Instructions When the Number of Iterations is Unknown

In the previous section, you created a macro that repeated a set of macro instructions a specific number of times based on the fact that you knew how many times the set of instructions needed to be executed. Sometimes you may not know how many times a set of macro instructions needs to be repeated.

You created that macro in the last section to add the numbers in column A and column B for a row and enter the sum in column C of the row. You assumed that you knew the number of rows in which numbers appeared in columns A and B. In this section, you will create a macro for solving this problem that is general enough so that it will work properly whenever you do not know the exact number of rows that have values in columns A and B.

The {if}, {quit} and {branch} commands will be used in the macro that you develop to solve the problem. These commands will allow you to loop through a set of instructions when the number of times they need to be repeated is not known prior to executing the macro. They also permit you to change the program flow within a macro.

For this exercise, erase the worksheets on your screen and create a worksheet that looks like Figure 12-20.

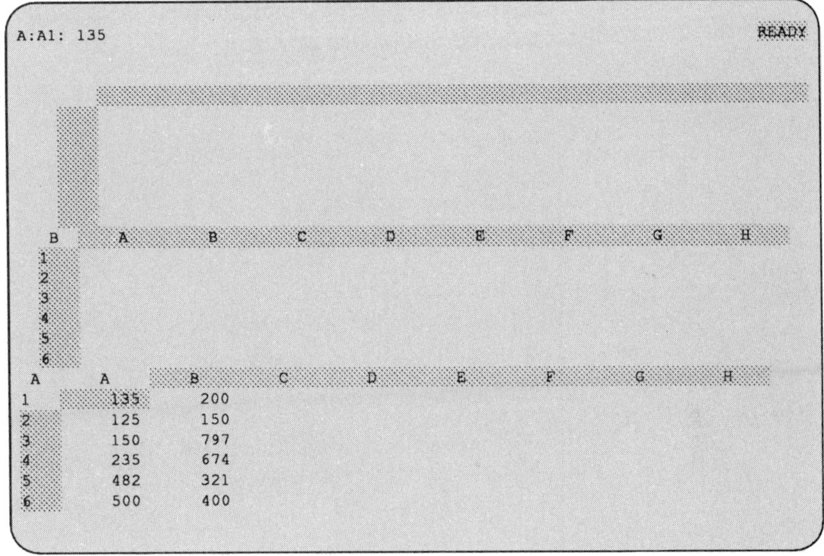

Figure 12-20

The steps necessary to solve this problem are:

1. Move the cell pointer to the proper starting position.

2. Add the two numbers in column A and B and enter the sum in column C.

3. Move the cell pointer down one cell in column C and then to the left once so the cell pointer is in column B.

4. Create a test range consisting of the cell in column B and immediately above it. Recall that the cell above the one in column B has a number in it.

5. Move the cell pointer to the right once so the cell pointer is in column C. Note that this cell is the cell in which you will place a sum if the cell immediately to the left of column B has a number in it.

6. Use the @COUNT function to determine the number of nonblank cells in the test range. If the count equals one, then the cell in column B is blank and, therefore, does not have a number in it. The macro then needs to stop executing. If the count is two, the instructions for adding the cells in column A and B need to be repeated.

Before entering the macro instructions, enter the title of the macro and macro name information that appear in Figure 12-21.

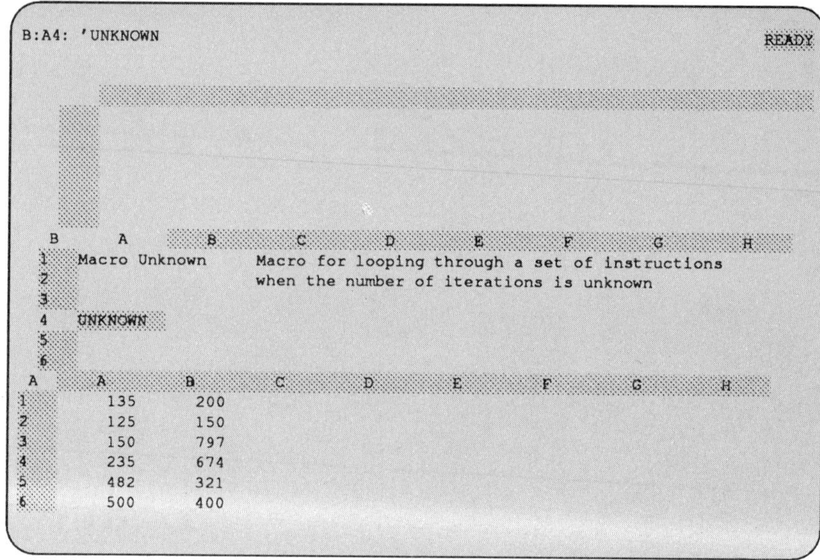

Figure 12-21

Assume that the values in columns A and B always begin with row 1 in the worksheet on which the macro is used. To specify C1 as the location for the first sum:

Move the cell pointer to cell B:B4

Enter {goto}A:C1~

To include a macro instruction for adding the numbers for the present row in columns A and B and entering the sum in column C for the row:

Move the cell pointer to cell B:B5

Enter '+{left}{left}+{left}~

To define a macro instruction that moves the cell pointer down one row and to the left one cell so the cell pointer will be in column B:

Move the cell pointer to cell B:B6

Enter {down} {left}

To enter a macro instruction that creates a test range consisting of the cell in column A and the one immediately above it:

Move the cell pointer to cell B:B7

Enter '/rncTEST~{up}~

To include a macro instruction for moving the cell pointer to the right once so it will be in column C again:

Move the cell pointer to cell B:B8

Enter {right}

At this point you need to specify a macro instruction that determines if the range name TEST has a count = 1.

Move the cell pointer to cell B:B9

Enter {if @COUNT(TEST) =1}{branch END}

Note that if the count for the range name TEST equals 1, control will be transferred to the initial cell in the range named END. In this situation, the cell in column B is blank, and the macro needs to be terminated.

If the count for the range name TEST equals 2, then there are numbers in column A and B that need to be summed. You also will need to delete the range name TEST so it can be created again to determine whether the macro needs to stop executing.

To include a macro instruction for deleting the range name TEST:

Move the cell pointer to cell B:B10

Enter '/rndTEST~

To specify a macro instruction that shows control needs to be transferred to the macro instruction that sums the numbers in columns A and B:

Move the cell pointer to cell B:B11

Enter {branch ADD}

At this point, you need to:

Move the cell pointer to cell B:A5

Enter ADD

Create the name range ADD and specify its range to be cell B:B5. Note that cell B:B5 includes the macro instruction for summing the numbers in columns A and B, and then entering the total in column C.

Here, you need to place the macro instructions for ending the macro on the macro worksheet. You must define the location of the range name END so the {branch END} command named earlier will execute properly, delete the range name TEST, move the cell pointer to cell A:A1 and quit. To define the location of the range name END and to delete the range name TEST:

Move the cell pointer to cell B:A13

Enter END

Move the cell pointer to cell B:B13

Enter '/rndTEST~

Now, create the range name END and define its range as cell B:B13. Note that the identifiers ADD and END are not actually required, but the use of such labels clarifies the macro instruction execution flow.

To include the macro instruction that moves the cell pointer to cell A:A1 after all of the sets of numbers in columns A and B have been summed:

Move the cell pointer to cell B:B14

Enter {goto}A:A1~

You could have used {home} instead of {goto}A:A1~.

To define the macro instruction that stops the execution of the macro:

Move the cell pointer to cell B:B15

Enter {quit}

The {quit} command in this macro is not essential since the macro would end when a blank cell was encountered. However, the {quit} command clarifies the ending point for the macro.

So you can see the complete macro, use the **Worksheet Window Clear** command sequence to display only worksheet B. Your screen should look like Figure 12-22.

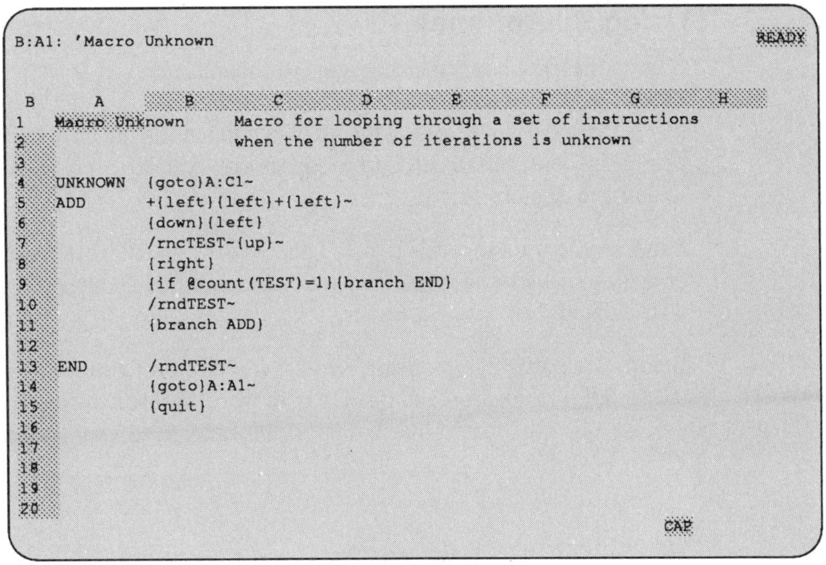

```
B:A1: 'Macro Unknown                                                    READY

B      A           B        C        D        E        F        G        H
1   Macro Unknown     Macro for looping through a set of instructions
2                     when the number of iterations is unknown
3
4   UNKNOWN   {goto}A:C1~
5   ADD       +{left}{left}+{left}~
6             {down}{left}
7             /rncTEST~{up}~
8             {right}
9             {if @count(TEST)=1}{branch END}
10            /rndTEST~
11            {branch ADD}
12
13  END       /rndTEST~
14            {goto}A:A1~
15            {quit}
16
17
18
19
20
                                                              CAP
```

Figure 12-22

After you compare your macro with Figure 12-22 and make any necessary modifications, name your macro using the name UNKNOWN. Save the worksheets using the file name UNKNOMAC.

Move the cell pointer to cell A:A1. Notice that you have six sets of numbers to sum. Execute the macro UNKNOWN. Your screen should look like Figure 12-23. You do not need to save the results after the macro is executed.

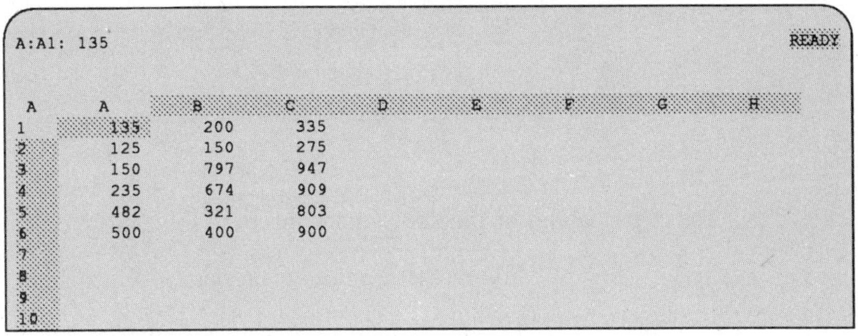

```
A:A1: 135                                                           READY

A      A        B        C        D        E        F        G        H
1       135      200      335
2       125      150      275
3       150      797      947
4       235      674      909
5       482      321      803
6       500      400      900
7
8
9
10
```

Figure 12-23

Using Subroutines

Subroutines are independent sets of instructions that can be called at any point in a macro. One advantage of using a subroutine is that the set of instructions can be easily called from any place in the macro so that the set of commands do not have to be duplicated in the macro. Another advantage of using a subroutine is that it can be called from several different locations within one or more macros.

Suppose you want to create a macro that permits you to input a code that designates whether or not you want to print the loan amortization schedule after the monthly payment amount is calculated.

Before you solve this problem, retrieve file AMORT, insert an additional worksheet after the AMORT worksheet and display both worksheets on your screen. When you finish this process, enter the macro title and name information so your screen looks like Figure 12-24.

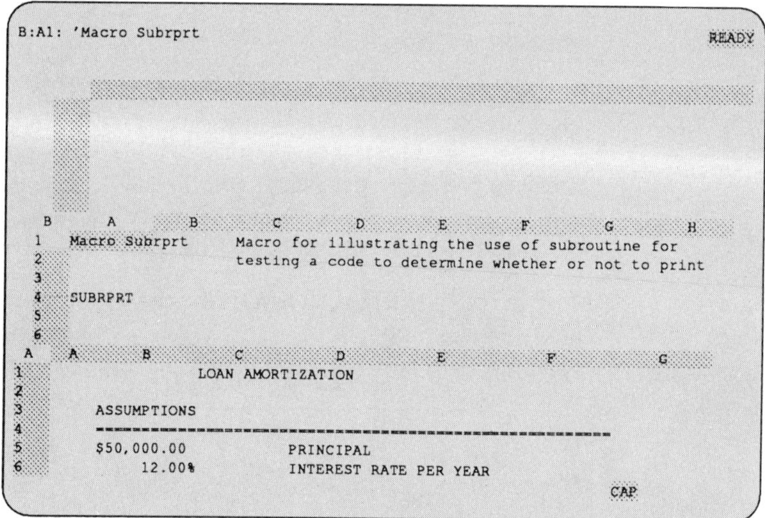

Figure 12-24

The steps that must be included in the macro to solve this problem are:

1. Prompt the user to enter the data on principal, interest rate and time period.

2. Calculate the loan payment using the data input for principal, interest rate and time period.

3. Prompt the user to enter a code to indicate whether the person wants to print the loan amortization schedule.

4. Test the code and, if appropriate, print the loan amortization schedule.

So you can see all of the macro instructions on your screen, display only worksheet B.

To make sure the macro executes on the loan amortization schedule, place an instruction in the macro to move the cell pointer to cell A:A1.

Move the cell pointer to cell B:B4

Enter {goto}A:A1~

You could have used {firstcell} or {fc} instead of {goto}A:A1~.

At a later point in the macro, you enter a message prompting the user to input the code to determine whether to print the loan amortization schedule. To ensure that the range of cells used are blank when the macro executes:

Move the cell pointer to cell B:B5

Enter '/reI1.I5~

To place the instructions for prompting the user to enter the principal, interest rate and time period in your macro:

Move the cell pointer to cell B:B6

Enter {getnumber "Enter Principal Amount: ",B5}~

Move the cell pointer to cell B:B7

Enter {getnumber "Enter Interest Rate in Decimal Form: ",B6}~

Move the cell pointer to cell B:B8

Enter {getnumber "Enter Time Period in Months: ",B7}~

To call the subroutine that prompts the user to enter the code for printing, that tests the value of the code, and, if appropriate, prints the loan amortization schedule:

Move the cell pointer to cell B:B9

Enter {CHKCODE}

To include instructions that will move the cell pointer to cell A:A1:

Move the cell pointer to cell B:B10

Enter {goto}A:A1~

To place a command in the macro that terminates execution of the macro:

Move the cell pointer to cell B:B11

Enter {quit}

At this point, you need to create the set of instructions that are included in the CHKCODE subroutine.

To place the subroutine name on the macro worksheet, and to name a location to enter the code:

Move the cell pointer to cell B:A16

Enter CHKCODE

Move the cell pointer to cell B:B16

Enter {goto}I1~

You now need to create the range name CHKCODE and include B:B16 as its range. When the macro instruction in B:B9 is executed, control will be transferred to cell B:B16.

To include the instructions for prompting the user to input the print code:

Move the cell pointer to cell B:B17

Enter If you wish to print the schedule: {down}

Move the cell pointer to cell B:B18

Enter type a 1 and press enter {down}

Move the cell pointer to cell B:B19

Enter If you do not wish to print the schedule: {down}

Move the cell pointer to cell B:B20

Enter type 2 and press enter {down}

To include a command that causes the macro to pause and wait for the user to enter the print code:

Move the cell pointer to cell B:B21

Enter {?}~

After the code is input, you need to include instructions to make sure a valid code is specified. If the code is invalid, the instructions for entering the code must be repeated. If the code is valid, then the code needs to be tested to see whether or not it is appropriate to print the loan amortization schedule.

To test whether the code that was input is valid:

Move the cell pointer to B:B22

Enter {if I5=1#or#I5=2} {branch TEST}

If cell I5 has a value of 1 or 2, control transfers to the initial cell in range name TEST to determine whether the loan amortization schedule needs to be printed.

When the code is not valid, the input range (I1..I5) needs to be erased and control needs to be transferred to the first instruction in the subroutine so the user can be prompted to enter the code again. To place these instructions in your macro:

Move the cell pointer to cell B:B23

Enter '/reI1.I5~

Move the cell pointer to cell B:B24

Enter {CHKCODE}

At this point, you need to enter the instructions for testing the code. If the code has a value of 1, then you do need to print the loan amortization schedule. If the code has a value of 2, you do not print the schedule.

To include the instructions for testing the code and printing:

Move the cell pointer to cell B:A26

Enter TEST

Move the cell pointer to cell B:B26

Enter {if I5=2} {return}

This {if} command tests to the code value to see if it is 2. When the code has the value of 2, the {return} command transfers control to the first macro command after the subroutine was called. In such a situation, the loan amortization schedule will not be printed.

If the value in I5 is a 1, then the loan amortization schedule needs to be printed. To print the schedule:

Move the cell pointer to cell B27

Enter '/pprA1.G77~

Move the cell pointer to cell B28

Enter agppq

To include an instruction to return to the command immediately following the command which called the subroutine:

Move	the cell pointer to cell B:B29
Enter	{return}

At this point, create the range name TEST and include cell B:B26 in its range. Your macro should look like the one illustrated in Parts 1 and 2 of Figure 12-25.

```
B:A1: 'Macro Subrprt                                                        READY

B     A         B         C         D         E         F         G         H
1   Macro Subrprt     Macro for illustrating the use of subroutine for
2                     testing a code to determine whether or not to print
3
4   SUBRPRT   {goto}A:A1~
5             /wgrm
6             /reI1.I5~
7             {getnumber "Enter Principal Amount:  ",B5}~
8             {getnumber "Enter Interest Rate in Decimal Form:  ",B6}~
9             {getnumber "Enter Time Period in Months:  ",B7}~
10            {calc}
11            {CHKCODE}
12            {calc}
13            {goto}A:A1~
14            {quit}
15
16  CHKCODE   {goto}I1~
17            If you wish to print the schedule: {down}
18            type a 1 and press enter {down}
19            If you do not wish to print the schedule: {down}
20            type a 2 and press enter {down}
```

Figure 12-25, Part 1

```
B:A21:                                                                      READY

B     A         B         C         D         E         F         G         H
21            {?}~
22            {if I5=1#or#I5=2}{branch TEST}
23            /reI1.I5~
24            {CHKCODE}
25
26  TEST      {if I5=2}{return}
27            /pprA1.G77~
28            agppq
29            {return}
30
31
32
```

Figure 12-25, Part 2

After you compare your macro with the one appearing in Figure 12-25 Parts 1 and 2, and make any necessary changes, name your macro using the name SUBPRT and save the worksheets using the file name PRCHK.

Move the cell pointer to cell A:A1. Execute the macro SUBPRT using $10,000 for the principal amount, 9 percent for the interest rate, and 60 months for the time period. When you are prompted for the print code, enter the number 1. Your screen should look like Figure 12-26 after the macro executes properly and you move the cell pointer to A:A9. You also should have printed the loan amortization schedule.

```
A:A9: [W5]                                                              READY

B      A         B          C          D          E          F          G          H
4   SUBPRT    {goto}A:A1~
5             /wgrm
6             /reI1.I5~
7             {getnumber "Enter Principal Amount:  ",B5}~
8             {getnumber "Enter Interest Rate in Decimal Form:  ",B6}~
9             {getnumber "Enter Time Period in Months:  ",B7}~
A     A         B          C          D          E          F          G
4       ---------------------------------------------------------------
5       $10,000.00          PRINCIPAL
6            9.00%          INTEREST RATE PER YEAR
7               60          TIME PERIOD IN MONTHS
8            0.75%          MONTHLY INTEREST RATE
9           207.58          CALCULATED PAYMENT AMOUNT
```

Figure 12-26

Execute the macro again, using a value of 2 for the print code. Finally execute the macro using 3 for the print code. Notice that you are prompted for a print code until you enter a 1 or a 2.

Do not save the results after the macro is executed.

Creating User-Designed Menus

In some situations, individuals may want to design their own menus using the Lotus 1-2-3 command language. The process for preparing a menu includes the following:

1. Write a *menu-processing* macro that initiates the execution of the user-designed menu.
2. Determine the entries for the menu line and the description line.
3. Write the macro commands for each menu option.

The following guidelines can be used in developing a user-designed menu:

1. Find a portion of the spreadsheet that has at least as many blank columns as there are menu options.
2. The first row of the user-designed menu contains the menu options as they will appear on the screen.
3. The row below the menu options includes a description of each menu option that will appear on the screen when a menu option is highlighted.
4. The macro commands for each menu option can be placed immediately below the menu item or in a range of cells at another location on the spreadsheet.
5. A menu-processing macro must be placed on the macro worksheet that contains the menu.

Some cautionary guidelines for creating menus follow:

1. Do not place more than 8 menu options in the first row of the menu you are designing.
2. The cell immediately to the right of the last menu option must be blank.
3. The options on the menu line should be short enough to make sure they will appear on the screen.
4. Make sure the options on a menu do not start with the same first character so that a menu option can be selected by typing the first character of the menu option.
5. Do not leave blank entries between the menu options.

Single-Tiered Menu

Suppose that you want to design a menu for the loan amortization schedule worksheet that permits you to calculate the monthly payment and print the appropriate schedule for a one- or a five-year time period. For this example, assume that the loan amount is $50,000 and the interest rate is 12 percent. When you finish this exercise, your screen will look like Figure 12-27 Part 1.

```
B:A1: [W6] 'Macro Single                                                      READY

 B   A      B            C             D             E             F
1   Macro Single       Macro for illustrating the design and use
2                      of a one-tier menu
3
4   SINGLE{menubranch MAIN}
5
6   MAIN  1-year       Print-1       Five-year     5-Print       Quit
7         1 year term  1 year sched 5 year term   5-year sched Quit process
8         {goto}A:B7~  /pprA:A1.A:G2{goto}A:B7~   /pprA:A1.A:G7/reA:B7~
9         12~          agppq         60~           agppq         {quit}
10        {goto}A:A1~  {menubranch M{goto}A:A1~   {menubranch MAIN}
11        {menubranch MAIN}          {menubranch MAIN}
12
13
```

Figure 12-27
Part 1

The complete contents of the cells are illustrated in Figure 12-27 Part 2.

B	A	B	C	D	E	F
1	Macro Single		Macro for illustrating the design and use			
2			of a one-tier menu			
3						
4	SINGLE{menubranch MAIN}					
5						
6	MAIN	1-year	Print-1	Five-year	5-Print	Quit
7		1-year term	1-year sched	5-year term	5-year sched	Quit process
8		{goto}A:B7~	/pprA:A1.A:G29~	{goto}A:B7~	/pprA:A1.A:G77~	/reA:B7~
9		12~	agppq	60~	agppq	{quit}
10		{goto}A:A1	{menubranch MAIN}	{goto}A:A1~	{menubranch MAIN}	
11		{menubranch MAIN}		{menubranch MAIN}		
12						
13						

Figure 12-27
Part 2

To complete this exercise, retrieve the file AMORT and insert an additional worksheet for the single-tiered menu macro. After placing the title and macro name on your worksheet, your screen should look like Figure 12-28.

```
B:A4: 'SINGLE                                                    READY

   B    A        B         C         D         E         F         G         H
   1  Macro Single      Macro for illustrating the design and use
   2                    of a one-tier menu
   3
   4  SINGLE
   5
   6
  A   A        B          C          D          E          F          G
  1                   LOAN AMORTIZATION
  2
  3     ASSUMPTIONS
  4     ===========================================================
  5     $50,000.00             PRINCIPAL
  6         12.00%             INTEREST RATE PER YEAR
```

Figure 12-28

When you execute a user-designed menu macro, you must include a {menubranch} command to indicate to 1-2-3 on which menu you want to start. To include this command on the macro worksheet:

Move	the cell pointer to cell B:B4
Enter	{menubranch MAIN}

To enter the label MAIN in your macro:

Move	the cell pointer to cell B:A6
Enter	MAIN

The five menu options to be included are 1-year, Print-1, Five-year, 5-Print and Quit. If the 1-year menu option is selected, then the loan amortization schedule will be computed using 12 months as the time period. When the Print-1 option is selected, the loan amortization schedule for a one-year (12 months) time period will be printed.

If the Five-year menu option is chosen, the loan amortization schedule will be calculated using a 60-month time period. When the 5-Print menu option is chosen, the loan amortization schedule for a five-year (60 months) time period will be printed. When the Quit menu option is selected, execution of the macro will stop.

To include the five menu options in your macro:

Move the cell pointer to cell B:B6

Enter '1-year

Move the cell pointer to cell B:C6

Enter Print-1

Move the cell pointer to cell B:D6

Enter Five-year

Move the cell pointer to cell B:E6

Enter '5-Print

Move the cell pointer to cell B:F6

Enter Quit

So you can see more of the information on your screen, reduce the column width of column A to 7. Then widen columns B through F so each column displays 13 characters.

At this point, you have placed the menu options on the macro worksheet. You now create the range name MAIN and include the location of the first menu option, B:B6, as its range.

The second row of your menu macro includes the description for each menu option that will appear in the control panel when the menu pointer is highlighting it. To enter the descriptive information for each of the menu options:

Move the cell pointer to cell B:B7

Enter '1-year term

Move the cell pointer to cell B:C7

Enter '1-year sched

Move the cell pointer to cell B:D7

Enter	'5-year term
Move	the cell pointer to cell B:E7
Enter	'5-year sched
Move	the cell pointer to cell B:F7
Enter	Quit process

The macro instructions that are to be executed when a menu option is selected can appear immediately below the description of the menu option or in a range at another location on the macro worksheet. For this example you will place the macro instructions immediately below each menu option.

For the 1-year menu option you need to enter macro instructions that enter the number 12 for the time period in cell A:B7, place the menu pointer in cell A:A1 and branch to the main menu. To include these instructions below the first menu option:

Move	the cell pointer to cell B:B8
Enter	{goto}A:B7~
Move	the cell pointer to cell B:B9
Enter	'12~
Move	the cell pointer to cell B:B10
Enter	{goto}A:A1~
Move	the cell pointer to cell B:B11
Enter	{menubranch MAIN}

When the Print-1 option is selected, you must include instructions that select the proper range of cells and prints a 12-month loan amortization schedule. Then, you must specify that control is to be transferred to the main menu.

To place the appropriate macro instructions under the second menu option:

Move	the cell pointer to cell B:C8
Enter	'/pprA:A1.A:G29~
Move	the cell pointer to cell B:C9
Enter	agppq
Move	the cell pointer to cell B:C10

Enter {menubranch MAIN}

The Five-year menu option requires the same set of instructions as the 1-year option, except the number 60 must be entered for the time period in cell A:B7. To include the instructions that must appear below the Five-year menu option:

Move the cell pointer to cell B:D8

Enter {goto}A:B7~

Move the cell pointer to cell B:D9

Enter '60~

Move the cell pointer to cell B:D10

Enter {goto}A:A1~

Move the cell pointer to cell B:D11

Enter {menubranch MAIN}

The set of instructions that must be included below the 5-Print menu option are the same as the Print-1 menu option, except the print range must include 60 months of data instead of 12. To place the appropriate instructions under the 5-Print menu option:

Move the cell pointer to cell B:E8

Enter '/pprA:A1.A:G77~

Move the cell pointer to cell B:E9

Enter agppq

Move the cell pointer to cell B:E10

Enter {menubranch MAIN}

The final menu option is Quit. For this menu option, you need to enter instructions to erase cell A:B7, where you placed the time period data, and end the execution of the macro. To place these instructions below the Quit menu:

Move the cell pointer to cell B:F8

Enter '/reA:B7~

Move the cell pointer to cell B:F9

Enter {quit}

Your screen should now look like Figure 12-29, Part 1.

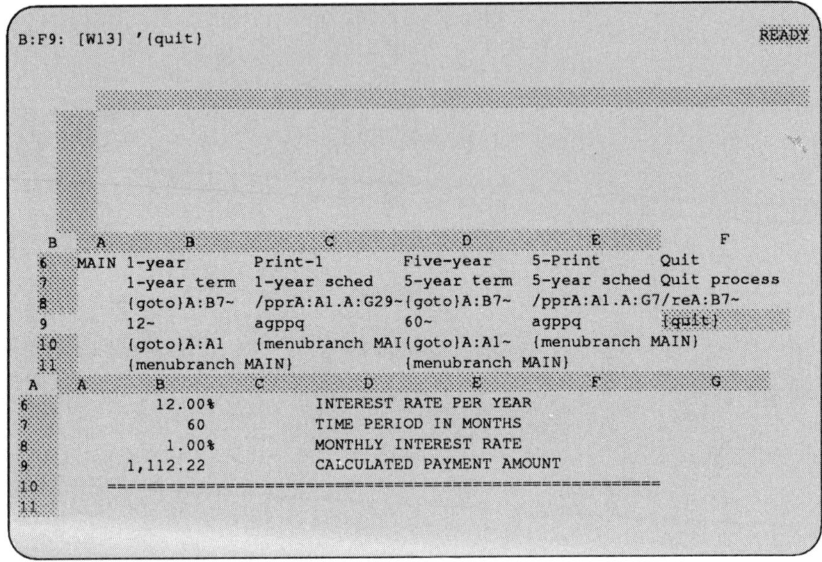

Figure 12-29
Part 1

B	A	B	C	D	E	F
1	Macro Single		Macro for illustrating the design and use			
2			of a one-tier menu			
3						
4	SINGLE{menubranch MAIN}					
5						
6	MAIN	1-year	Print-1	Five-year	5-Print	Quit
7		1-year term	1-year sched	5-year term	5-year sched	Quit process
8		{goto}A:B7~	/pprA:A1.A:G29~	{goto}A:B7~	/pprA:A1.A:G77~	/reA:B7~
9		12~	agppq	60~	agppq	{quit}
10		{goto}A:A1	{menubranch MAIN}	{goto}A:A1~	{menubranch MAIN}	
11		{menubranch MAIN}		{menubranch MAIN}		
12						
13						

Figure 12-29
Part 2

After comparing the menu you designed with Figure 12-29 Part 1 and with the information appearing in Figure 12-29 Part 2, make any necessary changes. Name your macro SINGLE. Include the cell B:B4 as the range for the macro SINGLE, and save the worksheets using the file name SINGLMAC.

Move the cell pointer to cell A:B7 and erase the contents of the cell. The ERR indicator will appear in some of the worksheet cells. When you execute the macro SINGLE, the ERR indicator will disappear from the cells. Make sure the principal amount is $50,000 and the interest rate is 12 percent. If necessary, change the values.

Execute the macro SINGLE and select the 1-year menu option. Figure 12-30 Part 1 includes the menu when it initially appears on the screen. Figure 12-30 Part 2 illustrates the appearance of the screen after the 1-year option is selected. Note that the macro is designed so the menu will continue to appear on the screen until you select the QUIT menu option. Figure 12-30 Part 3 displays the screen after the QUIT option is selected from the menu.

```
A:B7: (F0) [W11]                                                        MENU
1-year  Print-1  Five-year  5-Print  Quit
1 year term
 A    A        B         C           D           E           F          G
 1                    LOAN AMORTIZATION
 2
 3       ASSUMPTIONS
 4       ========================================================
 5       $50,000.00                 PRINCIPAL
 6           12.00%                 INTEREST RATE PER YEAR
 7                                  TIME PERIOD IN MONTHS
 8            1.00%                 MONTHLY INTEREST RATE
 9              ERR                 CALCULATED PAYMENT AMOUNT
10       ========================================================
11
12 ************************************************************************
13                                                     PRINCIPAL   INTEREST
14   PMT   PAYMENT  PRINCIPAL  INTEREST   PRINCIPAL      PAID        PAID
15   NUM   AMOUNT     AMOUNT    AMOUNT     BALANCE     TO DATE     TO DATE
16 ************************************************************************
17                                         50,000.00
18     1       ERR       ERR     500.00         ERR         ERR     500.00
19     2       ERR       ERR        ERR         ERR         ERR        ERR
20     3       ERR       ERR        ERR         ERR         ERR        ERR
                                     CMD
```

Figure 12-30
Part 1

```
A:A1: [W5]                                                                 MENU
1-year  Print-1  Five-year  5-Print  Quit
1 year term
 A   A        B          C          D          E           F           G
1                    LOAN AMORTIZATION
2
3       ASSUMPTIONS
4       ==========================================================
5       $50,000.00           PRINCIPAL
6            12.00%          INTEREST RATE PER YEAR
7               12           TIME PERIOD IN MONTHS
8             1.00%          MONTHLY INTEREST RATE
9         4,442.44           CALCULATED PAYMENT AMOUNT
10      ==========================================================
11
12 ************************************************************************
13                                                     PRINCIPAL   INTEREST
14  PMT   PAYMENT  PRINCIPAL  INTEREST   PRINCIPAL       PAID        PAID
15  NUM   AMOUNT     AMOUNT    AMOUNT     BALANCE      TO DATE     TO DATE
16 ************************************************************************
17                                       50,000.00
18    1  4,442.44  3,942.44     500.00   46,057.56    3,942.44      500.00
19    2  4,442.44  3,981.86     460.58   42,075.70    7,924.30      960.58
20    3  4,442.44  4,021.68     420.76   38,054.01   11,945.99    1,381.33
                                         CMD
```

Figure 12-30
Part 2

```
A:A1: [W5]                                                                 READY


 A   A        B          C          D          E           F           G
1                    LOAN AMORTIZATION
2
3       ASSUMPTIONS
4       ==========================================================
5       $50,000.00           PRINCIPAL
6            12.00%          INTEREST RATE PER YEAR
7                            TIME PERIOD IN MONTHS
8             1.00%          MONTHLY INTEREST RATE
9              ERR           CALCULATED PAYMENT AMOUNT
10      ==========================================================
11
12 ************************************************************************
13                                                     PRINCIPAL   INTEREST
14  PMT   PAYMENT  PRINCIPAL  INTEREST   PRINCIPAL       PAID        PAID
15  NUM   AMOUNT     AMOUNT    AMOUNT     BALANCE      TO DATE     TO DATE
16 ************************************************************************
17                                       50,000.00
18    1       ERR       ERR     500.00         ERR         ERR      500.00
19    2       ERR       ERR        ERR         ERR         ERR         ERR
20    3       ERR       ERR        ERR         ERR         ERR         ERR
```

Figure 12-30
Part 3

Multiple-Tiered Menus

User-designed menus can be linked together to form a *tiered* menu structure. The example here is an extension of the single-tiered menu in the previous section that allowed you to select a one-or five-year time period and then print the amortization schedule for a loan with a principal amount of $50,000 and an interest rate of 12 percent.

Suppose you want to allow a user of the loan amortization schedule worksheet the flexibility to specify the principal amount, interest rate and time period in one menu and then print the amortization schedule from a second menu. It is assumed for this example that you will be entering either 12 or 60 months for the time period; therefore, you will have the options to print a one- or a five-year loan amortization schedule.

Parts 1 and 2 of Figure 12-31 illustrate what the two-tier menu will look like when you finish this exercise. Notice in this example there are two menus: MENU1 and MENU2. The first menu includes options for entering the principal amount, interest rate, time period, transferring control to the second menu to print the appropriate loan amortization schedule and for stopping the execution of the macro. Figure 12-31 Part 3 includes the exact contents of each cell.

```
B:A21: [W6] 'MENU2                                                   READY

B   A      B                   C                   D
21  MENU2  Print-1             5-Print             Quit
22         1 year sched        5 year sched        Quit process
23         {branch PRINT_1}    {branch 5_PRINT}    {branch QUIT}
24
25
26
27         Print-1             5-Print             Quit
28
29         /pprA:A1.A:G29~     /pprA:A1.A:G77~     /reA:B5.A:B7~
30         agppq               agppq               {calc}
31         /reA:B5.A:B7~       /reA:B5.A:B7~       {goto}A:A1~
32         {calc}              {calc}              {quit}
33         {menubranch MENU1}  {menubranch MENU1}
34
35
```

Figure 12-31
Part 1

B:A21: [W6] 'MENU2 READY

B	A	B	C	D
21	MENU2	Print-1	5-Print	Quit
22		1 year sched	5 year sched	Quit process
23		{branch PRINT_1}	{branch 5_PRINT}	{branch QUIT}
24				
25				
26				
27		Print-1	5-Print	Quit
28				
29		/pprA:A1.A:G29~	/pprA:A1.A:G77~	/reA:B5.A:B7~
30		agppq	agppq	{calc}
31		/reA:B5.A:B7~	/reA:B5.A:B7~	{goto}A:A1~
32		{calc}	{calc}	{quit}
33		{menubranch MENU1}	{menubranch MENU1}	
34				
35				

Figure 12-31
Part 2

B	A	B	C	D	E	F
1	Macro Multi		Macro for illustrating the use of			
2			multiple-tiered menus			
3						
4	MULTI	{menubranch MENU1}				
5						
6	MENU	Principal	Int-Rate	Time	Schedule	End
7		Loan amount	Interest rate	Loan period	Print-sched	Quit process
8		{branch PRINCIPAL}	{branch INT-RATE}	{branch TIME}	{branch SCHEDULE}	{branch END}
9						
10		Principal	Int-Rate	Time	Schedule	End
11						
12		/wgrm	/wgrm	/wgrm	{calc}	/reA:B5.A:B7~
13		{goto}A:B5~	{goto}A:B6~	{goto}A:B7~	{menubranch MENU2}	{calc}
14		{?}~	{?}~	{?}~		{goto}A:A1~
15		{goto}A:A1~	{goto}A:A1~	{goto}A:A1~		{quit}
16		{menubranch MENU1}	{menubranch MENU1}	{menubranch MENU1}		
17						
18						
19						
20						
21	MENU	Print-1	5-Print	Quit		
22		1 year sched	5 year sched	Quit process		
23		{branch PRINT-1}	{branch 5-PRINT}	{branch QUIT}		
24						
25						
26						
27		Print-1	5-Print	Quit		
28						
29		/pprA:A1.A:G29~	/pprA:A1.A:G77~	/reA:B5.A:B7~		
30		agppq	agppq	{calc}		
31		/reA:B5.A:B7~	/reA:B5.A:B7~	{goto}A:A1~		
32		{calc}	{calc}	{quit}		
33		{menubranch MENU1}	{menubranch MENU1}			

Figure 12-31
Part 3

To complete this exercise, retrieve the file AMORT and insert an additional worksheet after the AMORT worksheet for the two-tiered menu macro. After placing the title and macro name on your worksheet, your screen should look like Figure 12-32. To see more of what appears in the columns, change the column width for column A to 6 and widen columns B through F so each column will display 13 characters.

```
B:A1: 'Macro Multi                                                    READY

 B    A          B          C          D          E          F          G          H
 1   Macro Multi       Macro for illustrating the use of
 2                     multiple-tiered menus
 3
 4   MULTI
 5
 6
```

Figure 12-32

When you execute a user-designed menu macro, you must include a {menubranch} command to indicate to 1-2-3 on which menu you want to start. To include this command on the macro worksheet:

Move	the cell pointer to cell B:B4
Enter	{menubranch MENU1}

To place the MENU1 label in your macro:

Move	the cell pointer to cell B:A6
Enter	MENU1

To include the MENU1 menu options in your macro:

Move	the cell pointer to cell B:B6
Enter	Principal
Move	the cell pointer to cell B:C6
Enter	Int-Rate
Move	the cell pointer to cell B:D6
Enter	Time
Move	the cell pointer to cell B:E6
Enter	Schedule

Move the cell pointer to cell B:F6

Enter End

At this point, you have placed the menu options for MENU1 on the macro worksheet. You now need to create the range name MENU1 and include the location of the first menu option, B:B6, as its range.

To place the description for each menu option that will appear in the control panel when the menu option is highlighted by the menu pointer:

Move the cell pointer to cell B:B7

Enter Loan amount

Move the cell pointer to cell B:C7

Enter Interest rate

Move the cell pointer to cell B:D7

Enter Loan period

Move the cell pointer to cell B:E7

Enter Print-sched

Move the cell pointer to cell B:F7

Enter Quit process

In the single-tier menu example, you placed the macro instructions for each option immediately below the description of the menu option. For this exercise, you place the instructions several cells below the macro options to illustrate another approach for entering them.

To start the process for placing the instructions for the macro options:

Copy the menu options in cells B:B6..B:E6 to cells B:B10..B:E10

You now need to define the range names for Principal, Int-Rate, Time, Schedule and End. Include the individual cells B:B12 through B:F12, respectively, as the range for each of the menu option range names. For example, the range name Principal should have cell B:B12 as its range and End should have cell B:F12 as its range.

Here, you need to enter the instructions for the various menu options below the menu option identifiers that appear in row 10. The instructions for the Principal menu option must state that the manual calculation mode is to be used, the cell pointer needs to be moved to the cell for the user to enter the principal amount A:B5, the macro must pause for the user to enter the principal value and control is to be transferred to MENU1 after the principal amount is entered.

To place the appropriate instructions on your macro worksheet:

Move the cell pointer to cell B:B12

Enter '/wgrm

Move the cell pointer to cell B:B13

Enter {goto}A:B5~

Move the cell pointer to cell B:B14

Enter {?}~

Move the cell pointer to cell B:B15

Enter {goto}A:A1~

Move the cell pointer to cell B:B16

Enter {menubranch MENU1}

The macro instructions for the Int-Rate and Time menu options are exactly the same as for the Principal menu option except for the cell in which the appropriate data is to be entered.

To place the instructions for the Int-Rate menu option on your macro worksheet:

Move the cell pointer to cell B:C12

Enter '/wgrm

Move the cell pointer to cell B:C13

Enter {goto}A:B6~

Move the cell pointer to cell B:C14

Enter {?}~

Move the cell pointer to cell B:C15

Enter {goto}A:A1~

Move	the cell pointer to cell B:C16
Enter	{menubranch MENU1}

To include the instructions for the Time menu option in your macro:

Move	the cell pointer to cell B:D12
Enter	'/wgrm
Move	the cell pointer to cell B:D13
Enter	{goto}A:B7~
Move	the cell pointer to cell B:D14
Enter	{?}~
Move	the cell pointer to cell B:D15
Enter	{goto}A:A1~
Move	the cell pointer to cell B:D16
Enter	{menubranch MENU1}

For the Schedule menu option you need instructions for calculating the loan amortization schedule and transferring control to the menu for printing the schedule. To place these instructions on your macro worksheet:

Move	the cell pointer to cell B:E12
Enter	{calc}
Move	the cell pointer to cell B:E13
Enter	{menubranch MENU2}

The final menu option for MENU1 to consider is END. For this menu option, you must enter instructions for erasing the principal, interest rate and time period values, removing the CALC indicator from the screen, moving the cell pointer to cell A:A1 and stopping the execution of the macro. To incorporate these instructions on your macro worksheet:

Move	the cell pointer to cell B:F12
Enter	'/reA:B5.A:B7~
Move	the cell pointer to cell B:F13
Enter	{calc}

Move the cell pointer to cell B:F14

Enter {goto}A:A1~

Move the cell pointer to cell B:F15

Enter {quit}

Now you need to place {branch} commands in the cells immediately below the descriptions for the menu options so control will be transferred to the appropriate macro instructions for the various menu options. To place these branch commands in the proper cells:

Move the cell pointer to cell B:B8

Enter {branch PRINCIPAL}

Move the cell pointer to cell B:C8

Enter {branch INT-RATE}

Move the cell pointer to cell B:D8

Enter {branch TIME}

Move the cell pointer to cell B:E8

Enter {branch SCHEDULE}

Move the cell pointer to cell B:F8

Enter {branch END}

Execution is transferred to MENU2 when you select the Schedule menu option on MENU1. The Print-1 and 5-Print menu options on MENU2 provide you with the capability to print a 1-year or 5-year amortization schedule.

You are now ready to place the macro instructions for MENU2 on your macro worksheet. Use the information in Figure 12-33 to enter the macro instructions for MENU2.

B	A	B	C	D	E	F
1	Macro Multi		Macro for illustrating the use of			
2			multiple-tiered menus			
3						
4	MULTI	{menubranch MENU1}				
5						
6	MENU	Principal	Int-Rate	Time	Schedule	End
7		Loan amount	Interest rate	Loan period	Print-sched	Quit process
8		{branch PRINCIPAL}	{branch INT-RATE}	{branch TIME}	{branch SCHEDULE}	{branch END}
9						
10		Principal	Int-Rate	Time	Schedule	End
11						
12		/wgrm	/wgrm	/wgrm	{calc}	/reA:B5.A:B7~
13		{goto}A:B5~	{goto}A:B6~	{goto}A:B7~	{menubranch MENU2}	{calc}
14		{?}~	{?}~	{?}~		{goto}A:A1~
15		{goto}A:A1~	{goto}A:A1~	{goto}A:A1~		{quit}
16		{menubranch MENU1}	{menubranch MENU1}	{menubranch MENU1}		
17						
18						
19						
20						
21	MENU	Print-1	5-Print	Quit		
22		1 year sched	5 year sched	Quit process		
23		{branch PRINT-1}	{branch 5-PRINT}	{branch QUIT}		
24						
25						
26						
27		Print-1	5-Print	Quit		
28						
29		/pprA:A1.A:G29~	/pprA:A1.A:G77~	/reA:B5.A:B7~		
30		agppq	agppq	{calc}		
31		/reA:B5.A:B7~	/reA:B5.A:B7~	{goto}A:A1~		
32		{calc}	{calc}	{quit}		
33		{menubranch MENU1}	{menubranch MENU1}			

Figure 12-33

After you have entered the information, be sure to create range names as follows:

Range Name	Cell to Include in the Range
MENU2	B:B21
PRINT-1	B:B29
5-PRINT	B:C29
QUIT	B:D29

After you have compared the multi-tiered menu you designed with Figure 12-33, make any necessary changes. Name your macro MULTI. Include the cell B:B4 as the range for the macro range name, MULTI and save the worksheets using the file name MULTIMAC.

Move the cell pointer to cell A:B5 and erase the cells A:B5 through A:B7. The ERR indicator may appear in some of the worksheet cells. When you execute the macro MULTI, the ERR indicator will disappear from the cells. Execute the macro MULTI. Figure 12-34 Part 1 includes the menu when it initially appears on the screen.

```
A:B5: (C2) [W11]                                                          MENU
Principal  Int-Rate  Time  Schedule  End
Loan amount
 A   A        B        C          D          E          F          G
 1                   LOAN AMORTIZATION
 2
 3       ASSUMPTIONS
 4       ======================================================
 5                             PRINCIPAL
 6                             INTEREST RATE PER YEAR
 7                             TIME PERIOD IN MONTHS
 8             0.83%           MONTHLY INTEREST RATE
 9           531.18            CALCULATED PAYMENT AMOUNT
10       ======================================================
11
12  **********************************************************************
13                                                 PRINCIPAL   INTEREST
14   PMT   PAYMENT  PRINCIPAL  INTEREST  PRINCIPAL    PAID        PAID
15   NUM   AMOUNT     AMOUNT    AMOUNT    BALANCE    TO DATE    TO DATE
16  **********************************************************************
17                                      25,000.00
18    1   531.18    322.84    208.33   24,677.16    322.84     208.33
19    2   531.18    325.53    205.64   24,351.62    648.38     413.98
20    3   531.18    328.25    202.93   24,023.38    976.62     616.91
                                      CMD      CALC
```

Figure 12-34
Part 1

To illustrate the use of the macro:

Select	Principal
Enter	50000
Select	Int-Rate
Enter	.10
Select	Time
Enter	12

To print the resulting amortization schedule:

Select	Schedule

Figure 12-34 Part 2 illustrates the screen after the Schedule option is selected.

```
A:A1: [W5]                                                          MENU
Print-1  5-Print  Quit
1 year sched
 A    A       B          C          D          E          F          G
1                     LOAN AMORTIZATION
2
3        ASSUMPTIONS
4        ========================================================
5        $50,000.00              PRINCIPAL
6             10.00%             INTEREST RATE PER YEAR
7                 12             TIME PERIOD IN MONTHS
8              0.83%             MONTHLY INTEREST RATE
9           4,395.79             CALCULATED PAYMENT AMOUNT
10       ========================================================
11
12  *************************************************************************
13                                                   PRINCIPAL    INTEREST
14   PMT   PAYMENT  PRINCIPAL  INTEREST   PRINCIPAL     PAID        PAID
15   NUM   AMOUNT     AMOUNT    AMOUNT     BALANCE     TO DATE     TO DATE
16  *************************************************************************
17                                        50,000.00
18     1  4,395.79  3,979.13     416.67   46,020.87    3,979.13      416.67
19     2  4,395.79  4,012.29     383.51   42,008.59    7,991.41      800.17
20     3  4,395.79  4,045.72     350.07   37,962.86   12,037.14    1,150.25
                                          CMD
```

Figure 12-34
Part 2

Select Print-1

After the schedule is printed:

Select End

Your screen should look like Figure 12-34 Part 3.

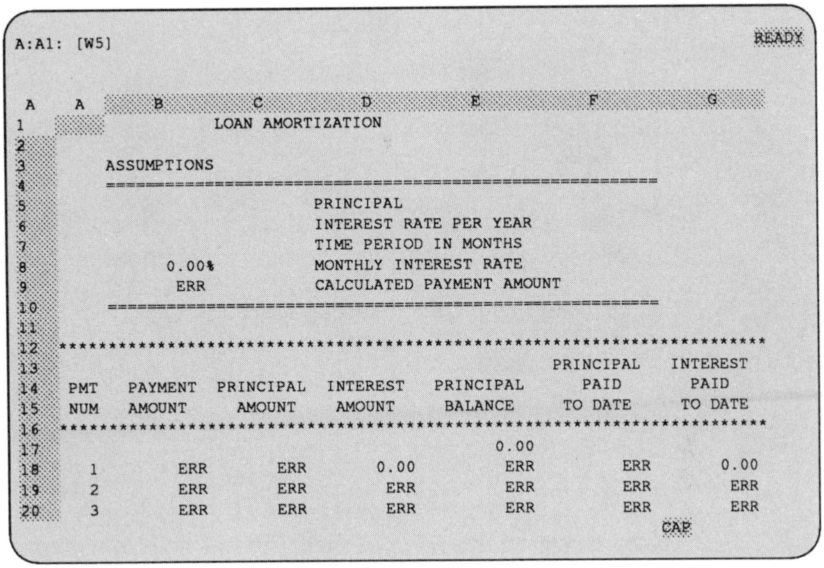

```
A:A1: [W5]                                                         READY

A   A      B          C          D          E          F          G
1                   LOAN AMORTIZATION
2
3       ASSUMPTIONS
4       =========================================================
5                                    PRINCIPAL
6                                    INTEREST RATE PER YEAR
7                                    TIME PERIOD IN MONTHS
8              0.00%                 MONTHLY INTEREST RATE
9               ERR                  CALCULATED PAYMENT AMOUNT
10      =========================================================
11
12 ***************************************************************************
13                                                        PRINCIPAL    INTEREST
14  PMT   PAYMENT  PRINCIPAL  INTEREST   PRINCIPAL          PAID         PAID
15  NUM   AMOUNT     AMOUNT    AMOUNT     BALANCE         TO DATE      TO DATE
16 ***************************************************************************
17                                             0.00
18   1       ERR        ERR       0.00          ERR           ERR         0.00
19   2       ERR        ERR        ERR          ERR           ERR          ERR
20   3       ERR        ERR        ERR          ERR           ERR          ERR
                                                          CAP
```

Figure 12-34
Part 3

■ /X COMMANDS

The /x commands were included in Lotus 1-2-3 Release 1A. These commands provided users with some programming capability. In Lotus 1-2-3 Release 3 there are equivalent commands available that are easier to understand. The /x commands are available in later releases of 1-2-3 to maintain compatibility with macros developed using Lotus 1-2-3 Release 1A.

/xg	goto programming command
/xm	menu processing command
/xi	if-then programming command
/xn	message command to prompt user to input a number
/xl	message command to prompt user to input a label
/xc	subroutine call command
/xr	return to macro from subroutine command
/xq	quit programming command

/xg

The /xg command transfers control to a specific cell in a macro sequence. Execution then continues at the specified location.

The /xg command has the following format:

```
/xg location~
```

The equivalent advanced macro command in later versions of 1-2-3 is {branch}.

/xm

The /xm command is used to direct control to a user-designed menu in a specified location.

The /xm command has the following format:

```
/xm location~
```

The equivalent advanced macro command in later versions of 1-2-3 is {menubranch}.

/xi

The /xi command is used to execute different steps in a macro depending on a specified condition.

The /xi command has the following format:

```
/xi condition~
```

If the condition is true, the macro commands to the right of the condition are executed. If the condition is false, the macro cell in the row immediately below the /xi command is executed. The equivalent advanced macro command in later versions of 1-2-3 is {if}.

/xn

The /xn command is used to prompt an individual to enter a number that will be placed in the cell specified by the location. The prompt appears at the top of the screen.

The /xn command has the following format:

```
/xn message~location~
```

The equivalent advanced macro command in later versions of 1-2-3 is {getnumber}.

/xl

The /xl command is similar to the /xn command, except a user is prompted to enter a string of characters. The characters are placed in the cell specified by the location. A maximum of 39 characters can be included in the message.

The /xl command has the following format:

```
/xl message~location~
```

The equivalent advanced macro command in later versions of 1-2-3 is {getlabel}.

/xc

The /xc command directs control to a location where a subroutine appears. A subroutine is a set of macro steps located outside of the main macro. Subroutines are often used when a specific condition is satisfied within a macro. The /xc command is used within the main macro to indicate where the subroutine appears on the spreadsheet.

The /xc command has the following format:

```
/xc location~
```

The equivalent advanced macro command in later versions of 1-2-3 is {subroutine}.

/xr

The /xr command is used in conjunction with the /xc command. The /xr command is used to indicate that a subroutine operation has been completed and it is time to return to the main macro. When an /xr command is encountered in a subroutine, control is transferred to the macro cell immediately following the /xc command that called the subroutine. Execution of the main macro then continues.

The /xr command has the following format:

```
/xr
```

The equivalent advanced macro command in later versions of 1-2-3 is {return}.

/xq

The /xq command stops the execution of the macro.

The /xq command has the following format:

```
/xq
```

The equivalent advanced macro command in later versions is {quit}.

Another way to stop a macro is by holding the Ctrl key down and then pressing the Break key.

SUMMARY

Macros provide an efficient way of automating repetitive procedures. They can be used for operations such as combining files, printing a spreadsheet, completing a data query, sorting data and restricting input to specific cells. Advanced macro commands can be used to enter sequences of numbers, to execute a loop of instructions, to prompt users to enter labels and numeric data, to create subroutines and to develop user-designed menus. Macros provide users of Lotus 1-2-3 with immense flexibility in developing various applications.

KEY CONCEPTS

Advanced macro commands
Debugging a macro
Interactive macros
Looping through a sequence of macro commands
Macro
Macro symbols
Multiple-tiered menus
Single-tiered menus
Subroutines
User-designed menus
/X commands

CHAPTER TWELVE
EXERCISE 1

INSTRUCTIONS: Circle T if the statement is True and F is the statement is False.

T F 1. You cannot use macros to place a sequence of values on a worksheet.

T F 2. A macro can be automatically executed when a file is retrieved by naming the macro ZERO.

T F 3. A series of macro instructions can be repeated only if you know how many times the instructions need to be repeated.

T F 4. A maximum of 10 menu options can be included in any user-designed menu.

T F 5. The /X commands have equivalent macro commands available in later releases of Lotus 1-2-3 that are easier to understand.

T F 6. Macros can be used to restrict the input by a user of a worksheet to a specific set of cells.

T F 7. The only way to use an interactive macro is if you force the macro to execute when the file containing the macro is retrieved.

T F 8. Macros can be written that prompt the user to input information.

T F 9. At most, five tiers can be incorporated in a user-designed menu.

CHAPTER TWELVE
EXERCISE 2
Creating a Macro to Query a Database Table

INSTRUCTIONS: Retrieve the file PERSON you created as an exercise in Chapter 8.

Write a macro that extracts the last names and first names for the individuals living in New York or San Antonio with the last name Adams. Include a print macro that prints the database table and the extracted records.

Place the macros for extracting the appropriate records and printing the results along with the database table on a separate worksheet. The macros should be properly documented.

Print the worksheet containing the database table and extracted records. Also, print the worksheet containing the macros you created.

CHAPTER TWELVE
EXERCISE 3
Creating a Macro for Entering Numbers

INSTRUCTIONS: Make sure you have a blank worksheet on your screen.

Create a macro that permits you to enter numbers across a row of a worksheet so that you do not have to move to the next cell after you press the ↵ key. Place the macro on a separate worksheet. Document the macro properly.

Enter the numbers 100, 25, 125 and 200 in cells B10 through E10 using the macro.

Print the worksheet containing the numbers you input. Also, print the worksheet containing the macro for entering the numbers.

CHAPTER TWELVE
EXERCISE 4
Executing a Loop of Instructions When the Number of Iterations is Known

INSTRUCTIONS: Make sure you have a blank worksheet on your screen.

Enter the following data on a worksheet.

Cell	Value
A1	10
B1	15
C1	5
A2	15
B2	20
C2	25
A3	30
B3	20
C3	10
A4	5
B4	15
C4	25
A5	15
B5	25
C5	10

Create a macro that computes for each row the sum of the cells in column A and column B and then multiplies the sum by the value in column C. Place the results in column D of each row. You can assume that you know to repeat the calculation procedure five times.

Prepare a macro that prints the worksheet with the final results. Place the macros for computing and printing the results on a separate worksheet. Document the macros properly.

Print the worksheet containing the values you entered and the resulting computations. Also, print the worksheet that includes the macros.

CHAPTER TWELVE
EXERCISE 5
Executing a Loop of Instructions When the Number of Iterations is Unknown

INSTRUCTIONS: Make sure you have a blank worksheet on your screen.

Enter the following data on a worksheet.

Cell	Value
A1	20
B1	25
C1	15
A2	25
B2	30
C2	35
A3	40
B3	30
C3	20
A4	15
B4	25
C4	35
A5	25
B5	35
C5	20

Create a macro that subtracts for each row the value in column B from the value in column A and then divides the difference by the value in column C. Place the results in column D of each row. Assume that you do not know the number of times needed to repeat the calculation procedure.

Prepare a macro that prints the worksheet with the final results. Place the macros for computing and printing the results on a separate worksheet. Document the macros properly.

Print the worksheet containing the values you entered and the resulting computations. Also, print the worksheet that includes the macros.

CHAPTER TWELVE
EXERCISE 6
Prompting a User to Enter Labels and Numeric Data

INSTRUCTIONS: Create an application of your own for prompting a user to enter labels and numeric data.

Print the worksheets containing the application you prepare and the macro you create. Document the macro properly.

CHAPTER TWELVE
EXERCISE 7
Creating a Single-Tier Menu

INSTRUCTIONS: Create an application of your own for using a single-tier menu.

Print the worksheets containing the application you prepare and the single-tier menu macro you create. Document the macro properly.

CHAPTER TWELVE
EXERCISE 8
Creating a Two-Tier Menu

INSTRUCTIONS: Create an application of your own for using a two-tier menu.

Print the worksheets containing the application you prepare and the two-tier menu macro you create. Document the macro properly.

CHAPTER TWELVE
EXERCISE 9
Creating a Three-Tier Menu

INSTRUCTIONS: Create an application of your own for using a three-tier menu.

Print the worksheets containing the application you prepare and the three-tier menu macro you create. Document the macro properly.

CHAPTER THIRTEEN

SIMPLE TEXT PROCESSING

OBJECTIVES

In this chapter, you will learn to:

- Write notes on a worksheet
- Manipulate labels to create a letter

CHAPTER OVERVIEW

Although Lotus 1-2-3 does not have **true** word processing capabilities, it does provide a way to perform simple text processing tasks by manipulating labels in the worksheet environment. You can use text processing to provide documentation on a worksheet or even to create a letter or memorandum. The first exercise in this chapter shows how to use 1-2-3 to include notes on a worksheet. The second exercise shows you how to create a letter.

WRITING NOTES ON A WORKSHEET

In the following exercise, notes will be entered below a worksheet.

Entering Text on a Worksheet

In this exercise, text will be placed on the BUDGET worksheet. Retrieve the file BUDGET.

To input the text:

Move	the cell pointer to cell A35

At this point, the CAPS indicator should be off.

Type	If desired, the growth rate assumptions can be changed by modifying the data in cells C25 through E28
Press	↵
Move	the cell pointer to cell A36

Do not attempt to correct any typographical errors at this time. Your screen should look like Figure 13-1.

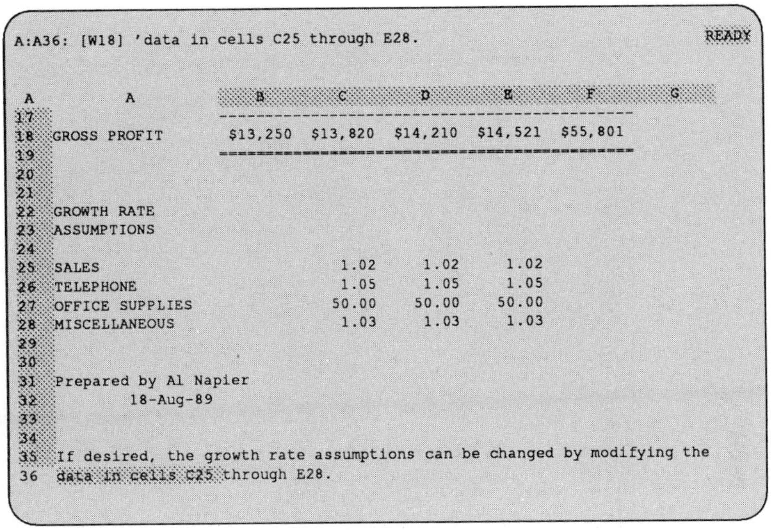

```
A:A36: [W18] 'data in cells C25 through E28.                              READY

A         A           B         C         D         E         F         G
17                 -------------------------------------------------
18 GROSS PROFIT      $13,250   $13,820   $14,210   $14,521   $55,801
19                 =================================================
20
21
22 GROWTH RATE
23 ASSUMPTIONS
24
25 SALES                       1.02      1.02      1.02
26 TELEPHONE                   1.05      1.05      1.05
27 OFFICE SUPPLIES            50.00     50.00     50.00
28 MISCELLANEOUS               1.03      1.03      1.03
29
30
31 Prepared by Al Napier
32         18-Aug-89
33
34
35 If desired, the growth rate assumptions can be changed by modifying the
36 data in cells C25 through E28.
```

Figure 13-1

To justify the text:

Press	/
Select	Range
Select	Justify

When prompted for the range to justify:

Press	(Esc)
Move	the cell pointer to cell A35
Type	.
Move	the cell pointer to cell G35
Press	↵

The text should now be justified below the worksheet and your screen should look like Figure 13-2. If you are inserting text above a worksheet, be sure to highlight the entire range in which the text is to appear rather than highlighting only the first row when specifying the Justify range. If the Justify range is not large enough, columns in the worksheet may be disturbed when executing the **R**ange **J**ustify command sequence.

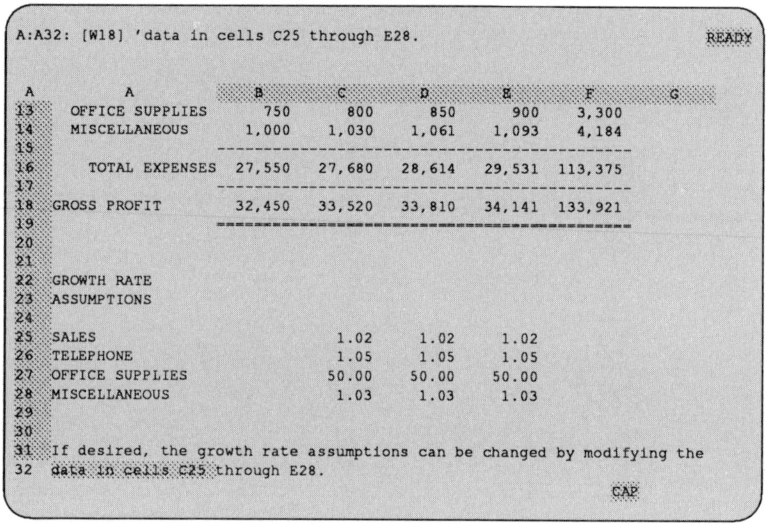

A:A32: [W18] 'data in cells C25 through E28. READY

A	A	B	C	D	E	F	G
13	OFFICE SUPPLIES	750	800	850	900	3,300	
14	MISCELLANEOUS	1,000	1,030	1,061	1,093	4,184	
15		----------	----------	----------	----------	----------	
16	TOTAL EXPENSES	27,550	27,680	28,614	29,531	113,375	
17		----------	----------	----------	----------	----------	
18	GROSS PROFIT	32,450	33,520	33,810	34,141	133,921	
19		==========	==========	==========	==========	==========	
20							
21							
22	GROWTH RATE						
23	ASSUMPTIONS						
24							
25	SALES		1.02	1.02	1.02		
26	TELEPHONE		1.05	1.05	1.05		
27	OFFICE SUPPLIES		50.00	50.00	50.00		
28	MISCELLANEOUS		1.03	1.03	1.03		
29							
30							
31	If desired, the growth rate assumptions can be changed by modifying the						
32	data in cells C25 through E28.						

CAP

Figure 13-2

Correcting Typographical Errors

A summary of how to correct errors follows:

- Move to the line where the typographical error appears.
- The cell pointer must be in the column where the label was input. For example, if the label was input in column A; all editing will be from column A.
- Press the [F2] key.
- When the [F2] key is pressed, the label appears in the control panel so that it can be edited. If necessary, the [F2] key can be used to continue typing after the last word entered on a line. For example, a paragraph exceeding 512 characters forces you to press [↵] and justify the paragraph before continuing. Move to the last line of text and use the [F2] key to continue typing text.
- Use the directional arrow keys to move to the typographical error.
- To insert text at this point, begin to type the desired text. To delete text at this point, use the backspace key or the [Del] key. [Del] means **Delete**.
- You can press the [Ins] key to *toggle* between inserting text or replacing text. [Ins] stands for **Insert**. For example, to insert text, press the [Ins] key. Begin to type. 1-2-3

is in *OVR* (overstrike) mode and all entered text will be typed over existing text. Press the [Ins] key again. Begin to type. All entered text is inserted without typing over existing text.

- After editing the line, press ↵
- Use the **R**ange **J**ustify command repeatedly to wrap text appropriately and to take into account any editing that was completed.

The steps above will have to be executed for *every* line that needs to be edited.

TEXT MANIPULATION USING 1-2-3

The following exercise demonstrates how to prepare a letter using 1-2-3. A printout of the completed letter is displayed in Figure 13-3.

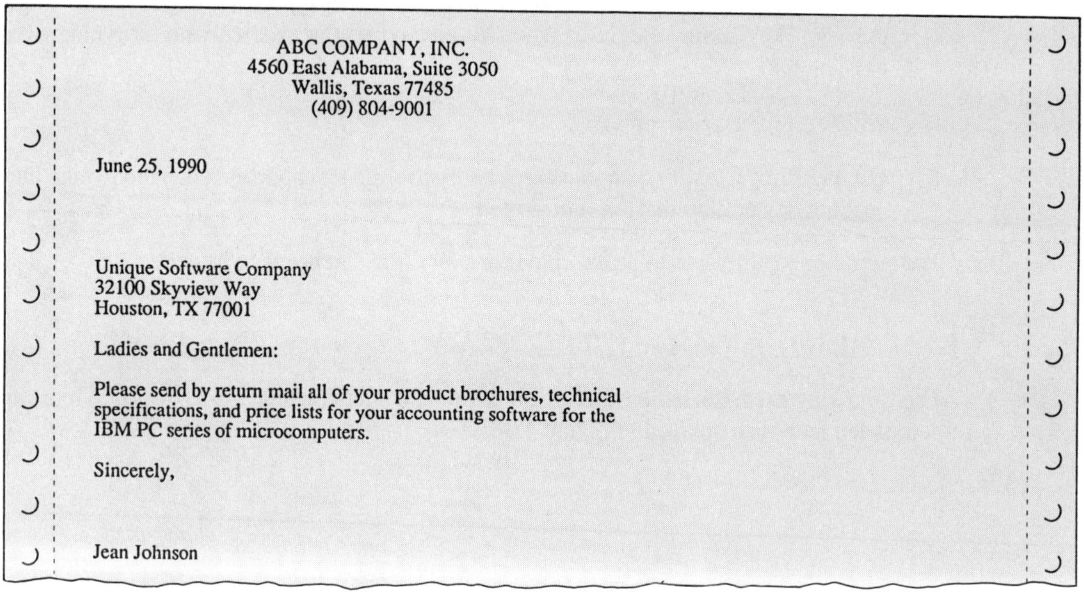

ABC COMPANY, INC.
4560 East Alabama, Suite 3050
Wallis, Texas 77485
(409) 804-9001

June 25, 1990

Unique Software Company
32100 Skyview Way
Houston, TX 77001

Ladies and Gentlemen:

Please send by return mail all of your product brochures, technical specifications, and price lists for your accounting software for the IBM PC series of microcomputers.

Sincerely,

Jean Johnson

Figure 13-3

Start with a blank worksheet on your screen.

Widening Column A

The cell pointer should be in cell A1. To widen column A:

Press /

Select	Worksheet
Select	Column
Select	Set-Width
Type	72
Press	↵

It is not necessary to widen column A to write a letter, but doing so makes it much easier to determine how many characters are on each line. Your screen should look like Figure 13-4. Only column A should be visible on the screen.

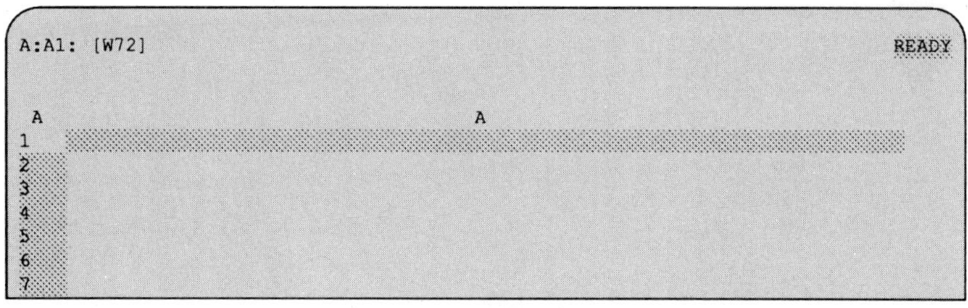

Figure 13-4

Creating a Simple Letter

In this section, you will create a simple letter using 1-2-3.

Entering the Return Address

To input the return address:

Move	the cell pointer to cell A1
Make	sure the CAP indicator is on
Type	^ABC COMPANY, INC.

The ^ symbol centers ABC COMPANY, INC in column A.

Press	↓

To turn the CAP indicator off:

Press	Caps Lock

The following text will not be typed in capital letters.

Type ^4560 East Alabama, Suite 3050

Press ↓

Type ^Wallis, Texas 77485

Press ↓

Type ^(409) 804-9001

Press ↵

The address should now be entered in cells A1 through A4. Your screen should look like Figure 13-5.

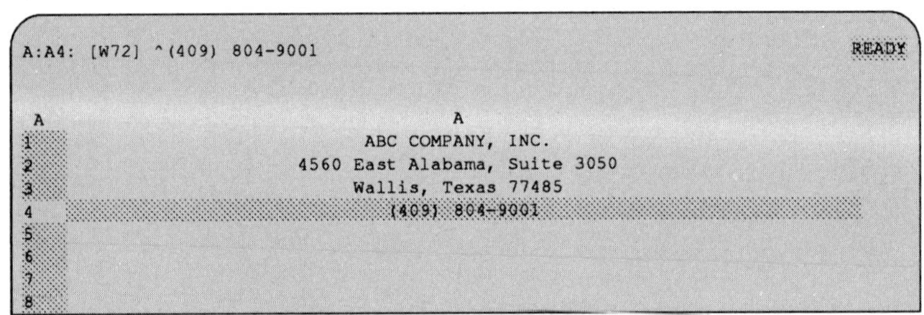

Figure 13-5

Entering the Date, Company Address and Salutation

To input the date:

Move the cell pointer to cell A7

Type June 25, 1990

Press ↵

To input the company address:

Move the cell pointer to cell A12

Type Unique Software Company

Press ↓

Type '32100 Skyview Way

The apostrophe is the label prefix and is located on the key with the double quote. The use of the apostrophe is necessary for the entry **32100 Skyview Way** to indicate that the cell entry is to be treated as a label and not a value. If the apostrophe is not included, 1-2-3 will not allow the text to be entered (it will "beep" when ↵ is pressed). The "beeping" occurs because Lotus identifies cell entries as a value or a label by the first character. Since **32100 Skyview Way** begins with a value, but also has nonnumeric characters (Skyview Way, in addition to spaces), Lotus will not accept the entry as a legitimate value.

Press ↓

Type Houston, TX 77001

Press ↵

To input the salutation:

Move the cell pointer to cell A16

Type Ladies and Gentlemen:

Press ↵

Your screen should look like Figure 13-6.

```
A:A16: [W72] 'Ladies and Gentlemen:                                        READY

 A                                    A
 1                              ABC COMPANY, INC.
 2                        4560 East Alabama, Suite 3050
 3                              Wallis, Texas 77485
 4                                (409) 804-9001
 5
 6
 7   June 25, 1990
 8
 9
10
11
12   Unique Software Company
13   32100 Skyview Way
14   Houston, TX 77001
15
16   Ladies and Gentlemen:
17
18
19
20
```

Figure 13-6

Entering the Body of the Letter

Without pressing the ↵ key, type the body of the letter:

Move the cell pointer to cell A18

Type Please send by return mail all of your product brochures, technical specifications, and price lists for your accounting software for the IBM PC series of microcomputers.

As the text is typed, it will scroll across the top of the screen. Do not attempt to correct any typographical errors at this time. When you are through typing the text:

Press ↵

Move the cell pointer to cell A21

The text is entered as one long label in cell A18. Your screen should look like Figure 13-7.

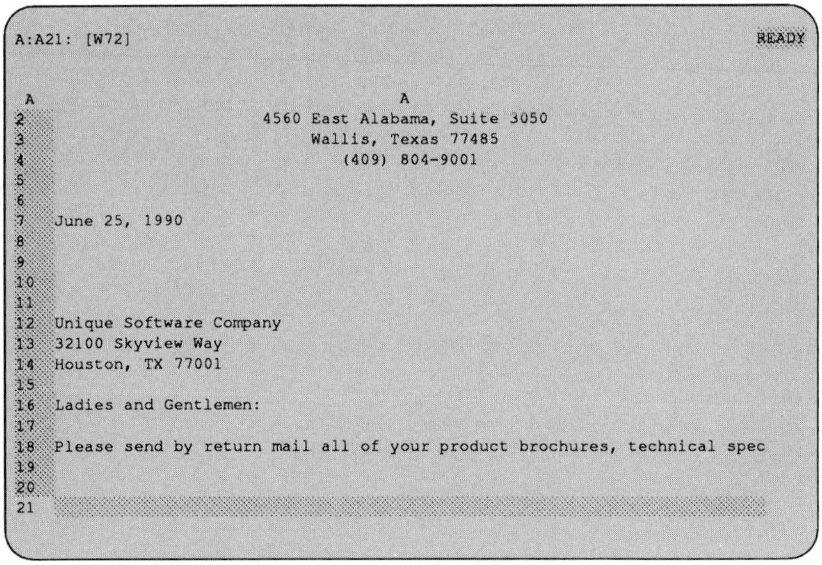

```
A:A21: [W72]                                                    READY

 A                              A
 2                  4560 East Alabama, Suite 3050
 3                       Wallis, Texas 77485
 4                          (409) 804-9001
 5
 6
 7   June 25, 1990
 8
 9
10
11
12   Unique Software Company
13   32100 Skyview Way
14   Houston, TX 77001
15
16   Ladies and Gentlemen:
17
18   Please send by return mail all of your product brochures, technical spec
19
20
21
```

Figure 13-7

Justifying or "Wrapping" the Text

To make the text "wrap" to the rows below:

Move the cell pointer to cell A18

Press /

Select Range

Select Justify

When prompted for the range to justify:

Press ↵

The text now has "wrapped" to the rows below. The text consists of three labels —one label each in cells A18, A19 and A20 respectively. Except for possible typographical errors, your screen should look like Figure 13-8.

```
A:A20: [W72] 'IBM PC series of microcomputers.                         READY

 A                                A
 1                          ABC COMPANY, INC.
 2                    4560 East Alabama, Suite 3050
 3                         Wallis, Texas 77485
 4                            (409) 804-9001
 5
 6
 7  June 25, 1990
 8
 9
10
11
12  Unique Software Company
13  32100 Skyview Way
14  Houston, TX 77001
15
16  Ladies and Gentlemen:
17
18  Please send by return mail all of your product brochures, technical
19  specifications, and price lists for your accounting software for the
20  IBM PC series of microcomputers.
```

Figure 13-8

Entering the Closing

To complete the letter:

Move the cell pointer to cell A22

Type Sincerely,

Press ↵

Move the cell pointer to cell A26

Type Jean Johnson

Press ↵

Except for possible typographical errors, your screen should look like Figure 13-9.

```
A:A26: [W72] 'Jean Johnson                                          READY

 A                                    A
 7  June 25, 1990
 8
 9
10
11
12  Unique Software Company
13  32100 Skyview Way
14  Houston, TX 77001
15
16  Ladies and Gentlemen:
17
18  Please send by return mail all of your product brochures, technical
19  specifications, and price lists for your accounting software for the
20  IBM PC series of microcomputers.
21
22  Sincerely,
23
24
25
26  Jean Johnson
```

Figure 13-9

If there are errors that need to be corrected, follow the instructions in the previous section titled Correcting Typographical Errors to edit the letter.

SUMMARY

Simple word processing capability is available in Lotus 1-2-3. Letters or memos and worksheet documentation can be written using the **R**ange **J**ustify command sequence to cause the text to "word wrap."

KEY CONCEPTS

Editing Text
Range Justify
Wrapping Text

CHAPTER THIRTEEN
EXERCISE 1

INSTRUCTIONS: Circle T if the statement is true and F if the statement is false.

T F 1. A column on a worksheet has to have a width of 72 before text can be justified.

T F 2. Each line of text is a separate label after the **R**ange **J**ustify command is executed.

T F 3. To edit a line of text that has been justified with the **R**ange **J**ustify command, use the F2 key.

T F 4. If the **R**ange **J**ustify command is executed with text above an existing worksheet, the Justify range should include enough space to justify the text without disturbing the worksheet below.

T F 5. The **R**ange **J**ustify command only performs if the Justify range consists of one column and text is not displayed under other columns.

CHAPTER THIRTEEN
EXERCISE 2
Editing Text

INSTRUCTIONS: Make sure you have a blank worksheet on your screen.

Enter the following text in cell A1:

```
Now is the time for all good men, women, and children
to come to the aid of their country.
```

Justify the sentence to appear across columns A-G.

Copy the text to cell A6.

Edit the text so the sentence reads as follows:

```
Now is the time for all good men and women to come
to the aid of their country.
```

Print the results.

CHAPTER THIRTEEN
EXERCISE 3
Creating a Memo

INSTRUCTIONS: Make sure you have a blank worksheet on your screen.

Enter the following text beginning in cell A1.

```
TO:
```

Enter the following text beginning in cell A3.

```
FROM:
```

Enter the following text in cell A5.

```
It has come to my attention that a number of new employees
have not yet attended the Lotus training seminars that
are currently available.  Please schedule as many
Beginning Lotus 1-2-3 seminars as necessary to provide
training for every new employee.  Furthermore, please
see that DOS classes for beginners are also scheduled.
```

Justify the text so that the text in cell A5 is displayed in columns A-G.

In cells B1 and B2, insert *Samantha Goldwyn* as the author of the memo and *All Training Coordinators* as the recipients.

Print the memo.

CHAPTER FOURTEEN

SUMMARY

As mentioned in the Introduction, the design of this book is intended for individuals who need to learn the capabilities of Lotus 1-2-3. Each chapter could be lengthened to include additional 1-2-3 capabilities for the features being discussed and an endless variety of applications could be added. However, the chapters are deliberately limited to the essential, basic concepts. Stressing the basics allows you to concentrate on the main idea of each exercise without being distracted by a multitude of other issues. At the same time, the examples are comprehensive and thorough enough to provide you with the tools you need to create larger, more complex spreadsheets. The next logical step is to apply the skills you learned in this book to your own applications.

APPENDIX A

LOTUS 1-2-3 COMMAND TREES

There are many Lotus 1-2-3 commands. The commands available in 1-2-3 are included on the command trees appearing in this appendix.

The menu below is the main menu that appears when the menu structure is entered. The pages following include the menu structure for the various menu options.

Worksheet	Range	Copy	Move	File	Print	Graph	Data	System	Quit

Worksheet Commands

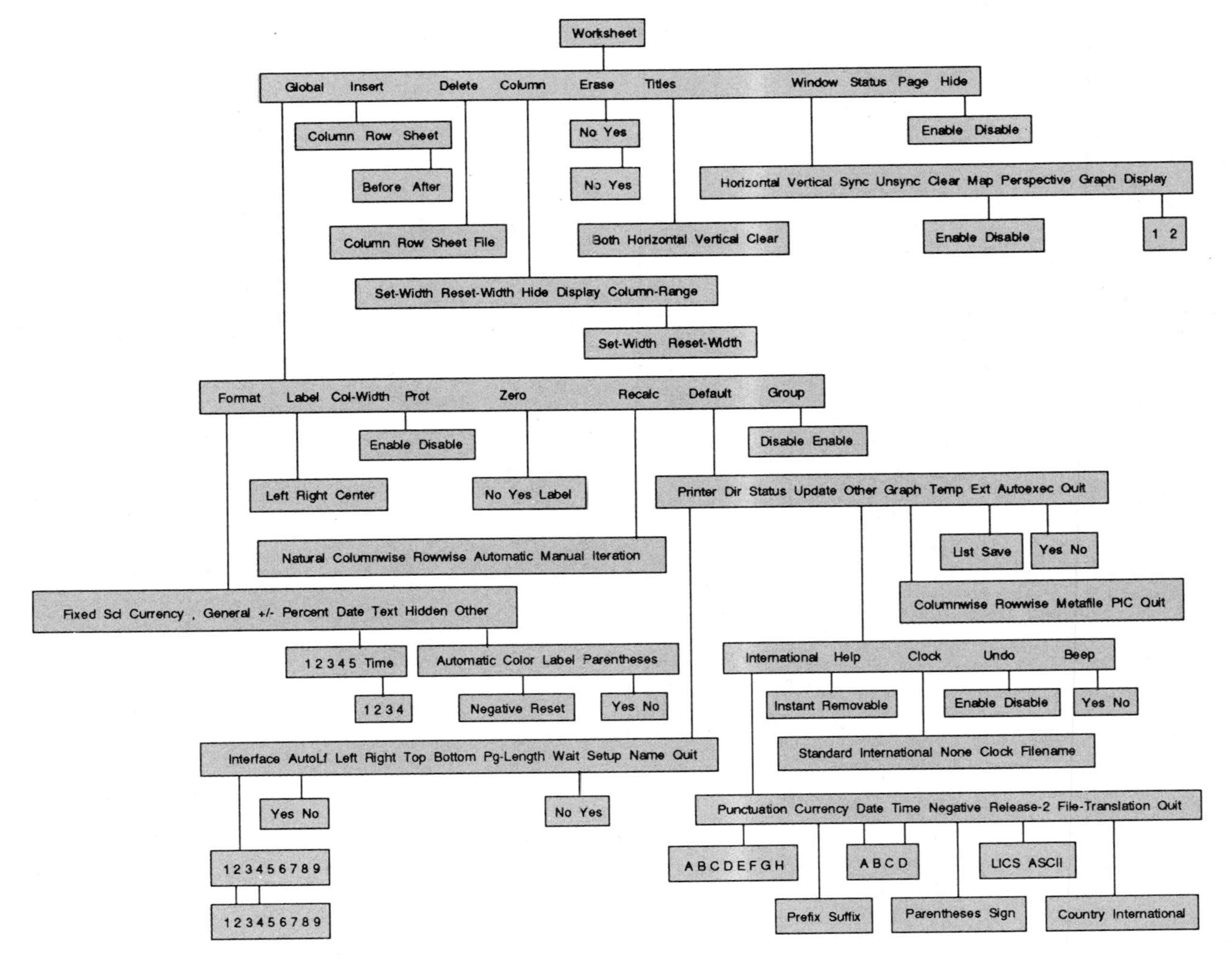

Range Commands

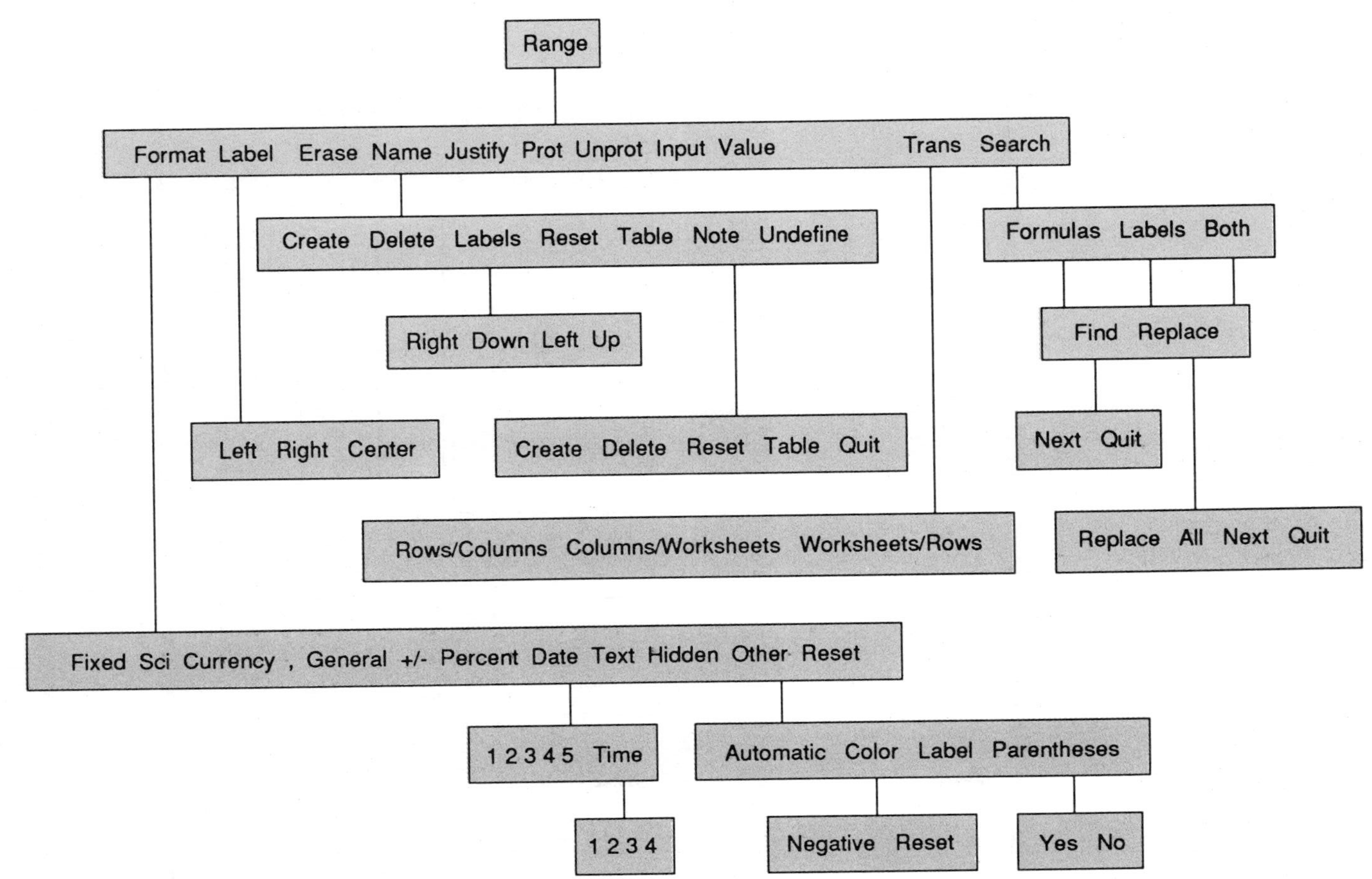

File Commands

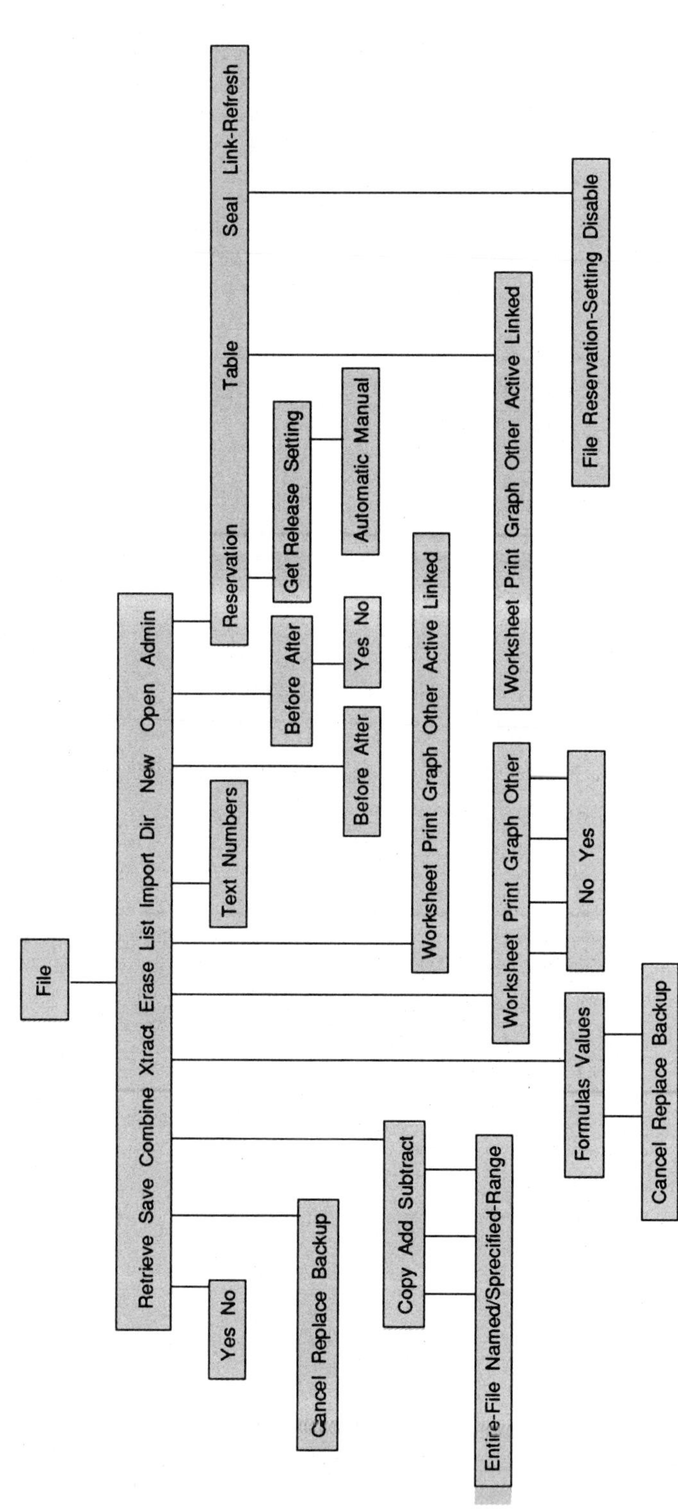

LOTUS 1-2-3 COMMAND TREES 727

Print Commands

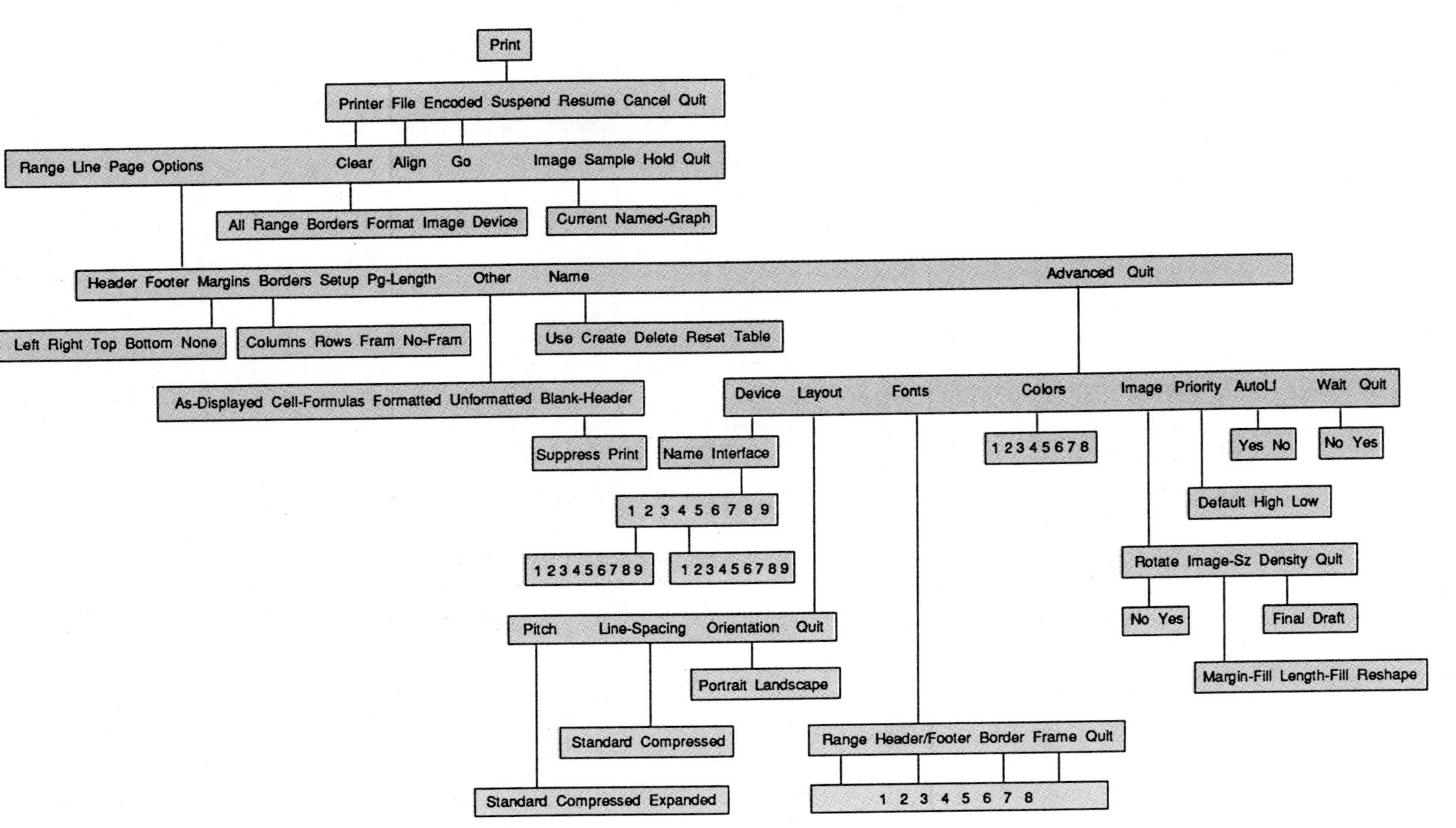

Graph Commands

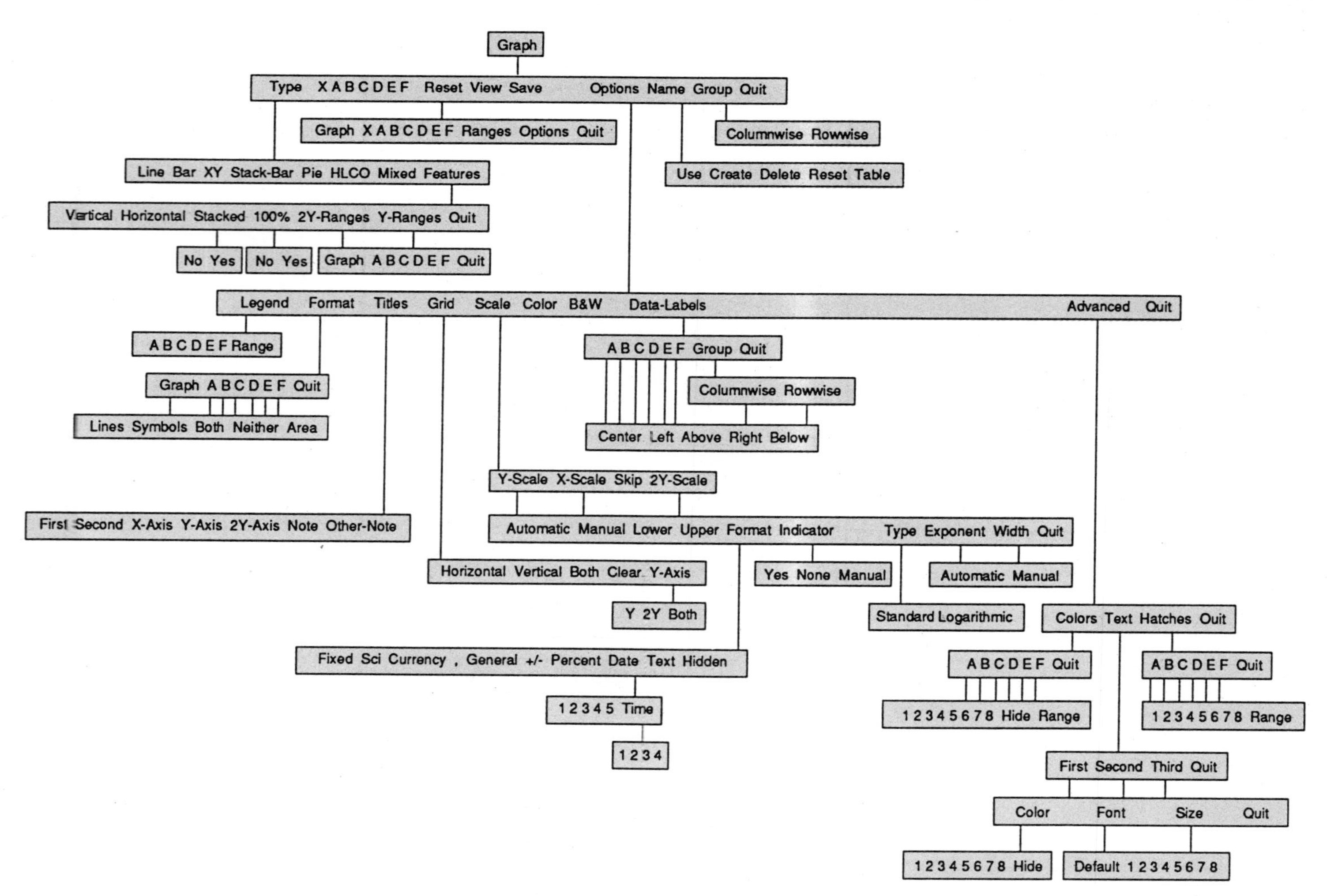

Data Commands

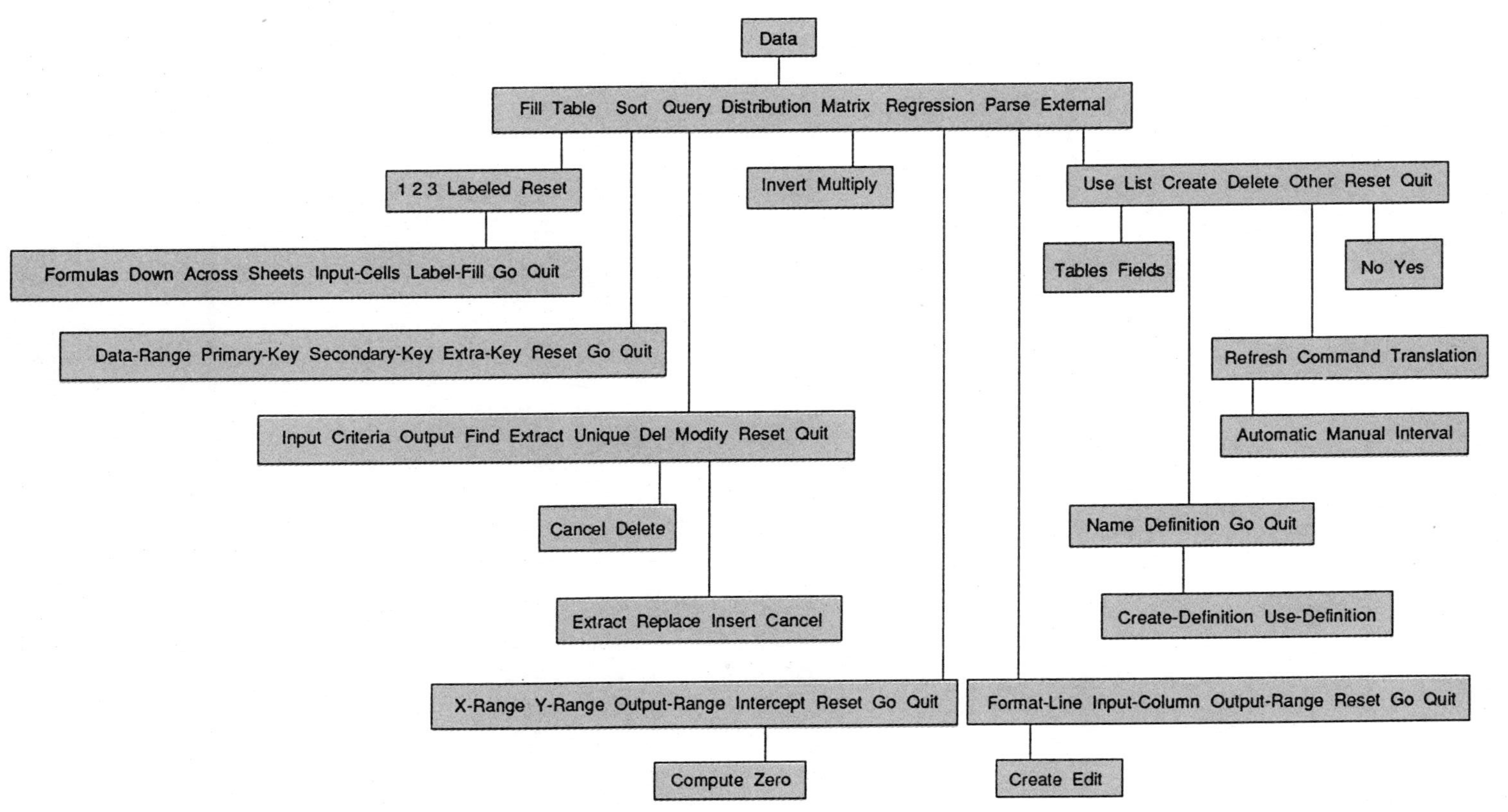

APPENDIX B

SUMMARY OF COMMANDS COVERED IN THIS BOOK

As indicated by the previous diagrams, there are many types of commands available in Lotus 1-2-3. Below is a summary of the functionality of the commands covered in this book. This summary is useful when a person knows what needs to be done but does not know what command to use. A complete list of the functionality of the 1-2-3 commands can be found in the Lotus 1-2-3 reference manual that comes with the software.

The keystrokes required for each command sequence are in bold and a description of the command sequence are included.

Data Analysis

Determine a frequency distribution for some data in a range of cells

/DD /**D**ata **D**istribution

Change formulas into values

/RV /**R**ange **V**alue

Create graphs from data in a spreadsheet

/G /**G**raph

Sort data in a spreadsheet

/DS /**D**ata **S**ort

Modifying the Appearance of the Spreadsheet

Change the format of a specific cell or group of cells in the spreadsheet

/RF /**R**ange **F**ormat

Restore the format for a range of cells to the original format

/RFR /**R**ange **F**ormat **R**eset

Change the default format for numeric values in the spreadsheet

/WGF /**W**orksheet **G**lobal **F**ormat

Format multiple worksheets using the group option

/WGGE /**W**orksheet **G**lobal **G**roup **E**nable

Change the width for a specific column in the spreadsheet

/WCS /**W**orksheet **C**olumn **S**et-Width

Return a column to its original width

/WCR /**W**orksheet **C**olumn **R**eset-Width

Widen multiple columns

/WCCS /**W**orksheet **C**olumn **C**olumn-Range **S**et-Width

Change the column default width

/WGC /**W**orksheet **G**lobal **C**olumn-Width

Copy information from one portion of the spreadsheet to another section of the spreadsheet

/C /**C**opy

Show formulas instead of numbers

/RFT /**R**ange **F**ormat **T**ext

Erase a specific cell or range of cells in the spreadsheet

/RE /**R**ange **E**rase

Erase the entire spreadsheet

/WEY /**W**orksheet **E**rase **Y**es

Format a range of cells automatically

/RFOA **/R**ange **F**ormat **O**ther **A**utomatic

Format a worksheet using automatic formatting

/WGFOA **/W**orksheet **G**lobal **F**ormat **O**ther **A**utomatic

Hide a column or group of columns in the spreadsheet

/WCH **/W**orksheet **C**olumn **H**ide

Hide a range of cells

/RFH **/R**ange **F**ormat **H**idden

Insert a blank row or rows in a spreadsheet

/WIR **/W**orksheet **I**nsert **R**ow

Insert a blank column or columns in a spreadsheet

/WIC **/W**orksheet **I**nsert **C**olumn

Insert a worksheet on the screen

/WIS **/W**orksheet **I**nsert **S**heet

Keep row labels or column headings on the monitor

/WT **/W**orksheet **T**itles

Move information from one section on the spreadsheet to another section on the spreadsheet

/M **/M**ove

To see multiple worksheets on the screen

/WWP **/W**orksheet **W**indow **P**erspective

To see one worksheet on the screen

/WWC **/W**orksheet **W**indow **C**lear

Modify the arrangement of text in a spreadsheet

/RJ **/R**ange **J**ustify

Change the alignment of a label or group of labels

/RL **/R**ange **L**abel

Display previously hidden column

/WCD /Worksheet Column Display

Delete a row or rows from a spreadsheet

/WDR /Worksheet Delete Row

Delete a column or columns from a spreadsheet

/WDC /Worksheet Delete Column

Divide the spreadsheet on the screen into two parts or windows

/WW /Worksheet Window

Suppress from view all cells that have a value of exactly 0

/WGZ /Worksheet Global Zero

Copying Data

Copy information from one portion of the spreadsheet to another section of the spreadsheet

/C /Copy

Change formulas into values

/RV /Range Value

Include data from another spreadsheet file into the spreadsheet in the memory

/FC /File Combine

Erasing Data

Delete a row or rows from a spreadsheet

/WDR /Worksheet Delete Row

Delete a column or columns from a spreadsheet

/WDC /Worksheet Delete Column

Erase the contents of one or more specific cells

/RE /Range Erase

Erase the spreadsheet presently being used if no changes have been made since the last time the worksheet was saved

/WEY	/**W**orksheet **E**rase **Y**es

Erase the worksheet if it has not been saved previously or if changes have been made since the last time it was saved

/WEYY	/**W**orksheet **E**rase **Y**es **Y**es

Graphing Data

Indicate the type of graph desired

/GT	/**G**raph **T**ype

Specify the data to appear on the X-axis in a graph

/GX	/**G**raph **X**

Specify the data to be graphed (six variables can be graphed at a time)

/GA	/**G**raph **A**
/GB	/**G**raph **B**
/GC	/**G**raph **C**
/GD	/**G**raph **D**
/GE	/**G**raph **E**
/GF	/**G**raph **F**

Create a graph using a group

/GG	/**G**raph **G**roup

Display the graph on the monitor screen

/GV	/**G**raph **V**iew

Change graph features

/GTF	/**G**raph **T**ype **F**eatures

Indicate various graphic settings

/GO	/**G**raph **O**ptions

Specify legend labels for variables being graphed

/GOL	/**G**raph **O**ptions **L**egend

Specify title lines for the graph

/GOTF	/**G**raph **O**ptions **T**itles **F**irst
/GOTS	/**G**raph **O**ptions **T**itles **S**econd

Specify labels for X-Axis and Y-Axis

/GOTX	/**G**raph **O**ptions **T**itles **X**-Axis
/GOTY	/**G**raph **O**ptions **T**itles **Y**-Axis

Place labels on data points

/GOD	/**G**raph **O**ptions **D**ata-Labels

Place horizontal, vertical or both horizontal and vertical lines on the graph

/GOG	/**G**raph **O**ptions **G**rid

Fill the area between lines on a line graph

/GOFGA	/**G**raph **O**ptions **F**ormat **G**raph **A**rea

Name a graph

/GN	/**G**raph **N**ame

Save a graph on a file for later printing

/GS	/**G**raph **S**ave

Print or plot the graph

/PPI	/**P**rint **P**rinter **I**mage

Print a graph with advanced options

/GOA	/**G**raph **O**ptions **A**dvanced

Reset or cancel some or all of the graph settings

/GR	/**G**raph **R**eset

List the graph files

/FLG	/**F**ile **L**ist **G**raph

Display a graph in a window

/WWG	/**W**orksheet **W**indow **G**raph

Hiding Data

Restrict the display of a column or columns

/WCH /**W**orksheet **C**olumn **H**ide

Display a column that had previously been hidden

/WCD /**W**orksheet **C**olumn **D**isplay

Suppress from view all cells that have a value of exactly 0

/WGZ /**W**orksheet **G**lobal **Z**ero

Loading Data

Load a spreadsheet file into the memory of the microcomputer

/FR /**F**ile **R**etrieve

Include data from another spreadsheet file into the spreadsheet in the memory

/FC /**F**ile **C**ombine

Moving Data

Move information from one section on the spreadsheet to another section on the spreadsheet

/M /**M**ove

Insert a blank row or rows in a spreadsheet

/WIR /**W**orksheet **I**nsert **R**ow

Insert a blank column or columns in a spreadsheet

/WIC /**W**orksheet **I**nsert **C**olumn

Delete a row or rows from a spreadsheet

/WDR /**W**orksheet **D**elete **R**ow

Delete a column or columns from a spreadsheet

/WDC /**W**orksheet **D**elete **C**olumn

Printing a Portion or an Entire Spreadsheet

Specify the range of data to print

/PPR /Print Printer Range

Indicate top of page setting

/PPA /Print Printer Align

Initiate printing

/PPG /Print Printer Go

Advance printer paper to top of next page

/PPP /Print Printer Page

Place spreadsheet on a text (ASCII) file

/PF /Print File

Print with column letters and row numbers framing the spreadsheet

/PPOBF /Print Printer Options Border Frame

Alter present printing settings

/PPO /Print Printer Options

Put a column border on each page

/PPOBC /Print Printer Options Border Columns

Place a footer at the bottom of each page

/PPOF /Print Printer Options Footer

Place a header at the top of each page

/PPOH /Print Printer Options Header

Changing the font

/PPOAF /Print Printer Options Advanced Fonts

Specify margins for printing page

/PPOM /Print Printer Options Margins

Print cell formulas instead of numeric values

/PPOOC /**P**rint **P**rinter **O**ptions **O**ther **C**ell-Formulas

Print what appears on the screen if cell formulas were previously used

/PPOOA /**P**rint **P**rinter **O**ptions **O**ther **A**s-Displayed

Insert a page break

/WP /**W**orksheet **P**age

Prioritize print jobs

/PPOAP /**P**rint **P**rinter **O**ptions **A**dvanced **P**riority

Change paper orientation

/PPOALO /**P**rint **P**rinter **O**ptions **A**dvanced **L**ayout **O**rientation

Print or plot a graph

/PPI /**P**rint **P**rinter **I**mage

Saving a Spreadsheet or Graph

Save a spreadsheet on a file

/FS /**F**ile **S**ave

Save a graph

/GS **G**raph **S**ave

Database Commands

Indicate input range of the database

/DQI /**D**ata **Q**uery **I**nput

Indicate the criterion to be used

/DQC /**D**ata **Q**uery **C**riterion

Indicate the information to be output if the criterion is satisfied

/DQO /**D**ata **Q**uery **O**utput

Find and highlight records in the database that satisfy the criterion

/DQF /Data Query Find

Copy the data from the records that satisfy the criterion to the output range

/DQE /Data Query Extract

Copy the data from the records that satisfy the criterion to the output range and eliminate duplicate data

/DQU /Data Query Unique

Delete records from the database that satisfy the criterion

/DQD /Data Query Delete

Enter a sequence of values, dates or times on a worksheet or multiple worksheets

/DF /Data Fill

Sort records in a database

/DS /Data Sort

Specify data range to be sorted

/DSD /Data Sort Data-Range

Specify the primary sort key

/DSP /Data Sort Primary-Key

Specify the secondary sort key

/DSS /Data Sort Secondary-Key

Specify extra sort keys

/DSE /Data Sort Extra-Key

Initiate sorting process

/DSG /Data Sort Go

Reset data sort settings

/DSR /Data Sort Reset

Initiate data table options

/DT /**D**ata **T**able

Access an external database table

/DE /**D**ata **E**xternal

List the fields in an external database table

/DELF /**D**ata **E**xternal **L**ist **F**ields

File Operations

Retrieve or load a file

/FR /**F**ile **R**etrieve

Open an existing file without erasing the current file

/FO /**F**ile **O**pen

Open a new file without erasing the current file

/FN /**F**ile **N**ew

Save a spreadsheet on a file

/FS /**F**ile **S**ave

Change the drive or path from which files are retrieved and saved

/FD /**F**ile **D**irectory

Change the default drive or path from which files are retrieved and saved

/WGDD /**W**orksheet **G**lobal **D**efault **D**ir

Save a spreadsheet in a text (ASCII) file

/PF /**P**rint **F**ile

Include data from another spreadsheet file into the spreadsheet in the memory

/FC /**F**ile **C**ombine

Seal reservation settings

/FASR /**F**ile **A**dmin **S**eal **R**eservation-Setting

Remove a password

/FASD /**F**ile **A**dmin **S**eal **D**isable

Create a table of file names

/FAT /**F**ile **A**dmin **T**able

Display names of files in current directory

/FL /**F**ile **L**ist

Remove or erase a file

/FE /**F**ile **E**rase

Save a graph for printing at a later time

/GS /**G**raph **S**ave

Saving a file or a graph to make a backup (BAK) file

/FSB /**F**ile **S**ave **B**ackup

Using Named Ranges

Create a named range for a cell or group of cells

/RNC /**R**ange **N**ame **C**reate

Annotate a range name

/RNNC /**R**ange **N**ame **N**ote **C**reate

View notes and range names

/RNNT /**R**ange **N**ame **N**ote **T**able

Delete a named range

/RND /**R**ange **N**ame **D**elete

Remove or delete all range names

/RNR /**R**ange **N**ame **R**eset

Working with Numeric Values

Modify the default format of all numbers

/WGF /Worksheet Global Format

Modify the format of a cell or group of cells

/RF /Range Format

Check the recalculation settings

/WS /Worksheet Status

Indicate how and when recalculation of formulas occurs

/WGR /Worksheet Global Recalculation

Suppress from view all cells that have a value of exactly 0

/WGZ /Worksheet Global Zero

Modify the column width when asterisks appear in a cell

/WCS /Worksheet Column Set-Width

Associate a range name with a number or set of numbers

/RNC /Range Name Create

Convert a cell or group of cells with a formula(s) to a value(s)

/RV /Range Value

Determine a frequency distribution for some data in a range of cells

/DD /Data Distribution

Protecting Cells in a Worksheet

Protecting all cells in a worksheet

/WGPE /Worksheet Global Prot Enable

Unprotect a worksheet

/WGPD /Worksheet Global Prot Disable

Protect a range of cells

/RP /**R**ange **P**rot

Unprotect a range of cells

/RU /**R**ange **U**nprot

Miscellaneous Commands

Display amount of memory available and current default settings for format, column width, cell protection, zero suppression and so on

/WS /**W**orksheet **S**tatus

Display current configuration for the printer, directory, margins and so on

/WGDS /**W**orksheet **G**lobal **D**efault **S**tatus

Change configuration settings for the printer, directory, margins and so on

/WGD /**W**orksheet **G**lobal **D**efault

Change spreadsheet settings for format, column width, recalculation, protection and so on

/WG /**W**orksheet **G**lobal

Indicate how and when recalculation of formulas occurs

/WGR /**W**orksheet **G**lobal **R**ecalculation

Exit to the operating system

/S /**S**ystem

Quit using 1-2-3

/Q /**Q**uit

Create a map of cell information

/WWME /**W**orksheet **W**indow **M**ap **E**nable

Search and Replace

/RS /**R**ange **S**earch

Turn the UNDO feature on

/WGDOUE /**W**orksheet **G**lobal **D**efault **O**ther **U**ndo **E**nable

UNDO a change

Alt-F4

Turn the UNDO feature off

/WGDOUD /**W**orksheet **G**lobal **D**efault **O**ther **U**ndo **D**isable

APPENDIX C

ANSWERS TO ODD-NUMBERED EXERCISES

CHAPTER ONE/EXERCISE 1 ANSWERS

INSTRUCTIONS: Answer the following questions in the space provided.

1. Define the following terms:

   a. Worksheet—the letter that appears at the intersection of the horizontal and vertical borders near the top left corner of the screen.
   b. Row Numbers—the row of numbers on the left border of the worksheet screen.
   c. Column Letters—the letters that appear across the top border of the worksheet screen.
   d. Cell—the area on a worksheet that occurs at the intersection of a column and a row.
   e. Cell Pointer—rectangular item that is used to highlight a cell.
   f. Current Cell—the cell that is highlighted by the cell pointer. When information is entered into a worksheet, it is placed in the cell highlighted by the cell pointer.
   g. Cell Address—the location of a cell. It is defined by a worksheet letter and column letter followed by a row number.
   h. Control Panel—the area above the column letter section of the worksheet.
   i. Mode Indicator—appears in the top right corner of the control panel of the worksheet.
   j. Status Indicator—specifies the condition of certain keys or of the program.

k. Date Indicator—current date being used by Lotus 1-2-3 that appears in the lower left-hand corner of the worksheet screen.
l. Time Indicator—current time being used by Lotus 1-2-3 that appears in the lower left-hand corner of the worksheet screen.
m. Worksheet—a term that is used interchangeably with the word spreadsheet.
n. Worksheet Frame—the area above and to the left of the worksheet that includes the row and column letter borders.

2. Describe the standard way of using the 1-2-3 menu structure.

   The first action is to press the / key (sometimes called the command key). The menu pointer is then moved to whatever menu option is desired and the ↵ (return or enter) key is pressed. The process is continued until the command sequence desired by the user is completed.

3. Describe the alternative method of using the 1-2-3 menu structure.

   The only difference in using the alternative method instead of the standard method is that the first letter of the menu option can be typed rather than moving the menu pointer to the desired menu option and pressing the ↵ key.

4. Describe the purpose of using the function keys F1 through F10.

   The function keys have been "programmed" to perform specific operations. These keys let the user perform specific actions such as going to a particular cell without having to use the arrow (directional) keys.

Note: Exercise 3 does not require an answer key.

CHAPTER TWO/EXERCISE 1 ANSWERS

INSTRUCTIONS: Circle T if the statement is true and F if the statement is false.

T	F	1. One way to correct incorrect data is to move to the incorrect data's cell, retype the data correctly, and press the ↵ to enter the correction.
T	**F**	2. The formula SUM(A..A7) will add the data in cells A1 through A7.
T	**F**	3. To round a number to two decimal places, you use the **R**ange **F**ormat command.
T	F	4. The **W**orksheet **E**rase **Y**es command sequence erases the worksheet currently in use from memory.
T	F	5. A print range must be specified before a spreadsheet can be printed.
T	F	6. The "@" character must precede special functions such as the SUM and ROUND functions.
T	**F**	7. Lotus 1-2-3 will automatically save changes that are made to a spreadsheet file.

T F 8. The **F**ile **R**etrieve command is used to look at a previously saved file.

T **F** 9. "BUDGET 1" is an acceptable file name.

T **F** 10. The letter "X" is the symbol for multiplication when using Lotus 1-2-3.

T **F** 11. Fonts cannot be changed.

T F 12. Column letters and row numbers can be used to form a "frame" when a spreadsheet is printed.

CHAPTER TWO/EXERCISE 3 ANSWERS

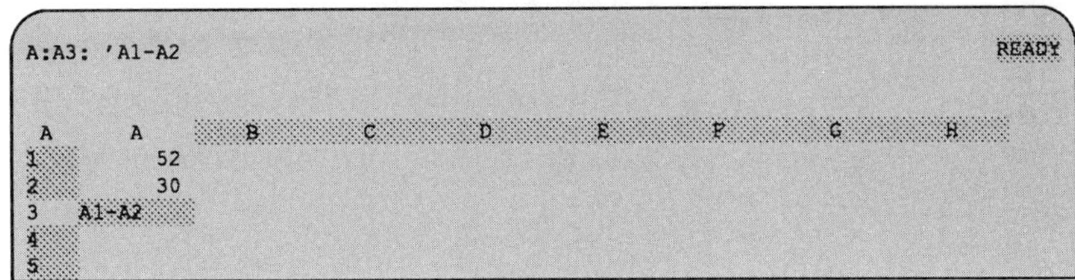

Exercise 2-3

1. What caused the error in cell A3?

   Because A1-A2 begins with an alphabetic character, the formula was read by Lotus as a label.

2. How can the error be corrected?

   Retype or edit the formula to be +A1-A2. Since the formula now begins with an arithmetic operator, the formula will calculate correctly.

CHAPTER TWO/EXERCISE 5 ANSWERS

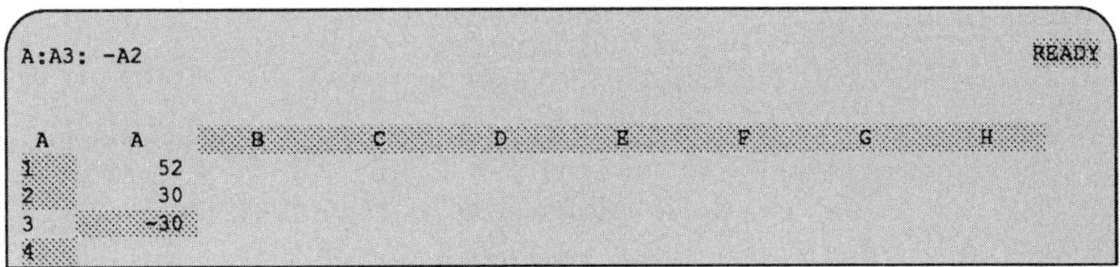

Exercise 2-5

1. What caused the error in computing A1-A2?

   +A1 was typed in and ↵ was pressed before the formula was completely typed in; at this point, +A1 was entered as the complete formula. -A2 was typed and the ↵ was pressed again, which resulted in -A2 being entered in cell A3. -A2 results in the answer -30, since 30 is the number in cell A2.

2. How can the error be corrected?

   Do not press ↵ before the entire formula is written.

Note: Exercises 7, 9 and 11 do not require answer keys.

CHAPTER THREE/EXERCISE 1 ANSWERS

INSTRUCTIONS: Circle T if the statement is true and F if the statement is false.

T	F	1. An absolute cell reference means that the reference is kept constant, even when copied.
T	F	2. The F2 key allows you to correct a cell entry without having to retype the entire entry.
T	**F**	3. **W**orksheet **T**itles allows you to center titles on a spreadsheet.
T	F	4. **W**orksheet **W**indow allows you to view two different areas of a spreadsheet at the same time.
T	F	5. **W**orksheet **P**age creates a page break in a spreadsheet.
T	F	6. If column D is hidden on a worksheet using **W**orksheet **C**olumn **H**ide, column D will not appear if the worksheet is printed.
T	F	7. **W**orksheet **G**lobal **R**ecalculation **M**anual is activated so that data can be entered without the worksheet recalculating after each new entry.
T	F	8. Changing the **F**ile **D**irectory changes the drive designation or path to which 1-2-3 saves and retrieves files.
T	**F**	9. **F**ile **E**rase erases a file from memory.
T	**F**	10. The **S**ystem command permanently returns you to the operating system.
T	F	11. Formulas and data in cells can be annotated.
T	**F**	12. After initiating a printing activity, you must wait until the printing is completed before issuing any command.
T	**F**	13. Only one cell at a time can be erased.

<u>T</u> F 14. Automatic formatting of cells is permitted.

<u>T</u> F 15. The width for multiple columns that are contiguous to each other can be changed to the same width at the same time.

CHAPTER THREE/EXERCISE 3 ANSWERS

1. How can the formula in cell C1 be changed so that cells D1 and E1 also refer to cell B2 for the projected revenue rate?

   Change the formula +B1*B2 in cell C1 to +B1*$B$2 so that B2 is an absolute cell reference. This can be accomplished by editing the formula to add the dollar signs to B2. Another method is to reenter the formula and, after highlighting cell B2 (or typing B2), press the (Abs) key to add the dollar signs. After changing the formula in cell C1, copy the formula to cells D1 and E1. Your screen should look like the one below.

```
A:C1: +B1*(1+$B$2)                                                        READY

A          A              B        C        D        E        F        G
1   REVENUE             10000    11500    13225 15208.75
2   ASSUMED REV RATE     0.15
3
4
```

Exercise 3-3

CHAPTER THREE/EXERCISE 5, 7, 9, 13, 15, 17 ANSWERS

```
A:A1: PR [W18]                                                            READY

A          A              B        C        D        E        F        G
1                                 PROJECTED PROFITS
2
3                        YEAR 1   YEAR 2   YEAR 3   YEAR 4   YEAR 5    TOTAL
4
5   REVENUE              25,000   27,000   28,350   31,185   33,368  144,903
6   EXPENSES              9,500    6,750    7,088    7,796    8,342   39,476
7                    ----------------------------------------------------
8   PROFIT BEFORE TAX    15,500   20,250   21,262   23,389   25,026  105,427
9   TAXES                 6,200    8,100    8,505    9,356   10,010   42,171
10                   ----------------------------------------------------
11  PROFIT AFTER TAX      9,300   12,150   12,757   14,033   15,016   63,256
12                   ====================================================
13  ASSUMPTIONS
14  REVENUE GROWTH RATE               8%       5%      10%       7%
15  EXPENSE RATE                     25%      25%      25%      25%
16  TAX RATE                         40%      40%      40%      40%
17
18
19
20
```

Exercise 3-5

```
A:A1: (,0) [W10] 12000                                              READY

A      A        B      C      D      E      F      G
1       12,000
2   $9,700.00
3        28.5%
4
5
```

Exercise 3-7

```
A:A1:                                                               READY

A      A        B      C      D      E      F      G      H
1               123
2
3         123
4
5               ABC
6
7         XYZXYZXYZ
8
9             ABC
10
11
```

Exercise 3-9

```
A:A1: [W18]                                                              READY

A          A              B        C        D        E        F        G
1
2                                                              ABC COMPANY
3                                                                BUDGET
4
5                       YEAR 1   YEAR 2   YEAR 3   YEAR 4   YEAR 5   YEAR 6
6
7   SALES               60,000   61,200   62,424   63,672   64,945   66,244
8
9   EXPENSES
10    SALARIES          35,000   35,500   36,200   37,000   37,000   37,000
11    RENT               9,000    9,000    9,000    9,000    9,000    9,000
12    TELEPHONE          1,000    1,050    1,103    1,158    1,216    1,277
13    OFFICE SUPPLIES      750      800      850      900      950    1,000
14    MISCELLANEOUS      1,000    1,030    1,061    1,093    1,126    1,160
15                    ----------------------------------------------------
16      TOTAL EXPENSES  46,750   47,380   48,214   49,151   49,292   49,437
17                    ----------------------------------------------------
18  GROSS PROFIT        13,250   13,820   14,210   14,521   15,653   16,807
19                    ====================================================
20
```

Exercise 3-13

A:B1: [W11] READY

A	A	B	C	D	E	F
1			ABC COMPANY			
2			BUDGET			
3						
4						
5		QTR1	QTR2	QTR3	QTR4	YR TOTAL
6						
7	SALES	$60,000	$61,200	$62,424	$63,672	$247,296
8						
9	EXPENSES					
10	SALARIES	35,000	35,500	36,200	37,000	143,700
11	RENT	9,000	9,000	9,000	9,000	36,000
12	TELEPHONE	1,000	1,050	1,103	1,158	4,311
13	OFFICE SUPPLIES	750	800	850	900	3,300
14	MISCELLANEOUS	1,000	1,030	1,061	1,093	4,184
15		----------	----------	----------	----------	----------
16	TOTAL EXPENSES	46,750	47,380	48,214	49,151	191,495
17		----------	----------	----------	----------	----------
18	GROSS PROFIT	$13,250	$13,820	$14,210	$14,521	$55,801
19		==========	==========	==========	==========	==========
20						

Exercise 3-15

A:B5: 0 READY

A	A	B	C	D	E	F	G
1			PROJECTED PROFITS				
2							
3		YEAR 1	YEAR 2	YEAR 3	YEAR 4	YEAR 5	TOTAL
4							
5	REVENUE						
6	EXPENSES	9,500					9,500
7		----------	----------	----------	----------	----------	----------
8	PROFIT BEFORE TAX	(9,500)					(9,500)
9	TAXES	(3,800)					(3,800)
10		----------	----------	----------	----------	----------	----------
11	PROFIT AFTER TAX	(5,700)					(5,700)
12		==========	==========	==========	==========	==========	==========
13	ASSUMPTIONS						
14	REVENUE GROWTH RATE		6%	6%	6%	6%	
15	EXPENSE RATE		25%	25%	25%	25%	
16	TAX RATE		40%	40%	40%	40%	
17							
18							
19							
20							

Exercise 3-17

Note: Exercise 11 does not require an answer key.

CHAPTER FOUR/EXERCISE 1 ANSWERS

INSTRUCTIONS: Circle T if the statement is true and F if the statement is false.

T F 1. A Lotus 1-2-3 graph can contain up to six different data ranges.

T F 2. To change a bar graph into a line graph, change the **G**raph **T**ype from **B**ar to **L**ine.

T F 3. If numbers are changed on the spreadsheet, the graph will reflect the changes when the graph is viewed again on the screen.

T **F** 4. If numbers are changed on the spreadsheet, the changes will be automatically reflected on any graph file that was previously created from the worksheet.

T F 5. It is possible to create three completely different graphs with data from one worksheet.

T F 6. If **F**ile **S**ave is not executed after a graph is made, the graph settings will not be saved.

T **F** 7. If a computer is not configured to show graphics on the screen, it is not possible to create and print a Lotus 1-2-3 graph.

T **F** 8. A color graph on the screen displays the colors in which the graph will be printed on a color printer or plotter.

T F 9. A pie graph displays the data in data range A.

T F 10. An XY graph is different from other Lotus graphs because it graphs data for variable X.

T **F** 11. High-Low-Close-Open graphs cannot be created using 1-2-3.

T **F** 12. Only one Y-axis can be used in 1-2-3.

T F 13. The scale indicator can be changed or deleted.

T **F** 14. Bar and line graphs cannot be combined on one chart.

T T 15. Data ranges can be graphed as a percentage of the total.

CHAPTER FOUR/EXERCISES 3, 5, 7 ANSWERS

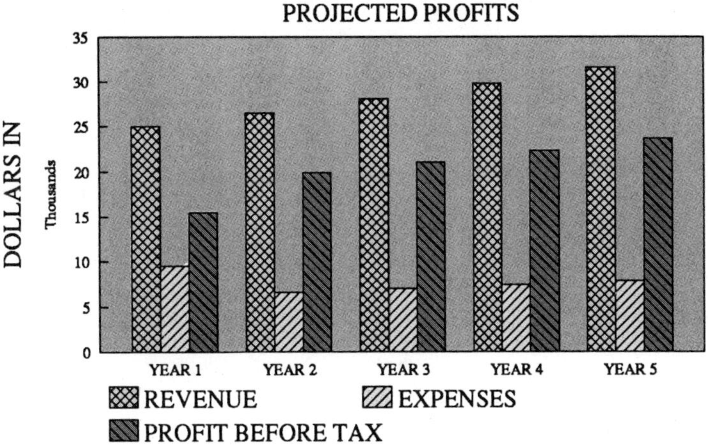

Exercise 4-3

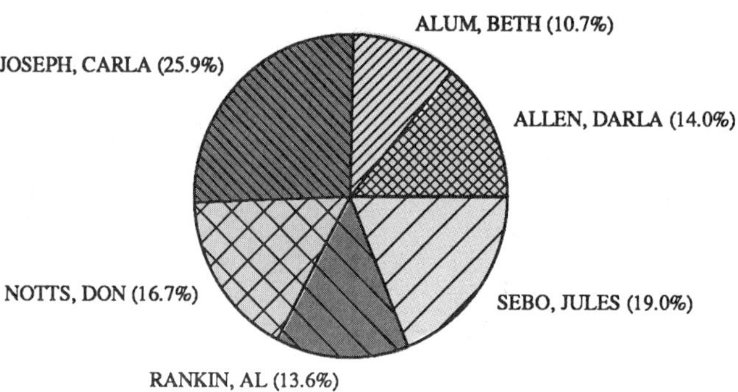

Exercise 4-5

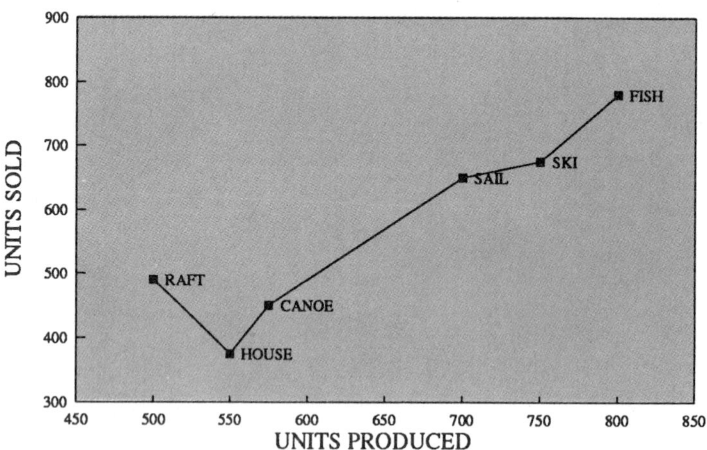

Exercise 4-7

Note: Exercise 9 does not require an answer key.

CHAPTER FIVE/EXERCISE 1 ANSWERS

INSTRUCTIONS: Circle T if the statement is true and F if the statement is false.

T <u>F</u> 1. In Lotus 1-2-3, a template file must be combined with another file containing data to generate a new spreadsheet.

<u>T</u> F 2. A template is a good way to keep spreadsheets standardized.

T <u>F</u> 3. When data is added to a template in memory, it is automatically added to the template file on the disk.

<u>T</u> F 4. A template can be used to create multiple worksheets.

<u>T</u> F 5. After adding data to a template in order to create a new spreadsheet, the worksheet should be saved using a name other than the template file name.

Note: Exercise 3 does not require an answer key.

CHAPTER SIX/EXERCISE 1 ANSWERS

INSTRUCTIONS: Circle T if the statement is true and F if the statement is false.

T <u>F</u> 1. At most three worksheets can be placed in a file in Lotus 1-2-3.

<u>T</u> F 2. One or more worksheets can be inserted before or after a worksheet existing in the memory of a computer.

<u>T</u> F 3. The F5 key can be used to move between multiple worksheets in a file.

<u>T</u> F 4. Cells can be copied from one worksheet to another.

T <u>F</u> 5. Cells cannot be copied from one file to another.

T <u>F</u> 6. When multiple worksheets exist in a file, only one worksheet at a time can be viewed on the screen.

<u>T</u> F 7. More than one file can be open at one time.

T <u>F</u> 8. The GROUP mode option available in 1-2-3 allows you to format more than one worksheet or file at one time.

```
A:A1: [W14]                                                            READY

     C      A            B          C          D          E          F          G
     1
     2
     3
     4  HOUSTON:         JUNE       JULY      AUGUST      TOTAL
     5
     6  TRAINING         20,000     15,000    22,000     57,000
    B       A            B          C          D          E          F          G
    1
    2
    3
    4  CHICAGO:          JUNE       JULY      AUGUST      TOTAL
    5
    6  TRAINING          12,000     15,000    14,000     41,000
   A        A            B          C          D          E          F          G
   1                     XYZ CONSULTING COMPANY
   2
   3
   4  NEW YORK:          JUNE       JULY      AUGUST      TOTAL
   5
   6  TRAINING           15,000     19,000    17,000     51,000
```

Exercise 6-3

Note: Exercise 5 does not require an answer key.

CHAPTER SEVEN/EXERCISE 1 ANSWERS

INSTRUCTIONS: Circle T if the statement is true and F if the statement is false.

T F 1. A template can be used to create several worksheets very rapidly.

T F 2. Worksheets in a file can be linked together through the use of formulas.

T **F** 3. While worksheets can be linked by formulas, files cannot be linked in the same manner.

T F 4. Multiple worksheets make it easy to combine information between the worksheets.

T **F** 5. Only two files can be open at one time, but many worksheets can be open within one file.

```
E:A1: [W11] 'XYZ COMPANY SUMMARY                                   READY

   E      A          B         C         D         E         F         G
   1   XYZ COMPANY SUMMARY
   2
   3
   4                 JUNE      JULY    AUGUST     TOTAL
   5
   6   NEW YORK     29,000    34,000   36,000    99,000
  D      A          B         C         D         E         F         G
  1
  2
  3
  4   LOS ANGELES:   JUNE      JULY    AUGUST     TOTAL
  5
  6   TRAINING      13,000    12,000   15,000    40,000
 C      A          B         C         D         E         F         G
 1
 2
 3
 4   HOUSTON:      JUNE      JULY    AUGUST     TOTAL
 5
 6   TRAINING     20,000    15,000   22,000    57,000
```

Exercise 7-3
Part 1

```
D:A1:                                                              READY

   D      A         B         C         D         E         F         G         H
   1                       ABC COMPANY
   2                       DIVISION 4
   3
   4
   5   PRODUCT  Q1        Q2        Q3        Q4        YR TOTAL
   6   ----------------------------------------------------
  C      A         B         C         D         E         F         G         H
  1                       ABC COMPANY
  2                       DIVISION 3
  3
  4
  5   PRODUCT  Q1        Q2        Q3        Q4        YR TOTAL
  6   ----------------------------------------------------
 B      A         B         C         D         E         F         G         H
 1                       ABC COMPANY
 2                       DIVISION 2
 3
 4
 5   PRODUCT  Q1        Q2        Q3        Q4        YR TOTAL
 6   ----------------------------------------------------
```

Exercise 7-3
Part 2

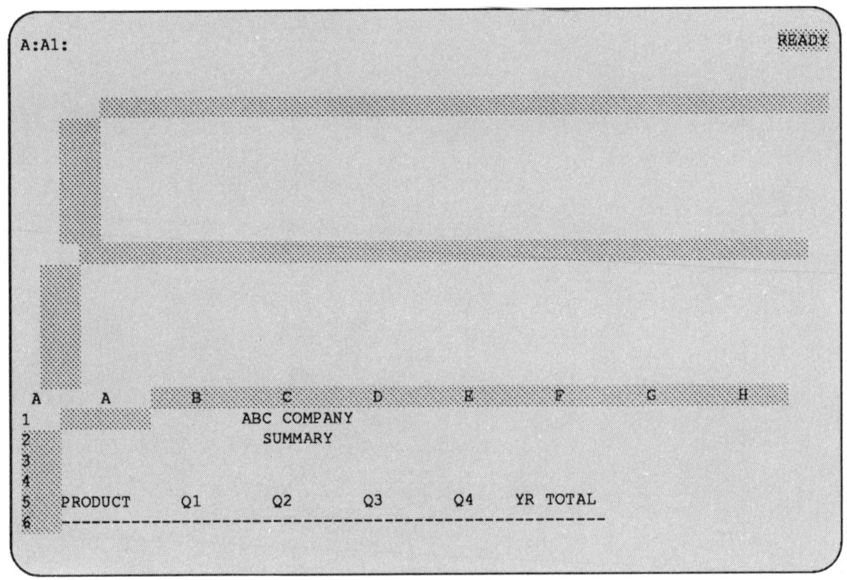

Exercise 7-3
Part 3

Note: Exercise 5 does not require an answer key.

CHAPTER EIGHT/EXERCISE 1 ANSWERS

INSTRUCTIONS: Circle T if the statement is true and F if the statement is false.

T **F** 1. When sorting a database in Lotus 1-2-3, the data-range must include the field titles.

T F 2. The field titles must be located in the line directly above the first record of the database for the **D**ata **Q**uery command sequence to work properly.

T **F** 3. It is appropriate to have more than one line consisting of field titles designated in the input range.

T F 4. Each criteria consists of two cells (a field title and the actual criteria).

T F 5. The input range, criteria, and output range must be manually set up on the worksheet and then identified through the menu options.

T F 6. The output range allows you to copy the desired fields that match the criteria to another area on the worksheet.

T **F** 7. When designating the output range, you may highlight only the field names that are desired; the records will appear directly below the field names on the worksheet in the output range when the **Q**uery **F**ind is executed.

T F 8. The QUERY key allows you to perform a query based upon previously set ranges.

T **F** 9. The criteria for a worksheet can be set by setting the bin range.

T **F** 10. The **Q**uery **U**nique command deletes multiple records in a database.

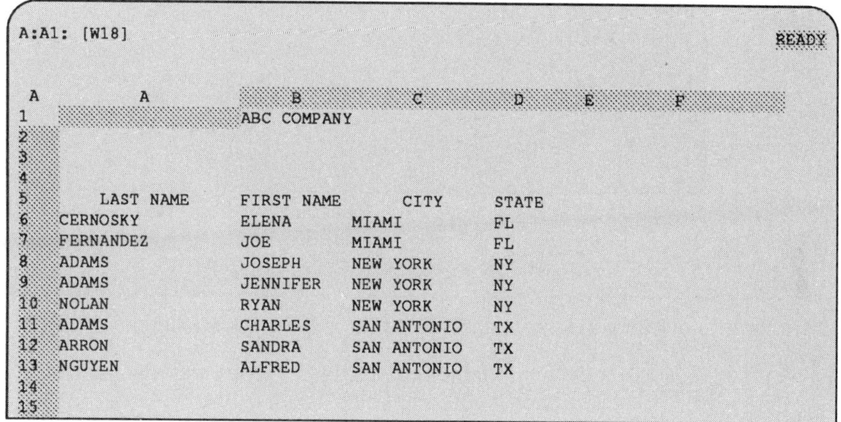

A:A1: [W18] READY

A	A	B	C	D	E	F
1		ABC COMPANY				
2						
3						
4						
5	LAST NAME	FIRST NAME	CITY	STATE		
6	CERNOSKY	ELENA	MIAMI	FL		
7	FERNANDEZ	JOE	MIAMI	FL		
8	ADAMS	JOSEPH	NEW YORK	NY		
9	ADAMS	JENNIFER	NEW YORK	NY		
10	NOLAN	RYAN	NEW YORK	NY		
11	ADAMS	CHARLES	SAN ANTONIO	TX		
12	ARRON	SANDRA	SAN ANTONIO	TX		
13	NGUYEN	ALFRED	SAN ANTONIO	TX		
14						
15						

Exercise 8-3

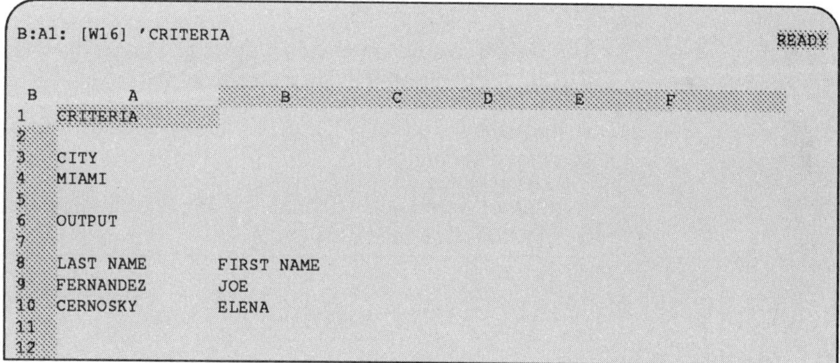

B:A1: [W16] 'CRITERIA READY

B	A	B	C	D	E	F
1	CRITERIA					
2						
3	CITY					
4	MIAMI					
5						
6	OUTPUT					
7						
8	LAST NAME	FIRST NAME				
9	FERNANDEZ	JOE				
10	CERNOSKY	ELENA				
11						
12						

Exercise 8-5

```
B:A1: [W16] 'CRITERIA                                                    READY

B       A                B          C          D          E          F
1   CRITERIA
2
3   CITY              LAST NAME
4   NEW YORK          ADAMS
5
6
7   OUTPUT
8
9   LAST NAME         FIRST NAME
10  ADAMS             JOSEPH
11  ADAMS             JENNIFER
12
13
```

Exercise 8-7

CHAPTER NINE/EXERCISE 1 ANSWERS

INSTRUCTIONS: Circle T if the statement is true and F if the statement is false.

T F 1. Database tables created by database management software packages can be accessed using Lotus 1-2-3.

T **F** 2. Sequences of numbers or times cannot be placed on multiple worksheets at one time.

T F 3. The **D**ata **T**able option makes it possible to analyze changes in variables that impact decision-making situations.

T F 4. A frequency distribution can be created using the **D**ata **D**istribution command sequence.

T **F** 5. A graph of a frequency distribution can be prepared by using the **G**raph **D**istribution command sequence.

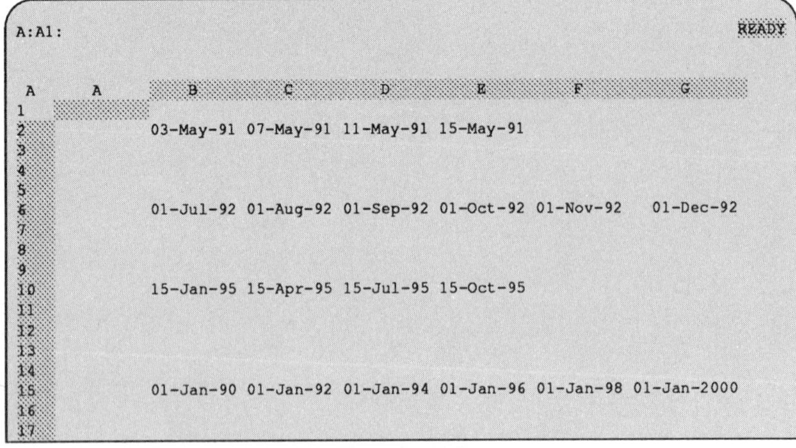

```
A:A1:                                                                    READY

A    A        B         C         D         E         F         G
1
2          03-May-91 07-May-91 11-May-91 15-May-91
3
4
5
6          01-Jul-92 01-Aug-92 01-Sep-92 01-Oct-92 01-Nov-92  01-Dec-92
7
8
9
10         15-Jan-95 15-Apr-95 15-Jul-95 15-Oct-95
11
12
13
14
15         01-Jan-90 01-Jan-92 01-Jan-94 01-Jan-96 01-Jan-98 01-Jan-2000
16
17
```

Exercise 9-3

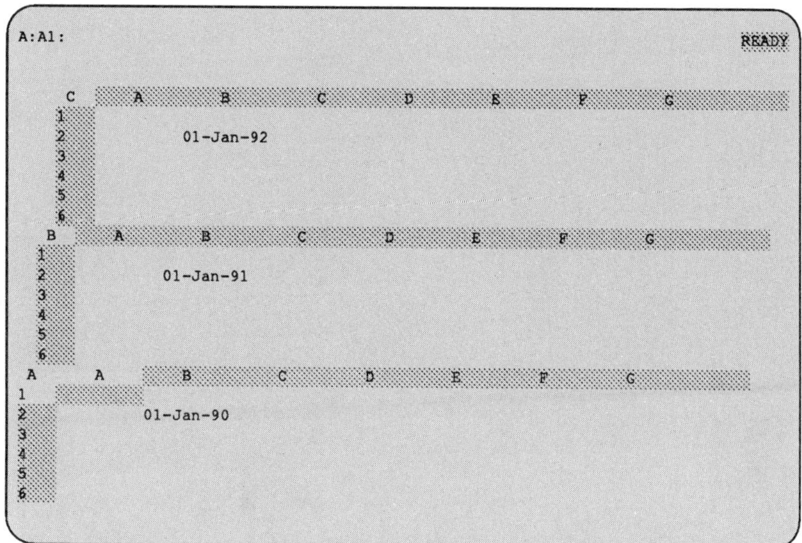

Exercise 9-5

```
A:A1: 'ASSUMPTIONS                                                    READY

A      A       B        C        D        E        F        G        H
1   ASSUMPTIONS
2
3    $50,000          PRINCIPAL
4         9%          ANNUAL INTEREST RATE
5         30          PERIOD IN YEARS
6      0.75%          MONTHLY INTEREST RATE
7    $402.31          CALCULATED MONTHLY PAYMENT
8
9
10  PRINCIPAL                   INTEREST RATE
11
12    402.31      9.0%     9.5%    10.0%    10.5%    11.0%
13    50,000    402.31   420.43   438.79   457.37   476.16
14    55,000    442.54   462.47   482.66   503.11   523.78
15    60,000    482.77   504.51   526.54   548.84   571.39
16    65,000    523.00   546.56   570.42   594.58   619.01
17    70,000    563.24   588.60   614.30   640.32   666.63
18
19
20
```

Exercise 9-7

```
A:A1: [W6]                                                        READY

A   A       B            C            D                   E        F      G
1       CRITERIA
2                     CITY
3       +EMP NO=EMPNO HOUSTON
4
5   EMP NO  LAST NAME    FIRST NAME        ADDRESS            CITY    STATE ZIP
6      123 LYLIE         SUSAN        2800 FOUNDREN        HOUSTON    TX    77063
7      239 ARMOUR        CYNTHIA      6450 CLARA           HOUSTON    TX    77041
8      390 CHIN          TOMMY        7110 BRITTMORE RD    HOUSTON    TX    77041
9      833 JONES         NINA         654 GESSNER          HOUSTON    TX    77024
10     898 VALETTI       GEORGE       109 MOUNTAIN DALE    HOUSTON    TX    77024
11     972 JOHNSON       SANDRA       11467 POST OAK       HOUSTON    TX    77098
12
13
```

Exercise 9-9

ABC COMPANY

DIVISION FREQUENCY DISTRIBUTION

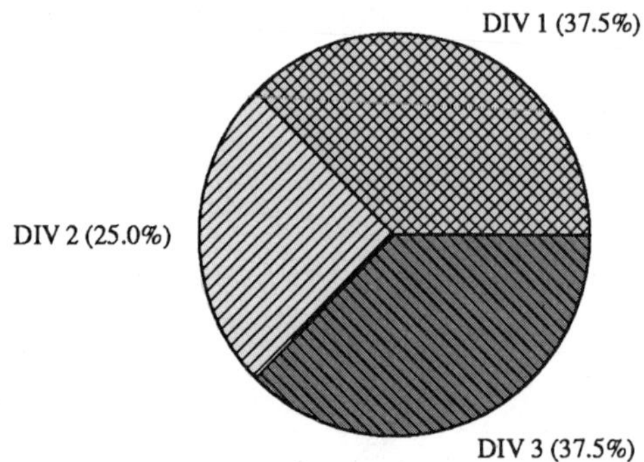

Exercise 9-11

CHAPTER TEN/EXERCISE 1 ANSWERS

INSTRUCTIONS: Circle T if the statement is true and F if the statement is false.

T <u>F</u> 1. @MIN determines the minute for a given serial number.

<u>T</u> F 2. Multiple items in a range may be listed individually (e.g., the syntax in the formula @COUNT(B1,B3,B4) is correct).

T <u>F</u> 3. Arguments within an @ function may be placed in any order desired by the user.

<u>T</u> F 4. Extra spaces are not acceptable within @ functions.

<u>T</u> F 5. A label has a value of 0 and will be counted as such if included in a range for an @ function.

<u>T</u> F 6. It is possible to alter an @ function with arithmetic operations to get the desired results (e.g., the formula @PMT(B1,B2/12,B3*12) is syntactically correct).

<u>T</u> F 7. If a worksheet file containing the @NOW function (formatted to show the date) is retrieved from a file and actively recalculates, the @NOW function will display the *current* system date.

T <u>F</u> 8. A single-cell item in an argument may not be entered directly into the formula (e.g., the formula @NPV(A1,B1..B6) cannot be entered as @NPV(.1,B1..B6).

<u>T</u> F 9. More than one @ function may be used in a formula.

<u>T</u> F 10. The @IF statement allows you to test one or more conditions in a worksheet and provide appropriate responses for either a true result or a false result.

<u>T</u> F 11. Date and time special functions are available in 1-2-3.

T <u>F</u> 12. XLOOKUP allows you to look up values in a row or a table.

<u>T</u> F 13. You can modify the appearance of a series of characters using the string functions.

T <u>F</u> 14. Data queries cannot be accomplished using special functions.

```
A:A10: @SUMPRODUCT(A3..A6,D3..D6)                                    READY

 A      A        B         C         D         E         F         G         H
 1
 2
 3        10                           5
 4        25                          10
 5        15                          20
 6
 7
 8
 9
10       600
11
12
```

Exercise 10-3

```
A:A1: (D1) [W10] @DATE(89,1,19)                                      READY

 A      A          B         C          D           E         F         G
 1   19-Jan-89         8          11:32:59 AM
 2    09:49 PM        14
 3         555        10
 4         604
 5   30-Aug-89
 6
 7
```

Exercise 10-5

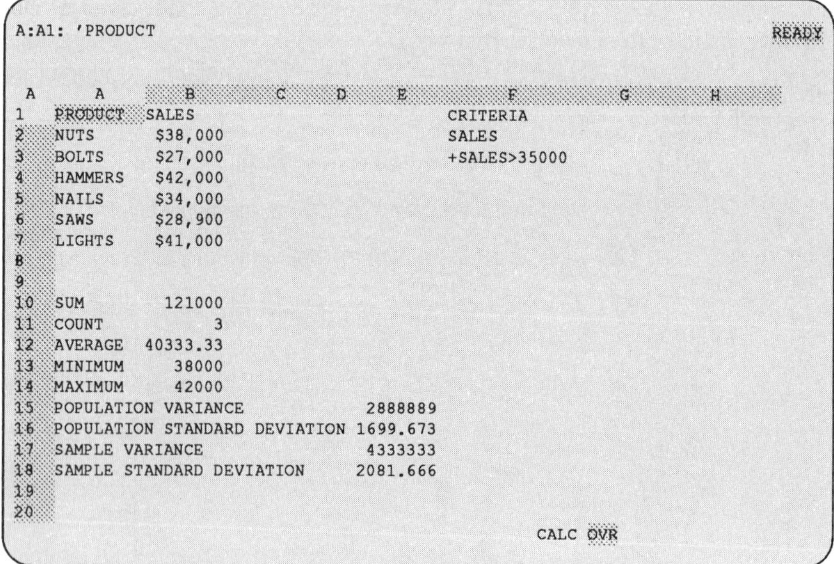

```
A:A1: 'PRODUCT                                                       READY

 A      A        B        C      D      E         F          G        H
 1   PRODUCT  SALES                            CRITERIA
 2   NUTS       $38,000                        SALES
 3   BOLTS      $27,000                        +SALES>35000
 4   HAMMERS    $42,000
 5   NAILS      $34,000
 6   SAWS       $28,900
 7   LIGHTS     $41,000
 8
 9
10   SUM          121000
11   COUNT             3
12   AVERAGE  40333.33
13   MINIMUM     38000
14   MAXIMUM     42000
15   POPULATION VARIANCE              2888889
16   POPULATION STANDARD DEVIATION 1699.673
17   SAMPLE VARIANCE                  4333333
18   SAMPLE STANDARD DEVIATION     2081.666
19
20
                                                    CALC OVR
```

Exercise 10-7

```
A:A1:                                                                  READY

A      A        B        C        D        E        F        G        H
1                                 A2
2         25
3                       25
4
5         11
6
7    C:$D$1
8
9        232
10
11         5
12
13
14       ERR       10        0
15
16        NA      100
17
```

Exercise 10-9

```
A:A1: @REPEAT("GRAPH ",6)                                              READY

A      A        B        C        D        E        F        G        H
1    GRAPH GRAPH GRAPH GRAPH GRAPH GRAPH
2
3    Lotus 1-2-3 is a great software package
4                 17           Lotus 1-2-3              39
5
6             software
7
8    Lotus 1-2-3 is a wonderful software package
9             software package
10
11   Fall is a beautiful time of year
12   fall is a beautiful time of year
13   FALL IS A BEAUTIFUL TIME OF YEAR
14   Fall Is A Beautiful Time Of Year
15
16
```

Exercise 10-11

CHAPTER ELEVEN/EXERCISE 1 ANSWERS

INSTRUCTIONS: Circle T if the statement is true and F if the statement is false.

T **F** 1. The range name for a macro must be taken from a label already existing on the worksheet.

T **F** 2. The range name for a macro must begin with a forward slash and a letter of the alphabet.

T F 3. A macro is a way to automate a repetitive procedure.

T F 4. Certain keystrokes in a macro must be enclosed in braces (the { and } characters).

T **F** 5. In a macro, the tilde (the ~ symbol) represents pressing the forward slash (the command key /).

T **F** 6. To execute the macro named \ Z, you must hold down the Ctrl key and tap the letter Z.

T F 7. A named range for a macro must contain the first macro step as the first line in the range.

T **F** 8. When entering data on a worksheet manually, the tilde can be used instead of pressing ↵.

T **F** 9. Either apostrophe (the ' or the ') can be used to preface a macro step.

T **F** 10. Documentation must be included in a macro.

T F 11. You can automatically record macro keystrokes.

T F 12. Macro libraries can be used to store macros that are applicable to more than one worksheet.

T **F** 13. Macro instructions can be executed one step at a time by using Alt-F1.

T **F** 14. It does not matter where you place macros on a worksheet.

```
A:A1: 'ABC COMPANY DIVISION SUMMARY                                  READY

 A      A          B          C          D          E          F          G          H
 1   ABC COMPANY DIVISION SUMMARY
 2
 3   PRODUCT      Q1         Q2         Q3         Q4     YR TOTAL
 4   ------------------------------------------------------
 5   DIV 1       8,000     17,000     22,000     14,000     61,000
 6   DIV 2       9,000     18,000     23,000     16,000     66,000
 7   DIV 3       7,000     19,000     23,000     11,000     60,000
 8   ------------------------------------------------------
 9   TOTAL      24,000     54,000     68,000     41,000    187,000
10   ======================================================
11
12
```

Exercise 11-3
Part 1

```
\I      {goto}A:A1~                 MOVE TO WORKSHEET A
        /wisb~                      INSERT A NEW SHEET BEFORE
        {goto}A:A3~                 COPY THE HEADINGS
        /fccnHEADING~               FROM THE RANGE NAME HEADINGS
        DIVSALES~                   IN THE DIVSALES FILE
        {goto}A:A5~                 ENTER LABELS FOR THE DIVISIONS
        DIV 1~{down}
        DIV 2~{down}
        DIV 3~{down}
        \-~                         ENTER A SUBTOTAL LINE
        /c~{right}.{right 4}~       COPY THE SUBTOTAL LINE
        {goto}A:B5~                 COMBINE RANGE NAMES FOR DIVISION
        /fcanDIV1TOTAL~             TOTALS ONTO THE NEW SHEET
        DIVSALES~
        {down}
        /fcanDIV2TOTAL~
        DIVSALES~
        {down}
        /fcanDIV3TOTAL~
        DIVSALES~
        {goto}A:A9~
        TOTAL{right}@sum(b5.b8)~    ENTER THE SUM FUNCTION TO GET A
        /c~{right}.{right 3}~       TOTAL FOR ALL DIVISIONS
        /rf,0~{right 4}~            COPY AND FORMAT THE FORMULA
        {down}{left}
        \=~                         ENTER THE TOTAL LINE
        /c~{right}.{right 4}~       COPY THE TOTAL LINE
        {home}
        ABC COMPANY DIVISION        ENTER A WORKSHEET HEADING
        SUMMARY~
        /wwc                        VIEW THE SUMMARY WORKSHEET ONLY

\P      {goto}A:A1~                 MOVE TO CELL A1 OF WORKSHEET A
        /ppr.{end}{home}~           PRINT RANGE IS THE WHOLE WORKSHEET
        agcrq                       PRINT AND CLEAR THE PRINT RANGE
        {goto}B:A1~                 MOVE TO CELL A1 OF WORKSHEET B
        /ppr.{end}{home}~           PRINT RANGE IS THE WHOLE WORKSHEET
        gcrq                        PRINT AND CLEAR THE PRINT RANGE
        {goto}C:A1~                 MOVE TO CELL A1 OF WORKSHEET C
        /ppr.{end}{home}~           PRINT RANGE IS THE WHOLE WORKSHEET
        gcrq                        PRINT AND CLEAR THE PRINT RANGE
        {goto}D:A1~                 MOVE TO CELL A1 OF WORKSHEET D
        /ppr.{end}{home}~           PRINT RANGE IS THE WHOLE WORKSHEET
        gpcaq                       PRINT AND CLEAR THE PRINT RANGE
        {goto}A:A1~                 MOVE TO A1 OF WORKSHEET A
```

Exercise 11-3
Part 2

```
A:A1: [W18]                                                          READY

A          A             B        C        D        E        F        G
1                                 PROJECTED PROFITS
2
3                        YEAR 1   YEAR 2   YEAR 3   YEAR 4   YEAR 5     TOTAL
4
5    REVENUE             25,000   26,500   28,090   29,775   31,561   140,926
6    EXPENSES             9,500    6,625    7,023    7,444    7,890    38,482
7                        ----------------------------------------------------
8    PROFIT BEFORE TAX   15,500   19,875   21,067   22,331   23,671   102,444
9    TAXES                6,200    7,950    8,427    8,932    9,468    40,977
10                       ----------------------------------------------------
11   PROFIT AFTER TAX     9,300   11,925   12,640   13,399   14,203    61,467
12                       ====================================================
13   ASSUMPTIONS
14   REVENUE GROWTH RATE                6%       6%       6%       6%
15   EXPENSE RATE                      25%      25%      25%      25%
16   TAX RATE                          40%      40%      40%      40%
17
18
```

Exercise 11-5
Part 1

```
B:A1: '\G                                                            READY

B    A         B        C        D        E        F        G        H
1    \G        {goto}A:A1~                MOVE TO A:A1
2              /grg                       RESET PREVIOUS GRAPH SETTINGS
3              tb                         MAKE TYPE BAR
4              xLABELS~                   X RANGE IS RANGE NAME LABELS
5              aREVENUE~                  A RANGE IS RANGE NAME REVENUE
6              bBEFORE_TAX~               B RANGE IS RANGE NAME BEFORE_TAX
7              cAFTER_TAX~                C RANGE IS RANGE NAME AFTER_TAX
8              olaREVENUE~                DEFINE LEGEND FOR EACH RANGE
9              lbPROFIT BEFORE TAX~
10             lcPROFIT AFTER TAX~
11             tfABC COMPANY~             SPECIFY FIRST, SECOND AND
12             tsPROJECTED PROFITS~       Y-AXIS TITLES
13             tyDOLLARS IN~
14             bqv                        VIEW IN BLACK AND WHITE
15
16   \P        {goto}A:A1~                MOVE TO CELL A:A1
17             /ppic                      PRINT CURRENT IMAGE
18             agpq                       GO AND QUIT
19
20
```

Exercise 11-5
Part 2

CHAPTER TWELVE/EXERCISE 1 ANSWERS

INSTRUCTIONS: Circle T if the statement is True and F is the statement is False.

T **F** 1. You cannot use macros to place a sequence of values on a worksheet.

T **F** 2. A macro can be automatically executed when a file is retrieved by naming the macro ZERO.

T **F** 3. A series of macro instructions can be repeated only if you know how many times the instructions need to be repeated.

T **F** 4. A maximum of 10 menu options can be included in any user-designed menu.

T F 5. The /X commands have equivalent macro commands available in later releases of Lotus 1-2-3 that are easier to understand.

T F 6. Macros can be used to restrict the input by a user of a worksheet to a specific set of cells.

T **F** 7. The only way to use an interactive macro is if you force the macro to execute when the file containing the macro is retrieved.

T F 8. Macros can be written that prompt the user to input information.

T **F** 9. At most, five tiers can be incorporated in a user-designed menu.

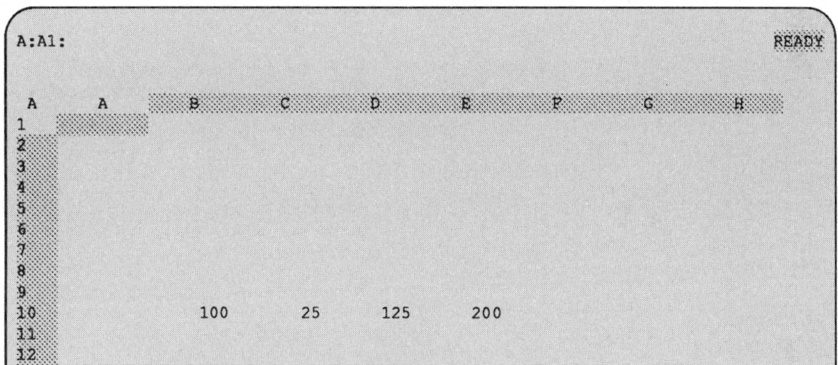

Exercise 12-3
Part 1

```
B:D5:                                                              READY

B     A        B        C        D        E        F        G        H
1  INPUT    {goto}A:B10~       MOVE TO FIRST CELL
2  NUMBERS  {?}~               ENTER A NUMBER
3           {right}            MOVE THE POINTER TO THE RIGHT
4           {branch NUMBERS}   BRANCH UP TO NUMBERS
5
6
```

Exercise 12-3
Part 2

```
A:A1: 20                                                           READY

A      A        B        C        D        E        F        G        H
1       20       25       15 -0.33333
2       25       30       35 -0.14286
3       40       30       20      0.5
4       15       25       35 -0.28571
5       25       35       20     -0.5
6
7
```

Exercise 12-5
Part 1

```
B:F13:                                                             READY

B     A          B        C        D        E        F        G
1  CALCULATE  {goto}A:D1~                           MOVE TO FIRST CELL
2  COMPUTE    +({left 3}-{left 2})/{left}~          ENTER FORMULA
3             {down}{left}                          MOVE TO COLUMN C
4             /rncTEST~{up}~                        CREATE TEST RANGE
5             {right}                               MOVE TO COLUMN D
6             {if @count(TEST)=1}{branch END}       BRANCH TO END IF THROUGH
7             /rndTEST~                             DELETE RANGE NAME TEST
8             {branch COMPUTE}                      ENTER NEXT FORMULA
9
10 END        /rndTEST~                             DELETE RANGE NAME TEST
11            {goto}A:A1~                           MOVE TO CELL A1
12            {quit}                                END OF MACRO
13
14
```

Exercise 12-5
Part 2

Note: Exercises 7 and 9 do not require an answer key.

CHAPTER THIRTEEN/EXERCISE 1 ANSWERS

INSTRUCTIONS: Circle T if the statement is true and F if the statement is false.

T **F** 1. A column on a worksheet has to have a width of 72 before text can be justified.

T F 2. Each line of text is a separate label after the **R**ange **J**ustify command is executed.

T F 3. To edit a line of text that has been justified with the **R**ange **J**ustify command, use the F2 key.

T F 4. If the **R**ange **J**ustify command is executed with text above an existing worksheet, the Justify range should include enough space to justify the text without disturbing the worksheet below.

T **F** 5. The **R**ange **J**ustify command only performs if the Justify range consists of one column and text is not displayed under other columns.

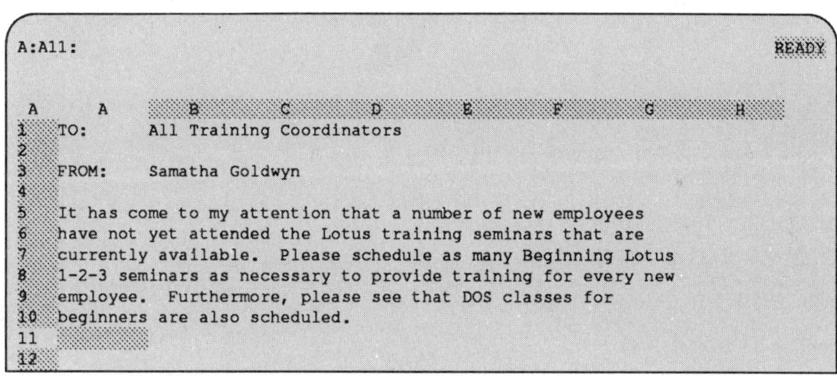

Exercise 13-3

ORDER INFORMATION AND FACULTY SUPPORT INFORMATION

For the quickest service, refer to the map below for the South-Western Regional Office serving your area.

1 ORDER INFORMATION

5101 Madison Road
Cincinnati, OH 45227-1490
General Telephone–513-527-6945
Telephone: 1-800-543-8440
FAX: 513-527-6979
Telex: 214371

FACULTY SUPPORT INFORMATION

5101 Madison Road
Cincinnati, OH 45227-1490
General Telephone–513-527-6950
Telephone: 1-800-543-8444

Alabama	Massachusetts	Pennsylvania
Connecticut	Michigan (Lower)**	Rhode Island
Delaware	Mississippi	South Carolina
Florida	New Hampshire	Tennessee
Georgia	New Jersey	Vermont
Indiana*	New York	Virginia
Kentucky	North Carolina	West Virginia
Maine	Ohio	District of Columbia
Maryland		

*Except for ZIP Code Areas 463, 464. These areas contact Region 2 Office.
**Except for the Upper Peninsula. This area contacts Region 2 Office.

2 ORDER INFORMATION and FACULTY SUPPORT INFORMATION

355 Conde Street
West Chicago, IL 60185
General Telephone–312-231-6000
Telephone: 1-800-543-7972

Illinois	Minnesota	North Dakota
Indiana*	Missouri	South Dakota
Iowa	Nebraska	Wisconsin
Michigan (Upper)**		

*Only for ZIP Code Areas 463, 464. Other areas contact Region 1 office.
**Only for Upper Peninsula. Other areas contact Region 1 office.

3 ORDER INFORMATION

13800 Senlac Drive
Suite 100
Dallas, TX 75234
General Telephone–214-241-8541
Telephone: 1-800-543-7972

FACULTY SUPPORT INFORMATION

5101 Madison Road
Cincinnati, OH 45227-1490
General Telephone–513-527-6950
Telephone: 1-800-543-8444

Arkansas	Louisiana	Texas
Colorado	New Mexico	Wyoming
Kansas	Oklahoma	

4 ORDER INFORMATION and FACULTY SUPPORT INFORMATION

6185 Industrial Way
Livermore, CA 94550
General Telephone–415-449-2280
Telephone: 1-800-543-7972

Alaska	Idaho	Oregon
Arizona	Montana	Utah
California	Nevada	Washington
Hawaii		

INDEX

1-2-3 COMMANDS

1-2-3 FUNCTIONS

1-2-3 ADVANCED MACRO COMMANDS